THE STORY

THE STORY
READERS AND WRITERS OF FICTION

DAVID BERGMAN
Towson State University

Macmillan Publishing Company
New York

Printed in the United States of America

Macmillan Publishing Company
866 Third Avenue, New York, New York 10022

Library of Congress Cataloging-in-Publication Data

The Story : readers and writers of fiction.

Includes index.
1. Authorship--Technique. 2. Fiction--Technique.
3. Short story. I. Bergman, David, 1950-
PN181.S76 1988 808.3'1 87-31492
ISBN 0-02-308360-3

Printing: 2 3 4 5 6 7 Year: 0 1 2 3 4

ACKNOWLEDGMENTS

Beacon Press. JAMES BALDWIN, "Autobiographical Notes," from *Notes of a Native Son* by James Baldwin. Copyright © 1955, renewed 1983, by James Baldwin. Reprinted by permission of Beacon Press.

Dell Publishing Co., Inc. KATHERINE ANNE PORTER, from "Three Statements about Writing," from *The Days Before.*

Doubleday & Company, Inc. CHINUA ACHEBE, "Dead Men's Path," from *Girls at War and Other Stories.* Copyright © 1972, 1973 by Chinua Achebe. Reprinted by permission of Doubleday & Company. JAMES BALDWIN, "The Rockpile," from the book *Going to Meet the Man.* Copyright © 1948, 1951, 1957, 1958, 1960, 1965 by James Baldwin. Reprinted by permission of Doubleday & Company. JOHN BARTH, "Autobiography," from *Lost in the Funhouse.* Copyright © 1968 by John Barth. Reprinted by permission of Doubleday & Company. JOSEPH CONRAD, "The Secret Sharer," from *Twixt Land and Sea;* "Preface to Twixt Land and Sea" from *Twixt Land and Sea.* Reprinted by permission of Doubleday & Company. MARCEL PROUST, "A Dinner in Society," from *Pleasures and Days.* Copyright © 1957 by F. W. Dupee and Barbara Dupee and copyright 1948 by Lear Publishers, Inc. Reprinted by Doubleday Publishing, a division of Bantam, Doubleday, Dell Publishing Group.

Farrar, Straus & Giroux, Inc. SHIRLEY JACKSON, "The Lottery," from *The Lottery* by Shirley Jackson. Copyright 1948, 1949 by Shirley Jackson. Copyright renewed © 1976, 1977 by Laurence Hyman, Barry Hyman, Mrs. Sarah Webster and Mrs. Joanne Schnurer. Originally appeared in *The New Yorker.* Reprinted by permission of Farrar, Straus and Giroux, Inc. FLANNERY O'CONNOR, "A Reasonable Use of the Unreasonable," Excerpt from "On Her Own Work," from *Mystery and Manners* by Flannery O'Connor, edited by Sally and Robert Fitzgerald. Copyright © 1957, 1961, 1963, 1966, 1967, 1968 by the Estate of Mary Flannery O'Connor. Reprinted by permission of Farrar, Straus and Giroux, Inc. BERNARD MALAMUD, "The Jewbird," from *Idiots First* by Bernard Malamud. Copyright © 1961, 1963 by Bernard Malamud. Reprinted by permission of Farrar, Straus and Giroux, Inc. GRACE PALEY, "A Conversation with My Father," from *Enormous Changes at the Last Minute* by Grace Paley. Copyright © 1972, 1974 by Grace Paley. Reprinted by permission of Farrar, Straus and Giroux, Inc.

Harcourt Brace Jovanovich, Inc. FLANNERY O'CONNOR, "A Good Man Is Hard to Find." Copyright 1953 by Flannery O'Connor; renewed 1981 by Mrs. Regina O'Connor. Reprinted from *A Good Man Is Hard to Find and Other Stories* by Flannery O'Connor by permission of Harcourt Brace Jovanovich, Inc. KATHERINE ANNE PORTER, "The Jilting of Granny Weatherall." Copyright 1930, 1958 by Katherine Anne Porter. Reprinted from her volume *Flowering Judas and Other Stories* by permission of Harcourt Brace Jovanovich, Inc. ALICE WALKER, "The Black Writer and the Southern Experience," from *In Search of Our Mother's Gardens.* Copyright © 1983 by Alice Walker. Reprinted by permission of Harcourt Brace Jovanovich, Inc. "To Hell with Dying," from *In Love and Trouble* by Alice Walker. EUDORA WELTY, "Why I Live at the P.O." Copyright 1941, 1969 by Eudora Welty.

Reprinted from her volume *A Curtain of Green and Other Stories* by permission of Harcourt Brace Jovanovich, Inc. VIRGINIA WOOLF, "Lappin and Lapinova," from *A Haunted House & Other Short Stories* by Virginia Woolf. Copyright 1944, 1972 by Harcourt Brace Jovanovich, Inc. Reprinted by permission of the publisher. "Professions for Women," from *The Death of the Moth and Other Essays* by Virginia Woolf, copyright 1942 by Harcourt Brace Jovanovich, Inc.; renewed 1970 by Marjorie T. Parsons, Executrix. Reprinted by permission of the publisher.

Harper & Row, Publishers, Inc. GABRIEL GARCIA MARQUEZ, "A Very Old Man with Enormous Wings," from *Collected Stories* by Gabriel Garcia Marquez. Copyright © 1971 by Gabriel Garcia Marquez. Reprinted by permission of Harper & Row, Publishers, Inc.

Harvard University Press. EUDORA WELTY, Excerpt from *One Writer's Beginnings.* Copyright © 1983, 1984 by Eudora Welty. Reprinted by permission.

Alfred A. Knopf, Inc. JULIO CORTÁZAR, "Continuity of Parks," pages 63–65, from *End of the Game and Other Stories* by Julio Cortázar. Copyright © 1967 by Random House, Inc. Reprinted by permission of Random House, Inc. E. M. FORSTER, "The Other Side of the Hedge," from *The Celestial Omnibus* by E. M. Forster. Published 1947 by Alfred A. Knopf, Inc. MILAN KUNDERA, "The Golden Apple of Eternal Desire," pages 95–117, from *Laughable Loves* by Milan Kundera, translated by Suzanne Rappaport. Copyright © 1974 by Alfred A. Knopf, Inc. Reprinted by permission of Alfred A. Knopf, Inc. V. S. NAIPAUL, "Bogart," from pages 9–16, from *Miguel Street.* Copyright © 1959 by V. S. Naipaul. Reprinted from *Three Novels: The Mystic Masseur, The Suffrage of Elvira, Miguel Street,* by permission of Alfred A. Knopf, Inc.

McGraw-Hill Book Company. RAYMOND CARVER, "The Student's Wife," from *Will You Be Quiet, Please?* Reprinted by permission of the author.

The New Yorker. ANNE TYLER, "Your Place Is Empty." Copyright © 1976 by Anne Tyler. Reprinted by permission of Russell and Volkening, Inc. as agents for the author.

New Directions Publishing Corporation. JORGE LUIS BORGES, "Borges and I" from *Labyrinths.* Copyright © 1964 by New Directions Publishing Corporation.

W. W. Norton & Company, Inc. ANNE TYLER, "Still Just Writing" is reprinted from *The Writer on Her Work,* edited by Janet Sternburg, by permission of W. W. Norton & Company, Inc. Copyright © 1980 by Janet Sternburg.

Penguin Books Ltd. ANTON CHEKHOV, "Lady with Lapdog," from *Lady with Lapdog and Other Stories* by Anton Chekhov, translated with an introduction by David Magarshack (Penguin Classics, 1964), copyright © David Magarshack, pp. 264–281.

S. G. Phillips, Inc. ISAAC BABEL, "My First Goose." Reprinted by permission of S. G. Phillips, Inc. from *The Collected Stories of Isaac Babel.* Copyright © 1955 by S. G. Phillips, Inc.

Random House, Inc. WILLIAM FAULKNER, "A Rose for Emily." Copyright 1930 and renewed 1958 by William Faulkner. Reprinted from *Collected Stories* by William Faulkner, by permission of Random House, Inc. Nobel Prize Address from *Essays, Speeches and Public Letters* by William Faulkner. V. S. NAIPAUL, "Bogart," from *Miguel Street.*

Sanford J. Greenburger Associates Inc. VLADIMIR NABOKOV, "Cloud, Castle, Lake" from *Nabokov's Dozen.* Copyright © 1941 by Atlantic Monthly Press, copyright renewed in 1968 by Vladimir Nabokov; published by permission of the Estate of Valdimir Nabokov.

Schocken Books Inc. FRANZ KAFKA, "Before the Law." Reprinted by permission of Schocken Books from *The Penal Colony* by Franz Kafka, trans. by Willa and Edwin Muir. Copyright © 1948, 1976 by Schocken Books Inc.

Charles Scribner's Sons. F. SCOTT FITZGERALD, "The Diamond as Big as the Ritz," from *Tales of the Jazz Age.* Copyright 1922 Charles Scribner's Sons; copyright renewed 1950 Frances Scott Fitzgerald Lanahan. Reprinted with the permission of Charles Scribner's Sons, a division of Macmillan, Inc.; "Babylon Revisited," from *Taps at Reveille.* Copyright 1931 The Curtis Publishing Company; copyright renewed © 1959 Frances Scott Fitzgerald Lanahan. Reprinted with the permission of Charles Scribner's Sons, a division of Macmillan, Inc. ERNEST HEMINGWAY, "The Killers," from *Men Without Women.* Copyright 1927 Charles Scribner's Sons; copyright renewed 1955 Ernest Hemingway. Reprinted with the permission of Charles Scribner's Sons, a division of Macmillan, Inc. ERNEST HEMINGWAY, "The Short Happy Life of Francis MacComber," from *Short Stories of Ernest Hemingway.* Copyright 1936 Ernest Hemingway; Copyright renewed © 1964 Mary Hemingway. Reprinted with permission of Charles Scribner's Sons, a div. of Macmillan, Inc. EDITH WHARTON, excerpt from "Telling a Short Story," from *The Writing of Fiction.* Copyright 1925 Charles Scribner's Sons; copyright renewed 1953 Frederic R. King. Reprinted with the permission of Charles Scribner's Sons, a division of Macmillan, Inc.; EDITH WHARTON, "Roman Fever," from *Roman Fever and Other Stories.* Copyright 1934 Liberty Magazine; copyright renewed © 1962 William R. Tyler. Reprinted with permission of Charles Scribner's Sons, a div. of Macmillan, Inc.

For my parents
whose stories are the
beginning of all the fiction
I will ever know

PREFACE

In the past, the reading process has often been separated from the writing process, as though writing and reading were entirely different activities. Student writers, of course, have been encouraged to think about their readers. But frequently readers have been urged to pretend that they are simply peripheral to what they read, that the story has no need for them, and that they have only a passive part to play as the audience. It is as if stories were discovered under cabbages without parentage or purpose.

In this book I have tried to bring the writing and reading process together in several ways that I hope will help students become better and more engaged readers and finer and more engaging writers. Some of these ways may appear new to you, although they are techniques that teachers have always used.

First, I have included essays, interviews and memoirs of various writers in the belief that their statements about their own work shed light on how it is to be read, the kind of reader they had in mind when writing, and the process by which they came to write as they did. These statements will also give students a better understanding of the authors and of the writing process. After these essays I have included a number of questions and subjects for students to think about either alone or in classroom discussion. These questions generally focus on the relationship between writers' ideas and the work they produce. These questions can also be the germ for an essay.

Second, at the end of each chapter's introductory material I have included four sets of questions and suggestions. The first of these sets of questions are more "Questions to Think About." These should raise basic philosophic issues about the concepts in the introduction and how they might apply to other areas of human experience. The second set of questions are "Essay Topics" to help students, the vast majority of whom will use this book in classes in which they must write essays. Indeed many of the statements in the introductory material of each chapter are designed to help students see the relationship between what happens to them as readers and what they do as writers. The third set contains not questions but suggestions for creative writing. These may be used in creative writing classes, by teachers who want to try some alternative writing assignments or by students who wish to write stories on their own. I have made these questions and suggestions fairly open, so that students and teachers may adapt them to their own particular needs and circumstances. The fourth set of questions are "Literary Essays." These writing assignments are not separate; the same issues will often reappear under various rubrics so that students will be able to consider them in different contexts and modes.

I should note that I have selected the stories to help teachers and students see the relationship between writing and reading. I have included only those stories that I have enjoyed reading over and over again, and many of these stories have become classics in the classroom for their broad appeal to students and their effectiveness as teaching tools. Others are not widely known, but I have found them so stimulating that I have good reason to believe they will appeal to a broad readership. I have always found it easier to write about works I have enjoyed, and I hope by providing stimulating reading I will have made the writing process less burdensome.

But I have also chosen stories for their variety. In each chapter I have endeavored to include stories by non-American authors, women authors, and representatives of minority ethnic groups. In such a way, readers should find in this collection at least one author who speaks out of their particular background and experience, an author, so to speak, who writes for them. Conversely all students will have to encounter writers who come from different countries and cultures and whose intended readers are very different from themselves. Such diversity should help students stretch their imaginative powers and yet not feel alienated from the acts of reading and writing. This book represents the pluralism which forms the heritage of American life and distinguishes American education. As such it constitutes not a departure from tradition, but an extension of it.

I would like to thank a number of people who helped me on this project. Gordon Lester-Massman urged me to undertake the project, and Jennifer Crewe was instrumental in helping me develop the project. Barbara Heinssen has been generous in taking over so difficult a project. Daniel Mark Epstein, Donald Craver of Towson State University, Alma Nugent of Goucher College and Richard Katz of Kean College have been excellent sounding boards and advisors. I have been particularly lucky in finding so many good critics who have carefully read and analyzed the manuscript as it travelled through its various stages. I want especially to thank Nancy G. Anderson, Auburn University at Montgomery; Brenda R. Bell, East Texas State University; Paula Ann Buss, William Rainey Harper College; Carol Fairbanks, University of Wisconsin at Eau Claire; Michael Hogan, University of New Mexico at Albuquerque; Catharine B. Kloss, University of Pittsburgh at Johnstown; Lois A. Marchino, University of Texas at El Paso; Peter Sherer, William Rainey Harper College; and Stacy W. Thompson, Central Michigan University.

All teachers learn from their students, but I have been especially fortunate to have such generous, hard working and wise students. I want to thank those in my 1986 Writing for Literature class, particularly Brenda Piskor, Michael Kliewer, Randall Ails, Shelley McPherson, Kurt Schwartz, Martha McCormick, Carol Sipes, Alison Chang, Dana Kraft, Heidi Kappeler, Andrew Merz, Lisa Monroe, Terri Sevick, Christopher Hires and Beth Gehl. Finally, I am indebted to John Lessner, not only for his material assistance during the far longer than expected composition of this book, but also for his psychological support—his patience, forbearance, and equanimity.

DB

CONTENTS

1
THE AUDIENCE

Every storyteller needs a listener, and in many ways the listener is as important as the teller. After all, without listeners or readers, there would be no stories or books. If you weren't reading this chapter now, I wouldn't be sitting at my desk writing it. My success as a writer depends to a large extent on whether I can interest you in the subject and provide you with the information you need in a clear and lively manner.

Consequently, I've done a lot of thinking about who you are and what you might need. This assessment has been made simpler by all the students I've known over the years. I have a composite picture of you in my mind. Most of you are in your late teens or older. No doubt some of you are returning to school after a number of years absence. Many of you have done a fair amount of reading and know a lot about stories and storytelling. A few of you may wish to become writers. You know how books can be exciting, frightening, romantic and informative; in short you have experienced the pleasures of reading. Others of you have not found pleasure in reading. For you reading is difficult and confusing, especially when you have been assigned specific material to read. Stories may not seem to have anything to do with your life. I know that both kinds of readers are my audience, and I want them both to come away from this book feeling that they are readers who can take more pleasure and get more understanding from the works they read.

Am I alone in my concern for my readers? Not at all. Eudora Welty, whose short story, "Why I Live at the P.O.," is included in this chapter, has written about how she feels about the reader.

> I think we write stories in the ultimate hope of communicating, but so do we make jelly in that hope. Communicating and hope of it are conditions of life itself. . . . We hope somebody will taste our jelly and eat it with even more pleasure than it deserves and ask for another helping—no more can we hope for in writing a story. Always in the back of our heads and in our hearts are such hopes, and attendant fears that we may fail—we do everything out of the energy of some form of love or desire to please.

For Eudora Welty, writing is an act of love. She is moved to write—just as she is moved to make jelly—out of the desire to communicate with people she hopes to please. But no one can please everyone, and few writers—or jelly makers—attempt to do so. Writers choose their audiences in much the same way as readers choose what they read.

THE VARIETY OF AUDIENCES

People who write for television or the movies usually write for large, general audiences, while those who write for magazines such as *Byte* or *The Harvard Business Journal* have a small, specialized audience. But writers usually don't have a single readership. Carl Sagan, for example, the noted astronomer who has authored articles for scientific journals, has also written the television series *Cosmos* for the general audience. How he wrote and what he wrote differed depending on his audience.

Audiences differ along certain lines. Gender, social class, geographic region, educational level, and age are categories often used to classify readers. Certain works are written primarily for women, others for men. Some books are written expressly for children; others for adults. Many major cities across the nation have developed regional magazines that cater to the specific interests of people in the area. A magazine such as *The National Review* is an organ of conservative opinion: *The New York Review of Books,* in contrast, has a tradition of being a journal of liberal opinion. Many political, ethnic, religious and professional groups have specific journals, publishing houses and audiences. Writers adapt their styles to suit their specific readers.

There's nothing necessarily "phoney" or hypocritical about changing one's style to suit one's audience. Such adaptation is polite as well as practical. It represents a sincere concern for meeting the needs and feelings of other people. You probably change the way you write and talk depending on your audience. For example, you speak differently when addressing a teacher, a fellow student, an employer or a co-worker. You might be informal when talking to a friend and more formal when addressing a teacher or employer. What may be a perfectly acceptable way of chatting with a buddy after class may be an entirely unacceptable way to speak to a teacher in class.

HOW TO DETERMINE AN AUDIENCE

Writers ask at least four questions about their audience: (1) Who is my audience? (2) What does the audience know? (3) What is the audience interested in hearing? (4) What does the audience expect? Sometimes the answers to these questions are clear, but often writers must guess at them.

For example the publishers of romance novels, stories of love that fill the bookstands at drugstores and supermarkets, have studied what their readers want and expect. The publishers have devised "tip sheets" which specify which features authors should include in their novels. The specifications are often quite precise. They will tell the author such things as whether the heroine may be married, may hold a job or travel to foreign countries, or even kiss the hero before their marriage. Authors who wish to please their readers and their publishers will follow these guidelines.

Other kinds of novels have less rigid rules, but readers of adventure and spy novels usually expect a lot of violent action. They want simple sentences with simple words. They usually want characters who are fairly stereotypical, with clear straightforward motives. They prefer stories in which "good guys" triumph over "bad guys." Successful writers of spy thrillers and adventure novels will give readers what they want and expect.

Writers of non-fiction also must be concerned about the desires, expectations and knowledge levels of their audiences. A writer for *The Wall Street Journal,* whose readers are business people, would not explain what "preferred stock" is in an article. But the same writer preparing an article for a local Sunday supplement may need to explain the term.

THE AUDIENCE FOR LITERATURE

Because westerns, romances, spy novels and adventure stories have such clearly indicated requirements, they are sometimes called "formula fiction." The readers of romance fiction expect certain elements (such as happy endings) when they buy a book, and they will feel "cheated" if the author fails to supply those elements. Readers of formula fiction usually read quickly, on the go, when they are tired, and for entertainment. They expect the author to do most of the work for them. For example, tired readers don't want to figure out a character's complex motivations and prefer authors who give clear and simple explanations. Similarly, readers who are on the go don't want to have to look up words in a dictionary. They want the vocabulary and sentence structure to be simple and straightforward. Because formula fiction is made to be read quickly and easily, the elements are frequently reduced to simple, straightforward and predictable patterns.

Of course, good writers have tried their hands at formula fiction, often enjoying the framework and possibilities such forms have to offer. Dorothy Sayers, who wrote a fine verse translation of Dante's *Divine Comedy,* wrote a popular series of detective novels. The classicist and poet C. Day Lewis, under the name of Nicholas Blake, also wrote detective novels. The English historian, Antonia Frazier and the American literary scholar Carolyn Heilbrun are noted authors of mysteries.

You can see why some readers grow tired of reading only formula fiction. Because such popular writing repeats the same patterns and reduces elements to their simplest forms, informed readers find a steady diet of formula fiction unsatisfactory. They also want works that challenge them and provide other sorts of pleasures and experiences. Rather than rushing through the works they read, informed readers tend to read slowly, enjoying precise and effective uses of language, and complexity and subtlety of character and plot. Informed readers seek out works that are different and unpredictable and that escape the patterns of formula fiction.

Informed readers are as demanding as, if not more demanding than, the readers of formula fiction. But the two types of readers look for different elements from stories. The informed reader appreciates beauty of language, complexity of thought, subtlety of characterization and freshness of organization and frequently is willing to take the time to savor these qualities. The formula reader generally wants simplicity of language and thought, directness of character and predictability of organization.

Of course, a person generally isn't one sort of reader, limited to only one sort of book, magazine or newspaper. The computer programmer who reads *Byte* at work may read *USA Today* during lunch and a detective novel before going to sleep. Many an English professor is addicted to who-done-its. President Kennedy, who won the Pulitzer prize for *Profiles in Courage,* found time in his busy schedule to read Ian Fleming's James Bond spy thrillers. This book aims at making you a better informed reader of all types of writing.

However, the stories in this book were written, by and large, for demanding readers. They were not written to any recipe—like so many batches of biscuits. Nor were the stories in this volume made like consumer items, to be used once and thrown away. Rather, they were meant to be read and re-read, to be thought about and enjoyed. We might say that one of the differences between literature and popular formula writing has to do with the expectations of readers. Readers of literature expect to be challenged by what they read. They expect that literature will not be exhausted by one quick reading but will need reflection and consideration. Readers consume formula fiction; while literature consumes its readers.

WHAT KIND OF READER ARE YOU?

People who are readers of formula fiction often have difficulty adjusting to the demands of literature. They become frustrated when a story is not clear the first time it is read. They do not take the time to try to imagine the setting or to contemplate the characters' motivation. They frequently skip long passages of scenic description. They ignore complex sentences or stylistic devices and are frustrated when too little physical action takes place.

Does this mean that formula fiction is bad and that the readers of formula fiction are bad readers? No. It simply means that formula fiction is a different kind of writing and its readers have different kinds of skills. The highest praise a formula writer can get is "I couldn't put your book down." But many writers of literature expect their readers to pause and reflect on the action of the story.

If you are a reader only of formula fiction, you will need to learn to adjust to the different demands of literature. You will have to give yourself more time to read, and you may have to read the story several times without skipping any passages. You will have to use your imagination and start trying to understand why the characters act the way they do. In short there is a lot more work involved if you are going to enjoy yourself, but the rewards will also be longer lasting.

QUESTIONS TO THINK ABOUT

1. How do you read? Do you pay attention to the author's language? Do you simply want to be carried away by a good story? Do you stop yourself in reading and ask why certain things occur in the story? Do you try to imagine what the characters and the setting look like? Do you flip to the end of a story to see how the plot turns out? Do you identify with characters or remain aloof from the action?
2. For whom do you write? Try to imagine your reader. What does your reader expect to find? What does your reader know? What does your reader want to discover? Do you do a good job in satisfying your reader. For example, do you try to write in a lively and interesting manner to keep your reader engaged? Do you define technical or unusual words so your reader can understand you? What do you expect from your reader? Do you expect the reader to figure out what you mean? If so, how is the reader to figure out your meaning?

ESSAY TOPICS

1. Discuss some of your more pleasurable reading experiences. What did those experiences have in common? What was different about them? If you've never derived pleasure from reading discuss why.
2. Discuss the problems you have communicating. What do you want people to understand? Why don't they understand you?
3. Narrate an incident you experienced or observed when a misunderstanding had amusing or calamitous results.

CREATIVE WRITING EXERCISES

1. Write letters to a friend, your parents and a bank asking to borrow $500. Try to vary the content and style as much as possible.
2. Discuss your ideal readers. What do your readers look like? Where do they read? What other attributes do they possess?
3. Pretend you are a famous fictional character writing a letter to the person who created you. For example you could be Hamlet writing to Shakespeare or Mickey Mouse writing to Walt Disney. What questions might you ask? Would you be pleased at what your creator did to you? Would you like what the audience thinks of you? How would you like to change?

LITERARY ESSAYS

1. The narrators of "Why I Live at the P.O." and "The Cask of Amontillado" both explain their actions to an implied listener. Compare these listeners and the motivations of the narrators for telling their stories.
2. Jealousy and revenge are motives that run through Welty's, Poe's and Cortázar's stories. How do these authors depict these basic human emotions?
3. Of the stories in the chapter, which one seems the easiest and hardest to respond to? What factors governed your response? Language? Tone? Situation? Character? How do you account for the differences?

EUDORA WELTY

WHY I LIVE AT THE P.O.

Born in 1909, Eudora Welty has spent most of her life in her native home of Jackson, Mississippi, though she received her B.A. from the University of Wisconsin and worked and studied in New York City. Like Faulkner who drew his inspiration from Oxford, Mississippi, Welty has set virtually all of her work in the South with an unerring eye for local detail and a pitch-perfect ear for voice. Nevertheless, her small-town gossips and dirt-poor farmers have something to say to all people about the human condition.

Welty has written several novels including Losing Battles *and* The Optimist's Daughter, *but her finest work has been in the short story where her uncanny sense of psychology and her off-beat sense of humor can find swift, sure expression.*

I was getting along fine with Mama, Papa-Daddy and Uncle Rondo until my sister Stella-Rondo just separated from her husband and came back home again. Mr. Whitaker! Of course I went with Mr. Whitaker first, when he first appeared here in China Grove, taking "Pose Yourself" photos, and Stella-Rondo broke us up. Told him I was one-sided. Bigger on one side than the other, which is a deliberate, calculated falsehood: I'm the same. Stella-Rondo is exactly twelve months to the day younger than I am and for that reason she's spoiled.

She's always had anything in the world she wanted and then she'd throw it away. Papa-Daddy gave her this gorgeous Add-a-Pearl necklace when she was eight years old and she threw it away playing baseball when she was nine, with only two pearls.

So as soon as she got married and moved away from home the first thing she did was separate! From Mr. Whitaker! This photographer with the popeyes she said she trusted. Came home from one of those towns up in Illinois and to our complete surprise brought this child of two.

Mama said she like to made her drop dead for a second. "Here you had this marvelous blonde child and never so much as wrote your mother a word about it," says Mama. "I'm thoroughly ashamed of you." But of course she wasn't.

Stella-Rondo just calmly takes off this *hat,* I wish you could see it. She says, "Why, Mama, Shirley-T.'s adopted, I can prove it."

"How?" says Mama, but all I says was, "H'm!" There I was over the hot stove, trying to stretch two chickens over five people and a completely unexpected child into the bargain, without one moment's notice.

"What do you mean—'H'm!'?" says Stella-Rondo, and Mama says, "I heard that, Sister."

I said that oh, I didn't mean a thing, only that whoever Shirley-T. was, she was the spit-image of Papa-Daddy if he'd cut off his beard, which of course he'd never do in the world. Papa-Daddy's Mama's papa and sulks.

Stella-Rondo got furious! She said, "Sister, I don't need to tell you you got a lot of nerve and always did have and I'll thank you to make no future reference to my adopted child whatsoever."

"Very well," I said. "Very well, very well. Of course I noticed at once she looks like Mr. Whitaker's side too. That frown. She looks like a cross between Mr. Whitaker and Papa-Daddy."

"Well, all I can say is she isn't."

"She looks exactly like Shirley Temple[1] to me," says Mama, but Shirley-T. just ran away from her.

So the first thing Stella-Rondo did at the table was turn Papa-Daddy against me.

"Papa-Daddy," she says. He was trying to cut up his meat. "Papa-

[1] Shirley Temple Black (1928–) was a child movie actress who sang and danced in such films as *Rebecca of Sunnybrook Farm* and *Little Miss Broadway.* She was known for her dimpled smile and blond curls.

Daddy!" I was taken completely by surprise. Papa-Daddy is about a million years old and's got this long-long beard. "Papa-Daddy, Sister says she fails to understand why you don't cut off your beard."

So Papa-Daddy l-a-y-s down his knife and fork! He's real rich. Mama says he is, he says he isn't. So he says, "Have I heard correctly? You don't understand why I don't cut off my beard?"

"Why," I says, "Papa-Daddy, of course I understand, I did not say any such of a thing, the idea!"

He says, "Hussy!"

I says, "Papa-Daddy, you know I wouldn't any more want you to cut off your beard than the man in the moon. It was the farthest thing from my mind! Stella-Rondo sat there and made that up while she was eating breast of chicken."

But he says, "So the postmistress fails to understand why I don't cut off my beard. Which job I got you through my influence with the government. 'Bird's nest'—is that what you call it?"

Not that it isn't the next to smallest P.O. in the entire state of Mississippi.

I says, "Oh, Papa-Daddy," I says, "I didn't say any such of a thing, I never dreamed it was a bird's nest, I have always been grateful though this is the next to smallest P.O. in the state of Mississippi, and I do not enjoy being referred to as a hussy by my own grandfather."

But Stella-Rondo says, "Yes, you did say it too. Anybody in the world could of heard you, that had ears."

"Stop right there," says Mama, looking at *me.*

So I pulled my napkin straight back through the napkin ring and left the table.

As soon as I was out of the room Mama says, "Call her back, or she'll starve to death," but Papa-Daddy says, "This is the beard I started growing on the Coast when I was fifteen years old." He would of gone on till nightfall if Shirley-T. hadn't lost the Milky Way she ate in Cairo.

So Papa-Daddy says, "I am going out and lie in the hammock, and you can all sit here and remember my words: I'll never cut off my beard as long as I live, even one inch, and I don't appreciate it in you at all." Passed right by me in the hall and went straight out and got in the hammock.

It would be a holiday. It wasn't five minutes before Uncle Rondo suddenly appeared in the hall in one of Stella-Rondo's flesh-colored kimonos, all cut on the bias, like something Mr. Whitaker probably thought was gorgeous.

"Uncle Rondo!" I says. "I didn't know who that was! Where are you going?"

"Sister," he says, "get out of my way, I'm poisoned."

"If you're poisoned stay away from Papa-Daddy," I says. "Keep out of the hammock. Papa-Daddy will certainly beat you on the head if you come within forty miles of him. He thinks I deliberately said he ought to cut off his beard after he got me the P.O., and I've told him and told him and told him, and he acts like he just don't hear me. Papa-Daddy must of gone stone deaf."

"He picked a fine day to do it then," says Uncle Rondo, and before you could say "Jack Robinson" flew out in the yard.

What he'd really done, he'd drunk another bottle of that prescription. He does it every single Fourth of July as sure as shooting, and it's horribly expensive. Then he falls over in the hammock and snores. So he insisted on zigzagging right on out to the hammock, looking like a half-wit.

Papa-Daddy woke up with this horrible yell and right there without moving an inch he tried to turn Uncle Rondo against me. I heard every word he said. Oh, he told Uncle Rondo I didn't learn to read till I was eight years old and he didn't see how in the world I ever got the mail put up at the P.O., much less read it all, and he said if Uncle Rondo could only fathom the lengths he had gone to to get me that job! And he said on the other hand he thought Stella-Rondo had a brilliant mind and deserved credit for getting out of town. All the time he was just lying there swinging as pretty as you please and looping out his beard, and poor Uncle Rondo was *pleading* with him to slow down the hammock, it was making him as dizzy as a witch to watch it. But that's what Papa-Daddy likes about a hammock. So Uncle Rondo was too dizzy to get turned against me for the time being. He's Mama's only brother and is a good case of a one-track mind. Ask anybody. A certified pharmacist.

Just then I heard Stella-Rondo raising the upstairs window. While she was married she got this peculiar idea that it's cooler with the windows shut and locked. So she has to raise the window before she can make a soul hear her outdoors.

So she raises the window and says, *"Oh!"* You would have thought she was mortally wounded.

Uncle Rondo and Papa-Daddy didn't even look up, but kept right on with what they were doing. I had to laugh.

I flew up the stairs and threw the door open! I says, "What in the wide world's the matter, Stella-Rondo? You mortally wounded?"

"No," she says, "I am not mortally wounded but I wish you would do me the favor of looking out that window there and telling me what you see."

So I shade my eyes and look out the window.

"I see the front yard," I says.

"Don't you see any human beings?" she says.

"I see Uncle Rondo trying to run Papa-Daddy out of the hammock," I says. "Nothing more. Naturally, it's so suffocating-hot in the house, with all the windows shut and locked, everybody who cares to stay in their right mind will have to go out and get in the hammock before the Fourth of July is over."

"Don't you notice anything different about Uncle Rondo?" asks Stella-Rondo.

"Why, no, except he's got on some terrible-looking flesh-colored contraption I wouldn't be found dead in, is all I can see," I says.

"Never mind, you won't be found dead in it, because it happens to be part of my trousseau, and Mr. Whitaker took several dozen photographs of me in it," says Stella-Rondo. "What on earth could Uncle Rondo *mean* by wearing part of my trousseau out in the broad open daylight without saying so much as 'Kiss my foot,' *knowing* I only got home this morning after my separation and hung my negligee up on the bathroom door, just as nervous as I could be?"

"I'm sure I don't know, and what do you expect me to do about it?" I says. "Jump out the window?"

"No, I expect nothing of the kind. I simply declare that Uncle Rondo looks like a fool in it, that's all," she says. "It makes me sick to my stomach."

"Well, he looks as good as he can," I says. "As good as anybody in reason could." I stood up for Uncle Rondo, please remember. And I said to Stella-Rondo, "I think I would do well not to criticize so freely if I were you and came home with a two-year-old child I had never said a word about, and no explanation whatever about my separation."

"I asked you the instant I entered this house not to refer one more time to my adopted child, and you gave me your word of honor you would not," was all Stella-Rondo would say, and started pulling out every one of her eyebrows with some cheap Kress tweezers.

So I merely slammed the door behind me and went down and made some green-tomato pickle. Somebody had to do it. Of course Mama had turned both the niggers loose; she always said no earthly power could hold one anyway on the Fourth of July, so she wouldn't even try. It turned out that Jaypan fell in the lake and came within a very narrow limit of drowning.

So Mama trots in. Lifts up the lid and says, "H'm! Not very good for your Uncle Rondo in his precarious condition, I must say. Or poor little adopted Shirley-T. Shame on you!"

That made me tired. I says, "Well, Stella-Rondo had better thank her lucky stars it was her instead of me came trotting in with that very peculiar-looking child. Now if it had been me that trotted in from Illinois and brought a peculiar-looking child of two, I shudder to think of the reception I'd of got, much less controlled the diet of an entire family."

"But you must remember, Sister, that you were never married to Mr. Whitaker in the first place and didn't go up to Illinois to live," says Mama, shaking a spoon in my face. "If you had I would of been just as overjoyed to see you and your little adopted girl as I was to see Stella-Rondo, when you wound up with your separation and came on back home."

"You would not," I says.

"Don't contradict me, I would," says Mama.

But I said she couldn't convince me though she talked till she was blue in the face. Then I said, "Besides, you know as well as I do that that child is not adopted."

"She most certainly is adopted," says Mama, stiff as a poker.

I says, "Why, Mama, Stella-Rondo had her just as sure as anything in this world, and just too stuck up to admit it."

"Why, Sister," said Mama. "Here I thought we were going to have a pleasant Fourth of July, and you start right out not believing a word your own baby sister tells you!"

"Just like Cousin Annie Flo. Went to her grave denying the facts of life," I remind Mama.

"I told you if you ever mentioned Annie Flo's name I'd slap your face," says Mama, and slaps my face.

"All right, you wait and see," I says.

"I," says Mama, "*I* prefer to take my children's word for anything when it's humanly possible." You ought to see Mama, she weighs two hundred pounds and has real tiny feet.

Just then something perfectly horrible occurred to me.

"Mama," I says, "can that child talk?" I simply had to whisper! "Mama, I wonder if that child can be—you know—in any way? Do you realize," I says, "that she hasn't spoken one single, solitary word to a human being up to the minute? This is the way she looks," I says, and I looked like this.

Well, Mama and I just stood there and stared at each other. It was horrible!

"I remember well that Joe Whitaker frequently drank like a fish," says Mama. "I believed to my soul he drank *chemicals*." And without another word she marches to the foot of the stairs and calls Stella-Rondo.

"Stella-Rondo? O-o-o-o-o! Stella-Rondo!"

"What?" says Stella-Rondo from upstairs. Not even the grace to get up off the bed.

"Can that child of yours talk?" asks Mama.

Stella-Rondo says, "Can she what?"

"Talk! Talk!" says Mama. "Burdyburdyburdyburdy!"

So Stella-Rondo yells back, "Who says she can't talk?"

"Sister says so," says Mama.

"You didn't have to tell me, I know whose word of honor don't mean a thing in this house," says Stella-Rondo.

And in a minute the loudest Yankee voice I ever heard in my life yells out, "OE'm Pop-OE the Sailor-r-r-r Ma-a-an!" and then somebody jumps up and down in the upstairs hall. In another second the house would of fallen down.

"Not only talks, she can tap-dance!" calls Stella-Rondo. "Which is more than some people I won't name can do."

"Why, the little precious darling thing!" Mama says, so surprised. "Just as smart as she can be!" Starts talking baby talk right there. Then she turns on me. "Sister, you ought to be thoroughly ashamed! Run upstairs this instant and apologize to Stella-Rondo and Shirley-T."

"Apologize for what?" I says. "I merely wondered if the child was normal, that's all. Now that she's proved she is, why, I have nothing further to say."

But Mama just turned on her heel and flew out, furious. She ran right upstairs and hugged the baby. She believed it was adopted. Stella-Rondo hadn't done a thing but turn her against me from upstairs while I stood there helpless over the hot stove. So that made Mama, Papa-Daddy and the baby all on Stella-Rondo's side.

Next, Uncle Rondo.

I must say that Uncle Rondo has been marvelous to me at various times in the past and I was completely unprepared to be made to jump out of my skin, the way it turned out. Once Stella-Rondo did something perfectly horrible to him—broke a chain letter from Flanders Field—and he took the radio back he had given her and gave it to me. Stella-Rondo was furious! For six months we all had to call her Stella instead of Stella-Rondo, or she wouldn't answer. I always thought Uncle Rondo had all the brains of the entire family. Another time he sent me to Mammoth Cave, with all expenses paid.

But this would be the day he was drinking that prescription, the Fourth of July.

So at supper Stella-Rondo speaks up and says she thinks Uncle Rondo ought to try to eat a little something. So finally Uncle Rondo said he would try a little cold biscuits and ketchup, but that was all. So *she* brought it to him.

"Do you think it wise to disport with ketchup in Stella-Rondo's flesh-colored kimono?" I says. Trying to be considerate! If Stella-Rondo couldn't watch out for her trousseau, somebody had to.

"Any objections?" asks Uncle Rondo, just about to pour out all the ketchup.

"Don't mind what she says, Uncle Rondo," says Stella-Rondo. "Sister has been devoting this solid afternoon to sneering out my bedroom window at the way you look."

"What's that?" says Uncle Rondo. Uncle Rondo has got the most terrible temper in the world. Anything is liable to make him tear the house down if it comes at the wrong time.

So Stella-Rondo says, "Sister says, 'Uncle Rondo certainly does look like a fool in that pink kimono!' "

Do you remember who it was that really said that?

Uncle Rondo spills out all the ketchup and jumps out of his chair and tears off the kimono and throws it down on the dirty floor and puts his foot on it. It had to be sent all the way to Jackson[2] to the cleaners and re-pleated.

"So that's your opinion of your Uncle Rondo, is it?" he says. "I look like a fool, do I? Well, that's the last straw. A whole day in this house with nothing to do, and then to hear you come out with a remark like that behind my back!"

"I didn't say any such of a thing, Uncle Rondo," I says, "and I'm not saying who did, either. Why, I think you look all right. Just try to take care of yourself and not talk and eat at the same time," I says. "I think you better go lie down."

"Lie down my foot," says Uncle Rondo. I ought to of known by that he was fixing to do something perfectly horrible.

So he didn't do anything that night in the precarious state he was in—just played Casino with Mama and Stella-Rondo and Shirley-T. and gave Shirley-T. a nickel with a head on both sides. It tickled her nearly to death, and she called him "Papa." But at 6:30 A.M. the next morning, he threw a whole five-cent package of some unsold one-inch firecrackers from the store as hard as he could into my bedroom and they every one went off. Not one bad one in the string. Anybody else, there'd be one that wouldn't go off.

Well, I'm just terribly susceptible to noise of any kind, the doctor has always told me I was the most sensitive person he had ever seen in his whole life, and I was simply prostrated. I couldn't eat! People tell me they heard it as far as the cemetery, and old Aunt Jep Patterson, that had been holding her own so good, thought it was Judgment Day and she was going to meet her whole family. It's usually so quiet here.

And I'll tell you it didn't take me any longer than a minute to make up my mind what to do. There I was with the whole entire house on Stella-Rondo's side and turned against me. If I have anything at all I have pride.

So I just decided I'd go straight down to the P.O. There's plenty of room there in the back, I says to myself.

Well! I made no bones about letting the family catch on to what I was up to. I didn't try to conceal it.

The first thing they knew, I marched in where they were all playing Old Maid and pulled the electric oscillating fan out by the plug, and everything got real hot. Next I snatched the pillow I'd done the needlepoint on right off the davenport from behind Papa-Daddy. He went

[2] Jackson, Mississippi, the state capital.

"Ugh!" I beat Stella-Rondo up the stairs and finally found my charm bracelet in her bureau drawer under a picture of Nelson Eddy.[3]

"So that's the way the land lies," says Uncle Rondo. There he was, piecing on the ham. "Well, Sister, I'll be glad to donate my army cot if you got any place to set it up, providing you'll leave right this minute and let me get some peace." Uncle Rondo was in France.

"Thank you kindly for the cot and 'peace' is hardly the word I would select if I had to resort to firecrackers at 6:30 A.M. in a young girl's bedroom," I says back to him. "And as to where I intend to go, you seem to forget my position as postmistress of China Grove, Mississippi," I says. "I've always got the P.O."

Well, that made them all sit up and take notice.

I went out front and started digging up some four o'clocks to plant around the P.O.

"Ah-ah-ah!" says Mama, raising the window. "Those happen to be my four-o'clocks. Everything planted in that star is mine. I've never known you to make anything grow in your life."

"Very well," I says. "But I take the fern. Even you, Mama, can't stand there and deny that I'm the one watered that fern. And I happen to know where I can send in a box top and get a packet of one thousand mixed seeds, no two the same kind, free."

"Oh, where?" Mama wants to know.

But I says, "Too late. You 'tend to your house, and I'll 'tend to mine. You hear things like that all the time if you know how to listen to the radio. Perfectly marvelous offers. Get anything you want free."

So I hope to tell you I marched in and got that radio, and they could of all bit a nail in two, especially Stella-Rondo, that it used to belong to, and she well knew she couldn't get it back, I'd sue for it like a shot. And I very politely took the sewing-machine motor I helped pay the most on to give Mama for Christmas back in 1929, and a good big calendar, with the first-aid remedies on it. The thermometer and the Hawaiian ukulele certainly were rightfully mine, and I stood on the step-ladder and got all my watermelon-rind preserves and every fruit and vegetable I'd put up, every jar. Then I began to pull the tacks out of the bluebird wall vases on the archway to the dining room.

"Who told you you could have those, Miss Priss?" says Mama, fanning as hard as she could.

"I bought 'em and I'll keep track of 'em," I says. "I'll tack 'em up one on each side the post-office window, and you can see 'em when you come to ask me for your mail, if you're so dead to see 'em."

"Not I! I'll never darken the door to that post office again if I live

[3] Nelson Eddy (1901–1967) was a singer and screen actor who appeared with Jeanette MacDonald in many film musicals. He was known for his good looks and light operatic voice.

to be a hundred," Mama says. "Ungrateful child! After all the money we spent on you at the Normal."[4]

"Me either," says Stella-Rondo. "You can just let my mail lie there and *rot,* for all I care. I'll never come and relieve you of a single, solitary piece."

"I should worry," I says. "And who you think's going to sit down and write you all those big fat letters and postcards, by the way? Mr. Whitaker? Just because he was the only man ever dropped down in China Grove and you got him—unfairly—is he going to sit down and write you a lengthy correspondence after you come home giving no rhyme nor reason whatsoever for your separation and no explanation for the presence of that child? I may not have your brilliant mind, but I fail to see it."

So Mama says, "Sister, I've told you a thousand times that Stella-Rondo simply got homesick, and this child is far too big to be hers," and she says, "Now, why don't you all just sit down and play Casino?"

Then Shirley-T. sticks out her tongue at me in this perfectly horrible way. She has no more manners than the man in the moon. I told her she was going to cross her eyes like that some day and they'd stick.

"It's too late to stop me now," I says. "You should have tried that yesterday. I'm going to the P.O. and the only way you can possibly see me is to visit me there."

So Papa-Daddy says, "You'll never catch me setting foot in that post office, even if I should take a notion into my head to write a letter some place." He says, "I won't have you reachin' out of that little old window with a pair of shears and cuttin' off any beard of mine. I'm too smart for you!"

"We all are," says Stella-Rondo.

But I said, "If you're so smart, where's Mr. Whitaker?"

So then Uncle Rondo says, "I'll thank you from now on to stop reading all the orders I get on postcards and telling everybody in China Grove what you think is the matter with them," but I says, "I draw my own conclusions and will continue in the future to draw them." I says, "If people want to write their inmost secrets on penny postcards, there's nothing in the wide world you can do about it, Uncle Rondo."

"And if you think we'll ever *write* another postcard you're sadly mistaken," says Mama.

"Cutting off your nose to spite your face then," I says. "But if you're all determined to have no more to do with the U.S. mail, think of this: What will Stella-Rondo do now, if she wants to tell Mr. Whitaker to come after her?"

"Wah!" says Stella-Rondo. I knew she'd cry. She had a conniption fit right there in the kitchen.

[4] Normal is short for Normal School or Teachers College.

"It will be interesting to see how long she holds out," I says. "And now—I am leaving."

"Good-bye," says Uncle Rondo.

"Oh, I declare," says Mama, "to think that a family of mine should quarrel on the Fourth of July, or the day after, over Stella-Rondo leaving old Mr. Whitaker and having the sweetest little adopted child! It looks like we'd all be glad!"

"Wah!" says Stella-Rondo, and has a fresh conniption fit.

"*He* left *her*—you mark my words," I says. "That's Mr. Whitaker. I know Mr. Whitaker. After all, I knew him first. I said from the beginning he'd up and leave her. I foretold every single thing that's happened."

"Where did he go?" asks Mama.

"Probably to the North Pole, if he knows what's good for him," I says.

But Stella-Rondo just bawled and wouldn't say another word. She flew to her room and slammed the door.

"Now look what you've gone and done, Sister," says Mama. "You go apologize."

"I haven't got time, I'm leaving," I says.

"Well, what are you waiting around for?" asks Uncle Rondo.

So I just picked up the kitchen clock and marched off, without saying "Kiss my foot" or anything, and never did tell Stella-Rondo good-bye.

There was a nigger girl going along on a little wagon right in front.

"Nigger girl," I says, "come help me haul these things down the hill, I'm going to live in the post office."

Took her nine trips in her express wagon. Uncle Rondo came out on the porch and threw her a nickel.

And that's the last I've laid eyes on any of my family or my family laid eyes on me for five solid days and nights. Stella-Rondo may be telling the most horrible tales in the world about Mr. Whitaker, but I haven't heard them. As I tell everybody, I draw my own conclusions.

But oh, I like it here. It's ideal, as I've been saying. You see, I've got everything cater-cornered, the way I like it. Hear the radio? All the war news. Radio, sewing machine, book ends, ironing board and that great big piano lamp—peace, that's what I like. Butter-bean vines planted all along the front where the strings are.

Of course, there's not much mail. My family are naturally the main people in China Grove, and if they prefer to vanish from the face of the earth, for all the mail they get or the mail they write, why, I'm not going to open my mouth. Some of the folks here in town are taking up for me and some turned against me. I know which is which. There are always people who will quit buying stamps just to get on the right side of Papa-Daddy.

But here I am, and here I'll stay. I want the world to know I'm happy.

And if Stella-Rondo should come to me this minute, on bended knees, and *attempt* to explain the incidents of her life with Mr. Whitaker, I'd simply put my fingers in both my ears and refuse to listen.

QUESTIONS

1. Who is the speaker of the story? What do you imagine is Eudora Welty's attitude toward the narrator?
2. To whom is the narrator talking? What sort of listener is implied by her tale? Does the narrator believe the listener is on her side or Papa-Daddy's side of this family squabble?
3. For whom did Eudora Welty intend this story? What kind of reader do you think Welty had in mind? Are you that type of reader?
4. What is the speaker's attitude toward Stella-Rondo? Is her attitude unusual for a sister?
5. Why does the narrator live at the P.O.? Could she live anywhere else?
6. The narrator says that she listens to the "war news" on the radio. When is the story set? Does the historical setting change your attitude toward the family feud? Is there any sense in which the narrator has already "put [her] fingers in both [her] ears and refuse[d] to listen"?

EUDORA WELTY

from ONE WRITER'S BEGINNINGS

In that vanished time in small-town Jackson,[1] most of the ladies I was familiar with, the mothers of my friends in the neighborhood, were busiest when they were sociable. In the afternoons there was regular visiting up and down the little grid of residential streets. Everybody had calling cards, even certain children; and newborn babies themselves were properly announced by sending out their tiny engraved calling cards attached with a pink or blue bow to those of their parents. Graduation presents to high-school pupils were often "card cases." On the hall table in every house the first thing you saw was a silver tray waiting to receive more calling cards on top of the stack already piled up like jackstraws; they were never thrown away.

My mother let none of this idling, as she saw it, pertain to her; she went her own way with or without her calling cards, and though she was fond of her friends and they were fond of her, she had little time for small talk. At first, I hadn't known what I'd missed.

When we at length bought our first automobile, one of our neighbors was often invited to go with us on the family Sunday afternoon ride. In Jackson it was counted an affront to the neighbors to start out for anywhere with an empty seat in the car. My mother sat in the back

[1] Jackson is the capital of Mississippi.

with her friend, and I'm told that as a small child I would ask to sit in the middle, and say as we started off, "Now *talk.*"

There was dialogue throughout the lady's accounts to my mother. "I said" . . . "He said" . . . "And I'm told she very plainly said" . . . "It was midnight before they finally heard, and what do you think it *was?*"

What I loved about her stories was that everything happened in *scenes.* I might not catch on to what the root of the trouble was in all that happened, but my ear told me it was dramatic. Often she said, "The crisis had come!"

This same lady was one of Mother's callers on the telephone who always talked a long time. I knew who it was when my mother would only reply, now and then, "Well, I declare," or "You don't say so," or "Surely not." She'd be standing at the wall telephone, listening against her will, and I'd sit on the stairs close by her. Our telephone had a little bar set into the handle which had to be pressed and held down to keep the connection open, and when her friend had said goodbye, my mother needed me to prize her fingers loose from the little bar; her grip had become paralyzed. "What did she say?" I asked.

"She wasn't *saying* a thing in this world," sighed my mother. "She was just ready to talk, that's all."

My mother was right. Years later, beginning with my story "Why I Live at the P.O.," I wrote reasonably often in the form of a monologue that takes possession of the speaker. How much more gets told besides!

This lady told everything in her sweet, marveling voice, and meant every word of it kindly. She enjoyed my company perhaps even more than my mother's. She invited me to catch her doodlebugs; under the trees in her backyard were dozens of their holes. When you stuck a broom straw down one and called, "Doodlebug, doodlebug, your house is on fire and all your children are burning up," she believed this is why the doodlebug came running out of the hole. This was why I loved to call up her doodlebugs instead of ours.

My mother could never have told me her stories, and I think I knew why even then: my mother didn't believe them.

THINGS TO THINK ABOUT

1. While you were growing up, did you know any unusual adults who were memorable characters? What were they like? What did you learn from them?
2. Did you ever eavesdrop on your parents' conversations with their friends? What did they talk about? What did you hope to hear? What did you learn?
3. Some of the most interesting people to listen to are people who may

not be telling the truth. Have you ever known fascinating liars? What were they like? What was the biggest "whopper" you have ever heard? What's the biggest whopper you've ever told?

4. What makes one person more interesting to listen to than another? Think about the teachers you've had in the past. What made one teacher more interesting than another?

EDGAR ALLAN POE

THE CASK OF AMONTILLADO

Edgar Allan Poe (1809–1849) has come to represent the epitome of the decadent, impoverished, drunken writer, and his life has been made to seem as lurid as his fiction. Orphaned as a child (his parents had been travelling actors), he was informally adopted by John Allen, a wealthy Southern merchant. He studied at The University of Virginia and West Point, and was thrown out of both. He married his cousin Virginia Clemm, who was then only thirteen, and whose death eleven years later sent Poe into a physical and emotional decline from which he never recovered. At the age of forty, he was found unconscious on a street in Baltimore—whether from alcohol or foul play it has never been determined—and he died a few days after.

In his short life he contributed to three different literary forms. As a critic, he developed ideas of composition which were to influence not only American, but also French literature. As a short story writer, he not only helped create its modern form, but almost single-handed brought into existence the detective story. As a poet, he undertook experiments in sound and prosody that influenced Baudelaire, Mallarmé and others. During his brief, fragmented and harried life, he was unusually productive and influential.

The thousand injuries of Fortunato I had borne as I best could, but when he ventured upon insult, I vowed revenge. You, who so well know the nature of my soul, will not suppose, however, that I gave utterance to a threat. *At length* I would be avenged; this was a point definitely settled—but the very definitiveness with which it was resolved precluded the idea of risk. I must not only punish, but punish with impunity. A wrong is unredressed when retribution overtakes its redresser. It is equally unredressed when the avenger fails to make himself felt as such to him who has done the wrong.

It must be understood that neither by word nor deed had I given Fortunato cause to doubt my good will. I continued, as was my wont, to smile in his face, and he did not perceive that my smile *now* was at the thought of his immolation.

He had a weak point—this Fortunato—although in other regards he was a man to be respected and even feared. He prided himself on his connoisseurship in wine. Few Italians have the true virtuoso spirit. For the most part their enthusiasm is adopted to suit the time and opportunity to practice imposture upon the British and Austrian *millionaires*. In painting and gemmary[1] Fortunato, like his countrymen, was a quack, but in the matter of old wines he was sincere. In this respect I did not differ from him materially;—I was skillful in the Italian vintages myself, and bought largely whenever I could.

It was about dusk, one evening during the supreme madness of the carnival season, that I encountered my friend. He accosted me with excessive warmth, for he had been drinking much. The man wore motley. He had on a tight-fitting parti-striped dress, and his head was surmounted by the conical cap and bells.[2] I was so pleased to see him, that I thought I should never have done wringing his hand.

I said to him—"My dear Fortunato, you are luckily met. How remarkably well you are looking to-day! But I have received a pipe[3] of what passes for Amontillado,[4] and I have my doubts."

"How?" said he, "Amontillado? A pipe? Impossible! And in the middle of the carnival?"[5]

"I have my doubts," I replied; "and I was silly enough to pay the full Amontillado price without consulting you in the matter. You were not to be found, and I was fearful of losing a bargain."

"Amontillado!"

"I have my doubts."

"Amontillado!"

"And I must satisfy them."

"Amontillado!"

"As you are engaged, I am on my way to Luchesi. If any one has a critical turn, it is he. He will tell me—"

"Luchesi cannot tell Amontillado from Sherry."

"And yet some fools will have it that his taste is a match for your own."

"Come, let us go."

"Whither?"

"To your vaults."

"My friend, no; I will not impose upon your good nature. I perceive you have an engagement. Luchesi—"

"I have no engagement; come."

"My friend, no. It is not the engagement, but the severe cold with which I perceive you are afflicted. The vaults are insufferably damp. They are encrusted with nitre."[6]

"Let us go, nevertheless. The cold is merely nothing. Amontillado!

[1] Gemmary is the art of gem cutting and gem engraving.

[2] In short, he is dressed like a clown.

[3] A pipe is a wine cask.

[4] Amontillado is a specific type of sherry made from grapes grown on the slopes of the Sierra de Montilla, south of Córdoba, Spain.

[5] The carnival or *Mardi Gras* is a yearly festival celebrated before Lent.

[6] Nitre is a mineral of potassium nitrate, appearing as a saltlike crust on rocks and stone.

You have been imposed upon; and as for Luchesi, he cannot distinguish Sherry from Amontillado."

Thus speaking, Fortunato possessed himself of my arm. Putting on a mask of black silk, and drawing a *roquelaure*[7] closely about my person, I suffered him to hurry me to my palazzo.[8]

There were no attendants at home; they had absconded to make merry in honor of the time. I had told them that I should not return until the morning, and had given them explicit orders not to stir from the house. These orders were sufficient, I well knew, to insure their immediate disappearance, one and all, as soon as my back was turned.

I took from their sconces two flambeaux, and giving one to Fortunato, bowed him through several suites of rooms to the archway that led into the vaults. I passed down a long and winding staircase, requesting him to be cautious as he followed. We came at length to the foot of the descent, and stood together on the damp ground of the catacombs of the Montresors.

The gait of my friend was unsteady, and the bells upon his cap jingled as he strode.

"The pipe," said he.

"It is farther on," said I; "but observe the white web-work which gleams from these cavern walls."

He turned towards me, and looked into my eyes with two filmy orbs that distilled the rheum of intoxication.

"Nitre?" he asked, at length.

"Nitre," I replied. "How long have you had that cough?"

"Ugh! ugh! ugh!—ugh! ugh! ugh!—ugh! ugh! ugh!—ugh! ugh! ugh!—ugh! ugh! ugh!"

My poor friend found it impossible to reply for many minutes.

"It is nothing," he said, at last.

"Come," I said, with decision, "we will go back; your health is precious. You are rich, respected, admired, beloved; you are happy, as once I was. You are a man to be missed. For me it is no matter. We will go back; you will be ill, and I cannot be responsible. Besides, there is Luchesi—"

"Enough," he said; "the cough is a mere nothing; it will not kill me. I shall not die of a cough."

"True—true," I replied; "and, indeed, I had no intention of alarming you unnecessarily—but you should use all proper caution. A draught of this Medoc[9] will defend us from the damps."

Here I knocked off the neck of a bottle which I drew from a long row of its fellows that lay upon the mould.

"Drink," I said, presenting him the wine.

[7] A roquelaure is a short cape.

[8] A palatial residence; a mansion.

[9] Medoc is a red Bordeaux wine made in the Medoc region of southwestern France.

He raised it to his lips with a leer. He paused and nodded to me familiarly, while his bells jingled.

"I drink," he said, "to the buried that repose around us."

"And I to your long life."

He again took my arm, and we proceeded.

"These vaults," he said, "are extensive."

"The Montresors," I replied, "were a great and numerous family."

"I forget your arms."

"A huge human foot d'or, in a field azure; the foot crushes a serpent rampant whose fangs are imbedded in the heel."

"And the motto?"

"Nemo me impune lacessit."[10]

"Good!" he said.

The wine sparkled in his eyes and the bells jingled. My own fancy grew warm with the Medoc. We had passed through walls of piled bones, with casks and puncheons intermingling, into the inmost recesses of the catacombs. I paused again, and this time I made bold to seize Fortunato by an arm above the elbow.

"The nitre!" I said; "see, it increases. It hangs like moss upon the vaults. We are below the river's bed. The drops of moisture trickle among the bones. Come, we will go back ere it is too late. Your cough—"

"It is nothing," he said; "let us go on. But first, another draught of the Medoc."

I broke and reached him a flagon of De Grâve.[11] He emptied it at a breath. His eyes flashed with a fierce light. He laughed and threw the bottle upwards with a gesticulation I did not understand.

I looked at him in surprise. He repeated the movement—a grotesque one.

"You do not comprehend?" he said.

"Not I," I replied.

"Then you are not of the brotherhood."[12]

"How?"

"You are not of the masons."

"Yes, yes," I said, "yes, yes."

"You? Impossible! A mason?"

"A mason," I replied.

"A sign," he said.

"It is this," I answered, producing a trowel from beneath the folds of my *roquelaure.*

"You jest," he exclaimed, recoiling a few paces. "But let us proceed to the Amontillado."

[10] The motto *"Nemo me impune lacessit"* means "No one dare attack me with impunity."

[11] De Grave is another French wine.

[12] The Freemasons are a secret sect of mystical persuasion whose origins go back at least to the 14th century. They were often hounded and imprisoned.

"Be it so," I said, replacing the tool beneath the cloak, and again offering him my arm. He leaned upon it heavily. We continued our route in search of the Amontillado. We passed through a range of low arches, descended, passed on, and descending again, arrived at a deep crypt, in which the foulness of the air caused our flambeaux rather to glow than flame.

At the most remote end of the crypt there appeared another less spacious. Its walls had been lined with human remains piled to the vault overhead, in the fashion of the great catacombs of Paris. Three sides of this interior crypt were still ornamented in this manner. From the fourth the bones had been thrown down, and lay promiscuously upon the earth, forming at one point a mound of some size. Within the wall thus exposed by the displacing of the bones, we perceived a still interior recess, in depth about four feet, in width three, in height six or seven. It seemed to have been constructed for no especial use within itself, but formed merely the interval between two of the colossal supports of the roof of the catacombs, and was backed by one of their circumscribing walls of solid granite.

It was in vain that Fortunato, uplifting his dull torch, endeavored to pry into the depths of the recess. Its termination the feeble light did not enable us to see.

"Proceed," I said; "herein is the Amontillado. As for Luchesi—"

"He is an ignoramus," interrupted my friend, as he stepped unsteadily forward, while I followed immediately at his heels. In an instant he had reached the extremity of the niche, and finding his progress arrested by the rock, stood stupidly bewildered. A moment more and I had fettered him to the granite. In its surface were two iron staples, distant from each other about two feet, horizontally. From one of these depended a short chain, from the other a padlock. Throwing the links about his waist, it was but the work of a few seconds to secure it. He was too much astounded to resist. Withdrawing the key I stepped back from the recess.

"Pass your hand," I said, "over the wall; you cannot help feeling the nitre. Indeed it is *very* damp. Once more let me *implore* you to return. No? Then I must positively leave you. But I must first render you all the little attentions in my power."

"The Amontillado!" ejaculated my friend, not yet recovered from his astonishment.

"True," I replied; "the Amontillado."

As I said these words I busied myself among the pile of bones of which I have before spoken. Throwing them aside, I soon uncovered a quantity of buildingstone and mortar. With these materials and with the aid of my trowel, I began vigorously to wall up the entrance of the niche.

I had scarcely laid the first tier of masonry when I discovered that the intoxication of Fortunato had in a great measure worn off. The earliest indication I had of this was a low moaning cry from the depth of the recess. It was *not* the cry of a drunken man. There was then a long and obstinate silence. I laid the second tier, and the third, and the fourth; and then I heard the furious vibrations of the chain. The noise lasted for several minutes, during which, that I might hearken to it with the more satisfaction, I ceased my labors and sat down upon the bones. When at last the clanking subsided, I resumed the trowel, and finished without interruption the fifth, the sixth, and the seventh tier. The wall was now nearly upon a level with my breast. I again paused, and holding the flambeaux over the masonwork, threw a few feeble rays upon the figure within.

A succession of loud and shrill screams, bursting suddenly from the throat of the chained form, seemed to thrust me violently back. For a brief moment I hesitated—I trembled. Unsheathing my rapier, I began to grope with it about the recess; but the thought of an instant reassured me. I placed my hand upon the solid fabric of the catacombs, and felt satisfied. I reapproached the wall. I replied to the yells of him who clamored. I re-echoed—I aided—I surpassed them in volume and in strength. I did this, and the clamorer grew still.

It was now midnight, and my task was drawing to a close. I had completed the eighth, the ninth, and the tenth tier. I had finished a portion of the last and the eleventh; there remained but a single stone to be fitted and plastered in. I struggled with its weight; I placed it partially in its destined position. But now there came from out the niche a low laugh that erected the hairs upon my head. It was succeeded by a sad voice, which I had difficulty in recognizing as that of the noble Fortunato. The voice said—

"Ha! ha! ha!—he! he! he!—a very good joke indeed—an excellent jest. We will have many a rich laugh about it at the palazzo—he! he! he!—over our wine—he! he! he!"

"The Amontillado!" I said.

"He! he! he!—he! he! he!—yes, the Amontillado. But is it not getting late? Will not they be awaiting us at the palazzo, the Lady Fortunato and the rest? Let us be gone."

"Yes," I said, "let us be gone."

"For the love of God, Montresor!"

"Yes," I said, "for the love of God!"

But to these words I hearkened in vain for a reply. I grew impatient. I called aloud;

"Fortunato!"

No answer. I called again;

"Fortunato!"

No answer still, I thrust a torch through the remaining aperture and let it fall within. There came forth in return only a jingling of the bells. My heart grew sick—on account of the dampness of the catacombs.

I hastened to make an end of my labor. I forced the last stone into its position; I plastered it up. Against the new masonry I reerected the old rampart of bones. For the half of a century no mortal had disturbed them. *In pace requiescat!*[13]

QUESTIONS

1. Who is the speaker of this story? What is the relationship between the narrator and Poe? Do Poe and the narrator necessarily hold the same notions?
2. To whom is the narrator speaking? Can we tell why he is speaking? Does the narrator provide an adequate motive for revenge?
3. For whom is Poe writing? Are the narrator's listeners and Poe's readers the same people? If not the same, how are they different? Is this difference greater than the similarities?
4. "The Cask of Amontillado" is set in Italy rather than in America. To Americans of the nineteenth century Italy was a distant land of intrigue and brutal passion. How would that attitude affect the readers of this story?
5. Would the effect of "The Cask of Amontillado" be heightened or lessened if set, for instance, in New Orleans?

EDGAR ALLAN POE

UNITY OF EFFECT

The tale proper, in my opinion, affords unquestionably the fairest field for the exercise of the loftiest talent which can be afforded by the wide domains of mere prose. Were I bidden to say how the highest genius could be most advantageously employed for the best display of its own powers, I should answer, without hesitation—in the composition of a rhymed poem, not to exceed in length what might be perused in an hour. Within this limit alone can the highest order of true poetry exist. I need only here say, upon this topic, that, in almost all classes of composition, the unity of effect or impression is a point of the greatest importance. It is clear, moreover, that this unity cannot be thoroughly preserved in productions whose perusal cannot be completed at one sitting. We may continue the reading of a prose composition, from the very nature of prose itself, much longer than we can persevere, to any good purpose, in the perusal of a poem. This latter, if truly fulfilling the demands of the poetic sentiment, induces an exaltation of the soul which cannot be long sustained. All high excitements are necessarily transient. Thus a long poem is a paradox. And, without unity of impression, the deepest effects cannot be brought about. Epics were the offspring of an imperfect sense of Art, and their reign is no more. A poem *too* brief may produce a vivid, but never an intense or enduring impression. Without a certain

[13] The Latin *"in pace requiescat"* means "May he rest in peace."

continuity of effect—without a certain duration or repetition of purpose—the soul is never deeply moved. There must be the dropping of the water upon the rock. De Beranger has wrought brilliant things—pungent and spirit-stirring—but, like all immassive bodies, they lack *momentum,* and thus fail to satisfy the Poetic Sentiment. They sparkle and excite, but, from want of continuity, fail deeply to impress. Extreme brevity will degenerate into epigrammatism; but the sin of extreme length is even more unpardonable. *In medio tutissimus ibis.*

Were I called upon, however, to designate that class of composition which, next to such a poem as I have suggested should best fulfil the demands of high genius—should offer it the most advantageous field of exertion—I should unhesitatingly speak of the prose tale. . . .

I allude to the short prose narrative, requiring from a half-hour to one or two hours in its perusal. The ordinary novel is objectionable, from its length, for reasons already stated in substance. As it cannot be read at one sitting, it deprives itself, of course, of the immense force derivable from *totality.* Worldly interests intervening during the pauses of perusal, modify, annul, or counteract, in a greater or less degree, the impressions of the book. But simple cessation in reading would, of itself, be sufficient to destroy the true unity. In the brief tale, however, the author is enabled to carry out the fulness of his intention, be it what it may. During the hour of perusal the soul of the reader is at the writer's control. There are no external or extrinsic influences—resulting from weariness or interruption.

A skilful literary artist has constructed a tale. If wise, he has not fashioned his thoughts to accommodate his incidents; but having conceived, with deliberate care, a certain unique or single *effect* to be wrought out, he then invents such incidents—he then combines such events as may best aid him in establishing this preconceived effect. If his very initial sentence tends not to the outbringing of this effect, then he has failed in his first step. In the whole composition there should be no word written, of which the tendency, direct or indirect, is not to the one pre-established design. And by such means, with such care and skill, a picture is at length painted which leaves in the mind of him who contemplates it with a kindred art, a sense of the fullest satisfaction. The idea of the tale has been presented unblemished, because undisturbed; and this is an end unattainable by the novel. Undue brevity is just as exceptionable here as in the poem; but undue length is yet more to be avoided.

We have said that the tale has a point of superiority even over the poem. In fact, while the *rhythm* of this latter is an essential aid in the development of the poem's highest idea—the idea of the Beautiful—the artificialities of this rhythm are an inseparable bar to the development of all points of thought or expression which have their basis in *Truth.* But Truth is often, and in very great degree, the aim of the tale. Some of the finest tales are tales of ratiocination. Thus the field of this species of composition, if not in so elevated a region on the Mountain of Mind, is a table-land of far vaster extent than the domain of the mere poem. Its products are never so rich but infinitely more numerous, and more appreciable by the mass of mankind. The writer of the prose tale, in short, may bring to his theme a vast variety of modes or inflections of thought and expression—(the ratiocinative, for example, the sarcastic, or the humorous) which are not only antagonistical to the nature of the poem, but absolutely forbidden by one of its most peculiar and indispensable adjuncts; we allude, of course, to rhythm. It may be added, here, *par parenthèse,* that the author who aims at the purely beautiful in a prose tale is labouring at a great disadvantage. For Beauty can be better treated in the poem. Not so with terror, or passion, or horror, or a multitude of such other points. And here it will be seen how full of prejudice are the usual animadversions against those *tales of effect.* . . .

The impressions produced were wrought in a legitimate sphere of action, and constituted a legitimate although sometimes an exaggerated interest. They were relished by every man of genius: although there were found many men of genius who condemned them without just ground. The true critic will but demand that the design intended be accomplished, to the fullest extent, by the means most advantageously applicable.

THINGS TO THINK ABOUT

1. What effect do you think Poe intended to have on his readers of "The Cask of Amontillado"? Was he successful in creating that effect in you?
2. What sort of elements are in the story that heighten Poe's desired effect? Are there any details that seem to contradict or dilute the effect?
3. What effects do you hope to achieve in your writing? What elements would best achieve those effects? Why do you want to achieve such effects? Are the effects worth achieving?

JULIO CORTÁZAR

CONTINUITY OF PARKS

Julio Cortázar (1914–1984) was born in Brussels, Belgium, but reared in Argentina, and he became the first of the great South American novelists to gain recognition in the United States. However, after 1951 and the rise of Juan Peron, he moved to Paris where he lived most of the remaining years of his life.

Like Borges—a fellow Argentinean—and Kafka, Cortázar is a relentless experimenter whose work has a dream-like wonder and horror. The chapters of his most famous novel Hopscotch *can be read in a number of sequences and were designed so that one could "hopscotch" through the book. But for all his playfulness, Cortázar was a serious and affecting writer.*

He had begun to read the novel a few days before. He had put it down because of some urgent business conferences, opened it again on his way back to the estate by train; he permitted himself a slowly growing interest in the plot, in the characterizations. That afternoon, after writing a letter giving his power of attorney and discussing a matter of joint ownership with the manager of his estate, he returned to the book in the tranquillity of his study which looked out upon the park with its oaks. Sprawled in his favorite armchair, its back toward the door—even the possibility of an intrusion would have irritated him, had he thought of it—he let his left hand caress repeatedly the green velvet upholstery and set to reading the final chapters. He remembered effortlessly the names and his mental image of the characters; the novel spread its glamour over him almost at once. He tasted the almost perverse pleasure of disengaging himself line by line from the things around him, and at the same time feeling his head rest comfortably on the green velvet of the chair with its high back, sensing that the cigarettes rested within reach of his hand, that beyond the great windows the air of afternoon danced under the oak trees in the park. Word by word, licked up by the sordid dilemma of the hero and heroine, letting himself be absorbed to the point where the images settled down and took on color and movement, he was witness to the final encounter in the mountain cabin. The woman arrived first, apprehensive; now the lover came in, his face cut by the backlash of a branch. Admirably, she stanched the blood with her kisses, but he rebuffed her caresses, he had not come to perform again the ceremonies of a secret passion, protected by a world of dry leaves and furtive paths through the forest. The dagger warmed itself against his chest, and underneath liberty pounded, hidden close. A lustful, panting dialogue raced down the pages like a rivulet of snakes, and one felt it had all been decided from eternity. Even to those caresses which writhed about the lover's body, as though wishing to keep him there, to dissuade him from it; they sketched abominably the frame of that other body it was necessary to destroy. Nothing had been forgotten: alibis, unforeseen hazards, possible mistakes. From this hour on, each instant had its use minutely assigned. The cold-blooded, twice-gone-over reexamination of the details was barely broken off so that a hand could caress a cheek. It was beginning to get dark.

Not looking at one another now, rigidly fixed upon the task which awaited them, they separated at the cabin door. She was to follow the trail that led north. On the path leading in the opposite direction, he turned for a moment to watch her running, her hair loosened and flying. He ran in turn, crouching among the trees and hedges until, in the yellowish fog of dusk, he could distinguish the avenue of trees which led up to the house. The dogs were not supposed to bark, they did not bark. The estate manager would not be there at this hour, and he was not there. He went up the three porch steps and entered. The woman's words reached him over the thudding of blood in his ears: first a blue chamber, then a hall, then a carpeted stairway. At the top, two doors. No one in the first room, no one in the second. The door of the salon, and then, the knife in hand, the light from the great windows, the high back of an armchair covered in green velvet, the head of the man in the chair reading a novel.

QUESTIONS

1. Did you find the end of "Continuity of Parks" a surprise? If so, where were you surprised? How has Cortázar arranged the events of the story in order to surprise the reader? If you were not surprised, how did Cortázar tip his hand to you?
2. Why do you suppose the main character—on the very afternoon he finishes the novel—writes "a letter giving his power of attorney" and discusses "a matter of joint ownership with the manager of the estate"? Is the ending of the novel as much a surprise to the main character as it is to you?
3. Is there any sense in which as readers of "Continuity of Parks" we become Cortázar's victims? How does the story depict the relationship between author and reader?
4. In what senses does identifying with characters in a story become a "fatal" way to read?
5. For what reader is the novel in "Continuity of Parks" written? Who are Cortázar's intended readers?
6. Has anything happened in recent South American affairs that would explain Cortázar's blurring of the relationship between fiction and reality?

2
FICTION AND EXPERIENCE

When I read for pleasure, I try to sit down in a quiet and comfortable place, a place where I can give my complete attention to my book. With the very first words I read a voice comes into my head. The voice can be a journalist's or a scientist's, an essayist's or a philosopher's. Or it could be the voice of a narrator telling me a story. The opening of a story is an invitation to go on a voyage of discovery, and if the narrator doesn't show that the voyage will be worth taking, I close the book and choose another one. Of course, I don't always have that luxury of closing a book. Like business people and students, I am often obliged to read assigned works, reports, papers, and articles. But novelists rarely, if ever, expect their books to become assigned reading. They know they must win over their readers.

If reading is a journey, where can the narrator take us? Anywhere. Since a story is fiction, the storyteller is not constrained by facts of history or geography. We can go back before the beginning of time or far into the future. We can meet with talking animals, extra-terrestrial creatures, the neighbor's cat or man-eating sharks. Narrators like Milton and Dante take us to Heaven and Hell, and Jules Verne takes us to the center of the earth. Space, time and the laws of physics and biology mean nothing to the fiction writer who is governed only by the conventions of literature and the dictates of the imagination.

FICTION AND ESCAPISM

The journey that readers take with the narrator is not an escape from life. The main character of Julio Cortázar's "Continuity of Parks" settles down with his book and tastes "the almost perverse pleasure of disengaging himself line by line from the things around him," but his sense of escape is illusory. In fact, the novel he reads is about his own life, and it will end with an account of his own death.

Writers, particularly of science fiction, will write about events far in the future to reveal the ultimate effects of developments in the present. Aldous Huxley wrote *Brave New World* about the effects of genetic engineering when such practices were not even in their infancy. Huxley's fantasy was meant to help people understand what implications new technology had for the future. His work is not an escape from life, but an exploration of what the human future might be. Similarly, some authors write about nearly perfect worlds, Utopias, as a way of imagining goals to which readers might strive or ideals readers might obtain. Finally, for political reasons, authors may find it easier to write about dictatorial wolves and defenceless sheep than to write about real dictators and terrorized citizens. This chapter includes Gabriel García Márquez's "A Very Old Man With Enormous Wings." It tells the story of a fallen angel. But though the story is fanciful, its implications are serious. It indicates how institutions try to deny what they can't control and how people ignore the truly miraculous things around them for the merely sensational and odd.

Moreover, people enjoy hearing stories that present a world that is more exciting, more awe-inspiring, more adventurous, and more peaceful than the one in which they live. Fictional worlds are not merely occasions for escaping the dull routine of everyday life, but can show us a better way to live, a vision of the future perhaps. The writer asks, "what if. . . ." What if we tried to build a better world, what would it be like? How would we behave if we met up with a murderer? A miracle? A mother-in-law from another culture? Or a dangerous social ritual?

THE RISE OF REALISM

Writers before the nineteenth century were generally unconcerned about the factual authenticity of their work. In his historical plays, Shakespeare takes enormous liberties with fact and seems entirely unbothered by documentary evidence. But in the nineteenth century, writers began to make a serious effort to restrict the events depicted in a story to those that might or could actually happen. These writers called themselves *realists,* and they worked hard to present accurately the time and place where the actions of their stories occurred. Writers began to do research before writing. They would check to make sure that geographic and historical references were correct. The novelist George Eliot compiled an entire notebook of historical data so that every detail of her masterpiece *Middlemarch* would be true to life. Working with a map of Dublin, a street car schedule and a stop watch, James Joyce kept track of his characters in his novel *Ulysses,* making certain they could move from place to place in the time allotted them in the novel. When he wanted a character to jump over a particular fence, he asked friends to check if such an action were possible. In the story "Araby," which appears in Chapter 7, Joyce sets the story in North Richmond Street. Neither the street, nor the details about it are invented. Joyce actually lived on the street and attended the school at its far end. Yet the main character is *not* James Joyce. "Araby" is fiction, not autobiography. The details have been drawn from life to enhance the story, make the action more believable, and increase the narrative's impact. Joyce's primary interest is on the psychology of the narrator, and the realistic details all contribute to our understanding of the character's mind.

AUTOBIOGRAPHICAL FICTION

One of the first pieces of advice young authors frequently receive is to write about what they know, the people they've encountered and the events that have happened to them. Fiction writers often borrow incidents from their own lives that they convert into fiction. Eudora Welty, in the passage from *One Writer's Beginning,* talks about how the voice of her mother's friend inspired "Why I Live at the P.O." Often a writer's life and a writer's fiction intersect at many points. From Anne Tyler's essay, "Still Just Writing," we can learn that some of the narrative details in her story, "Your Place is Empty," are drawn from personal experience. But as readers we should be careful not to equate the story with autobiography; we must not read a story as limited by the author's life. For the incident which inspires a story is its starting point, not its conclusion. Judging a story by autobiography is like judging an oak tree by an acorn.

In daily life we may know how the truth gets bent when we tell an anecdote to friends. People exaggerate, elaborate, invent, changing a simple incident into a saga. The old fisherman's story about The-One-That-Got-Away is a classic example of how supposedly autobiographical material gets transformed into fiction. Moreover, even when we wish to be faithful to our experiences we do not necessarily succeed in presenting the entire picture. We often emphasize those aspects of ourselves we would like our audience to appreciate and de-emphasize less attractive features of our personality. The face that a writer shows the public even in an autobiography is a carefully composed mask. Sometimes the mask is life-like, but we should not confuse the mask with the actual person.

NARRATIVE CONVENTIONS

Are realistic stories better than non-realistic stories? No. Both realistic and non-realistic writers have written great tales. Of course, some people prefer one type of story to another. But Shakespeare's *The Tempest* is not an inferior work because it contains a magician, a mythical seabeast and a spirit who has been imprisoned in a tree, and Joyce's "Araby" is not a great short story simply because it contains only realistic details.

The difference between realistic and non-realistic stories is that they are governed by different literary conventions. In a realistic story the author limits him– or herself to natural laws and historical probabilities. In a non-realistic story, authors can establish any rules they wish. But once the rules are established, the author must play by them in order to be consistent. For example, in *Peter Pan,* the author, Sir James Barrie, established the rule that no one grows older in Never-never Land. It would be inconsistent then if Peter began to grow a beard and develop arthritis. His aging is impermissable under the story's narrative rules. Similarly, if water is the only thing that can kill the Wicked Witch of the West, then Dorothy in *The Wizard of Oz* may not kill her with fire or a bullet.

We may think of these narrative rules or conventions as the rules of a game. For instance, only specific types of moves are allowed in chess, and the pleasure of the game is derived from working within the rules. The pleasure of fiction derives from the mutually agreed upon rules that determine what both writers and readers may do. Of course, writers may have enormous fun playing tricks within the rules of the game, or they may try to establish other rules that they believe are more interesting and pleasurable than the usual ones.

READERS AND NARRATIVE CONVENTIONS

How can readers know by what rules a story is governed? How can a reader know whether a story is realistic or non-realistic? Frequently, authors let their readers know quite quickly. In the opening lines of a story, authors frequently establish what sort of story they are writing. For example, "A Very Old Man With Enormous Wings" opens with the sentence: "On the third day of rain they had killed so many crabs inside the house that Pelayo had to cross the drenched courtyard and throw them into the sea, because the newborn child had a temperature all night and they thought it was due to the stench." Such a sentence, although it does not contain anything entirely impossible, talks about events that are so extraordinary that the reader is immediately put on notice that the story will not be limited to realistic detail. If the reader had any doubts the next sentence would reinforce the reader's assumption. Márquez writes: "The world had been sad since Tuesday." The sentence uses two poetic devices: *personification* and *hyperbole.* The narrator has turned the world into a person who has feeling, that is, he has personified the world into a sad human. The statement is also exaggerated or hyperbolic. Instead of saying, "this part of the world was saddening," the narrator has made the entire world sad. In these ways Márquez has alerted the reader to a heightened sense of reality. Critics have spoken about Márquez's "magical realism."

Writers, however, like to play with readers' expectations. In "A Continuity of Parks," Cortázar leads the reader to expect that the story will be a fairly realistic tale about a rich landowner who loves to read. At the end of the story, the reader discovers that these are false expectations. If we complained to Cortázar, he would probably respond by saying that he never claimed that the story was realistic. It is we who had made the wrong assumption.

QUESTIONS TO THINK ABOUT

1. How is your understanding of the world influenced by those around you? How do your parents, your friends, your teachers or others in authority influence your beliefs and values?
2. How do you judge between contradictory explanations of events? Have you ever been asked to arbitrate a disagreement between two friends, or between brothers and sisters? How do you decide who is narrating the actual sequence of events? Can you? How do you make your judgment?
3. Do you need to share the author's beliefs to enjoy the writer's stories? For example, do you need to believe in angels to enjoy Márquez's story? Would the story be more enjoyable if the reader did not believe in angels? Does it matter?

ESSAY TOPICS

1. Do you know any particularly good storytellers? When they tell stories how do they make them interesting? Are they faithful to what actually happened or do they exaggerate and elaborate by "embroidering" the story? Do the exaggerations, if they occur, harm the enjoyment of the story or obscure the deeper truth the stories exemplify? Discuss how the storyteller handles actual events.
2. In politics elected officials frequently present events in ways that justify the wisdom of their actions while their opponents try to present "the other side" of the story. Choose a recent political controversy about what a politician allegedly did or did not do, and discuss the differences between how the two sides narrated the events.
3. Some people believe that their attitudes toward their lives would be very different if they were either very rich or very poor. Discuss whether your attitude toward education would change if you were either a multi-millionaire or homeless.
4. Some people have argued that men's and women's perspectives of daily life are very different. Try to envision your average day if you were born of the opposite sex.

CREATIVE WRITING EXERCISES

1. Take a simple incident in your life and narrate it, then retell the story by exaggerating the details. For example, take a story of why you were late to class—perhaps because you had car trouble—and by exaggerating the details turn it into a big adventure. The garage mechanic could be a real monkey instead of being a "grease monkey"; the mud on the side of the road could be turned into quick sand.
2. Take an incident that occurs between people of the opposite sex and narrate it from *both* the male and female perspectives. For example, you may take the incident of someone asking another person out for a date. How does the male view the incident? How does the female?
3. Take an incident that occurs between people of different classes and narrate it from *both* perspectives. For example, you might narrate how a beggar sees the world and then how a millionaire sees the beggar. You might have an unemployed steel worker meet a yuppie at a maternity ward in which their wives both had babies. How would they view their children's, their marriages', and their own futures?

LITERARY ESSAYS

1. There is an old expression: "Truth is stranger than fiction." Discuss how authors make supernatural events seem believable or how they make ordinary events seem unusual and unbelievable. Pick episodes from stories in this chapter.
2. Do any of the stories in this chapter remind you of incidents in your own life? For example, did you ever look forward to a visit only to have it turn into a disaster? Compare your experiences to the events in the story. How were they different? How were they the same? Has the story taught you anything about your experience?
3. In several of these stories our final responses to the situations are very different from our first impressions. Many stories that start out ordinary turn rather strange at the end. Compare your responses and expectations at the beginning to your responses at the end of the story. Then try to indicate why, how and when these responses changed.

ANNE TYLER

YOUR PLACE IS EMPTY

Anne Tyler (b. 1941) was born in Minneapolis, Minnesota, but she lived in a number of Quaker communities in the Midwest and the South during her childhood. At sixteen, she entered Duke University and fell under the influence of the novelist Reynolds Price, who with Eudora Welty became her greatest literary influence.

Having published her first novel in her twenties, she has now produced a large number of works that have won her increasing respect and popularity. Her major works include Celestial Navigation, Dinner at the Homesick Restaurant, *and* The Accidental Tourist.

She lives with her husband, Taghi Modarressi, an Iranian-born psychiatrist and novelist, and their two daughters in Baltimore, the scene of most of her novels.

Early in October, Hassan Ardavi invited his mother to come from Iran for a visit. His mother accepted immediately. It wasn't clear how long the visit was to last. Hassan's wife thought three months would be a good length of time. Hassan himself had planned on six months, and said so in his letter of invitation. But his mother felt that after such a long trip six months would be too short, and she was counting on staying a year. Hassan's little girl, who wasn't yet two, had no idea of time at all. She was told that her grandmother was coming but she soon forgot about it.

Hassan's wife was named Elizabeth, not an easy word for Iranians to pronounce. She would have been recognized as American the world over—a blond, pretty girl with long bones and an ungraceful way of walking. One of her strong points was an ability to pick up foreign languages, and before her mother-in-law's arrival she bought a textbook and taught herself Persian. *"Salaam aleikum,"* she told the mirror every morning. Her daughter watched, startled, from her place on the potty-chair. Elizabeth ran through possible situations in her mind and looked up the words for them. "Would you like more tea? Do you take sugar?" At suppertime she spoke Persian to her husband, who looked amused at the new tone she gave his language, with her flat, factual American voice. He wrote his mother and told her Elizabeth had a surprise for her.

Their house was a three-story brick Colonial, but only the first two stories were in use. Now they cleared the third of its trunks and china barrels and *National Geographics,* and they moved in a few pieces of furniture. Elizabeth sewed flowered curtains for the window. She was unusually careful with them; to a foreign mother-in-law, fine seams might matter. Also, Hassan bought a pocket compass, which he placed in the top dresser drawer. "For her prayers," he said. "She'll want to face Mecca. She prays three times a day."

"But which direction is Mecca from here?" Elizabeth asked.

Hassan only shrugged. He had never said the prayers himself, not even as a child. His earliest memory was of tickling the soles of his mother's feet while she prayed steadfastly on; everyone knew it was forbidden to pause once you'd started.

Mrs. Ardavi felt nervous about the descent from the plane. She inched down the staircase sideways, one hand tight on the railing, the other clutching her shawl. It was night, and cold. The air seemed curiously opaque. She arrived on solid ground and stood collecting herself—a small, stocky woman in black, with a kerchief over her smooth gray hair. She held her back very straight, as if she had just had her feelings hurt. In picturing this moment she had always thought Hassan would be waiting beside the plane, but there was no sign of him. Blue lights dotted the darkness behind her, an angular terminal loomed ahead, and an official was herding the passengers toward a plate-glass door. She followed, entangled in a web of meaningless sounds such as those you might hear in a fever dream.

Immigration. Baggage Claims. Customs. To all she spread her hands and beamed and shrugged, showing she spoke no English. Meanwhile her fellow-passengers waved to a blur of faces beyond a glass wall. It seemed they all knew people here; she was the only one who didn't. She had issued from the plane like a newborn baby, speechless and friendless. And the customs official didn't seem pleased with her. She had brought too many gifts. She had stuffed her bags with them, discarding all but the most necessary pieces of her clothing so that she would have more room. There were silver tea sets and gold jewelry for her daughter-in-law, and for her granddaughter a doll dressed in the complicated costume of a nomad tribe, an embroidered sheepskin vest, and two religious medals on chains—one a disc inscribed with the name of Allah, the other a tiny gold Koran, with a very effective prayer for long life folded up within it. The customs official sifted gold through his fingers like sand and frowned at the Koran. "Have I done something wrong?" she asked. But of course he didn't understand her. Though you'd think, really, that if he would just *listen* hard enough, just meet her eyes once . . . it was a very simple language, there was no reason why it shouldn't come through to him.

For Hassan, she'd brought food. She had gathered all his favorite foods and put them in a drawstring bag embroidered with peacocks. When the official opened the bag he said something under his breath and called another man over. Together they unwrapped tiny newspaper packets and sniffed at various herbs. "Sumac," she told them. "Powder of lemons. Shambahleh." They gazed at her blankly. They untied a small cloth sack and rummaged through the kashk she had brought for soup. It rolled beneath their fingers and across the counter—hard white balls of yogurt curd, stuck with bits of sheep hair and manure. Some peasant had labored for hours to make that kashk. Mrs. Ardavi picked up one piece and replaced it firmly in the sack. Maybe the official understood her meaning: she was running out of patience. He threw up his hands. He slid her belongings down the counter. She was free to go.

Free to go where?

Dazed and stumbling, a pyramid of knobby parcels and bags, scraps of velvet and brocade and tapestry, she made her way to the glass wall.

A door opened out of nowhere and a stranger blocked her path. "Khanom Jun," he said. It was a name that only her children would use, but she passed him blindly and he had to touch her arm before she would look up.

He had put on weight. She didn't know him. The last time she'd seen him he was a thin, stoop-shouldered medical student disappearing into an Air France jet without a backward glance. "Khanom Jun, it's me," this stranger said, but she went on searching his face with cloudy eyes. No doubt he was a bearer of bad news. Was that it? A recurrent dream had warned her that she would never see her son again—that he would die on his way to the airport, or had already been dead for months but no one wanted to break the news; some second or third cousin in America had continued signing Hassan's name to his cheerful, anonymous letters. Now here was this man with graying hair and a thick mustache, his clothes American but his face Iranian, his eyes sadly familiar, as if they belonged to someone else. "Don't you believe me?" he said. He kissed her on both cheeks. It was his smell she recognized first—a pleasantly bitter, herblike smell that brought her the image of Hassan as a child, reaching thin arms around her neck. "It's you, Hassan," she said, and then she started crying against his gray tweed shoulder.

They were quiet during the long drive home. Once she reached over to touch his face, having wanted to do so for miles. None of the out-of-focus snapshots he'd sent had prepared her for the way he had aged. "How long has it been?" she asked. "Twelve years?" But both of them knew to the day how long it had been. All those letters of hers: "My dear Hassan, ten years now and still your place is empty." "Eleven years and still . . ."

Hassan squinted through the windshield at the oncoming headlights. His mother started fretting over her kerchief, which she knew she ought not to have worn. She'd been told so by her youngest sister, who had been to America twice. "It marks you," her sister had said. But that square of silk was the last, shrunken reminder of the veil she used to hide beneath, before the previous Shah had banished such things. At her age, how could she expose herself? And then her teeth; her teeth were a problem too. Her youngest sister had said, "You ought to get dentures made, I'm sure there aren't three whole teeth in your head." But Mrs. Ardavi was scared of dentists. Now she covered her mouth with one hand and looked sideways at Hassan, though so far he hadn't seemed to notice. He was busy maneuvering his car into the right-hand lane.

This silence was the last thing she had expected. For weeks she'd been saving up stray bits of gossip, weaving together the family stories she would tell him. There were three hundred people in her family—most of them related to each other in three or four different ways, all leading intricate and scandalous lives she had planned to discuss in detail, but instead she stared sadly out the window. You'd think Hassan would ask. You'd think they could have a better conversation than this, after such a long time. Disappointment made her cross, and now she stubbornly refused to speak even when she saw something she wanted to comment on, some imposing building or unfamiliar brand of car sliding past her into the darkness.

By the time they arrived it was nearly midnight. None of the houses were lit but Hassan's—worn brick, older than she would have expected. "Here we are," said Hassan. The competence with which he parked the car, fitting it neatly into a small space by the curb, put him firmly on the other side of the fence, the American side. She would have to face her daughter-in-law alone. As they climbed the front steps she whispered, "How do you say it again?"

"Say what?" Hassan asked.

"Her name. Lizabet?"

"Elizabeth. Like Elizabeth Taylor. *You* know."

"Yes, yes, of course," said his mother. Then she lifted her chin, holding tight to the straps of her purse.

Elizabeth was wearing bluejeans and a pair of fluffy slippers. Her hair was blond as corn silk, cut short and straight, and her face had the grave, sleepy look of a child's. As soon as she had opened the door she said, *"Salaam aleikum."* Mrs. Ardavi, overcome with relief at the Persian greeting, threw her arms around her and kissed both cheeks. Then they led her into the living room, which looked comfortable but a little too plain. The furniture was straight-edged, the rugs uninteresting, though the curtains had a nice figured pattern that caught her eye. In one corner sat a shiny red kiddie car complete with license plates. "Is that the child's?" she asked. "Hilary's?" She hesitated over the name. "Could I see her?"

"Now?" said Hassan.

But Elizabeth told him, "That's all right." (Women understood these things.) She beckoned to her mother-in-law. They climbed the stairs together, up to the second floor, into a little room that smelled of milk and rubber and talcum powder, smells she would know anywhere. Even in the half-light from the hallway, she could tell that Hilary was beautiful. She had black, tumbling hair, long black lashes, and skin of a tone they called wheat-colored, lighter than Hassan's. "There," said Elizabeth. "Thank you," said Mrs. Ardavi. Her voice was formal, but this was her first grandchild and it took her a moment to recover herself. Then they stepped back into the hallway. "I brought her some medals," she whispered. "I hope you don't mind."

"Medals?" said Elizabeth. She repeated the word anxiously, mispronouncing it.

"Only an Allah and a Koran, both very tiny. You'll hardly know they're there. I'm not used to seeing a child without a medal. It worries me."

Automatically her fingers traced a chain around her neck, ending in the hollow of her collarbone. Elizabeth nodded, looking relieved. "*Oh* yes. Medals," she said.

"Is that all right?"

"Yes, of course."

Mrs. Ardavi took heart. "Hassan laughs," she said. "He doesn't believe in these things. But when he left I put a prayer in his suitcase pocket, and you see he's been protected. Now if Hilary wore a medal, I could sleep nights."

"Of course," Elizabeth said again.

When they re-entered the living room, Mrs. Ardavi was smiling, and she kissed Hassan on the top of his head before she sat down.

American days were tightly scheduled, divided not into morning and afternoon but into 9:00, 9:30, and so forth, each half hour possessing its own set activity. It was marvellous. Mrs. Ardavi wrote her sisters: "They're more organized here. My daughter-in-law never wastes a minute." How terrible, her sisters wrote back. They were all in Teheran, drinking cup after cup of tea and idly guessing who might come and visit. "No, you misunderstand," Mrs. Ardavi protested. "I like it this way. I'm fitting in wonderfully." And to her youngest sister she wrote, "You'd think I was American. No one guesses otherwise." This wasn't true, of course, but she hoped it would be true in the future.

Hassan was a doctor. He worked long hours, from six in the morning until six at night. While she was still washing for her morning prayers she could hear him tiptoe down the stairs and out the front door. His car would start up, a distant rumble far below her, and from her bathroom window she could watch it swing out from beneath a tatter of red leaves and round the corner and disappear. Then she would sigh and return to her sink. Before prayers she had to wash her face, her hands, and the soles of her feet. She had to draw her wet fingers down the part in her hair. After that she returned to her room, where she swathed herself tightly in her long black veil and knelt on a beaded velvet prayer mat. East was where the window was, curtained by chintz and misted over. On the east wall she hung a lithograph of the Caliph Ali and a color snapshot of her third son, Babak, whose marriage she had arranged just a few months before this visit. If Babak hadn't married, she never could have come. He was the youngest, spoiled by being the only son at home. It had taken her three years to find a wife for him. (One was too modern, one too lazy, one so perfect she had been suspicious.) But finally the proper girl had turned up, modest and well-mannered and sufficiently wide of hip, and Mrs. Ardavi and the bridal couple had settled in a fine new house on the outskirts of Teheran. Now every time she prayed, she added a word of thanks that at last she had a home for her old age. After that, she unwound her veil and laid it carefully in a drawer. From another drawer she took thick cotton stockings and elastic garters; she stuffed her swollen feet into open-toed vinyl sandals. Unless she was going out, she wore a housecoat. It amazed her how wasteful Americans were with their clothing.

Downstairs, Elizabeth would have started her tea and buttered a piece of toast for her. Elizabeth and Hilary ate bacon and eggs, but bacon of course was unclean and Mrs. Ardavi never accepted any. Nor had it even been offered to her, except once, jokingly, by Hassan. The distinctive, smoky smell rose to meet her as she descended the stairs. "What does it taste like?" she always asked. She was dying to know. But Elizabeth's vocabulary didn't cover the taste of bacon; she only said it was salty and then laughed and gave up. They had learned very early to travel a well-worn conversational path, avoiding the dead ends caused by unfamiliar words. "Did you sleep well?" Elizabeth always asked in her funny, childish accent, and Mrs. Ardavi answered, "So-so." Then they would turn and watch Hilary, who sat on a booster seat eating scrambled eggs, a thin chain of Persian gold crossing the back of her neck. Conversation was easier, or even unnecessary, as long as Hilary was there.

In the mornings Elizabeth cleaned house. Mrs. Ardavi used that time for letter writing. She had dozens of letters to write, to all her aunts and uncles and her thirteen sisters. (Her father had had three wives, and a surprising number of children even for that day and age.) Then there was Babak. His wife was in her second month of pregnancy, so Mrs. Ardavi wrote long accounts of the American child-rearing methods. "There are some things I don't agree with," she wrote. "They let Hilary play outdoors by herself, with not even a servant to keep an eye on her." Then she would trail off and gaze thoughtfully at Hilary, who sat on the floor watching a television program called "Captain Kangaroo."

Mrs. Ardavi's own childhood had been murky and grim. From the age of nine she was wrapped in a veil, one corner of it clenched in her teeth to hide her face whenever she appeared on the streets. Her father, a respected man high up in public life, used to chase servant girls through the halls and trap them, giggling, in vacant bedrooms. At the age of ten she was forced to watch her mother bleed to death in childbirth, and when she screamed the midwife had struck her across the face and held her down till she had properly kissed her mother goodbye. There seemed no connection at all between her and this little overalled American. At times, when Hilary had one of her temper tantrums, Mrs. Ardavi waited in horror for Elizabeth to slap her and then, when no slap came, felt a mixture of relief and anger. "In Iran—" she would begin, and if Hassan was there he always said, "But this is not Iran, remember?"

After lunch Hilary took a nap, and Mrs. Ardavi went upstairs to say her noontime prayers and take a nap as well. Then she might do a little laundry in her bathtub. Laundry was a problem here. Although she liked Elizabeth, the fact was that the girl was a Christian, and therefore unclean; it would never do to have a Christian wash a Moslem's clothes. The automatic dryer was also unclean, having contained, at some point, a Christian's underwear. So she had to ask Hassan to buy her a drying rack. It came unassembled. Elizabeth put it together for her, stick by stick, and then Mrs. Ardavi held it under her shower and rinsed it off, hoping that would be enough to remove any taint. The Koran didn't cover this sort of situation.

When Hilary was up from her nap they walked her to the park—Elizabeth in her eternal bluejeans and Mrs. Ardavi in her kerchief and shawl, taking short painful steps in small shoes that bulged over her bunions. They still hadn't seen to her teeth, although by now Hassan had noticed them. She was hoping he might forget about the dentist, but then she saw him remembering every time she laughed and revealed her five brown teeth set wide apart.

At the park she laughed a great deal. It was her only way of communicating with the other women. They sat on the benches ringing the playground, and while Elizabeth translated their questions Mrs. Ardavi laughed and nodded at them over and over. "They want to know if you like it here," Elizabeth said. Mrs. Ardavi answered at length, but Elizabeth's translation was very short. Then gradually the other women forgot her, and conversation rattled on while she sat silent and watched each speaker's lips. The few recognizable words—"telephone," "television," "radio"—gave her the impression that American conversations were largely technical, even among women. Their gestures were wide and slow, disproving her youngest sister's statement that in America everyone was in a hurry. On the contrary, these women were dreamlike, moving singly or in twos across wide flat spaces beneath white November skies when they departed.

Later, at home, Mrs. Ardavi would say, "The red-haired girl, is she pregnant? She looked it, I thought. Is the fat girl happy in her marriage?" She asked with some urgency, plucking Elizabeth's sleeve when she was slow to answer. People's private lives fascinated her. On Saturday trips to the supermarket she liked to single out some interesting stranger. "What's the matter with that *jerky*-moving man? That girl, is she one of your dark-skinned people?" Elizabeth answered too softly, and never seemed to follow Mrs. Ardavi's pointing finger.

Supper was difficult; Mrs. Ardavi didn't like American food. Even when Elizabeth made something Iranian, it had an American taste to it—the vegetables still faintly crisp, the onions transparent rather than nicely blackened. "Vegetables not thoroughly cooked retain a certain acidity," Mrs. Ardavi said, laying down her fork. "This is a cause of constipation and stomach aches. At night I often have heartburn. It's been three full days since I moved my bowels." Elizabeth merely bent over her plate, offering no symptoms of her own in return. Hassan said, "At the table, Khanom? At the table?"

Eventually she decided to cook supper herself. Over Elizabeth's protests she began at three every afternoon, filling the house with the smell of dillweed and arranging pots on counters and cabinets and finally, when there was no more space, on the floor. She squatted on the floor with her skirt tucked between her knees and stirred great bowls of minced greens while behind her, on the gas range, four different pots of food bubbled and steamed. The kitchen was becoming more homelike, she thought. A bowl of yogurt brewed beside the stove, a kettle of rice soaked in the sink, and the top of the dishwasher was curlicued with the yellow dye from saffron. In one corner sat the pudding pan, black on the bottom from the times she had cooked down sugar to make a sweet for her intestines. "Now, this is your rest period," she always told Elizabeth. "Come to the table in three hours and be surprised." But Elizabeth only hovered around the kitchen, disturbing the serene, steam-filled air with clatter and slams as she put away pots, or pacing between stove and sink, her arms folded across her chest. At supper she ate little; Mrs. Ardavi wondered how Americans got so tall on such small suppers. Hassan, on the other hand, had second and third helpings. "I must be gaining five pounds a week," he said. "None of my clothes fit."

"That's good to hear," said his mother. And Elizabeth added something but in English, which Hassan answered in English also. Often now they broke into English for paragraphs at a time—Elizabeth speaking softly, looking at her plate, and Hassan answering at length and sometimes reaching across the table to cover her hand.

At night, after her evening prayers, Mrs. Ardavi watched television on the living-room couch. She brought her veil downstairs and wrapped it around her to keep the drafts away. Her shoes lay on the rug beneath her, and scattered down the length of the couch were her knitting bag, her sack of burned sugar, her magnifying glass, and *My First Golden Dictionary*. Elizabeth read novels in an easy chair, and Hassan watched TV so that he could translate the difficult parts of the plot. Not that Mrs. Ardavi had much trouble. American plots were easy to guess at, particularly the Westerns. And when the program was boring—a documentary or a special news feature—she could pass the time by talking to Hassan. "Your cousin Farah wrote," she said. "Do you remember her? A homely girl, too dark. She's getting a divorce and in my opinion it's fortunate; he's from a lower class. Do you remember Farah?"

Hassan only grunted, his eyes on the screen. He was interested in American politics. So was she, for that matter. She had wept for President Kennedy, and carried Jackie's picture in her purse. But these news programs were long and dry, and if Hassan wouldn't talk she was forced to turn at last to her *Golden Dictionary*.

In her childhood, she had been taught by expensive foreign tutors. Her mind was her great gift, the compensation for a large, plain face and a stocky figure. But now what she had learned seemed lost, forgotten utterly or fogged by years, so that Hassan gave a snort whenever she told him some fact that she had dredged up from her memory. It seemed that everything she studied now had to penetrate through a great thick layer before it reached her mind. "Tonk you," she practiced. "Tonk you. Tonk you." "Thank you," Hassan corrected her. He pointed out useful words in her dictionary—grocery-store words, household words—but she grew impatient with their woodenness. What she wanted was the language to display her personality, her famous courtesy, and her magical intuition about the inside lives of other people. Nightly she learned "salt," "bread," "spoon," but with an inner sense of dullness, and every morning when she woke her English was once again confined to "thank you" and "NBC."

Elizabeth, meanwhile, read on, finishing one book and reaching for the next without even glancing up. Hassan chewed a thumbnail and watched a senator. He shouldn't be disturbed, of course, but time after time his mother felt the silence and the whispery turning of pages stretching her nerves until she had to speak. "Hassan?"

"Hmm."

"My chest seems tight. I'm sure a cold is coming on. Don't you have a tonic?"

"No," said Hassan.

He dispensed medicines all day; he listened to complaints. Common sense told her to stop, but she persisted, encouraged by some demon that wouldn't let her tongue lie still. "Don't you have some syrup? What about that liquid you gave me for constipation? Would that help?"

"No, it wouldn't," said Hassan.

He drove her on, somehow. The less he gave, the more she had to ask. "Well, aspirin? Vitamins?" Until Hassan said, "Will you just let me *watch?*" Then she could lapse into silence again, or even gather up the clutter of her belongings and bid the two of them good night.

She slept badly. Often she lay awake for hours, fingering the edge of the sheet and staring at the ceiling. Memories crowded in on her, old grievances and fears, injustices that had never been righted. For the first time in years she thought of her husband, a gentle, weak man given to surprising outbursts of temper. She hadn't loved him when she married him, and at his death from a liver ailment six years later her main feeling had been resentment. Was it fair to be widowed so young, while other women were supported and protected? She had moved from her husband's home back to the old family estate, where five of her sisters still lived. There she had stayed till Babak's wedding, drinking tea all day with her sisters and pulling the strings by which the rest of the family was attached. Marriages were arranged, funerals attended, childbirth discussed in fine detail; servants' disputes were settled, and feuds patched up and then restarted. Her husband's face had quickly faded, leaving only a vacant spot in her mind. But now she could see him so clearly—a wasted figure on his deathbed, beard untrimmed, turban coming loose, eyes imploring her for something more than an absentminded pat on the cheek as she passed through his room on her way to check the children.

She saw the thin faces of her three small boys as they sat on the rug eating rice. Hassan was the stubborn, mischievous one, with perpetual scabs on his knees. Babak was the cuddly one. Ali was the oldest, who had caused so much worry—weak, like his father, demanding, but capable of turning suddenly charming. Four years ago he had died of a brain hemorrhage, slumping over a dinner table in faraway Shīrāz, where he'd gone to be free of his wife, who was also his double first cousin. Ever since he was born he had disturbed his mother's sleep, first because she worried over what he would amount to and now, after his death, because she lay awake listing all she had done wrong with him. She had been too lenient. No, too harsh. There was no telling. Mistakes she had made floated on the ceiling like ghosts—allowances she'd made when she knew she shouldn't have, protections he had not deserved, blows which perhaps he had not deserved either.

She would have liked to talk to Hassan about it, but any time she tried he changed the subject. Maybe he was angry about the way he had heard of Ali's death. It was customary to break such news gradually. She had started a series of tactful letters, beginning by saying that Ali was seriously ill when in truth he was already buried. Something in the letter had given her away—perhaps her plans for a rest cure by the seaside, which she never would have considered if she'd had an ailing son at home. Hassan had telephoned overseas, taking three nights to reach her. "Tell me what's wrong," he said. "I know there's something. When her tears kept her from answering, he asked, "Is he dead?" His voice sounded angry, but that might have been due to a poor connection. And when he hung up, cutting her off before she could say all she wanted, she thought, I should have told him straight out. I had forgotten that about him. Now when she spoke of Ali he listened politely, with his face frozen. She would have told him anything, all about the death and burial and that witch of a wife throwing herself, too late, into the grave; but Hassan never asked.

Death was moving in on her. Oh, not on her personally (the women in her family lived a century or longer, burying the men one by one) but on everybody around her, all the cousins and uncles and brothers-in-law. No sooner had she laid away her mourning clothes than it was time to bring them out again. Recently she had begun to feel she would outlive her two other sons as well, and she fought off sleep because of the dreams it brought—Babak lying stiff and cold in his grave, Hassan crumpled over in some dark American alley. Terrifying images would zoom at her out of the night. In the end she had to wrap herself in her veil and sleep instead on the Persian rug, which had the dusty smell of home and was, anyway, more comfortable than her unsteady foreign mattress.

At Christmas time, Hassan and Elizabeth gave Mrs. Ardavi a brightly colored American dress with short sleeves. She wore it to an Iranian party, even leaving off her kerchief in a sudden fit of daring. Everyone commented on how nice she looked. "Really you fit right in," a girl told her. "May I write to my mother about you? She was over here for a year and a half and never once stepped out of the house without her kerchief." Mrs. Ardavi beamed. It was true she would never have associated with these people at home—children of civil servants and bank clerks, newly rich now they'd finished medical school. The wives called their husbands "Doctor" even in direct address. But still it felt good to be speaking so much Persian; her tongue nearly ran away with her. "I see you're expecting a baby," she said to one of the wives. "Is it your first? I could tell by your eyes. Now don't be nervous. I had three myself; my mother had seven and never felt a pain in her life. She would squat down to serve my father's breakfast and 'Eh?' she would say. 'Aga Jun, it's the baby!' and there it would be on the floor between her feet, waiting for her to cut the cord and finish pouring the tea." She neglected to mention how her mother had died. All her natural tact came back to her, her gift with words and her knowledge of how to hold an audience. She bubbled and sparkled like a girl, and her face fell when it was time to go home.

After the party, she spent two or three days noticing more keenly than ever the loss of her language, and talking more feverishly when Hassan came home in the evening. This business of being a foreigner was something changeable. Boundaries kept shifting, and sometimes it was she who was the foreigner but other times Elizabeth, or even Hassan. (Wasn't it true, she often wondered, that there was a greater distance between men and women than between Americans and Iranians, or even *Eskimos* and Iranians?) Hassan was the foreigner when she and Elizabeth conspired to hide a miniature Koran in his glove compartment; he would have laughed at them. "You see," she told Elizabeth, "I know there's nothing to it, but it makes me feel better. When my sons were born I took them all to the bath attendant to have their blood let. People say it brings long life. I know that's superstition, but whenever afterward I saw those ridges down their backs I felt safe. Don't you understand?" And Elizabeth said, "Of course." She smuggled the Koran into the car herself, and hid it beneath the Texaco maps. Hassan saw nothing.

Hilary was a foreigner forever. She dodged her grandmother's yearning hands, and when the grownups spoke Persian she fretted and misbehaved and pulled on Elizabeth's sleeve. Mrs. Ardavi had to remind herself constantly not to kiss the child too much, not to reach out for a hug, not to offer her lap. In this country people kept more separate. They kept so separate that at times she felt hurt. They tried to be so subtle, so undemonstrative. She would never understand this place.

In January they took her to a dentist, who made clucking noises when he looked in her mouth. "What does he say?" she asked. "Tell me the worst." But Hassan was talking in a low voice to Elizabeth, and he waved her aside. They seemed to be having a misunderstanding of some sort. "What does he *say,* Hassan?"

"Just a minute."

She craned around in the high-backed chair, fighting off the dentist's little mirror. "I have to know," she told Hassan.

"He says your teeth are terrible. They have to be extracted and the gums surgically smoothed. He wants to know if you'll be here for another few months; he can't schedule you till later."

A cold lump of fear swelled in her stomach. Unfortunately she *would* be here; it had only been three months so far and she was planning to stay a year. So she had to watch numbly while her life was signed away, whole strings of appointments made, and little white cards filled out. And Hassan didn't even look sympathetic. He was still involved in whatever this argument was with Elizabeth. The two of them failed to notice how her hands were shaking.

It snowed all of January, the worst snow they had had in years. When she came downstairs in the mornings she found the kitchen icy cold, crisscrossed by drafts. "The sort of cold enters your bones," she told Elizabeth. "I'm sure to fall sick." Elizabeth only nodded. Some mornings now her face was pale and puffy, as if she had a secret worry, but Mrs. Ardavi had learned that it was better not to ask about it.

Early in February there was a sudden warm spell. Snow melted and all the trees dripped in the sunshine. "We're going for a walk," Elizabeth said, and Mrs. Ardavi said, "I'll come too." In spite of the warmth, she toiled upstairs for her woolen shawl. She didn't like to take chances. And she worried over Hilary's bare ears. "Won't she catch cold?" she asked. "I think we should cover her head."

"She'll be all right," said Elizabeth, and then shut her face in a certain stubborn way she had.

In the park, Elizabeth and Hilary made snowballs from the last of the snow and threw them at each other, narrowly missing Mrs. Ardavi, who stood watching with her arms folded and her hands tucked in her sleeves.

The next morning, something was wrong with Hilary. She sat at the breakfast table and cried steadily, refusing all food. "Now, now," her grandmother said, "won't you tell old Ka Jun what's wrong?" But when she came close Hilary screamed louder. By noon she was worse. Elizabeth called Hassan, and he came home immediately and laid a hand on Hilary's forehead and said she should go to the pediatrician. He drove them there himself. "It's her ears, I'm sure of it," Mrs. Ardavi said in the waiting room. For some reason Hassan grew angry. "Do you always know better than the experts?" he asked her. "What are we coming to the doctor for? We could have talked to you and saved the trip." His mother lowered her eyes and examined her purse straps. She understood that he was anxious, but all the same her feelings were hurt and when they rose to go into the office she stayed behind.

Later Hassan came back and sat down again. "There's an infection in her middle ear," he told her. "The doctor's going to give her a shot of penicillin." His mother nodded, careful not to annoy him by reminding him she had thought as much. Then Hilary started crying. She must be getting her shot now. Mrs. Ardavi herself was terrified of needles, and she sat gripping her purse until her fingers turned white, staring around the waiting room, which seemed pathetically cheerful, with its worn wooden toys and nursery-school paintings. Her own ear ached in sympathy. She thought of a time when she had boxed Ali's ears too hard and he had wept all that day and gone to sleep sucking his thumb.

While Hassan was there she was careful not to say anything, but the following morning at breakfast she said, "Elizabeth dear, do you remember that walk we took day before yesterday?"

"Yes," said Elizabeth. She was squeezing oranges for Hilary, who'd grown cheerful again and was eating a huge breakfast.

"Remember I said Hilary should wear a hat? Now you see you should have been more careful. Because of you she fell sick; she could have died. Do you see that now?"

"No," said Elizabeth.

Was her Persian that scanty? Lately it seemed to have shrunk and hardened, like a stale piece of bread. Mrs. Ardavi sighed and tried again. "Without a hat, you see—" she began. But Elizabeth had set down her orange, picked up Hilary, and walked out of the room. Mrs. Ardavi stared after her, wondering if she'd said something wrong.

For the rest of the day, Elizabeth was busy in her room. She was cleaning out bureaus and closets. A couple of times Mrs. Ardavi advanced as far as the doorway, where she stood awkwardly watching. Hilary sat on the floor playing with a discarded perfume bottle. Everything, it seemed, was about to be thrown away—buttonless blouses and stretched-out sweaters, stockings and combs and empty lipstick tubes. "Could I be of any help?" Mrs. Ardavi asked, but Elizabeth said, "Oh, no. Thank you very much." Her voice was cheerful. Yet when Hassan came home he went upstairs and stayed a long time, and the door remained shut behind him.

Supper that night was an especially fine stew, Hassan's favorite ever since childhood, but he didn't say a word about it. He hardly spoke at all, in fact. Then later, when Elizabeth was upstairs putting Hilary to bed, he said, "Khanoum Jun, I want to talk to you."

"Yes, Hassan," she said, laying aside her knitting. She was frightened by his seriousness, the black weight of his mustache, and her own father's deep black eyes. But what had she done? She knotted her hands and looked up at him, swallowing.

"I understand you've been interfering," he said.

"I, Hassan?"

"Elizabeth isn't the kind you can do that with. And she's raising the child just fine on her own."

"Well, of course she is," said his mother. "Did I ever say otherwise?"

"Show it, then. Don't offer criticisms."

"Very well," she said. She picked up her knitting and began counting stitches, as if she'd forgotten the conversation entirely. But that evening she was unusually quiet, and at nine o'clock she excused herself to go to bed. "So early?" Hassan asked.

"I'm tired," she told him, and left with her back very straight.

Her room surrounded her like a nest. She had built up layers of herself on every surface—tapestries and bits of lace and lengths of Paisley. The bureau was covered with gilt-framed pictures of the saints, and snapshots of her sisters at family gatherings. On the windowsill were little plants in orange and aqua plastic pots—her favorite American colors. Her bedside table held bottles of medicine, ivory prayer beads, and a tiny brick of holy earth. The rest of the house was bare and shiny, impersonal; this room was as comforting as her shawl.

Still, she didn't sleep well. Ghosts rose up again, tugging at her thoughts. Why did things turn out so badly for her? Her father had preferred her brothers, a fact that crushed her even after all these years. Her husband had had three children by her and then complained that she was cold. And what comfort were children? If she had stayed in Iran any longer Babak would have asked her to move; she'd seen it coming. There'd been some disrespect creeping into his bride's behavior, some unwillingness to take advice, which Babak had overlooked even when his mother pointed it out to him. And Hassan was worse—always so stubborn, much too independent. She had offered him anything if he would just stay in Iran but he had said no; he was set on leaving her. And he had flatly refused to take along his cousin Shora as his wife, though everyone pointed out how lonely he would be. He was so anxious to break away, to get *going*, to come to this hardhearted country and take up with a Christian girl. Oh, she should have laughed when he left, and saved her tears for someone more deserving. She never should have come here, she never should have asked anything of him again. When finally she went to sleep it seemed that her eyes remained open, burning large and dry beneath her lids.

In the morning she had a toothache. She could hardly walk for the pain. It was only Friday (the first of her dental appointments was for Monday), but the dentist made time for her during the afternoon and pulled the tooth. Elizabeth said it wouldn't hurt, but it did. Elizabeth treated it as something insignificant, merely a small break in her schedule, which required the hiring of a babysitter. She wouldn't even call Hassan home from work. "What could he do?" she asked.

So when Hassan returned that evening it was all a surprise to him—the sight of his mother with a bloody cotton cylinder hanging out over her lower lip like a long tooth. "What *happened* to you?" he asked. To make it worse, Hilary was screaming and had been all afternoon. Mrs. Ardavi put her hands over her ears, wincing. "Will you make that child hush?" Hassan told Elizabeth. "I think we should get my mother to bed." He guided her toward the stairs, and she allowed herself to lean on him. "It's mainly my heart," she said. "You know how scared I am of dentists." When he had folded back her bedspread and helped her to lie down she closed her eyes gratefully, resting one arm across her forehead. Even the comfort of hot tea was denied her; she had to stay on cold foods for twelve hours. Hassan fixed her a glass of ice water. He was very considerate, she thought. He seemed as shaken at the sight of her as Hilary had been. All during the evening he kept coming to check on her, and twice in the night she heard him climbing the stairs to listen at her door. When she moaned he called, "Are you awake?"

"Of course," she said.

"Can I get you anything?"

"No, no."

In the morning she descended the stairs with slow, groping feet, keeping a tight hold on the railing. "It was a very hard night," she said. "At four my gum started throbbing. Is that normal? I think these American pain pills are constipating. Maybe a little prune juice would restore my regularity."

"I'll get it," Hassan said. "You sit down. Did you take the milk of magnesia?"

"Oh, yes, but I'm afraid it wasn't enough," she said.

Elizabeth handed Hassan a platter of bacon, not looking at him.

After breakfast, while Hassan and his mother were still sitting over their tea, Elizabeth started cleaning the kitchen. She made quite a bit of noise. She sorted the silverware and then went through a tangle of utensils, discarding bent spatulas and rusty tongs. "May I help?" asked Mrs. Ardavi. Elizabeth shook her head. She seemed to have these fits of throwing things away. Now she was standing on the counter to take everything from the upper cabinets—crackers, cereals, half-empty bottles of spices. On the very top shelf was a flowered tin confectioner's box with Persian lettering on it, forgotten since the day Mrs. Ardavi had brought it. "My!" said Mrs. Ardavi. "Won't Hilary be surprised!" Elizabeth pried the lid off. Out flew a cloud of insects, grayish-brown with V-shaped wings. They brushed past Elizabeth's face and fluttered through her hair and swarmed toward the ceiling, where they dimmed the light fixture. Elizabeth flung the box as far from her as possible and climbed down from the counter. "Goodness!" said Mrs. Ardavi. "Why, *we* have those at home!" Hassan lowered his teacup. Mixed nuts and dried currants rolled every which way on the floor; more insects swung toward the ceiling. Elizabeth sat on the nearest chair and buried her head in her hands. "Elizabeth?" said Hassan.

But she wouldn't look at him. In the end she simply rose and went upstairs, shutting the bedroom door with a gentle, definite click, which they heard all the way down in the kitchen because they were listening so hard.

"Excuse me," Hassan said to his mother.

She nodded and stared into her tea.

After he was gone she went to find Hilary, and she set her on her knee, babbling various folk rhymes to her while straining her ears toward the silence overhead. But Hilary squirmed off her lap and went to play with a truck. Then Hassan came downstairs again. He didn't say a word about Elizabeth.

On the following day, when Mrs. Ardavi's tooth was better, she and Hassan had a little talk upstairs in her room. They were very polite with each other. Hassan asked his mother how long they could hope for her to stay. His mother said she hadn't really thought about it. Hassan said that in America it was the custom to have house guests for three months only. After that they moved to a separate apartment nearby, which he'd be glad to provide for her as soon as he could find one, maybe next week. "Ah, an apartment," said his mother, looking impressed. But she had never lived alone a day in her life, and so after a suitable pause she said that she would hate to put him to so much expense. "Especially," she said, "when I'm going in such a short time anyway, since I'm homesick for my sisters."

"Well, then," said Hassan.

At supper that night, Hassan announced that his mother was missing her sisters and would like to leave. Elizabeth lowered her glass. "Leave?" she said.

Mrs. Ardavi said, "And Babak's wife, of course, will be asking for me when the baby arrives."

"Well . . . but what about the dentist? You were supposed to start your appointments on Monday."

"It's not important," Mrs. Ardavi said.

"But we set up all those—"

"There are plenty of dentists she can see at home," Hassan told Elizabeth. "We have dentists in Iran, for God's sake. Do you imagine we're barbarians?"

"No," Elizabeth said.

On the evening of the third of March, Hassan drove his mother to the airport. He was worrying about the road, which was slippery after a snowfall. He couldn't find much to say to his mother. And once they had arrived, he deliberately kept the conversation to trivia—the verifying of tickets, checking of departure times, weighing of baggage. Her baggage was fourteen pounds overweight. It didn't make sense; all she had were her clothes and a few small gifts for her sisters. "Why is it so heavy?" Hassan asked. "What have you got in there?" But his mother only said, "I don't know," and straightened her shawl, looking elsewhere. Hassan bent to open a tooled-leather suitcase. Inside he found three empty urn-shaped wine bottles, the permanent-press sheets from her bed, and a sample box of detergent that had come in yesterday's mail. "Listen," said Hassan, "do you know how much I'd have to pay to fly these things over? What's the matter with you?"

"I wanted to show my sisters," his mother said.

"Well, forget it. Now, what else have you got?"

But something about her—the vague, childlike eyes set upon some faraway object—made him give in. He opened no more bags. He even regretted his sharpness, and when her flight was announced he hugged her closely and kissed the top of her head. "Go with God," he said.

"Goodbye, Hassan."

She set off down the corridor by herself, straggling behind a line of businessmen. They all wore hats. His mother wore her scarf, and of all the travelers she alone, securely kerchiefed and shawled, setting her small shoes resolutely on the gleaming tiles, seemed undeniably a foreigner.

QUESTIONS

1. In this story what Persian or Iranian practices differ from American practices? How do these differences look to the American characters? How do the American practices look to Mrs. Ardavi?
2. Did Tyler have American or Persian in mind as her readers? As an American, how did you perceive Mrs. Ardavi's actions? Did she seem exotic? Silly? Insensitive? Abnormal? Did your attitude to Mrs. Ardavi change in the course of the story?
3. As an American, how did you perceive Elizabeth's actions? Did she seem exotic? Silly? Insensitive? Abnormal? Did your attitude toward Elizabeth change during the story?
4. Should Elizabeth make Hilary wear a hat in cold weather to avoid ear infections? Why does Elizabeth get angry at Mrs. Ardavi's suggestion?

5. Mrs. Ardavi is accused of "interfering." Does she think she is interfering? In Persia would her conduct be criticized?
6. Tyler writes that "This business of being a foreigner is something changeable." What does Tyler mean? In what sense are all the characters foreigners?
7. The story ends with Dr. Ardavi watching his mother board a jet back to Iran. Does Dr. Ardavi's perception of his mother change during the course of the story? Mrs. Ardavi fantasizes at the beginning of the story that she will never see her son alive. Is there a sense in which that is true? Can Dr. Ardavi ever fill his empty place again?

ANNE TYLER

STILL JUST WRITING

While I was painting the downstairs hall I thought of a novel to write. Really I just thought of a character; he more or less wandered into my mind, wearing a beard and a broad-brimmed leather hat. I figured that if I sat down and organized this character on paper, a novel would grow up around him. But it was March and the children's spring vacation began the next day, so I waited.

After spring vacation the children went back to school, but the dog got worms. It was a little complicated at the vet's and I lost a day. By then it was Thursday; Friday is the only day I can buy the groceries, pick up new cedar chips for the gerbils, scrub the bathrooms. I waited till Monday. Still, that left me four good weeks in April to block out the novel.

By May I was ready to start actually writing, but I had to do it in patches. There was the follow-up treatment at the vet, and then a half-day spent trailing the dog with a specimen tin so the lab could be sure the treatment had really worked. There were visits from the washing machine repairman and the Davey tree man, not to mention briefer interruptions by the meter reader, five Jehovah's Witnesses, and two Mormons. People telephoned wanting to sell me permanent light bulbs and waterproof basements. An Iranian cousin of my husband's had a baby; then the cousin's uncle died; then the cousin's mother decided to go home to Iran and needed to know where to buy a black American coat before she left. There *are* no black American coats; don't Americans wear mourning? I told her no, but I checked around at all the department stores anyway because she didn't speak English. Then I wrote chapters one and two. I had planned to work till three-thirty every day, but it was a month of early quittings: once for the children's dental appointment, once for the cat's rabies shot, once for our older daughter's orthopedist, and twice for her gymnastic meets. Sitting on the bleachers in the school gymnasium, I told myself I could always use this in a novel someplace, but I couldn't really picture writing a novel about twenty little girls in leotards trying to walk the length of a wooden beam without falling off. By the time I'd written chapter three, it was Memorial Day and the children were home again.

I knew I shouldn't expect anything from June. School was finished then and camp hadn't yet begun. I put the novel away. I closed down my mind and planted some herbs and played cribbage with the children. Then on the 25th, we drove one child to a sleep-away camp in Virginia and entered the other in a day camp, and I was ready to start work again. First I had to take my car in for repairs and the mechanics lost it, but I didn't get diverted. I sat in the garage on a folding chair while they hunted my car all one afternoon, and I hummed a calming tune and tried to remember what I'd planned to do next in my novel. Or even what the novel was about, for that matter. My character wandered in again in his beard and his broad-brimmed hat. He looked a little pale and knuckly, like someone scrabbling at a cliff edge so as not to fall away entirely.

I had high hopes for July, but it began with a four-day weekend, and on Monday night we had a long-distance call from our daughter's camp in Virginia. She was seriously ill in a Charlottesville hospital. We left our youngest with friends and drove three hours in a torrent of rain. We found our daughter frightened and crying, and another child (the only other child I knew in all of Virginia) equally frightened and crying down in the emergency room with possible appendicitis, so I spent that night alternating between a chair in the pediatric wing and a chair in the emergency room. By morning, it had begun to seem that our daughter's illness was typhoid fever. We loaded her into the car and took her back to Baltimore, where her doctor put her on drugs and prescribed a long bed-rest. She lay in bed six days, looking wretched and calling for fluids and cold cloths. On the seventh day she got up her same old healthy self, and the illness was declared to be not typhoid fever after all but a simple virus, and we shipped her back to Virginia on the evening train. The next day I was free to start writing again but sat, instead, on the couch in my study, staring blankly at the wall.

I could draw some conclusions here about the effect that being a woman/wife/mother has upon my writing, except that I am married to a writer who is also a man/husband/father. He published his first novel while he was a medical student in Iran; then he came to America to finish his training. His writing fell by the wayside, for a long while. You can't be on call in the emergency room for twenty hours and write a novel during the other four. Now he's a child psychiatrist, full-time, and he writes his novels in the odd moments here and there—when he's not preparing a lecture, when he's not on the phone with a patient, when he's not attending classes at the psychoanalytic institute. He writes in Persian, still, in those black-and-white speckled composition books. Sometimes one of the children will interrupt him in English and he will answer in Persian, and they'll say, "What?" and he'll look up blankly, and it seems a sheet has to fall from in front of his eyes before he remembers where he is and switches to English. Often, I wonder what he would be doing now if he didn't have a family to support. He cares deeply about his writing and he's very good at it, but every morning at five-thirty he gets up and puts on a suit and tie and drives in the dark to the hospital. Both of us, in different ways, seem to be hewing our creative time in small, hard chips from our living time.

Occasionally, I take a day off. I go to a friend's house for lunch, or weed the garden, or rearrange the linen closet. I notice that at the end of one of these days, when my husband asks me what I've been doing, I tend to exaggerate any hardships I may have encountered. ("A pickup nearly sideswiped me on Greenspring Avenue. I stood in line an hour just trying to buy the children some flip-flops.") It seems sinful to have lounged around so. Also, it seems sinful that I have more choice than my husband as to whether or not to undertake any given piece of work. I can refuse to do an article if it doesn't appeal to me, refuse to change a short story, refuse to hurry a book any faster than it wants to go—all luxuries. My husband, on the other hand, is forced to rise and go off to that hospital every blessed weekday of his life. *His* luxury is that no one expects him to drop all else for two weeks when a child has chicken pox. The only person who has no luxuries at all, it seems to me, is the woman writer who is the sole support of her children. I often think about how she must manage. I think that if I were in that position, I'd have to find a job involving manual labor. I have spent so long erecting partitions around the part of me that writes—learning how to close the door on it when ordinary life intervenes, how to close the door on ordinary life when it's time to start writing again—that I'm not sure I could fit the two parts of me back together now.

Before we had children I worked in a library. It was a boring job, but I tend to like doing boring things. I would sit on a stool alphabetizing Russian catalogue cards and listening to the other librarians talking around me. It made me think of my adolescence, which was spent listening to the tobacco stringers while I handed tobacco. At night I'd go home from the library and write. I never wrote what the librarians said, exactly, but having those voices in my ears all day helped me summon up my own characters' voices. Then our first baby came along—an insomniac. I quit work and stayed home all day with her and walked her all night. Even if I had found the time to write, I wouldn't have had the insides. I felt drained; too much care and feeling were being drawn out of me. And the only voices I heard now were by appointment—people who came to dinner, or invited us to dinner, and who therefore felt they had to make deliberate conversation. That's one thing writers never have, and I still miss it: the easy-going, on-again-off-again, gossipy murmurs of people working alongside each other all day.

I enjoyed tending infants (though I've much preferred the later ages), but it was hard to be solely, continually in their company and not to be able to write. And I couldn't think of any alternative. I know it must be possible to have a child raised beautifully by a housekeeper, but every such child I've run into has seemed dulled and doesn't use words well. So I figured I'd better stick it out. As it happened, it wasn't that long—five years, from the time our first daughter was born till our second started nursery school and left me with my mornings free. But while I was going through it I thought it would be a lot longer. I couldn't imagine any end to it. I felt that everything I wanted to write was somehow coagulating in my veins and making me fidgety and slow. Then after a while I didn't have anything to write anyhow, but I still had the fidgets. I felt useless, no matter how many diapers I washed or strollers I pushed. The only way I could explain my life to myself was to imagine that I was living in a very small commune. I had spent my childhood in a commune, or what would nowadays be called a commune, and I was used to the idea of division of labor. What we had here, I told myself, was a perfectly sensible arrangement: one member was the liaison with the outside world, bringing in money; another was the caretaker, reading the Little Bear books to the children and repairing the electrical switches. This second member might have less physical freedom, but she had much more freedom to arrange her own work schedule. I must have sat down a dozen times a week and very carefully, consciously thought it all through. Often, I was merely trying to convince myself that I really did pull my own weight.

This Iranian cousin who just had the baby: she sits home now and cries a lot. She was working on her master's degree and is used to being out in the world more. "Never mind," I tell her, "you'll soon be out again. This stage doesn't last long."

"How long?" she asks.

"Oh . . . three years, if you just have the one."

"Three years!"

I can see she's appalled. Her baby is beautiful, very dark and Persian; and what's more, he sleeps—something I've rarely seen a baby do. What I'm trying to say to her (but of course, she'll agree without really hearing me) is that he's worth it. It seems to me that since I've had children, I've grown richer and deeper. They may have slowed down my writing for a while, but when I did write, I had more of a self to speak from. After all, who else in the world do you *have* to love, no matter what? Who else can you absolutely not give up on? My life seems more intricate. Also more dangerous.

After the children started school, I put up the partitions in my mind. I would rush around in the morning braiding their hair, packing their lunches; then the second they were gone I would grow quiet and climb the stairs to my study. Sometimes a child would come home early and I would feel a little tug between the two parts of me; I'd be absentminded and short-tempered. Then gradually I learned to make the transition more easily. It feels like a sort of string that I tell myself to loosen. When the children come home, I drop the string and close the study door and that's the end of it. It doesn't always work perfectly, of course. There are times when it doesn't work at all: if a child is sick, for instance, I can't possibly drop the children's end of the string, and I've learned not to try. It's easier just to stop writing for a while. Or if they're home but otherwise occupied, I no longer attempt to sneak off to my study to finish that one last page; I know that instantly, as if by magic, assorted little people will be pounding on my door requiring Band-Aids, tetanus shots, and a complete summation of the facts of life.

Last spring, I bought a midget tape recorder to make notes on. I'd noticed that my best ideas came while I was running the vacuum cleaner, but I was always losing them. I thought this little recorder would help. I carried it around in my shirt pocket. But I was ignoring the partitions, is what it was; I was letting one half of my life intrude upon the other. A child would be talking about her day at school and suddenly I'd whip out the tape recorder and tell it, "Get Morgan out of that cocktail party; he's not the type to drink." "Huh?" the child would say. Both halves began to seem ludicrous, unsynchronized. I took the recorder back to Radio Shack.

A few years ago, my parents went to the Gaza Strip to work for the American Friends Service Committee. It was a lifelong dream of my father's to do something with the AFSC as soon as all his children were grown, and he'd been actively preparing for it for years. But almost as soon as they got there, my mother fell ill with a mysterious fever that neither the Arab nor the Israeli hospitals could diagnose. My parents had to come home for her treatment, and since they'd sublet their house in North Carolina, they had to live with us. For four months, they stayed here—but only on a week-to-week basis, not knowing when they were going back, or whether they were going back at all, or how serious my mother's illness was. It was hard for her, of course, but it should have been especially hard in another way for my father, who had simply to hang in suspended animation for four months while my mother was whisked in and out of hospitals. However, I believe he was as pleased with life as he always is. He whistled Mozart and puttered around insulating our windows. He went on long walks collecting firewood. He strolled over to the meetinghouse and gave a talk on the plight of the Arab refugees. "Now that we seem to have a little time," he told my mother, "why not visit the boys?" and during one of her outpatient periods he took her on a gigantic cross-country trip to see all my brothers and any other relatives they happened upon. Then my mother decided she ought to go to a faith healer. (She wouldn't usually do such a thing, but she was desperate.) "Oh. Okay," my father said, and he took her to a faith healer, whistling all the way. And when the faith healer didn't work, my mother said, "I think this is psychosomatic. Let's go back to Gaza." My father said, "Okay," and reserved two seats on the next plane over. The children and I went to see them the following summer: my mother's fever was utterly gone, and my father drove us down the Strip, weaving a little Renault among the tents and camels, cheerfully whistling Mozart.

I hold this entire, rambling set of events in my head at all times, and remind myself of it almost daily. It seems to me that the way my father lives (infinitely adapting, and looking around him with a smile to say, "Oh! So *this* is where I am!") is also the way to slip gracefully through a choppy life of writing novels, plastering the dining room ceiling, and presiding at slumber parties. I have learned, bit by bit, to accept a school snow-closing as an unexpected holiday, an excuse to play seventeen rounds of Parcheesi instead of typing up a short story. When there's a midweek visitation of uncles from Iran (hordes of great, bald, yellow men calling for their glasses of tea, sleeping on guest beds, couches, two armchairs pushed together, and discarded crib mattresses), I have decided that I might as well listen to what they have to say, and work on my novel tomorrow instead. I smile at the uncles out of a kind of clear, swept space inside me. What this takes, of course, is a sense of limitless time, but I'm getting that. My life is beginning to seem unusually long. And there's a danger to it: I could wind up as passive as a piece of wood on a wave. But I try to walk a middle line.

I was standing in the schoolyard waiting for a child when another mother came up to me. "Have you found work yet?" she asked. "Or are you still just writing?"

Now, how am I supposed to answer that?

I could take offense, come to think of it. Maybe the reason I didn't is that I halfway share her attitude. They're *paying* me for this? For just writing down untruthful stories? I'd better look around for more permanent employment. For I do consider writing to be a finite job. I expect that any day now, I will have said all I have to say; I'll have used up all my characters, and then I'll be free to get on with my real life. When I make a note of new ideas on index cards, I imagine I'm clearing out my head, and that soon it will be empty and spacious. I file the cards in a little blue box, and I can picture myself using the final card one day—ah! through at last!—and throwing the blue box away. I'm like a dentist who continually fights tooth decay, working toward the time when he's conquered it altogether and done himself out of a job. But my head keeps loading up again; the little blue box stays crowded and messy. Even when I feel I have no ideas at all, and can't possibly start the next chapter, I have a sense of something still bottled in me, trying to get out.

People have always seemed funny and strange to me, and touching in unexpected ways. I can't shake off a sort of mist of irony that hangs over whatever I see. Probably that's what I'm trying to put across when I write; I may believe that I'm the one person who holds this view of things. And I'm always hurt when a reader says that I choose only bizarre or eccentric people to write about. It's not a matter of choice; it just seems to me that even the most ordinary person, in real life, will turn out to have something unusual at his center. I like to think that I might meet up with one of my past characters at the very next street corner. The odd thing is, sometimes I have. And if I were remotely religious, I'd believe that a little gathering of my characters would be waiting for me in heaven when I died. "*Then* what happened?" I'd ask them. "How have things worked out, since the last time I saw you?"

I think I was born with the impression that what happened in books was much more reasonable, and interesting, and *real,* in some ways, than what happened in life. I hated childhood, and spent it sitting behind a book waiting for adulthood to arrive. When I ran out of books I made up my own. At night, when I couldn't sleep, I made up stories in the dark. Most of my plots involved girls going west in covered wagons. I was truly furious that I'd been born too late to go west in a covered wagon.

I know a poet who says that in order to be a writer, you have to have had rheumatic fever in your childhood. I've never had rheumatic fever, but I believe that any kind of setting-apart situation will do as well. In my case, it was emerging from that commune—really an experimental Quaker community in the wilderness—and trying to fit into the outside world. I was eleven. I had never used a telephone and could strike a match on the soles of my bare feet. All the children in my new school looked very peculiar to me, and I certainly must have looked peculiar to them. I am still surprised, to this day, to find myself where I am. My life is so streamlined and full of modern conveniences. How did I get here? I have given up hope, by now, of ever losing my sense of distance; in fact, I seem to have come to cherish it. Neither I nor any of my brothers can stand being out among a crowd of people for any length of time at all.

I spent my adolescence planning to be an artist, not a writer. After all, books had to be about major events, and none had ever happened to me. All I knew were tobacco workers, stringing the leaves I handed them and talking up a storm. Then I found a book of Eudora Welty's short stories in the high school library. She was writing about Edna Earle, who was so slow-witted she could sit all day just pondering how the tail of the *C* got through the loop of the *L* on the Coca-Cola sign. Why, I knew Edna Earle. You mean you could *write* about such people? I have always meant to send Eudora Welty a thank-you note, but I imagine she would find it a little strange.

I wanted to go to Swarthmore College, but my parents suggested Duke instead, where I had a full scholarship, because my three brothers were coming along right behind me and it was more important for boys to get a good education than for girls. That was the first and last time that my being female was ever a serious issue. I still don't think it was just, but I can't say it ruined my life. After all, Duke had Reynolds Price, who turned out to be the only person I ever knew who could actually teach writing. It all worked out, in the end.

I believe that for many writers, the hardest time is that dead spot after college (where they're wonder-children, made much of) and before their first published work. Luckily, I didn't notice that part; I was so vague about what I wanted to do that I could hardly chafe at not yet doing it. I went to graduate school in Russian studies; I scrubbed decks on a boat in Maine; I got a job ordering books from the Soviet Union. Writing was something that crept in around the edges. For a while I lived in New York, where I became addicted to riding any kind of train or subway, and while I rode I often felt I was nothing but an enormous eye, taking things in and turning them over and sorting them out. But who would I tell them to, once I'd sorted them? I have never had more than three or four close friends, at any period of my life; and anyway, I don't talk well. I am the kind of person who wakes up at four in the morning and suddenly thinks of what she should have said yesterday at lunch. For me, writing something down was the only road out.

You would think, since I waited so long and so hopefully for adulthood, that it would prove to be a disappointment. Actually, I figure it was worth the wait. I like everything about it but the paperwork—the income tax and protesting the Sears bill and renewing the Triple-A membership. I always did count on having a husband and children, and here they are. I'm surprised to find myself a writer but have fitted it in fairly well, I think. The only real trouble that writing has ever brought me is an occasional sense of being invaded by the outside world. Why do people imagine that writers, having chosen the most private of professions, should be any good at performing in public, or should have the slightest desire to tell their secrets to interviewers from ladies' magazines? I feel I am only holding myself together by being extremely firm and decisive about what I will do and what I will not do. I will write my books and raise the children. Anything else just fritters me away. I know this makes me seem narrow, but in fact, I *am* narrow. I like routine and rituals and I hate leaving home; I have a sense of digging my heels in. I refuse to drive on freeways. I dread our annual vacation. Yet I'm continually prepared for travel: it is physically impossible for me to buy any necessity without buying a travel-sized version as well. I have a little toilet kit, with soap and a nightgown, forever packed and ready to go. How do you explain that?

As the outside world grows less dependable, I keep buttressing my inside world, where people go on meaning well and surprising other people with little touches of grace. There are days when I sink into my novel like a pool and emerge feeling blank and bemused and used up. Then I drift over to the schoolyard, and there's this mother wondering if I'm doing anything halfway useful yet. Am I working? Have I found a job? No, I tell her.

I'm still just writing.

THINGS TO THINK ABOUT

1. What autobiographical details recorded in "Still Just Writing" appear in Anne Tyler's story, "Your Place is Empty"? How have these details been transformed?
2. Do you know any professional writers? If so, how do they spend their days? How is their work regarded by the rest of the community? Does Tyler's life surprise you? Does she live in the way you imagined a writer would live? Does her life seem especially "dangerous" to you?
3. Tyler wrote, "People have always seemed funny and strange to me, and touching in unexpected ways." Can you detect any of this attitude in her story "Your Place Is Empty"?
4. Tyler suggests that it is necessary for a writer to have as a child some "kind of setting-apart situation." Why does she think such an experience is necessary? Do you think such an experience is necessary? Why?
5. Tyler says she believes "that even the most ordinary person, in real life, will turn out to have something unusual at his center." If this is true, what happens to the notions of "ordinary" and "unusual"? Do you share her beliefs? If so, why? If not, why?

GABRIEL GARCÍA MÁRQUEZ

A VERY OLD MAN WITH ENORMOUS WINGS

Gabriel García Márquez (b. 1928) a winner of The Nobel Prize for Literature has emerged as the most important living South American writer. His novel One Hundred Years of Solitude *has influenced an entire generation of writers who have copied "the magic realism" of his work.*

García Márquez was born in Aracataca, Colombia and studied journalism and law. He worked as a journalist throughout Latin America and in Europe and the United States. Like many other Latin American writers, he lives for political reasons outside of his native country. He now resides in Mexico.

On the third day of rain they had killed so many crabs inside the house that Pelayo had to cross his drenched courtyard and throw them into the sea, because the newborn child had a temperature all night and they thought it was due to the stench. The world had been sad since

Tuesday. Sea and sky were a single ash-gray thing and the sands of the beach, which on March nights glimmered like powdered light, had become a stew of mud and rotten shellfish. The light was so weak at noon that when Pelayo was coming back to the house after throwing away the crabs, it was hard for him to see what it was that was moving and groaning in the rear of the courtyard. He had to go very close to see that it was an old man, a very old man, lying face down in the mud, who, in spite of his tremendous efforts, couldn't get up, impeded by his enormous wings.

Frightened by that nightmare, Pelayo ran to get Elisenda, his wife, who was putting compresses on the sick child, and he took her to the rear of the courtyard. They both looked at the fallen body with mute stupor. He was dressed like a ragpicker. There were only a few faded hairs left on his bald skull and very few teeth in his mouth, and his pitiful condition of a drenched great-grandfather had taken away any sense of grandeur he might have had. His huge buzzard wings, dirty and half-plucked, were forever entangled in the mud. They looked at him so long and so closely that Pelayo and Elisenda very soon overcame their surprise and in the end found him familiar. Then they dared speak to him, and he answered in an incomprehensible dialect with a strong sailor's voice. That was how they skipped over the inconvenience of the wings and quite intelligently concluded that he was a lonely castaway from some foreign ship wrecked by the storm. And yet, they called in a neighbor woman who knew everything about life and death to see him, and all she needed was one look to show them their mistake.

"He's an angel," she told them. "He must have been coming for the child, but the poor fellow is so old that the rain knocked him down."

On the following day everyone knew that a flesh-and-blood angel was held captive in Pelayo's house. Against the judgment of the wise neighbor woman for whom angels in those times were the fugitive survivors of a celestial conspiracy, they did not have the heart to club him to death. Pelayo watched over him all afternoon from the kitchen, armed with his bailiff's club, and before going to bed he dragged him out of the mud and locked him up with the hens in the wire chicken coop. In the middle of the night, when the rain stopped, Pelayo and Elisenda were still killing crabs. A short time afterward the child woke up without a fever and with a desire to eat. Then they felt magnanimous and decided to put the angel on a raft with fresh water and provisions for three days and leave him to his fate on the high seas. But when they went out into the courtyard with the first light of dawn, they found the whole neighborhood in front of the chicken coop having fun with the angel, without the slightest reverence, tossing him things to eat through the openings in the wire as if he weren't a supernatural creature but a circus animal.

Father Gonzaga arrived before seven o'clock, alarmed at the strange news. By that time onlookers less frivolous than those at dawn had already arrived and they were making all kinds of conjectures concerning the captive's future. The simplest among them thought that he should be named mayor of the world. Others of sterner mind felt that he should be promoted to the rank of five-star general in order to win all wars. Some visionaries hoped that he could be put to stud in order to implant on earth a race of winged wise men who could take charge of the universe. But Father Gonzaga, before becoming a priest, had been a robust woodcutter. Standing by the wire, he reviewed his catechism in an instant and asked them to open the door so that he could take a close look at that pitiful man who looked more like a huge decrepit hen among the fascinated chickens. He was lying in a corner drying his open wings in the sunlight among the fruit peels and breakfast leftovers that the early risers had thrown him. Alien to the impertinences of the world, he only lifted his antiquarian eyes and murmured something in his dialect when Father Gonzaga went into the chicken coop and said good morning to him in Latin. The parish priest had his first suspicion of an imposter when he saw that he did not understand the language of God or know how to greet His ministers. Then he noticed that seen close up he was much too human: he had an unbearable smell of the outdoors, the back side of his wings was strewn with parasites and his main feathers had been mistreated by terrestrial winds, and nothing about him measured up to the proud dignity of angels. Then he came out of the chicken coop and in a brief sermon warned the curious against the risks of being ingenuous. He reminded them that the devil had the bad habit of making use of carnival tricks in order to confuse the unwary. He argued that if wings were not the essential element in determining the difference between a hawk and an airplane, they were even less so in the recognition of angels. Nevertheless, he promised to write a letter to his bishop so that the latter would write to his primate so that the latter would write to the Supreme Pontiff in order to get the final verdict from the highest courts.

His prudence fell on sterile hearts. The news of the captive angel spread with such rapidity that after a few hours the courtyard had the bustle of a marketplace and they had to call in troops with fixed bayonets to disperse the mob that was about to knock the house down. Elisenda, her spine all twisted from sweeping up so much marketplace trash, then got the idea of fencing in the yard and charging five cents admission to see the angel.

The curious came from far away. A traveling carnival arrived with a flying acrobat who buzzed over the crowd several times, but no one paid any attention to him because his wings were not those of an angel but, rather, those of a sidereal bat. The most unfortunate invalids on earth came in search of health: a poor woman who since childhood had been counting her heartbeats and had run out of numbers; a Portuguese man who couldn't sleep because the noise of the stars disturbed him; a sleepwalker who got up at night to undo the things he had done while awake; and many others with less serious ailments. In the midst of that shipwreck disorder that made the earth tremble, Pelayo and Elisenda were happy with fatigue, for in less than a week they had crammed their rooms with money and the line of pilgrims waiting their turn to enter still reached beyond the horizon.

The angel was the only one who took no part in his own act. He spent his time trying to get comfortable in his borrowed nest, befuddled by the hellish heat of the oil lamps and sacramental candles that had been placed along the wire. At first they tried to make him eat some mothballs, which, according to the wisdom of the wise neighbor woman, were the food prescribed for angels. But he turned them down, just as he turned down the papal lunches that the penitents brought him, and they never found out whether it was because he was an angel or because he was an old man that in the end he ate nothing but eggplant mush. His only supernatural virtue seemed to be patience. Especially during the first days, when the hens pecked at him, searching for the stellar parasites that proliferated in his wings, and the cripples pulled out feathers to touch their defective parts with, and even the most merciful threw stones at him, trying to get him to rise so they could see him standing. The only time they succeeded in arousing him was when they burned his side with an iron for branding steers, for he had been motionless for so many hours that they thought he was dead. He awoke with a start, ranting in his hermetic language and with tears in his eyes, and he flapped his wings a couple of times, which brought on a whirlwind of chicken dung and lunar dust and a gale of panic that did not seem to be of this world. Although many thought that his reaction had been one not of rage but of pain, from then on they were careful not to annoy him, because the majority understood that his passivity was not that of a hero taking his ease but that of a cataclysm in repose.

Father Gonzaga held back the crowd's frivolity with formulas of maidservant inspiration while awaiting the arrival of a final judgment on the nature of the captive. But the mail from Rome showed no sense of urgency. They spent their time finding out if the prisoner had a navel, if his dialect had any connection with Aramaic, how many times he could fit on the head of a pin, or whether he wasn't just a Norwegian with wings. Those meager letters might have come and gone until the end of time if a providential event had not put an end to the priest's tribulations.

It so happened that during those days, among so many other carnival attractions, there arrived in town the traveling show of the woman who had been changed into a spider for having disobeyed her parents. The admission to see her was not only less than the admission to see the angel, but people were permitted to ask her all manner of questions about her absurd state and to examine her up and down so that no one would ever doubt the truth of her horror. She was a frightful tarantula the size of a ram and with the head of a sad maiden. What was most heartrending, however, was not her outlandish shape but the sincere affliction with which she recounted the details of her misfortune. While still practically a child she had sneaked out of her parents' house to go to a dance, and while she was coming back through the woods after having danced all night without permission, a fearful thunderclap rent the sky in two and through the crack came the lightning bolt of brimstone that changed her into a spider. Her only nourishment came from the meatballs that charitable souls chose to toss into her mouth. A spectacle like that, full of so much human truth and with such a fearful lesson, was bound to defeat without even trying that of a haughty angel who scarcely deigned to look at mortals. Besides, the few miracles attributed to the angel showed a certain mental disorder, like the blind man who didn't recover his sight but grew three new teeth, or the paralytic who didn't get to walk but almost won the lottery, and the leper whose sores sprouted sunflowers. Those consolation miracles, which were more like mocking fun, had already ruined the angel's reputation when the woman who had been changed into a spider finally crushed him completely. That was how Father Gonzaga was cured forever of his insomnia and Pelayo's courtyard went back to being as empty as during the time it had rained for three days and crabs walked through the bedrooms.

The owners of the house had no reason to lament. With the money they saved they built a two-story mansion with balconies and gardens and high netting so that crabs wouldn't get in during the winter, and with iron bars on the windows so that angels wouldn't get in. Pelayo also set up a rabbit warren close to town and gave up his job as bailiff for good, and Elisenda bought some satin pumps with high heels and many dresses of iridescent silk, the kind worn on Sunday by the most desirable women in those times. The chicken coop was the only thing that didn't receive any attention. If they washed it down with creolin and burned tears of myrrh inside it every so often, it was not in homage to the angel but to drive away the dungheap stench that still hung everywhere like a ghost and was turning the new house into an old one. At first, when the child learned to walk, they were careful that he not get too close to the chicken coop. But then they began to lose their fears and got used to the smell, and before the child got his second teeth he'd gone inside the chicken coop to play, where the wires were falling apart. The angel was no less standoffish with him than with other mortals, but he tolerated the most ingenious infamies with the patience of a dog who had no illusions. They both came down with chicken pox at the same time. The doctor who took care of the child couldn't resist the temptation to listen to the angel's heart, and he found so much whistling in the heart and so many sounds in his kidneys that it seemed impossible for him to be alive. What surprised him most, however, was the logic of his wings. They seemed so natural on that completely human organism that he couldn't understand why other men didn't have them too.

When the child began school it had been some time since the sun and rain had caused the collapse of the chicken coop. The angel went dragging himself about here and there like a stray dying man. They would drive him out of the bedroom with a broom and a moment later find him in the kitchen. He seemed to be in so many places at the same time that they grew to think that he'd been duplicated, that he was reproducing himself all through the house, and the exasperated and unhinged Elisenda shouted that it was awful living in that hell full of angels. He could scarcely eat and his antiquarian eyes had also become so foggy that he went about bumping into posts. All he had left were the bare cannulae[1] of his last feathers. Pelayo threw a blanket over him and extended him the charity of letting him sleep in the shed, and only then did they notice that he had a temperature at night, and was delirious with the tongue twisters of an old Norwegian. That was one of the few times they became alarmed, for they thought he was going to die and not even the wise neighbor woman had been able to tell them what to do with dead angels.

And yet he not only survived his worst winter, but seemed improved with the first sunny days. He remained motionless for several days in the farthest corner of the courtyard, where no one would see him, and at the beginning of December some large, stiff feathers began to grow on his wings, the feathers of a scarecrow, which looked more like another misfortune of decrepitude. But he must have known the reason for those changes, for he was quite careful that no one should notice them, that no one should hear the sea chanteys that he sometimes sang under the stars. One morning Elisenda was cutting some bunches of onions for lunch when a wind that seemed to come from the high seas blew into the kitchen. Then she went to the window and caught the angel in his first attempts at flight. They were so clumsy that his fingernails opened a furrow in the vegetable patch and he was on the point of knocking the shed down with the ungainly flapping that slipped on the light and couldn't get a grip on the air. But he did manage to gain altitude. Elisenda let out a sigh of relief, for herself and for him, when she saw him pass over the last houses, holding himself up in some way with the risky flapping of a senile vulture. She kept watching him even when she was through cutting onions and she kept on watching until it was no longer possible for her to see him, because then he was no longer an annoyance in her life but an imaginary dot on the horizon of the sea.

[1] Cannulae are the reedlike shafts of feathers.

QUESTIONS

1. Do any of the characters treat the Very Old Man with the reverence due a human or angel? What kind of interest do people show him?
2. How does Father Gonzaga and the church hierarchy respond to the Very Old Man? How do they expect angels to look and act? Are their reactions reasonable?
3. Why is the spider-woman more popular than the Very Old Man?
4. The narrator speaks of the Very Old Man as responsible for "consolation miracles" instead of cures. What is the difference? Why would the Old Man produce such consolations instead of cures? Does he produce any miracles?
5. What do people expect of the Old Man? What did you as a reader expect of him? What would he have to do to prove that he is a sacred being? If he showed up at the student union, how would people react?
6. Why does Elisenda think of the Old Man as an "annoyance"? Why is she happy when he is gone? Is this the response you would have expected of someone who had a winged man drop in on her? Is her response unreasonable given human nature?

SHIRLEY JACKSON

THE LOTTERY

Shirley Jackson (1919–1965) wrote in two different styles. She had a comic style to tell realistic domestic stories and a gothic style for horror stories. "The Lottery" is her most famous tale, and when it first appeared in The New Yorker, *many readers wrote to the magazine believing the story to be a factual account.*

Shirley Jackson was born in San Francisco and educated at Syracuse University. She married the novelist and critic Stanley Edgar Hyman and had four children before her untimely death.

The morning of June 27th was clear and sunny with the fresh warmth of a full-summer day; the flowers were blossoming profusely and the grass was richly green. The people of the village began to gather in the square, between the post office and the bank, around ten o'clock; in some towns there were so many people that the lottery took two days and had to be started on June 26th, but in this village, where there were only about three hundred people, the whole lottery took less than two hours, so it could begin at ten o'clock in the morning and still be through in time to allow the villagers to get home for noon dinner.

The children assembled first, of course. School was recently over for the summer, and the feeling of liberty sat uneasily on most of them; they tended to gather together quietly for a while before they broke into boisterous play, and their talk was still of the classroom and the teacher, of books and reprimands. Bobby Martin had already stuffed his pockets full of stones, and the other boys soon followed his example, selecting the smoothest and roundest stones; Bobby and Harry Jones and Dickie Delacroix—the villagers pronounced this name "Dellacroy"—eventually made a great pile of stones in one corner of the square and guarded it against the raids of the other boys. The girls stood aside, talking among themselves, looking over their shoulders at the boys, and the very small children rolled in the dust or clung to the hands of their older brothers or sisters.

Soon the men began to gather, surveying their own children, speaking of planting and rain, tractors and taxes. They stood together, away from the pile of stones in the corner, and their jokes were quiet and they smiled rather than laughed. The women, wearing faded house dresses and sweaters, came shortly after their menfolk. They greeted one another and exchanged bits of gossip as they went to join their husbands. Soon the women, standing by their husbands, began to call to their children, and the children came reluctantly, having to be called four or five times. Bobby Martin ducked under his mother's grasping hand and ran, laughing, back to the pile of stones. His father spoke up sharply, and Bobby came quickly and took his place between his father and his oldest brother.

The lottery was conducted—as were the square dances, the teenage club, the Halloween program—by Mr. Summers, who had time and energy to devote to civic activities. He was a round-faced, jovial man and he ran the coal business, and people were sorry for him, because he had no children and his wife was a scold. When he arrived in the square, carrying the black wooden box, there was a murmur of conversation among the villagers, and he waved and called, "Little late today, folks." The postmaster, Mr. Graves, followed him, carrying a three-legged stool, and the stool was put in the center of the square and Mr. Summers set the black box down on it. The villagers kept their distance, leaving a space between themselves and the stool, and when Mr. Summers said, "Some of you fellows want to give me a hand?" there was a hesitation before two men, Mr. Martin and his oldest son, Baxter, came forward to hold the box steady on the stool while Mr. Summers stirred up the papers inside it.

The original paraphernalia for the lottery had been lost long ago, and the black box now resting on the stool had been put into use even before Old Man Warner, the oldest man in town, was born. Mr. Summers spoke frequently to the villagers about making a new box, but no one liked to upset even as much tradition as was represented by the black box. There was a story that the present box had been made with some pieces of the box that had preceded it, the one that had been constructed when the first people settled down to make a village here. Every year, after the lottery, Mr. Summers began talking again about a new box, but every year the subject was allowed to fade off without anything's being done. The black box grew shabbier each year; by now it was no longer completely black but splintered badly along one side to show the original wood color, and in some places faded or stained.

Mr. Martin and his oldest son, Baxter, held the black box securely on the stool until Mr. Summers had stirred the papers thoroughly with his hand. Because so much of the ritual had been forgotten or discarded, Mr. Summers had been successful in having slips of paper substituted for the chips of wood that had been used for generations. Chips of wood, Mr. Summers had argued, had been all very well when the village was tiny, but now that the population was more than three hundred and likely to keep on growing, it was necessary to use something that would fit more easily into the black box. The night before the lottery, Mr. Summers and Mr. Graves made up the slips of paper and put them in the box, and it was then taken to the safe of Mr. Summers' coal company and locked up until Mr. Summers was ready to take it to the square next morning. The rest of the year, the box was put away, sometimes one place, sometimes another; it had spent one year in Mr. Graves's barn and another year underfoot in the post office, and sometimes it was set on a shelf in the Martin grocery and left there.

There was a great deal of fussing to be done before Mr. Summers declared the lottery open. There were the lists to make up—of heads of families, heads of households in each family, members of each household in each family. There was the proper swearing-in of Mr. Summers by the postmaster, as the official of the lottery; at one time, some people remembered, there had been a recital of some sort, performed by the official of the lottery, a perfunctory, tuneless chant that had been rattled off duly each year; some people believed that the official of the lottery used to stand just so when he said or sang it, others believed that he was supposed to walk among the people, but years and years ago this part of the ritual had been allowed to lapse. There had been, also, a ritual salute, which the official of the lottery had had to use in addressing each person who came up to draw from the box, but this also had changed with time, until now it was felt necessary only for the official to speak to each person approaching Mr. Summers was very good at all this; in his clean white shirt and blue jeans, with one hand resting carelessly on the black box, he seemed very proper and important as he talked interminably to Mr. Graves and the Martins.

Just as Mr. Summers finally left off talking and turned to the assembled villagers, Mrs. Hutchinson came hurriedly along the path to the square, her sweater thrown over her shoulders, and slid into place in the back of the crowd. "Clean forgot what day it was," she said to Mrs. Delacroix, who stood next to her, and they both laughed softly. "Thought my old man was out back stacking wood," Mrs. Hutchinson went on, "and then I looked out the window and the kids was gone, and then I remembered it was the twenty-seventh and came a-running." She dried her hands on her apron, and Mrs. Delacroix said, "You're in time, though. They're still talking away up there."

Mrs. Hutchinson craned her neck to see through the crowd and found her husband and children standing near the front. She tapped Mrs. Delacroix on the arm as a farewell and began to make her way through the crowd. The people separated good-humoredly to let her through; two or three people said, in voices just loud enough to be heard across the crowd, "Here comes your Missus, Hutchinson," and "Bill, she made it after all." Mrs. Hutchinson reached her husband, and Mr. Summers, who had been waiting, said cheerfully, "Thought we were going to have to get on without you, Tessie." Mrs. Hutchinson said, grinning, "Wouldn't have me leave m'dishes in the sink, now, would you, Joe?," and soft laughter ran through the crowd as the people stirred back into position after Mrs. Hutchinson's arrival.

"Well, now," Mr. Summers said soberly, "guess we better get started, get this over with, so's we can go back to work. Anybody ain't here?"

"Dunbar," several people said. "Dunbar, Dunbar."

Mr. Summers consulted his list. "Clyde Dunbar," he said. "That's right. He's broke his leg, hasn't he? Who's drawing for him?"

"Me, I guess," a woman said, and Mr. Summers turned to look at her. "Wife draws for her husband," Mr. Summers said. "Don't you have a grown boy to do it for you, Janey?" Although Mr. Summers and everyone else in the village knew the answer perfectly well, it was the business of the official of the lottery to ask such questions formally. Mr. Summers waited with an expression of polite interest while Mrs. Dunbar answered.

"Horace's not but sixteen yet," Mrs. Dunbar said regretfully. "Guess I gotta fill in for the old man this year."

"Right," Mr. Summers said. He made a note on the list he was holding. Then he asked, "Watson boy drawing this year?"

A tall boy in the crowd raised his hand. "Here," he said. "I'm drawing for m'mother and me." He blinked his eyes nervously and ducked his head as several voices in the crowd said things like "Good fellow, Jack," and "Glad to see your mother's got a man to do it."

"Well," Mr. Summers said, "guess that's everyone. Old Man Warner make it?"

"Here," a voice said, and Mr. Summers nodded.

A sudden hush fell on the crowd as Mr. Summers cleared his throat and looked at the list. "All ready?" he called. "Now, I'll read the names—heads of families first—and the men come up and take a paper out of the box. Keep the paper folded in your hand without looking at it until everyone has had a turn. Everything clear?"

The people had done it so many times that they only half listened to the directions; most of them were quiet, wetting their lips, not looking around. Then Mr. Summers raised one hand high and said, "Adams." A man disengaged himself from the crowd and came forward. "Hi, Steve," Mr. Summers said, and Mr. Adams said, "Hi, Joe." They grinned at one another humorlessly and nervously. Then Mr. Adams reached into the black box and took out a folded paper. He held it firmly by one corner as he turned and went hastily back to his place in the crowd, where he stood a little apart from his family, not looking down at his hand.

"Allen," Mr. Summers said. "Anderson . . . Bentham."

"Seems like there's no time at all between lotteries any more," Mrs. Delacroix said to Mrs. Graves in the back row. "Seems like we got through with the last one only last week."

"Times sure goes fast," Mrs. Graves said.

"Clark . . . Delacroix."

"There goes my old man," Mrs. Delacroix said. She held her breath while her husband went forward.

"Dunbar," Mr. Summers said, and Mrs. Dunbar went steadily to the box while one of the women said, "Go on, Janey," and another said, "There she goes."

"We're next," Mrs. Graves said. She watched while Mr. Graves came around from the side of the box, greeted Mr. Summers gravely, and selected a slip of paper from the box. By now, all through the crowd there were men holding the small folded papers in their large hands, turning them over and over nervously. Mrs. Dunbar and her two sons stood together, Mrs. Dunbar holding the slip of paper.

"Harburt . . . Hutchinson."

"Get up there, Bill," Mrs. Hutchinson said, and the people near her laughed.

"Jones."

"They do say," Mr. Adams said to Old Man Warner, who stood next to him, "that over in the north village they're talking of giving up the lottery."

Old Man Warner snorted. "Pack of crazy fools," he said. "Listening to the young folks, nothing's good enough for *them.* Next thing you know, they'll be wanting to go back to living in caves, nobody work any more, live *that* way for a while. Used to be a saying about 'Lottery in June, corn be heavy soon.' First thing you know, we'd all be eating stewed chickweed and acorns. There's *always* been a lottery," he added petulantly. "Bad enough to see young Joe Summers up there joking with everybody."

"Some places have already quit lotteries," Mrs. Adams said.

"Nothing but trouble in *that,*" Old Man Warner said stoutly. "Pack of young fools."

"Martin." And Bobby Martin watched his father go forward. "Overdyke . . . Percy."

"I wish they'd hurry," Mrs. Dunbar said to her older son. "I wish they'd hurry."

"They're almost through," her son said.

"You get ready to run tell Dad," Mrs. Dunbar said.

Mr. Summers called his own name and then stepped forward precisely and selected a slip from the box. Then he called, "Warner."

"Seventy-seventh year I been in the lottery," Old Man Warner said as he went through the crowd. "Seventy-seventh time."

"Watson." The tall boy came awkwardly through the crowd. Someone said, "Don't be nervous, Jack," and Mr. Summers said, "Take your time, son."

"Zanini."

After that, there was a long pause, a breathless pause, until Mr. Summers, holding his slip of paper in the air, said, "All right, fellows." For a minute, no one moved, and then all the slips of paper were opened. Suddenly, all the women began to speak at once, saying, "Who is it?," "Who's got it?," "Is it the Dunbars?," "Is it the Watsons?" Then the voices began to say, "It's Hutchinson. It's Bill," "Bill Hutchinson's got it."

"Go tell your father," Mrs. Dunbar said to her older son.

People began to look around to see the Hutchinsons. Bill Hutchinson was standing quiet staring down at the paper in his hand. Suddenly, Tessie Hutchinson shouted to Mr. Summers. "You didn't give him time enough to take any paper he wanted. I saw you. It wasn't fair."

"Be a good sport, Tessie," Mrs. Delacroix called, and Mrs. Graves said, "All of us took the same chance."

"Shut up, Tessie," Bill Hutchinson said.

"Well, everyone," Mr. Summers said, "that was done pretty fast, and now we've got to be hurrying a little more to get done in time." He consulted his next list. "Bill," he said, "you draw for the Hutchinson family. You got any other households in the Hutchinsons?"

"There's Don and Eva," Mrs. Hutchinson yelled. "Make *them* take their chance!"

"Daughters draw with their husbands' families, Tessie," Mr. Summers said gently. "You know that as well as anyone else."

"It wasn't *fair,*" Tessie said.

"I guess not, Joe," Bill Hutchinson said regretfully. "My daughter draws with her husband's family, that's only fair. And I've got no other family except the kids."

"Then, as far as drawing for families is concerned, it's you," Mr. Summers said in explanation, "and as far as drawing for households is concerned, that's you, too. Right?"

"Right," Bill Hutchinson said.

"How many kids, Bill?" Mr. Summers asked formally.

"Three," Bill Hutchinson said. "There's Bill, Jr., and Nancy, and little Dave. And Tessie and me."

"All right, then," Mr. Summers said. "Harry, you got their tickets back?"

Mr. Graves nodded and held up the slips of paper. "Put them in the box, then," Mr. Summers directed. "Take Bill's and put it in."

"I think we ought to start over," Mrs. Hutchinson said, as quietly as she could. "I tell you it wasn't *fair.* You didn't give him time enough to choose. *Every*body saw that."

Mr. Graves had selected the five slips and put them in the box, and he dropped all the papers but those onto the ground, where the breeze caught them and lifted them off.

"Listen, everybody," Mrs. Hutchinson was saying to the people around her.

"Ready, Bill?" Mr. Summers asked, and Bill Hutchinson, with one quick glance around at his wife and children, nodded.

"Remember," Mr. Summers said, "take the slips and keep them folded until each person has taken one. Harry, you help little Dave." Mr. Graves took the hand of the little boy, who came willingly with him up to the box. "Take a paper out of the box, Davy," Mr. Summers said. Davy put his hand into the box and laughed. "Take just *one* paper," Mr. Summers said. "Harry, you hold it for him." Mr. Graves took the child's hand and removed the folded paper from the tight fist and held it while little Dave stood next to him and looked up at him wonderingly.

"Nancy next," Mr. Summers said. Nancy was twelve, and her school friends breathed heavily as she went forward, switching her skirt, and took a slip daintily from the box. "Bill, Jr.," Mr. Summers said, and Billy, his face red and his feet over-large, nearly knocked the box over as he got a paper out. "Tessie," Mr. Summers said. She hesitated for a minute, looking around defiantly, and then set her lips and went up to the box. She snatched a paper out and held it behind her.

"Bill," Mr. Summers said, and Bill Hutchinson reached into the box and felt around, bringing his hand out at last with the slip of paper in it.

The crowd was quiet. A girl whispered, "I hope it's not Nancy," and the sound of the whisper reached the edges of the crowd.

"It's not the way it used to be," Old Man Warner said clearly. "People ain't the way they used to be."

"All right," Mr. Summers said. "Open the papers. Harry, you open little Dave's."

Mr. Graves opened the slip of paper and there was a general sigh through the crowd as he held it up and everyone could see that it was blank. Nancy and Bill, Jr., opened theirs at the same time, and both beamed and laughed, turning around to the crowd and holding their slips of paper above their heads.

"Tessie," Mr. Summers said. There was a pause, and then Mr. Summers looked at Bill Hutchinson, and Bill unfolded his paper and showed it. It was blank.

"It's Tessie," Mr. Summers said, and his voice was hushed. "Show us her paper, Bill."

Bill Hutchinson went over to his wife and forced the slip of paper out of her hand. It had a black spot on it, the black spot Mr. Summers had made the night before with the heavy pencil in the coal company office. Bill Hutchinson held it up, and there was a stir in the crowd.

"All right, folks," Mr. Summers said. "Let's finish quickly."

Although the villagers had forgotten the ritual and lost the original black box, they still remembered to use stones. The pile of stones the boys had made earlier was ready; there were stones on the ground with the blowing scraps of paper that had come out of the box. Mrs. Delacroix selected a stone so large she had to pick it up with both hands and turned to Mrs. Dunbar. "Come on," she said. "Hurry up."

Mrs. Dunbar had small stones in both hands, and she said, gasping for breath, "I can't run at all. You'll have to go ahead and I'll catch up with you."

The children had stones already, and someone gave little Davy Hutchinson a few pebbles.

Tessie Hutchinson was in the center of a cleared space by now, and she held her hands out desperately as the villagers moved in on her. "It isn't fair," she said. A stone hit her on the side of the head.

Old Man Warner was saying, "Come on, come on, everyone." Steve Adams was in the front of the crowd of villagers, with Mrs. Graves beside him.

"It isn't fair, it isn't right," Mrs. Hutchinson screamed, and then they were upon her.

QUESTIONS

1. What details in the early parts of the story suggest that "The Lottery" will be a realistic story? Does Jackson suggest in the opening of the story anything about the lottery which would make you suspicious of its deadly purpose?
2. How does the narrator suggest the ritual nature of the lottery? What other sorts of rituals is it compared to? What part does ritual play in the life of a community?
3. At what point in the story did you as a reader begin to suspect that the lottery was a deadly ritual? What alerted you to the prospect? Did the suspicion come suddenly, or did it build up gradually?
4. What details in the early part of the story appeared at first innocent but proved—as you read to the end—to be sinister or deadly? Why didn't they seem sinister at first?
5. Do you know anyone in your community, block or dormitory who has been singled out for abuse or punishment? What did the person do to elicit the

abuse? Is the abuse justified by the person's actions? Are they in any sense a scapegoat?

HENRY JAMES

THE REAL THING

Henry James (1843–1916) grew up under remarkable circumstances. His father was a wealthy man of philosophical tendency who wished to rear his children under conditions most advantageous to the development of their minds and spirits. He sent them to the best school in Europe and America; they travelled a good deal both here and abroad; they were introduced to the most stimulating people their father could find. His experiment was not without its success.

Henry's brother William, after flirting with a career as a painter became one of the greatest psychologists of his age, writing such classic studies The Principles of Psychology *and* The Varieties of Religious Experience. *Their sister Alice was a talented writer as well. Her diaries are one of the most remarkable products of their kind, exhibiting the qualities of sensibility—moral earnestness, comic penetration, and psychological subtlety—that mark the works of her brothers.*

Throughout his long career in which he resided chiefly in England, Henry James wrote many different kinds of works. His greatest achievement is his novels—particularly Portrait of a Lady, The Ambassadors, *and* The Wings of the Dove*—but he also wrote plays, biographies, memoirs, a travel book recounting his return trip to America, and criticism. He is regarded as one of the greatest writers of short tales whose linguistic density and deftness are matched by their psychological sureness and subtlety.*

When the porter's wife (she used to answer the house-bell), announced "A gentleman—with a lady, sir," I had, as I often had in those days, for the wish was father to the thought, an immediate vision of sitters. Sitters my visitors in this case proved to be; but not in the sense I should have preferred. However, there was nothing at first to indicate that they might have come for a portrait. The gentleman, a man of fifty, very high and very straight, with a moustache slightly grizzled and a dark gray walking-coat admirably fitted, both of which I noted professionally—I don't mean as a barber or yet as a tailor—would have struck me as a celebrity if celebrities often were striking. It was a truth of which I had for some time been conscious that a figure with a good deal of frontage was, as one might say, almost never a public institution. A glance at the lady helped to remind me of this paradoxical law: she also looked too distinguished to be a "personality." Moreover one would scarcely come across two variations together.

Neither of the pair spoke immediately—they only prolonged the preliminary gaze which suggested that each wished to give the other a chance. They were visibly shy; they stood there letting me take them in—which, as I afterwards perceived, was the most practical thing they could have done. In this way their embarrassment served their cause. I had seen people painfully reluctant to mention that they desired anything so gross as to be represented on canvas; but the scruples of my new friends appeared almost insurmountable. Yet the gentleman might have said "I should like a portrait of my wife," and the lady might have said "I should like a portrait of my husband." Perhaps they were not husband and wife—this naturally would make the matter more delicate. Perhaps they wished to be done together—in which case they ought to have brought a third person to break the news.

"We come from Mr. Rivet," the lady said at last, with a dim smile which had the effect of a moist sponge passed over a "sunk" piece of painting, as well as of a vague allusion to vanished beauty. She was as tall and straight, in her degree, as her companion, and with ten years less to carry. She looked as sad as a woman could look whose face was not charged with expression; that is, her tinted oval mask showed friction as an exposed surface shows it. The hand of time had played over her freely, but only to simplify. She was slim and stiff, and so well-dressed, in dark blue cloth, with lappets and pockets and buttons, that it was clear she employed the same tailor as her husband. The couple had an indefinable air of prosperous thrift—they evidently got a good deal of luxury for their money. If I was to be one of their luxuries it would behove me to consider my terms.

"Ah, Claude Rivet recommended me?" I inquired; and I added that it was very kind of him, though I could reflect that, as he only painted landscape, this was not a sacrifice.

The lady looked very hard at the gentleman, and the gentleman looked round the room. Then staring at the floor a moment and stroking his moustache, he rested his pleasant eyes on me with the remark: "He said you were the right one."

"I try to be, when people want to sit."

"Yes, we should like to," said the lady anxiously.

"Do you mean together?"

My visitors exchanged a glance. "If you could do anything with *me,* I suppose it would be double," the gentleman stammered.

"Oh, yes, there's naturally a higher charge for two figures than for one."

"We should like to make it pay," the husband confessed.

"That's very good of you," I returned, appreciating so unwonted a sympathy—for I supposed he meant pay the artist.

A sense of strangeness seemed to dawn on the lady. "We mean for the illustrations—Mr. Rivet said you might put one in."

"Put one in—an illustration?" I was equally confused.

"Sketch her off, you know," said the gentleman, colouring.

It was only then that I understood the service Claude Rivet had rendered me; he had told them that I worked in black and white, for magazines, for storybooks, for sketches of contemporary life, and consequently had frequent employment for models. These things were true, but it was not less true (I may confess it now—whether because the aspiration was to lead to everything or to nothing I leave the reader to guess), that I couldn't get the honours, to say nothing of the emoluments, of a great painter of portraits out of my head. My "illustrations" were my pot-boilers; I looked to a different branch of art (far and away the most interesting it had always seemed to me), to perpetuate my fame. There was no shame in looking to it also to make my fortune; but that fortune was by so much further from being made from the moment my visitors wished to be "done" for nothing. I was disappointed; for in the pictorial sense I had immediately *seen* them. I had seized their type—I had already settled what I would do with it. Something that wouldn't absolutely have pleased them, I afterwards reflected.

"Ah, you're—you're—a—?" I began, as soon as I had mastered my surprise. I couldn't bring out the dingy word "models"; it seemed to fit the case so little.

"We haven't had much practice," said the lady.

"We've got to *do* something, and we've thought that an artist in your line might perhaps make something of us," her husband threw off. He further mentioned that they didn't know many artists and that they had gone first, on the off-chance (he painted views of course, but sometimes put in figures—perhaps I remembered), to Mr. Rivet, whom they had met a few years before at a place in Norfolk where he was sketching.

"We used to sketch a little ourselves," the lady hinted.

"It's very awkward, but we absolutely *must* do something," her husband went on.

"Of course, we're not so *very* young," she admitted, with a wan smile.

With the remark that I might as well know something more about them, the husband had handed me a card extracted from a neat new pocket-book (their appurtenances were all of the freshest) and inscribed with the words "Major Monarch." Impressive as these words were they didn't carry my knowledge much further; but my visitor presently added: I've left the army, and we've had the misfortune to lose our money. In fact our means are dreadfully small."

"It's an awful bore," said Mrs. Monarch.

They evidently wished to be discreet—to take care not to swagger because they were gentlefolks. I perceived they would have been willing to recognise this as something of a drawback, at the same time that I guessed at an underlying sense—their consolation in adversity—that they *had* their points. They certainly had; but these advantages struck me as preponderantly social; such for instance as would help to make a drawing-room look well. However, a drawing-room was always, or ought to be, a picture.

In consequence of his wife's allusion to their age Major Monarch observed: "Naturally, it's more for the figure that we thought of going in. We can still hold ourselves up." On the instant I saw that the figure was indeed their strong point. His "naturally" didn't sound vain, but it lighted up the question. "*She* has got the best," he continued, nodding at his wife, with a pleasant after-dinner absence of circumlocution. I could only reply, as if we were in fact sitting over our wine, that this didn't prevent his own from being very good; which led him in turn to rejoin: "We thought that if you ever have to do people like us, we might be something like it. *She,* particularly—for a lady in a book, you know."

I was so amused by them that, to get more of it, I did my best to take their point of view; and though it was an embarrassment to find myself appraising physically, as if they were animals on hire or useful blacks, a pair whom I should have expected to meet only in one of the relations in which criticism is tacit, I looked at Mrs. Monarch judicially enough to be able to exclaim, after a moment, with conviction: "Oh yes, a lady in a book!" She was singularly like a bad illustration.

"We'll stand up, if you like," said the Major; and he raised himself before me with a really grand air.

I could take his measure at a glance—he was six feet two and a perfect gentleman. It would have paid any club in process of formation and in want of a stamp to engage him at a salary to stand in the principal window. What struck me immediately was that in coming to me they had rather missed their vocation; they could surely have been turned to better account for advertising purposes. I couldn't of course see the thing in detail, but I could see them make someone's fortune—I don't mean their own. There was something in them for a waistcoatmaker, an hotel-keeper or a soap-vendor. I could imagine "We always use it" pinned on their bosoms with the greatest effect; I had a vision of the promptitude with which they would launch a table d'hôte.[1]

Mrs. Monarch sat still, not from pride but from shyness, and presently her husband said to her: "Get up my dear and show how smart you are." She obeyed, but she had no need to get up to show it. She walked to the end of the studio, and then she came back blushing, with her fluttered eyes on her husband. I was reminded of an incident I had accidentally had a glimpse of in Paris—being with a friend there, a dramatist about to produce a play—when an actress came to him to ask to be intrusted with a part. She went through her paces before him, walked up and down as Mrs. Monarch was doing. Mrs. Monarch did it quite as well, but I abstained from applauding. It was very odd to see such people apply for such poor pay. She looked as if she had ten thousand a year. Her husband had used the word that described her: she was, in the London current jargon, essentially and typically

[1] *Table d'hôte* is a table where the residents of a hotel dine together.

"smart." Her figure was, in the same order of ideas, conspicuously and irreproachably "good." For a woman of her age her waist was surprisingly small; her elbow moreover had the orthodox crook. She held her head at the conventional angle; but why did she come to *me?* She ought to have tried on jackets at a big shop. I feared my visitors were not only destitute, but "artistic"—which would be a great complication. When she sat down again I thanked her, observing that what a draughtsman most valued in his model was the faculty of keeping quiet.

"Oh, *she* can keep quiet," said Major Monarch. Then he added, jocosely: "I've always kept her quiet."

"I'm not a nasty fidget, am I?" Mrs. Monarch appealed to her husband.

He addressed his answers to me. "Perhaps it isn't out of place to mention—because we ought to be quite business-like, oughtn't we?—that when I married her she was known as the Beautiful Statue."

"Oh dear!" said Mrs. Monarch, ruefully.

"Of course I should want a certain amount of expression," I rejoined.

"Of *course!*" they both exclaimed.

"And then I suppose you know that you'll get awfully tired."

"Oh, we *never* get tired!" they eagerly cried.

"Have you had any kind of practice?"

They hesitated—they looked at each other. "We've been photographed, *immensely,*" said Mrs. Monarch.

"She means the fellows have asked us," added the Major.

"I see—because you're so good-looking."

"I don't know what they thought, but they were always after us."

"We always got our photographs for nothing," smiled Mrs. Monarch.

"We might have brought some, my dear," her husband remarked.

"I'm not sure we have any left. We've given quantities away," she explained to me.

"With our autographs and that sort of thing," said the Major.

"Are they to be got in the shops?" I inquired, as a harmless pleasantry.

"Oh, yes; *hers*—they used to be."

"Not now," said Mrs. Monarch, with her eyes on the floor.

II

I could fancy the "sort of thing" they put on the presentation-copies of their photographs, and I was sure they wrote a beautiful hand. It was odd how quickly I was sure of everything that concerned them. If they were now so poor as to have to earn shillings and pence, they never had had much of a margin. Their good looks had been their capital, and they had good-humouredly made the most of the career that this resource marked out for them. It was in their faces, the blankness, the deep intellectual repose of the twenty years of country-house visiting which had given them pleasant intonations. I could see the sunny drawing-rooms, sprinkled with periodicals she didn't read, in which Mrs. Monarch had continuously sat; I could see the wet shrubberies in which she had walked, equipped to admiration for either exercise. I could see the rich covers the Major had helped to shoot and the wonderful garments in which, late at night, he repaired to the smoking-room to talk about them. I could imagine their leggings and waterproofs,[2] their knowing tweeds and rugs, their rolls of sticks and cases of tackle and neat umbrellas; and I could evoke the exact appearance of their servants and the compact variety of their luggage on the platforms of country stations.

They gave small tips but they were liked; they didn't do anything themselves, but they were welcome. They looked so well everywhere; they gratified the general relish for stature, complexion and "form." They knew it without fatuity or vulgarity, and they respected themselves in consequence. They were not superficial; they were thorough and kept themselves up—it had been their line. People with such a taste for activity had to have some line. I could feel how, even in a dull house, they could have been counted upon for cheerfulness. At present something had happened—it didn't matter what, their little income had grown less, it had grown least—and they had to do something for pocket-money. Their friends liked them, but didn't like to support them. There was something about them that represented credit—their clothes, their manners, their type; but if credit is a large empty pocket in which an occasional chink reverberates, the chink at least must be audible. What they wanted of me was to help to make it so. Fortunately they had no children—I soon divined that. They would also perhaps wish our relations to be kept secret: this was why it was "for the figure"—the reproduction of the face would betray them.

I liked them—they were so simple; and I had no objection to them if they would suit. But, somehow, with all their perfections I didn't easily believe in them. After all they were amateurs, and the ruling passion of my life was the detestation of the amateur. Combined with this was another perversity—an innate preference for the represented subject over the real one: the defect of the real one was so apt to be a lack of representation. I liked things that appeared; then one was sure. Whether they *were* or not was a subordinate and almost a profitless question. There were other considerations, the first of which was that I already had two or three people in use, notably a young person with big feet, in alpaca, from Kilburn, who for a couple of years had come to me regularly for my illustrations and with whom I was still—perhaps ignobly—satisfied. I frankly explained to my visitors how the case stood; but they had taken more precautions than I supposed. They had reasoned

[2] Waterproofs are raincoats.

out their opportunity, for Claude Rivet had told them of the projected *édition de luxe*[3] of one of the writers of our day—the rarest of the novelists—who, long neglected by the multitudinous vulgar and dearly prized by the attentive (need I mention Philip Vincent?) had had the happy fortune of seeing, late in life, the dawn and then the full light of a higher criticism—an estimate in which, on the part of the public, there was something really of expiation. The edition in question, planned by a publisher of taste, was practically an act of high reparation; the woodcuts with which it was to be enriched were the homage of English art to one of the most independent representatives of English letters. Major and Mrs. Monarch confessed to me that they had hoped I might be able to work *them* into my share of the enterprise. They knew I was to do the first of the books, "Rutland Ramsay," but I had to make clear to them that my participation in the rest of the affair—this first book was to be a test—was to depend on the satisfaction I should give. If this should be limited my employers would drop me without a scruple. It was therefore a crisis for me, and naturally I was making special preparations, looking about for new people, if they should be necessary, and securing the best types. I admitted however that I should like to settle down to two or three good models who would do for everything.

"Should we have often to—a—put on special clothes?" Mrs. Monarch timidly demanded.

"Dear, yes—that's half the business."

"And should we be expected to supply our own costumes?"

"Oh, no; I've got a lot of things. A painter's models put on—or put off—anything he likes."

"And do you mean—a—the same?"

"The same?"

Mrs. Monarch looked at her husband again.

"Oh, she was just wondering," he explained, "if the costumes are in *general* use." I had to confess that they were, and I mentioned further that some of them (I had a lot of genuine, greasy last-century things), had served their time, a hundred years ago, on living, world-stained men and women. "We'll put on anything that *fits,*" said the Major.

"Oh, I arrange that—they fit in the pictures."

"I'm afraid I should do better for the modern books. I would come as you like," said Mrs. Monarch.

"She has got a lot of clothes at home: they might do for contemporary life," her husband continued.

"Oh, I can fancy scenes in which you'd be quite natural." And indeed I could see the slipshod rearrangements of stale properties—the stories I tried to produce pictures for without the exasperation of reading them—

[3] *Édition de luxe* is French for deluxe edition, usually consisting of finely bound and illustrated volumes.

whose sandy tracts the good lady might help to people. But I had to return to the fact that for this sort of work—the daily mechanical grind—I was already equipped; the people I was working with were fully adequate.

"We only thought we might be more like *some* characters," said Mrs. Monarch mildly, getting up.

Her husband also rose; he stood looking at me with a dim wistfulness that was touching in so fine a man. "Wouldn't it be rather a pull sometimes to have—a—to have—?" He hung fire;[4] he wanted me to help him by phrasing what he meant. But I couldn't—I didn't know. So he brought it out, awkwardly: "The *real* thing; a gentleman, you know, or a lady." I was quite ready to give a general assent—I admitted that there was a great deal in that. This encouraged Major Monarch to say, following up his appeal with an unacted gulp: "It's awfully hard—we've tried everything." The gulp was communicative; it proved too much for his wife. Before I knew it Mrs. Monarch had dropped again upon a divan and burst into tears. Her husband sat down beside her, holding one of her hands; whereupon she quickly dried her eyes with the other, while I felt embarrassed as she looked up at me. "There isn't a confounded job I haven't applied for—waited for—prayed for. You can fancy we'd be pretty bad first. Secretaryships and that sort of thing? You might as well ask for a peerage. I'd be *anything*—I'm strong; a messenger or a coalheaver. I'd put on a gold-laced cap and open carriage-doors in front of the haberdasher's; I'd hang about a station, to carry portmanteaus; I'd be a postman. But they won't look at you; there are thousands as good as yourself, already on the ground. *Gentlemen,* poor beggars, who have drunk their wine, who have kept their hunters!"

I was as reassuring as I knew how to be, and my visitors were presently on their feet again while, for the experiment, we agreed on an hour. We were discussing it when the door opened and Miss Churm came in with a wet umbrella. Miss Churm had to take the omnibus to Maida Vale and then walk half-a-mile. She looked a trifle blowsy and slightly splashed. I scarcely ever saw her come in without thinking afresh how odd it was that, being so little in herself, she should yet be so much in others. She was a meagre little Miss Churm, but she was an ample heroine of romance. She was only a freckled cockney, but she could represent everything, from a fine lady to a shepherdess; she had the faculty, as she might have had a fine voice or long hair. She couldn't spell, and she loved beer, but she had two or three "points," and practice, and a knack, and mother-wit, and a kind of whimsical sensibility, and a love of the theatre, and seven sisters, and not an ounce of respect, especially for the *h*.[5] The first thing my visitors saw was that her umbrella

[4] Hung fire means hesitated.
[5] In the cockney accent the *h* is omitted; thus Miss Churme has no "respect" for it.

was wet, and in their spotless perfection they visibly winced at it. The rain had come on since their arrival.

"I'm all in a soak; there *was* a mess of people in the bus. I wish you lived near a stytion," said Miss Churm. I requested her to get ready as quickly as possible, and she passed into the room in which she always changed her dress. But before going out she asked me what she was to get into this time.

"It's the Russian princess, don't you know?" I answered; "the one with the 'golden eyes,' in black velvet, for the long thing in the *Cheapside*."

"Golden eyes? I *say!*" cried Miss Churm, while my companions watched her with intensity as she withdrew. She always arranged herself, when she was late, before I could turn round; and I kept my visitors a little, on purpose, so that they might get an idea, from seeing her, what would be expected of themselves. I mentioned that she was quite my notion of an excellent model—she was really very clever.

"Do you think she looks like a Russian princess?" Major Monarch asked, with lurking alarm.

"When I make her, yes."

"Oh, if you have to *make* her—!" he reasoned, acutely.

"That's the most you can ask. There are so many that are not make-able."

"Well now, *here's* a lady"—and with a persuasive smile he passed his arm into his wife's—"who's already made!"

"Oh, I'm not a Russian princess," Mrs. Monarch protested, a little coldly. I could see that she had known some and didn't like them. There, immediately, was a complication of a kind that I never had to fear with Miss Churm.

This young lady came back in black velvet—the gown was rather rusty and very low on her lean shoulders—and with a Japanese fan in her red hands. I reminded her that in the scene I was doing she had to look over someone's head. "I forget whose it is; but it doesn't matter. Just look over a head."

"I'd rather look over a stove," said Miss Churm; and she took her station near the fire. She fell into position, settled herself into a tall attitude, gave a certain backward inclination to her head and a certain forward droop to her fan, and looked, at least to my prejudiced sense, distinguished and charming, foreign and dangerous. We left her looking so, while I went downstairs with Major and Mrs. Monarch.

"I think I could come about as near it as that," said Mrs. Monarch.

"Oh, you think she's shabby, but you must allow for the alchemy of art."

However, they went off with an evident increase of comfort, founded on their demonstrable advantage in being the real thing. I could fancy them shuddering over Miss Churm. She was very droll about them when I went back, for I told her what they wanted.

"Well, if *she* can sit I'll tyke to bookkeeping," said my model.

"She's very lady-like," I replied, as an innocent form of aggravation.

"So much the worse for *you.* That means she can't turn round."

"She'll do for the fashionable novels."

"Oh yes, she'll *do* for them!" my model humorously declared. "Ain't they bad enough without her?" I had often sociably denounced them to Miss Churm.

III

It was for the elucidation of a mystery in one of these works that I first tried Mrs. Monarch. Her husband came with her, to be useful if necessary—it was sufficiently clear that as a general thing he would prefer to come with her. At first I wondered if this were for "propriety's" sake—if he were going to be jealous and meddling. The idea was too tiresome, and if it had been confirmed it would speedily have brought our acquaintance to a close. But I soon saw there was nothing in it and that if he accompanied Mrs. Monarch it was (in addition to the chance of being wanted), simply because he had nothing else to do. When she was away from him his occupation was gone—she never *had* been away from him. I judged, rightly, that in their awkward situation their close union was their main comfort and that this union had no weak spot. It was a real marriage, an encouragement to the hesitating, a nut for pessimists to crack. Their address was humble (I remember afterwards thinking it had been the only thing about them that was really professional), and I could fancy the lamentable lodgings in which the Major would have been left alone. He could bear them with his wife—he couldn't bear them without her.

He had too much tact to try and make himself agreeable when he couldn't be useful; so he simply sat and waited, when I was too absorbed in my work to talk. But I liked to make him talk—it made my work, when it didn't interrupt it, less sordid, less special. To listen to him was to combine the excitement of going out with the economy of staying at home. There was only one hindrance: that I seemed not to know any of the people he and his wife had known. I think he wondered extremely, during the term of our intercourse, whom the deuce I *did* know. He hadn't a stray sixpence of an idea to fumble for; so we didn't spin it very fine—we confined ourselves to questions of leather and even of liquor (saddlers and breeches-makers and how to get good claret cheap), and matters like "good trains" and the habits of small game. His lore on these last subjects was astonishing, he managed to interweave the station-master with the ornithologist. When he couldn't talk about greater things he could talk cheerfully about smaller, and since I couldn't accompany him into reminiscences of the fashionable world he could lower the conversation without a visible effort to my level.

So earnest a desire to please was touching in a man who could so easily have knocked one down. He looked after the fire and had an opinion on the draught of the stove, without my asking him, and I could see that he thought many of my arrangements not half clever enough. I remember telling him that if I were only rich I would offer him a salary to come and teach me how to live. Sometimes he gave a random sigh, of which the essence was: "Give me even such a bare old barrack as *this,* and I'd do something with it!" When I wanted to use him he came alone; which was an illustration of the superior courage of women. His wife could bear her solitary second floor, and she was in general more discreet; showing by various small reserves that she was alive to the propriety of keeping our relations markedly professional—not letting them slide into sociability. She wished it to remain clear that she and the Major were employed, not cultivated, and if she approved of me as a superior, who could be kept in his place, she never thought me quite good enough for an equal.

She sat with great intensity, giving the whole of her mind to it, and was capable of remaining for an hour almost as motionless as if she were before a photographer's lens. I could see she had been photographed often, but somehow the very habit that made her good for that purpose unfitted her for mine. At first I was extremely pleased with her lady-like air, and it was a satisfaction, on coming to follow her lines, to see how good they were and how far they could lead the pencil. But after a few times I began to find her too insurmountably stiff; do what I would with it my drawing looked like a photograph or a copy of a photograph. Her figure had no variety of expression—she herself had no sense of variety. You may say that this was my business, was only a question of placing her. I placed her in every conceivable position, but she managed to obliterate their differences. She was always a lady certainly, and into the bargain was always the same lady. She was the real thing, but always the same thing. There were moments when I was oppressed by the serenity of her confidence that she *was* the real thing. All her dealings with me and all her husband's were an implication that this was lucky for *me.* Meanwhile I found myself trying to invent types that approached her own, instead of making her own transform itself—in the clever way that was not impossible; for instance, to poor Miss Churm. Arrange as I would and take the precautions I would, she always, in my pictures, came out too tall—landing me in the dilemma of having represented a fascinating woman as seven feet high, which, out of respect perhaps to my own very much scantier inches, was far from my idea of such a personage.

The case was worse with the Major—nothing I could do would keep *him* down, so that he became useful only for the representation of brawny giants. I adored variety and range, I cherished human accidents, the illustrative note; I wanted to characterise closely, and the thing in the world I most hated was the danger of being ridden by a type. I had quarrelled with some of my friends about it—I had parted company with them for maintaining that one *had* to be, and that if the type was beautiful (witness Raphael and Leonardo), the servitude was only a gain. I was neither Leonardo nor Raphael; I might only be a presumptuous young modern searcher, but I held that everything was to be sacrificed sooner than character. When they averred that the haunting type in question could easily *be* character, I retorted, perhaps superficially: "Whose?" It couldn't be everybody's—it might end in being nobody's.

After I had drawn Mrs. Monarch a dozen times I perceived more clearly than before that the value of such a model as Miss Churm resided precisely in the fact that she had no positive stamp, combined of course with the other fact that what she did have was a curious and inexplicable talent for imitation. Her usual appearance was like a curtain which she could draw up at request for a capital performance. This performance was simply suggestive; but it was a word to the wise—it was vivid and pretty. Sometimes, even, I thought it, though she was plain herself, too insipidly pretty; I made it a reproach to her that the figures drawn from her were monotonously (*bêtement,*[6] as we used to say) graceful. Nothing made her more angry: it was so much her pride to feel that she could sit for characters that had nothing in common with each other. She would accuse me at such moments of taking away her "reputy-tion."

It suffered a certain shrinkage, this queer quantity, from the repeated visits of my new friends. Miss Churm was greatly in demand, never in want of employment, so I had no scruple in putting her off occasionally, to try them more at my ease. It was certainly amusing at first to do the real thing—it was amusing to do Major Monarch's trousers. They *were* the real thing, even if he did come out colossal. It was amusing to do his wife's back hair (it was so mathematically neat,) and the particular "smart" tension of her tight stays. She lent herself especially to positions in which the face was somewhat averted or blurred; she abounded in ladylike back views and *profils perdus.*[7] When she stood erect she took naturally one of the attitudes in which court-painters represent queens and princesses; so that I found myself wondering whether, to draw out this accomplishment, I couldn't get the editor of the *Cheapside* to publish a really royal romance, "A Tale of Buckingham Palace." Sometimes, however, the real thing and the make-believe came into contact; by which I mean that Miss Churm, keeping an appointment or coming to make one on days when I had much work in hand, encountered her invidious rivals. The encounter was not on their part, for they noticed

[6] *Bêtement* is French for "foolishly."

[7] *Profils perdus* is French for "lost profiles"; it refers to a painting in which a figure is seen from behind, showing chiefly the contours of the cheek and the back.

her no more than if she had been the housemaid; not from intentional loftiness, but simply because, as yet, professionally, they didn't know how to fraternise, as I could guess that they would have liked—or at least that the Major would. They couldn't talk about the omnibus—they always walked; and they didn't know what else to try—she wasn't interested in good trains or cheap claret. Besides, they must have felt—in the air—that she was amused at them, secretly derisive of their ever knowing how. She was not a person to conceal her scepticism if she had had a chance to show it. On the other hand Mrs. Monarch didn't think her tidy; for why else did she take pains to say to me (it was going out of the way, for Mrs. Monarch), that she didn't like dirty women?

One day when my young lady happened to be present with my other sitters (she even dropped in, when it was convenient, for a chat), I asked her to be so good as to lend a hand in getting tea—a service with which she was familiar and which was one of a class that, living as I did in a small way, with slender domestic resources, I often appealed to my models to render. They liked to lay hands on my property, to break the sitting, and sometimes the china—I made them feel Bohemian. The next time I saw Miss Churm after this incident she surprised me greatly by making a scene about it—she accused me of having wished to humiliate her. She had not resented the outrage at the time, but had seemed obliging and amused, enjoying the comedy of asking Mrs. Monarch, who sat vague and silent, whether she would have cream and sugar, and putting an exaggerated simper into the question. She had tried intonations—as if she too wished to pass for the real thing; till I was afraid my other visitors would take offence.

Oh, *they* were determined not to do this; and their touching patience was the measure of their great need. They would sit by the hour, uncomplaining, till I was ready to use them; they would come back on the chance of being wanted and would walk away cheerfully if they were not. I used to go to the door with them to see in what magnificent order they retreated. I tried to find other employment for them—I introduced them to several artists. But they didn't "take," for reasons I could appreciate, and I became conscious, rather anxiously, that after such disappointments they fell back upon me with a heavier weight. They did me the honour to think that it was I who was most *their* form. They were not picturesque enough for the painters, and in those days there were not so many serious workers in black and white. Besides, they had an eye to the great job I had mentioned to them—they had secretly set their hearts on supplying the right essence for my pictorial vindication of our fine novelist. They knew that for this undertaking I should want no costume-effects, none of the frippery of past ages—that it was a case in which everything would be contemporary and satirical and, presumably, genteel. If I could work them into it their future would be assured, for the labour would of course be long and the occupation steady.

One day Mrs. Monarch came without her husband—she explained his absence by his having had to go to the City. While she sat there in her usual anxious stiffness there came, at the door, a knock which I immediately recognised as the subdued appeal of a model out of work. It was followed by the entrance of a young man whom I easily perceived to be a foreigner and who proved in fact an Italian acquainted with no English word but my name, which he uttered in a way that made it seem to include all others. I had not then visited his country, nor was I proficient in his tongue; but as he was not so meanly constituted—what Italian is?—as to depend only on that member for expression he conveyed to me, in familiar but graceful mimicry, that he was in search of exactly the employment in which the lady before me was engaged. I was not struck with him at first, and while I continued to draw I emitted rough sounds of discouragement and dismissal. He stood his ground, however, not importunately, but with a dumb, dog-like fidelity in his eyes which amounted to innocent impudence—the manner of a devoted servant (he might have been in the house for years), unjustly suspected. Suddenly I saw that this very attitude and expression made a picture, whereupon I told him to sit down and wait till I should be free. There was another picture in the way he obeyed me, and I observed as I worked that there were others still in the way he looked wonderingly, with his head thrown back, about the high studio. He might have been crossing himself in St. Peter's. Before I finished I said to myself: "The fellow's a bankrupt orangemonger, but he's a treasure."

When Mrs. Monarch withdrew he passed across the room like a flash to open the door for her, standing there with the rapt, pure gaze of the young Dante[8] spellbound by the young Beatrice. As I never insisted, in such situations, on the blankness of the British domestic, I reflected that he had the making of a servant (and I needed one, but couldn't pay him to be only that), as well as of a model; in short I made up my mind to adopt my bright adventurer if he would agree to officiate in the double capacity. He jumped at my offer, and in the event my rashness (for I had known nothing about him) was not brought home to me. He proved a sympathetic though a desultory ministrant, and had in a wonderful degree the *sentiment de la pose*.[9] It was uncultivated, instinctive; a part of the happy instinct which had guided him to my door and helped him to spell out my name on the card nailed to it. He had had no other introduction to me than a guess, from the shape of my high north window, seen outside, that my place was a studio and that as a studio it would contain an artist. He had wandered to England in search of fortune, like other itinerants, and had embarked, with a partner and

[8] Dante Alighieri (1265–1321), the greatest Italian poet, fell in love with Beatrice when they were both youths. It is she who leads Dante through Paradise in *The Divine Comedy*.
[9] *Sentiment de la pose* is French for "the feeling of the pose," as when models strike a suitable attitude or gesture.

a small green handcart, on the sale of penny ices. The ices had melted away and the partner had dissolved in their train. My young man wore tight yellow trousers with reddish stripes and his name was Oronte. He was sallow but fair, and when I put him into some old clothes of my own he looked like an Englishman. He was as good as Miss Churm, who could look, when required, like an Italian.

IV

I thought Mrs. Monarch's face slightly convulsed when, on her coming back with her husband, she found Oronte installed. It was strange to have to recognise in a scrap of a lazzarone[10] a competitor to her magnificent Major. It was she who scented danger first, for the Major was anecdotically unconscious. But Oronte gave us tea, with a hundred eager confusions (he had never seen such a queer process), and I think she thought better of me for having at last an "establishment." They saw a couple of drawings that I had made of the establishment, and Mrs. Monarch hinted that it never would have struck her that he had sat for them. "Now the drawings you make from *us,* they look exactly like us," she reminded me, smiling in triumph; and I recognised that this was indeed just their defect. When I drew the Monarchs I couldn't, somehow, get away from them—get into the character I wanted to represent; and I had not the least desire my model should be discovered in my picture. Miss Churm never was, and Mrs. Monarch thought I hid her, very properly, because she was vulgar; whereas if she was lost it was only as the dead who go to heaven are lost—in the gain of an angel the more.

By this time I had got a certain start with "Rutland Ramsay," the first novel in the great projected series; that is I had produced a dozen drawings, several with the help of the Major and his wife, and I had sent them in for approval. My understanding with the publishers, as I have already hinted, had been that I was to be left to do my work, in this particular case, as I liked, with the whole book committed to me; but my connection with the rest of the series was only contingent. There were moments when, frankly, it *was* comfort to have the real thing under one's hand; for there were characters in "Rutland Ramsay" that were very much like it. There were people presumably as straight as the Major and women of as good a fashion as Mrs. Monarch. There was a great deal of country-house life—treated, it is true, in a fine, fanciful, ironical, generalised way—and there was a considerable implication of knickerbockers and kilts. There were certain things I had to settle at the outset; such things for instance as the exact appearance of

[10] A lazzarone is one of the homeless beggars of Naples.

the hero, the particular bloom of the heroine. The author of course gave me a lead, but there was a margin for interpretation. I took the Monarchs into my confidence, I told them frankly what I was about, I mentioned my embarrassments and alternatives. "Oh, take *him!*" Mrs. Monarch murmured sweetly, looking at her husband; and "What could you want better than my wife?" the Major inquired, with the comfortable candour that now prevailed between us.

I was not obliged to answer these remarks—I was only obliged to place my sitters. I was not easy in mind, and I postponed, a little timidly perhaps, the solution of the question. The book was a large canvas, the other figures were numerous, and I worked off at first some of the episodes in which the hero and the heroine were not concerned. When once I had set *them* up I should have to stick to them—I couldn't make my young man seven feet high in one place and five feet nine in another. I inclined on the whole to the latter measurement, though the Major more than once reminded me that *he* looked about as young as anyone. It was indeed quite possible to arrange him, for the figure, so that it would have been difficult to detect his age. After the spontaneous Oronte had been with me a month, and after I had given him to understand several different times that his native exuberance would presently constitute an insurmountable barrier to our further intercourse, I waked to a sense of his heroic capacity. He was only five feet seven, but the remaining inches were latent. I tried him almost secretly at first, for I was really rather afraid of the judgment my other models would pass on such a choice. If they regarded Miss Churm as little better than a snare, what would they think of the representation by a person so little the real thing as an Italian street-vendor of a protagonist formed by a public school?

If I went a little in fear of them it was not because they bullied me, because they had got an oppressive foothold, but because in their really pathetic decorum and mysteriously permanent newness they counted on me so intensely. I was therefore very glad when Jack Hawley came home: he was always of such good counsel. He painted badly himself, but there was no one like him for putting his finger on the place. He had been absent from England for a year; he had been somewhere—I don't remember where—to get a fresh eye. I was in a good deal of dread of any such organ, but we were old friends; he had been away for months and a sense of emptiness was creeping into my life. I hadn't dodged a missile for a year.

He came back with a fresh eye, but with the same old black velvet blouse, and the first evening he spent in my studio we smoked cigarettes till the small hours. He had done no work himself, he had only got the eye; so the field was clear for the production of my little things. He wanted to see what I had done for the *Cheapside,* but he was disappointed in the exhibition. That at least seemed the meaning of two or three comprehensive groans which, as he lounged on my big divan, on a folded leg, looking at my latest drawings, issued from his lips with the smoke of the cigarette.

"What's the matter with you?" I asked.

"What's the matter with *you!*"

"Nothing save that I'm mystified."

"You are indeed. You're quite off the hinge. What's the meaning of this new fad?" And he tossed me, with visible irreverence, a drawing in which I happened to have depicted both my majestic models. I asked if he didn't think it good, and he replied that it struck him as execrable, given the sort of thing I had always represented myself to him as wishing to arrive at; but I let that pass, I was so anxious to see exactly what he meant. The two figures in the picture looked colossal, but I supposed this was *not* what he meant, inasmuch as, for aught he knew to the contrary, I might have been trying for that. I maintained that I was working exactly in the same way as when he last had done me the honour to commend me. "Well, there's a big hole somewhere," he answered; "wait a bit and I'll discover it." I depended upon him to do so: where else was the fresh eye? But he produced at last nothing more luminous than "I don't know—I don't like your types." This was lame, for a critic who had never consented to discuss with me anything but the question of execution, the direction of strokes and the mystery of values.

"In the drawings you've been looking at I think my types are very handsome."

"Oh, they won't do!"

"I've had a couple of new models."

"I see you have. *They* won't do."

"Are you very sure of that?"

"Absolutely—they're stupid."

"You mean *I* am—for I ought to get round that."

"You *can't*—with such people. Who are they?"

I told him, as far as was necessary, and he declared, heartlessly: "*Ce sont des gens qu'il faut mettre à la porte.*"[11]

"You've never seen them; they're awfully good," I compassionately objected.

"Not seen them? Why, all this recent work of yours drops to pieces with them. It's all I want to see of them."

"No one else has said anything against it—the *Cheapside* people are pleased."

"Everyone else is an ass, and the *Cheapside* people are the biggest asses of all. Come, don't pretend, at this time of day, to have pretty

[11] *Ce sont des gens qu'il faut mettre à la porte* is French for "Those are the sort of people one must put out the door."

illusions about the public, especially about publishers and editors. It's not for *such* animals you work—it's for those who know, *coloro che sanno;*[12] so keep straight for *me* if you can't keep straight for yourself. There's a certain sort of thing you tried for from the first—and a very good thing it is. But this twaddle isn't *in* it." When I talked with Hawley later about "Rutland Ramsay" and its possible successors he declared that I must get back into my boat again or I would go to the bottom. His voice in short was the voice of warning.

I noted the warning, but I didn't turn my friends out of doors. They bored me a good deal; but the very fact that they bored me admonished me not to sacrifice them—if there was anything to be done with them—simply to irritation. As I look back at this phase they seem to me to have pervaded my life not a little. I have a vision of them as most of the time in my studio, seated, against the wall, on an old velvet bench to be out of the way, and looking like a pair of patient courtiers in a royal ante-chamber. I am convinced that during the coldest weeks of the winter they held their ground because it saved them fire. Their newness was losing its gloss, and it was impossible not to feel that they were objects of charity. Whenever Miss Churm arrived they went away, and after I was fairly launched in "Rutland Ramsay" Miss Churm arrived pretty often. They managed to express to me tacitly that they supposed I wanted her for the low life of the book, and I let them suppose it, since they had attempted to study the work—it was lying about the studio—without discovering that it dealt only with the highest circles. They had dipped into the most brilliant of our novelists without deciphering many passages. I still took an hour from them, now and again, in spite of Jack Hawley's warning: it would be time enough to dismiss them, if dismissal should be necessary, when the rigour of the season was over. Hawley had made their acquaintance—he had met them at my fireside—and thought them a ridiculous pair. Learning that he was a painter they tried to approach him, to show him too that they were the real thing; but he looked at them, across the big room, as if they were miles away; they were a compendium of everything that he most objected to in the social system of his country. Such people as that, all convention and patent-leather, with ejaculations that stopped conversation, had no business in a studio. A studio was a place to learn to see, and how could you see through a pair of feather beds?

The main inconvenience I suffered at their hands was that, at first, I was shy of letting them discover how my artful little servant had begun to sit to me for "Rutland Ramsay." They knew that I had been odd enough (they were prepared by this time to allow oddity to artists,) to pick a foreign vagabond out of the streets, when I might have had a

[12] *Coloro che sanno* is a misquotation of Dante's phrase, "el maestro di color che sanno," which means "the master of those who know."

person with whiskers and credentials; but it was some time before they learned how high I rated his accomplishments. They found him in an attitude more than once, but they never doubted I was doing him as an organ-grinder. There were several things they never guessed, and one of them was that for a striking scene in the novel, in which a footman briefly figured, it occurred to me to make use of Major Monarch as the menial. I kept putting this off, I didn't like to ask him to don the livery—besides the difficulty of finding a livery to fit him. At last, one day late in the winter, when I was at work on the despised Oronte (he caught one's idea in an instant), and was in the glow of feeling that I was going very straight, they came in, the Major and his wife, with their society laugh about nothing (there was less and less to laugh at), like country-callers—they always reminded me of that—who have walked across the park after church and are presently persuaded to stay to luncheon. Luncheon was over, but they could stay to tea—I knew they wanted it. The fit was on me, however, and I couldn't let my ardour cool and my work wait, with the fading daylight, while my model prepared it. So I asked Mrs. Monarch if she would mind laying it out—a request which, for an instant, brought all the blood to her face. Her eyes were on her husband's for a second, and some mute telegraphy passed between them. Their folly was over the next instant; his cheerful shrewdness put an end to it. So far from pitying their wounded pride, I must add, I was moved to give it as complete a lesson as I could. They bustled about together and got out the cups and saucers and made the kettle boil. I know they felt as if they were waiting on my servant, and when the tea was prepared I said: "He'll have a cup, please—he's tired." Mrs. Monarch brought him one where he stood and he took it from her as if he had been a gentleman at a party, squeezing a crush-hat with an elbow.

Then it came over me that she had made a great effort for me—made it with a kind of nobleness—and that I owed her a compensation. Each time I saw her after this I wondered what the compensation could be. I couldn't go on doing the wrong thing to oblige them. Oh, it *was* the wrong thing, the stamp of the work for which they sat—Hawley was not the only person to say it now. I sent in a large number of the drawings I had made for "Rutland Ramsay," and I received a warning that was more to the point than Hawley's. The artistic adviser of the house for which I was working was of opinion that many of my illustrations were not what had been looked for. Most of these illustrations were the subjects in which the Monarchs had figured. Without going into the question of what *had* been looked for, I saw at this rate I shouldn't get the other books to do. I hurled myself in despair upon Miss Churm, I put her through all her paces. I not only adopted Oronte publicly as my hero, but one morning when the Major looked in to see if I didn't require him to finish a figure for the *Cheapside*, for which he had begun to sit the week before, I told him that I had changed my mind—I would do the drawing from my man. At this my visitor turned pale and stood looking at me. "Is *he* your idea of an English gentleman?" he asked.

I was disappointed, I was nervous, I wanted to get on with my work; so I replied with irritation: "Oh, my dear Major—I can't be ruined for *you!*"

He stood another moment; then, without a word, he quitted the studio. I drew a long breath when he was gone, for I said to myself that I shouldn't see him again. I had not told him definitely that I was in danger of having my work rejected, but I was vexed at his not having felt the catastrophe in the air, read with me the moral of our fruitless collaboration, the lesson that, in the deceptive atmosphere of art, even the highest respectability may fail of being plastic.

I didn't owe my friends money, but I did see them again. They reappeared together, three days later, and under the circumstances there was something tragic in the fact. It was a proof to me that they could find nothing else in life to do. They had threshed the matter out in a dismal conference—they had digested the bad news that they were not in for the series. If they were not useful to me even for the *Cheapside* their function seemed difficult to determine, and I could only judge at first that they had come, forgivingly, decorously, to take a last leave. This made me rejoice in secret that I had little leisure for a scene; for I had placed both my other models in position together and I was pegging away at a drawing from which I hoped to derive glory. It had been suggested by the passage in which Rutland Ramsay, drawing up a chair to Artemisia's piano-stool, says extraordinary things to her while she ostensibly fingers out a difficult piece of music. I had done Miss Churm at the piano before—it was an attitude in which she knew how to take on an absolutely poetic grace. I wished the two figures to "compose" together, intensely, and my little Italian had entered perfectly into my conception. The pair were vividly before me, the piano had been pulled out; it was a charming picture of blended youth and murmured love, which I had only to catch and keep. My visitors stood and looked at it, and I was friendly to them over my shoulder.

They made no response, but I was used to silent company and went on with my work, only a little disconcerted (even though exhilarated by the sense that *this* was at least the ideal thing), at not having got rid of them after all. Presently I heard Mrs. Monarch's sweet voice beside, or rather above me: "I wish her hair was a little better done." I looked up and she was staring with a strange fixedness at Miss Churm whose back was turned to her. "Do you mind my just touching it?" she went on—a question which made me spring up for an instant, as with the instinctive fear that she might do the young lady a harm. But she quieted me with a glance I shall never forget—I confess I should like to have been able to paint *that*—and went for a moment to my model. She spoke to her softly, laying a hand upon her shoulder and bending over her; and as the girl, understandingly, gratefully assented, she disposed her rough curls, with a few quick passes, in such a way to make Miss Churm's head twice as charming. It was one of the most heroic personal services I have ever seen rendered. Then Mrs. Monarch turned away with a low sigh and, looking about her as if for something to do, stooped to the floor with a noble humility and picked up a dirty rag that had dropped out of my paint-box.

The Major meanwhile had also been looking for something to do and, wandering to the other end of the studio, saw before him my breakfast things, neglected, unremoved. "I say, can't I be useful *here?*" he called out to me with an irrepressible quaver. I assented with a laugh that I fear was awkward and for the next ten minutes, while I worked, I heard the light clatter of china and the tinkle of spoons and glass. Mrs. Monarch assisted her husband—they washed up my crockery, they put it away. They wandered off into my little scullery, and I afterwards found that they had cleaned my knives and that my slender stock of plate had an unprecedented surface. When it came over me, the latent eloquence of what they were doing, I confess that my drawing was blurred for a moment—the picture swam. They had accepted their failure, but they couldn't accept their fate. They had bowed their heads in bewilderment to the perverse and cruel law in virtue of which the real thing could be so much less precious than the unreal; but they didn't want to starve. If my servants were my models, my models might be my servants. They would reverse the parts—the others would sit for the ladies and gentlemen, and *they* would do the work. They would still be in the studio—it was an intense dumb appeal to me not to turn them out. "Take us on," they wanted to say—"we'll do *anything*."

When all this hung before me the *afflatus*[13] vanished—my pencil dropped from my hand. My sitting was spoiled and I got rid of my sitters, who were also evidently rather mystified and awestruck. Then, alone with the Major and his wife, I had a most uncomfortable moment. He put their prayer into a single sentence: "I say, you know—just let *us* do for you, can't you?" I couldn't—it was dreadful to see them emptying my slops; but I pretended I could, to oblige them, for about a week. Then I gave them a sum of money to go away; and I never saw them again. I obtained the remaining books, but my friend Hawley repeats that Major and Mrs. Monarch did me a permanent harm, got me into a second-rate trick. If it be true I am content to have paid the price—for the memory.

QUESTIONS

1. The narrator tells the Monarchs, on their first visit, that they "must allow for the alchemy of art." What does he mean? Why *must* they make room for it?

2. How is the Monarchs's marriage "a real marriage"?
3. The narrator tells us that he "admired variety and range." He adds, "I wanted to characterize closely, and the thing in the world I most hated was the danger of being ridden by a type." What according to the narrator is the difference between "character" and "type"? Are the Monarchs characters or types?
4. Jack Hawley tells the narrator that the Monarchs are "a compendium of everything I most objected to in the social system of [England]." What does Hawley mean? In what ways are the Monarchs objectionable? Is Hawley alone in his opinion?
5. In what sense is an artist studio "a place to learn to see"?
6. The narrator describes Mrs. Monarch's rearrangement of Miss Churm's hair as "one of the most heroic personal services I have ever seen rendered." How is the action heroic? Is Mrs. Monarch the hero of the story? Does the story contain a hero?
7. In what way is "the real thing . . . much less precious than the unreal"? Why are the Monarchs no good at being models? Why are they no use as servants? What value do the Monarchs have?

3
AUTHORS AND NARRATORS

Imagine that we are at the scene of an auto accident. Two cars—one yellow, the other blue—are angled into each other at the intersection. A crowd has gathered, and two police officers, who are responsible for filing an accident report, are questioning people to ascertain what happened.

The driver of the yellow car says, "I was trying to make a left turn. I waited for the traffic to clear, and while I was making the turn I saw this car dart out into the street and swipe me."

After the first officer writes down the driver's account, he returns to his partner. "What did the driver of the yellow car say?" the partner asks.

"The driver was trying to make a left turn and was waiting for the intersection to clear before proceeding. When the intersection was open, the driver proceeded left. Then the blue car smashed into the yellow one."

"The driver is a liar!" shouts the operator of the blue vehicle. "I'll tell you the truth. I was waiting at the corner for the light to change green. When the light changed, I proceeded across. I thought the yellow car had stopped at the red light, but no. All of a sudden the yellow car took off and hit me in the side."

"Did anyone else see the accident?"

"I did," says a worker who watched the incident from a third story window of the building on the corner. "The yellow car waited for the traffic to clear before making the left turn. The blue car waited at the red light and began to move when the light turned green. The yellow car was too far into the intersection to see that the light had turned red. But the blue car did not permit the yellow car to complete the turn."

TYPES OF NARRATION

We can learn a good deal about the problems of narration from this rather commonplace incident. The most important lesson is that narration is largely determined by where the narrator stands in relation to the action and to the participants. The participants in an event—the two drivers—tend to see things from a limited point of view. People tend to think of themselves as being in the right, and we expect to hear each driver blame the other for the accident. Even those less involved have limited perspectives. The police understand the incident only through the conflicting testimony of the two drivers. Only the observer on the third floor, in the God-like position of looking down on the action and with no personal knowledge of the drivers, can give an impartial, informed report on the entire event.

Literary scholars have given names to these various narrative perspectives. The stories that the two drivers give are called "first person narratives." In a first person narrative, a participant in an event speaks for him or herself. The first police officer, who tells his partner what the driver of the yellow car thought and did, gives a "limited third person narrative," because although the officer was not a participant in the accident, his perspective is not fundamentally different from the driver's. The observer on the third floor of the office building gave an "omniscient third person narrative." This observer saw everything, knows everything that is important about the action and is utterly trustworthy.

OMNISCIENT NARRATORS

If you were the police officers, you would be pleased to get the omniscient narrator's story. From the omniscient narrator's point of view, one gets all the narrative details presented in an orderly and authoritative manner. The reader and the police officer have all the work done for them, and they don't have to bother figuring out who is responsible for the accident because the omniscient narrator has determined responsibility. Many formula stories are told from the omniscient perspective because it provides a simple, clear, untroubled way to view the action.

Omniscient narratives, however, have several drawbacks. Only God is truly omniscient, and writers frequently hesitate from assuming the god-like stance of the all-knowing narrator. Moreover, the subject of much of literature is the process by which we come to understand events. Since omniscient narrators know everything, they do not help us learn the process by which humans make sense of existence. Finally—and perhaps most fundamentally—omniscience takes away a good deal of the excitement of discovery, and discovery is one of the essential joys of reading. For example, many detective novels begin after a murder has been committed. If the reader knew the identity of the murderer, much of the excitement and suspense would be lost. Being kept in the dark heightens the suspense and surprise of a story.

LIMITED THIRD PERSON NARRATIVES

The most frequently used narrative perspective is the limited third person. In this kind of story, the narrator—who is not a participant in the story—chooses a character and recounts the events as though looking over the character's shoulder. It's as though the narrator were a camera mounted to the character's back and with special access to the character's mind. Sometimes this character is called a "reflector" because it is through the character that the actions of the story are reflected.

Edith Wharton, whose story, "Roman Fever" is included in this chapter, discusses the importance of the reflector as a means of giving unity to a short story. She warns young writers

> never to let the character who serves as reflector record anything not naturally within his register. It should be the storyteller's first care to choose this reflecting mind deliberately, as one would choose a building site, or decide upon the orientation of one's house, and when this is done, to live inside the mind chosen, trying to feel, see and react exactly as the latter would, no more, no less, and above all, no otherwise. Only thus can the writer avoid attributing incongruities of thought and metaphor to his chosen interpreter.

The reflectors, according to Wharton, should be carefully chosen because they will give the story its shape and form. But the reflector does not know everything, and the writer must be extremely careful not to ascribe to the reflector knowledge or feelings the reflector could not or would not have. For example, the reflector cannot know for certain what goes on in the minds of the other characters. However, the reflector can guess what the other characters think and feel.

In the limited third person narratives, the reader, the narrator and the reflector all have about the same understanding of the events of the story. As readers, we are dependent on the reflector for an understanding of the events. However, authors will occasionally let us look beyond the limitations of the reflector. For example, a character who is in love may recognize the faults of the beloved long after the reader has become aware of them. The reflector's closeness to the action may interfere with the character's understanding of the events, but the reader, viewing the story from a distance, may see events more clearly.

In detective stories, or who-done-its, this tension between what the reader guesses and what the detective discovers provides a great deal of the excitement. Involved readers often try to guess who-done-it before the private eye. In any case, limited third person narratives give readers a chance to make discoveries on their own while following the reflector's efforts to make sense of the action. Together, reader and reflector pass through events they only partially understand.

FIRST PERSON NARRATIVES

First person narrators tell their own stories in their own words. Although at first they seem to be the most straightforward of all narratives, they can be among the trickiest to read because many readers fail to distinguish between the author's point of view and the narrator's perspective.

Authors frequently prefer telling a story in a character's voice. They admire other people's narrative abilities, and often an author wishes to capture a character's manner of speech and vividness of recall and the insights others may have about life. Eudora Welty, for example, was so taken with the non-stop monologues of her mother's friends that in her story "Why I Live In The P.O.," Welty sought to capture those peculiar narrative gifts. But though Welty is fascinated with the voice of the narrator, she does not necessarily share the narrator's opinions and feelings. Similarly, the narrator of "The Cask of Amontillado," who is a murderer and sees nothing wrong with burying his enemy alive, does not speak for Poe. But Poe wishes us to look into the mind of a man obsessed with revenge, to understand the nature of his madness. The narrator of "The Cask of Amontillado" is called an "unreliable narrator," and the author invites us to question the validity of his perceptions, sanity and emotions.

Unreliable narrators force readers to make judgments on their own; they free readers to act critically. Although we all have been told not to believe everything we hear, most of us maintain a dim faith in what we see in print. But authors of unreliable narratives want readers to be skeptical of the narrator's opinions, to try to isolate what seems reasonable and true from what seems false and immoral. As readers, we must reach these judgments—not on the basis of what a narrator tells us to believe—but on the values we hold as reasonable, moral, and caring individuals.

Not all first person narrators are unreliable. Frequently they appear to articulate the values and beliefs of the author. For example, the narrator of John Updike's "A & P" quits his job for reasons that Updike generally approves of—the unwillingness to humiliate people just because they are different. But we should always be careful not to confuse a writer's life with the narrator's life even when the author approves of his narrator's views. As far as I know, John Updike never worked as a check-out clerk in an A & P, nor did he live as a boy in Massachusetts. Updike may agree with his narrator's values, but we can never say he *is* the narrator.

THE READER'S ATTITUDE TOWARD THE NARRATOR

Most stories begin with a voice—a narrator's voice—and the voice tells us a story. On occasion, narrators will formally introduce themselves, but usually readers will have to figure out who is speaking from clues dropped along the way. As of any stranger, we should be a little wary of believing what the narrator tells us, but like any polite listener, we should give the speaker our attention and our sympathy. If in the process of the story we suspect that the narrator is a cheat, a liar or a mad person, we can go back and reevaluate what we have heard, deciding what seems reasonable or false. We may not discount all we've heard; the best liars weave a large number of truths into the fabric of their lies. But we should become more aware of how experience is shaped by the perceiver. Indeed that awareness may be a fundamental lesson of all fiction: each of us constructs his or her own version of experience.

However, we must not as readers merely rely on our prejudices to determine the reliability of a narrator. One of the impulses that drives people to write and to read is the desire to encounter people and events we would not encounter on our own. Some people respond with fear and contempt to anything or anyone who is different or unusual. Authors often wish us to understand people before we judge them, to try to see the world as they see it before we impose our own standards.

In this way we can learn a lot not only about others, but about ourselves.

SYMPATHY AND JUDGMENT

As readers and as human beings we are caught between two impulses: sympathy and judgment. Often we view these impulses as separate—that if we sympathize with someone's feelings, we will not be able to judge them fairly and objectively. Some people contend that judgment can only be exercised by remaining outside of the action. The reader stands between the two views, being both involved in the action, by imaginatively reconstructing it, yet remaining detached from the story's actual events. Without a sympathetic understanding of the character's feelings, we will not be able to judge adequately. If we identify too thoroughly with a character, however, we may lose our objectivity. Literature is one of the testing grounds in which we learn the difficult process of both sympathizing and judging, of understanding someone else's feelings and evaluating the propriety of their actions.

We may now be ready to distinguish between propaganda and literature. Propaganda does not wish to aid a reader in forming an independent and free conclusion. It trades on fears and prejudices to lead the reader to a prearranged position. In literature, the author may have strong convictions that he or she wishes to convey to the reader, but the reader is always treated as an independent, moral person who must finally come to a judgment based on a free, thoughtful, and engaged assessment of the story.

QUESTIONS TO THINK ABOUT

1. How do you decide whom to believe and whom not to believe? Is this judgment made on the basis of prejudice or is it a well-considered analysis? For example, if you were lost what sorts of people might you ask for direction? What sorts of people would you avoid asking?
2. Does a speaker have to be truthful to be interesting to listen to? Do you know anyone who tells tall tales in such an amusing or vivid way that they are fun to listen to? How do they make their stories interesting? Why are some people more interesting than others?

ESSAY TOPICS

1. What qualities does a convincing speaker have? Classify those elements of personal appearance, tone and content that make one speaker more believable than another.
2. At some time in our lives most of us have been deceived by someone, a friend whom we discovered was no friend at all, a person who took advantage of our good will. Narrate the incident and analyze the reasons you were taken in.
3. Have you ever known anyone with "the gift of gab?" Describe the person. What did the person sound like? What sorts of stories did the person tell? How did the person affect you and those around you? How did the person use that gift?

CREATIVE WRITING EXERCISES

1. Take a small anecdote and write it first in the first person, then in the limited third person, and finally from the omniscient point of view. How did your anecdote change? What way was the most interesting?
2. If you know anyone with a particularly vivid way of telling stories, try to recount one of the person's tales using the person's own voice? If you don't know anyone, invent a character and have that character tell one of your stories.
3. Write a story in which the narrator is of a different sex than you. If you are a man, tell a story from a woman's perspective. If you are a

woman, tell a story from a man's perspective. What difficulties do you find? What do you learn from such an exercise?

LITERARY ESSAYS

1. Compare Charlotte Perkins Gilman's experience with doctors to their treatment of the narrator of "The Yellow Wallpaper." The differences are as important as the similarities in indicating why Gilman was able to go on as a writer while her narrator appears to be slipping deeper into insanity.
2. Distinguish between the author's, the narrator's and the main character's attitudes in "Giving Birth." Why does Atwood divide these points-of-view?
3. Compare Atwood's use of multiple perspectives in "Giving Birth" to Joyce's perspectives in "Araby." Who handles the multiple perspectives more effectively, subtly or movingly?

EDITH WHARTON

ROMAN FEVER

Edith Wharton (1862–1937) wrote chiefly about the people she knew best—wealthy Americans who travelled easily and well on both sides of the Atlantic. She was born into a rich New York socialite family, and from the age of five until she was eleven, she lived and travelled in Europe. She married Edward Wharton, a rich and well-connected Bostonian, who proved to be dull and unsympathetic to her artistic desires. In 1913 she divorced him.

Edith Wharton's first works met with little critical regard, but with the encouragement of Henry James, she produced The House of Mirth, *which brought her recognition. Her other major works include* The Age of Innocence, Ethan Frome, *and* The Custom of the Country. *The French government awarded her the Cross of the Legion of Honor for her work with wounded soldiers during the First World War.*

1

From the table at which they had been lunching two American ladies of ripe but well-cared-for middle age moved across the lofty terrace of the Roman restaurant and, leaning on its parapet, looked first at each other, and then down on the outspread glories of the Palatine and the Forum, with the same expression of vague but benevolent approval.

As they leaned there a girlish voice echoed up gaily from the stairs leading to the court below. "Well, come along, then," it cried, not to them but to an invisible companion, "and let's leave the young things to their knitting"; and a voice as fresh laughed back: "Oh, look here, Babs, not actually *knitting*—" "Well, I mean figuratively," rejoined the first. "After all, we haven't left our poor parents much else to do . . ." and at that point the turn of the stairs engulfed the dialogue.

The two ladies looked at each other again, this time with a tinge of smiling embarrassment, and the smaller and paler one shook her head and coloured slightly.

"Barbara!" she murmured, sending an unheard rebuke after the mocking voice in the stairway.

The other lady, who was fuller, and higher in colour, with a small determined nose supported by vigorous black eyebrows, gave a good-humoured laugh. "That's what our daughters think of us!"

Her companion replied by a deprecating gesture. "Not of us individually. We must remember that. It's just the collective modern idea of Mothers. And you see—" Half guiltily she drew from her handsomely mounted black hand-bag a twist of crimson silk run through by two fine knitting needles. "One never knows," she murmured. "The new system has certainly given us a good deal of time to kill; and sometimes I get tired just looking—even at this." Her gesture was now addressed to the stupendous scene at their feet.

The dark lady laughed again, and they both relapsed upon the view, contemplating it in silence, with a sort of diffused serenity which might have been borrowed from the spring effulgence of the Roman skies. The luncheon-hour was long past, and the two had their end of the vast terrace to themselves. At its opposite extremity a few groups, detained by a lingering look at the outspread city, were gathering up guide-books and fumbling for tips. The last of them scattered, and the two ladies were alone on the air-washed height.

"Well, I don't see why we shouldn't just stay here," said Mrs. Slade, the lady of the high colour and energetic brows. Two derelict basket-chairs stood near, and she pushed them into the angle of the parapet, and settled herself in one, her gaze upon the Palatine. "After all, it's still the most beautiful view in the world."

"It always will be, to me," assented her friend Mrs. Ansley, with no slight a stress on the "me" that Mrs. Slade, though she noticed it, wondered if it were not merely accidental, like the random underlinings of old-fashioned letter-writers.

"Grace Ansley was always old-fashioned," she thought; and added aloud, with a retrospective smile: "It's a view we've both been familiar with for a good many years. When we first met here we were younger than our girls are now. You remember?"

"Oh, yes, I remember," murmured Mrs. Ansley, with the same undefinable stress.—"There's that head-waiter wondering," she interpolated. She was evidently far less sure than her companion of herself and of her rights in the world.

"I'll cure him of wondering," said Mrs. Slade, stretching her hand toward a bag as discreetly opulent-looking as Mrs. Ansley's. Signing to the head-waiter, she explained that she and her friend were old lovers of Rome, and would like to spend the end of the afternoon looking down on the view—that is, if it did not disturb the service? The head-waiter, bowing over her gratuity, assured her that the ladies were most welcome, and would be still more so if they would condescend to remain for dinner. A full moon night, they would remember . . .

Mrs. Slade's black brows drew together, as though references to the moon were out-of-place and even unwelcome. But she smiled away her frown as the head-waiter retreated. "Well, why not? We might do worse. There's no knowing, I suppose, when the girls will be back. Do you even know back from *where?* I don't!"

Mrs. Ansley again coloured slightly. "I think those young Italian aviators we met at the Embassy invited them to fly to Tarquinia for tea. I suppose they'll want to wait and fly back by moonlight."

"Moonlight—moonlight! What a part it still plays. Do you suppose they're as sentimental as we were?"

"I've come to the conclusion that I don't in the least know what they are," said Mrs. Ansley. "And perhaps we didn't know much more about each other."

"No; perhaps we didn't."

Her friend gave her a shy glance. "I never should have supposed you were sentimental, Alida."

"Well, perhaps I wasn't." Mrs. Slade drew her lids together in retrospect; and for a few moments the two ladies, who had been intimate since childhood, reflected how little they knew each other. Each one, of course, had a label ready to attach to the other's name; Mrs. Delphin Slade, for instance, would have told herself, or any one who asked her, that Mrs. Horace Ansley, twenty-five years ago, had been exquisitely lovely—no, you wouldn't believe it, would you? . . . though, of course, still charming, distinguished . . . Well, as a girl she had been exquisite; far more beautiful than her daughter Barbara, though certainly Babs, according to the new standards at any rate, was more effective—had more *edge,* as they say. Funny where she got it, with those two nullities as parents. Yes; Horace Ansley was—well, just the duplicate of his wife. Museum specimens of old New York. Good-looking, irreproachable, exemplary. Mrs. Slade and Mrs. Ansley had lived opposite each other—actually as well as figuratively—for years. When the drawing-room curtains in No. 20 East 73rd Street were renewed, No. 23, across the way, was always aware of it. And of all the movings, buyings, travels, anniversaries, illnesses—the tame chronicle of an estimable pair. Little of it escaped Mrs. Slade. But she had grown bored with it by the time her husband made his big *coup* in Wall Street, and when they bought in upper Park Avenue had already begun to think: "I'd rather live opposite a speak-easy for a change; at least one might see it raided." The idea of seeing Grace raided was so amusing that (before the move) she launched it at a woman's lunch. It made a hit, and went the rounds—she sometimes wondered if it had crossed the street, and reached Mrs. Ansley. She hoped not, but didn't much mind. Those were the days when respectability was at a discount, and it did the irreproachable no harm to laugh at them a little.

A few years later, and not many months apart, both ladies lost their husbands. There was an appropriate exchange of wreaths and condolences, and a brief renewal of intimacy in the half-shadow of their mourning; and now, after another interval, they had run across each other in Rome, at the same hotel, each of them the modest appendage of a salient daughter. The similarity of their lot had again drawn them together, lending itself to mild jokes, and the mutual confession that, if in old days it must have been tiring to "keep up" with daughters, it was now, at times, a little dull not to.

No doubt, Mrs. Slade reflected, she felt her unemployment more than poor Grace ever would. It was a big drop from being the wife of Delphin Slade to being his widow. She had always regarded herself (with a certain conjugal pride) as his equal in social gifts, as contributing her full share to the making of the exceptional couple they were: but the difference after his death was irremediable. As the wife of the famous corporation lawyer, always with an international case or two on hand, every day brought its exciting and unexpected obligation: the impromptu entertaining of eminent colleagues from abroad, the hurried dashes on legal business to London, Paris or Rome, where the entertaining was so handsomely reciprocated; the amusement of hearing in her wake: "What, that handsome woman with the good clothes and the eyes is Mrs. Slade—*the* Slade's wife? Really? Generally the wives of celebrities are such frumps."

Yes; being *the* Slade's widow was a dullish business after that. In living up to such a husband all her faculties had been engaged; now she had only her daughter to live up to, for the son who seemed to have inherited his father's gifts had died suddenly in boyhood. She had fought through that agony because her husband was there, to be helped and to help; now, after the father's death, the thought of the boy had become unbearable. There was nothing left but to mother her daughter; and dear Jenny was such a perfect daughter that she needed no excessive mothering. "Now with Babs Ansley I don't know that I *should* be so quiet," Mrs. Slade sometimes half-enviously reflected; but Jenny, who was younger than her brilliant friend, was that rare accident, an extremely pretty girl who somehow made youth and prettiness seem as safe as their absence. It was all perplexing—and to Mrs. Slade a little boring. She wished that Jenny would fall in love—with the wrong man, even; that she might have to be watched, outmanoeuvred, rescued.

And instead, it was Jenny who watched her mother, kept her out of draughts, made sure that she had taken her tonic . . .

Mrs. Ansley was much less articulate than her friend, and her mental portrait of Mrs. Slade was slighter, and drawn with fainter touches. "Alida Slade's awfully brilliant; but not as brilliant as she thinks," would have summed it up; though she would have added, for the enlightenment of strangers, that Mrs. Slade had been an extremely dashing girl; much more so than her daughter, who was pretty, of course, and clever in a way, but had none of her mother's—well, "vividness," some one had once called it. Mrs. Ansley would take up current words like this, and cite them in quotation marks, as unheard-of audacities. No; Jenny was not like her mother. Sometimes Mrs. Ansley thought Alida Slade was disappointed; on the whole she had had a sad life. Full of failures and mistakes; Mrs. Ansley had always been rather sorry for her . . .

So these two ladies visualized each other, each through the wrong end of her little telescope.

2

For a long time they continued to sit side by side without speaking. It seemed as though, to both, there was a relief in laying down their somewhat futile activities in the presence of the vast Memento Mori which faced them. Mrs. Slade sat quite still, her eyes fixed on the golden slope of the Palace of the Caesars, and after a while Mrs. Ansley ceased to fidget with her bag, and she too sank into meditation. Like many intimate friends, the two ladies had never before had occasion to be silent together, and Mrs. Ansley was slightly embarrassed by what seemed, after so many years, a new stage in their intimacy, and one with which she did not yet know how to deal.

Suddenly the air was full of that deep clangour of bells which periodically covers Rome with a roof of silver. Mrs. Slade glanced at her wristwatch. "Five o'clock already," she said, as though surprised.

Mrs. Ansley suggested interrogatively: "There's bridge at the Embassy at five." For a long time Mrs. Slade did not answer. She appeared to be lost in contemplation, and Mrs. Ansley thought the remark had escaped her. But after a while she said, as if speaking out of a dream: "Bridge, did you say? Not unless you want to . . . But I don't think I will, you know."

"Oh, no," Mrs. Ansley hastened to assure her. "I don't care to at all. It's so lovely here; and so full of old memories, as you say." She settled herself in her chair, and almost furtively drew forth her knitting. Mrs. Slade took sideway note of this activity, but her own beautifully cared-for hands remained motionless on her knee.

"I was just thinking," she said slowly, "what different things Rome stands for to each generation of travellers. To our grandmothers, Roman fever; to our mothers, sentimental dangers—how we used to be guarded!—to our daughters, no more dangers than the middle of Main Street. They don't know it—but how much they're missing!"

The long golden light was beginning to pale, and Mrs. Ansley lifted her knitting a little closer to her eyes. "Yes; how we were guarded!"

"I always used to think," Mrs. Slade continued, "that our mothers had a much more difficult job than our grandmothers. When Roman fever stalked the streets it must have been comparatively easy to gather in the girls at the danger hour; but when you and I were young, with such beauty calling us, and the spice of disobedience thrown in, and no worse risk than catching cold during the cool hour after sunset, the mothers used to be put to it to keep us in—didn't they?"

She turned again toward Mrs. Ansley, but the latter had reached a delicate point in her knitting. "One, two, three—slip two; yes, they must have been," she assented, without looking up.

Mrs. Slade's eyes rested on her with a deepened attention. "She can knit—in the face of *this!* How like her . . ."

Mrs. Slade leaned back, brooding, her eyes ranging from the ruins which faced her to the long green hollow of the Forum, the fading glow of the church fronts beyond it, and the outlying immensity of the Colosseum. Suddenly she thought: "It's all very well to say that our girls have done away with sentiment and moonlight. But if Babs Ansley isn't out to catch that young aviator—the one who's a Marchese—then I don't know anything. And Jenny has no chance beside her. I know that too. I wonder if that's why Grace Ansley likes the two girls to go everywhere together? My poor Jenny as a foil—!" Mrs. Slade gave a hardly audible laugh, and at the sound Mrs. Ansley dropped her knitting.

"Yes—?"

"I—oh, nothing, I was only thinking how your Babs carries everything before her. That Campolieri boy is one of the best matches in Rome. Don't look so innocent, my dear—you know he is. And I was wondering, ever so respectfully, you understand . . . wondering how two such exemplary characters as you and Horace had managed to produce anything quite so dynamic." Mrs. Slade laughed again, with a touch of asperity.

Mrs. Ansley's hands lay inert across her needles. She looked straight out at the great accumulated wreckage of passion and splendour at her feet. But her small profile was almost expressionless. At length she said: "I think you overrate Babs, my dear."

Mrs. Slade's tone grew easier. "No; I don't. I appreciate her. And perhaps envy you. Oh, my girl's perfect; if I were a chronic invalid I'd—well, I think I'd rather be in Jenny's hands. There must be times . . . but there! I always wanted a brilliant daughter . . . and never quite understood why I got an angel instead."

Mrs. Ansley echoed her laugh in a faint murmur. "Babs is an angel too."

"Of course—of course! But she's got rainbow wings. Well, they're wandering by the sea with their young men; and here we sit . . . and it all brings back the past a little too acutely."

Mrs. Ansley had resumed her knitting. One might almost have imagined (if one had known her less well, Mrs. Slade reflected) that, for her also, too many memories rose from the lengthening shadows of those august ruins. But no; she was simply absorbed in her work. What was there for her to worry about? She knew that Babs would almost certainly come back engaged to the extremely eligible Campolieri. "And she'll sell the New York house, and settle down near them in Rome, and never be in their way . . . she's much too tactful. But she'll have an excellent cook, and just the right people in for bridge and cocktails . . . and a perfectly peaceful old age among her grandchildren."

Mrs. Slade broke off this prophetic flight with a recoil of self-disgust. There was no one of whom she had less right to think unkindly than of Grace Ansley. Would she never cure herself of envying her? Perhaps she had begun too long ago.

She stood up and leaned against the parapet, filling her troubled eyes with the tranquillizing magic of the hour. But instead of tranquillizing her the sight seemed to increase her exasperation. Her gaze turned toward the Colosseum. Already its golden flank was drowned in purple shadow, and above it the sky curved crystal clear, without light or colour. It was the moment when afternoon and evening hang balanced in mid-heaven.

Mrs. Slade turned back and laid her hand on her friend's arm. The gesture was so abrupt that Mrs. Ansley looked up, startled.

"The sun's set. You're not afraid, my dear?"

"Afraid—?"

"Of Roman fever or pneumonia? I remember how ill you were that winter. As a girl you had a very delicate throat, hadn't you?"

"Oh, we're all right up here. Down below, in the Forum, it does get deathly cold, all of a sudden . . . but not here."

"Ah, of course you know because you had to be so careful." Mrs. Slade turned back to the parapet. She thought: "I must make one more effort not to hate her." Aloud she said: "Whenever I look at the Forum from up here, I remember that story about a great-aunt of yours, wasn't she? A dreadfully wicked great-aunt?"

"Oh, yes; Great-aunt Harriet. The one who was supposed to have sent her young sister out to the Forum after sunset to gather a night-blooming flower for her album. All our great-aunts and grand-mothers used to have albums of dried flowers."

Mrs. Slade nodded. "But she really sent her because they were in love with the same man—"

"Well, that was the family tradition. They said Aunt Harriet confessed it years afterward. At any rate, the poor little sister caught the fever and died. Mother used to frighten us with the story when we were children."

"And you frightened *me* with it, that winter when you and I were here as girls. The winter I was engaged to Delphin."

Mrs. Ansley gave a faint laugh. "Oh, did I? Really frightened you? I don't believe you're easily frightened."

"Not often; but I was then. I was easily frightened because I was too happy. I wonder if you know what that means?"

"I—yes . . ." Mrs. Ansley faltered.

"Well, I suppose that was why the story of your wicked aunt made such an impression on me. And I thought: 'There's no more Roman fever, but the Forum is deathly cold after sunset—especially after a hot day. And the Colosseum's even colder and damper'."

"The Colosseum—?"

"Yes. It wasn't easy to get in, after the gates were locked for the night. Far from easy. Still, in those days it could be managed; it *was* managed, often. Lovers met there who couldn't meet elsewhere. You knew that?"

"I—I daresay. I don't remember."

"You don't remember? You don't remember going to visit some ruins or other one evening, just after dark, and catching a bad chill? You were supposed to have gone to see the moon rise. People always said that expedition was what caused your illness."

There was a moment's silence; then Mrs. Ansley rejoined: "Did they? It was all so long ago."

"Yes. And you got well again—so it didn't matter. But I suppose it struck your friends—the reason given for your illness, I mean—because everybody knew you were so prudent on account of your throat, and your mother took such care of you . . . You *had* been out late sight-seeing, hadn't you, that night?"

"Perhaps I had. The most prudent girls aren't always prudent. What made you think of it now?"

Mrs. Slade seemed to have no answer ready. But after a moment she broke out: "Because I simply can't bear it any longer—!"

Mrs. Ansley lifted her head quickly. Her eyes were wide and very pale. "Can't bear what?"

"Why—your not knowing that I've always known why you went."

"Why I went—?"

"Yes. You think I'm bluffing, don't you? Well, you went to meet the man I was engaged to—and I can repeat every word of the letter that took you there."

While Mrs. Slade spoke Mrs. Ansley had risen unsteadily to her feet. Her bag, her knitting and gloves, slid in a panic-stricken heap to the ground. She looked at Mrs. Slade as though she were looking at a ghost.

"No, no—don't," she faltered out.

"Why not? Listen, if you don't believe me. 'My one darling, things can't go on like this. I must see you alone. Come to the Colosseum immediately after dark tomorrow. There will be somebody to let you in. No one whom you need fear will suspect'—but perhaps you've forgotten what the letter said?"

Mrs. Ansley met the challenge with an unexpected composure. Steadying herself against the chair she looked at her friend, and replied: "No; I know it by heart too."

"And the signature? 'Only *your* D.S.' Was that it? I'm right, am I? That was the letter that took you out that evening after dark?"

Mrs. Ansley was still looking at her. It seemed to Mrs. Slade that a slow struggle was going on behind the voluntarily controlled mask of her small quiet face. "I shouldn't have thought she had herself so well in hand," Mrs. Slade reflected, almost resentfully. But at this moment Mrs. Ansley spoke. "I don't know how you knew. I burnt that letter at once."

"Yes; you would, naturally—you're so prudent!" The sneer was open now. "And if you burnt the letter you're wondering how on earth I know what was in it. That's it, isn't it?"

Mrs. Slade waited, but Mrs. Ansley did not speak.

"Well, my dear, I know what was in that letter because I wrote it!"

"You wrote it?"

"Yes."

The two women stood for a minute staring at each other in the last golden light. Then Mrs. Ansley dropped back into her chair. "Oh," she murmured, and covered her face with her hands.

Mrs. Slade waited nervously for another word or movement. None came, and at length she broke out: "I horrify you."

Mrs. Ansley's hands dropped to her knee. The face they uncovered was streaked with tears. "I wasn't thinking of you. I was thinking—it was the only letter I ever had from him!"

"And I wrote it. Yes; I wrote it! But I was the girl he was engaged to. Did you happen to remember that?"

Mrs. Ansley's head drooped again. "I'm not trying to excuse myself . . . I remembered . . ."

"And still you went?"

"Still I went."

Mrs. Slade stood looking down on the small bowed figure at her side. The flame of her wrath had already sunk, and she wondered why she had ever thought there would be any satisfaction in inflicting so purposeless a wound on her friend. But she had to justify herself.

"You do understand? I'd found out—and I hated you, hated you. I knew you were in love with Delphin—and I was afraid; afraid of you, of your quiet ways, your sweetness . . . your . . . well, I wanted you out of the way, that's all. Just for a few weeks; just till I was sure of him. So in a blind fury I wrote that letter . . . I don't know why I'm telling you now."

"I suppose," said Mrs. Ansley slowly, "it's because you've always gone on hating me."

"Perhaps. Or because I wanted to get the whole thing off my mind." She paused. "I'm glad you destroyed the letter. Of course I never thought you'd die."

Mrs. Ansley relapsed into silence, and Mrs. Slade, leaning above her, was conscious of a strange sense of isolation, of being cut off from the warm current of human communion. "You think me a monster!"

"I don't know . . . It was the only letter I had, and you say he didn't write it?"

"Ah, how you care for him still!"

"I cared for that memory," said Mrs. Ansley.

Mrs. Slade continued to look down on her. She seemed physically reduced by the blow—as if, when she got up, the wind might scatter her like a puff of dust. Mrs. Slade's jealousy suddenly leapt up again at the sight. All these years the woman had been living on that letter. How she must have loved him, to treasure the mere memory of its ashes! The letter of the man her friend was engaged to. Wasn't it she who was the monster?

"You tried your best to get him away from me, didn't you? But you failed; and I kept him. That's all."

"Yes. That's all."

"I wish now I hadn't told you. I'd no idea you'd feel about it as you do; I thought you'd be amused. It all happened so long ago, as you say; and you must do me the justice to remember that I had no reason to think you'd ever taken it seriously. How could I, when you were married to Horace Ansley two months afterward? As soon as you could get out of bed your mother rushed you off to Florence and married you. People were rather surprised—they wondered at its being done so quickly; but I thought I knew. I had an idea you did it out of *pique*—to be able to say you'd got ahead of Delphin and me. Girls have such silly reasons for doing the most serious things. And your marrying so soon convinced me that you'd never really cared."

"Yes. I suppose it would," Mrs. Ansley assented.

The clear heaven overhead was emptied of all its gold. Dusk spread over it, abruptly darkening the Seven Hills. Here and there lights began to twinkle through the foliage at their feet. Steps were coming and going on the deserted terrace—waiters looking out of the doorway at the head of the stairs, then reappearing with trays and napkins and flasks of wine. Tables were moved, chairs straightened. A feeble string of electric lights flickered out. Some vases of faded flowers were carried away, and brought back replenished. A stout lady in a dust-coat suddenly appeared, asking in broken Italian if any one had seen the elastic band which held together her tattered Baedeker. She poked with her stick under the table at which she had lunched, the waiters assisting.

The corner where Mrs. Slade and Mrs. Ansley sat was still shadowy and deserted. For a long time neither of them spoke. At length Mrs. Slade began again: "I suppose I did it as a sort of joke—"

"A joke?"

"Well, girls are ferocious sometimes, you know. Girls in love especially. And I remember laughing to myself all that evening at the idea that you were waiting around there in the dark, dodging out of sight, listening for every sound, trying to get in—. Of course I was upset when I heard you were so ill afterward."

Mrs. Ansley had not moved for a long time. But now she turned slowly toward her companion. "But I didn't wait. He'd arranged everything. He was there. We were let in at once," she said.

Mrs. Slade sprang up from her leaning position. "Delphin there? They let you in?—Ah, now you're lying!" She burst out with violence.

Mrs. Ansley's voice grew clearer, and full of surprise. "But of course he was there. Naturally he came—"

"Came? How did he know he'd find you there? You must be raving!"

Mrs. Ansley hesitated, as though reflecting. "But I answered the letter. I told him I'd be there. So he came."

Mrs. Slade flung her hands up to her face. "Oh, God—you answered! I never thought of your answering . . ."

"It's odd you never thought of it, if you wrote the letter."

"Yes. I was blind with rage."

Mrs. Ansley rose, and drew her fur scarf about her. "It is cold here. We'd better go . . . I'm sorry for you," she said, as she clasped the fur about her throat.

The unexpected words sent a pang through Mrs. Slade. "Yes; we'd better go." She gathered up her bag and cloak. "I don't know why you should be sorry for me," she muttered.

Mrs. Ansley stood looking away from her toward the dusky secret mass of the Colosseum. "Well—because I didn't have to wait that night."

Mrs. Slade gave an unquiet laugh. "Yes; I was beaten there. But I oughtn't to begrudge it to you, I suppose. At the end of all these years. After all, I had everything; I had him for twenty-five years. And you had nothing but that one letter that he didn't write."

Mrs. Ansley was again silent. At length she turned toward the door of the terrace. She took a step, and turned back, facing her companion.

"I had Barbara," she said, and began to move ahead of Mrs. Slade toward the stairway.

QUESTIONS

1. Although the narrator of "Roman Fever" enters the minds of both Mrs. Slade and Mrs. Ansley, one of these characters constitutes the principal "reflector" of the story? Who is the narrator's "reflector"? Why did Wharton choose that character as the "reflector"?
2. As a reader, did your attitude change toward the characters during the course of the story? If so, how did your attitude change? Was the change gradual or sudden?
3. How does the narrator prepare the reader for the revelation that Babs is the illegitimate daughter of Mr. Slade?
4. Mrs. Slade speaks about how Americans have changed their attitude toward Rome. How has that attitude changed? What are the contemporary attitudes toward Rome? Is it regarded as a place of danger, romance and fun? How does the setting add to the story?
5. Poe's "Cask of Amontillado" also contains an Italian setting. Do the stories contain other similarities in the way the authors use Italian atmosphere? Would the stories be different if they were set in London, Chicago or Salt Lake City?

EDITH WHARTON

from TELLING A SHORT STORY

It remains to try to see what constitutes (in any permanent sense) the underlying norm of the "good short story."

A curious distinction between the successful tale and the successful novel at once presents itself. It is safe to say (since the surest way of measuring achievement in art is by survival) that the test of the novel is that its people should be *alive.* No subject in itself, however fruitful, appears to be able to keep a novel alive; only the characters in it can. Of the short story the same cannot be said. Some of the greatest short stories owe their vitality entirely to the dramatic rendering of a situation. Undoubtedly the characters engaged must be a little more than puppets; but apparently, also, they may be a little less than individual human beings. In this respect the short story, rather than the novel, might be called the direct descendant of the old epic or ballad—of those earlier forms of fiction in all of which action was the chief affair, and the character, if they did not remain mere puppets, seldom or never became more than types—such as the people, for instance, in Molière. The reason for the difference is obvious. Type, general character, may be set forth in a few strokes, but the progression, the unfolding of personality, of which the reader instinctively feels the need if the actors in the tale are to retain their individuality for him through a succession of changing circumstances—this slow but continuous growth requires space, and therefore belongs by definition to a larger, a symphonic plan.

The chief technical difference between the short story and the novel may therefore be summed up by saying that situation is the main concern of the short story, character of the novel; and it follows that the effect produced by the short story depends almost entirely on its form, or presentation. Even more—yes, and much more—than in the construction of the novel, the impression of vividness, of *presentness,* in the affair narrated, has to be sought, and made sure of beforehand, by that careful artifice which is the real carelessness of art. The short-story writer must not only know from what angle to present his anecdote if it is to give out all its fires, but must understand just *why* that particular angle and no other is the right one. He must therefore have turned his subject over and over, walked around it, so to speak, and applied to it those laws of perspective which Paolo Uccello called "so beautiful," before it can be offered to the reader as a natural unembellished fragment of experience, detached like a ripe fruit from the tree.

The moment the writer begins to grope in the tangle of his "material," to hesitate between one and another of the points that any actual happening thrusts up in such disorderly abundance, the reader feels a corresponding hesitancy, and the illusion of reality vanishes. The non-observance of the optics of the printed page results in the same failure to make the subject "carry" as the non-observance of the optics of the stage in presenting a play. By all means let the writer of short stories reduce the technical trick to its minimum—as the cleverest actresses put on the least paint; but let him always bear in mind that the surviving minimum is the only bridge between the reader's imagination and his.

* * *

Nothing but deep familiarity with his subject will protect the short-story writer from another danger: that of contenting himself with a mere sketch of the episode selected. The temptation to do so is all the greater because some critics, in their resentment of the dense and the prolix, have tended to overestimate the tenuous and the tight. Mérimée's tales are often cited as models of the *conte;* but they are rather the breathless summaries of longer tales than the bold fore-shortening of an episode from which all the significance it has to give has been adroitly extracted. It is easy to be brief and sharply outlined if one does away with one or more dimensions; the real achievement, as certain tales of Flaubert's and Turgenev's, of Stevenson's and of Maupassant's show, is to suggest illimitable air within a narrow space.

The stories of the German "romantic," Heinrich von Kleist, have likewise been praised for an extreme economy of material, but they should rather be held up as an awful warning against waste, for in their ingenious dovetailing of improbable incidents, the only economy practised is that of leaving out all that would have enriched the subject, visually or emotionally. One, indeed, "The Marquise d'O" (thrift is carried so far that the characters are known merely by their initials), has in it the making of a good novel, not unlike Goethe's "Elective Affinities"; but reduced to the limits of a short story it offers a mere skeleton of its subject.

The phrase "economy of material" suggests another danger to which the novelist and the writer of short stories are equally exposed. Such economy is, in both cases, nearly always to be advised in the multiplication of accidental happenings, minor episodes, surprises and contrarieties. Most beginners crowd into their work twice as much material of this sort as it needs. The reluctance to look deeply enough into a subject leads to the indolent habit of decorating its surface. I was once asked to read a manuscript on the eternal theme of a lovers' quarrel. The quarreling pair made up, and the reasons for dispute and reconciliation were clearly inherent in their characters and situation; but the author, being new at the trade, felt obliged to cast about for an additional, a fortuitous, pretext for their reunion—so he sent them for a drive, made the horses run away, and caused the young man to save the young lady's life. This is a crude example of a frequent fault. Again and again the novelist passes by the real meaning of a situation simply for lack of letting it reveal all its potentialities instead of dashing this way and that in quest of fresh effects. If, when once drawn to a subject, he would let it grow slowly in his mind instead of hunting about for arbitrary combinations of circumstance, his tale would have the warm scent and flavor of a fruit ripened in the sun instead of the insipidity of one forced in a hothouse.

There is a sense in which the writing of fiction may be compared to the administering of a fortune. Economy and expenditure must each bear a part in it, but they should never degenerate into parsimony or waste. True economy consists in the drawing out of one's subject of every drop of significance it can give, true expenditure in devoting time, meditation and patient labor to the process of extraction and representation.

It all comes back to a question of expense: expense of time, of patience, of study, of thought, of letting hundreds of stray experiences accumulate and group themselves in the memory, till suddenly one of the number emerges and throws its sharp light on the subject which solicits you. It has been often, and inaccurately, said that the mind of a creative artist is a mirror, and the work of art the reflection of life in it. The mirror, indeed, is the artist's mind, with all his experiences reflected in it; but the work of art, from the smallest to the greatest, should be something projected, not reflected, something on which his mirrored experiences, at the right conjunction of the stars, are to be turned for its full illumination.

THINGS TO THINK ABOUT

1. How does "Roman Fever" exemplify the qualities of a good short story that Wharton discusses in her essay? Are the characters in "Roman Fever" more than types? Is the story filled with extraneous actions? Is there economy of expression?

2. Wharton compares writing to "administering a fortune." What does this comparison indicate about the intended readers of her essay? How does the metaphor of "administering a fortune" differ from "making a fortune"?
3. Wharton uses economic metaphors throughout her essay on "Telling a Short Story." In what ways is such language appropriate to the writer, a woman writer, or the writer about high society?

JAMES JOYCE

ARABY

Although James Joyce (1882–1941) left Dublin in 1904 to live on the continent and visited his native city only briefly afterwards. Dublin is the imaginative locale of all his fiction. He rejected his hometown as "the center of paralysis," but he never could leave it completely behind.

Joyce was a rebel and tireless experimenter. On graduation from University College, Dublin, he made his first trip to the continent, living in Paris for a year. When he returned to Europe after his mother's death, he settled first in Italy, then in Switzerland (during the First World War) and finally in Paris. When the Nazis invaded Paris, Joyce, sick and virtually blind, escaped again to Switzerland where he soon died.

Joyce wrote poetry, a play, journalism, a book of short stories, and three novels The Portrait of the Artist as a Young Man, Ulysses, *and* Finnegan's Wake. *Many people consider him the finest twentieth-century novelist in English.*

North Richmond Street, being blind,[1] was a quiet street except at the hour when the Christian Brothers' School set the boys free. An uninhabited house of two stories stood at the blind end, detached from its neighbours in a square ground. The other houses of the street, conscious of decent lives within them, gazed at one another with brown imperturbable faces.

The former tenant of our house, a priest, had died in the back drawing-room. Air, musty from having been long enclosed, hung in all the rooms, and the waste room behind the kitchen was littered with old useless papers. Among these I found a few paper-covered books, the pages of which were curled and damp: *The Abbot,* by Walter Scott, *The Devout Communicant,* and *The Memoirs of Vidocq.*[2] I liked the last best because its leaves were yellow. The wild garden behind the house contained a central apple tree and a few straggling bushes under one of which I found the late tenant's rusty bicycle pump. He had been a very charitable priest; in his will he had left all his money to institutions and the furniture of his house to his sister.

[1] A blind street is a dead-end street.

[2] François-Eugène Vidocq (1775–1857) helped create the French security police. *The Abbot* is one of Sir Walter Scott's Scottish historical romances. *The Devout Communicant* is a Catholic devotional manual.

When the short days of winter came dusk fell before we had well eaten our dinners. When we met in the street the houses had grown sombre. The space of sky above us was the colour of ever-changing violet and towards it the lamps of the street lifted their feeble lanterns. The cold air stung us and we played till our bodies glowed. Our shouts echoed in the silent street. The career of our play brought us through the dark muddy lanes behind the houses where we ran the gauntlet of the rough tribes from the cottages to the back doors of the dark dripping gardens where odours arose from the ash-pits, to the dark odorous stables where a coachman smoothed and combed the horse or shook music from the buckled harness. When we returned to the street, light from the kitchen windows had filled the areas. If my uncle was seen turning the corner we hid in the shadow until we had seen him safely housed. Or if Mangan's sister came out on the doorstep to call her brother in to his tea we watched her from our shadow peer up and down the street. We waited to see whether she would remain or go in and, if she remained, we left our shadow and walked up to Mangan's steps resignedly. She was waiting for us, her figure defined by the light from the half-opened door. Her brother always teased her before he obeyed and I stood by the railings looking at her. Her dress swung as she moved her body and the soft rope of her hair tossed from side to side.

Every morning I lay on the floor in the front parlour watching her door. The blind was pulled down to within an inch of the sash so that I could not be seen. When she came out on the doorstep my heart leaped. I ran to the hall, seized my books and followed her. I kept her brown figure always in my eye and, when we came near the point at which our ways diverged, I quickened my pace and passed her. This happened morning after morning. I had never spoken to her, except for a few casual words, and yet her name was like a summons to all my foolish blood.

Her image accompanied me even in places the most hostile to romance. On Saturday evenings when my aunt went marketing I had to go to carry some of the parcels. We walked through the flaring streets, jostled by drunken men and bargaining women, amid the curses of labourers, the shrill litanies of shop-boys who stood on guard by the barrels of pigs' cheeks, the nasal chanting of street-singers, who sang a *come-all-you* about O'Donovan Rossa,[3] or a ballad about the troubles in our native land. These noises converged in a single sensation of life for me: I imagined that I bore my chalice safely through a throng of foes. Her name sprang to my lips at moments in strange prayers and praises which I myself did not understand. My eyes were often full of tears. I

[3] Jeremiah Donovan (1831–1915), commonly called O'Donovan Rossa, was an Irish nationalist celebrated in street songs or *come-all-you's*.

could not tell why and at times a flood from my heart seemed to pour itself out into my bosom. I thought little of the future. I did not know whether I would ever speak to her or not or, if I spoke to her, how I could tell her of my confused adoration. But my body was like a harp and her words and gestures were like fingers running upon the wires.

One evening I went into the back drawing-room in which the priest had died. It was a dark rainy evening and there was no sound in the house. Through one of the broken panes I heard the rain impinge upon the earth, the fine incessant needles of water playing in the sodden beds. Some distant lamp or lighted window gleamed below me. I was thankful that I could see so little. All my senses seemed to desire to veil themselves and, feeling that I was about to slip from them, I pressed the palms of my hands together until they trembled, murmuring: *"O love! O love!"* many times.

At last she spoke to me. When she addressed the first words to me I was so confused that I did not know what to answer. She asked me was I going to *Araby*. I forgot whether I answered yes or no. It would be a splendid bazaar, she said she would love to go.

"And why can't you?" I asked.

While she spoke she turned a silver bracelet round and round her wrist. She could not go, she said, because there would be a retreat that week in her convent. Her brother and two other boys were fighting for their caps and I was alone at the railings. She held one of the spikes, bowing her head towards me. The light from the lamp opposite our door caught the white curve of her neck, lit up her hair that rested there and, falling, lit up the hand upon the railing. It fell over one side of her dress and caught the white border of a petticoat, just visible as she stood at ease.

"It's well for you," she said.

"If I go," I said, "I will bring you something."

What innumerable follies laid waste my waking and sleeping thoughts after the evening! I wished to annihilate the tedious intervening days. I chafed against the work of school. At night in my bedroom and by day in the classroom her image came between me and the page I strove to read. The syllables of the word *Araby* were called to me through the silence in which my soul luxuriated and cast an Eastern enchantment over me. I asked for leave to go to the bazaar on Saturday night. My aunt was surprised and hoped it was not some Freemason[4] affair. I answered few questions in class. I watched my master's face pass from amiability to sternness; he hoped I was not beginning to idle. I could not call my wandering thoughts together. I had hardly any patience

[4] Freemason societies, because they were secret, were frequently considered dangerous gatherings.

with the serious work of life which, now that it stood between me and my desire, seemed to me child's play, ugly monotonous child's play.

On Saturday morning I reminded my uncle that I wished to go to the bazaar in the evening. He was fussing at the hall-stand, looking for the hat brush, and answered me curtly:

"Yes, boy, I know."

As he was in the hall I could not go into the front parlour and lie at the window. I left the house in bad humour and walked slowly towards the school. The air was pitilessly raw and already my heart misgave me.

When I came home to dinner my uncle had not yet been home. Still it was early. I sat staring at the clock for some time and, when its ticking began to irritate me, I left the room. I mounted the staircase and gained the upper part of the house. The high cold empty gloomy rooms liberated me and I went from room to room singing. From the front window I saw my companions playing below in the street. Their cries reached me weakened and indistinct and, leaning my forehead against the cool glass, I looked over at the dark house where she lived. I may have stood there for an hour, seeing nothing but the brown-clad figure cast by my imagination, touched discreetly by the lamplight at the curved neck, at the hand upon the railings and at the border below the dress.

When I came downstairs again I found Mrs. Mercer sitting at the fire. She was an old garrulous woman, a pawnbroker's widow, who collected used stamps for some pious purpose. I had to endure the gossip of the tea-table. The meal was prolonged beyond an hour and still my uncle did not come. Mrs. Mercer stood up to go: she was sorry she couldn't wait any longer, but it was after eight o'clock and she did not like to be out late, as the night air was bad for her. When she had gone I began to walk up and down the room, clenching my fists. My aunt said:

"I'm afraid you may put off your bazaar for this night of Our Lord."

At nine o'clock I heard my uncle's latchkey in the hall-door. I heard him talking to himself and heard the hall-stand rocking when it had received the weight of his overcoat. I could interpret these signs. When he was midway through his dinner I asked him to give me the money to go to the bazaar. He had forgotten.

"The people are in bed and after their first sleep now," he said.

I did not smile. My aunt said to him energetically:

"Can't you give him the money and let him go? You've kept him late enough as it is."

My uncle said he was very sorry he had forgotten. He said he believed in the old saying: "All work and no play makes Jack a dull boy." He asked me where I was going and, when I had told him a second time, he asked me did I know *The Arab's Farewell to his Steed.*[5] When I left the kitchen he was about to recite the opening lines of the piece to my aunt.

I held a florin tightly in my hand as I strode down Buckingham Street towards the station. The sight of the streets thronged with buyers and glaring with gas recalled to me the purpose of my journey. I took my seat in a third-class carriage of a deserted train. After an intolerable delay the train moved out of the station slowly. It crept onward among ruinous houses and over the twinkling river. At Westland Row Station a crowd of people pressed to the carriage doors; but the porters moved them back, saying that it was a special train for the bazaar. I remained alone in the bare carriage. In a few minutes the train drew up beside an improvised wooden platform. I passed out on the road and saw by the lighted dial of a clock that it was ten minutes to ten. In front of me was a large building which displayed the magical name.

I could not find any sixpenny entrance and, fearing that the bazaar would be closed, I passed in quickly through a turnstile, handing a shilling to a weary-looking man. I found myself in a big hall girdled at half its height by a gallery. Nearly all the stalls were closed and the greater part of the hall was in darkness. I recognized a silence like that which pervades a church after a service. I walked into the center of the bazaar timidly. A few people were gathered about the stalls which were still open. Before a curtain, over which the words *Café Chantant* were written in coloured lamps, two men were counting money on a salver. I listened to the fall of the coins.

Remembering with difficulty why I had come I went over to one of the stalls and examined porcelain vases and flowered tea-sets. At the door of the stall a young lady was talking and laughing with two young gentlemen. I remarked their English accents and listened vaguely to their conversation.

"O, I never said such a thing!"

"O, but you did!"

"O, but I didn't!"

"Didn't she say that?"

"Yes. I heard her."

"O, there's a . . . fib!"

Observing me, the young lady came over and asked me did I wish to buy anything. The tone of her voice was not encouraging; she seemed to have spoken to me out of a sense of duty. I looked humbly at the great jars that stood like eastern guards at either side of the dark entrance to the stall and murmured:

"No, thank you."

[5] A poem by Caroline Norton (1808–1877).

The young lady changed the position of one of the vases and went back to the two young men. They began to talk of the same subject. Once or twice the young lady glanced at me over her shoulder.

I lingered before her stall, though I knew my stay was useless, to make my interest in her wares seem the more real. Then I turned away slowly and walked down the middle of the bazaar. I allowed the two pennies to fall against the sixpence in my pocket. I heard a voice call from one end of the gallery that the light was out. The upper part of the hall was now completely dark.

Gazing up into the darkness I saw myself as a creature driven and derided by vanity; and my eyes burned with anguish and anger.

QUESTIONS

1. Based on the language used in the story, would you describe the narrator as well or poorly educated? When he writes, "I bore my chalice safely through throngs of foe" what sorts of language is he borrowing? Do most boys use such language?
2. How does the narrator view his relationship to Dublin society? Is he a realist or an idealist?
3. How would you describe his relationship to Mangan's sister? How well does he know her? Do her action and speech justify his attitude toward her?
4. At the conclusion of the story, the narrator describes himself as "a creature driven and derided by vanity." What does he mean? Is that a realistic evaluation of his condition?
5. What is the relationship between the older, presumably more mature narrator and his younger self?

CHARLOTTE PERKINS GILMAN

THE YELLOW WALL-PAPER

Charlotte Perkins Gilman (1860–1935) was a major writer on women's issues in her day. Her fictional writing make up only a small part of her output. Her first major work was Woman and Economics, *which argued for the economic independence of women. She also wrote about child care, international peace and labor issues.*

But Gilman was not merely a writer, she was an activist as well. In 1915, she helped found the Women's Peace Party and throughout her life lectured and spoke for the various causes she championed. She committed suicide in 1935.

It is very seldom that mere ordinary people like John and myself secure ancestral halls for the summer.

A colonial mansion, a hereditary estate, I would say a haunted house, and reach the height of romantic felicity—but that would be asking too much of fate!

Still I will proudly declare that there is something queer about it.

Else, why should it be let so cheaply? And why have stood so long untenanted?

John laughs at me, of course, but one expects that in marriage.

John is practical in the extreme. He has no patience with faith, an intense horror of superstition, and he scoffs openly at any talk of things not to be felt and seen and put down in figures.

John is a physician, and *perhaps*—(I would not say it to a living soul, of course, but this is dead paper and a great relief to my mind)—*perhaps* that is one reason I do not get well faster.

You see he does not believe I am sick!

And what can one do?

If a physician of high standing, and one's own husband, assures friends and relatives that there is really nothing the matter with one but temporary nervous depression—a slight hysterical tendency—what is one to do?

My brother is also a physician, and also of high standing, and he says the same thing.

So I take phosphates or phosphites—whichever it is, and tonics, and journeys, and air, and exercise, and am absolutely forbidden to "work" until I am well again.

Personally, I disagree with their ideas.

Personally, I believe that congenial work, with excitement and change, would do me good.

But what is one to do?

I did write for a while in spite of them; but it *does* exhaust me a good deal—having to be so sly about it, or else meet with heavy opposition.

I sometimes fancy that in my condition if I had less opposition and more society and stimulus—but John says the very worst thing I can do is to think about my condition, and I confess it always makes me feel bad.

So I will let it alone and talk about the house.

The most beautiful place! It is quite alone, standing well back from the road, quite three miles from the village. It makes me think of English places that you read about, for there are hedges and walls and gates that lock, and lots of separate little houses for the gardeners and people.

There is a *delicious* garden! I never saw such a garden—large and shady, full of box-bordered paths, and lined with long grape-covered arbors with seats under them.

There were greenhouses, too, but they are all broken now.

There was some legal trouble, I believe, something about the heirs and coheirs; anyhow, the place has been empty for years.

That spoils my ghostliness, I am afraid, but I don't care—there is something strange about the house—I can feel it.

I even said so to John one moonlight evening, but he said what I felt was a *draught,* and shut the window.

I get unreasonably angry with John sometimes. I'm sure I never used to be sensitive. I think it is due to this nervous condition.

But John says if I feel so, I shall neglect proper self-control; so I take pains to control myself—before him, at least, and that makes me very tired.

I don't like our room a bit. I wanted one downstairs that opened on the piazza and had roses all over the window, and such pretty old-fashioned chintz hangings! but John would not hear of it.

He said there was only one window and not room for two beds, and no near room for him if he took another.

He is very careful and loving, and hardly lets me stir without special direction.

I have a schedule prescription for each hour in the day; he takes all care from me, and so I feel basely ungrateful not to value it more.

He said we came here solely on my account, that I was to have perfect rest and all the air I could get. "Your exercise depends on your strength, my dear," said he, "and your food somewhat on your appetite; but air you can absorb all the time." So we took the nursery at the top of the house.

It is a big, airy room, the whole floor nearly, with windows that look all ways, and air and sunshine galore. It was nursery first and then playroom and gymnasium, I should judge; for the windows are barred for little children, and there are rings and things in the walls.

The paint and paper look as if a boys' school had used it. It is stripped off—the paper—in great patches all around the head of my bed, about as far as I can reach, and in a great place on the other side of the room low down. I never saw a worse paper in my life.

One of those sprawling flamboyant patterns committing every artistic sin.

It is dull enough to confuse the eye in following, pronounced enough to constantly irritate and provoke study, and when you follow the lame uncertain curves for a little distance they suddenly commit suicide—plunge off at outrageous angles, destroy themselves in unheard of contradictions.

The color is repellent, almost revolting; a smouldering unclean yellow, strangely faded by the slow-turning sunlight.

It is a dull yet lurid orange in some places, a sickly sulphur tint in others.

No wonder the children hated it! I should hate it myself if I had to live in this room long.

There comes John, and I must put this away,—he hates to have me write a word.

We have been here two weeks, and I haven't felt like writing before, since that first day.

I am sitting by the window now, up in this atrocious nursery, and there is nothing to hinder my writing as much as I please, save lack of strength.

John is away all day, and even some nights when his cases are serious.

I am glad my case is not serious!

But these nervous troubles are dreadfully depressing.

John does not know how much I really suffer. He knows there is no *reason* to suffer, and that satisfies him.

Of course it is only nervousness. It does weigh on me so not to do my duty in any way!

I meant to be such a help to John, such a real rest and comfort, and here I am a comparative burden already!

Nobody would believe what an effort it is to do what little I am able,—to dress and entertain, and order things.

It is fortunate Mary is so good with the baby. Such a dear baby!

And yet I *cannot* be with him, it makes me so nervous.

I suppose John never was nervous in his life. He laughs at me so about this wall-paper!

At first he meant to repaper the room, but afterwards he said that I was letting it get the better of me, and that nothing was worse for a nervous patient than to give way to such fancies.

He said that after the wall-paper was changed it would be the heavy bedstead, and then the barred windows, and then that gate at the head of the stairs, and so on.

"You know the place is doing you good," he said, "and really, dear, I don't care to renovate the house just for a three months' rental."

"Then do let us go downstairs," I said, "there are such pretty rooms there."

Then he took me in his arms and called me a blessed little goose, and said he would go down to the cellar, if I wished, and have it whitewashed into the bargain.

But he is right enough about the beds and windows and things.

It is an airy and comfortable room as any one need wish, and, of course, I would not be so silly as to make him uncomfortable just for a whim.

I'm really getting quite fond of the big room, all but that horrid paper.

Out of one window I can see the garden, those mysterious deep-shaded arbors, the riotous old-fashioned flowers, and bushes and gnarly trees.

Out of another I get a lovely view of the bay and a little private wharf belonging to the estate. There is a beautiful shaded lane that runs down there from the house. I always fancy I see people walking in these numerous paths and arbors, but John has cautioned me not to give way to fancy in the least. He says that with my imaginative power and habit of story-making, a nervous weakness like mine is sure to lead to all manner of excited fancies, and that I ought to use my will and good sense to check the tendency. So I try.

I think sometimes that if I were only well enough to write a little it would relieve the press of ideas and rest me.

But I find I get pretty tired when I try.

It is so discouraging not to have any advice and companionship about my work. When I get really well, John says we will ask Cousin Henry and Julia down for a long visit; but he says he would as soon put fireworks in my pillowcase as to let me have those stimulating people about now.

I wish I could get well faster.

But I must not think about that. This paper looks to me as if it *knew* what a vicious influence it had!

There is a recurrent spot where the pattern lolls like a broken neck and two bulbous eyes stare at you upside down.

I get positively angry with the impertinence of it and the everlastingness. Up and down and sideways they crawl, and those absurd, unblinking eyes are everywhere. There is one place where two breadths didn't match, and the eyes go all up and down the line, one a little higher than the other.

I never saw so much expression in an inanimate thing before, and we all know how much expression they have! I used to lie awake as a child and get more entertainment and terror out of blank walls and plain furniture than most children could find in a toy-store.

I remember what a kindly wink the knobs of our big, old bureau used to have, and there was one chair that always seemed like a strong friend.

I used to feel that if any of the other things looked too fierce I could always hop into that chair and be safe.

The furniture in this room is no worse than inharmonious, however, for we had to bring it all from downstairs. I suppose when this was used as a playroom they had to take the nursery things out, and no wonder! I never saw such ravages as the children have made here.

The wall-paper, as I said before, is torn off in spots, and it sticketh closer than a brother—they must have had perseverance as well as hatred.

Then the floor is scratched and gouged and splintered, the plaster itself is dug out here and there, and this great heavy bed which is all we found in the room, looks as if it had been through the wars.

But I don't mind it a bit—only the paper.

There comes John's sister. Such a dear girl as she is, and so careful of me! I must not let her find me writing.

She is a perfect and enthusiastic housekeeper, and hopes for no better profession. I verily believe she thinks it is the writing which made me sick!

But I can write when she is out, and see her a long way off from these windows.

There is one that commands the road, a lovely shaded winding road, and one that just looks off over the country. A lovely country, too, full of great elms and velvet meadows.

This wall-paper has a kind of sub-pattern in a different shade, a particularly irritating one, for you can only see it in certain lights, and not clearly then.

But in the places where it isn't faded and where the sun is just so— I can see a strange, provoking, formless sort of figure, that seems to skulk about behind that silly and conspicuous front design.

There's sister on the stairs!

Well, the Fourth of July is over! The people are all gone and I am tired out. John thought it might do me good to see a little company, so we just had mother and Nellie and the children down for a week.

Of course I didn't do a thing. Jennie sees to everything now.

But it tired me all the same.

John says if I don't pick up faster he shall send me to Weir Mitchell in the fall.

But I don't want to go there at all. I had a friend who was in his hands once, and she says he is just like John and my brother, only more so!

Besides, it is such an undertaking to go so far.

I don't feel as if it was worth while to turn my hand over for anything, and I'm getting dreadfully fretful and querulous.

I cry at nothing, and cry most of the time.

Of course I don't when John is here, or anybody else, but when I am alone.

And I am alone a good deal just now. John is kept in town very often by serious cases, and Jennie is good and lets me alone when I want her to.

So I walk a little in the garden or down that lovely lane, sit on the porch under the roses, and lie down up here a good deal.

I'm getting really fond of the room in spite of the wall-paper. Perhaps *because* of the wall-paper.

It dwells in my mind so!

I lie here on this great immovable bed—it is nailed down, I believe— and follow that pattern about by the hour. It is as good as gymnastics, I assure you. I start, we'll say, at the bottom, down in the corner over there where it has not been touched, and I determine for the thousandth time that I *will* follow that pointless pattern to some sort of a conclusion.

I know a little of the principle of design, and I know this thing was not arranged on any laws of radiation, or alternation, or repetition, or symmetry, or anything else that I ever heard of.

It is repeated, of course, by the breadths, but not otherwise.

Looked at in one way each breadth stands alone, the bloated curves and flourishes—a kind of "debased Romanesque" with *delirium tremens*—go waddling up and down in isolated columns of fatuity.

But, on the other hand, they connect diagonally, and the sprawling outlines run off in great slanting waves of optic horror, like a lot of wallowing seaweeds in full chase.

The whole thing goes horizontally, too, at least it seems so, and I exhaust myself in trying to distinguish the order of its going in that direction.

They have used a horizontal breadth for a frieze, and that adds wonderfully to the confusion.

There is one end of the room where it is almost intact, and there, when the crosslights fade and the low sun shines directly upon it, I can almost fancy radiation after all,—the interminable grotesques seem to form around a common centre and rush off in headlong plunges of equal distraction.

It makes me tired to follow it. I will take a nap I guess.

I don't know why I should write this.

I don't want to.

I don't feel able.

And I know John would think it absurd. But I *must* say what I feel and think in some way—it is such a relief!

But the effort is getting to be greater than the relief.

Half the time now I am awfully lazy, and lie down ever so much.

John says I mustn't lose my strength, and has me take cod liver oil and lots of tonics and things, to say nothing of ale and wine and rare meat.

Dear John! He loves me very dearly, and hates to have me sick. I tried to have a real earnest reasonable talk with him the other day, and tell him how I wish he would let me go and make a visit to Cousin Henry and Julia.

But he said I wasn't able to go, nor able to stand it after I got there; and I did not make out a very good case for myself, for I was crying before I had finished.

It is getting to be a great effort for me to think straight. Just this nervous weakness I suppose.

And dear John gathered me up in his arms, and just carried me upstairs and laid me on the bed, and sat by me and read to me till it tired my head.

He said I was his darling and his comfort and all he had, and that I must take care of myself for his sake, and keep well.

He says no one but myself can help me out of it, that I must use my will and self-control and not let any silly fancies run away with me.

There's one comfort, the baby is well and happy, and does not have to occupy this nursery with the horrid wall-paper.

If we had not used it, that blessed child would have! What a fortunate escape! Why, I wouldn't have a child of mine, an impressionable little thing, live in such a room for worlds.

I never thought of it before, but it is lucky that John kept me here after all, I can stand it so much easier than a baby, you see.

Of course I never mention it to them any more—I am too wise,—but I keep watch of it all the same.

There are things in that paper that nobody knows but me, or ever will.

Behind that outside pattern the dim shapes get clearer every day.

It is always the same shape, only very numerous.

And it is like a woman stooping down and creeping about behind that pattern. I don't like it a bit. I wonder—I begin to think—I wish John would take me away from here!

It is so hard to talk with John about my case, because he is so wise, and because he loves me so.

But I tried it last night.

It was moonlight. The moon shines in all around just as the sun does.

I hate to see it sometimes, it creeps so slowly, and always comes in by one window or another.

John was asleep and I hated to waken him, so I kept still and watched the moonlight on that undulating wall-paper till I felt creepy.

The faint figure behind seemed to shake the pattern, just as if she wanted to get out.

I got up softly and went to feel and see if the paper *did* move, and when I came back John was awake.

"What is it, little girl?" he said. "Don't go walking about like that—you'll get cold."

I thought it was a good time to talk, so I told him that I really was not gaining here, and that I wished he would take me away.

"Why darling!" said he, "our lease will be up in three weeks, and I can't see how to leave before.

"The repairs are not done at home, and I cannot possibly leave town just now. Of course if you were in any danger, I could and would, but you really are better, dear, whether you can see it or not. I am a doctor, dear, and I know. You are gaining flesh and color, your appetite is better, I feel really much easier about you."

"I don't weigh a bit more," said I, "nor as much; and my appetite may be better in the evening when you are here, but it is worse in the morning when you are away!"

"Bless her little heart!" said he with a big hug, "she shall be as sick as she pleases! But now let's improve the shining hours by going to sleep, and talk about it in the morning!"

"And you won't go away?" I asked gloomily.

"Why, how can I, dear? It is only three weeks more and then we will take a nice little trip of a few days while Jennie is getting the house ready. Really dear you are better!"

"Better in body perhaps—" I began, and stopped short, for he sat up straight and looked at me with such a stern, reproachful look that I could not say another word.

"My darling," said he, "I beg of you, for my sake and for our child's sake, as well as for your own, that you will never for one instant let that idea enter your mind! There is nothing so dangerous, so fascinating, to a temperament like yours. It is a false and foolish fancy. Can you not trust me as a physician when I tell you so?"

So of course I said no more on that score, and we went to sleep before long. He thought I was asleep first, but I wasn't, and lay there for hours trying to decide whether that front pattern and the back pattern really did move together or separately.

On a pattern like this, by daylight, there is a lack of sequence, a defiance of law, that is a constant irritant to a normal mind.

The color is hideous enough, and unreliable enough, and infuriating enough, but the pattern is torturing.

You think you have mastered it, but just as you get well underway in following, it turns a back-somersault and there you are. It slaps you in the face, knocks you down, and tramples upon you. It is like a bad dream.

The outside pattern is a florid arabesque, reminding one of a fungus. If you can imagine a toadstool in joints, an interminable string of toadstools, budding and sprouting in endless convolutions—why, that is something like it.

That is, sometimes!

There is one marked peculiarity about this paper, a thing nobody seems to notice but myself, and that is that it changes as the light changes.

When the sun shoots in through the east window—I always watch for that first long, straight ray—it changes so quickly that I never can quite believe it.

That is why I watch it always.

By moonlight—the moon shines in all night when there is a moon—I wouldn't know it was the same paper.

At night in any kind of light, in twilight, candle light, lamplight, and worst of all by moonlight, it becomes bars! The outside pattern I mean, and the woman behind it is as plain as can be.

I didn't realize for a long time what the thing was that showed behind, that dim sub-pattern, but now I am quite sure it is a woman.

By daylight she is subdued, quiet. I fancy it is the pattern that keeps her so still. It is so puzzling. It keeps me quiet by the hour.

I lie down ever so much now. John says it is good for me, and to sleep all I can.

Indeed he started the habit by making me lie down for an hour after each meal.

It is a very bad habit I am convinced, for you see I don't sleep.

And that cultivates deceit, for I don't tell them I'm awake—O no!

The fact is I am getting a little afraid of John.

He seems very queer sometimes, and even Jennie has an inexplicable look.

It strikes me occasionally, just as a scientific hypothesis,—that perhaps it is the paper!

I have watched John when he did not know I was looking, and come into the room suddenly on the most innocent excuses, and I've caught him several times *looking at the paper!* And Jennie too. I caught Jennie with her hand on it once.

She didn't know I was in the room, and when I asked her in a quiet, a very quiet voice, with the most restrained manner possible, what she was doing with the paper—she turned around as if she had been caught stealing, and looked quite angry—asked me why I should frighten her so!

Then she said that the paper stained everything it touched, that she had found yellow smooches on all my clothes and John's, and she wished we would be more careful!

Did not that sound innocent? But I know she was studying that pattern, and I am determined that nobody shall find it out but myself!

Life is very much more exciting now than it used to be. You see I have something more to expect, to look forward to, to watch. I really do eat better, and am more quiet than I was.

John is so pleased to see me improve! He laughed a little the other day, and said I seemed to be flourishing in spite of my wall-paper.

I turned it off with a laugh. I had no intention of telling him it was *because* of the wall-paper—he would make fun of me. He might even want to take me away.

I don't want to leave now until I have found it out. There is a week more, and I think that will be enough.

I'm feeling ever so much better! I don't sleep much at night, for it is so interesting to watch developments; but I sleep a good deal in the daytime.

In the daytime it is tiresome and perplexing.

There are always new shoots on the fungus, and new shades of yellow all over it. I cannot keep count of them, though I have tried conscientiously.

It is the strangest yellow, that wall-paper! It makes me think of all the yellow things I ever saw—not beautiful ones like buttercups, but old foul, bad yellow things.

But there is something else about that paper—the smell! I noticed it the moment we came into the room, but with so much air and sun it was not bad. Now we have had a week of fog and rain, and whether the windows are open or not, the smell is here.

It creeps all over the house.

I find it hovering in the dining-room, skulking in the parlor, hiding in the hall, lying in wait for me on the stairs.

It gets into my hair.

Even when I go to ride, if I turn my head suddenly and surprise it—there is that smell!

Such a peculiar odor, too! I have spent hours in trying to analyze it, to find what it smelled like.

It is not bad—at first, and very gentle, but quite the subtlest, most enduring odor I ever met.

In this damp weather it is awful, I wake up in the night and find it hanging over me.

It used to disturb me at first. I thought seriously of burning the house—to reach the smell.

But now I am used to it. The only thing I can think of that it is like is the *color* of the paper! A yellow smell.

There is a very funny mark on this wall, low down, near the mopboard. A streak that runs round the room. It goes behind every piece of furniture, except the bed, a long, straight, even *smooch,* as if it had been rubbed over and over.

I wonder how it was done and who did it, and what they did it for. Round and round and round—round and round and round—it makes me dizzy!

I really have discovered something at last.

Through watching so much at night, when it changes so, I have finally found out.

The front pattern *does* move—and no wonder! The woman behind shakes it!

Sometimes I think there are a great many women behind, and sometimes only one, and she crawls around fast, and her crawling shakes it all over.

Then in the very bright spots she keeps still, and in the very shady spots she just takes hold of the bars and shakes them hard.

And she is all the time trying to climb through. But nobody could climb through that pattern—it strangles so; I think that is why it has so many heads.

They get through, and then the pattern strangles them off and turns them upside down, and makes their eyes white!

If those heads were covered or taken off it would not be half so bad.

I think that woman gets out in the daytime!

And I'll tell you why—privately—I've seen her!

I can see her out of every one of my windows!

It is the same woman, I know, for she is always creeping, and most women do not creep by daylight.

I see her on that long road under the trees, creeping along, and when a carriage comes she hides under the blackberry vines.

I don't blame her a bit. It must be very humiliating to be caught creeping by daylight!

I always lock the door when I creep by daylight. I can't do it at night, for I know John would suspect something at once.

And John is so queer now, that I don't want to irritate him. I wish he would take another room! Besides, I don't want anybody to get that woman out at night but myself.

I often wonder if I could see her out of all the windows at once.

But, turn as fast as I can, I can only see out of one at one time.

And though I always see her, she *may* be able to creep faster than I can turn!

I have watched her sometimes away off in the open country, creeping as fast as a cloud shadow in a high wind.

If only that top pattern could be gotten off from the under one! I mean to try it, little by little.

I have found out another funny thing, but I shan't tell it this time! It does not do to trust people too much.

There are only two more days to get this paper off, and I believe John is beginning to notice. I don't like the look in his eyes.

And I heard him ask Jennie a lot of professional questions about me. She had a very good report to give.

She said I slept a good deal in the daytime.

John knows I don't sleep very well at night, for all I'm so quiet!

He asked me all sorts of questions, too, and pretended to be very loving and kind.

As if I couldn't see through him!

Still, I don't wonder he acts so, sleeping under this paper for three months.

It only interests me, but I feel sure John and Jennie are secretly affected by it.

Hurrah! This is the last day, but it is enough. John to stay in town over night, and won't be out until this evening.

Jennie wanted to sleep with me—the sly thing! but I told her I should undoubtedly rest better for a night all alone.

That was clever, for really I wasn't alone a bit! As soon as it was moonlight and that poor thing began to crawl and shake the pattern, I got up and ran to help her.

I pulled and she shook, I shook and she pulled, and before morning we had peeled off yards of that paper.

A strip about as high as my head and half around the room.

And then when the sun came and that awful pattern began to laugh at me, I declared I would finish it to-day!

We go away to-morrow, and they are moving all my furniture down again to leave things as they were before.

Jennie looked at the wall in amazement, but I told her merrily that I did it out of pure spite at the vicious thing.

She laughed and said she wouldn't mind doing it herself, but I must not get tired.

How she betrayed herself that time!

But I am here, and no person touches this paper but me,—not *alive!*

She tried to get me out of the room—it was too patent! But I said it was so quiet, and empty and clean now that I believed I would lie down again and sleep all I could; and not to wake me even for dinner—I would call when I woke.

So now she is gone, and the servants are gone, and the things are gone, and there is nothing left but that great bedstead nailed down, with the canvas mattress we found on it.

We shall sleep downstairs to-night, and take the boat home to-morrow.

I quite enjoy the room, now it is bare again.

How those children did tear about here!

This bedstead is fairly gnawed!

But I must get to work.

I have locked the door and thrown the key down into the front path.

I don't want to go out, and I don't want to have anybody come in, till John comes.

I want to astonish him.

I've got a rope up here that even Jennie did not find. If that woman does get out, and tries to get away, I can tie her!

But I forgot I could not reach far without anything to stand on!

This bed will *not* move!

I tried to lift and push it until I was lame, and then I got so angry I bit off a little piece at one corner—but it hurt my teeth.

Then I peeled off all the paper I could reach standing on the floor. It sticks horribly and the pattern just enjoys it! All those strangled heads and bulbous eyes and waddling fungus growths just shriek with derision!

I am getting angry enough to do something desperate. To jump out of the window would be admirable exercise, but the bars are too strong even to try.

Besides I wouldn't do it. Of course not. I know well enough that a step like that is improper and might be misconstrued.

I don't like to *look* out of the windows even—there are so many of those creeping women, and they creep so fast.

I wonder if they all come out of that wall-paper as I did?

But I am securely fastened now by my well-hidden rope—you don't get *me* out in the road there!

I suppose I shall have to get back behind the pattern when it comes night, and that is hard!

It is so pleasant to be out in this great room and creep around as I please!

I don't want to go outside. I won't, even if Jennie asks me to.

For outside you have to creep on the ground, and everything is green instead of yellow.

But here I can creep smoothly on the floor, and my shoulder just fits in that long smooch around the wall, so I cannot lose my way.

Why there's John at the door!

It is no use, young man, you can't open it!

How he does call and pound!

Now he's crying for an axe.

It would be a shame to break down that beautiful door!

"John dear!" said I in the gentlest voice, "the key is down by the front steps, under a plantain leaf!"

That silenced him for a few moments.

Then he said—very quietly indeed, "Open the door, my darling!"

"I can't," said I. "The key is down by the front door under a plantain leaf!"

And then I said it again, several times, very gently and slowly, and said it so often that he had to go and see, and he got it of course, and came in. He stopped short by the door.

"What is the matter?" he cried. "For God's sake, what are you doing!"

I kept on creeping just the same, but I looked at him over my shoulder.

"I've got out at last," said I, "in spite of you and Jane. And I've pulled off most of the paper, so you can't put me back!"

Now why should that man have fainted? But he did, and right across my path by the wall, so that I had to creep over him every time!

QUESTIONS

1. For whom is the narrator writing? Does she think of her reader as more sympathetic or less sympathetic than her husband or Jennie?
2. The narrator says that she cannot get better because her husband is a doctor. What does she mean by this seemingly paradoxical statement? What about his treatment makes her ill? How would you treat her were you a doctor? Her husband?
3. Is there anything significant in the fact that the narrator particularly objects to the color of the wallpaper? What associations do you have with the color yellow? What happens to the color of yellow wallpaper as it ages? What is the significance of the pattern?
4. At what point in the story did you recognize that the narrator has gone insane? Did you come to that recognition slowly, or did it happen suddenly?

Is she insane at the start of the story, or does she gradually grow insane? How can you tell?

5. What is the relationship between Charlotte Perkins Gilman and the narrator? Is Gilman insane? Does she stand in the same relationship to her narrator as Poe stands in relationship to the narrator of "The Cask of Amontillado"?

CHARLOTTE PERKINS GILMAN

from THE LIVING OF CHARLOTTE PERKINS GILMAN

This was a worse horror than before, for now I saw the stark fact—that I was well while away and sick while at home—a heartening prospect! Soon ensued the same utter prostration, the unbearable inner misery, the ceaseless tears. A new tonic had been invented, Essence of Oats, which was given me, and did some good for a time. I pulled up enough to do a little painting that fall, but soon slipped down again and stayed down. An old friend of my mother's, dear Mrs. Diman, was so grieved at this condition that she gave me a hundred dollars and urged me to go away somewhere and get cured.

At that time the greatest nerve specialist in the country was Dr. S. W. Mitchell of Philadelphia. Through the kindness of a friend of Mr. Stetson's living in that city, I went to him and took "the rest cure"; went with the utmost confidence, prefacing the visit with a long letter giving "the history of the case" in a way a modern psychologist would have appreciated. Dr. Mitchell only thought it proved self-conceit. He had a prejudice against the Beechers. "I've had two women of your blood here already," he told me scornfully. This eminent physician was well versed in two kinds of nervous prostration; that of the business man exhausted from too much work, and the society woman exhausted from too much play. The kind I had was evidently beyond him. But he did reassure me on one point—there was no dementia, he said, only hysteria.

I was put to bed and kept there. I was fed, bathed, rubbed, and responded with the vigorous body of twenty-six. As far as he could see there was nothing the matter with me, so after a month of this agreeable treatment he sent me home, with this prescription:

"Live as domestic a life as possible. Have your child with you all the time." (Be it remarked that if I did but dress the baby it left me shaking and crying—certainly far from a healthy companionship for her, to say nothing of the effect on me.) "Lie down an hour after each meal. Have but two hours' intellectual life a day. And never touch pen, brush or pencil as long as you live."

I went home, followed those directions rigidly for months, and came perilously near to losing my mind. The mental agony grew so unbearable that I would sit blankly moving my head from side to side—to get out from under the pain. Not physical pain, not the least "headache" even, just mental torment, and so heavy in its nightmare gloom that it seemed real enough to dodge.

I made a rag baby, hung it on a doorknob and played with it. I would crawl into remote closets and under beds—to hide from the grinding pressure of that profound distress. . . .

Finally, in the fall of '87, in a moment of clear vision, we agreed to separate, to get a divorce. There was no quarrel, no blame for either one, never an unkind word between us, unbroken mutual affection—but it seemed plain that if I went crazy it would do my husband no good, and be a deadly injury to my child.

What this meant to the young artist, the devoted husband, the loving father, was so bitter a grief and loss that nothing would have justified breaking the marriage save this worse loss which threatened. It was not a choice between going and staying, but between going, sane, and staying, insane. If I had been of the slightest use to him or to the child, I would have "stuck it," as the English say. But this progressive weakening of the mind made a horror unnecessary to face; better for that dear child to have separated parents than a lunatic mother.

We had been married four years and more. This miserable condition of mind, this darkness, feebleness and gloom, had begun in those difficult years of courtship, had grown rapidly worse after marriage, and was now threatening utter loss; whereas I had repeated proof that the moment I left home I began to recover. It seemed right to give up a mistaken marriage.

Our mistake was mutual. If I had been stronger and wiser I should never have been persuaded into it. Our suffering was mutual too, his unbroken devotion, his manifold cares and labors in tending a sick wife, his adoring pride in the best of babies, all coming to naught, ending in utter failure—we sympathized with each other but faced a bitter necessity. The separation must come as soon as possible, the divorce must wait for conditions.

If this decision could have been reached sooner it would have been much better for me, the lasting mental injury would have been less. Such recovery as I have made in forty years, and the work accomplished, seem to show that the fear of insanity was not fulfilled, but the effects of nerve bankruptcy remain to this day. So much of my many failures, of misplay and misunderstanding and "queerness" is due to this lasting weakness, and kind friends so unfailingly refuse to allow for it, to believe it, that I am now going to some length in stating the case.

THINGS TO THINK ABOUT

1. How does "The Yellow Wallpaper" use autobiographical information? What details from Gilman's life does the story contain? What details differ?
2. Is there any significance in the fact that in the story the narrator's husband

is also her physician while in Gilman's own case they were two different individuals?

3. What is the proper conduct of a physician toward his or her patient? Is it proper that Dr. Mitchell "had a prejudice against" Gilman's family? How might a physician's prejudices affect the treatment?
4. Why does Gilman recover while her narrator slips more deeply into madness?

MARGARET ATWOOD

GIVING BIRTH

Margaret Atwood (b. 1932) has emerged as one of the more important authors writing not just in Canada, but in the English-speaking world. She was born in Ottawa, attended the University of Toronto, Radcliffe College and Harvard University. She has worked as a cashier, waitress, market researcher, film writer and teacher.

She has written in a number of different genres. Beginning as a poet, she developed into a novelist and has subsequently produced works for scholars and children. In all, she has produced over twenty books including The Handmaid's Tale, You Are Happy, *and* Surfacing.

Atwood began writing as a child, and at sixteen felt that it was "the only thing [she] wanted to do." She says that her parents, though they did not encourage her as a writer, "expected me to make use of my intelligence and abilities," and such expectations were "a more important kind of support."

But who gives it? And to whom is it given? Certainly it doesn't feel like giving, which implies a flow, a gentle handing over, no coercion. But there is scant gentleness here; it's too strenuous, the belly like a knotted fist, squeezing, the heavy trudge of the heart, every muscle in the body tight and moving, as in a slow-motion shot of a high-jump, the faceless body sailing up, turning, hanging for a moment in the air, and then—back to real time again—the plunge, the rush down, the result. Maybe the phrase was made by someone viewing the result only: in this case, the rows of babies to whom birth has occurred, lying like neat packages in their expertly wrapped blankets, pink or blue, with their labels Scotch Taped to their clear plastic cots, behind the plate-glass window.

No one ever says *giving death,* although they are in some ways the same, events, not things. And *delivering,* that act the doctor is generally believed to perform: who delivers what? Is it the mother who is delivered, like a prisoner being released? Surely not; nor is the child delivered to the mother like a letter through a slot. How can you be both the sender and the receiver at once? Was someone in bondage, is someone made free? Thus language, muttering in its archaic tongues of something, yet one more thing, that needs to be re-named.

It won't be by me, though. These are the only words I have, I'm stuck with them, stuck in them. (That image of the tar sands, old tableau in the Royal Ontario Museum, second floor north, how persistent it is. Will I break free, or will I be sucked down, fossilized, a sabre-toothed tiger or lumbering brontosaurus who ventured out too far? Words ripple at my feet, black, sluggish, lethal. Let me try once more, before the sun gets me, before I starve or drown, while I can. It's only a tableau after all, it's only a metaphor. See, I can speak, I am not trapped, and you on your part can understand. So we will go ahead as if there were no problem about language.)

This story about giving birth is not about me. In order to convince you of that I should tell you what I did this morning, before I sat down at this desk—a door on top of two filing cabinets, radio to the left, calendar to the right, these devices by which I place myself in time. I got up at twenty-to-seven, and, halfway down the stairs, met my daughter, who was ascending, autonomously she thought, actually in the arms of her father. We greeted each other with hugs and smiles; we then played with the alarm clock and the hot water bottle, a ritual we go through only on the days her father has to leave the house early to drive into the city. This ritual exists to give me the illusion that I am sleeping in. When she finally decided it was time for me to get up, she began pulling my hair. I got dressed while she explored the bathroom scales and the mysterious white altar of the toilet. I took her downstairs and we had the usual struggle over her clothes. Already she is wearing miniature jeans, miniature T-shirts. After this she fed herself: orange, banana, muffin, porridge.

We then went out to the sun porch, where we recognized anew, and by their names, the dog, the cats and the birds, blue jays and goldfinches at this time of year, which is winter. She puts her fingers on my lips as I pronounce these words; she hasn't yet learned the secret of making them. I am waiting for her first word: surely it will be miraculous, something that has never yet been said. But if so, perhaps she's already said it and I, in my entrapment, my addiction to the usual, have not heard it.

In her playpen I discovered the first alarming thing of the day. It was a small naked woman, made of that soft plastic from which jiggly spiders and lizards and the other things people hang in their car windows are also made. She was given to my daughter by a friend, a woman who does props for movies, she was supposed to have been a prop but she wasn't used. The baby loved her and would crawl around the floor holding her in her mouth like a dog carrying a bone, with the head sticking out one side and the feet out the other. She seemed chewy and harmless, but the other day I noticed that the baby had managed to make a tear in the body with her new teeth. I put the woman into the cardboard box I use for toy storage.

But this morning she was back in the playpen and the feet were gone. The baby must have eaten them, and I worried about whether or not the plastic would dissolve in her stomach, whether it was toxic. Sooner or later, in the contents of her diaper, which I examine with the usual amount of maternal brooding, I knew I would find two small pink plastic feet. I removed the doll and later, while she was still singing to the dog outside the window, dropped it into the garbage. I am not up to finding tiny female arms, breasts, a head, in my daughter's disposable diapers, partially covered by undigested carrots and the husks of raisins, like the relics of some gruesome and demented murder.

Now she's having her nap and I am writing this story. From what I have said, you can see that my life (despite these occasional surprises, reminders of another world) is calm and orderly, suffused with that warm, reddish light, those well-placed blue highlights and reflecting surfaces (mirrors, plates, oblong window-panes) you think of as belonging to Dutch genre paintings; and like them it is realistic in detail and slightly sentimental. Or at least it has an aura of sentiment. (Already I'm having moments of muted grief over those of my daughter's baby clothes which are too small for her to wear any more. I will be a keeper of hair, I will store things in trunks, I will weep over photos.) But above all it's solid, everything here has solidity. No more of those washes of light, those shifts, nebulous effects of cloud, Turner sunsets, vague fears, the impalpables Jeanie used to concern herself with.

I call this woman Jeanie after the song. I can't remember any more of the song, only the title. The point (for in language there are always these "points," these reflections; this is what makes it so rich and sticky, this is why so many have disappeared beneath its dark and shining surface, why you should never try to see your own reflection in it; you will lean over too far, a strand of your hair will fall in and come out gold, and, thinking it is gold all the way down, you yourself will follow, sliding into those outstretched arms, towards the mouth you think is opening to pronounce your name but instead, just before your ears fill with pure sound, will form a word you have never heard before. . . .)

The point, for me, is in the hair. My own hair is not light brown, but Jeanie's was. This is one difference between us. The other point is the dreaming; for Jeanie isn't real in the same way that I am real. But by now, and I mean your time, both of us will have the same degree of reality, we will be equal: wraiths, echoes, reverberations in your own brain. At the moment though Jeanie is to me as I will someday be to you. So she is real enough.

Jeanie is on her way to the hospital, to give birth, to be delivered. She is not quibbling over these terms. She's sitting in the back seat of the car, with her eyes closed and her coat spread over her like a blanket. She is doing her breathing exercises and timing her contractions with a stopwatch. She has been up since two-thirty in the morning, when she took a bath and ate some lime Jell-O, and it's now almost ten. She has learned to count, during the slow breathing, in numbers (from one to ten while breathing in, from ten to one while breathing out) which she can actually see while she is silently pronouncing them. Each number is a different colour and, if she's concentrating very hard, a different typeface. They range from plain roman to ornamented circus numbers, red with gold filigree and dots. This is a refinement not mentioned in any of the numerous books she's read on the subject. Jeanie is a devotee of handbooks. She has at least two shelves of books that cover everything from building kitchen cabinets to auto repairs to smoking your own hams. She doesn't do many of these things, but she does some of them, and in her suitcase, along with a washcloth, a package of lemon Life Savers, a pair of glasses, a hot water bottle, some talcum powder and a paper bag, is the book that suggested she take along all of these things.

(By this time you may be thinking that I've invented Jeanie in order to distance myself from these experiences. Nothing could be further from the truth. I am, in fact, trying to bring myself closer to something that time has already made distant. As for Jeanie, my intention is simple: I am bringing her back to life.)

There are two other people in the car with Jeanie. One is a man, whom I will call A., for convenience. A. is driving. When Jeanie opens her eyes, at the end of every contraction, she can see the back of his slightly balding head and his reassuring shoulders. A. drives well and not too quickly. From time to time he asks her how she is, and she tells him how long the contractions are lasting and how long there is between them. When they stop for gas he buys them each a Styrofoam container of coffee. For months he has helped her with the breathing exercises, pressing on her knee as recommended by the book, and he will be present at the delivery. (Perhaps it's to him that the birth will be given, in the same sense that one gives a performance.) Together they have toured the hospital maternity ward, in company with a small group of other pairs like them: one thin solicitous person, one slow bulbous person. They have been shown the rooms, shared and private, the sitz-baths, the delivery room itself, which gave the impression of being white. The nurse was light-brown, with limber hips and elbows; she laughed a lot as she answered questions.

"First they'll give you an enema. You know what it is? They take a tube of water and put it up your behind. Now, the gentlemen must put on this—and these, over your shoes. And these hats, this one for those with long hair, this for those with short hair."

"What about those with no hair?" says A.

The nurse looks up at his head and laughs. "Oh, you still have some," she says. "If you have a question, do not be afraid to ask."

They have also seen the film made by the hospital, a full-colour film of a woman giving birth to, can it be a baby? "Not all babies will be this large at birth," the Australian nurse who introduces the movie says.

Still, the audience, half of which is pregnant, doesn't look very relaxed when the lights go on. ("If you don't like the visuals," a friend of Jeanie's has told her, "you can always close your eyes.") It isn't the blood so much as the brownish-red disinfectant that bothers her. "I've decided to call this whole thing off," she says to A., smiling to show it's a joke. He gives her a hug and says, "Everything's going to be fine."

And she knows it is. Everything will be fine. But there is another woman in the car. She's sitting in the front seat, and she hasn't turned or acknowledged Jeanie in any way. She, like Jeanie, is going to the hospital. She too is pregnant. She is not going to the hospital to give birth, however, because the words, the words, are too alien to her experience, the experience she is about to have, to be used about it at all. She's wearing a cloth coat with checks in maroon and brown, and she has a kerchief tied over her hair. Jeanie has seen her before, but she knows little about her except that she is a woman who did not wish to become pregnant, who did not choose to divide herself like this, who did not choose any of these ordeals, these initiations. It would be no use telling her that everything is going to be fine. The word in English for unwanted intercourse is rape. But there is no word in the language for what is about to happen to this woman.

Jeanie has seen this woman from time to time throughout her pregnancy, always in the same coat, always with the same kerchief. Naturally, being pregnant herself has made her more aware of other pregnant women, and she has watched them, examined them covertly, every time she has seen one. But not every other pregnant woman is this woman. She did not, for instance, attend Jeanie's pre-natal classes at the hospital, where the women were all young, younger than Jeanie.

"How many will be breast-feeding?" asks the Australian nurse with the hefty shoulders.

All hands but one shoot up. A modern group, the new generation, and the one lone bottle-feeder, who might have (who knows?) something wrong with her breasts, is ashamed of herself. The others look politely away from her. What they want most to discuss, it seems, are the differences between one kind of disposable diaper and another. Sometimes they lie on mats and squeeze each other's hands, simulating contractions and counting breaths. It's all very hopeful. The Australian nurse tells them not to get in and out of the bathtub by themselves. At the end of an hour they are each given a glass of apple juice.

There is only one woman in the class who has already given birth. She's there, she says, to make sure they give her a shot this time. They delayed it last time and she went through hell. The others look at her with mild disapproval. *They* are not clamouring for shots, they do not intend to go through hell. Hell comes from the wrong attitude, they feel. The books talk about *discomfort.*

"It's not discomfort, it's pain, baby," the woman says.

The others smile uneasily and the conversation slides back to disposable diapers.

Vitaminized, conscientious, well-read Jeanie, who has managed to avoid morning sickness, varicose veins, stretch marks, toxemia and depression, who has had no aberrations of appetite, no blurrings of vision—why is she followed, then, by this other? At first it was only a glimpse now and then, at the infants' clothing section in Simpson's Basement, in the supermarket lineup, on street corners as she herself slid by in A.'s car: the haggard face, the bloated torso, the kerchief holding back the too-sparse hair. In any case, it was Jeanie who saw her, not the other way around. If she knew she was following Jeanie she gave no sign.

As Jeanie has come closer and closer to this day, the unknown day on which she will give birth, as time has thickened around her so that it has become something she must propel herself through, a kind of slush, wet earth underfoot, she has seen this woman more and more often, though always from a distance. Depending on the light, she has appeared by turns as a young girl of perhaps twenty to an older woman of forty or forty-five, but there was never any doubt in Jeanie's mind that it was the same woman. In fact it did not occur to her that the woman was not real in the usual sense (and perhaps she was, originally, on the first or second sighting, as the voice that causes an echo is real), until A. stopped for a red light during this drive to the hospital and the woman, who had been standing on the corner with a brown paper bag in her arms, simply opened the front door of the car and got in. A. didn't react, and Jeanie knows better than to say anything to him. She is aware that the woman is not really there: Jeanie is not crazy. She could even make the woman disappear by opening her eyes wider, by staring, but it is only the shape that would go away, not the feeling. Jeanie isn't exactly afraid of this woman. She is afraid for her.

When they reach the hospital, the woman gets out of the car and is through the door by the time A. has come around to help Jeanie out of the back seat. In the lobby she is nowhere to be seen. Jeanie goes through Admission in the usual way, unshadowed.

There has been an epidemic of babies during the night and the maternity ward is overcrowded. Jeanie waits for her room behind a dividing screen. Nearby someone is screaming, screaming and mumbling between screams in what sounds like a foreign language. Portuguese, Jeanie thinks. She tells herself that for them it is different, you're supposed to scream, you're regarded as queer if you don't scream, it's a required part of giving birth. Nevertheless she knows that the woman screaming is the other woman and she is screaming from pain. Jeanie listens to the other voice, also a woman's, comforting, reassuring: her mother? A nurse?

A. arrives and they sit uneasily, listening to the screams. Finally Jeanie is sent for and she goes for her prep. Prep school, she thinks. She takes off her clothes—when will she see them again?—and puts on the hospital gown. She is examined, labelled around the wrist and given an enema. She tells the nurse she can't take Demerol because she's allergic to it, and the nurse writes this down. Jeanie doesn't know whether this is true or not but she doesn't want Demerol, she has read the books. She intends to put up a struggle over her pubic hair—surely she will lose her strength if it is all shaved off—but it turns out the nurse doesn't have very strong feelings about it. She is told her contractions are not far enough along to be taken seriously, she can even have lunch. She puts on her dressing gown and rejoins A., in the freshly vacated room, eats some tomato soup and a veal cutlet, and decides to take a nap while A. goes out for supplies.

Jeanie wakes up when A. comes back. He has brought a paper, some detective novels for Jeanie and a bottle of Scotch for himself. A. reads the paper and drinks Scotch, and Jeanie reads *Poirot's Early Cases.* There is no connection between Poirot and her labour, which is now intensifying, unless it is the egg-shape of Poirot's head and the vegetable marrows he is known to cultivate with strands of wet wool (placentae? umbilical cords?). She is glad the stories are short; she is walking around the room now, between contractions. Lunch was definitely a mistake.

"I think I have back labour," she says to A. They get out the handbook and look up the instructions for this. It's useful that everything has a name. Jeanie kneels on the bed and rests her forehead on her arms while A. rubs her back. A. pours himself another Scotch, in the hospital glass. The nurse, in pink, comes, looks, asks about the timing, and goes away again. Jeanie is beginning to sweat. She can only manage half a page or so of Poirot before she has to clamber back up on the bed again and begin breathing and running through the coloured numbers.

When the nurse comes back, she has a wheelchair. It's time to go down to the labour room, she says. Jeanie feels stupid sitting in the wheelchair. She tells herself about peasant women having babies in the fields, Indian women having them on portages with hardly a second thought. She feels effete. But the hospital wants her to ride, and considering the fact that the nurse is tiny, perhaps it's just as well. What if Jeanie were to collapse, after all? After all her courageous talk. An image of the tiny pink nurse, antlike, trundling large Jeanie through the corridors, rolling her along like a heavy beach ball.

As they go by the check-in desk a woman is wheeled past on a table, covered by a sheet. Her eyes are closed and there's a bottle feeding into her arm through a tube. Something is wrong. Jeanie looks back—she thinks it was the other woman—but the sheeted table is hidden now behind the counter.

In the dim labour room Jeanie takes off her dressing gown and is helped up onto the bed by the nurse. A. brings her suitcase, which is not a suitcase actually but a small flight bag, the significance of this has not been lost on Jeanie, and in fact she now has some of the apprehensive feelings she associates with planes, including the fear of a crash. She takes out her Life Savers, her glasses, her washcloth and the other things she thinks she will need. She removes her contact lenses and places them in their case, reminding A. that they must not be lost. Now she is purblind.

There is something else in her bag that she doesn't remove. It's a talisman, given to her several years ago as a souvenir by a travelling friend of hers. It's a rounded oblong of opaque blue glass, with four yellow-and-white eye shapes on it. In Turkey, her friend has told her, they hang them on mules to protect against the Evil Eye. Jeanie knows this talisman probably won't work for her, she is not Turkish and she isn't a mule, but it makes her feel safer to have it in the room with her. She had planned to hold it in her hand during the most difficult part of labour but somehow there is no longer any time for carrying out plans like this.

An old woman, a fat old woman dressed all in green, comes into the room and sits beside Jeanie. She says to A., who is sitting on the other side of Jeanie, "That is a good watch. They don't make watches like that any more." She is referring to his gold pocket watch, one of his few extravagances, which is on the night table. Then she places her hand on Jeanie's belly to feel the contraction. "This is good," she says, her accent is Swedish or German. "This, I call a contraction. Before, it was nothing." Jeanie can no longer remember having seen her before. "Good. Good."

"When will I have it?" Jeanie asks, when she can talk, when she is no longer counting.

The old woman laughs. Surely that laugh, those tribal hands, have presided over a thousand beds, a thousand kitchen tables . . . "A long time yet," she says. "Eight, ten hours."

"But I've been *doing* this for twelve hours already," Jeanie says.

"Not hard labour," the woman says. "Not good, like this."

Jeanie settles into herself for the long wait. At the moment she can't remember why she wanted to have a baby in the first place. That decision was made by someone else, whose motives are now unclear. She remembers the way women who had babies used to smile at one another, mysteriously, as if there was something they knew that she didn't, the way they would casually exclude her from their frame of reference. What was the knowledge, the mystery, or was having a baby really no more inexplicable than having a car accident or an orgasm? (But these too were indescribable, events of the body, all of them; why should the mind distress itself trying to find a language for them?) She has sworn she will never do that to any woman without children, engage in those passwords and exclusions. She's old enough, she's been put through enough years of it to find it tiresome and cruel.

But—and this is the part of Jeanie that goes with the talisman hidden in her bag, not with the part that longs to build kitchen cabinets and smoke hams—she is, secretly, hoping for a mystery. Something more than this, something else, a vision. After all she is risking her life, though it's not too likely she will die. Still, some women do. Internal bleeding, shock, heart failure, a mistake on the part of someone, a nurse, a doctor. She deserves a vision, she deserves to be allowed to bring something back with her from this dark place into which she is now rapidly descending.

She thinks momentarily about the other woman. Her motives, too, are unclear. Why doesn't she want to have a baby? Has she been raped, does she have ten other children, is she starving? Why hasn't she had an abortion? Jeanie doesn't know, and in fact it no longer matters why. *Uncross your fingers,* Jeanie thinks to her. Her face, distorted with pain and terror, floats briefly behind Jeanie's eyes before it too drifts away.

Jeanie tries to reach down to the baby, as she has many times before, sending waves of love, colour, music, down through her arteries to it, but she finds she can no longer do this. She can no longer feel the baby as a baby, its arms and legs poking, kicking, turning. It has collected itself together, it's a hard sphere, it does not have time right now to listen to her. She's grateful for this because she isn't sure anyway how good the message would be. She no longer has control of the numbers either, she can no longer see them, although she continues mechanically to count. She realizes she has practised for the wrong thing, A. squeezing her knee was nothing, she should have practised for this, whatever it is.

"Slow down," A. says. She's on her side now, he's holding her hand. "Slow it right down."

"I can't. I can't do it, I can't do this."

"Yes, you can."

"Will I sound like that?"

"Like what?" A. says. Perhaps he can't hear it: it's the other woman, in the room next door or the room next door to that. She's screaming and crying, screaming and crying. While she cries she is saying, over and over, "It hurts. It hurts."

"No, you won't," he says. So there is someone, after all.

A doctor comes in, not her own doctor. They want her to turn over on her back.

"I can't," she says. "I don't like it that way." Sounds have receded, she has trouble hearing them. She turns over and the doctor gropes with her rubber-gloved hand. Something wet and hot flows over her thighs.

"It was just ready to break," the doctor says. "All I had to do was touch it. Four centimetres," she says to A.

"Only *four?*" Jeanie says. She feels cheated; they must be wrong. The doctor says her own doctor will be called in time. Jeanie is outraged at them. They have not understood, but it's too late to say this and she slips back into the dark place, which is not hell, which is more like being inside, trying to get out. *Out,* she says or thinks. Then she is floating, the numbers are gone, if anyone told her to get up, go out of the room, stand on her head, she would do it. From minute to minute she comes up again, grabs for air.

"You're hyperventilating," A. says. "Slow it down." He is rubbing her back now, hard, and she takes his hand and shoves it viciously further down, to the right place, which is not the right place as soon as his hand is there. She remembers a story she read once, about the Nazis tying the legs of Jewish women together during labour. She never really understood before how that could kill you.

A nurse appears with a needle. "I don't want it," Jeanie says.

"Don't be hard on yourself," the nurse says. "You don't have to go through pain like that." What pain? Jeanie thinks. When there is no pain she feels nothing, when there is pain, she feels nothing because there is no *she.* This, finally, is the disappearance of language. *You don't remember afterwards,* she has been told by almost everyone.

Jeanie comes out of a contraction, gropes for control. "Will it hurt the baby?" she says.

"It's a mild analgesic," the doctor says. "We wouldn't allow anything that would hurt the baby." Jeanie doesn't believe this. Nevertheless she is jabbed, and the doctor is right, it is very mild, because it doesn't seem to do a thing for Jeanie, though A. later tells her she has slept briefly between contractions.

Suddenly she sits bolt upright. She is wide awake and lucid. "You have to ring that bell right now," she says. "This baby is being born."

A. clearly doesn't believe her. "I can feel it, I can feel the head," she says. A. pushes the button for the call bell. A nurse appears and checks, and now everything is happening too soon, nobody is ready. They set off down the hall, the nurse wheeling Jeanie feels fine. She watches the corridors, the edges of everything shadowy because she doesn't have her glasses on. She hopes A. will remember to bring them. They pass another doctor.

"Need me?" she asks.

"Oh no," the nurse answers breezily. "Natural childbirth."

Jeanie realizes that this woman must have been the anaesthetist. "What?" she says, but it's too late now, they are in the room itself, all those glossy surfaces, tubular strange apparatus like a science-fiction movie, and the nurse is telling her to get onto the delivery table. No one else is in the room.

"You must be crazy," Jeanie says.

"Don't push," the nurse says.

"What do you mean?" Jeanie says. This is absurd. Why should she wait, why should the baby wait for them because they're late?

"Breathe through your mouth," the nurse says. "Pant," and Jeanie finally remembers how. When the contraction is over she uses the nurse's arm as a lever and hauls herself across onto the table.

From somewhere her own doctor materializes, in her doctor suit already, looking even more like Mary Poppins than usual, and Jeanie says, "Bet you weren't expecting to see me so soon!" The baby is being born when Jeanie said it would, though just three days ago the doctor said it would be at least another week, and this makes Jeanie feel jubilant and smug. Not that she knew, she'd believed the doctor.

She's being covered with a green tablecloth, they are taking far too long, she feels like pushing the baby out now, before they are ready. A. is there by her head, swathed in robes, hats, masks. He has forgotten her glasses. "Push now," the doctor says. Jeanie grips with her hands, grits her teeth, face, her whole body together, a snarl, a fierce smile, the baby is enormous, a stone, a boulder, her bones unlock, and, once, twice, the third time, she opens like a birdcage turning slowly inside out.

A pause; a wet kitten slithers between her legs. "Why don't you look?" says the doctor, but Jeanie still has her eyes closed. No glasses, she couldn't have seen a thing anyway. "Why don't you look?" the doctor says again.

Jeanie opens her eyes. She can see the baby, who has been wheeled up beside her and is fading already from the alarming birth purple. A good baby, she thinks, meaning it as the old woman did: *a good watch,* well-made, substantial. The baby isn't crying; she squints in the new light. Birth isn't something that has been given to her, nor has she taken it. It was just something that has happened so they could greet each other like this. The nurse is stringing beads for her name. When the baby is bundled and tucked beside Jeanie, she goes to sleep.

As for the vision, there wasn't one. Jeanie is conscious of no special knowledge; already she's forgetting what it was like. She's tired and very cold; she is shaking, and asks for another blanket. A. comes back to the room with her; her clothes are still there. Everything is quiet, the other woman is no longer screaming. Something has happened to her, Jeanie knows. Is she dead? Is the baby dead? Perhaps she is one of those casualties (and how can Jeanie herself be sure, yet, that she will not be among them) who will go into postpartum depression and never come out. "You see, there was nothing to be afraid of," A. says before he leaves, but he was wrong.

The next morning Jeanie wakes up when it's light. She's been warned about getting out of bed the first time without the help of a nurse, but she decides to do it anyway (peasant in the field! Indian on the portage!). She's still running adrenaline, she's also weaker than she thought, but she wants very much to look out the window. She feels she's been inside too long, she wants to see the sun come up. Being awake this early always makes her feel a little unreal, a little insubstantial, as if she's partly transparent, partly dead.

(It was to me, after all, that the birth was given, Jeanie gave it, I am the result. What would she make of me? Would she be pleased?)

The window is two panes with a venetian blind sandwiched between them; it turns by a knob at the side. Jeanie has never seen a window like this before. She closes and opens the blind several times. Then she leaves it open and looks out.

All she can see from the window is a building. It's an old stone building, heavy and Victorian, with a copper roof oxidized to green. It's solid, hard, darkened by soot, dour, leaden. But as she looks at this building, so old and seemingly immutable, she sees that it's made of water. Water, and some tenuous jelly-like substance. Light flows through it from behind (the sun is coming up), the building is so thin, so fragile, that it quivers in the slight dawn wind. Jeanie sees that if the building is this way (a touch could destroy it, a ripple of the earth, why has no one noticed, guarded it against accidents?) then the rest of the world must be like this too, the entire earth, the rocks, people, trees, everything needs to be protected, cared for, tended. The enormity of this task defeats her; she will never be up to it, and what will happen then?

Jeanie hears footsteps in the hall outside her door. She thinks it must be the other woman, in her brown-and-maroon-checked coat, carrying her paper bag, leaving the hospital now that her job is done. She has seen Jeanie safely through, she must go now to hunt through the streets of the city for her next case. But the door opens, it's a nurse, who is just in time to catch Jeanie as she sinks to the floor, holding on to the edge of the air-conditioning unit. The nurse scolds her for getting up too soon.

After that the baby is carried in, solid, substantial, packed together like an apple, Jeanie examines her, she is complete, and in the days that follow Jeanie herself becomes drifted over with new words, her hair slowly darkens, she ceases to be what she was and is replaced, gradually, by someone else.

QUESTIONS

1. What do we know about the narrator of "Giving Birth"? What is her relationship to Jeanie? Why does she work so hard to establish their separateness? What assumption is the narrator afraid that the reader will make?
2. What is the relationship between Jeanie and The Other Woman? Why doesn't the Other Woman have a name?
3. What is the relationship between the narrator and Margaret Atwood? Can we tell?
4. What sort of vision is Jeanie expecting? The narrator says that Jeanie did not have a vision. Is that statement entirely true?

5. The narrator suggests that the narrator is the birth which Jeanie has given. What does the narrator mean by such a statement?
6. In what ways has the Other Woman "seen Jeanie safely through" her delivery?
7. How do we change? What experience would be necessary to make you a different person? Would going to war, committing a murder, losing your money, taking a trip, or having a baby be a significant enough event to alter your personality? Are there any experiences that could fundamentally change your identity?

JORGE LUIS BORGES

BORGES AND I

Jorge Luis Borges (1899–1986) suffered from political difficulties and physical handicaps to produce works of uncommon forcefulness and precision. Although born in a shabby section of Buenos Aires, Argentina, Borges came from a distinguished family which included British ancestors. Consequently, he learned English even before he knew Spanish and later became a professor of English and American literature at the University of Buenos Aires.

Just before World War I, Borges left with his family for Geneva where he added German and French to his repertoire of languages. He returned to Argentina in 1921, and published his first book, a volume of poetry in 1925. He took up fiction slowly and hesitantly, only after he had written critical and literary essays.

In the late nineteen thirties, Borge accepted a major post at the Buenos Aires Library from which he was removed by the dictator, Juan Peron. After Peron's deposition, Borges was made director of the national library. However, by that time he was already blind from a hereditary disease. His later works were dictated to relatives, secretaries and friends.

The other one, the one called Borges, is the one things happen to. I walk through the streets of Buenos Aires and stop for a moment, perhaps mechanically now, to look at the arch of an entrance hall and the grillwork on the gate; I know of Borges from the mail and see his name on a list of professors or in a biographical dictionary. I like hourglasses, maps, eighteenth-century typography, the taste of coffee and the prose of Stevenson;[1] he shares these preferences, but in a vain way that turns them into the attributes of an actor. It would be an exaggeration to say that ours is a hostile relationship; I live, let myself go on living, so that Borges may contrive his literature, and this literature justifies me. It is no effort for me to confess that he has achieved some valid pages, but those pages cannot save me, perhaps because what is good belongs to no one, not even to him, but rather to the language and to tradition. Besides, I am destined to perish, definitively, and only some instant of myself can survive in him. Little by little, I am giving over everything to him, though I am quite aware of his perverse custom of falsifying and magnifying things. Spinoza knew that all things long to persist in their being; the stone eternally wants to be a stone and the tiger a tiger. I shall remain in Borges, not in myself (if it is true that I am someone), but I recognize myself less in his books than in many others or in the laborious strumming of a guitar. Years ago I tried to free myself from him and went from the mythologies of the suburbs to the games with time and infinity, but those games belong to Borges now and I shall have to imagine other things. Thus my life is a flight and I lose everything and everything belongs to oblivion, or to him.

I do not know which of us has written this page.

QUESTIONS

1. What is the relationship between Borges and the "I" of this story? If their relationship isn't "hostile," what is it?
2. Why does the "I" doubt that he "is someone"?
3. Why does the "I" recognize itself less in Borges' books than in "the laborious strumming of a guitar"?
4. "I am destined to perish," the speaker tells the reader. What does he mean by that? Is his fate unusual? Is it unusual for a writer?
5. Why doesn't the speaker know who wrote this piece?

4

PLOT AND ACTION

Stories are so familiar that we often don't consider how they differ from other types of writing, such as essays, sermons or scientific papers. Stories recount events; they tell us what happens. Of course, storytellers can also relate why actions happened, how they happened, and what was the consequence of their happening. But these features are extra. The storyteller's one obligation is to relate events.

Simple enough? It turns out to be very complicated, and the best way to appreciate the complexity is to look at a very simple story. Here is one only two sentences long:

THE OBEDIENT DOG

by Ignacy Krasicki

> All night a dog barked to keep thieves from entering its master's house; in the morning the sleepless master beat the dog. The next night the thieves returned, and the following day, the dog was beaten again.

Let us ask two basic narrative questions: (1) What were the conditions prior to the narrated events? (2) What happened? The answer to the first question is that a man lived quietly with his obedient dog. The answer to the second question is that on two successive nights robbers attempted to enter his house.

But we can break down the event into smaller, but inter-related actions: (a) thieves arrive; (b) the dog barks; (c) the master beats the dog; (d) the thieves return; (e) the master beats the dog again. Even the simplest event is made up of many separate actions. Indeed most events contain so many separate actions that no one could report them all. Writers must omit unimportant actions or those which readers can infer from the rest of the story.

In even the simplest story, the reader must fill in details. For example, Krasicki does not bother to relate how the master beat the dog. Did he use his hands? A rolled up newspaper? A whip? A belt? Nor are readers told how the thieves entered the house. Did they pry up a window? A door? Slide down a chimney? Authors "flesh out a story" by adding these missing details.

READER INFERENCES

Krasicki omits certain actions because he trusts that his readers will be able to infer them from the action. Many of us like riddles, and stories often require us to solve riddle-like omissions. The first riddle is why does the master beat his dog on the first morning? The answer may be found in the word "sleepless." Apparently, the master was ignorant of the thieves' presences, and beat the dog for keeping him awake. The second riddle is why does the master beat the dog on the second night? The answer is because the house has been robbed. The robbery is another inference the reader must make.

Having made these two inferences, the reader can understand the story's moral. The dog is continually punished for his obedience. The first morning he is beaten for obediently barking at the thieves and on the second morning for obediently remaining silent while the house was being robbed. The dog suffers for its obedience, and—by extension, Krasicki warns us—we also suffer for our blind obedience to foolish and insensitive superiors.

What an awful lot of work for a two sentence story! How much more effort is involved in a longer work? How do we ever make sense of a novel? Fortunately we do much of this work automatically. Writers, luckily, do not consciously have to decide whether to narrate each and every action. They, too, have an intuitive sense of what to put in and what to leave out.

FOLLOWING STORIES

Writers are concerned about their readers' ability to follow along with a story. They take pains so that their intended readers will be able to draw the larger inferences from the work and to make the imaginative and logical leaps needed to enjoy the story. Writers make this assessment first by considering the readers. If the reader is uninformed, poorly educated or lazy, the reader will be able to make only obvious inferences. If, however, the reader is energetic, informed and well-educated, then the writer can move more quickly or more subtly.

The second way of assessing whether readers can follow a story is by having other people go over it. Writers have editors, friends and relatives read over their work, and these intelligent, sensitive and sympathetic readers are one of the writer's best tools. In the preface to this book you will find a long list of individuals who have helped me become a better writer. Of course, in the end, writers must make their own decisions about how to tell a story. But these decisions are rarely made without consulting good readers.

ORDERING EVENTS

If we drew a timeline of the actions in "The Obedient Dog," it would look something like this:

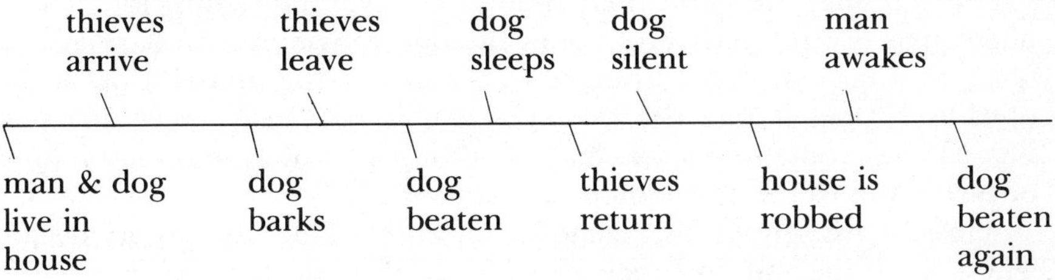

As we discussed, some of these events are not explicitly stated in the story but must be inferred from other actions. Moreover, these events are not always narrated in order of their occurrence. Take the opening of the story: "All night a dog barked to keep thieves from entering its master's home. . . ." The sentence begins by stating that the dog barked and then proceeds to tell us that thieves are trying to enter the master's house. As readers we know that the actual order was the other way around: the thieves' attempt to enter the house aroused the dog who started barking.

Very rarely do storytellers relate an event in strictly chronological order. Most writers begin in the middle of things—what is called in Latin *in medias res*—and then alternatively can move backwards and forwards as the storyteller needs to recount events.

You may be thinking that this is an awkward and confusing way to tell stories. You may be asking why don't writers start at the beginning and go step-by-step to the end. There are several reasons writers don't follow this simple method. First, it would be boring. Second it would eliminate surprise and suspense. Third, it is impossible to do because events have neither a clear beginning and end, nor a clear number of steps.

Where, for example, does the story of "The Obedient Dog" properly begin? Krasicki begins it with the dog barking, but someone else might have begun it with the arrival of the thieves. But the thieves would not have come unless the house contained property worth stealing. So the story—one could argue—properly begins when the dog's master bought the house and acquired sufficient property to warrant a watchdog. But where did the man come from? Where did he get that property? How did he get the dog? Don't these need to be explained? I hope you can see now that if Krasicki tried to answer all these questions, he would be pushed back further and further in time in an infinite regression. Therefore, one of the major decisions a writer must make is where to start a story. Readers should pay close attention to how and where a story begins. As you know from your own writing experience, the opening paragraph of a story or essay is very difficult to write and a successful opening makes the entire work easier to organize and understand.

If beginnings are hard, then endings are even more difficult. Where does this story properly end? Does the dog refuse ever to bark again? Or does it bark at every stranger who walks by the house? Does it die of abuse? Does it bite the master? Does it run away? We can't tell. Krasicki has come to his conclusion, but it is one of an infinite number of places where the story could have ended.

Three central questions come to mind: (1) How do writers decide where to begin and end their stories? (2) How do authors decide the order in which they will narrate events? (3) What events are worth narrating? The remainder of this chapter will explore some of the answers to these questions.

ENDINGS AND BEGINNINGS

I have compared the story to a journey that the reader takes with the narrator. But there are two sorts of journeys. In one we wander about aimlessly with no discernable goal. In the other type of journey we have a destination, and the path there may be twisting and filled with many obstacles.

Good stories—as well as good essays and poems—are usually the second sort of journey. Although the narrator or the characters may never explicitly state the goal, nevertheless, the story has an end to which it is moving. Indeed the journey is a common pattern in short stories. Flannery O'Connor's "A Good Man Is Hard To Find," Joseph Conrad's "The Secret Sharer," and Ernest Hemingway's "The Short Happy Life of Francis MacComber" are organized around journeys.

Readers should pay attention to the goals of the characters. In "The Obedient Dog," there are two goals: The thieves' goal to rob the house, and the dog's goal to be obedient to its master. These two goals are in conflict. The action of stories frequently revolve around either the obstacles placed in the path of a goal or the conflict between competing goals.

Stories, then, frequently begin with a character formulating a goal or encountering some conflict in achieving that goal. The story ends when the character either succeeds in achieving or fails to achieve the goal.

Scholars have given various names to the parts of a story, names that come primarily from dramatic criticism. Often in the early parts of a story, the reader encounters the major characters, the story's setting and the background information necessary for understanding the ensuing action. This information is called the exposition, and though in some stories it appears as a big lump, most writers parcel it out so as not to bore or confuse the reader. The exposition is said to come to an end when the main character has established his or her purpose.

As the character attempts to achieve the goal, he or she runs into obstacles of various sorts—natural, human, supernatural, psychic, or a combination of all four. This part of the story is called the conflict, and it continues usually with ever-increasing intensity until the climax or turning point when the reader recognizes whether the character will succeed or fail in the goal. Yet even after readers can foresee the character's success or failure, the story continues to its final resolution in which we see how the character responds to his or her success or failure. Exciting sporting events frequently have a similar structure. First we are introduced to the various players and size up their strategies. This opening corresponds to the exposition. Then the teams play in earnest against one another, fighting it out until it is clear who will win. If the viewers surmise the winner too early in the game, they become bored. But even when the outcome is clear, a game can remain interesting if the underdog continues to wage a good fight. In the end, the game has its resolution, and the players either celebrate their victory or accept their defeat. Of course in fiction as in life, winners and losers are not always so easily defined, and characters can achieve some of their goals or recognize that their goals were not worth achieving.

SUSPENSE AND SURPRISE

As we travel on these imaginative journeys, authors know unless they can keep readers occupied and interested that readers will grow restless and bored or—if the journey is very tedious—stop reading all together.

One way writers keep readers interested is by packing surprises into the journey. In Conrad's "The Secret Sharer," for example, a man unexpectedly pulls himself out of the water as the ship lays in anchor in the midst of the Gulf of Siam. In "A Good Man Is Hard to Find," a family not only has an automobile accident, but meets up with a band of desperate fugitives. The fictional journey, like life, is full of surprises. And just as in life, the initial delight, horror or excitement of a narrative surprise is soon over. Surprises, then, are good for giving the reader a jolt, but they cannot sustain interest.

Suspense, however, provides a sustained source of interest and pleasure. Suspense keeps a story going. The goal of the story provides an author (and the reader) with the central core of suspense—will the character or narrator achieve his or her goal? We know the crude delights of suspense from comic books and horror films. Will Superman be able to stop the mad scientist from taking over the world? Will the monster destroy Tokyo? We hurriedly turn the pages or sit at the edge of our seats to find the answer. In subtler ways, all stories have suspense.

Suspense occurs when the reader has only partial knowledge about events. The best explanation of the difference between surprise and suspense is by Alfred Hitchcock, the cinematic master. In an interview with the French director and critic Francois Truffaut, Hitchcock explains the difference this way:

> There is a distinction between "suspense" and "surprise," and yet many [people] continually confuse the two. I'll explain what I mean. We are now having an innocent little chat. Let us suppose that there is a bomb underneath this table between us. Nothing happens, and then all of a sudden "Boom!" There is an explosion. The audience is surprised, but prior to the surprise, it is an absolutely ordinary scene, of no special consequence. Now let us take a suspense situation. The bomb is underneath the table and the public knows it, probably because they have seen the anarchist place it there. The public is aware that the bomb is going to explode at one o'clock and there is a clock in the decor. The public can see that it is a quarter to one. In these conditions the same innocuous conversation becomes fascinating because the public is participating in the scene. The audience is longing to warn the characters on the screen: "You shouldn't be talking about such trivial matters. There's a bomb beneath you and it's about to explode!"
>
> In the first case we have given the public fifteen seconds of surprise at the moment of the explosion. In the second case we have provided them with fifteen minutes of suspense. The conclusion is that whenever possible the public must be informed. Except when the surprise is a twist, that is, when the unexpected ending is, in itself, the highlight of the story.

The art of suspense is the reader's—or in Hitchcock's term "the public's"—partial knowledge of what will happen. Only the author—or the director—will know whether there will be an explosion or not.

The action in a plot is ordered to allow the reader some knowledge. We can now see the advantages of the limited third person perspective. By limiting the reader's understanding to one character's point of view, the author has built in an excellent means of creating surprise and suspense.

WHAT IS SIGNIFICANT ACTION?

Readers come to a story with prejudices about what is interesting and what isn't. Some people find the exploits of cowboys interesting; others the daily lives of homemakers. Some people are curious only about violent action; others are interested in the workings of the mind. We come to literature, therefore, with certain preconceptions about what is a "significant action." For some it may be winning a ballgame, averting a war, or saving the life of a child. But it may be confronting one's own death, falling in love or freeing oneself from old fears and habits.

Writers like to play with our sense of what is significant. Hitchcock shows how an "innocuous" little chat can be "fascinating." But authors like to draw our attention to the events in life we tend to overlook. They often want to show us what we miss by being so busy, unobservant, complaisant or self-involved. Before criticizing a work for being boring, readers should first reflect on whether they have failed to appreciate the significance of the subject or the author's handling of the subject.

ESSAY TOPICS

1. Choose a story, and discuss how the beginning and the end of the story relate to the characters' or the narrator's purpose.
2. Have you ever suddenly become struck by a simple, everyday object or occurrence such as a fallen leaf, dogs playing in the yard, the elegance of a can opener? Describe such an event. Discuss why that object or event suddenly became of interest. What did you learn by your observation?
3. Discuss a story that you found particularly interesting. Was it the subject matter alone that held your attention, or did the organization and structure also contribute to making the story interesting?
4. Discuss a story that you found particularly dull. Was it the subject matter or the author's treatment of the subject which bored you? What would you do to make the story more interesting?
5. Make a time line such as the one on p. 157 of the events in a story, and discuss how the author has rearranged those events in the narrative. Has the story been improved by the rearrangement?

CREATIVE WRITING EXERCISES

1. Narrate an event in such a way that it is utterly boring. Then narrate the same event in a way that creates or heightens the suspense. For example you might describe the end of a ballgame. How would you give the play-by-play in the most boring and most exciting manners? How would you narrate a wedding, a date, a political event?
2. Take an everyday event like making breakfast, going to class, or doing homework and narrate it in such a way that it is interesting.
3. Are any of your stories boring to your readers? Analyze whether you have given your characters a clear goal. Then see if you have created suspense. Where is the story defective? Rewrite the story to clarify the character's goal and to increase the suspense.

LITERARY ESSAYS

1. "The Horse Dealer's Daughter" may be said to contain two surprises: (1) Mabel's attempted suicide, and (2) her declaration of Ferguson's love. Are both events wholly unexpected? Do either of them make sense? Discuss how Lawrence prepares the reader for these two surprises.
2. "A Good Man Is Hard To Find" contains one big surprise—the family's encounter with The Misfit. Compare O'Connor's to Lawrence's handling of narrative surprise. Are the two surprises equally unexpected? To the reader? To the characters?
3. In "The Rockpile" James Baldwin is more concerned with suspense than surprise. How does he build suspense? Why is Baldwin more concerned with keeping his readers informed of his character's thoughts than either Lawrence of O'Connor?

JAMES BALDWIN

THE ROCKPILE

The son of a preacher, James Baldwin (b. 1924) was raised in Harlem, New York where he absorbed the life of the city and the rich black culture which had developed there. In the 1950s and early 1960s, he was considered by many people to be the most articulate, penetrating and passionate writer on the condition of blacks in America. Ironically in 1948, he left the United States to settle in France, where he has lived ever since.

Baldwin has written plays, essays, short stories and novels. He first achieved fame for his novel Go Tell It On the Mountain, *which was followed by the collections of essays* Autobiographical Notes *and* Notes of a Native Son. *He has also worked as a handyman, dishwasher, journalist, and film director.*

Across the street from their house, in an empty lot between two houses, stood the rockpile. It was a strange place to find a mass of natural rock jutting out of the ground; and someone, probably Aunt Florence, had once told them that the rock was there and could not be taken away because without it the subway cars underground would fly apart, killing all the people. This, touching on some natural mystery concerning the surface and the center of the earth, was far too intriguing an explanation to be challenged, and it invested the rockpile, moreover, with such mysterious importance that Roy felt it to be his right, not to say his duty, to play there.

Other boys were to be seen there each afternoon after school and all day Saturday and Sunday. They fought on the rockpile. Sure footed, dangerous, and reckless, they rushed each other and grappled on the heights, sometimes disappearing down the other side in a confusion of dust and screams and upended, flying feet. "It's a wonder they don't kill themselves," their mother said, watching sometimes from the fire escape. "You children stay away from there, you hear me?" Though she said "children" she was looking at Roy, where he sat beside John on the fire escape. "The good Lord knows," she continued, "I don't want you to come home bleeding like a hog every day the Lord sends." Roy shifted impatiently, and continued to stare at the street, as though in this gazing he might somehow acquire wings. John said nothing. He had not really been spoken to: he was afraid of the rockpile and of the boys who played there.

Each Saturday morning John and Roy sat on the fire escape and watched the forbidden street below. Sometimes their mother sat in the room behind them, sewing, or dressing their younger sister, or nursing the baby, Paul. The sun fell across them and across the fire escape with a high, benevolent indifference; below them, men and women, and boys and girls, sinners all, loitered; sometimes one of the church-members passed and saw them and waved. Then, for the moment that they waved decorously back, they were intimidated. They watched the saint, man or woman, until he or she had disappeared from sight. The passage of one of the redeemed made them consider, however vacantly, the wickedness of the street, their own latent wickedness in sitting where they sat; and made them think of their father, who came home early on Saturdays and who would soon be turning this corner and entering the dark hall below them.

But until he came to end their freedom, they sat, watching and longing above the street. At the end of the street nearest their house was the bridge which spanned the Harlem River and led to a city called the Bronx; which was where Aunt Florence lived. Nevertheless, when they saw her coming, she did not come from the bridge, but from the opposite end of the street. This, weakly, to their minds, she explained by saying that she had taken the subway, not wishing to walk, and that, besides, she did not live in *that* section of the Bronx. Knowing that the Bronx was across the river, they did not believe this story ever, but, adopting toward her their father's attitude, assumed that she had just left some sinful place which she dared not name, as, for example, a movie palace.

In the summertime boys swam in the river, diving off the wooden dock, or wading in from the garbage-heavy bank. Once a boy, whose name was Richard, drowned in the river. His mother had not known where he was; she had even come to their house, to ask if he was there. Then, in the evening, at six o'clock, they had heard from the street a woman screaming and wailing; and they ran to the windows and looked out. Down the street came the woman, Richard's mother, screaming, her face raised to the sky and tears running down her face. A woman walked beside her, trying to make her quiet and trying to hold her up. Behind them walked a man, Richard's father, with Richard's body in his arms. There were two white policemen walking in the gutter, who did not seem to know what should be done. Richard's father and Richard were wet, and Richard's body lay across his father's arms like a cotton baby. The woman's screaming filled all the street; cars slowed down and the people in the cars stared; people opened their windows and looked out and came rushing out of doors to stand in the gutter, watching. Then the small procession disappeared within the house which stood beside the rockpile. Then, "*Lord, Lord, Lord!*" cried Elizabeth, their mother, and slammed the window down.

One Saturday, an hour before his father would be coming home, Roy was wounded on the rockpile and brought screaming upstairs. He and John had been sitting on the fire escape and their mother had gone into the kitchen to sip tea with Sister McCandless. By and by Roy became bored and sat beside John in restless silence; and John began drawing into his school-book a newspaper advertisement which featured a new electric locomotive. Some friends of Roy passed beneath the fire escape and called him. Roy began to fidget, yelling down to them through the bars. Then a silence fell. John looked up. Roy stood looking at him.

"I'm going downstairs," he said.

"You better stay where you is, boy. You know Mama don't want you going downstairs."

"I be right *back.* She won't even know I'm gone, less you run and tell her."

"I ain't *got* to tell her. What's going to stop her from coming in here and looking out the window?"

"She's talking," Roy said. He started into the house.

"But Daddy's going to be home soon!"

"I be back before *that.* What you all the time got to be so *scared* for?" He was already in the house and he now turned, leaning on the windowsill, to swear impatiently, "I be back in *five* minutes."

John watched him sourly as he carefully unlocked the door and disappeared. In a moment he saw him on the sidewalk with his friends. He did not dare to go and tell his mother that Roy had left the fire escape because he had practically promised not to. He started to shout, *Remember, you said five minutes!* but one of Roy's friends was looking up at the fire escape. John looked down at his schoolbook: he became engrossed again in the problem of the locomotive.

When he looked up again he did not know how much time had passed, but now there was a gang fight on the rockpile. Dozens of boys fought each other in the harsh sun: clambering up the rocks and battling hand to hand, scuffed shoes sliding on the slippery rock; filling the bright air with curses and jubilant cries. They filled the air, too, with flying weapons: stones, sticks, tin cans, garbage, whatever could be picked up and thrown. John watched in a kind of absent amazement—until he remembered that Roy was still downstairs, and that he was one of the boys on the rockpile. Then he was afraid; he could not see his brother among the figures in the sun; and he stood up, leaning over the fire-escape railing. Then Roy appeared from the other side of the rocks; John saw that his shirt was torn; he was laughing. He moved until he stood at the very top of the rockpile. Then, something, an empty tin can, flew out of the air and hit him on the forehead, just above the eye. Immediately, one side of Roy's face ran with blood, he fell and rolled on his face down the rocks. Then for a moment there was no movement at all, no sound, the sun, arrested, lay on the street and the sidewalk and the arrested boys. Then someone screamed or shouted; boys began to run away, down the street, toward the bridge. The figure on the ground, having caught its breath and felt its own blood, began to shout. John cried, "Mama! Mama!" and ran inside.

"Don't fret, don't fret," panted Sister McCandless as they rushed down the dark, narrow, swaying stairs, "don't fret. Ain't a boy been born don't get his knocks every now and again. *Lord!*" they hurried into the sun. A man had picked Roy up and now walked slowly toward them. One or two boys sat silent on their stoops; at either end of the street there was a group of boys watching. "He ain't hurt bad," the man said, "wouldn't be making this kind of noise if he was hurt real bad."

Elizabeth, trembling, reached out to take Roy, but Sister McCandless, bigger, calmer, took him from the man and threw him over her shoulder as she once might have handled a sack of cotton. "God bless you," she said to the man, "God bless you, son." Roy was still screaming. Elizabeth stood behind Sister McCandless to stare at his bloody face.

"It's just a flesh wound," the man kept saying, "just broke the skin, that's all." They were moving across the sidewalk, toward the house. John, not now afraid of the staring boys, looked toward the corner to see if his father was yet in sight.

Upstairs, they hushed Roy's crying. They bathed the blood away, to find, just above the left eyebrow, the jagged, superficial scar. "Lord, have mercy," murmured Elizabeth, "another inch and it would've been his eye." And she looked with apprehension toward the clock. "Ain't it the truth," said Sister McCandless, busy with bandages and iodine.

"When did he go downstairs?" his mother asked at last.

Sister McCandless now sat fanning herself in the easy chair, at the head of the sofa where Roy lay, bound and silent. She paused for a moment to look sharply at John. John stood near the window, holding the newspaper advertisement and the drawing he had done.

"We was sitting on the fire escape," he said. "Some boys he knew called him."

"When?"

"He said he'd be back in five minutes."

"Why didn't you tell me he was downstairs?"

He looked at his hands, clasping his notebook, and did not answer.

"Boy," said Sister McCandless, "you hear your mother a-talking to you?"

He looked at his mother. He repeated:

"He said he'd be back in five minutes."

"He said he'd be back in five minutes," said Sister McCandless with scorn, "don't look to me like that's no right answer. You's the man of the house, you supposed to look after your baby brothers and sisters—you ain't supposed to let them run off and get half-killed. But I expect," she added, rising from the chair, dropping the cardboard fan, "your Daddy'll make you tell the truth. Your Ma's way too soft with you."

He did not look at her, but at the fan where it lay in the dark red, depressed seat where she had been. The fan advertised a pomade for the hair and showed a brown woman and her baby, both with glistening hair, smiling happily at each other.

"Honey," said Sister McCandless, "I got to be moving along. Maybe I drop in later tonight. I don't reckon you going to be at Tarry Service tonight?"

Tarry Service was the prayer meeting held every Saturday night at church to strengthen believers and prepare the church for the coming of the Holy Ghost on Sunday.

"I don't reckon," said Elizabeth. She stood up; she and Sister McCandless kissed each other on the cheek. "But you be sure to remember me in your prayers."

"I surely will do that." She paused, with her hand on the door knob, and looked down at Roy and laughed. "Poor little man," she said, "reckon he'll be content to sit on the fire escape *now.*"

Elizabeth laughed with her. "It sure ought to be a lesson to him. You don't reckon," she asked nervously, still smiling, "he going to keep that scar, do you?"

"Lord, no," said Sister McCandless, "ain't nothing but a scratch. I declare, Sister Grimes, you worse than a child. Another couple of weeks and you won't be able to *see* no scar. No, you go on about your housework, honey, and thank the Lord it weren't no worse." She opened the door; they heard the sound of feet on the stairs. "I expect that's the Reverand," said Sister McCandless, placidly, "I *bet* he going to raise cain."

"Maybe it's Florence," Elizabeth said. "Sometimes she get here about this time." They stood in the doorway, staring, while the steps reached the landing below and began again climbing to their floor. "No," said Elizabeth then, "that ain't her walk. That's Gabriel."

"Well, I'll just go on," said Sister McCandless, "and kind of prepare his mind." She pressed Elizabeth's hand as she spoke and started into the hall, leaving the door behind her slightly ajar. Elizabeth turned slowly back into the room. Roy did not open his eyes, or move; but she knew that he was not sleeping; he wished to delay until the last possible moment any contact with his father. John put his newspaper and his notebook on the table and stood, leaning on the table, staring at her.

"It wasn't my fault," he said. "I couldn't stop him from going downstairs."

"No," she said, "you ain't got nothing to worry about. You just tell your Daddy the truth."

He looked directly at her, and she turned to the window, staring into the street. What was Sister McCandless saying? Then from her bedroom she heard Delilah's thin wail and she turned, frowning, looking toward the bedroom and toward the still open door. She knew that John was watching her. Delilah continued to wail, she thought, angrily, *Now that girl's getting too big for that,* but she feared that Delilah would awaken Paul and she hurried into the bedroom. She tried to soothe Delilah back to sleep. Then she heard the front door open and close—too loud, Delilah raised her voice, with an exasperated sigh Elizabeth picked the child up. Her child and Gabriel's, her children and Gabriel's: Roy, Delilah, Paul. Only John was nameless and a stranger, living, unalterable testimony to his mother's days in sin.

"What happened?" Gabriel demanded. He stood, enormous, in the center of the room, his black lunchbox dangling from his hand, staring at the sofa where Roy lay. John stood just before him, it seemed to her astonished vision just below him, beneath his fist, his heavy shoe. The child stared at the man in fascination and terror—when a girl down home she had seen rabbits stand so paralyzed before the barking dog. She hurried past Gabriel to the sofa, feeling the weight of Delilah in her arms like the weight of a shield, and stood over Roy, saying:

"Now, ain't a thing to get upset about, Gabriel. This boy sneaked downstairs while I had my back turned and got hisself hurt a little. He's alright now."

Roy, as though in confirmation, now opened his eyes and looked gravely at his father. Gabriel dropped his lunchbox with a clatter and knelt by the sofa.

"How you feel, son? Tell your Daddy what happened?"

Roy opened his mouth to speak and then, relapsing into panic, began to cry. His father held him by the shoulder.

"You don't want to cry. You's Daddy's little man. Tell your Daddy what happened."

"He went downstairs," said Elizabeth, "where he didn't have no business to be, and got to fighting with them bad boys playing on that rockpile. That's what happened and it's a mercy it weren't nothing worse."

He looked up at her. "Can't you let this boy answer me for hisself?"

Ignoring this, she went on, more gently: "He got cut on the forehead, but it ain't nothing to worry about."

"You call a doctor? How you know it ain't nothing to worry about?"

"Is you got money to be throwing away on doctors? No, I ain't called no doctor. Ain't nothing wrong with my eyes that I can't tell whether he's hurt bad or not. He got a fright more'n anything else, and you ought to pray God it teaches him a lesson."

"You got a lot to say *now,*" he said, "but I'll have *me* something to say in a minute. I'll be wanting to know when all this happened, what you was doing with your eyes *then.*" He turned back to Roy, who had lain quietly sobbing eyes wide open and body held rigid: and who now, at his father's touch, remembered the height, the sharp, sliding rock beneath his feet, the sun, the explosion of the sun, his plunge into darkness and his salty blood; and recoiled, beginning to scream, as his father touched his forehead. "Hold still, hold still," crooned his father, shaking, "hold still. Don't cry. Daddy ain't going to hurt you, he just wants to see this bandage, see what they've done to his little man." But Roy continued to scream and would not be still and Gabriel dared not lift the bandage for fear of hurting him more. And he looked at Elizabeth in fury: "Can't you put that child down and help me with this boy? John, take your baby sister from your mother—don't look like neither of you got good sense."

John took Delilah and sat down with her in the easy chair. His mother bent over Roy, and held him still, while his father, carefully—but still Roy screamed—lifted the bandage and stared at the wound. Roy's sobs began to lessen. Gabriel readjusted the bandage. "You see," said Elizabeth, finally, "he ain't nowhere near dead."

"It sure ain't your fault that he ain't dead." He and Elizabeth considered each other for a moment in silence. "He came mightly close to losing an eye. Course, his eyes ain't as big as your'n, so I reckon you don't think it matters so much." At this her face hardened; he smiled. "Lord, have mercy," he said, "you think you ever going to learn to do right? Where was you when all this happened? Who let him go downstairs?"

"Ain't nobody let him go downstairs, he just went. He got a head just like his father, it got to be broken before it'll bow. I was in the kitchen."

"Where was Johnnie?"

"He was in here?"

"Where?"

"He was on the fire escape."

"Didn't he know Roy was downstairs?"

"I reckon."

"What you mean, you reckon? He ain't got your big eyes for nothing, does he?" He looked over at John. "Boy, you see your brother go downstairs?"

"Gabriel, ain't no sense in trying to blame Johnnie. You know right well if you have trouble making Roy behave, he ain't going to listen to his brother. He don't hardly listen to me."

"How come you didn't tell your mother Roy was downstairs?"

John said nothing, staring at the blanket which covered Delilah.

"Boy, you hear me? You want me to take a strap to you?"

"No, you ain't," she said. "You ain't going to take no strap to this boy, not today you ain't. Ain't a soul to blame for Roy's lying up there now but you—you because you done spoiled him so that he thinks he can do just anything and get away with it. I'm here to tell you that ain't no way to raise no child. You don't pray to the Lord to help you do better than you been doing, you going to live to shed bitter tears that the Lord didn't take his soul today." And she was trembling. She moved, unseeing, toward John and took Delilah from his arms. She looked back at Gabriel, who had risen, who stood near the sofa, staring at her. And she found in his face not fury alone, which would not have surprised her; but hatred so deep as to become insupportable in its lack of personality. His eyes were struck alive, unmoving, blind with malevolence—she felt, like the pull of the earth at her feet, his longing to witness her perdition. Again, as though it might be propitiation, she moved the child in her arms. And at this his eyes changed, he looked at Elizabeth, the mother of his children, the helpmeet given by the Lord. Then her eyes clouded; she moved to leave the room; her foot struck the lunchbox lying on the floor.

"John," she said, "pick up your father's lunchbox like a good boy."

She heard, behind her, his scrambling movement as he left the easy chair, the scrape and jangle of the lunchbox as he picked it up, bending his dark head near the toe of his father's heavy shoe.

QUESTIONS

1. What is Roy's goal? What goals, if any, does John have? Are these goals ever in conflict?
2. Why does Elizabeth defend John? Why does she believe her husband will be particularly harsh with John?
3. What is John's relationship with Gabriel? Why do you suppose Baldwin waits so long in the story to inform the reader that John is not Gabriel's son?
4. When does Baldwin make clear that the Grimeses are a black family? Why does Baldwin wait so long?
5. What significance does the rockpile have? Why does Roy believe the pile "to be his right"?
6. What kind of world do the Grimeses live in? How successful is Elizabeth Grimes's attempt to keep the children from that world?

JAMES BALDWIN

AUTOBIOGRAPHICAL NOTES

I was born in Harlem thirty-one years ago. I began plotting novels at about the time I learned to read. The story of my childhood is the usual bleak fantasy, and we can dismiss it with the unrestrained observation that I certainly would not consider living it again. In those days my mother was given to the exasperating and mysterious habit of having babies. As they were born, I took them over with one hand and held a book with the other. The children probably suffered, though they have since been kind enough to deny it, and in this way I read *Uncle Tom's Cabin* and *A Tale of Two Cities* over and over and over again; in this way, in fact, I read just about everything I could get my hands on—except the Bible, probably because it was the only book I was encouraged to read. I must also confess that I wrote—a great deal—and my first professional triumph, in any case, the first effort of mine to be seen in print, occurred at the age of twelve or thereabouts, when a short story I had written about the Spanish revolution won some sort of prize in an extremely short-lived church newspaper. I remember the story was censored by the lady editor, though I don't remember why, and I was outraged.

Also wrote plays, and songs, for one of which I received a letter of congratulations from Mayor La Guardia, and poetry, about which the less said, the better. My mother was delighted by all these goings-on, but my father wasn't; he wanted me to be a preacher. When I was fourteen I became a preacher, and when I was seventeen I stopped. Very shortly thereafter I left home. For God knows how long I struggled with the world of commerce and industry—I guess they would say they struggled with *me*—and when I was about twenty-one I had enough done of a novel to get a Saxton Fellowship. When I was twenty-two the fellowship was over, the novel turned out to be unsalable, and I started waiting on tables in a Village restaurant and writing book reviews—mostly, as it turned out, about the Negro problem, concerning which the color of my skin made me automatically an expert. Did another book, in company with photographer Theodore Pelatowski, about the store-front churches in Harlem. This book met exactly the same fate as my first—fellowship, but no sale. (It was a Rosenwald Fellowship.) By the time I was twenty-four I had decided to stop reviewing books about the Negro problem—which, by this time, was only slightly less horrible in print than it was in life—and I packed my bags and went to France, where I finished, God knows how, *Go Tell It on the Mountain.*

Any writer, I suppose, feels that the world into which he was born is nothing less than a conspiracy against the cultivation of his talent—which attitude certainly has a great deal to support it. On the other hand, it is only because the world looks on his talent with such a frightening indifference that the artist is compelled to make his talent important. So that any writer, looking back over even so short a span of time as I am here forced to assess, finds that the things which hurt him and the things which helped him cannot be divorced from each other; he could be helped in a certain way only because he was hurt in a certain way; and his help is simply to be enabled to move from one conundrum to the next—one is tempted to say that he moves from one disaster to the next. When one begins looking for influences one finds them by the score. I haven't thought much about my own, not enough anyway; I hazard that the King James Bible, the rhetoric of the store-front church, something ironic and violent and perpetually understated in Negro speech—and something of Dickens' love for bravura—have something to do with me today; but I wouldn't stake my life on it. Likewise, innumerable people have helped me in many ways; but finally, I suppose, the most difficult (and most rewarding) thing in my life has been the fact that I was born a Negro and was forced, therefore, to effect some kind of truce with this reality. (Truce, by the way, is the best one can hope for.)

One of the difficulties about being a Negro writer (and this is not special pleading, since I don't mean to suggest that he has it worse than anybody else) is that the Negro problem is written about so widely. The bookshelves groan under the weight of information, and everyone therefore considers himself informed. And this information, furthermore, operates usually (generally, popularly) to reinforce traditional attitudes. Of traditional attitudes there are only two—For or Against—and I, personally, find it difficult to say which attitude has caused me the most pain. I am perfectly aware that the change from ill-will to good-will, however motivated, however imperfect, however expressed, is better than no change at all.

But it is part of the business of the writer—as I see it—to examine attitudes, to go beneath the surface, to tape the source. From this point of view the Negro problem is nearly inaccessible. It is not only written about so widely; it is written about so badly. It is quite possible to say that the price a Negro pays for becoming articulate is to find himself, at length, with nothing to be articulate about. ("You taught me the language," says Caliban to Prospero, "and my profit on't is I know how to curse.") Consider: the tremendous social activity that this problem generates imposes on whites and Negroes alike the necessity of looking forward, of working to bring about a better day. This is fine, it keeps the waters troubled; it is all, indeed, that has made possible the Negro's progress. Nevertheless, social affairs are not generally speaking the writer's prime concern, whether they ought to be or not; it is absolutely necessary that he establish between himself and these affairs a distance that will allow, at least, for clarity, so that before he can look forward in any meaningful sense, he must first be allowed to take a long look back. In the context of the Negro problem neither whites nor blacks, for excellent reasons of their own, have the faintest desire to look back; but I think that the past is all that makes the present coherent, and further, that the past will remain horrible for exactly as long as we refuse to assess it honestly.

I know, in any case, that the most crucial time in my own development came when I was forced to recognize that I was a kind of bastard of the West; when I followed the line of my past I did not find myself in Europe but in Africa. And this meant that in some subtle way, in a really profound way, I brought to Shakespeare, Bach, Rembrandt, to the stones of Paris, to the cathedral at Chartres, and to the Empire State Building, a special attitude. These were not really my creations, they did not contain my history; I might search in them in vain forever for any reflection of myself. I was an interloper; this was not my heritage. At the same time I had no other heritage which I could possibly hope to use—I had certainly been unfitted for the jungle or the tribe. I would have to appropriate these white centuries, I would have to make them mine—I would have to accept my special attitude, my special place in this scheme—otherwise I would have no place in *any* scheme. What was the most difficult was the fact that I was forced to admit something I had always hidden from myself, which the American Negro has had to hide from himself as the price of his public progress; that I hated and feared white people. This did not mean that I loved black people; on the contrary, I despised them, possibly because they failed to produce Rembrandt. In effect, I hated and feared the world. And this meant, not only that I thus gave the world an altogether murderous power over me, but also that in such a self-destroying limbo I could never hope to write.

One writes out of one thing only—one's own experience. Everything depends on how relentlessly one forces from this experience the last drop, sweet or bitter, it can possibly give. This is the only real concern of the artist, to recreate out of the disorder of life that order which is art. The difficulty then, for me, of being a Negro writer was the fact that I was, in effect, prohibited from examining my own experience too closely by the tremendous demands and the very real dangers of my social situation.

I don't think the dilemma outlined above is uncommon. I do think, since writers work in the disastrously explicit medium of language, that it goes a little way towards explaining why, out of the enormous resources of Negro speech and life, and despite the example of Negro music, prose written by Negroes has been generally speaking so pallid and so harsh. I have not written about being a Negro at such length because I expect that to be my only subject, but only because it was the gate I had to unlock before I could hope to write about anything else. I don't think that the Negro problem in America can be even discussed coherently without bearing in mind its context; its context being the history, traditions, customs, the moral assumptions and preoccupations of the country; in short, the general social fabric. Appearances to the contrary, no one in America escapes its effects and everyone in America bears some responsibility for it. I believe this the more firmly because it is the overwhelming tendency to speak of this problem as though it were a thing apart. But in the work of Faulkner, in the general attitude and certain specific passages in Robert Penn Warren, and, most significantly, in the advent of Ralph Ellison, one sees the beginnings—at least—of a more genuinely penetrating search. Mr. Ellison, by the way, is the first Negro novelist I have ever read to utilize in language, and brilliantly, some of the ambiguity and irony of Negro life.

About my interests: I don't know if I have any, unless the morbid desire to own a sixteen-millimeter camera and make experimental movies can be so classified. Otherwise, I love to eat and drink—it's my melancholy conviction that I've scarcely ever had enough to eat (this is because it's *impossible* to eat enough if you're worried about the next meal)—and I love to argue with people who do not disagree with me too profoundly, and I love to laugh. I do *not* like bohemia, or bohemians, I do not like people whose principal aim is pleasure, and I do not like people who are *earnest* about anything. I don't like people who like me because I'm a Negro; neither do I like people who find in the same accident grounds for contempt. I love America more than any other country in the world, and, exactly for this reason, I insist on the right to criticize her perpetually. I think all theories are suspect, that the finest principles may have to be modified, or may even be pulverized by the demands of life, and that one must find, therefore, one's own moral center and move through the world hoping that this center will guide one aright. I consider that I have many responsibilities, but none greater than this: to last, as Hemingway says, and get my work done.

I want to be an honest man and a good writer.

THINGS TO THINK ABOUT

1. What sorts of things in your background influenced your way of expressing yourself? If you express yourself best through physical action, what sorts of experiences influenced that tendency? If you express yourself best through music, how do you account for that? If you have trouble writing, is there something in your background that makes writing difficult?
2. Baldwin says that he may have been influenced by "something ironic and violent and perpetually understated in Negro speech." Do you find evidence of this influence in "The Rockpile"?
3. How does fear stop people from writing? Whom does a writer fear? Reader? Critics? The government? Him or herself? Does a black writer such as Baldwin have more to fear than a white writer? How is overcoming fear necessary before you can write? Does writing help the writer overcome fear?
4. Baldwin writes that because he "love[s] America more than any other country in the world" he has "the right to criticize her perpetually." In what ways does love give the right to criticize? In what way is love necessary for criticism? Do people who hate an object criticize it, or do they merely denounce it?

D. H. LAWRENCE

THE HORSE DEALER'S DAUGHTER

D[avid] H[erbert] Lawrence (1885–1930) was a man of enormous restless energy. Born in Nottingham, England to a coal miner and his refined wife, Lawrence grew up in an atmosphere both rough and delicate. He attended school on scholarship and graduated from Nottingham University where he met Frieda von Richthofen, the daughter of a German baron and the wife of a university professor, whom he married in 1914. The Lawrences lived a tumultuous life, residing in Italy, Australia, Mexico and the United States where his ashes are buried. In the last few years of Lawrence's life, his travels were necessitated by tuberculosis from which he died in his mid-forties.

D.H. Lawrence was a controversial writer. His novels, particularly The Rainbow *and* Lady Chatterley's Lover *were banned for obscenity and were the subject of extensive litigation. Lawrence was an early advocate of Jungian psychology, and his political views were considered extreme. But he earned followers for the powerful, sensuous, sometimes hypnotic quality of his prose and poetry.*

"Well, Mabel, and what are you going to do with yourself?" asked Joe, with foolish flippancy. He felt quite safe himself. Without listening for an answer, he turned aside, worked a grain of tobacco to the tip of his tongue and spat it out. He did not care about anything, since he felt safe himself.

The three brothers and the sister sat round the desolate breakfast table, attempting some sort of desultory consultation. The morning's post had given the final tap to the family fortune, and all was over. The dreary dining room itself, with its heavy mahogany furniture, looked as if it were waiting to be done away with.

But the consultation amounted to nothing. There was a strange air of ineffectuality about the three men, as they sprawled at table, smoking and reflecting vaguely on their own condition. The girl was alone, a rather short, sullen-looking young woman of twenty-seven. She did not share the same life as her brothers. She would have been goodlooking, save for the impassive fixity of her face, "bull-dog," as her brothers called it.

There was a confused tramping of horses' feet outside. The three men all sprawled round in their chairs to watch. Beyond the dark holly bushes that separated the strip of lawn from the highroad, they could see a cavalcade of shire horses swinging out of their own yard, being taken for exercise. This was the last time. These were the last horses that would go through their hands. The young men watched with critical, callous look. They were all frightened at the collapse of their lives, and the sense of disaster in which they were involved left them no inner freedom.

Yet they were three fine, well-set fellows enough. Joe, the eldest, was a man of thirty-three, broad and handsome in a hot, flushed way. His face was red, he twisted his black moustache over a thick finger, his eyes were shallow and restless. He had a sensual way of uncovering his teeth when he laughed, and his bearing was stupid. Now he watched the horses with a glazed look of helplessness in his eyes, a certain stupor of downfall.

The great draught-horses swung past. They were tied head to tail, four of them, and they heaved along to where a lane branched off from the highroad, planting their great hoofs floutingly in the fine black mud, swinging their great rounded haunches sumptuously, and trotting a few sudden steps as they were led into the lane, round the corner. Every movement showed a massive, slumbrous strength, and a stupidity which held them in subjection. The groom at the head looked back, jerking the leading rope. And the cavalcade moved out of sight up the lane, the tail of the last horse, bobbed up tight and stiff, held out taut from the swinging great haunches as they rocked behind the hedges in a motion-like sleep.

Joe watched with glazed hopeless eyes. The horses were almost like his own body to him. He felt he was done for now. Luckily he was engaged to a woman as old as himself, and therefore her father, who was steward of a neighboring estate, would provide him with a job. He would marry and go into harness. His life was over, he would be a subject animal now.

He turned uneasily aside, the retreating steps of the horses echoing in his ears. Then, with foolish restlessness, he reached for the scraps of bacon rind from the plates, and making a faint whistling sound, flung them to the terrier that lay against the fender. He watched the dog swallow them, and waited till the creature looked into his eyes. Then a faint grin came on his face, and in a high, foolish voice he said:

"You won't get much more bacon, shall you, you little bitch?"

The dog faintly and dismally wagged its tail, then lowered its haunches, circled round, and lay down again.

There was another helpless silence at the table. Joe sprawled uneasily in his seat, not willing to go till the family conclave was dissolved. Fred Henry, the second brother, was erect, clean-limbed, alert. He had watched the passing of the horses with more sang-froid. If he was an animal, like Joe, he was an animal which controls, not one which is controlled. He was master of any horse, and he carried himself with a well-tempered air of mastery. But he was not master of the situations of life. He pushed his coarse brown moustache upwards, off his lip, and glanced irritably at his sister, who sat impassive and inscrutable.

"You'll go and stop with Lucy for a bit, shan't you?" he asked. The girl did not answer.

"I don't see what else you can do," persisted Fred Henry.

"Go as a skivvy," Joe interpolated laconically.

The girl did not move a muscle.

"If I was her, I should go in for training for a nurse," said Malcolm, the youngest of them all. He was the baby of the family, a young man of twenty-two, with a fresh, jaunty *museau*.

But Mabel did not take any notice of him. They had talked at her and round her for so many years, that she hardly heard them at all.

The marble clock on the mantlepiece softly chimed the half-hour, the dog rose uneasily from the hearthrug and looked at the party at the breakfast table. But still they sat on in ineffectual conclave.

"Oh, all right," said Joe suddenly, apropos of nothing. "I'll get a move on."

He pushed back his chair, straddled his knees with a downward jerk, to get them free, in horsey fashion, and went to the fire. Still he did not go out of the room; he was curious to know what the others would do or say. He began to charge his pipe, looking down at the dog and saying, in a high, affected voice:

"Going wi' me? Going wi' me are ter? Tha'rt goin' further tha that counts on just now, dost hear?"

The dog faintly wagged its tail, the man stuck out his jaw and covered his pipe with his hands, and puffed intently, losing himself in the tobacco, looking down all the while at the dog with an absent brown eye. The dog looked at him in mournful distrust. Joe stood with his knees stuck out, in real horsey fashion.

"Have you had a letter from Lucy?" Fred Henry asked of his sister.

"Last week," came the neutral reply.

"And what does she say?"

There was no answer.

"Does she *ask* you to go and stop there?" persisted Fred Henry.

"She says I can if I like."

"Well, then, you'd better. Tell her you'll come on Monday."

This was received in silence.

"That's what you'll do then, is it?" said Fred Henry, in some exasperation.

But she made no answer. There was a silence of futility and irritation in the room. Malcolm grinned fatuously.

"You'll have to make up your mind between now and next Wednesday," said Joe loudly, "or else find yourself lodgings on the curbstone."

The face of the young woman darkened, but she sat on immutable.

"Here's Jack Fergusson!" exclaimed Malcolm, who was looking aimlessly out of the window.

"Where?" exclaimed Joe, loudly.

"Just gone past."

"Coming in?"

Malcolm craned his neck to see the gate.

"Yes," he said.

There was a silence. Mabel sat on like one condemned, at the head of the table. Then a whistle was heard from the kitchen. The dog got up and barked sharply. Joe opened the door and shouted:

"Come on."

After a moment a young man entered. He was muffled up in overcoat and a purple woolen scarf, and his tweed cap, which he did not remove, was pulled down on his head. He was of medium height, his face was rather long and pale, his eyes looked tired.

"Hello, Jack! Well, Jack!" exclaimed Malcolm and Joe. Fred Henry merely said, "Jack."

"What's doing?" asked the newcomer, evidently addressing Fred Henry.

"Same. We've got to be out by Wednesday. Got a cold?"

"I have—got it bad, too."

"Why don't you stop in?"

"*Me* stop in? When I can't stand on my legs, perhaps I shall have a chance." The young man spoke huskily. He had a slight Scotch accent.

"It's a knock-out, isn't it," said Joe, boisterously, "if a doctor goes round croaking with a cold. Looks bad for the patients, doesn't it?"

The young doctor looked at him slowly.

"Anything the matter with *you,* then?" he asked sarcastically.

"Not as I know of. Damn your eyes, I hope not. Why?"

"I thought you were very concerned about the patients, wondered if you might be one yourself."

"Damn it, no, I've never been patient to no flaming doctor, and hope I never shall be," returned Joe.

At this point Mabel rose from the table, and they all seemed to become aware of her existence. She began putting the dishes together. The young doctor looked at her, but did not address her. He had not greeted her. She went out of the room with the tray, her face impassive and unchanged.

"When are you off then, all of you?" asked the doctor.

"I'm catching the eleven-forty," replied Malcolm. "Are you goin' down wi' th' trap, Joe?"

"Yes, I've told you I'm going down wi' th' trap, haven't I?"

"We'd better be getting her in then. So long, Jack, if I don't see you before I go," said Malcolm, shaking hands.

He went out, followed by Joe, who seemed to have his tail between his legs.

"Well, this is the devil's own," exclaimed the doctor, when he was left alone with Fred Henry. "Going before Wednesday, are you?"

"That's the orders," replied the other.

"Where, to Northampton?"

"That's it."

"The devil!" exclaimed Fergusson, with quiet chagrin.

And there was silence between the two.

"All settled up, are you?" asked Fergusson.

"About."

There was another pause.

"Well, I shall miss yer, Freddy, boy," said the young doctor.

"And I shall miss thee, Jack," returned the other.

"Miss you like hell," mused the doctor.

Fred Henry turned aside. There was nothing to say. Mabel came in again, to finish clearing the table.

"What are *you* going to do, then, Miss Pervin?" asked Fergusson. "Going to your sister's, are you?"

Mabel looked at him with her steady, dangerous eyes, that always made him uncomfortable, unsettling his superficial ease.

"No," she said.

"Well, what in the name of fortune *are* you going to do? Say what you mean to do," cried Fred Henry, with futile intensity.

But she only averted her head, and continued her work. She folded the white table-cloth, and put on the chenille cloth.

"The sulkiest bitch that ever trod!" muttered her brother.

But she finished her task with perfectly impassive face, the young doctor watching her interestedly all the while. Then she went out.

Fred Henry stared after her, clenching his lips, his blue eyes fixing in sharp antagonism, as he made a grimace of sour exasperation.

"You could bray her into bits, and that's all you'd get out of her," he said in a small, narrowed tone.

The doctor smiled faintly.

"What's she *going* to do, then?" he asked.

"Strike me if *I* know!" returned the other.

There was a pause. Then the doctor stirred.

"I'll be seeing you to-night, shall I?" he said to his friend.

"Ay—where's it to be? Are we going over to Jessdale?"

"I don't know. I've got such a cold on me. I'll come round to the Moon and Stars, anyway."

"Let Lizzie and May miss their night for once, eh?"

"That's it—if I feel as I do now."

"All's one—"

The two young men went through the passage and down to the back door together. The house was large, but it was servantless now, and desolate. At the back was a small bricked house-yard, and beyond that a big square, graveled fine and red, and having stables on two sides. Sloping, dank, winter-dark fields stretched away on the open sides.

But the stables were empty. Joseph Pervin, the father of the family, had been a man of no education, who had become a fairly large horse dealer. The stables had been full of horses, there was a great turmoil and come-and-go of horses and of dealers and grooms. Then the kitchen was full of servants. But of late things had declined. The old man had married a second time, to retrieve his fortunes. Now he was dead and everything was gone to the dogs, there was nothing but debt and threatening.

For months, Mabel had been servantless in the big house, keeping the home together in penury for her ineffectual brothers. She had kept house for ten years. But previously it was with unstinted means. Then, however brutal and coarse everything was, the sense of money had kept her proud, confident. The men might be foul-mouthed, the women in the kitchen might have bad reputations, her brothers might have illegitimate children. But so long as there was money, the girl felt herself established, and brutally proud, reserved.

No company came to the house, save dealers and coarse men. Mabel had no associates of her own sex, after her sister went away. But she did not mind. She went regularly to church, she attended to her father. And she lived in the memory of her mother, who had died when she was fourteen, and whom she had loved. She had loved her father, too, in a different way, depending upon him, and feeling secure in him, until at the age of fifty-four he married again. And then she had set hard against him. Now he had died and left them all hopelessly in debt.

She had suffered badly during the period of poverty. Nothing, however, could shake the curious sullen, animal pride that dominated each member of the family. Now, for Mabel, the end had come. Still she would not cast about her. She would follow her own way just the same. She would always hold the keys of her own situation. Mindless and persistent, she endured from day to day. Why should she think? Why should she answer anybody? It was enough that this was the end, and there was no way out. She need not pass any more darkly along the main street of the small town, avoiding every eye. She need not demean herself any more, going into the shops and buying the cheapest food. This was at an end. She thought of nobody, not even of herself. Mindless and persistent, she seemed in a sort of ecstasy to be coming nearer to her fulfillment, her own glorification, approaching her dead mother, who was glorified.

In the afternoon she took a little bag, with shears and sponge and a small scrubbing brush, and went out. It was a gray, wintry day, with saddened, dark green fields and an atmosphere blackened by the smoke of foundries not far off. She went quickly, darkly along the causeway, heeding nobody, through the town to the churchyard.

There she always felt secure, as if no one could see her, although as a matter of fact she was exposed to the stare of every one who passed along under the churchyard wall. Nevertheless, once under the shadow of the great looming church, among the graves, she felt immune from the world, reserved within the thick churchyard wall as in another country.

Carefully she clipped the grass from the grave, and arranged the pinky white, small chrysanthemums in the tin cross. When this was done, she took an empty jar from a neighboring grave, brought water, and carefully, most scrupulously sponged the marble headstone and the coping-stone.

It gave her sincere satisfaction to do this. She felt in immediate contact with the world of her mother. She took minute pains, went through the park in a state bordering on pure happiness, as if in performing this task she came into a subtle, intimate connection with her mother. For the life she followed here in the world was far less real than the world of death she inherited from her mother.

The doctor's house was just by the church. Fergusson, being a mere hired assistant, was slave to the countryside. As he hurried now to attend to the outpatients in the surgery, glancing across the graveyard with his quick eyes, he saw the girl at her task at the grave. She seemed so intent and remote, it was like looking into another world. Some mystical element was touched in him. He slowed down as he walked, watching her as if spellbound.

She lifted her eyes, feeling him looking. Their eyes met. And each looked away again at once, each feeling, in some way, found out by the other. He lifted his cap and passed on down the road. There remained distinct in his consciousness, like a vision, the memory of her face, lifted from the tombstone in the churchyard, and looking at him with slow, large, portentous eyes. It *was* portentous, her face. It seemed to mesmerize him. There was a heavy power in her eyes which laid hold of his whole being, as if he had drunk some powerful drug. He had been feeling weak and done before. Now the life came back into him, he felt delivered from his own fretted, daily self.

He finished his duties at the surgery as quickly as might be, hastily filling up the bottle of the waiting people with cheap drugs. Then, in perpetual haste, he set off again to visit several cases in another part of his round, before teatime. At all times he preferred to walk if he could, but particularly when he was not well. He fancied the motion restored him.

The afternoon was falling. It was gray, deadened, and wintry, with a slow, moist, heavy coldness sinking in and deadening all the faculties. But why should he think or notice? He hastily climbed the hill and turned across the dark green fields, following the black cindertrack. In the distance, across a shallow dip in the country, the small town was clustered like smouldering ash, a tower, a spire, a heap of low, raw, extinct houses. And on the nearest fringe of the town, sloping into the dip, was Oldmeadow, the Pervins' house. He could see the stables and the outbuildings distinctly, as they lay towards him on the slope. Well, he would not go there many more times! Another resource would be lost to him, another place gone: the only company he cared for in the alien, ugly little town he was losing. Nothing but work, drudgery, constant hastening from dwelling to dwelling among the colliers and the iron-workers. It wore him out, but at the same time he had a craving for it. It was a stimulant to him to be in the homes of the working people, moving as it were through the innermost body of their life. His nerves were excited and gratified. He could come so near, into the very lives of the rough, inarticulate, powerfully emotional men and women. He grumbled, he said he hated the hellish hole. But as a matter of fact it excited him, the contact with the rough, strongly-feeling people was a stimulant applied direct to his nerves.

Below Oldmeadow, in the green, shallow, soddened hollow of fields, lay a square, deep pond. Roving across the landscape, the doctor's quick eye detected a figure in black passing through the gate of the field, down towards the pond. He looked again. It would be Mabel Pervin. His mind suddenly became alive and attentive.

Why was she going down there? He pulled up on the path on the slope above, and stood staring. He could just make sure of the small black figure moving in the hollow of the failing day. He seemed to see her in the midst of such obscurity, that he was like a clairvoyant, seeing rather with the mind's eye than with ordinary sight. Yet he could see her positively enough, while he kept his eye attentive. He felt, if he looked away from her, in the thick, ugly falling dusk, he would lose her altogether.

He followed her minutely as she moved, direct and intent, like something transmitted rather than stirring in voluntary activity, straight down the field towards the pond. There she stood on the bank for a moment. She never raised her head. Then she waded slowly into the water.

He stood motionless as the small black figure walked slowly and deliberately towards the center of the pond, very slowly, gradually moving deeper into the motionless water, and still moving forward as the water got up to her breast. Then he could see her no more in the dusk of the dead afternoon.

"There!" he exclaimed, "Would you believe it?"

And he hastened straight down, running over the wet, soddened fields, pushing through the hedges, down into the depression of callous wintry obscurity. It took him several minutes to come to the pond. He stood on the bank, breathing heavily. He could see nothing. His eyes seemed to penetrate the dead water. Yes, perhaps that was the dark shadow of her black clothing beneath the surface of the water.

He slowly ventured into the pond. The bottom was deep, soft clay, he sank in, and the water clasped dead cold round his legs. As he stirred he could smell the cold, rotten clay that fouled up into the water. It was objectionable in his lungs. Still, repelled and yet not heeding, he moved deeper into the pond. The cold water rose over his thighs, over his loins, upon his abdomen. The lower part of his body was all sunk in the hideous cold element. And the bottom was so deeply soft and uncertain he was afraid of pitching with his mouth underneath. He could not swim, and was afraid.

He crouched a little, spreading his hands under the water and moving them round, trying to feel for her. The dead cold pond swayed upon his chest. He moved again, a little deeper, and again, with his hands underneath, he felt all around under the water. And he touched her clothing. But it evaded his fingers. He made a desperate effort to grasp it.

And so doing he lost his balance and went under, horribly, suffocating in the foul earthy water, struggling madly for a few moments. At last, after what seemed an eternity, he got his footing, rose again into the air and looked around. He gasped, and knew he was in the world. Then he looked at the water. She had risen near him. He grasped her clothing, and drawing her nearer, turned to take his way to land again.

He went very slowly, carefully, absorbed in the slow progress. He rose higher, climbing out of the pond. The water was now only about his legs; he was thankful, full of relief to be out of the clutches of the pond. He lifted her and staggered on to the bank, out of the horror of wet, gray clay.

He laid her down on the bank. She was quite unconscious and running with water. He made the water come from her mouth, he worked to restore her. He did not have to work very long before he could feel the breathing begin again in her; she was breathing naturally. He worked a little longer. He could feel her live beneath his hands; she was coming back. He wiped her face, wrapped her in his overcoat, looked round into the dim, dark gray world, then lifted her and staggered down the bank and across the fields.

It seemed an unthinkably long way, and his burden so heavy he felt he would never get to the house. But at last he was in the stableyard, and then in the house-yard. He opened the door and went into the house. In the kitchen he laid her down on the hearthrug, and called. The house was empty. But the fire was burning in the grate.

Then again he kneeled to attend to her. She was breathing regularly, her eyes were wide open and as if conscious, but there seemed something missing in her look. She was conscious in herself, but unconscious of her surroundings.

He ran upstairs, took blankets from a bed, and put them before the fire to warm. Then he removed her saturated, earthy-smelling clothing, rubbed her dry with a towel, and wrapped her naked in the blankets. Then he went into the dining-room, to look for spirits. There was a little whisky. He drank a gulp himself, and put some into her mouth.

The effect was instantaneous. She looked full into his face, as if she had been seeing him for some time, and yet had only just become conscious of him.

"Dr. Fergusson?" she said.

"What?" he answered.

He was divesting himself of his coat, intending to find some dry clothing upstairs. He could not bear the smell of the dead, clayey water, and he was mortally afraid of his own health.

"What did I do?" she asked.

"Walked into the pond," he replied. He had begun to shudder like one sick, and could hardly attend to her. Her eyes remained full on him, he seemed to be going dark in his mind, looking back at her helplessly. The shuddering became quieter in him, his life came back in him, dark and unknowing, but strong again.

"Was I out of my mind?" she asked, while her eyes were fixed on him all the time.

"Maybe, for the moment," he replied. He felt quiet, because his strength came back. The strange fretful strain had left him.

"Am I out of my mind now?" she asked.

"Are you?" he reflected a moment. "No," he answered truthfully. "I don't see that you are." He turned his face aside. He was afraid now, because he felt dazed, and felt dimly that her power was stronger than his, in this issue. And she continued to look at him fixedly all the time. "Can you tell me where I shall find some dry things to put on?" he asked.

"Did you dive into the pond for me?" she asked.

"No," he answered. "I walked in. But I went in overhead as well."

There was silence for a moment. He hesitated. He very much wanted to go upstairs to get into dry clothing. But there was another desire in him. And she seemed to hold him. His will seemed to have gone to sleep, and left him, standing there slack before her. But he felt warm inside himself. He did not shudder at all, though his clothes were sodden on him.

"Why did you?" she asked.

"Because I didn't want you to do such a foolish thing," he said.

"It wasn't foolish," she said, still gazing at him as she lay on the floor, with a sofa cushion under her head. "It was the right thing to do. *I* knew best, then."

"I'll go and shift these wet things," he said. But still he had not the power to move out of her presence, until she sent him. It was as if she had the life of his body in her hands, and he could not extricate himself. Or perhaps he did not want to.

Suddenly she sat up. Then she became aware of her own immediate condition. She felt the blankets about her, she knew her own limbs.

For a moment it seemed as if her reason were going. She looked round, with wild eye, as if seeking something. He stood still with fear. She saw her clothing lying scattered.

"Who undressed me?" she asked, her eyes resting full and inevitable on his face.

"I did," he replied, "to bring you round."

For some moments she sat and gazed at him awfully, her lips parted.

"Do you love me, then?" she asked.

He only stood and stared at her, fascinated. His soul seemed to melt.

She shuffled forward on her knees, and put her arms round him, round his legs, as he stood there, pressing her breasts against his knees and thighs, clutching him with strange, convulsive certainty, pressing his thighs against her, drawing him to her face, her throat, as she looked up at him with flaring, humble eyes of transfiguration, triumphant in first possession.

"You love me," she murmured, in strange transport, yearning and triumphant and confident. "You love me. I know you love me, I know."

And she was passionately kissing his knees, through the wet clothing, passionately and indiscriminately kissing his knees, his legs, as if unaware of everything.

He looked down at the tangled wet hair, the wild, bare, animal shoulders. He was amazed, bewildered, and afraid. He had never thought of loving her. He had never wanted to love her. When he rescued her and restored her, he was a doctor, and she was a patient. He had had no single personal thought of her. Nay, this introduction of the personal element was very distasteful to him, a violation of his professional honor. It was horrible to have her there embracing his knees. It was horrible. He revolted from it, violently. And yet—and yet—he had not the power to break away.

She looked at him again, with the same supplication of powerful love, and that same transcendent, frightening light of triumph. In view of the delicate flame which seemed to come from her face like a light, he was powerless. And yet he had never intended to love her. He had never intended. And something stubborn in him could not give way.

"You love me," she repeated, in a murmur of deep, rhapsodic assurance. "You love me."

Her hands were drawing him, drawing him down to her. He was afraid, even a little horrified. For he had, really, no intention of loving her. Yet her hands were drawing him towards her. He put out his hand quickly to steady himself, and grasped her bare shoulder. A flame seemed to burn the hand that grasped her soft shoulder. He had no intention of loving her: his whole will was against his yielding. It was horrible. And yet wonderful was the touch of her shoulders, beautiful the shining of her face. Was she perhaps mad? He had a horror of yielding to her. Yet something in him ached also.

He had been staring away at the door, away from her. But his hand remained on her shoulder. She had gone suddenly very still. He looked down at her. Her eyes were now wide with fear, with doubt, the light was dying from her face, a shadow of terrible grayness was returning. He could not bear the touch of her eyes' question upon him, and the look of death behind the question.

With an inward groan he gave way, and let his heart yield towards her. A sudden gentle smile came on his face. And her eyes, which never left his face, slowly, slowly filled with tears. He watched the strange water rise in her eyes, like some slow fountain coming up. And his heart seemed to burn and melt away in his breast.

He could not bear to look at her any more. He dropped on his knees and caught her head with his arms and pressed her face against his throat. She was very still. His heart, which seemed to have broken, was burning with a kind of agony in his breast. And he felt her slow, hot tears wetting his throat. But he could not move.

He felt the hot tears wet his neck and the hollows of his neck, and he remained motionless, suspended through one of man's eternities. Only now it had become indispensable to him to have her face pressed close to him; he could never let her go again. He could never let her head go away from the close clutch of his arm. He wanted to remain like that for ever, with his heart hurting him in a pain that was also life to him. Without knowing, he was looking down on her damp, soft brown hair.

Then, as it were suddenly, he smelt the horrid stagnant smell of that water. And at the same moment she drew away from him and looked at him. Her eyes were wistful and unfathomable. He was afraid of them, and he fell to kissing her, not knowing what he was doing. He wanted her eyes not to have that terrible, wistful, unfathomable look.

When she turned her face to him again, a faint delicate flush was glowing, and there was again dawning that terrible shining of joy in her eyes, which really terrified him, and yet which he now wanted to see, because he feared the look of doubt still more.

"You love me?" she said, rather faltering.

"Yes." The word cost him a painful effort. Not because it wasn't true. But because it was too newly true, the *saying* seemed to tear open again his newly torn heart. And he hardly wanted it to be true, even now.

She lifted her face to him, and he bent forward and kissed her on the mouth, gently, with the one kiss that is an eternal pledge. And as he kissed her his heart strained again in his breast. He never intended to love her. But now it was over. He had crossed over the gulf to her, and all that he had left behind had shriveled and become void.

After the kiss, her eyes again slowly filled with tears. She sat still, away from him, with her face drooped aside, and her hands folded in her lap. The tears fell very slowly. There was complete silence. He too sat there motionless and silent on the hearthrug. The strange pain of his heart that was broken seemed to consume him. That he should love her? That this was love! That he should be ripped open in this way! Him, a doctor! How they would all jeer if they knew! It was agony to him to think they might know.

In the curious naked pain of the thought he looked again to her. She was sitting there drooped into a muse. He saw a tear fall, and his heart flared hot. He saw for the first time that one of her shoulders was quite uncovered, one arm bare, he could see one of her small breasts; dimly, because it had become almost dark in the room.

"Why are you crying?" he asked, in an altered voice.

She looked up at him, and behind her tears the consciousness of her situation for the first time brought a dark look of shame to her eyes.

"I'm not crying, really," she said, watching him half frightened.

He reached his hand, and softly closed it on her bare arm.

"I love you! I love you!" he said in a soft, low vibrating voice, unlike himself.

She shrank, and dropped her head. The soft, penetrating grip of his hand on her arm distressed her. She looked up at him.

"I want to go," she said. "I want to go and get you some dry things."

"Why?" he said. "I'm all right."

"But I want to go," she said. "And I want you to change your things."

He released her arm, and she wrapped herself in the blanket, looking at him rather frightened. And still she did not rise.

"Kiss me," she said wistfully.

He kissed her, but briefly, half in anger.

Then, after a second, she rose nervously, all mixed up in the blanket. He watched her in her confusion, as she tried to extricate herself and wrap herself up so that she could walk. He watched her relentlessly, as she knew. And as she went, the blanket trailing, and as he saw a glimpse of her feet and her white leg, he tried to remember her as she was when he had wrapped her in the blanket. But then he didn't want to remember, because she had been nothing to him then, and his nature revolted from remembering her as she was when she was nothing to him.

A tumbling, muffled noise from within the dark house startled him. Then he heard her voice:—"There are clothes." He rose and went to the foot of the stairs, and gathered up the garments she had thrown down. Then he came back to the fire, to rub himself down and dress. He grinned at his own appearance when he had finished.

The fire was sinking, so he put on coal. The house was now quite dark, save for the light of a street-lamp that shone in faintly from beyond the holly trees. He lit the gas with matches he found on the mantelpiece. Then he emptied the pockets of his own clothes, and threw all his wet things in a heap into the scullery. After which he gathered up her sodden clothes, gently, and put them in a separate heap on the copper-top in the scullery.

It was six o'clock on the clock. His own watch had stopped. He ought to go back to the surgery. He waited, and still she did not come down. So he went to the foot of the stairs and called:

"I shall have to go."

Almost immediately he heard her coming down. She had on her best dress of black voile, and her hair was tidy, but still damp. She looked at him—and in spite of herself, smiled.

"I don't like you in those clothes," she said.

"Do I look a sight?" he answered.

They were shy of one another.

"I'll make you some tea," she said.

"No, I must go."

"Must you?" And she looked at him again with the wide, strained, doubtful eyes. And again, from the pain of his breast, he knew how he loved her. He went and bent to kiss her, gently, passionately, with his heart's painful kiss.

"And my hair smells so horrible," she murmured in distraction. "And I'm so awful, I'm so awful! Oh, no, I'm too awful." And she broke into bitter, heartbroken sobbing. "You can't want to love me, I'm horrible."

"Don't be silly, don't be silly," he said, trying to comfort her, kissing her, holding her in his arms. "I want you, I want to marry you, we're going to be married, quickly, quickly—tomorrow if I can."

But she only sobbed terribly, and cried:

"I feel awful. I feel awful. I feel I'm horrible to you."

"No, I want you, I want you," was all he answered, blindly, with that terrible intonation which frightened her almost more than her horror lest he should *not* want her.

QUESTIONS

1. In the opening sentence, Joe asks, "Mabel . . . what are you going to do with yourself?" Is that a good place to begin the story? Does the opening serve to justify why the story concludes as it does?
2. Why is Joe concerned about Mabel's future? What opportunities did she have for employment?
3. Why does Mabel attempt suicide?
4. Why is Mabel convinced that Fergusson must love her? Is her assumption unfounded?
5. Does Fergusson love Mabel? If so what sort of love does he feel? Why would he be attracted to Mabel?

6. What kind of future does a marriage between Mabel and Fergusson have? Will theirs be a happy marriage? Are they terribly mismatched?

FLANNERY O'CONNOR

A GOOD MAN IS HARD TO FIND

Flannery O'Connor (1925–1964) was born in Savannah, Georgia, but except for brief periods in her life she lived in Millidgeville, a small town in Georgia where her mother's family had resided since before the Civil War. O'Connor described the area as "a real Bible Belt," and her stories are informed by a staunch, unyielding Roman Catholicism.

At an early age O'Connor contracted lupus, a deforming and debilitating disease from which she ultimately died. As a consequence her journeys away from Millidgeville grew less and less, and she became increasingly dependent on her devoted mother. One of her passions—especially toward the end of her life—was a flock of peacocks which she bred and sold.

O'Connor wrote only two novels Wise Blood, *and* The Violent Bear It Away. *A.L. Rowse called her "probably the greatest short-story writer of our time." Her lectures were published posthumously as* Mystery and Manners, *as were a collection of her letters* The Habit of Being.

The grandmother didn't want to go to Florida. She wanted to visit some of her connections in east Tennessee and she was seizing at every chance to change Bailey's mind. Bailey was the son she lived with, her only boy. He was sitting on the edge of his chair at the table, bent over the orange sports section of the *Journal.* "Now look here, Bailey," she said, "see here, read this," and she stood with one hand on her thin hip and the other rattling the newspaper at his bald head. "Here this fellow that calls himself The Misfit is aloose from the Federal Pen and headed toward Florida and you read here what it says he did to these people. Just you read it. I wouldn't take my children in any direction with a criminal like that aloose in it. I couldn't answer to my conscience if I did."

Bailey didn't look up from his reading so she wheeled around then and faced the children's mother, a young woman in slacks, whose face was as broad and innocent as a cabbage and was tied round with a green head-kerchief that had two points on the top like rabbit's ears. She was sitting on the sofa, feeding the baby his apricots out of a jar. "The children have been to Florida before," the old lady said. "You all ought to take them somewhere else for a change so they would see different parts of the world and be broad. They never have been to east Tennessee."

The children's mother didn't seem to hear her but the eight-year-old boy, John Wesley, a stocky child with glasses, said, "If you don't want to go to Florida, why dontcha stay at home?" He and the little girl, June Star, were reading the funny papers on the floor.

"She wouldn't stay at home to be queen for a day," June Star said without raising her yellow head.

"Yes and what would you do if this fellow, The Misfit, caught you?" the grandmother asked.

"I'd smack his face," John Wesley said.

"She wouldn't stay at home for a million bucks," June Star said. "Afraid she'd miss something. She has to go everywhere we go."

"All right, Miss," the grandmother said. "Just remember that the next time you want me to curl your hair."

June Star said her hair was naturally curly.

The next morning the grandmother was the first one in the car, ready to go. She had her big black valise that looked like the head of a hippopotamus in one corner, and underneath it she was hiding a basket with Pitty Sing, the cat, in it. She didn't intend for the cat to be left alone in the house for three days because he would miss her too much and she was afraid he might brush against one of the gas burners and accidentally asphyxiate himself. Her son, Bailey, didn't like to arrive at a motel with a cat.

She sat in the middle of the back seat with John Wesley and June Star on either side of her. Bailey and the children's mother and the baby sat in the front and they left Atlanta at eight forty-five with the mileage on the car at 55890. The grandmother wrote this down because she thought it would be interesting to say how many miles they had been when they got back. It took them twenty minutes to reach the outskirts of the city.

The old lady settled herself comfortably, removing her white cotton gloves and putting them up with her purse on the shelf in front of the back window. The children's mother still had on slacks and still had her head tied up in a green kerchief, but the grandmother had on a navy blue straw sailor hat with a bunch of white violets on the brim and a navy blue dress with a small white dot in the print. Her collar and cuffs were white organdy trimmed with lace and at her neckline she had pinned a purple spray of cloth violets containing a sachet. In case of an accident, anyone seeing her dead on the highway would know at once that she was a lady.

She said she thought it was going to be a good day for driving, neither too hot nor too cold, and she cautioned Bailey that the speed limit was fifty-five miles an hour and that the patrolmen hid themselves behind billboards and small clumps of trees and sped out after you before you had a chance to slow down. She pointed out interesting details of the scenery: Stone Mountain; the blue granite that in some places came up to both sides of the highway; the brilliant red clay banks slightly streaked with purple; and the various crops that made rows of green lace-work on the ground. The trees were full of silver-white sunlight and the meanest of them sparkled. The children were reading comic magazines and their mother had gone back to sleep.

"Let's go through Georgia fast so we won't have to look at it much," John Wesley said.

"If I were a little boy," said the grandmother, "I wouldn't talk about my native state that way. Tennessee has the mountains and Georgia has the hills."

"Tennessee is just a hillbilly dumping ground," John Wesley said, "and Georgia is a lousy state too."

"You said it," June Star said.

"In my time," said the grandmother, folding her thin veined fingers, "children were more respectful of their native states and their parents and everything else. People did right then. Oh look at the cute little pickaninny!" she said and pointed to a Negro child standing in the door of a shack. "Wouldn't that make a picture, now?" she asked and they all turned and looked at the little Negro out of the back window. He waved.

"He didn't have any britches on," June said.

"He probably didn't have any," the grandmother explained. "Little niggers in the country don't have things like we do. If I could paint, I'd paint that picture," she said.

The children exchanged comic books.

The grandmother offered to hold the baby and the children's mother passed him over the front seat to her. She set him on her knee and bounced him and told him about the things they were passing. She rolled her eyes and screwed up her mouth and stuck her leathery thin face into his smooth bland one. Occasionally he gave her a faraway smile. They passed a large cotton field with five or six graves fenced in the middle of it, like a small island. "Look at the graveyard!" the grandmother said, pointing it out. "That was the old family burying ground. That belonged to the plantation."

"Where's the plantation?" John Wesley asked.

"Gone With the Wind," said the grandmother. "Ha. Ha."

When the children finished all the comic books they had brought, they opened the lunch and ate it. The grandmother ate a peanut butter sandwich and an olive and would not let the children throw the box and the paper napkins out the window. When there was nothing else to do they played a game by choosing a cloud and making the other two guess what shape it suggested. John Wesley took one the shape of a cow and June Star guessed a cow and John Wesley said, no, an automobile, and June Star said he didn't play fair, and they began to slap each other over the grandmother.

The grandmother said she would tell them a story if they would keep quiet. When she told a story, she rolled her eyes and waved her head and was very dramatic. She said once when she was a maiden lady she had been courted by a Mr. Edgar Atkins Teagarden from Jasper, Georgia. She said he was a very good-looking man and a gentleman and that he brought her a watermelon every Saturday afternoon with his initials cut in it, E. A. T. Well, one Saturday, she said, Mr. Teagarden brought the watermelon and there was nobody at home and he left it on the front porch and returned in his buggy to Jasper, but she never got the watermelon, she said, because a nigger boy ate it when he saw the initials, E. A. T.! This story tickled John Wesley's funny bone and he giggled and giggled but June Star didn't think it was any good. She said she wouldn't marry a man that just brought her a watermelon on Saturday. The grandmother said she would have done well to marry Mr. Teagarden because he was a gentleman and had bought Coca-Cola stock when it first came out and that he had died only a few years ago, a very wealthy man.

They stopped at The Tower for barbecued sandwiches. The Tower was a part stucco and part wood filling station and dance hall set in a clearing outside of Timothy. A fat man named Red Sammy Butts ran it and there were signs stuck here and there on the building and for miles up and down the highway saying, TRY RED SAMMY'S FAMOUS BARBECUE. NONE LIKE FAMOUS RED SAMMY'S! RED SAM! THE FAT BOY WITH THE HAPPY LAUGH. A VETERAN! SAMMY'S YOUR MAN!

Red Sammy was lying on the bare ground outside The Tower with his head under a truck while a gray monkey about a foot high, chained to a small chinaberry tree, chattered nearby. The monkey sprang back into the tree and got on the highest limb as soon as he saw the children jump out of the car and run toward him.

Inside, The Tower was a long dark room with a counter at one end and tables at the other and dancing space in the middle. They all sat down at a broad table next to the nickelodeon and Red Sam's wife, a tall burnt-brown woman with hair and eyes lighter than her skin, came and took their order. The children's mother put a dime in the machine and played "The Tennessee Waltz," and the grandmother said that tune always made her want to dance. She asked Bailey if he would like to dance but he only glared at her. He didn't have a naturally sunny disposition like she did and trips made him nervous. The grandmother's brown eyes were very bright. She swayed her head from side to side and pretended she was dancing in her chair. June Star said play something she could tap to so the children's mother put in another dime and played a fast number and June Star stepped out onto the dance floor and did her tap routine.

"Ain't she cute?" Red Sam's wife said, leaning over the counter. "Would you like to come be my little girl?"

"No I certainly wouldn't," June Star said. "I wouldn't live in a broken-down place like this for a million bucks!" and she ran back to the table.

"Ain't she cute?" the woman repeated, stretching her mouth politely.

"Aren't you ashamed?" hissed the grandmother.

Red Sam came in and told his wife to quit lounging on the counter and hurry with these people's order. His khaki trousers reached just to his hip bones and his stomach hung over them like a sack of meal swaying under his shirt. He came over and sat down at a table nearby and let out a combination sigh and yodel. "You can't win," he said. "You can't win," and he wiped his sweating red face off with a gray handkerchief. "These days you don't know who to trust," he said. "Ain't that the truth?"

"People are certainly not nice like they used to be," said the grandmother.

"Two fellers come in here last week," Red Sammy said, "driving a Chrysler. It was a old beat-up car but it was a good one and these boys looked all right to me. Said they worked at the mill and you know I let them fellers charge the gas they bought? Now why did I do that?"

"Because you're a good man!" the grandmother said at once.

"Yes'm, I suppose so," Red Sam said as if he were struck with the answer.

His wife brought the orders, carrying the five plates all at once without a tray, two in each hand and one balanced on her arm. "It isn't a soul in this green world of God's that you can trust," she said. "And I don't count anybody out of that, not nobody," she repeated, looking at Red Sammy.

"Did you read about that criminal, The Misfit, that's escaped?" asked the grandmother.

"I wouldn't be a bit surprised if he didn't attact this place right here," said the woman. "If he hears about it being here, I wouldn't be none surprised to see him. If he hears it's two cent in the cash register, I wouldn't be a tall surprised if he . . ."

"That'll do," Red Sam said. "Go bring these people their Co'Colas," and the woman went off to get the rest of the order.

"A good man is hard to find," Red Sammy said. "Everything is getting terrible. I remember the day you could go off and leave your screen door unlatched. Not no more."

He and the grandmother discussed better times. The old lady said that in her opinion Europe was entirely to blame for the way things were now. She said the way Europe acted you would think we were made of money and Red Sam said it was no use talking about it, she was exactly right. The children ran outside into the white sunlight and looked at the monkey in the lacy chinaberry tree. He was busy catching fleas on himself and biting each one carefully between his teeth as if it were a delicacy.

They drove off again into the hot afternoon. The grandmother took cat naps and woke up every few minutes with her own snoring. Outside of Toombsboro she woke up and recalled an old plantation that she had visited in this neighborhood once when she was a young lady. She said the house had six white columns across the front and that there was an avenue of oaks leading up to it and two little wooden trellis arbors on either side in front where you sat down with your suitor after a stroll in the garden. She recalled exactly which road to turn off to get to it. She knew that Bailey would not be willing to lose any time looking at an old house, but the more she talked about it, the more she wanted to see it once again and find out if the little twin arbors were still standing. "There was a secret panel in this house," she said craftily, not telling the truth but wishing that she were, "and the story went that all the family silver was hidden in it when Sherman came through but it was never found . . ."

"Hey!" John Wesley said. "Let's go see it! We'll find it! We'll poke all the woodwork and find it! Who lives there? Where did you turn off at? Hey Pop, can't we turn off there?"

"We never have seen a house with a secret panel!" June Star shrieked. "Let's go to the house with the secret panel! Hey, Pop, can't we go see the house with the secret panel!"

"It's not far from here, I know," the grandmother said. "It wouldn't take over twenty minutes."

Bailey was looking straight ahead. His jaw was as rigid as a horseshoe. "No," he said.

The children began to yell and scream that they wanted to see the house with the secret panel. John Wesley kicked the back of the front seat and June Star hung over her mother's shoulder and whined desperately into her ear that they never had any fun even on their vacation, and that they could never do what THEY wanted to do. The baby began to scream and John Wesley kicked the back of the seat so hard that his father could feel the blows in his kidney.

"All right!" he shouted, and drew the car to a stop at the side of the road. "Will you all shut up? Will you all just shut up for one second? If you don't shut up, we won't go anywhere."

"It would be very educational for them," the grandmother murmured.

"All right," Bailey said, "but get this: this is the only time we're going to stop for anything like this. This is the one and only time."

"The dirt road that you have to turn down is about a mile back," the grandmother directed. "I marked it when we passed."

"A dirt road," Bailey groaned.

After they had turned around and were headed toward the dirt road, the grandmother recalled other points about the house, the beautiful glass over the front doorway and the candle-lamp in the hall. John Wesley said that the secret panel was probably in the fireplace.

"You can't go inside this house," Bailey said. "You don't know who lives there."

"While you all talk to the people in front, I'll run around behind and get in a window," John Wesley suggested.

"We'll all stay in the car," his mother said.

They turned onto the dirt road and the car raced roughly along in a swirl of pink dust. The grandmother recalled the times when there were no paved roads and thirty miles was a day's journey. The dirt road was hilly and there were sudden washes in it and sharp curves on dangerous embankments. All at once they would be on a hill, looking down over the blue tops of trees for miles around, then the next minute, they would be in a red depression with the dust-coated trees looking down on them.

"This place had better turn up in a minute," Bailey said, "or I'm going to turn around."

The road looked as if no one had traveled on it in months.

"It's not much farther," the grandmother said and just as she said it, a horrible thought came to her. The thought was so embarrassing that she turned red in the face and her eyes dilated and her feet jumped up, upsetting her valise in the corner. The instant the valise moved, the newspaper top she had over the basket under it rose with a snarl and Pitty Sing, the cat, sprang onto Bailey's shoulder.

The children were thrown to the floor and their mother, clutching the baby, was thrown out the door onto the ground, the old lady was thrown into the front seat. The car turned over once and landed right-side-up in a gulch on the side of the road. Bailey remained in the driver's seat with the cat—gray-striped with a broad white face and an orange nose—clinging to his neck like a caterpillar.

As soon as the children saw they could move their arms and legs, they scrambled out of the car, shouting. "We've had an ACCIDENT!" The grandmother was curled up under the dashboard, hoping she was injured so that Bailey's wrath would not come down on her all at once. The horrible thought she had had before the accident was that the house she had remembered so vividly was not in Georgia but in Tennessee.

Bailey removed the cat from his neck with both hands and flung it out the window against the side of a pine tree. Then he got out of the car and started looking for the children's mother. She was sitting against the side of the red gutted ditch, holding the screaming baby, but she only had a cut down her face and a broken shoulder. "We've had an ACCIDENT!" the children screamed in a frenzy of delight.

"But nobody's killed," June Star said with disappointment as the grandmother limped out of the car, her hat still pinned to her head but the broken front brim standing up at a jaunty angle and the violet spray hanging off the side. They all sat down in the ditch, except the children, to recover from the shock. They were all shaking.

"Maybe a car will come along," said the children's mother hoarsely.

"I believe I have injured an organ," said the grandmother, pressing her side, but no one answered her. Bailey's teeth were clattering. He had on a yellow sport shirt with bright blue parrots designed in it and his face was as yellow as the shirt. The grandmother decided that she would not mention that the house was in Tennessee.

The road was about ten feet above and they could see only the tops of the trees on the other side of it. Behind the ditch they were sitting in there were more woods, tall and dark and deep. In a few minutes they saw a car some distance away on top of a hill, coming slowly as if the occupants were watching them. The grandmother stood up and waved both arms dramatically to attract their attention. The car continued to come on slowly, disappeared around a bend and appeared again, moving even slower, on top of the hill they had gone over. It was a big black battered hearse-like automobile. There were three men in it.

It came to a stop just over them and for some minutes, the driver looked down with a steady expressionless gaze to where they were sitting, and didn't speak. Then he turned his head and muttered something to the other two and they got out. One was a fat boy in black trousers and a red sweat shirt with a silver stallion embossed on the front of it. He moved around on the right side of them and stood staring, his mouth partly open in a kind of loose grin. The other had on khaki pants and a blue striped coat and a gray hat pulled down very low, hiding most of his face. He came around slowly on the left side. Neither spoke.

The driver got out of the car and stood by the side of it, looking down at them. He was an older man than the other two. His hair was just beginning to gray and he wore silver-rimmed spectacles that gave him a scholarly look. He had a long creased face and didn't have on any shirt or undershirt. He had on blue jeans that were too tight for him and was holding a black hat and a gun. The two boys also had guns.

"We've had an ACCIDENT!" the children screamed.

The grandmother had the peculiar feeling that the bespectacled man was someone she knew. His face was familiar to her as if she had known him all her life but she could not recall who he was. He moved away from the car and began to come down the embankment, placing his feet carefully so that he wouldn't slip. He had on tan and white shoes and no socks, and his ankles were red and thin. "Good afternoon," he said. "I see you all had you a little spill."

"We turned over twice!" said the grandmother.

"Oncet," he corrected. "We seen it happen. Try their car and see will it run, Hiram," he said quietly to the boy with the gray hat.

"What you got that gun for?" John Wesley asked. "Whatcha gonna do with that gun?"

"Lady," the man said to the children's mother, "would you mind calling them children to sit down by you? Children make me nervous. I want all you all to sit down right together there where you're at."

"What are you telling us what to do for?" June Star asked.

Behind them the line of woods gaped like a dark open mouth. "Come here," said their mother.

"Look here now," Bailey began suddenly, "we're in a predicament! We're in . . ."

The grandmother shrieked. She scrambled to her feet and stood staring. "You're The Misfit!" she said. "I recognized you at once."

"Yes'm," the man said, smiling slightly as if he were pleased in spite of himself to be known, "but it would have been better for all of you, lady, if you hadn't of reckernized me."

Bailey turned his head sharply and said something to his mother that shocked even the children. The old lady began to cry and The Misfit reddened.

"Lady," he said, "don't you get upset. Sometimes a man says things he don't mean. I don't reckon he meant to talk to you thataway."

"You wouldn't shoot a lady, would you?" the grandmother said and removed a clean handkerchief from her cuff and began to slap at her eyes with it.

The Misfit pointed the toe of his shoe into the ground and made a little hole and then covered it up again. "I would hate to have to," he said.

"Listen," the grandmother almost screamed, "I know you're a good man. You don't look a bit like you have common blood. I know you must come from nice people!"

"Yes mam," he said, "finest people in the world." When he smiled he showed a row of strong white teeth. "God never made a finer woman than my mother and my daddy's heart was pure gold," he said. The boy with the red sweat shirt had come around behind them and was standing with his gun at his hip. The Misfit squatted down on the ground. "Watch them children, Bobby Lee," he said. "You know they make me nervous." He looked at the six of them huddled together in front of him and he seemed to be embarrassed as if he couldn't think of anything to say. "Ain't a cloud in the sky," he remarked, looking up at it. "Don't see no sun but don't see no cloud neither."

"Yes, it's a beautiful day," said the grandmother. "Listen," she said, "you shouldn't call yourself The Misfit because I know you're a good man at heart. I can just look at you and tell."

"Hush!" Bailey yelled. "Hush! Everybody shut up and let me handle this!" He was squatting in the position of a runner about to sprint forward but he didn't move.

"I pre-chate that, lady," The Misfit said and drew a little circle in the ground with the butt of his gun.

"It'll take a half a hour to fix this here car," Hiram called, looking over the raised hood of it.

"Well, first you and Bobby Lee get him and that little boy to step over yonder with you," The Misfit said, pointing to Bailey and John Wesley. "The boys want to ask you something," he said to Bailey. "Would you mind stepping back in them woods there with them?"

"Listen," Bailey began, "we're in a terrible predicament. Nobody realizes what this is," and his voice cracked. His eyes were as blue and intense as the parrots in his shirt and he remained perfectly still.

The grandmother reached up to adjust her hat brim as if she were going to the woods with him but it came off in her hand. She stood staring at it and after a second she let it fall on the ground. Hiram pulled Bailey up by the arm as if he were assisting an old man. John Wesley caught hold of his father's hand and Bobby Lee followed. They went off toward the woods and just as they reached the dark edge, Bailey turned and supporting himself against a gray naked pine trunk, he shouted, "I'll be back in a minute, Mamma, wait on me!"

"Come back this instant!" his mother shrilled but they all disappeared into the woods.

"Bailey Boy!" the grandmother called in a tragic voice but she found she was looking at The Misfit squatting on the ground in front of her. "I just know you're a good man," she said desperately. "You're not a bit common!"

"Nome, I ain't a good man," The Misfit said after a second as if he had considered her statement carefully, "but I ain't the worst in the world neither. My daddy said I was different breed of dog from my brothers and sisters. 'You know,' Daddy said, 'it's some that can live their whole life out without asking about it and it's others has to know why it is, and this boy is one of the latters. He's going to be into everything!' " He put on his black hat and looked up suddenly and then away deep into the woods as if he were embarrassed again. "I'm sorry I don't have on a shirt before you ladies," he said, hunching his shoulders slightly. "We buried our clothes that we had on when we escaped and we're just making do until we can get better. We borrowed these from some folks we met," he explained.

"That's perfectly all right," the grandmother said. "Maybe Bailey has an extra shirt in his suitcase."

"I'll look and see terrectly," The Misfit said.

"Where are they taking him?" the children's mother screamed.

"Daddy was a card himself," The Misfit said. "You couldn't put anything over on him. He never got in trouble with the Authorities though. Just had the knack of handling them."

"You could be honest too if you'd only try," said the grandmother. "Think how wonderful it would be to settle down and live a comfortable life and not have to think about somebody chasing you all the time."

The Misfit kept scratching in the ground with the butt of his gun as if he were thinking about it. "Yes'm, somebody is always after you," he murmured.

The grandmother noticed how thin his shoulder blades were just behind his hat because she was standing up looking down on him. "Do you ever pray?" she asked.

He shook his head. All she saw was the black hat wiggle between his shoulder blades. "Nome," he said.

There was a pistol shot from the woods, followed closely by another. Then silence. The old lady's head jerked around. She could hear the wind move through the tree tops like a long satisfied insuck of breath. "Bailey Boy!" she called.

"I was a gospel singer for a while," The Misfit said. "I been most everything. Been in the arm service, both land and sea, at home and abroad, been twict married, been an undertaker, been with the railroads, plowed Mother Earth, been in a tornado, seen a man burnt alive oncet," and he looked up at the children's mother and the little girl who were sitting close together, their faces white and their eyes glassy; "I even seen a woman flogged," he said.

"Pray, pray," the grandmother began, "pray, pray . . ."

"I never was a bad boy that I remember of," The Misfit said in an almost dreamy voice, "but somewheres along the line I done something wrong and got sent to the penitentiary. I was buried alive," and he looked up and held her attention to him by a steady stare.

"That's when you should have started to pray," she said. "What did you do to get sent to the penitentiary that first time?"

"Turn to the right, it was a wall," The Misfit said, looking up again at the cloudless sky. "Turn to the left, it was a wall. Look up it was a ceiling, look down it was a floor. I forgot what I done, lady. I set there and set there, trying to remember what it was I done and I ain't recalled it to this day. Oncet in a while, I would think it was coming to me, but it never come."

"Maybe they put you in by mistake," the old lady said vaguely.

"Nome," he said. "It wasn't no mistake. They had the papers on me."

"You must have stolen something," she said.

The Misfit sneered slightly. "Nobody had nothing I wanted," he said. "It was a head-doctor at the penitentiary said what I had done was kill my daddy but I know that for a lie. My daddy died in nineteen ought nineteen of the epidemic flu and I never had a thing to do with it. He was buried in the Mount Hopewell Baptist churchyard and you can go there and see for yourself."

"If you would pray," the old lady said, "Jesus would help you."

"That's right," The Misfit said.

"Well then, why don't you pray?" she asked trembling with delight suddenly.

"I don't want no hep," he said. "I'm doing all right by myself."

Bobby Lee and Hiram came ambling back from the woods. Bobby Lee was dragging a yellow shirt with bright blue parrots in it.

"Throw me that shirt, Bobby Lee," The Misfit said. The shirt came flying at him and landed on his shoulder and he put it on. The grandmother couldn't name what the shirt reminded her of. "No, lady," The Misfit said while he was buttoning it up. "I found out the crime don't matter. You can do one thing or you can do another, kill a man or take a tire off his car, because sooner or later you're going to forget what it was you done and just be punished for it."

The children's mother had begun to make heaving noises as if she couldn't get her breath. "Lady," he asked, "would you and that little girl like to step off yonder with Bobby Lee and Hiram and join your husband?"

"Yes, thank you," the mother said faintly. Her left arm dangled helplessly and she was holding the baby, who had gone to sleep, in the other. "Hep that lady up, Hiram," The Misfit said as she struggled to climb out of the ditch, "and Bobby Lee, you hold onto that little girl's hand."

"I don't want to hold hands with him," June Star said. "He reminds me of a pig."

The fat boy blushed and laughed and caught her by the arm and pulled her off into the woods after Hiram and her mother.

Alone with The Misfit, the grandmother found that she had lost her voice. There was not a cloud in the sky nor any sun. There was nothing around her but woods. She wanted to tell him that he must pray. She opened and closed her mouth several times before anything came out. Finally she found herself saying, "Jesus, Jesus," meaning Jesus will help you, but the way she was saying it, it sounded as if she might be cursing.

"Yes'm," The Misfit said as if he agreed. "Jesus thrown everything off balance. It was the same case with Him as with me except He hadn't committed any crime and they could prove I had committed one because they had the papers on me. Of course," he said, "they never shown me any papers. That's why I sign myself now. I said long ago, you get you a signature and sign everything you do and keep a copy of it. Then you'll know what you done and you can hold up the crime to the punishment and see do they match and in the end you'll have something to prove you ain't been treated right. I call myself The Misfit," he said, "because I can't make what all I done wrong fit what all I gone through in punishment."

There was a piercing scream from the woods, followed closely by a pistol report. "Does it seem right to you, lady, that one is punished a heap and another ain't punished at all?"

"Jesus!" the old lady cried. "You've got good blood! I know you wouldn't shoot a lady! I know you come from nice people! Pray! Jesus, you ought not to shoot a lady. I'll give you all the money I've got!"

"Lady," The Misfit said, looking beyond her far into the woods, "there never was a body that give the undertaker a tip."

There were two more pistol reports and the grandmother raised her head like a parched old turkey hen crying for water and called, "Bailey Boy, Bailey Boy!" as if her heart would break.

"Jesus was the only One that ever raised the dead," The Misfit continued, "and He shouldn't have done it. He thrown everything off balance. If He did what He said, then it's nothing for you to do but throw away everything and follow Him, and if He didn't, then it's nothing for you to do but enjoy the few minutes you got left the best way you can—by killing somebody or burning down his house or doing some other meanness to him. No pleasure but meanness," he said and his voice had become almost a snarl.

"Maybe He didn't raise the dead," the old lady mumbled, not knowing what she was saying and feeling so dizzy that she sank down in the ditch with her legs twisted under her.

"I wasn't there so I can't say He didn't," The Misfit said. "I wisht I had of been there," he said, hitting the ground with his fist. "It ain't right I wasn't there because if I had of been there I would of known. Listen lady," he said in a high voice, "if I had of been there I would of known and I wouldn't be like I am now." His voice seemed about to crack and the grandmother's head cleared for an instant. She saw the man's face twisted close to her own as if he were going to cry and she murmured, "Why you're one of my babies. You're one of my own children!" She reached out and touched him on the shoulder. The Misfit sprang back as if a snake had bitten him and shot her three times through the chest. Then he put his gun down on the ground and took off his glasses and began to clean them.

Hiram and Bobby Lee returned from the woods and stood over the ditch, looking down at the grandmother who half sat and half lay in a puddle of blood with her legs crossed under her like a child's and her face smiling up at the cloudless sky.

Without his glasses, The Misfit's eyes were red-rimmed and pale and defenseless-looking. "Take her off and thow her where you thown the others," he said, picking up the cat that was rubbing itself against his leg.

"She was a talker, wasn't she?" Bobby Lee said, sliding down the ditch with a yodel.

"She would of been a good woman," The Misfit said, "if it had been somebody there to shoot her every minute of her life."

"Some fun!" Bobby Lee said.

"Shut up, Bobby Lee," The Misfit said. "It's no real pleasure in life."

QUESTIONS

1. What is the grandmother's goal in the story? Does she achieve her goal?
2. The Baileys seem to have strayed from their path. Do they achieve their goal?
3. Do you find the Baileys likeable or unlikeable people? Do they deserve what happens to them? Is their fate justified by their sociablity or lack of sociability? How important in making moral decisions is a person's sociability?
4. What does the Misfit mean when he says that "Jesus thrown everything off balance"?
5. What does the grandmother mean when she calls the Misfit "one of my own children"? Why does she say it? Is it merely a trick to keep the Misfit from killing her?
6. What are the moral choices we have according to the Misfit? Are the Misfits ideas crazy or do they make theological sense?

FLANNERY O'CONNOR

A REASONABLE USE OF THE UNREASONABLE

Last fall I received a letter from a student who said she would be "graciously appreciative" if I would tell her "just what enlightenment" I expected her to get from each of my stories. I suspect she had a paper to write. I wrote her back to forget about the enlightenment and just try to enjoy them. I knew that was the most unsatisfactory answer I could have given because, of course, she didn't want to enjoy them, she just wanted to figure them out.

In most English classes the short story has become a kind of literary specimen to be dissected. Every time a story of mine appears in a Freshman anthology, I have a vision of it, with its little organs laid open, like a frog in a bottle.

I realize that a certain amount of this what-is-the-significance has to go on, but I think something has gone wrong in the process when, for so many students, the story becomes simply a problem to be solved, something which you evaporate to get Instant Enlightenment.

A story really isn't any good unless it successfully resists paraphrase, unless it hangs on and expands in the mind. Properly, you analyze to enjoy, but it's equally true that to analyze with any discrimination, you have to have enjoyed already, and I think that the best reason to hear a story read is that it should stimulate that primary enjoyment.

I don't have any pretensions to being an Aeschylus or Sophocles and providing you in this story with a cathartic experience out of your mythic background, though this story I'm going to read certainly calls up a good deal of the South's mythic background, and it should elicit from you a degree of pity and terror, even though its way of being serious is a comic one. I do think, though, that like the Greeks you should know what is going to happen in this story so that any element of suspense in it will be transferred from its surface to its interior.

I would be most happy if you had already read it, happier still if you knew it well, but since experience has taught me to keep my expectations along these lines modest, I'll tell you that this is the story of a family of six which, on its way driving to Florida, gets wiped out by an escaped convict who calls himself the Misfit. The family is made up of the Grandmother and her son, Bailey, and his children, John Wesley and June Star and the baby, and there is also the cat and the children's mother. The cat is named Pitty Sing, and the Grandmother is taking him with them, hidden in a basket.

Now I think it behooves me to try to establish with you the basis on which reason operates in this story. Much of my fiction takes its character from a reasonable use of the unreasonable, though the reasonableness of my use of it may not always be apparent. The assumptions that underlie this use of it, however, are those of the central Christian mysteries. These are assumptions to which a large part of the modern audience takes exception. About this I can only say that there are perhaps other ways than my own in which this story could be read, but none other by which it could have been written. Belief, in my own case anyway, is the engine that makes perception operate.

The heroine of this story, the Grandmother, is in the most significant position life offers the Christian. She is facing death. And to all appearances she, like the rest of us, is not too well prepared for it. She would like to see the event postponed. Indefinitely.

I've talked to a number of teachers who use this story in class and who tell their students that the Grandmother is evil, that in fact, she's a witch, even down to the cat. One of these teachers told me that his students, and particularly his Southern students, resisted this interpretation with a certain bemused vigor, and he didn't understand why. I had to tell him that they resisted it because they all had grandmothers or great-aunts just like her at home, and they knew, from personal experience, that the old lady lacked comprehension, but that she had a good heart. The Southerner is usually tolerant of those weaknesses that proceed from innocence, and he knows that a taste for self-preservation can be readily combined with the missionary spirit.

This same teacher was telling his students that morally the Misfit was several cuts above the Grandmother. He had a really sentimental attachment to the Misfit. But then a prophet gone wrong is almost always more interesting than your grandmother, and you have to let people take their pleasures where they find them.

It is true that the old lady is a hypocritical old soul; her wits are no match for the Misfit's, nor is her capacity for grace equal to his; yet I think the unprejudiced reader will feel that the Grandmother has a special kind of triumph in this story which instinctively we do not allow to someone altogether bad.

I often ask myself what makes a story work, and what makes it hold up as a story, and I have decided that it is probably some action, some gesture of a character that is unlike any other in the story, one which indicates where the real heart of the story lies. This would have to be an action or a gesture which was both totally right and totally unexpected; it would have to be one that was both in character and beyond character; it would have to suggest both the world and eternity. The action or gesture I'm talking about would have to be on the anagogical level, that is, the level which has to do with the Divine life and our participation in it. It would be a gesture that transcended any neat allegory that might have been intended or any pat moral categories a reader could make. It would be a gesture which somehow made contact with mystery.

There is a point in this story where such a gesture occurs. The Grandmother is at last alone, facing the Misfit. Her head clears for an instant and she realizes, even in her limited way, that she is responsible for the man before her and joined to him by ties of kinship which have their roots deep in the mystery she has been merely prattling about so far. And at this point, she does the right thing, she makes the right gesture.

I find that students are often puzzled by what she says and does here, but I think myself that if I took out this gesture and what she says with it, I would have no story. What was left would not be worth your attention. Our age not only does not have a very sharp eye for the almost imperceptible intrusions of grace, it no longer has much feeling for the nature of the violences which precede and follow them. The devil's greatest wile, Baudelaire has said, is to convince us that he does not exist.

I suppose the reasons for the use of so much violence in modern fiction will differ with each writer who uses it, but in my own stories I have found that violence is strangely capable of returning my characters to reality and preparing them to accept their moment of grace. Their heads are so hard that almost nothing else will do the work. This idea, that reality is something to which we must be returned at considerable cost, is one which is seldom understood by the casual reader, but it is one which is implicit in the Christian view of the world.

I don't want to equate the Misfit with the devil. I prefer to think that, however unlikely this may seem, the old lady's gesture, like the mustard-seed, will grow to be a great crow-filled tree in the Misfit's heart, and will be enough of a pain to him there to turn him into the prophet he was meant to become. But that's another story.

This story has been called grotesque, but I prefer to call it literal. A good story is literal in the same sense that a child's drawing is literal. When a child draws, he doesn't intend to distort but to set down exactly what he sees, and as his gaze is direct, he sees the lines that create motion. Now the lines of motion that interest the writer are usually invisible. They are lines of spiritual motion. And in this story you should be on the lookout for such things as the action of grace in the Grandmother's soul, and not for the dead bodies.

We hear many complaints about the prevalence of violence in modern fiction, and it is always assumed that this violence is a bad thing and meant to be an end in itself. With the serious writer, violence is never an end in itself. It is the extreme situation that best reveals what we are essentially, and I believe these are times when writers are more interested in what we are essentially than in the tenor of our daily lives. Violence is a force which can be used for good or evil, and among other things taken by it is the kingdom of heaven. But regardless of what can be taken by it, the man in the violent situation reveals those qualities least dispensable in his personality, those qualities which are all he will have to take into eternity with him; and since the characters in this story are all on the verge of eternity, it is appropriate to think of what they take with them. In any case, I hope that if you consider these points in connection with the story, you will come to see it as something more than an account of a family murdered on the way to Florida.

THINGS TO THINK ABOUT

1. Does O'Connor believe that her audience will share her religious and moral "assumptions"?
2. Why does O'Connor believe the grandmother is the hero?
3. Does O'Connor believe there are different ways to interprete the story?
4. According to O'Connor, what way does the the region, religion or education of readers affect their interpretation of the story and evaluation of the characters?
5. How does O'Connor believe she makes reasonable use of the unreasonable?

5
CHARACTER

Every story has at least one character—the person or thing that performs the action of the story. Usually characters are people, but they can be animals, robots, extraterrestrial beings, ghosts or natural phenomena such as storms, earthquakes and fires.

Authors treat their characters in a variety of ways. Sometimes we learn very little about characters. In "The Obedient Dog," for example, the readers learn only that the dog is obedient, the master harsh and the thieves persistent. None of these traits makes the characters stand out as individuals, and the author does not bother to give them names. Krasicki is interested in the action, not in the characters of his tale.

Other writers are very concerned about their characters, who they are and how they act and think. Many authors talk about their characters as though the characters were real people who could act independently of their creators. In "A Conversation With My Father," Grace Paley speaks about her characters as though they were neighbors living on her block whom she could visit and talk to. Paley's characters aren't stick figures with one or two traits, but complex individuals who seem to possess personal histories and diverse motives.

The novelist E.M. Forster, one of whose stories is included in this volume, distinguished between what he called *round* and *flat characters.* The distinction is analogous to the difference between the stick figures found in cartoons and the seemingly three-dimensional portraits found in an oil painting. According to Forster the test between a flat and round character is whether a character can be summed up in a single sentence. Flat characters can be described in a few words, but round characters demand at least several sentences. Some round characters elude complete description. The characters in Paley's story are *round characters* because they can't be summarized in a single sentence. The characters in Krasicki's "The Obedient Dog" are flat characters because they can be summed up in a word or two.

There is nothing wrong with flat characters, especially in stories where the reader's attention is supposed to be focused on action. But because round characters are harder to create and control, informed readers have come to value them as particularly important assets. Characters who exhibit complexity of motivation, subtlety of action, and individuality are given particular praise.

EVALUATING CHARACTERS

Some people pride themselves on being good judges of character. They believe that in a few minutes they can tell whether someone is trustworthy or irresponsible, honest or deceptive, nice or mean. But even those who don't jump to judgment must sooner or later make evaluations of other people, deciding whom to befriend and whom to trust. Making a mistake in evaluating character can be a painful and costly error.

How do we evaluate people? Our judgments are based on several types of observations: (1) how people look, (2) what they say, (3) how they behave, (4) what others say about them, and (5) how others treat them.

Not all these observations bear the same weight. We commonly believe that people's actions speak louder than their words. Consequently, we base our judgments more on what people do than on what they say. It is frequently best to ignore gossip, but the opinions of knowledgable and trustworthy people are important in forming a sound opinion of someone's character. Thus, businesses often request references when hiring new employees. We know that looks are deceiving, and we try to base our opinions of people's character on more substantial evidence than the cut of their clothes. Nevertheless, we are all affected by gossip and superficial considerations. In forming our opinions, we try to balance all the evidence about a person.

In reading stories we use many of the same principles for judging characters. Usually characters are described. As readers, we are given information about their height, weight, hair, eyes, and clothing. Through the plot, we have a chance to observe the characters' behavior. Through dialogue, we learn what they have to say for themselves and what other characters say about them. We might not hear every word, but a good author makes sure we get all the evidence necessary to form a clear enough picture.

In addition, fiction provides us at times with two means of understanding characters which we do not possess in real life. Often an omniscient narrator will evaluate a character for us. Of greater importance, we are often told what happens in a character's mind, in his or her inner–most, unexpressed thoughts and feelings. No one in real life can look into another person's mind, but in fiction we look into people's thoughts quite frequently. Perhaps this is the reason some fictional characters seem more alive than actual people.

In "fleshing out" a character, writers usually provide us with a great deal of concrete evidence by which we can form our own independent evaluation of the characters. However, the evidence is selected to give us help in the process. For example, in V. S. Naipaul's story "Bogart," the character derives this nickname because he tries to act like the tough screen star. By the end of the story, we recognize that this toughness is an act, a self-conscious attempt to play the macho man. Our judgment of the character will be based on how he appeared and what he actually did. Moreover we begin to see that his actions were a futile attempt to live up to appearances.

DYNAMIC AND STATIC CHARACTERS

It is useful to distinguish between two other classifications of character: *dynamic* and *static characters.* Static characters do not change during the course of a story. They possess the same traits at the end as they had at the beginning. Dynamic characters, however, change in the course of the action and often are changed by the very events and conflicts they encounter. As in life, the changes do not have to be major reversals of character; indeed, changes are often subtle and, therefore, difficult to detect. Because the capacity of real people to change is often limited and slow to develop, believable characters usually change only barely. Frequently good authors will indicate in the exposition that a character has the capacity to alter.

One of the criticisms often levelled against popular fiction is that characters change too quickly and too radically. In real life we tend to be suspicious of overnight transformations—the miser who suddenly becomes philanthropic, the juvenile delinquent who in the bat of an eye becomes a Boy Scout, the hardened criminal who turns to a life of saintly good deeds. Such transformations may happen, but we expect that there will be a correspondingly momentous event which initiated such a conversion. So, too, in literature, readers tend not to believe rapid character transformations unless the author has been particularly careful in justifying and preparing such changes.

CONFLICTS AND INCONSISTENCIES

Though fictional characters sometimes seem more alive than living people, it is important to realize the difference between actual humans and fictional characters. Fictional characters can never have the complexity of real people. Some of the most vivid characters are positively flat and one dimensional. Superman and Darth Vader have their power over our imaginations because they represent extremes of goodness and evil we don't encounter in real life. Real human beings are neither so good nor so bad. They inhabit some middle ground between the purely angelic and the absolutely demonic.

Consequently, when writers try to present realistic characters, they create characters that are a mixture of conflicting traits and desires. Indeed the stories they tell are frequently about the conflicts within characters and the way characters try to resolve those conflicts. Fictional characters, like real people, often behave strangely because of their emotional conflicts. For example, we probably all know students who want both to do well in school and to have a good time. Torn between these opposing desires, they study all night before an exam after having ignored their work for weeks. The result is lower grades and less satisfying work than had they studied on a regular basis. Similarly Bogart, V. S. Naipaul's character, behaves in an odd, seemingly mysterious way. Only toward the end of the story do we recognize the conflict that has led to his odd behavior—the desire to look like a he-man and the fear of being weak and ineffectual. We understand his actions as, first, trying to prove his masculinity to himself and, second, as proving it to his neighbors. Bogart is both a sad and a frightening character.

In judging a story, we must, however, distinguish between the conflicting impulses in a character and inconsistency of behavior. We traditionally praise writers for creating characters with conflicting traits or impulses, but we criticize writers who construct inconsistent characters. How can readers tell the difference between conflicts and inconsistencies?

Inconsistencies are unexplained or unmotivated differences in behavior. The author provides no indication why a character who has behaved in one fashion suddenly switches behavior. However, in good stories writers provide evidence to indicate why a character's behavior changes. For example, in Anne Tyler's "Your Place Is Empty," a mother who has waited twelve years to visit her son hurries back home before the expected end of her visit. Is this inconsistency? No. Tyler carefully indicates how the mother has angered the son and daughter-in-law by interfering in their affairs and why the mother's own feelings of being out of place and unwanted in her son's house drive her to shorten her visit. We come to understand that her desire to feel at home is stronger than her desire to be in the home of her son. We might say that the mother's feelings have changed, that the mother has grown and developed as a character. In good stories this change does not happen simply or at once. It occurs slowly over time, and it is exhibited by a number of incidents that indicate the gradual alterations in a character's outlook and attitude. Murderers who turn into saints after one emotional experience strike sophisticated readers as "unrealistic" and "unbelievable." Rapid alterations of character are usually viewed as narrative flaws.

REALISTIC AND FANTASTIC CHARACTERS

When we say that characters are "realistic," we do not mean that their lives are "normal" or even "average." We mean only that they behave plausibly under possible conditions. For example, few Americans are married to Iranians like the wife in "Your Place Is Empty," nor do most families meet murderers on their vacation as in "A Good Man Is Hard to Find." These are not "average" experiences. Yet they do occur to people. These stories are "realistic" because the events in the story correspond to events that could possibly happen and are consistent with human nature and natural law. The test of a character's "realism" is not whether the character resembles anyone you personally know, but whether the character acts in a way consistent with human nature and with natural law.

There is another kind of character—a fantastic character who acts in ways contrary to natural law. "The Very Old Man With Enormous Wings" is a fantastic character. Literature abounds with fantastic characters. In Shakespeare's plays there are elfs, gnomes, witches, sprites, mythological monsters and fairies.

Are fantastic characters free to behave in any way they like? No. Although they are freed from the constraints of natural law, they still must conform to conventions of literature. Since the Jewbird in Bernard Malamud's story can talk at one point in the story, he must be able to talk throughout the tale. He must consistently exhibit his character traits. Moreover, the Jewbird isn't free from all natural laws, only the law that says birds cannot converse. Like other birds, he is subject to gravity, hunger, disease and death. His magical attribute of speech does not free him from the common lot of crows.

One of the most unusual senses readers have is how fantastic beings ought to behave. We have a sense that if a bird could talk and be Jewish, that he'd sound very much like Malamud's Jewbird. Fantastic characters must obey this intuitive sense of correctness. It seems right that the Incrediable Hulk is Green. But we would not accept his character if he were polka-dotted. The imagination can be stretched, but only so far.

EMPATHY, SYMPATHY, AND JUDGMENT

The reader who remains emotionally unmoved by a story has not experienced the story. The reader may have read every word, understood every sentence, but until the reader has begun to feel emotion, the reader has not truly experienced the work. In this way, reading literature is different from reading a chemistry textbook. One sort of reading stimulates the intellect; the other stimulates both the intellect and the emotions.

One of the ways we begin to transform the intellectual medium of words into an emotional experience is by *empathizing* with one or more of the characters. I have never given birth to a child, but I have been afraid of pain or what might happen to my body, and I can empathize with Jeanie's mixed emotions in "Giving Birth." When readers empathize with a character, they put themselves in the character's place. Empathy is not only a good way to begin reading, but a corrective to our prejudice. Speaking of her story "A Good Man is Hard to Find," Flannery O'Connor remarks that many Northern readers consider the grandmother to be "evil, that in fact, she's a witch." O'Connor believes that Southern readers are better able to evaluate the grandmother. Southern readers, according to O'Connor, "all have grandmothers or great-aunts just like [the grandmother in the story] at home, and they knew from personal experience, that the old lady lacked comprehension, but that she had a good heart." O'Connor suggests that viewing the fictional grandmother in relation to one's own grandmother is useful because it will help the reader empathize with the character.

But there are hazards to reading only with empathy. If we empathize with every character and event, we merely see ourselves everywhere. We turn every story into a mirror of our own experience, and in the end we distort every story by making it fit the pattern of our own lives. Although each of us shares certain traits with all other human beings, everyone is different. Readers must remember how they differ from characters and how the characters' experiences differ from their own. Differences are as important as, if not more important than, similarities.

Empathetic understanding does not mean that we do not judge characters. Understanding why the Misfit murders people does not make it all right for him to murder. Understanding why the narrator of "The Yellow Wall-Paper" is driven insane does not make her insanity less horrible or more acceptable. But it does help us to recognize that murderers and the insane do not stop being people because of their actions. On the contrary, empathy makes us understand how close these acts and conditions are to us. The rule of thumb is that one cannot truly judge until one has understood. By delaying judgment until the reader has understood the characters, the reader will make sounder, juster and better informed decisions.

THINGS TO THINK ABOUT

1. Can any reader come to a story without preconceptions that will affect the way the story is read? How does the fact that the reader is a male or female affect the way that person reads? How does one's religious orientation affect the way one reads? Can you read works translated from French, German or Russian as easily as those originally written in English? If not, what accounts for the difference? What allowances must be made for the historical and cultural difference?
2. What sorts of qualities do you look for in a friend? How do you judge people? Do you think your way of judging people is effective, correct, limiting, or undiscriminating? On what basis do you hope people judge you? How do people judge you?

IDEAS FOR ESSAYS

1. Discuss a situation in which you seriously misjudged a person's character or motives either because you (a) thought the person was good when he or she wasn't, or (b) because you thought someone was bad when the person was, in fact, motivated by good intentions. Why did you make the error in judgment? How did you come to correct your misjudgment?
2. Do you judge the actions of men and women consistently? Do you hold men and women up to different standards of behavior? If an unmarried woman gets pregnant, do you judge her more harshly than the man who impregnated her? If a woman shows fear when faced with opposition, do you judge her less harshly than when a man displays fear? How do you account for the ways you judge men and women?

CREATIVE WRITING EXERCISES

1. Try to create a sympathetic character who is as far removed from you as possible. If you're a man, make the character a woman; if you're from the country, make the person an urbanite; if you're from the South, make the person a Northerner. How far can your sympathy stretch?
2. Describe a character at three stages of the character's life. Imagine the character as a child, a young adult and in old age. How has the character changed? How has the character stayed the same?
3. Create a scene in which a character is in conflict because of opposing desires. For example, narrate a scene in which a character wishes both to date someone disliked by the character's parents and to please those parents. How does your character resolve that conflict? Does the character act wisely?

LITERARY ESSAYS

1. In "To Hell With Dying" and "A Dinner in Society," the narrators are also characters in the story. Compare these two narrators and the way they function in their stories. How are our views of the narrators modified by their actions?
2. Discuss how the comments of minor characters in "Bogart" and "Sweat" affect our judgments of the major characters. How would our response to the major characters be changed without these comments?
3. Some people have stated that bad characters are more interesting to

read about than good ones. Do you find this to be true? Support your answer with examples from the stories in this chapter.

ALICE WALKER

TO HELL WITH DYING

Alice Walker (b. 1944) served a long apprenticeship before she achieved fame with her third novel The Color Purple, *which won both the Pulitzer Prize and The American Book Award before it was made into the popular motion picture. She was educated at Spelman College in Georgia and Sarah Lawrence College in New York and worked for Head Start in Mississippi and as a social worker in New York before beginning a career teaching at such schools as Wellsley College, Yale University, and the University of California at Berkeley.*

In addition to her novels and short stories, Alice Walker is also a distinguished poet and essayist. She has written a biography for children of the great black writer Langston Hughes and has edited a collection of writings by Zora Neale Hurston.

> "To hell with dying," my father would say, "these children want Mr. Sweet!"

Mr. Sweet was a diabetic and an alcoholic and a guitar player and lived down the road from us on a neglected cotton farm. My older brothers and sisters got the most benefit from Mr. Sweet, for when they were growing up he had quite a few years ahead of him and so was capable of being called back from the brink of death any number of times—whenever the voice of my father reached him as he lay expiring. . . . "To hell with dying, man," my father would say, pushing the wife away from the bedside (in tears although she knew the death was not necessarily the last one unless Mr. Sweet really wanted it to be), "the children want Mr. Sweet!" And they did want him, for at a signal from Father they would come crowding around the bed and throw themselves on the covers and whoever was the smallest at the time would kiss him all over his wrinkled brown face and begin to tickle him so that he would laugh all down in his stomach, and his moustache which was long and sort of straggly, would shake like Spanish moss and was also that color.

Mr. Sweet had been ambitious as a boy, wanted to be a doctor or lawyer or sailor, only to find that black men fare better if they are not. Since he could be none of those things he turned to fishing as his only earnest career and playing the guitar as his only claim to doing anything extraordinarily well. His son, the only one that he and his wife, Miss Mary, had, was shiftless as the day is long and spent money as if he were trying to see the bottom of the mint, which Mr. Sweet would tell him was the clean brown palm of his hand. Miss Mary loved her "baby," however, and worked hard to get him the "li'l necessaries" of life, which turned out mostly to be women.

Mr. Sweet was a tall, thinnish man with thick kinky hair going dead white. He was dark brown, his eyes were very squinty and sort of bluish, and he chewed Brown Mule tobacco. He was constantly on the verge of being blind drunk, for he brewed his own liquor and was not in the least a stingy sort of man, and was always very melancholy and sad, though frequently when he was "feelin' good" he'd dance around the yard with us, usually keeling over just as my mother came to see what the commotion was.

Toward all of us children he was very kind, and had the grace to be shy with us, which is unusual in grown-ups. He had great respect for my mother for she never held his drunkenness against him and would let us play with him even when he was about to fall in the fireplace from drink. Although Mr. Sweet would sometimes lose complete or nearly complete control of his head and neck so that he would loll in his chair, his mind remained strangely acute and his speech not too affected. His ability to be drunk and sober at the same time made him an ideal playmate, for he was as weak as we were and we could usually best him in wrestling, all the while keeping a fairly coherent conversation going.

We never felt anything of Mr. Sweet's age when we played with him. We loved his wrinkles and would draw some on our brows to be like him, and his white hair was my special treasure and he knew it and would never come to visit us just after he had had his hair cut off at the barbershop. Once he came to our house for something, probably to see my father about fertilizer for his crops, for although he never paid the slightest attention to his crops he liked to know what things would be best to use on them if he ever did. Anyhow, he had not come with his hair since he had just had it shaved off at the barbershop. He wore a huge straw hat to keep off the sun and also to keep his head away from me. But as soon as I saw him I ran up and demanded that he take me up and kiss me, with his funny beard which smelled so strongly of tobacco. Looking forward to burying my small fingers into his woolly hair I threw away his hat only to find he had done something to his hair, that it was no longer there! I let out a squall which made my mother think that Mr. Sweet had finally dropped me in the well or something and from that day I've been wary of men in hats. However, not long after, Mr. Sweet showed up with his hair grown out and just as white and kinky and impenetrable as it ever was.

Mr. Sweet used to call me his princess, and I believed it. He made me feel pretty at five and six, and simply outrageously devastating at the blazing age of eight and a half. When he came to our house with his guitar the whole family would stop whatever they were doing to sit around him and listen to him play. He liked to play "Sweet Georgia Brown," that was what he called me sometimes, and also he liked to play "Caldonia" and all sorts of sweet, sad, wonderful songs which he sometimes made up. It was from one of these songs that I learned that he had had to marry Miss Mary when he had in fact loved somebody else (now living in Chi'-ca-go, or De-stroy, Michigan). He was not sure that Joe Lee, her "baby," was also his baby. Sometimes he would cry and that was an indication that he was about to die again. And so we would all get prepared, for we were sure to be called upon.

I was seven the first time I remember actually participating in one of Mr. Sweet's "revivals"—my parents told me I had participated before, I had been the one chosen to kiss him and tickle him long before I knew the rite of Mr. Sweet's rehabilitation. He had come to our house, it was a few years after his wife's death, and he was very sad, and also, typically, very drunk. He sat on the floor next to me and my older brother, the rest of the children were grown-up and lived elsewhere, and began to play his guitar and cry. I held his woolly head in my arms and wished I could have been old enough to have been the woman he loved so much and that I had not been lost years and years ago.

When he was leaving my mother said to us that we'd better sleep light that night for we'd probably have to go over to Mr. Sweet's before daylight. And we did. For soon after we had gone to bed one of the neighbors knocked on our door and called my father and said that Mr. Sweet was sinking fast and if he wanted to get in a word before the crossover he'd better shake a leg and get over to Mr. Sweet's house. All the neighbors knew to come to our house if something was wrong with Mr. Sweet, but they did not know how we always managed to make him well, or at least stop him from dying, when he was often so near death. As soon as we heard the cry we got up, my brother and I and my mother and father, and put on our clothes. We hurried out of the house and down the road for we were always afraid that we might someday be too late and Mr. Sweet would get tired of dallying.

When we got to the house, a very poor shack really, we found the front room full of neighbors and relatives and someone met us at the door and said that it was all very sad that old Mr. Sweet Little (for Little was his family name although we mostly ignored it) was about to kick the bucket. My parents were advised not to take my brother and me into the "death-room" seeing we were so young and all, but we were so much more accustomed to the death-room than he that we ignored him and dashed in without giving his warning a second thought. I was almost in tears, for these deaths upset me fearfully, and the thought of how much depended on me and my brother (who was such a ham most of the time) made me very nervous.

The doctor was bending over the bed and turned back to tell us for at least the tenth time in the history of my family that alas, old Mr. Sweet Little was dying and that the children had best not see the face of implacable death (I didn't know what "implacable" was, but whatever it was, Mr. Sweet was not!). My father pushed him rather abruptly out of the way saying as he always did and very loudly for he was saying it to Mr. Sweet, "To hell with dying, man, these children want Mr. Sweet!" which was my cue to throw myself upon the bed and kiss Mr. Sweet all around the whiskers and under the eyes and around the collar of his nightshirt where he smelled so strongly of all sorts of things, mostly liniment.

I was very good at bringing him around, for as soon as I saw that he was struggling to open his eyes I knew he was going to be all right and so could finish my revival sure of success. As soon as his eyes were open he would begin to smile and that way I knew that I had surely won. Once though I got a tremendous scare for he could not open his eyes and later I learned that he had had a stroke and that one side of his face was stiff and hard to get into motion. When he began to smile I could tickle him in earnest for I was sure that nothing would get in the way of his laughter, although once he began to cough so hard that he almost threw me off his stomach, but that was when I was very small, little more than a baby, and my bushy hair had gotten in his nose.

When we were sure he would listen to us we would ask him why he was in bed and when he was coming to see us again and could we play with his guitar which more than likely would be leaning against the bed. His eyes would get all misty and he would sometimes cry out loud, but we never let it embarrass us for he knew that we loved him and that we sometimes cried too for no reason. My parents would leave the room to just the three of us; Mr. Sweet, by that time, would be propped up in bed with a number of pillows behind his head and with me sitting and lying on his shoulder and along his chest. Even when he had trouble breathing he would not ask me to get down. Looking into my eyes he would shake his white head and run a scratchy old finger all around my hairline, which was rather low down nearly to my eyebrows and for which some people said I looked like a baby monkey.

My brother was very generous in all this, he let me do all the reviving—he had done it for years before I was born and so was glad to be able to pass it on to someone new. What he would do while I talked to Mr. Sweet was pretend to play the guitar, in fact pretend that he was a young version of Mr. Sweet, and it always made Mr. Sweet glad to think that someone wanted to be like him—of course we did not know this then, we played the thing by ear, and whatever he seemed to like, we did. We were desperately afraid that he was just going to take off one day and leave us.

It did not occur to us that we were doing anything special; we had not learned that death was final when it did come. We thought nothing of triumphing over it so many times, and in fact became a trifle contemptuous of people who let themselves be carried away. It did not occur to us that if our own father had been dying we could not have stopped it, that Mr. Sweet was the only person over whom we had power.

When Mr. Sweet was in his eighties I was a young lady studying away in a university many miles from home. I saw him whenever I went home, but he was never on the verge of dying that I could tell and I began to feel that my anxiety for his health and psychological well-being was unnecessary. By this time he not only had a moustache but a long flowing snow-white beard which I loved and combed and braided for hours. He was still a very heavy drinker and was like an old Chinese opium-user, very peaceful, fragile, gentle, and the only jarring note about him was his old steel guitar which he still played in the old sad, sweet, downhome blues way.

On Mr. Sweet's ninetieth birthday I was finishing my doctorate in Massachusetts and had been making arrangements to go home for several weeks' rest. That morning I got a telegram telling me that Mr. Sweet was dying again and could I please drop everything and come home. Of course I could. My dissertation could wait and my teachers would understand when I explained to them when I got back. I ran to the phone, called the airport, and within four hours I was speeding along the dusty road to Mr. Sweet's.

The house was more dilapidated than when I was last there, barely a shack; but it was overgrown with yellow roses which my family had planted many years ago. The air was heavy and sweet and very peaceful. I felt strange walking through the gate and up the old rickety steps. But the strangeness left me as I caught sight of the long white beard I loved so well flowing down the thin body over the familiar quilt coverlet. Mr. Sweet!

His eyes were closed tight and his hands, crossed over his stomach, were thin and delicate, no longer rough and scratchy. I remembered how always before I had run and jumped up on him just anywhere; now I knew he would not be able to support my weight. I looked around at my parents, and was surprised to see that my father and mother also looked old and frail. My father, his own hair very gray, leaned over the quietly sleeping old man who, incidentally, smelled still of wine and tobacco, and said as he'd done so many times, "To hell with dying, man! My daughter is home to see Mr. Sweet!" My brother had not been able to come as he was in the war in Asia. I bent down and gently stroked the closed eyes and gradually they began to open. The closed, wine-stained lips twitched a little, then parted in a warm, slightly embarrassed smile. Mr. Sweet could see me and he recognized me and his eyes looked very spry and twinkly for a moment. I put my head down on the pillow next to his and we just looked at each other for a long time. Then he began to trace my peculiar hairline with a thin, smooth finger. I closed my eyes when his finger halted above my ear (he used to rejoice at the dirt in my ears when I was little), his hand stayed cupped around my cheek. When I opened my eyes, sure I had reached him in time, his were closed.

Even at twenty-four how could I believe that I had failed? that Mr.

Sweet was really gone? He had never gone before. But when I looked up at my parents I saw that they were holding back tears. They had loved him dearly. He was like a piece of rare and delicate china which was always being saved from breaking and which finally fell. I looked long at the old face, the wrinkled forehead, the red lips, the hands that still reached out to me. Soon I felt my father pushing something cool into my hands. It was Mr. Sweet's guitar. He had asked them months before to give it to me; he had known that even if I came next time he would not be able to respond in the old way. He did not want me to feel that my trip had been for nothing.

The old guitar! I plucked the strings, hummed "Sweet Georgia Brown." The magic of Mr. Sweet lingered still in the cool steel box. Through the window I could catch the fragrant delicate scent of tender yellow roses. The man on the high old-fashioned bed with the quilt coverlet and the flowing white beard had been my first love.

QUESTIONS

1. How would you describe Mr. Sweet's character? Can you describe it in a sentence or two? Is he a round or flat character? What does the narrator mean by comparing him to "a piece of rare and delicate china"?
2. Does Mr. Sweet's character change in the course of the story?
3. How would you describe the narrator's character? Is she a round or flat character?
4. Does the narrator's character change in the course of the story?
5. What is the narrator's final attitude toward death? Is it a typical attitude?
6. How does the narrator prepare us for the final statement, "The man . . . had been my first love"?

ALICE WALKER

THE BLACK WRITER AND THE SOUTHERN EXPERIENCE

My mother tells of an incident that happened to her in the thirties during the Depression. She and my father lived in a small Georgia town and had half a dozen children. They were sharecroppers, and food, especially flour, was almost impossible to obtain. To get flour, which was distributed by the Red Cross, one had to submit vouchers signed by a local official. On the day my mother was to go into town for flour she received a large box of clothes from one of my aunts who was living in the North. The clothes were in good condition, though well worn, and my mother needed a dress, so she immediately put on one of those from the box and wore it into town. When she reached the distribution center and presented her voucher she was confronted by a white woman who looked her up and down with marked anger and envy.

"What'd you come up here for?" the woman asked.

"For some flour," said my mother, presenting her voucher.

"Humph," said the woman, looking at her more closely and with unconcealed fury. "Anybody dressed up as good as you don't need to come here *begging* for food."

"I ain't begging," said my mother; "the government is giving away flour to those that need it, and I need it. I wouldn't be here if I didn't. And these clothes I'm wearing was given to me." But the woman had already turned to the next person in line, saying over her shoulder to the white man who was behind the counter with her, "The *gall* of niggers coming in here dressed better than me!" This thought seemed to make her angrier still, and my mother, pulling three of her small children behind her and crying from humiliation, walked sadly back into the street.

"What did you and Daddy do for flour that winter?" I asked my mother.

"Well," she said, "Aunt Mandy Aikens lived down the road from us and she got plenty of flour. We had a good stand of corn so we had plenty of meal. Aunt Mandy would swap me a bucket of flour for a bucket of meal. We got by all right."

Then she added thoughtfully, "And that old woman that turned me off so short got down so bad in the end that she was walking on *two* sticks." And I knew she was thinking, though she never said it: Here I am today, my eight children healthy and grown and three of them in college and me with hardly a sick day for years. Ain't Jesus wonderful?

In this small story is revealed the condition and strength of a people. Outcasts to be used and humiliated by the larger society, the Southern black sharecropper and poor farmer clung to his own kind and to a religion that had been given to pacify him as a slave but which he soon transformed into an antidote against bitterness. Depending on one another, because they had nothing and no one else, the sharecroppers often managed to come through "all right." And when I listen to my mother tell and retell this story I find that the white woman's vindictiveness is less important than Aunt Mandy's resourceful generosity or my mother's ready stand of corn. For their lives were not about that pitiful example of Southern womanhood, but about themselves.

What the black Southern writer inherits as a natural right is a sense of *community*. Something simple but surprisingly hard, especially these days, to come by. My mother, who is a walking history of our community, tells me that when each of her children was born the midwife accepted as payment such home-grown or homemade items as a pig, a quilt, jars of canned fruits and vegetables. But there was never any question that the midwife would come when she was needed, whatever the eventual payment for her services. I consider this each time I hear of a hospital that refuses to admit a woman in labor unless she can hand over a substantial sum of money, cash.

Nor am I nostalgic, as a French philosopher once wrote, for lost poverty. I am nostalgic for the solidarity and sharing a modest existence can sometimes bring. We knew, I suppose, that we were poor. Somebody knew; perhaps the landowner who grudgingly paid my father three hundred dollars a year for twelve months' labor. But we never considered ourselves to be poor, unless, of course, we were deliberately humiliated. And because we never believed we were poor, and therefore worthless, we could depend on one another without shame. And always there were the Burial Societies, the Sick-and-Shut-in Societies, that sprang up out of spontaneous need. And no one seemed terribly upset that black sharecroppers were ignored by white insurance companies. It went without saying, in my mother's day, that birth and death required assistance from the community, and that the magnitude of these events was lost on outsiders.

As a college student I came to reject the Christianity of my parents, and it took me years to realize that though they had been force fed a white man's palliative, in the form of religion, they had made it into something at once simple and noble. True, even today, they can never successfully picture a God who is not white, and that is a major cruelty, but their lives testify to a greater comprehension of the teachings of Jesus than the lives of people who sincerely believe a God *must* have a color and that there can be such a phenomenon as a "white" church.

The richness of the black writer's experience in the South can be remarkable, though some people might not think so. Once, while in college, I told a white middle-aged Northerner that I hoped to be a poet. In the nicest possible language, which still made me as mad as I've ever been, he suggested that a "farmer's daughter" might not be the stuff of which poets are made. On one level, of course, he had a point. A shack with only a dozen or so books is an unlikely place to discover a young Keats. But it is narrow thinking, indeed, to believe that a Keats is the only kind of poet one would want to grow up to be. One wants to write poetry that is understood by one's people, not by the Queen of England. Of course, should she be able to profit by it too, so much the better, but since that is not likely, catering to her tastes would be a waste of time.

For the black Southern writer, coming straight out of the country, as Wright did—Natchez and Jackson are still not as citified as they like to think they are—there is the world of comparisons; between town and country, between the ugly crowding and griminess of the cities and the spacious cleanliness (which actually seems impossible to dirty) of the country. A country person finds the city confining, like a too tight dress. And always, in one's memory, there remain all the rituals of one's growing up: the warmth and vividness of Sunday worship (never mind that you never quite believed) in a little church hidden from the road, and houses set so far back into the woods that at night it is impossible for strangers to find them. The daily dramas that evolve in such a private world are pure gold. But this view of a strictly private and hidden existence, with its triumphs, failures, grotesqueries, is not nearly as valuable to the socially conscious black Southern writer as his double vision is. For not only is he in a position to see his own world, and its close community ("Homecomings" on First Sundays, barbecues to raise money to send to Africa—one of the smaller ironies—the simplicity and eerie calm of a black funeral, where the beloved one is buried way in the middle of a wood with nothing to mark the spot but perhaps a wooden cross already coming apart), but also he is capable of knowing, with remarkably silent accuracy, the people who make up the larger world that surrounds and suppresses his own.

It is a credit to a writer like Ernest J. Gaines, a black writer who writes mainly about the people he grew up with in rural Louisiana, that he can write about whites and blacks exactly as he sees them and *knows* them, instead of writing of one group as a vast malignant lump and of the other as a conglomerate of perfect virtues.

In large measure, black Southern writers owe their clarity of vision to parents who refused to diminish themselves as human beings by succumbing to racism. Our parents seemed to know that an extreme negative emotion held against other human beings for reasons they do not control can be blinding. Blindness about other human beings, especially for a writer, is equivalent to death. Because of this blindness, which is, above all, racial, the works of many Southern writers have died. Much that we read today is fast expiring.

My own slight attachment to William Faulkner was rudely broken by realizing, after reading statements he made in *Faulkner in the University,* that he believed whites superior morally to blacks; that whites had a duty (which at their convenience they would assume) to "bring blacks along" politically, since blacks, in Faulkner's opinion, were "not ready" yet to function properly in a democratic society. He also thought that a black man's intelligence is directly related to the amount of white blood he has.

For the black person coming of age in the sixties, where Martin Luther King stands against the murderers of Goodman, Chaney, and Schwerner, there appears no basis for such assumptions. Nor was there any in Garvey's day, or in Du Bois's or in Douglass's or in Nat Turner's. Nor at any other period in our history, from the very founding of the country; for it was hardly incumbent upon slaves to be slaves and saints too. Unlike Tolstoy, Faulkner was not prepared to struggle to change the structure of the society he was born in. One might concede that in his fiction he did seek to examine the reasons for its decay, but unfortunately, as I have learned while trying to teach Faulkner to black students, it is not possible, from so short a range, to separate the man from his works.

One reads Faulkner knowing that his "colored" people had to come through "Mr. William's" back door, and one feels uneasy, and finally enraged that Faulkner did not burn the whole house down. When the provincial mind starts out *and continues* on a narrow and unprotesting course, "genius" itself must run on a track.

Flannery O'Connor at least had the conviction that "reality" is at best superficial and that the puzzle of humanity is less easy to solve than that of race. But Miss O'Connor was not so much of Georgia, as in it. The majority of Southern writers have been too confined by prevailing social customs to probe deeply into mysteries that the Citizens Councils insist must never be revealed.

Perhaps my Northern brothers will not believe me when I say there is a great deal of positive material I can draw from my "underprivileged" background. But they have never lived, as I have, at the end of a long road in a house that was faced by the edge of the world on one side and nobody for miles on the other. They have never experienced the magnificent quiet of a summer day when the heat is intense and one is so very thirsty, as one moves across the dusty cotton fields, that one learns forever that water is the essence of all life. In the cities it cannot be so clear to one that he is a creature of the earth, feeling the soil between the toes, smelling the dust thrown up by the rain, loving the earth so much that one longs to taste it and sometimes does.

Nor do I intend to romanticize the Southern black country life. I can recall that I hated it, generally. The hard work in the fields, the shabby houses, the evil greedy men who worked my father to death and almost broke the courage of that strong woman, my mother. No, I am simply saying that Southern black writers, like most writers, have a heritage of love and hate, but that they also have enormous richness and beauty to draw from. And, having been placed, as Camus says, "halfway between misery and the sun," they, too, know that "though all is not well under the sun, history is not everything."

No one could wish for a more advantageous heritage than that bequeathed to the black writer in the South: a compassion for the earth, a trust in humanity beyond our knowledge of evil, and an abiding love of justice. We inherit a great responsibility as well, for we must give voice to centuries not only of silent bitterness and hate but also of neighborly kindness and sustaining love.

THINGS TO THINK ABOUT

1. Walker argues that "the black Southern writer inherits as a natural right . . . a sense of *community*." Does her story "To Hell With Dying" exhibit that sense of "community"? Does Zora Neale Hurston's "Sweat" show that same sense of community? Does Baldwin's "The Rockpile"?

2. According to Walker "birth and death required assistance from the community." How does her story dramatize this theme of black Southern experience? To what extent has American society lost this sense?
3. Is educated language the only effective language for writing great literature? Was Shakespeare considered in his own day a well-educated person? Compare Walker's statements about the richness of black English to Baldwin's.
4. Are poor people not rich subjects for literature? What sorts of characters are most interesting to you? Are their race, sex, economic status or educational level important in determining their value as heroes?
5. Walker says that she "like most writers [has] a heritage of love and hate, but . . . also . . . enormous richness and beauty to draw from." List the things you have inherited; include both the positive and negative aspects of the heritage that are shaping you as a writer.

V. S. NAIPAUL

BOGART

V.S. Naipaul (b. 1932) is considered by many to be the finest writer in English to emerge from the former British colonies in the Third World. He was born in Trinidad of an Indian family and educated in Trinidad and at Oxford University in England. He has settled in England since 1950 and has adopted the manner of an Englishman. He is the brother of Shiva Naipaul, himself a distinguished writer.

Naipaul typically refuses comment on his work, asserting that "the work is there: the reader must see what meaning, if any, the work has for him." However, he insists that his nonfiction is "an integral part of my work." In addition to his novels In a Free State, A Bend in the River, *and* A House for Mr. Biswas, *he has also written* India: A Wounded Civilization *and* Among the Believers: An Islamic Journey.

Every morning when he got up Hat would sit on the banister of his back verandah and shout across, 'What happening there, Bogart?'

Bogart would turn in his bed and mumble softly, so that no one heard, 'What happening there, Hat?'

It was something of a mystery why he was called Bogart; but I suspect that it was Hat who gave him the name. I don't know if you remember the year the film *Casablanca* was made. That was the year when Bogart's fame spread like fire through Port of Spain and hundreds of young men began adopting the hardboiled Bogartian attitude.

Before they called him Bogart they called him Patience, because he played that game from morn till night. Yet he never liked cards.

Whenever you went over to Bogart's little room you found him sitting on his bed with the cards in seven lines on a small table in front of him.

'What happening there, man?' he would ask quietly, and then he would say nothing for ten or fifteen minutes. And somehow you felt you couldn't really talk to Bogart, he looked so bored and superior. His eyes were small and sleepy. His face was fat and his hair was gleaming black. His arms were plump. Yet he was not a funny man. He did everything with a captivating languor. Even when he licked his thumb to deal out the cards there was grace in it.

He was the most bored man I ever knew.

He made a pretence of making a living by tailoring, and he had even paid me some money to write a sign for him:

TAILOR AND CUTTER

Suits made to Order
Popular and Competitive Prices

He bought a sewing-machine and some blue and white and brown chalks. But I never could imagine him competing with anyone; and I cannot remember him making a suit. He was a little bit like Popo, the carpenter next door, who never made a stick of furniture, and was always planing and chiselling and making what I think he called mortises. Whenever I asked him, 'Mr Popo, what you making?' he would reply, 'Ha, boy! That's the question. I making the thing without a name.' Bogart was never even making anything like this.

Being a child, I never wondered how Bogart came by any money. I assumed that grown-ups had money as a matter of course. Popo had a wife who worked at a variety of jobs; and ended up by becoming the friend of many men. I could never think of Bogart as having mother or father; and he never brought a woman to his little room. This little room of his was called the servant-room but no servant to the people in the main house ever lived there. It was just an architectural convention.

It is still something of a miracle to me that Bogart managed to make friends. Yet he did make many friends; he was at one time quite the most popular man in the street. I used to see him squatting on the pavement with all the big men of the street. And while Hat or Edward or Eddoes was talking, Bogart would just look down and draw rings with his fingers on the pavement. He never laughed audibly. He never told a story. Yet whenever there was a fête or something like that, everybody would say, 'We must have Bogart. He smart like hell, that man.' In a way he gave them great solace and comfort, I suppose.

And so every morning, as I told you, Hat would shout, very loudly, 'What happening there, Bogart?'

And he would wait for the indeterminate grumble which was Bogart saying, 'What happening there, Hat?'

But one morning, when Hat shouted, there was no reply. Something which had appeared unalterable was missing.

Bogart had vanished; had left us without a word.

The men in the street were silent and sorrowful for two whole days.

They assembled in Bogart's little room. Hat lifted up the deck of cards that lay on Bogart's table and dropped two or three cards at a time reflectively.

Hat said, 'You think he gone Venezuela?'

But no one knew. Bogart told them so little.

And the next morning Hat got up and lit a cigarette and went to his back verandah and was on the point of shouting, when he remembered. He milked the cows earlier than usual that morning, and the cows didn't like it.

A month passed; then another month. Bogart didn't return.

Hat and his friends began using Bogart's room as their club-house. They played *wappee* and drank rum and smoked, and sometimes brought the odd stray woman to the room. Hat was presently involved with the police for gambling and sponsoring cock-fighting; and he had to spend a lot of money to bribe his way out of trouble.

It was as if Bogart had never come to Miguel Street. And after all Bogart had been living in the street only for four years or so. He had come one day with a single suitcase, looking for a room, and he had spoken to Hat who was squatting outside his gate, smoking a cigarette and reading the cricket scores in the evening paper. Even then he hadn't said much. All he said—that was Hat's story—was, 'You know any rooms?' and Hat had led him to the next yard where there was this furnished servant-room going for eight dollars a month. He had installed himself there immediately, brought out a pack of cards, and begun playing patience.

This impressed Hat.

For the rest he had always remained a man of mystery. He became Patience.

When Hat and everybody else had forgotten or nearly forgotten Bogart, he returned. He turned up one morning just about seven and found Eddoes and a woman on his bed. The woman jumped up and screamed. Eddoes jumped up, not so much afraid as embarrassed.

Bogart said, 'Move over. I tired and I want to sleep.'

He slept until five that afternoon, and when he woke up he found his room full of the old gang. Eddoes was being very loud and noisy to cover up his embarrassment. Hat had brought a bottle of rum.

Hat said, 'What happening there, Bogart?'

And he rejoiced when he found his cue taken up. 'What happening there, Hat?'

Hat opened the bottle of rum, and shouted to Boyee to go buy a bottle of soda water.

Bogart asked, 'How the cows, Hat?'

'They all right.'

'And Boyee?'

'He all right too. Ain't you just hear me call him?'

'And Errol?'

'He all right too. But what happening, Bogart? *You* all right?'

Bogart nodded, and drank a long Madrassi shot of rum. Then another, and another; and they had presently finished the bottle.

'Don't worry.' Bogart said. 'I go buy another.'

They had never seen Bogart drink so much; they had never heard him talk so much; and they were alarmed. No one dared to ask Bogart where he had been.

Bogart said, 'You boys been keeping my room hot all the time.'

'It wasn't the same without you,' Hat replied.

But they were all worried. Bogart was hardly opening his lips when he spoke. His mouth was twisted a little, and his accent was getting slightly American.

"Sure, sure,' Bogart said, and he had got it right. He was just like an actor.

Hat wasn't sure that Bogart was drunk.

In appearance, you must know, Hat recalled Rex Harrison, and he had done his best to strengthen the resemblance. He combed his hair backwards, screwed up his eyes, and he spoke very nearly like Harrison.

'Damn it, Bogart,' Hat said, and he became very like Rex Harrison. 'You may as well tell us everything right away.'

Bogart showed his teeth and laughed in a twisted, cynical way.

'Sure I'll tell,' he said, and got up and stuck his thumbs inside his waistband. 'Sure, I'll tell everything.'

He lit a cigarette, leaned back in such a way that the smoke got into his eyes; and, squinting, he drawled out his story.

He had got a job on a ship and had gone to British Guiana. There he had deserted, and gone into the interior. He became a cowboy on the Rupununi, smuggled things (he didn't say what) into Brazil, and had gathered some girls from Brazil and taken them to Georgetown. He was running the best brothel in the town when the police treacherously took his bribes and arrested him.

'It was a high-class place,' he said, 'no bums. Judges and doctors and big shot civil servants.'

'What happen?' Eddoes asked. 'Jail?'

'How you so stupid?' Hat said. 'Jail, when the man here with we. But why you people so stupid? Why you don't let the man talk?'

But Bogart was offended, and refused to speak another word.

From then on the relationship between these men changed. Bogart became the Bogart of the films. Hat became Harrison. And the morning exchange became this:

'Bogart!'

'Shaddup, Hat!'

Bogart now became the most feared man in the street. Even Big

Foot was said to be afraid of him. Bogart drank and swore and gambled with the best. He shouted rude remarks at girls walking by themselves in the street. He bought a hat, and pulled down the brim over his eyes. He became a regular sight, standing against the high concrete fence of his yard, hands in his pockets, one foot jammed against the wall, and an eternal cigarette in his mouth.

Then he disappeared again. He was playing cards with the gang in his room, and he got up and said, 'I'm going to the latrine.'

They didn't see him for four months.

When he returned, he had grown a little fatter but he had become a little more aggressive. His accent was now pure American. To complete the imitation, he began being expansive towards children. He called out to them in the streets, and gave them money to buy gum and chocolate. He loved stroking their heads, and giving them good advice.

The third time he went away and came back he gave a great party in his room for all the children or kids, as he called them. He bought cases of Solo and Coca-Cola and Pepsi-Cola and about a bushel of cakes.

Then Sergeant Charles, the policeman who lived up Miguel Street at number forty-five, came and arrested Bogart.

'Don't act tough, Bogart,' Sergeant Charles said.

But Bogart failed to take the cue.

'What happening, man? I ain't do anything.'

Sergeant Charles told him.

There was a little stir in the papers. The charge was bigamy; but it was up to Hat to find out all the inside details that the newspapers never mention.

'You see,' Hat said on the pavement that evening, 'the man leave his first wife in Tunapuna and come to Port of Spain. They couldn't have children. He remain here feeling sad and small. He go away, find a girl in Caroni and he give she a baby. In Caroni they don't make joke about that sort of thing and Bogart had to get married to the girl.'

'But why he leave she?' Eddoes asked.

'To be a man, among we men.'

QUESTIONS

1. How does Bogart change in the course of the story? Is there any significance to his change of name from "Patience" to "Bogart"?
2. Where does Bogart get his sense of masculine identity? What is the image that Bogart tries to live up to? Why does he believe it is important to live up to that image?
3. Is Bogart's image of masculinity a reasonable one? Is it a helpful one? Is it a common one?

4. Why does Bogart leave his first wife? Why does he leave his second wife? What value does Bogart put on women?
5. What is Bogart's attitude toward children? What is his attitude toward being a father? Is there any contradiction in these attitudes?
6. How would you judge Bogart's character? Is prison a punishment for Bogart or does it confirm his masculine image?
7. Would you describe Bogart as a "realistic" character?

JOHN BARTH

AUTOBIOGRAPHY: A SELF-RECORDED FICTION

John Barth (b. 1930) was born in the sleepy town of Cambridge on Maryland's eastern shore, the scene of a number of his works including The Floating Opera, *his first novel, which established his reputation. Since then, at regular intervals, Barth has published his novels which have become increasingly difficult and experimental, questioning the conventions and procedures—indeed the very status—of fiction.*

He began as a jazz musician, studying at the Julliard School of Music, then took a degree at The Johns Hopkins University where he now teaches writing.

You who listen give me life in a manner of speaking.

I won't hold you responsible.

My first words weren't my first words. I wish I'd begun differently.

Among other things I haven't a proper name. The one I bear's misleading, if not false. I didn't choose it either.

I don't recall asking to be conceived! Neither did my parents come to think of it. Even so. Score to be settled. Children are vengeance.

I seem to've known myself from the beginning without knowing I knew; no news is good news; perhaps I'm mistaken.

Now that I reflect I'm not enjoying this life: my link with the world.

My situation appears to me as follows: I speak in a curious, detached manner, and don't necessarily hear myself. I'm grateful for small mercies. Whether anyone follows me I can't tell.

Are you there? If so I'm blind and deaf to you, or you are me, or both're both. One may be imaginary; I've had stranger ideas. I hope I'm a fiction without real hope. Where there's a voice there's a speaker.

I see I see myself as a halt narrative: first person, tiresome. Pronoun sans ante or precedent, warrant or respite. Surrogate for the substantive; contentless form, interestless principle; blind eye blinking at nothing. Who am I. A little *crise d'identité*[1] for you.

I must compose myself.

Look, I'm writing. No, listen, I'm nothing but talk; I won't last long.

[1] A *crise d'identité* is French for "identity crisis."

The odds against my conception were splendid; against my birth excellent; against my continuance favorable. Are yet. On the other hand, if my sort are permitted a certain age and growth. God help us, our life expectancy's been known to increase at an obscene rate instead of petering out. Let me squeak on long enough, I just might live forever: a word to the wise.

My beginning was comparatively interesting, believe it or not. Exposition. I was spawned not long since in an American state and born in no better. Grew in no worse. Persist in a representative. Prohibition, Depression, Radicalism, Decadence, and what have you. An eye sir for an eye. It's alleged, now, that Mother was a mere passing fancy who didn't pass quickly enough; there's evidence also that she was a mere novel device, just in style, soon to become a commonplace, to which Dad resorted one day when he found himself by himself with pointless pen. In either case she was mere, Mom; at any event Dad dallied. He has me to explain. Bear in mind, I suppose he told her. A child is not its parents, but sum of their conjoined shames. A figure of speech. Their manner of speaking. No wonder I'm heterodoxical.

Nothing lasts longer than a mood. Dad's infatuation passed; I remained. He understood, about time, that anything conceived in so unnatural and fugitive a fashion was apt to be freakish, even monstrous—and an advertisement of his folly. His second thought therefore was to destroy me before I spoke a word. He knew how these things work; he went by the book. To expose ourselves publicly is frowned upon; therefore we do it to one another in private. He me, I him; one was bound to be the case. What fathers can't forgive is that their offspring receive and sow broadcast their shortcomings. From my conception to the present moment Dad's tried to turn me off; not ardently, not consistently, not successfully so far; but persistently, persistently, with at least half a heart. How do I know? I'm his bloody mirror!

Which is to say, upon reflection I reverse and distort him. For I suspect that my true father's sentiments are the contrary of murderous. That one only imagines he begot me; mightn't he be deceived and deadly jealous? In his heart of hearts he wonders whether I mayn't after all be the get of a nobler spirit, taken by beauty past his grasp. Or else, what comes to the same thing, to me, I've a pair of dads, to match my pair of moms. How account for my contradictions except as the vices of their versus? Beneath self-contempt, I particularly scorn my fondness for paradox. I despise pessimism, narcissism, solipsism,[2] truculence, word-play, and pusillanimity, my chiefer inclinations; loathe self-loathers *ergo me;*[3] have no pity for self-pity and so am free of that sweet baseness. I doubt I am. Being me's no joke.

[2] Narcissism is the love of oneself; solipsism is the philosophical position that nothing exists but the contents of one's own mind.
[3] *Ergo me* is Latin for "therefore me."

I continued the tale of my forebears. Thus my exposure; thus my escape. This cursed me, turned me out; that, curse him, saved me; right hand slipped me through left's fingers. Unless on a third hand I somehow preserved myself. Unless unless: the mercy-killing was successful. Buzzards let us say made brunch of me betimes but couldn't stomach my voice, which persists like the Nauseous Danaid.[4] We . . . monstrosities are easilier achieved than got rid of.

In sum I'm not what either parent or I had in mind. One hoped I'd be astonishing, forceful, triumphant—heroical in other words. One dead. I myself conventional. I turn out I. Not every kid thrown to the wolves ends a hero: for each survivor, a mountain of beast-baits; for every Oedipus, a city of feebs.[5]

So much for my dramatic exposition: seems not to've worked. Here I am, Dad: Your creature! Your caricature!

Unhappily, things get clearer as we go along. I perceive that I have no body. What's less, I've been speaking of myself without delight or alternative as self-consciousness pure and sour; I declare now that even that isn't true. I'm not aware of myself at all, as far as I know. I don't think . . . I know what I'm talking about.

Well, well, being well into my life as it's been called I see well how it'll end, unless in some meaningless surprise. If anything dramatic were going to happen to make me successfuller . . . agreeabler . . . endurabler . . . it should've happened by now, we will agree. A change for the better still isn't unthinkable; miracles can be cited. But the odds against a wireless *deus ex machina*[6] aren't encouraging.

Here, a confession: Early on I too aspired to immortality. Assumed I'd be beautiful, powerful, loving, loved. At least commonplace. Anyhow human. Even the revelation of my several defects—absence of presence to name one—didn't fetch me right to despair: crippledness affords its own heroisms, does it not; heroes are typically gimpish, are they not. But your crippled hero's one thing, a bloody hero after all; your heroic cripple another, etcetcetcetcetcet. Being an ideal's warped image, my fancy's own twist figure, is what undoes me.

I wonder if I repeat myself. One-track minds may lead to their origins. Perhaps I'm still in utero,[7] hung up in my delivery; my exposition and

[4] A Danaid is one of the mythical fifty daughters of Danaus, ruler of Argus, who ordered his daughters to murder their husbands on their wedding night.

[5] Oedipus is the mythical ruler of Thebes (rhymes with "feebs") who unknowingly kills his father and marries his mother. Oedipus was left out on a hillside (exposed) when born because his father, Laïos, wished to avoid the prophecy that he would be slain by his son. Oedipus was saved by shepherds, who raised him. See Sophocles' play on the subject, pages 922–61.

[6] *Deus ex machina* literally means "god from a machine," a stage device used in Greek drama which would lower an actor, dressed up as a god, to unravel complicated plots and bring about a happy ending.

[7] *In utero* is a medical term for "in the womb."

the rest merely foreshadow what's to come, the argument for an interrupted pregnancy.

Womb, coffin, can—in any case, from my viewless viewpoint I see no point in going further. Since Dad among his other failings failed to end me when he should've, I'll turn myself off if I can this instant.

Can't. *Then if anyone hears me, speaking from here inside like a sunk submariner, and has the means to my end, I pray him do us both a kindness.*

Didn't. Very well, my ace in the hole: *Father, have mercy, I dare you! Wretched old fabricator, where's your shame? Put an end to this, for pity's sake! Now! Now!*

So. My last trump, and I blew it. Not much in the way of a climax; more a climacteric. I'm not the dramatic sort. May the end come quietly, then, without my knowing it. In the course of any breath. In the heart of any word. This one. This one.

Perhaps I'll have a posthumous cautionary value, like gibbeted corpses, pickled freaks. Self-preservation, it seems, may smell of formaldehyde.

A proper ending wouldn't spin out so.

I suppose I might have managed things to better effect, in spite of the old boy. Too late now.

Basket case. Waste.

Shake up some memorable last words at least. There seems to be time.

Nonsense. I'll mutter to the end, one word after another, string the rascals out, mad or not, heard or not, my last words will be my last words.

QUESTIONS

1. Who is the speaker? Who is the speaker's father?
2. Why does the speaker believe his father wants to kill him?
3. Why does the speaker think he has "a pair of dads"? Who would his fathers be?
4. Why can't the speaker die or end his life?
5. In what senses is the speaker a "basket case"?
6. What does this story illustrate about how we read the narrator of a story?
7. Would you describe the narrator as a "realistic" character?

MARCEL PROUST

A DINNER IN SOCIETY

One of the great ironies of modern literature is that Marcel Proust (1871–1922), a man of fragile health and delicate sensibility should have written one of the longest novels of the period. Epic in length and intention, The Remembrance of Things Past *runs to seven volumes and chronicles an entire culture.*

Proust was born in Paris to a wealthy family. His father was a doctor and his mother—to whom he was extremely attached—was Jewish. He enjoyed, however, the privileges of high society about which he wrote both lovingly and satirically in all his work. At the age of nine he developed asthma from which he suffered with increasing severity throughout his life. From his thirties on, he lived as a semi-invalid. In addition to the short pieces collected as Pleasures and Days, *he also wrote the critical work* Contre Sainte-Beuve.

> "But who, Fundanius, shared with you the pleasures of that repast? I should very much like to know."
>
> —*Horace*

I

Honoré was late. He greeted his hosts, the guests he knew, was introduced to the others, and they went in to dinner. After a few moments, a very young man sitting next to him asked him to tell him the names of the other guests and something about them. Honoré had never seen him in society before. He was very handsome. The hostess kept throwing ardent glances his way which told plainly enough why he had been invited and that he would soon become a member of her circle. He was someone with a future, Honoré felt, but without envy and with good-natured courtesy he set about complying with his request. He looked around the table. Opposite him the two guests sitting side by side pointedly ignored each other. With blundering good intention, they had been invited together and seated next to each other because they were both engaged in literary pursuits. But besides this foremost reason for hating each other, they had another more personal one. The elder, being related to M. Paul Desjardins and to M. de Vogüé (doubly hypnotized) affected a contemptuous silence toward the younger one, disciple and favorite of M. Maurice Barrès, who in his turn assumed an ironic expression intended for the other. Indeed, the ill-will of each exaggerated quite involuntarily the importance of the other, as though the chief of scoundrels were confronted with the king of imbeciles. Farther down the table a superb Spanish woman was eating ferociously. She had, without hesitating, like a sensible person, sacrificed another engagement this evening in order to advance her social career by dining in a fashionable house. And her calculations had had every chance of being successful. The snobbery of Madame Fremer was for her friends, and that of her friends for her, sort of mutual guarantee against sinking into the bourgeois class. But chance would have it on this particular evening that Madame Fremer was getting rid of a stock of people she hadn't been able to dispose of before, but whom, for one reason or another, she felt obliged to entertain, and whom she had assembled tonight pell-mell. The whole lot, it is true, was topped by a duchess, but one whom the Spanish woman already knew and from whom she could expect no further advantage. She was also exchanging exasperated glances with her husband, whose guttural tones could be heard in any gathering saying successively, with a five-minute interval between each request well filled with other occupations: "Would you present me to the *Duc?*"—"*Monsieur le Duc,* would you present me to the *Duchesse?*"—"*Madame la Duchesse,* may I present my wife?" Annoyed at losing his time this evening, he had nevertheless resigned himself to the inevitable and entered into conversation with his neighbor, the partner of his host whom Fremer had been begging his wife to invite for over a year. She had finally yielded, tucking him in between the husband of the Spanish woman and a humanist. A voracious reader, the humanist was also a voracious eater. He abounded in quotations and ructations which disgusted his table companion on the other side, a noble commoner, Madame Lenoir. Without losing any time, Madame Lenoir had turned the conversation to the victories of the Prince de Buivres in Dahomey, saying in melting tones: "Dear boy, I am so glad he is such an honor to the family!" She was, it is true, a cousin of the Buivres, and they, all younger than she, treated her with all the deference due her age, her devotion to the royal family, her immense fortune and the unfailing sterility of her three marriages. Whatever family feeling she possessed she had settled on the Buivres. She felt personally dishonored by the Buivres whose misdeeds had forced his family to have a guardian appointed for him by the court, and around her right-thinking brow and Orleanist bandeaux she wore, of course, the laurels of the Buivres who was a general. An intruder in this family, hitherto so exclusive, she had become its head and, as it were, the dowager of the family. She really felt herself exiled in modern society, was always talking wistfully of "the ancient noblemen of the old days." Her snobbery was all imagination, and was, moreover, all the imagination she had. Names rich in history and glory having a strange power over her sensibilities, she found the same disinterested delight in dining with princes as in reading the memoirs of the ancient regime. Her bonnets with their grapes were as invariable as her principles. Her eyes shone with imbecility. Her smiling face was noble, her gesticulations excessive and insignificant. Trusting in God, she displayed the same flurry of optimistic excitement on the eve of a garden party or a revolution, apparently conjuring radicalism or bad weather with the same gestures. Her neighbor, the humanist, talked to her with tiresome elegance and with a terrible gift for volubility. He quoted Horace to excuse in other people's eyes, and to poetize for himself, his gluttony and drunkenness. Invisible roses, antique yet fresh, circled Madame Lenoir's narrow forehead. But with an equable courtesy (requiring no effort on her part since it represented for her the exercise of her power and respect, so rare today, for ancient traditions) every five minutes she would turn to speak to M. Fremer's partner. The latter certainly had no reason to complain. From the other end of the table Madame Fremer accorded him the most flattering attention. She wanted him to remember this dinner for many years, and, determined not to resuscitate this kill-joy for a long time to come, she set about killing him with kindness. As for M. Fremer, working all day at his bank and in the evening dragged by his wife into society or kept at home when they themselves entertained, always ready to take a person's head off, always muzzled, he had finally acquired for all circumstances, even the most benign, an expression which was a mixture of mute irritation, sulky resignation, controlled exasperation and profound and brutish insensibility. Yet this evening his wife made the financier's countenance beam with satisfaction every time her glances and his partner's met. And although traditionally he could not endure the man, he felt a certain fugitive but sincere affection for him, not because he had been able to dazzle him with his wealth, but because of that same obscure fraternity which we feel in foreign lands at the sight of a compatriot, no matter how unbearable. M. Fremer, so violently wrenched from his habits every evening, so unjustly deprived of his well-earned repose, so cruelly uprooted, felt a bond, detested ordinarily but strong, that at last linked him to someone, drew him out, extricated him from his fierce and desperate isolation. Opposite him, Madame Fremer could see her blond beauty reflected in the eyes of all the guests. The double reputation surrounding her was a deceptive prism through which everyone tried to make out her true character. Ambitious, given to intrigue, almost an adventuress, according to the financial circles she had deserted for a more brilliant destiny, she appeared on the contrary, in the eyes of the Faubourg and the royal family who had been seduced by her superior intelligence, an angel of sweetness and virtue. And, as a matter of fact, she never forgot her more humble former friends, remembered them particularly when they were sick or in mourning, touching circumstances, and which, moreover, since at such times one does not go into society, made it impossible for them to complain of not being invited. In this way she satisfied her charitable urges and was able to shed sincere tears in the presence of relatives and priests at the bedside of the dying, little by little killing the remorse that her too frivolous life inspired in her scrupulous heart.

But the most agreeable guest was the young Duchess de D . . . , whose vivacious and clear mind, that was never perplexed or troubled, contrasted strangely with the incurable melancholy of her beautiful eyes, the pessimism of her lips, the infinite and noble lassitude of her hands. This consummate lover of life in all its forms—charity, literature, the theatre, action, friendship—bit her beautiful red lips, like despised flowers, without withering them, while they curved ever so faintly in a smile. Her eyes seemed to betray a spirit forever shipwrecked on the forlorn waters of regret. How often in the street, at the theatre, thoughtful strangers had kindled their dream at those variable stars! The duchess, her thoughts at the moment busy with the recollection of some farce she had seen, or combining a new costume, continued nevertheless, sadly twisting her resigned and pensive fingers, and casting about her those deep disconsolate glances that drowned the impressionable guests in the torrent of their melancholy. Her exquisite conversation carelessly assumed the faded and charming elegances of an outmoded skepticism. There had just been a discussion, and this person, so positive in life and who held that there could only be one way to dress, kept repeating: "But why can't one say everything, think everything? I may be right, you may also be right. How terrible, how narrow to permit only one opinion." Her mind, unlike her body, was not dressed in the latest fashion, and she would readily make fun of the symbolists and fanatics. Her mind indeed was like those charming women who are beautiful and vivacious enough to be attractive even dressed in dowdy clothes. Perhaps another form of deliberate coquetry. Certain too crude ideas would have annihilated her mind just as certain colors were a calamity to her complexion.

Honoré had given his attractive neighbor a quick sketch of the different figures, but so good-naturedly that, in spite of their profound differences, they all appeared alike, the brilliant Madame de Torreno, the witty Duchess de D . . . , the beautiful Madame Lenoir. And he had neglected the one trait they had in common, or rather the same collective folly, the same prevalent epidemic with which they were all afflicted: snobbishness. And even snobbishness, according to the nature of each, took very different forms, and it was a far cry from the imaginative and poetic snobbishness of Madame Lenoir to the all-conquering snobbishness of Madame de Torreno who was as avid as a public official bent on getting to the top. And yet the terrible woman was capable of being rehumanized. The man sitting next to her had just finished telling her how he had admired her little daughter in the Parc Monceau. Immediately she broke her indignant silence. For this obscure accountant, she felt a grateful and pure sympathy which she would perhaps have been incapable of feeling for a prince. And they were chatting together now like old friends.

Madame Fremer presided over the conversation with a visible satisfaction due to her consciousness of the high mission she was accomplishing. Accustomed to presenting noted writers to duchesses, she seemed in her own eyes a sort of all powerful Foreign Minister exercising, even over the protocol, her sovereign judgment, just as a spectator at the theatre, as he digests his dinner, looks down upon, since he judges them, actors, audience, author, the rules of dramatic art, genius. As a matter of fact, the conversation was going along smoothly enough. The moment of the dinner had been reached when the gentlemen begin to touch knees under the table with the lady next to them, or to inquire about her literary preferences, depending on education and temperament, depending above all on the lady. Thus, for a second a hitch seemed inevitable. Honoré's handsome neighbor, with the imprudence of youth, having tried to insinuate that there was perhaps in the work of Heredia more thought than was generally supposed, the guests whose mental habits he had upset assumed a surly air. But Madame Fremer quickly exclaiming: "Oh, on the contrary, they are simply admirable cameos, gorgeous enamels, faultless specimens of the goldsmith's art," animation and satisfaction reappeared on every face. A discussion on anarchists was more serious. But Madame Fremer, as though bowing resignedly to the fatality of a natural law, said slowly: "What good would it do? Rich and poor we have always with us." And all these people, the poorest among them having an income of at least a hundred thousand pounds, impressed by the truth of her remark and relieved of their scruples, emptied with beaming cheerfulness their last glass of champagne.

II

After Dinner

Honoré, feeling his head a little giddy from the mixture of wines, took his departure without saying goodbye, found his coat downstairs, and started along the Champs Elysées on foot. He was overflowing with joy. The barriers of the impossible that usually keep our desires and our dreams from entering the field of reality had been broken down, and his thoughts, excited by their own motion, circulated joyously through the unattainable.

The mysterious avenues that stretch between human beings, at whose end a sun of unsuspected joy and desolation sets every evening, beckoned him. All the people he thought of became at once irresistibly sympathetic, and one after the other he took the streets where he might hope to meet them, and if his anticipations had been realized he would have greeted the unknown or indifferent person without fear and with an agreeable thrill. The stage-set too close to him having fallen, life stretched far away before him in all the charm of its novelty and its mystery in friendly landscapes that called to him. And regret that it was only the mirage or reality of a single evening filled him with despair. He would do nothing henceforth but dine and also drink, in order to see all these beautiful things again. He only suffered from his inability immediately to reach all the scenes scattered here and there in the infinitude of the distant perspective. But at that moment he became conscious of the sound of his own voice a trifle amplified, exaggerated, which for the last quarter of an hour had been repeating: "Life is sad, how idiotic!" (This last word was emphasized by an abrupt gesture of his right arm and he noticed the brusque movement of his cane.) He said sadly to himself that these mechanically uttered words were indeed a banal translation of such visions which were, perhaps, inexpressible.

"Alas! It is probably only the intensity of my pleasure and my regret that has been multiplied a hundred-fold, while the intellectual narrator remains the same. My happiness is nervous, personal, untranslatable for others, and if at this moment I were to write, my style would have the same merits and the same faults and alas! the same mediocrity as usual!" But the sensation of physical well-being kept the thought from bothering him, served indeed as a supreme consolation by completely effacing it from his memory. He had arrived on the boulevards. People passed by him and he offered them his sympathy, sure that it was reciprocated. He felt himself to be the glorious center of their attention; he opened his overcoat to let them admire his gleaming white shirt front, so very becoming to him, the dark red carnation in his buttonhole. Thus he offered himself to the admiration of the passers-by and to their affection which he so voluptuously shared.

QUESTIONS

1. What things join all the dinner guests together?
2. How does Honoré fit into the group? Is he an outsider? On what basis does he make his evaluations of character? Is he sympathetic or unsympathetic to the dinner guests?
3. Do the political opinions of the dinner guests reflect an objective analysis of the issues or do they reflect their financial and social positions?
4. Why is Honoré so joyous after the dinner? Why does he open his coat to the passersby?
5. What does Honoré mean by the words, "Life is sad, how idiotic!"?

ZORA NEALE HURSTON

SWEAT

Zora Neale Hurston (1903–1968) was one of the most controversial figures of the Harlem Renaissance, the group of black writers who congregated in the Harlem section of New York during the 1930s.

Hurston was born in Eatonville, Florida, but at sixteen she joined a travelling theatrical troupe which eventually brought her to New York. At Columbia University, she studied anthropology with Franz Boas, one of the more celebrated anthropologists of the time, and began collecting black folk material. Later she travelled to Haiti to study voodoo. She gave up on the more objective approaches of anthropology to involve herself personally in her studies.

In addition to her anthropological work, Hurston wrote a play with Langston Hughes, novels—the most important of which is Their Eyes Were Watching God*—collections of stories and folktales, and a memoir,* Dust Tracks in the Road.

It was eleven o'clock of a Spring night in Florida. It was Sunday. Any other night, Delia Jones would have been in bed for two hours by this time. But she was a washwoman, and Monday morning meant a great deal to her. So she collected the soiled clothes on Saturday when she returned the clean things. Sunday night after church, she sorted them and put the white things to soak. It saved her almost a half day's start. A great hamper in the bedroom held the clothes that she brought home. It was so much neater than a number of bundles lying around.

She squatted in the kitchen floor beside the great pile of clothes, sorting them into small heaps according to color, and humming a song in a mournful key, but wondering through it all where Sykes, her husband, had gone with her horse and buckboard.

Just then something long, round, limp and black fell upon her shoulders and slithered to the floor beside her. A great terror took hold of her. It softened her knees and dried her mouth so that it was a full minute before she could cry out or move. Then she saw that it was the big bull whip her husband liked to carry when he drove.

She lifted her eyes to the door and saw him standing there bent over with laughter at her fright. She screamed at him.

"Sykes, what you throw dat whip on me like dat? You know it would skeer me—looks just like a snake, an' you knows how skeered Ah is of snakes."

"Course Ah knowed it! That's how come Ah done it." He slapped his leg with his hand and almost rolled on the ground in his mirth. "If you such a big fool dat you got to have a fit over a earth worm or a string, Ah don't keer how bad Ah skeer you."

"You aint got no business doing it. Gawd knows it's a sin. Some day Ah'm gointuh drop dead from some of yo' foolishness. 'Nother thing, where you been wid mah rig? Ah feeds dat pony. He aint fuh you to be drivin' wid no bull whip."

"Yo sho is one aggravatin' nigger woman!" he declared and stepped into the room. She resumed her work and did not answer him at once. "Ah done tole you time and again to keep them white folks' clothes outa dis house."

He picked up the whip and glared down at her. Delia went on with her work. She went out into the yard and returned with a galvanized tub and set it on the washbench. She saw that Sykes had kicked all of the clothes together again, and now stood in her way truculently, his whole manner hoping, *praying*, for an argument. But she walked calmly around him and commenced to re-sort the things.

"Next time, Ah'm gointer to kick 'em outdoors," he threatened as he struck a match along the leg of his corduroy breeches.

Delia never looked up from her work, and her thin, stooped shoulders sagged further.

"Ah aint for no fuss t'night Sykes. Ah just come from taking sacrament at the church house."

He snorted scornfully. "Yeah, you just come from de church house on a Sunday night, but heah you is gone to work on them clothes. You ain't nothing but a hypocrite. One of them amen-corner Christians—sing, whoop, shout, then come home and wash white folks clothes on the Sabbath."

He stepped roughly upon the whitest pile of things, kicking them helter-skelter as he crossed the room. His wife gave a little scream of dismay, and quickly gathered them together again.

"Sykes, you quit grindin' dirt into these clothes! How can Ah git through by Sat'day if Ah don't start on Sunday?"

"Ah don't keer if you never git through. Anyhow, Ah done promised Gawd and a couple of other men, Ah aint gointer have it in mah house. Don't gimme no lip neither, else Ah'll throw 'em out and put mah fist up side yo' head to boot."

Delia's habitual meekness seemed to slip from her shoulders like a blown scarf. She was on her feet; her poor little body, her bare knuckly hands bravely defying the strapping hulk before her.

"Looka heah, Sykes, you done gone too fur. Ah been married to you fur fifteen years, and Ah been takin' in washin' for fifteen years. Sweat, sweat, sweat! Work and sweat, cry and sweat, pray and sweat!

"What's that got to do with me?" he asked brutally.

"What's it got to do with you, Sykes? Mah tub of suds is filled yo' belly with vittles more times than yo' hands is filled it. Mah sweat is done paid for this house and Ah reckon Ah kin keep on sweatin' in it."

She seized the iron skillet from the stove and struck a defensive pose, which act surprised him greatly, coming from her. It cowed him and he did not strike her as he usually did.

"Naw you won't," she panted, "that ole snaggle-toothed black woman you runnin' with aint comin' heah to pile up on *mah* sweat and blood. You aint paid for nothin' on this place, and Ah'm gointer stay right heah till Ah'm toted out foot foremost."

"Well, you better quit gittin' me riled up, else they'll be totin' you out sooner than you expect. Ah'm so tired of you Ah don't know whut to do. Gawd! how Ah hates skinny wimmen!"

A little awed by this new Delia, he sidled out of the door and slammed the back gate after him. He did not say where he had gone, but she knew too well. She knew very well that he would not return until nearly daybreak also. Her work over, she went on to bed but not to sleep at once. Things had come to a pretty pass!

She lay awake, gazing upon the debris that cluttered their matrimonial trail. Not an image left standing along the way. Anything like flowers had long ago been drowned in the salty stream that had been pressed from her heart. Her tears, her sweat, her blood. She had brought love to the union and he had brought a longing for the flesh. Two months after the wedding, he had given her the first brutal beating. She had the memory of numerous trips to Orlando with all of his wages when he had returned to her penniless, even before the first year had passed. She was young and soft then, but now she thought of her knotty, muscled limbs, her harsh knuckly hands, and drew herself up into an unhappy little ball in the middle of the big feather bed. Too late now to hope for love, even if it were not Bertha it would be someone else. This case differed from the others only in that she was bolder than the others. Too late for everything except her little home. She had built it for her old days, and planted one by one the trees and flowers there. It was lovely to her, lovely.

Somehow before sleep came, she found herself saying aloud: "Oh well, whatever goes over the Devil's back, is got to come under his belly. Sometime or ruther, Sykes, like everybody else, is gointer reap his sowing." After that she was able to build a spiritual earthworks against her husband. His shells could no longer reach her. *Amen.* She went to sleep and slept until he announced his presence in bed by kicking her feet and rudely snatching the cover away.

"Gimme some kivah heah, an' git yo' damn foots over on yo' own side! Ah oughter mash you in yo' mouf fuh drawing dat skillet on me."

Delia went clear to the rail without answering him. A triumphant indifference to all that he was or did.

The week was as full of work for Delia as all other weeks, and Saturday found her behind her little pony, collecting and delivering clothes.

It was a hot, hot day near the end of July. The village men on Joe Clarke's porch even chewed cane listlessly. They did not hurl the cane-knots as usual. They let them dribble over the edge of the porch. Even conversation had collapsed under the heat.

"Heah comes Delia Jones," Jim Merchant said, as the shaggy pony came 'round the bend of the road toward them. The rusty buckboard was heaped with baskets of crisp, clean laundry.

"Yep," Joe Lindsay agreed. "Hot or col', rain or shine, jes ez reg'lar ez de weeks roll roun' Delia carries 'em an' fetches 'em on Sat'day."

"She better if she wanter eat," said Moss. "Syke Jones aint wuth de shot an' powder hit would tek tuh kill 'em. Not to *bub* he aint."

"He sho' aint," Walter Thomas chimed in. "It's too bad, too, cause she wuz a right pritty lil trick when he got huh. Ah'd uh mah'ied huh mahseff if he hadnter beat me to it."

Delia nodded briefly at the men as she drove past.

"Too much knockin' will ruin *any* 'oman. He done beat huh 'nough tuh kill three women, let 'lone change they looks," said Elijah Mosely. "How Syke kin stommuck dat big black greasy Mogul he's layin' roun' wid, gits me. Ah swear dat eight-rock couldn't kiss a sardine can Ah done thowed out de back do' 'way las' yeah."

"Aw, she's fat, thass how come. He's allus been crazy 'bout fat women," put in Merchant. "He'd a' been tied up wid one long time ago if he could a' found one tuh have him. Did Ah tell yuh 'bout him come sidlin' roun *mah* wife—bringin' her a basket uh pee-cans outa his yard fuh a present? Yes-sir, mah wife! She tol' him tuh take 'em right straight back home, cause Delia works so hard ovah dat washtub she reckon everything en de place taste lak sweat an' soapsuds. Ah jus' wisht Ah'd a' caught 'im 'roun' dere! Ah'd a' made his hips ketch on fiah down dat shell road."

"Ah know he done it, too. Ah sees 'im grinnin' at every 'oman dat passes," Walter Thomas said. "But even so, he useter eat some mighty big hunks uh humble pie tuh git dat lil' 'oman he got. She wuz ez pritty ez a speckled pup! Dat wuz fifteen yeahs ago. He useter be so skeered uh losin' huh, she could make him do some parts of a husband's duty. Dey never wuz de same in de mind."

"There oughter be a law about him," said Lindsay. "He aint fit tuh carry guts tuh a bear."

Clarke spoke for the first time. "Taint no law on earth dat kin make a man be decent if it aint in 'im. There's plenty men dat takes a wife lak dey do a joint uh sugar-cane. It's round, juicy an' sweet when dey gits it. But dey squeeze an' grind, squeeze an' grind an' wring tell dey wring every drop uh pleasure dat's in 'em out. When dey's satisfied dat dey is wrung dry, dey treats 'em jes lak dey do a cane-chew. Dey thows 'em away. Dey knows whut dey is doin' while dey is at it, an' hates theirselves fuh it but they keeps on hangin' after huh tell she's empty. Den dey hates huh fuh bein' a cane-chew an' in de way."

"We oughter take Syke an' dat stray 'oman uh his'n down in Lake Howell swamp an' lay on de rawhide till they cain't say 'Lawd a'-mussy.' He allus wuz uh ovahbearin' niggah, but since dat white 'oman from up north done teached 'im how to run a automobile, he done got too biggety to live—an' we oughter kill 'im," Old Man Anderson advised.

A grunt of approval went around the porch. But the heat was melting their civic virtue and Elijah Moseley began to bait Joe Clarke.

"Come on, Joe, git a melon outa dere an' slice it up for yo' customers. We'se all sufferin' wid de heat. De bear's done got *me!*"

"Thass right, Joe, a watermelon is jes' whut Ah needs tuh cure de eppizudicks," Walter Thomas joined forces with Moseley. "Come on dere, Joe. We all is steady customers an' you aint set us up in a long time. Ah chooses dat long, bowlegged Floridy favorite."

"A god, an' be dough. You all gimme twenty cents and slice away," Clarke retorted. "Ah needs a col' slice m'self. Heah, everybody chip in. Ah'll lend y'll mah meat knife."

The money was quickly subscribed and the huge melon brought forth. At that moment, Sykes and Bertha arrived. A determined silence fell on the porch and the melon was put away again.

Merchant snapped down the blade of his jackknife and moved toward the store door.

"Come on in, Joe, an' gimme a slab uh sow belly an' uh pound uh coffee—almost fuhgot 'twas Sat'day. Got to git on home." Most of the men left also.

Just then Delia drove past on her way home, as Sykes was ordering magnificently for Bertha. It pleased him for Delia to see.

"Git whutsoever yo' heart desires, Honey. Wait a minute, Joe. Give huh two botles uh strawberry soda-water, uh quart uh parched ground-peas, an' a block uh chewin' gum."

With all this they left the store, with Sykes reminding Bertha that this was his town and she could have it if she wanted it.

The men returned soon after they left, and held their watermelon feast. "Where did Syke Jones git dat 'oman from nohow?" Lindsay asked.

"Ovah Apopka. Guess dey musta been cleanin' out de town when she lef'. She don't look lak a thing but a hunk uh liver wid hair on it."

"Well, she sho' kin squall," Dave Carter contributed. "When she gits ready tuh laff, she jes' opens huh mouf an' latches it back tuh de las' notch. No ole grandpa alligator down in Lake Bell ain't got nothin' on huh."

Bertha had been in town three months now. Sykes was still paying her room rent at Della Lewis'—the only house in town that would have taken her in. Sykes took her frequently to Winter Park to "stomps." He still assured her that he was the swellest man in the state.

"Sho' you kin have dat lil' ole house soon's Ah kin git dat 'oman outa dere. Everything b'longs tuh me an' you sho' kin have it. Ah sho' 'bominates uh skinny 'oman. Lawdy, you sho' is got one portly shape on you! You kin git *anything* you wants. Dis is *mah* town an' you sho' kin have it."

Delia's work-worn knees crawled over the earth in Gethsemane and on the rocks of Calvary many, many times during these months. She avoided the villagers and meeting places in her efforts to be blind and deaf. But Bertha nullified this to a degree, by coming to Delia's house to call Sykes out to her at the gate.

Delia and Sykes fought all the time now with no peaceful interludes. They slept and ate in silence. Two or three times Delia had attempted a timid friendliness, but she was repulsed each time. It was plain that the breaches must remain agape.

The sun had burned July to August. The heat streamed down like a million hot arrows, smiting all things living upon the earth. Grass withered, leaves browned, snakes went blind in shedding and men and dogs went mad. Dog days!

Delia came home one day and found Sykes there before her. She wondered, but started to go on into the house without speaking, even though he was standing in the kitchen door and she must either stoop under his arm or ask him to move. He made no room for her. She noticed a soap box beside the steps, but paid no particular attention to it, knowing that he must have brought it there. As she was stooping to pass under his outstretched arm, he suddenly pushed her backward, laughingly.

"Look in de box dere Delia, Ah done brung yuh somethin'!"

She nearly fell upon the box in her stumbling, and when she saw what it held, she all but fainted outright.

"Syke! Syke, mah Gawd! You take dat rattlesnake 'way from heah! You *gottuh.* Oh, Jesus, have mussy!"

"Ah aint gut tuh do nuthin' uh de kin'—fact is Ah aint got tuh do nothin' but die. Taint no use uh you puttin' on airs makin' out lak you sceered uh dat snake—he's gointer stay right heah tell he die. He wouldn't bite me cause Ah knows how tuh handle 'im. Nohow he wouldn't risk breakin' out his fangs 'gin *yo'* skinny laigs."

"Naw, now Syke, don't keep dat thing 'roun' heah tuh skeer me tuh death. You knows Ah'm even feared uh earth worms. Thass de biggest snake Ah evah did see. Kill 'im Syke, please."

"Doan ast me tuh do nothin' fuh yuh. Goin' 'roun' tryin' to be so damn asterperious. Naw, Ah aint' gonna kill it. Ah think uh damn sight mo' uh him dan you! Dat's a nice snake an' anybody doan lak 'im kin jes' hit de grit."

The village soon heard that Sykes had the snake, and came to see and ask questions.

"How de hen-fire did you ketch dat six-foot rattler, Syke?" Thomas asked.

"He's full uh frogs so he caint hardly move, thass how Ah eased up on 'm. But Ah'm a snake charmer an' knows how tuh handle 'em. Shux, dat aint nothin'. Ah could ketch one eve'y day if Ah so wanted tuh."

"Whut he needs is a heavy hick'ry club leaned real heavy on his head. Dat's de bes 'way tuh charm a rattlesnake."

"Naw, Walt, y'll jes' don't understand dese diamon' backs lak Ah do," said Sykes in a superior tone of voice.

The village agreed with Walter, but the snake stayed on. His box remained by the kitchen door with its screen wire covering. Two or three days later it had digested its meal of frogs and literally came to life. It rattled at every movement in the kitchen or the yard. One day as Delia came down the kitchen steps she saw his chalky-white fangs curved like scimitars hung in the wire meshes. This time she did not run away with averted eyes as usual. She stood for a long time in the doorway in a red fury that grew bloodier for every second that she regarded the creature that was her torment.

That night she broached the subject as soon as Sykes sat down to the table.

"Syke, Ah wants you tuh take dat snake 'way fum heah. You done starved me an' Ah put up widcher, you done beat me an Ah took dat, but you done kilt all mah insides bringin' dat varmint heah."

Sykes poured out a saucer full of coffee and drank it deliberately before he answered her.

"A whole lot Ah keer 'bout how you feels inside uh out. Dat snake aint goin' no damn wheah till Ah gits ready fuh 'im tuh go. So fur as beatin' is concerned, yuh aint took near all dat you gointer take ef yuh stay 'roun' *me.*"

Delia pushed back her plate and got up from the table. "Ah hates you, Sykes," she said calmly. "Ah hates you tuh de same degree dat Ah useter love yuh. Ah done took an' took till mah belly is full up tuh mah neck. Dat's de reason Ah got mah letter fum de church an' moved mah membership tuh Woodbridge—so Ah don't haftuh take no sacrament wid yuh. Ah don't wantuh see yuh 'round' me atall. Lay 'roun' wid dat 'oman all yuh wants tuh, but gwan 'way fum me an' mah house. Ah hates yuh lak uh suck-egg dog."

Sykes almost let the huge wad of corn bread and collard greens he was chewing fall out of his mouth in amazement. He had a hard time whipping himself to the proper fury to try to answer Delia.

"Well, Ah'm glad you does hate me. Ah'm sho' tiahed uh you hangin' ontuh me. Ah don't want yuh. Look at yuh stringey ole neck! Yo' rawbony laigs an' arms is enough tuh cut uh man tuh death. You looks jes' lak de devvul's doll-baby tuh *me.* You cain't hate me no worse dan Ah hates you. Ah been hatin' *you* fuh years.

"Yo' ole black hide don't look lak nothin' tuh me, but uh passle uh wrinkled up rubber, wid yo' big ole yeahs flappin' on each side lak up paih uh buzzard wings. Don't think Ah'm gointuh be run 'way fum mah house neither. Ah'm goin' tuh de white folks about *you,* mah young man, de very nex' time you lay yo' han's on me. Mah cup is done run ovah." Delia said this with no signs of fear and Sykes departed from the house, threatening her, but made not the slighest move to carry out any of them.

That night he did not return at all, and the next day being Sunday, Delia was glad that she did not have to quarrel before she hitched up her pony and drove the four miles to Woodbridge.

She stayed to the night service—"love feast"—which was very warm and full of spirit. In the emotional winds her domestic trials were borne far and wide so that she sang as she drove homeward,

"Jurden water, black an' col'
Chills de body, not de soul
An' Ah wantah cross Jurden in uh calm time."

She came from the barn to the kitchen door and stopped.

"Whut's de mattah, ol' satan, you aint kickin' up yo' racket?" She addressed the snake's box. Complete silence. She went on into the house with a new hope in its birth struggles. Perhaps her threat to go to the white folks had frightened Sykes! Perhaps he was sorry! Fifteen years of misery and suppression had brought Delia to the place where she would hope *anything* that looked towards a way over or through her wall of inhibitions.

She felt in the match safe behind the stove at once for a match. There was only one there.

"Dat niggah wouldn't fetch nothin' heah tuh save his rotten neck, but he kin run thew whut Ah brings quick enough. Now he done toted off nigh on tuh haff uh box uh matches. He done had dat 'oman heah in mah house, too."

Nobody but a woman could tell how she knew this even before she struck the match. But she did and it put her into a new fury.

Presently she brought in the tubs to put the white things to soak. This time she decided she need not bring the hamper out of the bedroom; she would go in there and do the sorting. She picked up the pot-bellied lamp and went in. The room was small and the hamper stood hard by the foot of the white iron bed. She could sit and reach through the bedposts—resting as she worked.

"Ah wantah cross Jurden in uh calm time." She was singing again. The mood of the "love feast" had returned. She threw back the lid of the basket almost gaily. Then, moved by both horror and terror, she sprang back toward the door. *There lay the snake in the basket!* He moved sluggishly at first, but even as she turned round and round, jumped up and down in an insanity of fear, he began to stir vigorously. She saw him pouring his awful beauty from the basket upon the bed, then she seized the lamp and ran as fast as she could to the kitchen. The wind from the open door blew out the light and the darkness added to her terror. She sped to the darkness of the yard, slamming the door after her before she thought to set down the lamp. She did not feel safe even on the ground, so she climbed up in the hay barn.

There for an hour or more she lay sprawled upon the hay a gibbering wreck.

Finally she grew quiet, and after that, coherent thought. With this, stalked through her a cold, bloody rage. Hours of this. A period of introspection, a space of retrospection, then a mixture of both. Out of this an awful calm.

"Well, Ah done de bes' Ah could. If things aint right, Gawd knows taint mah fault."

She went to sleep—a twitchy sleep—and woke up to a faint gray sky. There was a loud hollow sound below. She peered out. Sykes was at the wood-pile, demolishing a wire-covered box.

He hurried to the kitchen door, but hung outside there some minutes before he entered, and stood some minutes more inside before he closed it after him.

The gray in the sky was spreading. Delia descended without fear now, and crouched beneath the low bedroom window. The drawn shade shut out the dawn, shut in the night. But the thin walls held back no sound.

"Dat ol' scratch is woke up now!" She mused at the tremendous whirr inside, which every woodsman knows, is one of the sound illusions. The rattler is a ventriloquist. His whirr sounds to the right, to the left, straight ahead, behind, close under foot—everywhere but where it is. Woe to him who guesses wrong unless he is prepared to hold up his end of the argument! Sometimes he strikes without rattling at all.

Inside, Sykes heard nothing until he knocked a pot lid off the stove while trying to reach the match safe in the dark. He had emptied his pockets at Bertha's.

The snake seemed to wake up under the stove and Sykes made a quick leap into the bedroom. In spite of the gin he had had, his head was clearing now.

"Mah Gawd!" he chattereed, "ef Ah could on'y strack uh light!"

The rattling ceased for a moment as he stood paralyzed. He waited. It seemed that the snake waited also.

"Oh, fuh de light! Ah thought he'd be too sick"—Sykes was muttering to himself when the whirr began again, closer, right underfoot this time. Long before this, Sykes' ability to think had been flattened down to primitive instinct and he leaped—onto the bed.

Outside Delia heard a cry that might have come from a maddened chimpanzee, a stricken gorilla. All the terror, all the horror, all the rage that man possibly could express, without a recognizable human sound.

A tremendous stir inside there, another series of animal screams, the intermittent whirr of the reptile. The shade torn violently down from the window, letting in the red dawn, a huge brown hand seizing the window stick, great dull blows upon the wooden floor punctuating the gibberish of sound long after the rattle of the snake had abruptly subsided. All this Delia could see and hear from her place beneath the window, and it made her ill. She crept over to the four-o'clocks and stretched herself on the cool earth to recover.

She lay there. "Delia, Delia!" She could hear Sykes calling in a most despairing tone as one who expected no answer. The sun crept on up, and he called. Delia could not move—her legs were gone flabby. She never moved, he called, and the sun kept rising.

"Mah Gawd!" She heard him moan, "Mah Gawd fum Heben!" She heard him stumbling about and got up from her flower-bed. The sun was growing warm. As she approached the door she heard him call out hopefully, "Delia, is dat you Ah heah?"

She saw him on his hands and knees as soon as she reached the door. He crept an inch or two toward her—all that he was able, and she saw his horribly swollen neck and his one open eye shining with hope. A surge of pity too strong to support bore her away from that eye that must, could not, fail to see the tubs. He would see the lamp. Orlando with its doctors was too far. She could scarcely reach the Chinaberry tree, where she waited in the growing heat while inside she knew the cold river was creeping up and up to extinguish that eye which must know by now that she knew.

QUESTIONS

1. What had been Delia and Sykes relationship before the action of the story?
2. How has Bertha changed the relationship between Delia and Sykes?
3. How has Sykes controlled Delia? Is his strategy successful?
4. Has Delia's "habitual meekness" been used against her? Does Delia need to use violence to gain her freedom at the end? How does Delia change in the course of the story?
5. What principle of justice is involved in Sykes's death?
6. The village men who gather on Joe Clarke's porch have no direct role in the action of the story. Why do you suppose Hurston included them in the story? What is their function? How would the story be different if the men were omitted from the story?
7. What role do white people play in "Sweat"?

6

SETTINGS: PARTICULARS OF TIME AND PLACE

The story is a journey the reader takes with the author. Two questions people ask when they travel are "Where are we going?" and "What time will we get there?" The author tries to answer these questions through the story's setting.

A common reading habit of busy people is to skip over passages of scenic description to get to the action. Some consider such passages to be "filler," put in to pad a story. The opposite is true. Nothing in a good story is there by accident. A good storyteller includes only those elements that are essential for the reader's experience. Scenic description—those particulars of time and place—are essential to the story. They both limit and extend the significance of the action and help the reader to see events clearly and vividly.

THE CONCRETENESS OF THE FICTIONAL IMAGINATION

For most writers, stories are not primarily about abstract themes such as justice, morality and love. They are about particular people acting in particular ways during a particular time. Storytellers, unlike philosophers, think in concrete terms. They hope that their particular stories will have wider significance, that readers will find in the isolated incident larger implications. But their chief concern is to make the particular events of the story as vivid as possible in the readers' minds. Writers create this sense of their imagined world by providing settings to their stories.

A setting may not be presented all at once. When we first enter a room, we do not see all the details at one glance. We see the room piecemeal, noticing details only when they seem important. In stories writers will rarely bother to give a complete description of a room. When they do, readers should be particularly attentive. More frequently, they mention only those details that are important for a reader to notice and select particulars that will give readers special insight into the place, time, psychology of the characters and themes of the story.

READING FOR SETTING

Let us see how William Faulkner sets a scene in his story "A Rose for Emily." Emily Grierson is the daughter of one of the town's most important citizens. Her father, however, left her very little money when he died, and the chivalrous mayor "invented an involved tale" to justify remitting her taxes. When a new mayor is elected, he orders her to pay, and she refuses "without comment." The city council then send a delegation to visit Miss Emily:

> A deputation waited upon her, knocked at the door through which no visitor had passed since she ceased giving china-painting lessons eight or ten years earlier. They were admitted by the old Negro into a dim hall from which a stairway mounted into still more shadow. It smelled of dust and disuse—a close, dank smell. The Negro led them into the parlor. It was furnished in heavy, leather-covered furniture. When the Negro opened the blinds of one window, they could see that the leather was cracked; and when they sat down, a faint dust rose sluggishly about their thighs, spinning with slow motes in the single sun-ray. On a tarnished gilt easel before the fireplace stood a crayon portrait of Miss Emily's father.

This passage is written from a limited third person perspective. The reader follows closely behind the delegation. First, we knock at the door, wait, and then the delegation with the reader enter into the vestibule. The black servant leads us into the front parlor. We sniff the air which has an unpleasant smell of rooms rarely opened and poorly ventilated. On entering the parlor, the reader is allowed to see the heavy, leather furniture. Such furniture is expensive, and at first all we can take in is that the room has been richly furnished. It is too dark to see anything else. But when the servant opens the windows, we recognize that this former lavishness and wealth has gone to ruin—the leather is cracked and greasy with soot. Dust balls roll around on the unclean floors. Now we are allowed to see the picture that is meant to be impressive in its large golden frame placed before the fireplace. But we notice two details that limit the intended splendor: the gold has tarnished and the picture is made of crayon, not oil. The portrait is showy, but not made from the best materials.

We can learn several things from this short passage. Miss Emily's father had in his day a certain amount of wealth, but he was not as rich as he tried to make people believe, for the room is showy rather than furnished with the finest materials. Moreover, whatever was good has been ruined by neglect and disuse. As soon as light is thrown on these possessions their decay becomes evident. In many ways the environment mirrors the people who live in it, and Miss Emily is much like her front parlor—her former gentility is cracked, decaying and gone to ruin.

But it is also important to notice what Faulkner has left out. We may have the illusion—and fiction creates illusions—that the room is vividly portrayed, but Faulkner provides the readers with only a few well-chosen details. We learn only that the room contains an easel, a crayon portrait, a fireplace, dust and cracked leather furniture. But there must also be tables, a rug, lamps, and probably a cabinet or bookcase as well. Faulkner does not give us a complete accounting. A story, after all, is not an auction catalogue. Faulkner has found the right balance, giving just enough details so that we can visualize the room and not so many details that we are bored by unnecessary information.

Each item shows us something new about Miss Emily's parlor. The furniture indicates how her world is cracked by dry rot. The dust indicates the willful neglect of the room. The guilt frame indicates the desire to be showy, and the crayon drawing shows the need to make economies. Rather than being wordy, this passage is remarkably condensed. We can see how Faulkner has used concrete detail to communicate complex ideas.

How much detail is enough? An author must give enough detail to allow the reader to see imaginatively the action taking place and to understand the action. You might wish to compare Faulkner's description of the parlor with Joseph Conrad's description of the captain's quarters in "The Secret Sharer." Conrad is very precise, accounting for every item in the room. But Conrad needs such precision because he must prepare the reader for the difficulty of hiding Leggatt in the room.

BEYOND SPACE AND TIME

Storytellers are not limited to actual places to set their stories. Stories can take place anywhere and anytime, from prehistoric eras to distant galaxies far into the future. They can take place on magical islands or in the clouds. They can even take place beyond space and time.

The fable of "The Obedient Dog" does not mention or suggest any specific time or place. The reader learns no more than it took place in a house. Is the story marred by these omissions?

The virtue of "The Obedient Dog" is the simplicity and force of its action. The story strives to be universal, that is, applicable to all places and all times. Its actions occur in the dream-like landscape of the imagination. Some critics would call the story *archetypal;* the figures in the story are basic units of experience. The dog represents "dogness," the man represent "humanness," the thieves, the eternal robbers. Franz Kafka's tale "Before the Law," possesses the same archetypal quality.

ADVICE FOR WRITERS

You have probably been told to put more concrete details into your stories and essays. Why? As we have been discussing, good writing is more than getting your readers to understand what you want them to understand. Good writing is also getting readers to experience the action of the story or the context of the idea. To experience writing, readers must be provided with objects to see, sounds to hear, odors to smell and foods to taste. The readers' senses are engaged through concrete details. But the reader should not be burdened by long lists of items. The effective writer is obliged to choose only those specifics that are necessary for the reader to gain a sense of the whole.

IDEAS FOR DISCUSSION

1. Discuss the classroom and how it is organized. What does the condition of the classroom say about the institution? For example, if the building is new, does that mean the institution is new as well? If it is ugly, does that mean the institution does not care about the comfort and aesthetic pleasure of the students? What does the condition of the classroom say about the students and the teachers? Do you take pride in your environment? Why? How?
2. How do we express ourselves through our clothing and environment? What messages are you giving by wearing the clothes that you wear? What messages are you giving by the contents and condition of your room?

IDEAS FOR ESSAYS

1. Discuss how your environment has shaped your character. If you grew up in a city, how did that urban setting affect the way you see the world? If you grew up on a farm, how did rural life affect your perspective? If you grew up in the suburbs, what aspects of suburban life have affected your development?
2. How does technology alter our experience and our character? Imagine how automobiles, telephones, computers, and television have altered your life. How would your existence be altered without these inventions?

3. Are there experiences that are "universal"? Do people across time experience the same sorts of things? What happens to the experience of marriage when the marriage is arranged and the couple has met only once or twice under formal circumstances? How would such circumstances—which are common in many cultures—effect your attitude toward marriage and family?

CREATIVE WRITING EXERCISES

1. Try to give a reader a sense of your home by choosing only a half dozen items that suggest the environment. What items would you choose? What details about those items would you emphasize?
2. Describe your hometown at three different points in its history. Describe how it looked when it was founded, at some time in its past, and as it is today. Are there any details that remain constant? What changes have occurred?
3. If you had your choice, where would you live? Describe this place whether it is real or imaginary. Avoid abstract terms like "pretty," "peaceful," or "happy." Try to use all of your five senses.
4. Describe yourself as you looked as a baby, as you might look in five years and again in thirty years.
5. Describe what you might look like if you were born of the opposite sex.

LITERARY ESSAYS

1. Two of the stories in this chapter are set in the U.S. Two are set in foreign countries, and "Before the Law" is set in an entirely metaphysical locale. Which of the settings do you find the most vivid or easiest to imagine? How can you explain this vividness?
2. In most of the stories in this chapter the setting is realistic. Explain why an author has set the story in its specific location? How would the story be less effective if set elsewhere?
3. Discuss the way that nature mirrors human action in one or more of the stories in this chapter. For example, does it rain when characters are sad? Does the sun come out when they are happy?

WILLIAM FAULKNER

A ROSE FOR EMILY

For a short time after the First World War, William Faulkner (1897–1962) earned his living by stunt flying. In the flimsy biplanes of the early twenties, flying was reckless, daring, and very modern, an activity in which one's skill was only just the equal of chance. Faulkner's writing invited the same daring and modernity.

An indifferent student, He left high school and college before completing either. He made ends meet through odd jobs and was nearly thirty by the time he published his first novel Soldiers' Pay. *Slowly, he found his way to the material he would develop in his adult life—the interlocking saga of fictional Jefferson, Mississippi in the mythical Yoknapatawpha County, a place that bore a striking resemblance to his hometown of Oxford, Mississippi. His major works include* As I Lay Dying, The Sound and the Fury, *and* The Hamlet.

Faulkner was awarded the Nobel Prize for Literature in 1949.

I

When Miss Emily Grierson died, our whole town went to her funeral: the men through a sort of respectful affection for a fallen monument, the women mostly out of curiosity to see the inside of her house, which no one save an old manservant—a combined gardener and cook—had seen in at least ten years.

It was a big, squarish frame house that had once been white, decorated with cupolas and spires, and scrolled balconies in the heavily lightsome style of the seventies, set on what had once been our most select street. But garages and cotton gins had encroached and obliterated even the august names of that neighborhood; only Miss Emily's house was left, lifting its stubborn and coquettish decay above the cotton wagons and the gasoline pumps—an eyesore among eyesores. And now Miss Emily had gone to join the representatives of those august names where they lay in the cedar-bemused cemetery among the ranked and anonymous graves of Union and Confederate soldiers who fell at the battle of Jefferson.

Alive, Miss Emily had been a tradition, a duty, and a care; a sort of hereditary obligation upon the town, dating from that day in 1894 when Colonel Sartoris, the mayor—he who fathered the edict that no Negro woman should appear on the street without an apron—remitted her taxes, the dispensation dating from the death of her father on into perpetuity. Not that Miss Emily would have accepted charity. Colonel Sartoris invented an involved tale to the effect that Miss Emily's father had loaned money to the town, which the town, as a matter of business, preferred this way of repaying. Only a man of Colonel Sartoris' generation and thought could have invented it, and only a woman could have believed it.

When the next generation, with its more modern ideas, became mayors and aldermen, this arrangement created some little dissatisfaction. On the first of the year they mailed her a tax notice. February came, and there was no reply. They wrote her a formal letter, asking her to call at the sheriff's office at her convenience. A week later the mayor wrote her himself, offering to call or to send his car for her, and received in reply a note on paper of an archaic shape, in a thin, flowing calligraphy in faded ink, to the effect that she no longer went out at all. The tax notice was also enclosed, without comment.

They called a special meeting of the Board of Aldermen. A deputation waited upon her, knocked at the door through which no visitor had passed since she ceased giving china-painting lessons eight or ten years earlier. They were admitted by the old Negro into a dim hall from which a stairway mounted into still more shadow. It smelled of dust and disuse—a close, dank smell. The Negro led them into the parlor. It was furnished in heavy, leather-covered furniture. When the Negro opened the blinds of one window, they could see that the leather was cracked; and when they sat down, a faint dust rose sluggishly about their thighs, spinning with slow motes in the single sun-ray. On a tarnished gilt easel before the fireplace stood a crayon portrait of Miss Emily's father.

They rose when she entered—a small, fat woman in black, with a thin gold chain descending to her waist and vanishing into her belt, leaning on an ebony cane with a tarnished gold head. Her skeleton was small and spare; perhaps that was why what would have been merely plumpness in another was obesity in her. She looked bloated, like a body long submerged in motionless water, and of that pallid hue. Her eyes, lost in the fatty ridges of her face, looked like two small pieces of coal pressed into a lump of dough as they moved from one face to another while the visitors stated their errand.

She did not ask them to sit. She just stood in the door and listened quietly until the spokesman came to a stumbling halt. Then they could hear the invisible watch ticking at the end of the gold chain.

Her voice was dry and cold. "I have no taxes in Jefferson. Colonel Sartoris explained it to me. Perhaps one of you can gain access to the city records and satisfy yourselves."

"But we have. We are the city authorities, Miss Emily. Didn't you get a notice from the sheriff, signed by him?"

"I received a paper, yes," Miss Emily said. "Perhaps he considers himself the sheriff . . . I have no taxes in Jefferson."

"But there is nothing on the books to show that, you see. We must go by the—"

"See Colonel Sartoris. I have no taxes in Jefferson."

"But Miss Emily—"

"See Colonel Sartoris." (Colonel Sartoris had been dead almost ten years.) "I have no taxes in Jefferson. Tobe!" The Negro appeared. "Show these gentlemen out."

II

So she vanquished them, horse and foot, just as she had vanquished their fathers thirty years before about the smell. That was two years after her father's death and a short time after her sweetheart—the one we believed would marry her—had deserted her. After her father's death she went out very little; after her sweetheart went away, people hardly saw her at all. A few of the ladies had the temerity to call, but were not received, and the only sign of life about the place was the Negro man—a young man then—going in and out with a market basket.

"Just as if a man—any man—could keep a kitchen properly," the ladies said; so they were not surprised when the smell developed. It was another link between the gross, teeming world and the high and mighty Griersons.

A neighbor, a woman, complained to the mayor, Judge Stevens, eighty years old.

"But what will you have me do about it, madam?" he said.

"Why, send her word to stop it," the woman said. "Isn't there a law?"

"I'm sure that won't be necessary," Judge Stevens said. "It's probably just a snake or a rat that nigger of hers killed in the yard. I'll speak to him about it."

The next day he received two more complaints, one from a man who came in diffident deprecation. "We really must do something about it, Judge. I'd be the last one in the world to bother Miss Emily, but we've got to do something." That night the Board of Aldermen met—three graybeards and one younger man, a member of the rising generation.

"It's simple enough," he said. "Send her word to have her place cleaned up. Give her a certain time to do it in, and if she don't . . ."

"Dammit, sir," Judge Stevens said, "will you accuse a lady to her face of smelling bad?"

So the next night, after midnight, four men crossed Miss Emily's lawn and slunk about the house like burglars, sniffing along the base of the brickwork and at the cellar openings while one of them performed a regular sowing motion with his hand out of a sack slung from his shoulder. They broke open the cellar door and sprinkled lime there, and in all the outbuildings. As they recrossed the lawn, a window that had been dark was lighted and Miss Emily sat in it, the light behind her, and her upright torso motionless as that of an idol. They crept quietly across the lawn and into the shadow of the locusts that lined the street. After a week or two the smell went away.

That was when people had begun to feel really sorry for her. People in our town, remembering how old lady Wyatt, her great-aunt, had gone completely crazy at last, believed that the Griersons held themselves a little too high for what they really were. None of the young men were quite good enough for Miss Emily and such. We had long thought of them as a tableau, Miss Emily a slender figure in white in the background, her father a spraddled silhouette in the foreground, his back to her and clutching a horsewhip, the two of them framed by the back-flung front door. When she got to be thirty and was still single, we were not pleased exactly, but vindicated; even with insanity in the family she wouldn't have turned down all of her chances if they had really materialized.

When her father died, it got about that the house was all that was left to her; and in a way, people were glad. At last they could pity Miss Emily. Being left alone, and a pauper, she had become humanized. Now she too would know the old thrill and the old despair of a penny more or less.

The day after his death all the ladies prepared to call at the house and offer condolence and aid, as is our custom. Miss Emily met them at the door, dressed as usual and with no trace of grief on her face. She told them that her father was not dead. She did that for three days, with the ministers calling on her, and the doctors, trying to persuade her to let them dispose of the body. Just as they were about to resort to law and force, she broke down, and they buried her father quickly.

We did not say she was crazy then. We believed she had to do that. We remembered all the young men her father had driven away, and we knew that with nothing left, she would have to cling to that which had robbed her, as people will.

III

She was sick for a long time. When we saw her again, her hair was cut short, making her look like a girl, with a vague resemblance to those angels in colored church windows—sort of tragic and serene.

The town had just let the contracts for paving the sidewalks, and in the summer after her father's death they began to work. The construction company came with niggers and mules and machinery, and a foreman named Homer Barron, a Yankee—a big, dark, ready man, with a big voice and eyes lighter than his face. The little boys would follow in groups to hear him cuss the niggers, and the niggers singing in time to the rise and fall of picks. Pretty soon he knew everybody in town. Whenever you heard a lot of laughing anywhere about the square, Homer Barron would be in the center of the group. Presently we began to see him and Miss Emily on Sunday afternoons driving in the yellow-wheeled buggy and the matched team of bays from the livery stable.

At first we were glad that Miss Emily would have an interest, because the ladies all said, "Of course a Grierson would not think seriously of a Northerner, a day laborer." But there were still others, older people, who said that even grief could not cause a real lady to forget *noblesse oblige*—without calling it *noblesse oblige.* They just said, "Poor Emily. Her kinsfolk should come to her." She had some kin in Alabama; but years ago her father had fallen out with them over the estate of old lady Wyatt, the crazy woman, and there was no communication between the two families. They had not even been represented at the funeral.

And as soon as the old people said, "Poor Emily," the whispering began. "Do you suppose it's really so?" they said to one another. "Of course it is. What else could . . ." This behind their hands; rustling of craned silk and satin behind jalousies closed upon the sun of Sunday afternoon as the thin, swift clop-clop-clop of the matched team passed: "Poor Emily."

She carried her head high enough—even when we believed that she was fallen. It was as if she demanded more than ever the recognition of her dignity as the last Grierson; as if it had wanted that touch of earthiness to reaffirm her imperviousness. Like when she bought the rat poison, the arsenic. That was over a year after they had begun to say "Poor Emily," and while the two female cousins were visiting her.

"I want some poison," she said to the druggist. She was over thirty then, still a slight woman, though thinner than usual, with cold, haughty black eyes in a face the flesh of which was strained across the temples and about the eyesockets as you imagine a lighthousekeeper's face ought to look. "I want some poison," she said.

"Yes, Miss Emily. What kind? For rats and such? I'd recom—"

"I want the best you have. I don't care what kind."

The druggist named several. "They'll kill anything up to an elephant. But what you want is—"

"Arsenic," Miss Emily said. "Is that a good one?"

"Is . . . arsenic? Yes ma'am. But what you want—"

"I want arsenic."

The druggist looked down at her. She looked back at him, erect, her face like a strained flag. "Why, of course," the druggist said. "If that's what you want. But the law requires you to tell what you are going to use it for."

Miss Emily just stared at him, her head tilted back in order to look him eye for eye, until he looked away and went and got the arsenic and wrapped it up. The Negro delivery boy brought her the package; the druggist didn't come back. When she opened the package at home there was written on the box, under the skull and bones: "For rats."

IV

So the next day we all said, "She will kill herself"; and we said it would be the best thing. When she had first begun to be seen with Homer Barron, we had said, "She will marry him." Then we said, "She will persuade him yet," because Homer himself had remarked—he liked men, and it was known that he drank with the younger men in the Elk's Club—that he was not a marrying man. Later we said, "Poor Emily," behind the jalousies as they passed on Sunday afternoon in the glittering buggy, Miss Emily with her head high and Homer Barron with his hat cocked and a cigar in his teeth, reins and whip in a yellow glove.

Then some of the ladies began to say that it was a disgrace to the town and a bad example to the young people. The men did not want to interfere, but at last the ladies forced the Baptist minister—Miss Emily's people were Episcopal—to call upon her. He would never divulge what happened during that interview, but he refused to go back again. The next Sunday they again drove about the streets, and the following day the minister's wife wrote to Miss Emily's relations in Alabama.

So she had blood-kin under her roof again and we sat back to watch developments. At first nothing happened. Then we were sure that they were to be married. We learned that Miss Emily had been to the jeweler's and ordered a man's toilet set in silver, with the letters H.B. on each piece. Two days later we learned that she had bought a complete outfit of men's clothing, including a nightshirt, and we said, "They are married." We were really glad. We were glad because the two female cousins were even more Grierson than Miss Emily had ever been.

So we were surprised when Homer Barron—the streets had been finished some time since—was gone. We were a little disappointed that there was not a public blowing-off, but we believed that he had gone on to prepare for Miss Emily's coming, or to give a chance to get rid of the cousins. (By that time it was a cabal, and we were all Miss Emily's allies to help circumvent the cousins.) Sure enough, after another week they departed. And, as we had expected all along, within three days Homer Barron was back in town. A neighbor saw the Negro man admit him at the kitchen door at dusk one evening.

And that was the last we saw of Homer Barron. And of Miss Emily for some time. The Negro man went in and out with the market basket, but the front door remained closed. Now and then we would see her at a window for a moment, as the men did that night when they sprinkled the lime, but for almost six months she did not appear on the streets. Then we knew that this was to be expected too; as if that quality of her father which had thwarted her woman's life so many times had been too virulent and too furious to die.

When we next saw Miss Emily, she had grown fat and her hair was turning gray. During the next few years it grew grayer and grayer until it attained an even pepper-and-salt iron-gray, when it ceased turning. Up to the day of her death at seventy-four it was still that vigorous iron-gray, like the hair of an active man.

From that time on her front door remained closed, save for a period of six or seven years, when she was about forty, during which she gave lessons in china-painting. She fitted up a studio in one of the downstairs rooms, where the daughters and granddaughters of Colonel Sartoris' contemporaries were sent to her with the same regularity and in the same spirit that they were sent on Sundays with a twenty-five cent piece for the collection plate. Meanwhile her taxes had been remitted.

Then the newer generation became the backbone and the spirit of the town, and the painting pupils grew up and fell away and did not send their children to her with boxes of color and tedious brushes and pictures cut from the ladies' magazines. The front door closed upon the last one and remained closed for good. When the town got free postal delivery Miss Emily alone refused to let them fasten the metal numbers above her door and attach a mailbox to it. She would not listen to them.

Daily, monthly, yearly we watched the Negro grow grayer and more stooped, going in and out with the market basket. Each December we sent her a tax notice, which would be returned by the post office a week later, unclaimed. Now and then we would see her in one of the downstairs windows—she had evidently shut up the top floor of the house—like the carven torso of an idol in a niche, looking or not looking at us, we could never tell which. Thus she passed from generation to generation—dear, inescapable, impervious, tranquil, and perverse.

And so she died. Fell ill in the house filled with dust and shadows, with only a doddering Negro man to wait on her. We did not even know she was sick; we had long since given up trying to get any information from the Negro. He talked to no one, probably not even to her, for his voice had grown harsh and rusty, as if from disuse.

She died in one of the downstairs rooms, in a heavy walnut bed with a curtain, her gray head propped on a pillow yellow and moldy with age and lack of sunlight.

V

The Negro met the first of the ladies at the front door and let them in, with their hushed, sibilant voices and their quick, curious glances, and then he disappeared. He walked right through the house and out the back and was not seen again.

The two female cousins came at once. They held the funeral on the second day, with the town coming to look at Miss Emily beneath a mass of bought flowers, with the crayon face of her father musing profoundly above the bier and the ladies sibilant and macabre; and the very old men—some in their brushed Confederate uniforms—on the porch and the lawn, talking of Miss Emily as if she had been a con temporary of theirs, believing that they had danced with her and courted her perhaps, confusing time with its mathematical progression, as the old do, to whom all the past is not a diminishing road, but, instead, a huge meadow which no winter ever quite touches, divided from them now by the narrow bottleneck of the most recent decade of years.

Already we knew that there was one room in that region above stairs which no one had seen in forty years, and which would have to be forced. They waited until Miss Emily was decently in the ground before they opened it.

The violence of breaking down the door seemed to fill this room with pervading dust. A thin, acrid pall as of the tomb seemed to lie everywhere upon this room decked and furnished as for a bridal: upon the valance curtains of faded rose color, upon the rose-shaded lights, upon the dressing table, upon the delicate array of crystal and the man's toilet things backed with tarnished silver, silver so tarnished that the monogram was obscured. Among them lay a collar and tie, as if they had just been removed, which, lifted, left upon the surface a pale crescent in the dust. Upon a chair hung the suit, carefully folded; beneath it the two mute shoes and the discarded socks.

The man himself lay in the bed.

For a long while we just stood there, looking down at the profound and fleshless grin. The body had apparently once lain in the attitude of an embrace, but now the long sleep that outlasts love, that conquers even the grimace of love, had cuckolded him. What was left of him, rotted beneath what was left of the nightshirt, had become inextricable from the bed in which he lay; and upon him and upon the pillow beside him lay that even coating of the patient and biding dust.

Then we noticed that in the second pillow was the indentation of a head. One of us lifted something from it, and leaning forward, that faint and invisible dust dry and acrid in the nostrils, we saw a long strand of iron-gray hair.

QUESTIONS

1. The narrator says that "only a man of Colonel Sartoris' generation and thought could have invented" the story for remitting Miss Emily's taxes, but that "the next generation, with its more modern ideas" found "dissatisfaction" with the arrangement. What happened between the Colonel's generation and the supposedly modern generation of his followers? Is the modern generation an advancement?
2. In what ways have "the Griersons held themselves a little too high for what they really were"? How has Miss Emily attempted to keep up appearances? How does the house reflect the desire to show power and social status? How has the house decayed with the family?
3. What is the significance of the silver toiletry set?
4. Is the narrator surprised to find the skeleton in the bed? How has the town attempted to keep up appearances?
5. In his Nobel Prize speech, Faulkner says that the only theme worth writing about is "the human heart in conflict with itself." Does this theme appear in "A Rose for Emily"?

WILLIAM FAULKNER

ADDRESS UPON RECEIVING THE NOBEL PRIZE FOR LITERATURE

Stockholm, December 10, 1950

I feel that this award was not made to me as a man, but to my work—a life's work in the agony and sweat of the human spirit, not for glory and least of all for profit, but to create out of the materials of the human spirit something which did not exist before. So this award is only mine in trust. It will not be difficult to find a dedication for the money part of it commensurate with the purpose and significance of its origin. But I would like to do the same with the acclaim too, by using this moment as a pinnacle from which I might be listened to by the young men and women already dedicated to the same anguish and travail, among whom is already that one who will some day stand here where I am standing.

Our tragedy today is a general and universal physical fear so long sustained by now that we can even bear it. There are no longer problems of the spirit. There is only the question: When will I be blown up? Because of this, the young man or woman writing today has forgotten the problems of the human heart in conflict with itself which alone can make good writing because only that is worth writing about, worth the agony and the sweat.

He must learn them again. He must teach himself that the basest of all things is to be afraid; and, teaching himself that, forget it forever, leaving no room in his workshop for anything but the old verities and truths of the heart, the old universal truths lacking which any story is ephemeral and doomed—love and honor and pity and pride and compassion and sacrifice. Until he does so, he labors under a curse. He writes not of love but of lust, of defeats in which nobody loses anything of value, of victories without hope and, worst of all, without pity or compassion. His griefs grieve on no universal bones, leaving no scars. He writes not of the heart but of the glands.

Until he relearns these things, he will write as though he stood among and watched the end of man. I decline to accept the end of man. It is easy enough to say that man is immortal simply because he will endure: that when the last ding-dong of doom has clanged and faded from the last worthless rock hanging tideless in the last red and dying evening, that even then there will still be one more sound: that of his puny inexhaustible voice, still talking. I refuse to accept this. I believe that man will not merely endure: he will prevail. He is immortal, not because he alone among creatures has an inexhaustible voice, but because he has a soul, a spirit capable of compassion and sacrifice and endurance. The poet's, the writer's, duty is to write about these things. It is his privilege to help man endure by lifting his heart, by reminding him of the courage and honor and hope and pride and compassion and pity and sacrifice which have been the glory of his past. The poet's voice need not merely be the record of man, it can be one of the props, the pillars to help him endure and prevail.

THINGS TO THINK ABOUT

1. Faulkner says that young writers ask "only the question: When will I be blown up?" How is contemporary literature haunted by the notion of a nuclear holocaust? Is this a notion that can create great literature?
2. Faulkner claims that the only theme that "can make good writing" is "the problem of the human heart in conflict with itself." Why is that such a good theme? In what ways does the story "A Rose for Emily" illustrate that theme?
3. In what ways has contemporary literature become the work of a "puny inexhaustible voice still talking"? Examine John Barth's story "Autobiography" for evidence of Faulkner's prophecy.
4. How will a story such as "A Rose for Emily" become a pillar "to help [humans to] endure and prevail"?

JOSEPH CONRAD

THE SECRET SHARER

Loss and displacement are the two constants of Conrad's life (1857–1924). Born in a part of Poland under Russian control, Conrad (originally Korzeniowski) was exiled to Russia with his parents who were Polish nationalists. At twelve he was orphaned and returned to Cracow for his education, but at seventeen he went to sea in the French merchant service.

Not until he was in his twenties and had joined a British ship did Conrad start learning English, and he was nearly forty when he published in his adopted country his first novel, Almayer's Folly. *His masterpieces* Lord Jim, Nostrome, *and* The Secret Agent *followed.*

Writing was always a painful and laborious process for Conrad, who often stayed up around the clock to finish his work and achieve his goal, "a meticulous precision of statement."

1

On my right hand there were lines of fishing-stakes resembling a mysterious system of half-submerged bamboo fences, incomprehensible in its division of the domain of tropical fishes, and crazy of aspect as if abandoned for ever by some nomad tribe of fishermen now gone to the other end of the ocean; for there was no sign of human habitation as far as the eye could reach. To the left a group of barren islets, suggesting ruins of stone walls, towers, and block-houses, had its foundations set in a blue sea that itself looked solid, so still and stable did it lie below my feet; even the track of light from the westering sun shone smoothly, without that animated glitter which tells of an imperceptible ripple. And when I turned my head to take a parting glance at the tug which had just left us anchored outside the bar, I saw the straight line of the flat shore joined to the stable sea, edge to edge, with a perfect and unmarked closeness, in one leveled floor half brown, half blue under the enormous dome of the sky. Corresponding in their insignificance to the islets of the sea, two small clumps of trees, one on each side of the only fault in the impeccable joint, marked the mouth of the river Meinam[1] we had just left on the first preparatory stage of our homeward journey; and, far back on the inland level, a larger and loftier mass, the grove surrounding the great Paknam pagoda, was the only thing on which the eye could rest from the vain task of exploring the monotonous sweep of the horizon. Here and there gleams as of a few scattered pieces of silver marked the windings of the great river; and on the nearest of them, just within the bar, the tug steaming right into the land became lost to my sight, hull and funnel and masts, as though the impassive earth had swallowed her up without an effort, without a tremor. My eye followed the light cloud of her smoke, now here, now there, above the plain, according to the devious curves of the stream, but always fainter and farther away, till I lost it at last behind the mitre-shaped hill of the great pagoda. And then I was left alone with my ship, anchored at the head of the Gulf of Siam.

She floated at the starting-point of a long journey, very still in an immense stillness, the shadows of her spars flung far to the eastward by the setting sun. At that moment I was alone on her decks. There was not a sound in her—and around us nothing moved, nothing lived, not a canoe on the water, not a bird in the air, not a cloud in the sky. In this breathless pause at the threshold of a long passage we seemed to be measuring our fitness for a long and arduous enterprise, the appointed task of both our existences to be carried out, far from all human eyes, with only sky and sea for spectators and for judges.

There must have been some glare in the air to interfere with one's sight, because it was only just before the sun left us that my roaming eyes made out beyond the highest ridge of the principal islet of the group something which did away with the solemnity of perfect solitude. The tide of darkness flowed on swiftly; and with tropical suddenness a swarm of stars came out above the shadowy earth, while I lingered yet, my hand resting lightly on my ship's rail as if on the shoulder of a trusted friend. But, with all that multitude of celestial bodies staring down at one, the comfort of quiet communion with her was gone for good. And there were also disturbing sounds by this time—voices, footsteps forward; the steward flitted along the main deck, a busily ministering spirit; a hand-bell tinkled urgently under the poop deck.[2]

[1] Meinam, also called Chao Phraya, is the central river of Thailand and flows through the capital, Bangkok, whose lower port is called Paknam or Samut Prakan. The Gulf of Siam is now called the Gulf of Thailand.

[2] The poop deck is the short raised deck from which a ship is commanded.

I found my two officers waiting for me near the supper table, in the lighted cuddy.[3] We sat down at once, and as I helped the chief mate, I said:

"Are you aware that there is a ship anchored inside the islands? I saw her mast-heads above the ridge as the sun went down."

He raised sharply his simple face, overcharged by a terrible growth of whisker, and emitted his usual ejaculations, "Bless my soul, sir! You don't say so!"

My second mate was a round-cheeked, silent young man, grave beyond his years, I thought; but as our eyes happened to meet I detected a slight quiver on his lips. I looked down at once. It was not my part to encourage sneering on board my ship. It must be said, too, that I knew very little of my officers. In consequence of certain events of no particular significance, except to myself, I had been appointed to the command only a fortnight before. Neither did I know much of the hands forward. All these people had been together for eighteen months or so, and my position was that of the only stranger on board. I mention this because it has some bearing on what is to follow. But what I felt most was my being a stranger to the ship; and if all the truth must be told, I was somewhat of a stranger to myself. The youngest man on board (barring the second mate), and untried as yet by a position of the fullest responsibility, I was willing to take the adequacy of the others for granted. They had simply to be equal to their tasks; but I wondered how far I should turn out faithful to that ideal conception of one's own personality every man sets up for himself secretly.

Meantime the chief mate, with an almost visible effect of collaboration on the part of his round eyes and frightful whiskers, was trying to evolve a theory of the anchored ship. His dominant trait was to take all things into earnest consideration. He was of a painstaking turn of mind. As he used to say, he "liked to account to himself" for practically everything that came in his way, down to a miserable scorpion he had found in his cabin a week before. The why and the wherefore of that scorpion—how it got on board and came to select his room rather than the pantry (which was a dark place and more what a scorpion would be partial to), and how on earth it managed to drown itself in the inkwell of his writing-desk—had exercised him infinitely. The ship within the islands was much more easily accounted for; and just as we were about to rise from table he made his pronouncement. She was, he doubted not, a ship from home lately arrived. Probably she drew too much water to cross the bar except at the top of spring tides. Therefore she went into that natural harbor to wait for a few days in preference to remaining in an open roadstead.

"That's so," confirmed the second mate suddenly, in his slightly hoarse voice. "She draws over twenty feet. She's the Liverpool ship *Sephora*

[3] A cuddy is a small cabin.

with a cargo of coal. Hundred and twenty-three days from Cardiff."[4]

We looked at him in surprise.

"The tugboat skipper told me when he come on board for your letters, sir," explained the young man. "He expects to take her up the river the day after tomorrow."

After thus overwhelming us with the extent of his information he slipped out of the cabin. The mate observed regretfully that he "could not account for that young fellow's whims." What prevented him telling us all about it at once, he wanted to know.

I detained him as he was making a move. For the last two days the crew had had plenty of hard work, and the night before they had very little sleep. I felt painfully that I—a stranger—was doing something unusual when I directed him to let all hands turn in without setting an anchor-watch.[5] I proposed to keep on deck myself till one o'clock or thereabouts. I would get the second mate to relieve me at that hour.

"He will turn out the cook and the steward at four," I concluded, "and then give you a call. Of course at the slightest sign of any sort of wind we'll have the hands up and make a start at once."

He concealed his astonishment. "Very well, sir." Outside the cuddy he put his head in the second mate's door to inform him of my unheard-of caprice to take a five hours' anchor-watch on myself. I heard the other raise his voice incredulously—"What? The captain himself?" Then a few more murmurs, a door closed, then another. A few moments later I went on deck.

My strangeness, which had made me sleepless, had prompted that unconventional arrangement, as if I had expected in those solitary hours of the night to get on terms with the ship of which I knew nothing, manned by men of whom I knew very little more. Fast alongside a wharf, littered like any ship in port with a tangle of unrelated things, invaded by unrelated shore people, I had hardly seen her yet properly. Now, as she lay cleared for sea, the stretch of her main deck seemed to me very fine under the stars. Very fine, very roomy for her size, and very inviting. I descended the poop and paced the waist, my mind picturing to myself the coming passage through the Malay Archipelago, down the Indian Ocean, and up the Atlantic.[6] All its phases were familiar enough to me, every characteristic, all the alternatives which were likely to face me on the high seas—everything! . . . except the novel responsibility of command. But I took heart from the reasonable thought that the ship was like other ships, the men like other men, and that the sea was not likely to keep any special surprises expressly for my discomfiture.

[4] Liverpool is a port city in northwest England. Cardiff is a port city and capital of Wales.

[5] An anchor watch is a detail of one or more men who stand watch on deck at night when a vessel is at anchor.

[6] The ship is planning to return to England via a southwest route around Africa.

Arrived at that comforting conclusion, I bethought myself a cigar and went below to get it. All was still down there. Everybody at the after end of the ship was sleeping profoundly. I came out again on the quarter-deck, agreeably at ease in my sleeping suit[7] on that warm, breathless night, barefooted, a glowing cigar in my teeth, and, going forward, I was met by the profound silence of the fore end of the ship. Only as I passed the door of the forecastle I heard a deep, quiet, trustful sigh of some sleeper inside. And suddenly I rejoiced in the great security of the sea as compared with the unrest of the land, in my choice of that untempted life presenting no disquieting problems, invested with an elementary moral beauty by the absolute straightforwardness of its appeal and by the singleness of its purpose.

The riding-light[8] in the fore-rigging burned with a clear, untroubled, as if symbolic, flame, confident and bright in the mysterious shades of the night. Passing on my way aft along the other side of the ship, I observed that the rope side-ladder, put over, no doubt, for the master of the tug when he came to fetch away our letters, had not been hauled in as it should have been. I became annoyed at this, for exactitude in small matters is the very soul of discipline. Then I reflected that I had myself peremptorily dismissed my officers from duty, and by my own act had prevented the anchor-watch being formally set and things properly attended to. I asked myself whether it was wise ever to interfere with the established routine of duties even from the kindest of motives. My action might have made me appear eccentric. Goodness only knew how that absurdly whiskered mate would "account" for my conduct, and what the whole ship thought of that informality of their new captain. I was vexed with myself.

Not from compunction certainly, but, as it were mechanically, I proceeded to get the ladder in myself. Now a side-ladder of that sort is a light affair and comes in easily, yet my vigorous tug, which should have brought it flying on board, merely recoiled upon my body in a totally unexpected jerk. What the devil! . . . I was so astounded by the immovableness of that ladder that I remained stock-still, trying to account for it to myself like that imbecile mate of mine. In the end, of course, I put my head over the rail.

The side of the ship made an opaque belt of shadow on the darkling glassy shimmer of the sea. But I saw at once something elongated and pale floating very close to the ladder. Before I could form a guess a faint flash of phosphorescent light, which seemed to issue suddenly from the naked body of a man, flickered in the sleeping water with the elusive, silent play of summer lightning in a night sky. With a gasp I saw revealed to my stare a pair of feet, the long legs, a broad livid

[7] A sleeping-suit is a pajama with feet, a type often worn now by children.
[8] A riding-light is displayed when a ship is riding at anchor.

back immersed right up to the neck in a greenish cadaverous glow. One hand, awash, clutched the bottom rung of the ladder. He was complete but for the head. A headless corpse! The cigar dropped out of my gaping mouth with a tiny plop and a short hiss quite audible in the absolute stillness of all things under heaven. At that I suppose he raised up his face, a dimly pale oval in the shadow of the ship's side. But even then I could only barely make out down there the shape of his black-haired head. However, it was enough for the horrid, frost-bound sensation which had gripped me about the chest to pass off. The moment of vain exclamations was past too. I only climbed on the spare spar and leaned over the rail as far as I could, to bring my eyes nearer to that mystery floating alongside.

As he hung by the ladder, like a resting swimmer, the sea-lightning played about his limbs at every stir; and he appeared in it ghastly, silvery, fish-like. He remained as mute as a fish, too. He made no motion to get out of the water, either. It was inconceivable that he should not attempt to come on board, and strangely troubling to suspect that perhaps he did not want to. And my first words were prompted by just that troubled incertitude.

"What's the matter?" I asked in my ordinary tone, speaking down to the face upturned exactly under mine.

"Cramp," it answered, no louder. Then slightly anxious, "I say, no need to call any one."

"I was not going to," I said.

"Are you alone on deck?"

"Yes."

I had somehow the impression that he was on the point of letting go the ladder to swim away beyond my ken—mysterious as he came. But, for the moment, this being appearing as if he had risen from the bottom of the sea (it was certainly down there, tentatively:

"I suppose your captain's turned in?"

"I am sure he isn't," I said.

He seemed to struggle with himself, for I heard something like the low, bitter murmur of doubt. "What's the good?" His next words came out with a hesitating effort.

"Look here, my man. Could you call him out quietly?"

I thought the time had come to declare myself.

"*I* am the captain."

I heard a "By Jove!" whispered at the level of the water. The phosphorescence flashed in the swirl of the water all about his limbs, his other hand seized the ladder.

"My name's Leggatt."

The voice was calm and resolute. A good voice. The self-possession of that man had somehow induced a corresponding state in myself. It was very quietly that I remarked:

"You must be a good swimmer."

"Yes. I've been in the water practically since nine o'clock. The question for me now is whether I am to let go this ladder and go on swimming till I sink from exhaustion or—to come on board here."

I felt this was no mere formula of desperate speech, but a real alternative in the view of a strong soul. I should have gathered from this that he was young; indeed, it is only the young who are ever confronted by such clear issues. But at the time it was pure intuition on my part. A mysterious communication was established already between us two—in the face of that silent, darkened tropical sea. I was young, too; young enough to make no comment. The man in the water began suddenly to climb up the ladder, and I hastened away from the rail to fetch some clothes.

Before entering the cabin I stood still, listening in the lobby at the foot of the stairs. A faint snore came through the closed door of the chief mate's room. The second mate's door was on the hook, but the darkness in there was absolutely soundless. He, too, was young and could sleep like a stone. Remained the steward, but he was not likely to wake up before he was called. I got a sleeping suit out of my room, and, coming back on deck, saw the naked man from the sea sitting on the main-hatch, glimmering white in the darkness, his elbows on his knees and his head in his hands. In a moment he had concealed his damp body in a sleeping suit of the same gray-stripe pattern as the one I was wearing, and followed me like my double on the poop. Together we moved right aft, barefooted, silent.

"What is it?" I asked in a deadened voice, taking the lighted lamp out of the binnacle, and raising it to his face.

"An ugly business."

He had rather regular features; a good mouth; light eyes under somewhat heavy, dark eyebrows; a smooth, square forehead; no growth on his cheeks; a small, brown mustache, and a well-shaped, round chin. His expression was concentrated, meditative, under the inspecting light of the lamp I held up to his face; such as a man thinking hard in solitude might wear. My sleeping suit was just right for his size. A well-knit young fellow of twenty-five at most. He caught his lower lip with the edge of white, even teeth.

"Yes," I said, replacing the lamp in the binnacle. The warm, heavy tropical night closed upon his head again.

"There's a ship over there," he murmured.

"Yes, I know. The *Sephora*. Did you know of us?"

"Hadn't the slightest idea. I am the mate of her—" He paused and corrected himself. "I should say I *was*."

"Aha! Something wrong?"

"Yes. Very wrong indeed. I've killed a man."

"What do you mean? Just now?"

"No, on the passage. Weeks ago. Thirty-nine south. When I say a man—"

"Fit of temper," I suggested confidently.

The shadowy, dark head, like mine, seemed to nod imperceptibly above the ghostly gray of my sleeping suit. It was, in the night, as though I had been faced by my own reflection in the depths of a sombre and immense mirror.

"A pretty thing to have to own up to for a Conway boy,"[9] murmured my double distinctly.

"You're a Conway boy?"

"I am," he said, as if startled. Then, slowly . . . "Perhaps you too . . ."

It was so; but being a couple of years older I had left before he joined. After a quick interchange of dates a silence fell; and I thought suddenly of my absurd mate with his terrific whiskers and the "Bless my soul—you don't say so" type of intellect. My double gave me an inkling of his thoughts by saying:

"My father's a parson in Norfolk.[10] Do you see me before a judge and jury on that charge? For myself I can't see the necessity. There are fellows that an angel from heaven—And I am not that. He was one of those creatures that are just simmering all the time with a silly sort of wickedness. Miserable devils that have no business to live at all. He wouldn't do his duty and wouldn't let anybody else do theirs. But what's the good of talking! You know well enough the sort of ill-conditioned snarling cur . . ."

He appealed to me as if our experiences had been as identical as our clothes. And I knew well enough the pestiferous danger of such a character where there are no means of legal repression. And I knew well enough also that my double there was no homicidal ruffian. I did not think of asking him for details, and he told me the story roughly in brusque, disconnected sentences. I needed no more. I saw it all going on as though I were myself inside that other sleeping suit.

"It happened while we were setting a reefed foresail, at dusk. Reefed foresail! You understand the sort of weather. The only sail we had left to keep the ship running; so you may guess what it had been like for days. Anxious sort of job, that. He gave me some of his cursed insolence at the sheet. I tell you I was overdone with this terrific weather that seemed to have no end to it. Terrific, I tell you—and a deep ship. I believe the fellow himself was half crazed with funk. It was no time for gentlemanly reproof, so I turned round and felled him like an ox. He up and at me. We closed just as an awful sea made for the ship.

[9] The Conway was a training ship for young officers of the Royal Navy and merchant service.

[10] Norfolk is a maritime county in eastern England.

All hands saw it coming and took to the rigging, but I had him by the throat, and went on shaking him like a rat, the men above us yelling. 'Look out! Look out!' Then a crash as if the sky had fallen on my head. They say that for over ten minutes hardly anything was to be seen of the ship—just the three masts and a bit of the forecastle head and of the poop all awash driving along in a smother of foam. It was a miracle that they found us, jammed together behind the forebits. It's clear that I meant business, because I was holding him by the throat still when they picked us up. He was black in the face. It was too much for them. It seems they rushed us aft together, gripped as we were, screaming, 'Murder!' like a lot of lunatics, and broke into the cuddy. And the ship running for her life, touch and go all the time, any minute her last in a sea fit to turn your hair gray only a-looking at it. I understand that the skipper, too, started raving like the rest of them. The man had been deprived of sleep for more than a week, and to have this sprung on him at the height of a furious gale nearly drove him out of his mind. I wonder they didn't fling me overboard after getting the carcass of their precious shipmate out of my fingers. They had rather a job to separate us, I've been told. A sufficiently fierce story to make an old judge and a respectable jury sit up a bit. The first thing I heard when I came to myself was the maddening howling of that endless gale, and on that the voice of the old man. He was hanging on to my bunk, staring into my face out of his sou'wester.

" 'Mr. Leggatt, you have killed a man. You can act no longer as chief mate of this ship.' "

His care to subdue his voice made it sound monotonous. He rested a hand on the end of the skylight to steady himself with, and all that time did not stir a limb, so far as I could see. "Nice little tale for a quiet tea party," he concluded in the same tone.

One of my hands, too, rested on the end of the skylight; neither did I stir a limb, so far as I knew. We stood less than a foot from each other. It occurred to me that if old "Bless my soul—you don't say so" were to put his head up the companion and catch sight of us, he would think he was seeing double, or imagine himself come upon a scene of weird witchcraft: the strange captain having a quiet confabulation by the wheel with his own gray ghost. I became very much concerned to prevent anything of the sort. I heard the other's soothing undertone:

"My father's a parson in Norfolk," it said. Evidently he had forgotten he had told me this important fact before. Truly a nice little tale.

"You had better slip down into my stateroom now," I said, moving off stealthily. My double followed my movements; our bare feet made no sound; I let him in, closed the door with care, and after giving a call to the second mate, returned on deck for my relief.

"Not much sign of any wind yet," I remarked when he approached.

"No, sir. Not much," he assented sleepily in his hoarse voice, with just enough deference, no more, and barely suppressing a yawn.

"Well, that's all you have to look out for. You have got your orders."

"Yes, sir."

I paced a turn or two on the poop and saw him take up his position face forward with his elbow in the ratlines[11] of the mizzen-rigging[12] before I went below. The mate's faint snoring was still going on peacefully. The cuddy lamp was burning over the table on which stood a vase with flowers, a polite attention from the ship's provision merchant—the last flowers we should see for the next three months at the very least. Two bunches of bananas hung from the beam symmetrically, one on each side of the rudder-casing. Everything was as before in the ship—except that two of her captain's sleeping suits were simultaneously in use, one motionless in the cuddy, the other keeping very still in the captain's stateroom.

It must be explained here that my cabin had the form of the capital letter L, the door being within the angle and opening into the short part of the letter. A couch was to the left, the bedplace to the right; my writing-desk and the chronometers' table faced the door. But any one opening it, unless he stepped right inside, had no view of what I call the long (or vertical) part of the letter. It contained some lockers surmounted by a bookcase; and a few clothes, a thick jacket or two, caps, oilskin coat, and such-like, hung on hooks. There was at the bottom of that part a door opening into my bathroom, which could be entered also directly from the saloon. But that way was never used.

The mysterious arrival had discovered the advantage of this particular shape. Entering my room, lighted strongly by a big bulkhead lamp swung on gimbals above my writing-desk, I did not see him anywhere till he stepped out quietly from behind the coats hung in the recessed part.

"I heard somebody moving about, and went in there at once," he whispered. I, too, spoke under my breath.

"Nobody is likely to come in here without knocking and getting permission."

He nodded. His face was thin and the sunburn faded, as though he had been ill. And no wonder. He had been, I heard presently, kept under arrest in his cabin for nearly nine weeks. But there was nothing sickly in his eyes or in his expression. He was not a bit like me, really; yet, as we stood leaning over my bedplace, whispering side by side, with our dark heads together and our backs to the door, anybody bold enough to open it stealthily would have been treated to the uncanny sight of a double captain busy talking in whispers with his other self.

[11] Ratlines are footropes.

[12] The mizzen is the third mast aft on sailing ships carrying three or more masts.

"But all this doesn't tell me how you came to hang on to our side-ladder," I inquired, in the hardly audible murmurs we used, after he had told me something more of the proceedings on board the *Sephora* once the bad weather was over.

"When we sighted Java Head[13] I had had time to think all those matters out several times over. I had six weeks of doing nothing else, and with only an hour or so every evening for a tramp on the quarter-deck."

He whispered, his arms folded on the side of my bedplace, staring through the open port. And I could imagine perfectly the manner of this thinking out—a stubborn if not a steadfast operation; something of which I should have been perfectly incapable.

"I reckoned it would be dark before we closed with the land," he continued, so low that I had to strain my hearing, near as we were to each other, shoulder touching shoulder almost. "So I asked to speak to the old man. He always seemed very sick when he came to see me—as if he could not look me in the face. You know, that foresail saved the ship. She was too deep to have run long under bare poles. And it was I that managed to set it for him. Anyway, he came. When I had him in my cabin—he stood by the door looking at me as if I had the halter round my neck already—I asked him right away to leave my cabin door unlocked at night while the ship was going through Sunda Straits.[14] There would be the Java coast within two or three miles, off Anjer Point. I wanted nothing more. I've had a prize for swimming my second year in the Conway."

"I can believe it," I breathed out.

"God only knows why they locked me in every night. To see some of their faces you'd have thought they were afraid I'd go about at night strangling people. Am I a murdering brute? Do I look it? By Jove! if I had been he wouldn't have trusted himself like that into my room. You'll say I might have chucked him aside and bolted out, there and then—it was dark already. Well, no. And for the same reason I wouldn't think of trying to smash the door. There would have been a rush to stop me at the noise, and I did not mean to get into a confounded scrimmage. Somebody else might have got killed—for I would not have broken out only to get chucked back, and I did not want any more of that work. He refused, looking more sick than ever. He was afraid of the men, and also of that old second mate of his who had been sailing with him for years—a gray-headed old humbug; and his steward, too, had been with him devil knows how long—seventeen years or more—a dogmatic sort of loafer who hated me like poison, just because I was

[13] Java Head is the cape on the extreme western edge of Java and is the entrance to the Sunda Straits.

[14] The Sunda Straits is the body of water between Java and Sumatra.

the chief mate. No chief mate ever made more than one voyage in the *Sephora,* you know. Those two old chaps ran the ship. Devil only knows what the skipper wasn't afraid of (all his nerve went to pieces altogether in that hellish spell of bad weather we had)—of what the law would do to him—of his wife, perhaps. Oh yes! she's on board. Though I don't think she would have meddled. She would have been only too glad to have me out of the ship in any way. The 'brand of Cain' business, don't you see? That's all right. I was ready enough to go off wandering on the face of the earth—and that was price enough to pay for an Abel of that sort. Anyhow, he wouldn't listen to me. 'This thing must take its course. I represent the law here.' He was shaking like a leaf. 'So you won't?' 'No!' 'Then I hope you will be able to sleep on that,' I said, and turned my back on him. 'I wonder that *you* can,' cries he, and locks the door.

"Well, after that, I couldn't. Not very well. That was three weeks ago. We have had a slow passage through the Java Sea; drifted about Carimata for ten days. When we anchored here they thought, I suppose, it was all right. The nearest land (and that's five miles) is the ship's destination; the consul would soon set about catching me; and there would have been no object in bolting to these islets there. I don't suppose there's a drop of water on them. I don't know how it was, but tonight that steward, after bringing me my supper, went out to let me eat it, and left the door unlocked. And I ate it—all there was, too. After I had finished I strolled out on the quarter-deck. I don't know that I meant to do anything. A breath of fresh air was all I wanted, I believe. Then a sudden temptation came over me. I kicked off my slippers and was in the water before I had made up my mind fairly. Somebody heard the splash and they raised an awful hullabaloo. 'He's gone! Lower the boats! He's committed suicide! No, he's swimming.' Certainly I was swimming. It's not easy for a swimmer like me to commit suicide by drowning. I landed on the nearest islet before the boat left the ship's side. I heard them pulling about in the dark, hailing, and so on, but after a bit they gave up. Everything quieted down and the anchorage became as still as death. I sat down on a stone and began to think. I felt certain they would start searching for me at daylight. There was no place to hide on those stony things—and if there had been, what would have been the good? But now I was clear of that ship, I was not going back. So after a while I took off all my clothes, tied them up in a bundle with a stone inside, and dropped them in the deep water on the outer side of that islet. That was suicide enough for me. Let them think what they liked, but I didn't mean to drown myself. I meant to swim till I sank—but that's not the same thing. I struck out for another of these little islands, and it was from that one that I first saw your riding-light. Something to swim for. I went on easily, and on the way I came upon a flat rock a foot or two above water. In the daytime, I dare say, you might make it out with a glass from your poop. I scrambled up on it and rested myself for a bit. Then I made another start. That last spell must have been over a mile."

His whisper was getting fainter and fainter, and all the time he stared straight out through the porthole, in which there was not even a star to be seen. I had not interrupted him. There was something that made comment impossible, in his narrative, or perhaps in himself; a sort of feeling, a quality, which I can't find a name for. And when he ceased, all I found was a futile whisper, "So you swam for our light?"

"Yes—straight for it. It was something to swim for. I couldn't see any stars low down because the coast was in the way, and I couldn't see the land, either. The water was like glass. One might have been swimming in a confounded thousand feet deep cistern with no place for scrambling out anywhere; but what I didn't like was the notion of swimming round and round like a crazed bullock before I gave out; and as I didn't mean to go back . . . No. Do you see me being hauled back, stark naked, off one of these little islands by the scruff of the neck and fighting like a wild beast? Somebody would have got killed for certain, and I did not want any of that. So I went on. Then your ladder—"

"Why didn't you hail the ship?" I asked, a little louder.

He touched my shoulder lightly. Lazy footsteps came right over our heads and stopped. The second mate had crossed from the other side of the poop and might have been hanging over the rail, for all we knew.

"He couldn't hear us talking—could he?" My double breathed into my very ear anxiously.

His anxiety was an answer, a sufficient answer, to the question I had put to him. An answer containing all the difficulty of that situation. I closed the porthole quietly, to make sure. A louder word might have been overheard.

"Who's that?" he whispered then.

"My second mate. But I don't know much more of the fellow than you do."

And I told him a little about myself. I had been appointed to take charge while I least expected anything of the sort, not quite a fortnight ago. I didn't know either the ship or the people. Hadn't had the time in port to look about me or size anybody up. And as to the crew, all they knew was that I was appointed to take the ship home. For the rest, I was almost as much of a stranger on board as himself, I said. And at the moment I felt it most acutely. I felt that it would take very little to make me a suspect person in the eyes of the ship's company.

He had turned about meantime; and we, the two strangers in the ship, faced each other in identical attitudes.

"Your ladder—" he murmured, after a silence. "Who'd have thought of finding a ladder hanging over at night in a ship anchored out here! I felt just then a very unpleasant faintness. After the life I've been leading for nine weeks, anybody would have got out of condition. I wasn't capable of swimming round as far as your rudder-chains. And, lo and behold! there was a ladder to get hold of. After I gripped it I said to myself, 'What's the good?' When I saw a man's head looking over I thought I would swim away presently and leave him shouting—in whatever language it was. I didn't mind being looked at. I—I liked it. And then you speaking to me so quietly—as if you had expected me—made me hold on a little longer. It had been a confounded lonely time—I don't mean while swimming. I was glad to talk a little to somebody that didn't belong to the *Sephora.* As to asking for the captain, that was a mere impulse. It could have been no use, with all the ship knowing about me and the other people pretty certain to be round here in the morning. I don't know—I wanted to be seen, to talk with somebody, before I went on. I don't know what I would have said. . . . 'Fine night, isn't it?' or something of the sort."

"Do you think they will be round here presently?" I asked, with some incredulity.

"Quite likely," he said faintly.

He looked extremely haggard all of a sudden. His head rolled on his shoulders.

"H'm. We shall see then. Meantime get into that bed," I whispered. "Want help? There."

It was a rather high bedplace with a set of drawers underneath. This amazing swimmer really needed the lift I gave him by seizing his leg. He tumbled in, rolled over on his back, and flung one arm across his eyes. And then, with his face nearly hidden, he must have looked exactly as I used to look in that bed. I gazed upon my other self for a while before drawing across carefully the two green serge curtains which ran on a brass rod. I thought for a moment of pinning them together for greater safety, but I sat down on the couch, and once there I felt unwilling to rise and hunt for a pin. I would do it in a moment. I was extremely tired, in a peculiarly intimate way, by the strain of stealthiness, by the effort of whispering, and the general secrecy of this excitement. It was three o'clock by now, and I had been on my feet since nine, but I was not sleepy; I could not have gone to sleep. I sat there, fagged out,[15] looking at the curtains, trying to clear my mind of the confused sensation of being in two places at once, and greatly bothered by an exasperating knocking in my head. It was a relief to discover suddenly that it was not in my head at all, but on the outside of the door. Before I could collect myself, the words "Come in" were out of my mouth, and the steward entered with a tray, bringing in my morning coffee. I had slept,

[15] Fagged out is British slang for exhausted.

after all, and I was so frightened that I shouted, "This way! I am here, steward," as though he had been miles away. He put down the tray on the table next the couch and only then said, very quietly, "I can see you are here, sir." I felt him give me a keen look, but I dared not meet his eyes just then. He must have wondered why I had drawn the curtains of my bed before going to sleep on the couch. He went out, hooking the door open as usual.

I heard the crew washing decks above me. I knew I would have been told at once if there had been any wind. Calm, I thought, and I was doubly vexed. Indeed, I felt dual more than ever. The steward reappeared suddenly in the doorway. I jumped up from the couch so quickly that he gave a start.

"What do you want here?"

"Close your port, sir—they are washing decks."

"It is closed," I said, reddening.

"Very well, sir." But he did not move from the doorway and returned my stare in an extraordinary, equivocal manner for a time. Then his eyes wavered, all his expression changed, and in a voice unusually gentle, almost coaxingly.

"May I come in to take the empty cup away, sir?"

"Of course!" I turned my back on him while he popped in and out. Then I unhooked and closed the door and even pushed the bolt. This sort of thing could not go on very long. The cabin was as hot as an oven, too. I took a peep at my double, and discovered that he had not moved; his arm was still over his eyes; but his chest heaved, his hair was wet, his chin glistened with perspiration. I reached over him and opened the port.

"I must show myself on deck," I reflected.

Of course, theoretically, I could do what I liked, with no one to say nay to me within the whole circle of the horizon; but to lock my cabin door and take the key away I did not dare. Directly I put my head out of the companion I saw the group of my two officers, the second mate barefooted, the chief mate in long india-rubber boots, near the break of the poop, and the steward half-way down the poop ladder talking to them eagerly. He happened to catch sight of me and dived, the second ran down on the main deck shouting some order or other, and the chief mate came to meet me, touching his cap.

There was a sort of curiosity in his eye that I did not like. I don't know whether the steward had told them that I was "queer" only, or downright drunk, but I know the man meant to have a good look at me. I watched him coming with a smile which, as he got into point-blank range, took effect and froze his very whiskers. I did not give him time to open his lips.

"Square the yards by lifts and braces before the hands go to breakfast."

It was the first particular order I had given on board that ship; and

I stayed on deck to see it executed too. I had felt the need of asserting myself without loss of time. That sneering young cub got taken down a peg or two on that occasion, and I also seized the opportunity of having a good look at the face of every foremast man as they filed past me to go to the after braces. At breakfast time, eating nothing myself, I presided with such frigid dignity that the two mates were only too glad to escape from the cabin as soon as decency permitted, and all the time the dual working of my mind distracted me almost to the point of insanity. I was constantly watching myself, my secret self, as dependent on my actions as my own personality, sleeping in that bed, behind that door which faced me as I sat at the head of the table. It was very much like being mad, only it was worse, because one was aware of it.

I had to shake him for a solid minute, but when at last he opened his eyes it was in the full possession of his senses, with an inquiring look.

"All's well so far," I whispered. "Now you must vanish into the bathroom."

He did so, as noiseless as a ghost, and I then rang for the steward, and facing him boldly, directed him to tidy up my stateroom while I v having my bath—"and be quick about it." As my tone admitted of no excuses, he said, "Yes, sir," and ran off to fetch his dustpan and brushes. I took a bath and did most of my dressing, splashing, and whistling softly for the steward's edification, while the secret sharer of my life stood drawn bolt upright in that little space, his face looking very sunken in daylight, his eyelids lowered under the stern, dark line of his eyebrows drawn together by a slight frown.

When I left him there to go back to my room the steward was finishing dusting. I sent for the mate and engaged him in some insignificant conversation. It was, as it were, trifling with the terrific character of his whiskers; but my object was to give him an opportunity for a good look at my cabin. And then I could at last shut, with a clear conscience, the door of my stateroom and get my double back into the recessed part. There was nothing else for it. He had to sit still on a small folding stool, half smothered by the heavy coats hanging there. We listened to the steward going into the bathroom out of the saloon, filling the water-bottles there, scrubbing the bath, setting things to rights, whisk, bang, clatter—out again into the saloon—turn the key—click. Such was my scheme for keeping my second self invisible. Nothing better could be contrived under the circumstances. And there we sat: I at my writing-desk ready to appear busy with some papers, he behind me, out of sight of the door. It would not have been prudent to talk in daytime; and I could not have stood the excitement of that queer sense of whispering to myself. Now and then, glancing over my shoulder, I saw him far back there, sitting rigidly on the low stool, his bare feet close together, his arms folded, his head hanging on his breast—and perfectly still. Anybody would have taken him for me.

I was fascinated by it myself. Every moment I had to glance over my shoulder. I was looking at him when a voice outside the door said:

"Beg pardon, sir."

"Well!" . . . I kept my eyes on him, and so when the voice outside the door announced, "There's a ship's boat coming our way, sir," I saw him give a start—the first movement he had made for hours. But he did not raise his bowed head.

"All right. Get the ladder over."

I hesitated. Should I whisper something to him? But what? His immobility seemed to have been never disturbed. What could I tell him he did not know already? . . . Finally I went on deck.

2

The skipper of the *Sephora* had a thin, red whisker all round his face, and the sort of complexion that goes with hair of that color; also the particular, rather smeary shade of blue in the eyes. He was not exactly a showy figure; his shoulders were high, his stature but middling—one leg slightly more bandy than the other. He shook hands, looking vaguely around. A spiritless tenacity was his main characteristic, I judged. I behaved with a politeness which seemed to disconcert him. Perhaps he was shy. He mumbled to me as if he were ashamed of what he was saying; gave his name (it was something like Archbold—but at this distance of years I hardly am sure), his ship's name, and a few other particulars of that sort, in the manner of a criminal making a reluctant and doleful confession. He had had terrible weather on the passage out—terrible—terrible—wife aboard, too.

"What was that for—fun?" I asked with an appearance of polite interest.

"No!" he sighed. "Painful duty."

As he persisted in his mumbling and I wanted my double to hear every word, I hit upon the notion of informing him that I regretted to say I was hard of hearing.

"Such a young man too!" he nodded, keeping his smeary, blue, unintelligent eyes fastened upon me. "What was the cause of it—some disease?" he inquired, without the least sympathy and as if he thought that, if so, I'd got no more than I deserved.

"Yes; disease," I admitted in a cheerful tone which seemed to shock him. But my point was gained, because he had to raise his voice to give me his tale. It is not worth while to record that version. It was just over two months since all this had happened, and he had thought so much about it that he seemed completely muddled as to its bearings, but still immensely impressed.

"What would you think of such a thing happening on board your own ship? I've had the *Sephora* for these fifteen years. I am a well-known shipmaster."

He was densely distressed—and perhaps I should have sympathized with him if I had been able to detach my mental vision from the unsuspected sharer of my cabin as though he were my second self. There he was on the other side of the bulkhead, four or five feet from us, no more, as we sat in the saloon. I looked politely at Captain Archbold (if that was his name), but it was the other I saw, in a gray sleeping suit, seated on a low stool, his bare feet close together, his arms folded, and every word said between us falling into the ears of his dark head bowed on his chest.

"I have been at sea now, man and boy, for seven and thirty years, and I've never heard of such a thing happening in an English ship. And that it should be my ship. Wife on board, too."

I was hardly listening to him.

"Don't you think," I said, "that the heavy sea which, you told me, came aboard just then might have killed the man? I have seen the sheer weight of a sea kill a man very neatly, by simply breaking his neck."

"Good God!" he uttered impressively, fixing his smeary blue eyes on me. "The sea! No man killed by the sea ever looked like that." He seemed positively scandalized at my suggestion. And as I gazed at him, certainly not prepared for anything original on his part, he advanced his head close to mine and thrust his tongue out at me so suddenly that I couldn't help starting back.

After scoring over my calmness in this graphic way he nodded wisely. If I had seen the sight, he assured me, I would never forget it as long as I lived. The weather was too bad to give the corpse a proper sea burial. So next day at dawn they took it up on the poop, covering its face with a bit of bunting; he read a short prayer, and then, just as it was, in its oilskins and long boots, they launched it amongst those mountainous seas that seemed ready every moment to swallow up the ship herself and the terrified lives on board of her.

"That reefed foresail saved you," I threw in.

"Under God—it did," he exclaimed fervently. "It was by a special mercy, I firmly believe, that it stood some of those hurricane squalls."

"It was the setting of that sail which—" I began.

"God's own hand in it," he interrupted me. "Nothing less could have done it. I don't mind telling you that I hardly dared give the order. It seemed impossible that we could touch anything without losing it, and then our last hope would have been gone."

The terror of that gale was on him yet. I let him go on for a bit, then said casually—as if returning to a minor subject:

"You were very anxious to give up your mate to the shore people, I believe?"

He was. To the law. His obscure tenacity on that point had in it something incomprehensible and a little awful; something, as it were, mystical, quite apart from his anxiety that he should not be suspected of "countenancing any doings of that sort." Seven and thirty virtuous years at sea, of which over twenty of immaculate command, and the last fifteen in the *Sephora,* seemed to have laid him under some pitiless obligation.

"And you know," he went on, groping shamefacedly amongst his feelings, "I did not engage that young fellow. His people had some interest with my owners. I was in a way forced to take him on. He looked very smart, very gentlemanly, and all that. But do you know—I never liked him, somehow. I am a plain man. You see, he wasn't exactly the sort for the chief mate of a ship like the *Sephora.*"

I had become so connected in thoughts and impressions with the secret sharer of my cabin that I felt as if I, personally, were being given to understand that I, too, was not the sort that would have done for the chief mate of a ship like the *Sephora.* I had no doubt of it in my mind.

"Not at all the style of man. You understand," he insisted superfluously, looking hard at me.

I smiled urbanely. He seemed at a loss for a while.

"I suppose I must report a suicide."

"Beg pardon?"

"Sui-cide! That's what I'll have to write to my owners directly I get in."

"Unless you manage to recover him before tomorrow," I assented dispassionately. . . . "I mean, alive."

He mumbled something which I really did not catch, and I turned my ear to him in a puzzled manner. He fairly bawled:

"The land—I say, the mainland is at least seven miles off my anchorage."

"About that."

My lack of excitement, of curiosity, of surprise, of any sort of pronounced interest, began to arouse his distrust. But except for the felicitous pretense of deafness I had not tried to pretend anything. I had felt utterly incapable of playing the part of ignorance properly, and therefore was afraid to try. It is also certain that he had brought some ready-made suspicions with him, and that he viewed my politeness as a strange and unnatural phenomenon. And yet how else could I have received him? Not heartily! That was impossible for psychological reasons, which I need not state here. My only object was to keep off his inquiries. Surlily? Yes, but surliness might have provoked a point-blank question. From its novelty to him and from its nature, punctilious courtesy was the manner best calculated to restrain the man. But there was the danger of his breaking through my defense bluntly. I could not, I think, have met him by a direct lie, also for psychological (not moral) reasons. If he had only known how afraid I was of his putting my feeling of identity with the other to the test! But, strangely enough (I thought of it only afterward), I believe that he was not a little disconcerted by the reverse side of that weird situation, by something in me that reminded him of the man he was seeking—suggested a mysterious similitude to the young fellow he had distrusted and disliked from the first.

However that might have been, the silence was not very prolonged. He took another oblique step.

"I reckon I had no more than a two-mile pull to your ship. Not a bit more."

"And quite enough, too, in this awful heat," I said.

Another pause full of mistrust followed. Necessity, they say, is mother of invention, but fear, too, is not barren of ingenious suggestions. And I was afraid he would ask me point-blank for news of my other self.

"Nice little saloon, isn't it?" I remarked, as if noticing for the first time the way his eyes roamed from one closed door to the other. "And very well fitted out, too. Here, for instance," I continued, reaching over the back of my seat negligently and flinging the door open, "is my bathroom."

He made an eager movement, but hardly gave it a glance. I got up, shut the door of the bathroom, and invited him to have a look round, as if I were very proud of my accommodation. He had to rise and be shown round, but he went through the business without any raptures whatever.

"And now we'll have a look at my stateroom," I declared, in a voice as loud as I dared to make it, crossing the cabin to the starboard side with purposely heavy steps.

He followed me in and gazed around. My intelligent double had vanished. I played my part.

"Very convenient—isn't it?"

"Very nice. Very comf . . ." He didn't finish, and went out brusquely as if to escape from some unrighteous wiles of mine. But it was not to be. I had been too frightened not to feel vengeful; I felt I had him on the run, and I meant to keep him on the run. My polite insistence must have had something menacing in it, because he gave in suddenly. And I did not let him off a single item: mates' rooms, pantry, storerooms, the very sail-locker, which was also under the poop—he had to look into them all. When at last I showed him out on the quarter-deck he drew a long, spiritless sigh, and mumbled dismally that he must really be going back to his ship now. I desired my mate, who had joined us, to see to the captain's boat.

The man of whiskers gave a blast on the whistle which he used to wear hanging round his neck, and yelled, "*Sephora*'s away!" My double down there in my cabin must have heard, and certainly could not feel more relieved than I. Four fellows came running out from somewhere forward and went over the side, while my own men, appearing on deck too, lined the rail. I escorted my visitor to the gangway ceremoniously, and nearly overdid it. He was a tenacious beast. On the very ladder he lingered, and in that unique, guiltily conscientious manner of sticking to the point:

"I say . . . you . . . you don't think that—"

I covered his voice loudly.

"Certainly not. . . . I am delighted. Goodbye."

I had an idea of what he meant to say, and just saved myself by the privilege of defective hearing. He was too shaken generally to insist, but my mate, close witness of that parting, looked mystified and his face took on a thoughtful cast. As I did not want to appear as if I wished to avoid all communication with my officers, he had the opportunity to address me.

"Seems a very nice man. His boat's crew told our chaps a very extraordinary story, if what I am told by the steward is true. I suppose you had it from the captain, sir?"

"Yes. I had a story from the captain."

"A very horrible affair—isn't it, sir?"

"It is."

"Beats all these tales we hear about murders in Yankee ships."

"I don't think it beats them. I don't think it resembles them in the least."

"Bless my soul—you don't say so! But of course I've no acquaintance whatever with American ships, not I, so I couldn't go against your knowledge. It's horrible enough for me. . . . But the queerest part is that those fellows seemed to have some idea the man was hidden aboard here. They had really. Did you ever hear of such a thing?"

"Preposterous—isn't it?"

We were walking to and fro athwart the quarter-deck. No one of the crew forward could be seen (the day was Sunday), and the mate pursued:

"There was some little dispute about it. Our chaps took offense. 'As if we would harbor a thing like that,' they said. 'Wouldn't you like to look for him in our coal-hole?' Quite a tiff. But they made it up in the end. I suppose he did drown himself. Don't you, sir?"

"I don't suppose anything."

"You have no doubt in the matter, sir?"

"None whatever."

I left him suddenly. I felt I was producing a bad impression, but with my double down there it was most trying to be on deck. And it was almost as trying to be below. Altogether a nerve-trying situation. But on the whole I felt less torn in two when I was with him. There was no one in the whole ship whom I dared take into my confidence. Since the hands had got to know his story, it would have been impossible to pass him off for any one else, and an accidental discovery was to be dreaded now more than ever. . . .

The steward being engaged in laying the table for dinner, we could talk only with our eyes when I first went down. Later in the afternoon we had a cautious try at whispering. The Sunday quietness of the ship was against us; the stillness of air and water around her was against us; the elements, the men were against us—everything was against us in our secret partnership; time itself—for this could not go on for ever. The very trust in Providence was, I supposed, denied to his guilt. Shall I confess that this thought cast me down very much? And as to the chapter of accidents which counts for so much in the book of success, I could only hope that it was closed. For what favorable accident could be expected?

"Did you hear everything?" were my first words as soon as we took up our position side by side, leaning over my bedplace.

He had. And the proof of it was his earnest whisper, "The man told you he hardly dared to give the order."

I understood the reference to be to that saving foresail.

"Yes. He was afraid of it being lost in the setting."

"I assure you he never gave the order. He may think he did, but he never gave it. He stood there with me on the break of the poop after the maintopsail blew away, and whimpered about our last hope—positively whimpered about it and nothing else—and the night coming on! To hear one's skipper go on like that in such weather was enough to drive any fellow out of his mind. It worked me up into a sort of desperation. I just took it into my own hands and went away from him, boiling, and—But what's the use telling you? *You* know! . . . Do you think that if I had not been pretty fierce with them I should have got the men to do anything? Not it! The boss'en perhaps? Perhaps! It wasn't a heavy sea—it was a sea gone mad! I suppose the end of the world will be something like that; and a man may have the heart to see it coming once and be done with it—but to have to face it day after day . . . I don't blame anybody. I was precious little better than the rest. Only—I was an officer of that old coal-wagon, anyhow. . . ."

"I quite understand," I conveyed that sincere assurance into his ear. He was out of breath with whispering; I could hear him pant slightly. It was all very simple. The same strung-up force which had given twenty-four men a chance, at least, for their lives had, in a sort of recoil, crushed an unworthy mutinous existence.

But I had no leisure to weigh the merits of the matter—footsteps in the saloon, a heavy knock. "There's enough wind to get under way with, sir." Here was the call of a new claim upon my thoughts and even upon my feelings.

"Turn the hands up," I cried through the door. "I'll be on deck directly."

I was going out to make the acquaintance of my ship. Before I left the cabin our eyes met—the eyes of the only two strangers on board. I pointed to the recessed part where the little camp-stool awaited him and laid my finger on my lips. He made a gesture—somewhat vague—a little mysterious, accompanied by a faint smile, as if of regret.

This is not the place to enlarge upon the sensations of a man who feels for the first time a ship move under his feet to his own independent word. In my case they were not unalloyed. I was not wholly alone with my command; for there was that stranger in my cabin. Or, rather, I was not completely and wholly with her. Part of me was absent. That mental feeling of being in two places at once affected me physically as if the mood of secrecy had penetrated my very soul. Before an hour had elapsed since the ship had begun to move, having occasion to ask the mate (he stood by my side) to take a compass bearing of the Pagoda, I caught myself reaching up to his ear in whispers. I say I caught myself, but enough had escaped to startle the man. I can't describe it otherwise than by saying that he shied. A grave, preoccupied manner, as though he were in possession of some perplexing intelligence, did not leave him henceforth. A little later I moved away from the rail to look at the compass with such a stealthy gait that the helmsman noticed it—and I could not help noticing the unusual roundness of his eyes. These are trifling instances, though it's to no commander's advantage to be suspected of ludicrous eccentricities. But I was also more seriously affected. There are to a seaman certain words, gestures, that should in given conditions come as naturally, as instinctively, as the winking of a menaced eye. A certain order should spring on to his lips without thinking; a certain sign should get itself made, so to speak, without reflection. But all unconscious alertness had abandoned me. I had to make an effort of will to recall myself back (from the cabin) to the conditions of the moment. I felt that I was appearing an irresolute commander to those people who were watching me more or less critically.

And, besides, there were the scares. On the second day out, for instance, coming off the deck in the afternoon (I had straw slippers on my bare feet) I stopped at the open pantry door and spoke to the steward. He was doing something there with his back to me. At the sound of my voice he nearly jumped out of his skin as the saying is, and incidentally broke a cup.

"What on earth's the matter with you?" I asked, astonished.

He was extremely confused. "Beg your pardon, sir. I made sure you were in your cabin."

"You see I wasn't."

"No, sir. I could have sworn I had heard you moving in there not a moment ago. It's most extraordinary . . . very sorry, sir."

I passed on with an inward shudder. I was so identified with my secret double that I did not even mention the fact in those scanty, fearful whispers we exchanged. I suppose he had made some slight noise of some kind or other. It would have been miraculous if he hadn't at one time or another. And yet, haggard as he appeared, he looked always perfectly self-controled, more than calm—almost invulnerable. On my suggestion he remained almost entirely in the bathroom, which, upon the whole, was the safest place. There could be really no shadow of an excuse for any one ever wanting to go in there, once the steward had done with it. It was a very tiny place. Sometimes he reclined on the floor, his legs bent, his head sustained on one elbow. At others I would find him on the camp-stool, sitting in his gray sleeping suit and with his cropped dark hair like a patient, unmoved convict. At night I would smuggle him into my bedplace, and we would whisper together, with the regular footfalls of the officer of the watch passing and repassing over our heads. It was an infinitely miserable time. It was lucky that some tins of fine preserves were stowed in a locker in my stateroom; hard bread I could always get hold of; and so he lived on stewed chicken, pâté de foie gras, asparagus, cooked oysters, sardines—on all sorts of abominable sham-delicacies out of tins. My early morning coffee he always drank; and it was all I dared do for him in that respect.

Every day there was the horrible maneuvering to go through so that my room and then the bathroom should be done in the usual way. I came to hate the sight of the steward, to abhor the voice of that harmless man. I felt that it was he who would bring on the disaster of discovery. It hung like a sword over our heads.

The fourth day out, I think (we were then working down the east side of the Gulf of Siam, tack for tack, in light winds and smooth water)—the fourth day, I say, of this miserable juggling with the unavoidable, as we sat at our evening meal, that man, whose slightest movement I dreaded, after putting down the dishes ran up on deck busily. This could not be dangerous. Presently he came down again; and then it appeared that he had remembered a coat of mine which I had thrown over a rail to dry after having been wetted in a shower which had passed over the ship in the afternoon. Sitting stolidly at the head of the table I became terrified at the sight of the garment on his arm. Of course he made for my door. There was no time to lose.

"Steward!" I thundered. My nerves were so shaken that I could not govern my voice and conceal my agitation. This was the sort of thing that made my terrifically whiskered mate tap his forehead with his forefinger. I had detected him using that gesture while talking on deck with a confidential air to the carpenter. It was too far to hear a word, but I had no doubt that this pantomime could only refer to the strange new captain.

"Yes, sir," the pale-faced steward turned resignedly to me. It was this maddening course of being shouted at, checked without rhyme or reason, arbitrarily chased out of my cabin, suddenly called into it, sent flying out of his pantry on incomprehensible errands, that accounted for the growing wretchedness of his expression.

"Where are you going with that coat?"

"To your room, sir."

"Is there another shower coming?"

"I'm sure I don't know, sir. Shall I go up again and see, sir?"

"No! never mind."

My object was attained, as of course my other self in there would have heard everything that passed. During this interlude my two officers never raised their eyes off their respective plates; but the lip of that confounded cub, the second mate, quivered visibly.

I expected the steward to hook my coat on and come out at once. He was very slow about it; but I dominated my nervousness sufficiently not to shout after him. Suddenly I became aware (it could be heard plainly enough) that the fellow for some reason or other was opening the door of the bathroom. It was the end. The place was literally not big enough to swing a cat in. My voice died in my throat and I went stony all over. I expected to hear a yell of surprise and terror, and made a movement, but had not the strength to get on my legs. Everything remained still. Had my second self taken the poor wretch by the throat? I don't know what I could have done next moment if I had not seen the steward come out of my room, close the door, and then stand quietly by the sideboard.

"Saved," I thought. "But, no! Lost! Gone! He was gone!"

I laid my knife and fork down and leaned back in my chair. My head swam. After a while, when sufficiently recovered to speak in a steady voice, I instructed my mate to put the ship round at eight o'clock himself.

"I won't come on deck," I went on. "I think I'll turn in, and unless the wind shifts I don't want to be disturbed before midnight. I feel a bit seedy."

"You did look middling bad a little while ago," the chief mate remarked without showing any great concern.

They both went out, and I stared at the steward clearing the table. There was nothing to be read on that wretched man's face. But why did he avoid my eyes? I asked myself. Then I thought I should like to hear the sound of his voice.

"Steward!"

"Sir!" Startled as usual.

"Where did you hang up that coat?"

"In the bathroom, sir." The usual anxious tone. "It's not quite dry yet, sir."

For some time longer I sat in the cuddy. Had my double vanished as he had come? But of his coming there was an explanation, whereas his disappearance would be inexplicable. . . . I went slowly into my dark room, shut the door, lighted the lamp, and for a time dared not turn round. When at last I did I saw him standing bolt upright in the narrow recessed part. It would not be true to say I had a shock, but an irresistible doubt of his bodily existence flitted through my mind. Can it be, I asked myself, that he is not visible to other eyes than mine? It was like being haunted. Motionless, with a grave face, he raised his hands slightly at me in a gesture which meant clearly, "Heavens! what a narrow escape!" Narrow indeed. I think I had come creeping quietly as near insanity as any man who has not actually gone over the border. That gesture restrained me, so to speak.

The mate with the terrific whiskers was now putting the ship on the other tack. In the moment of profound silence which follows upon the hands going to their stations I heard on the poop his raised voice: "Hard alee!" and the distant shout of the order repeated on the main deck. The sails, in that light breeze, made but a faint fluttering noise. It ceased. The ship was coming round slowly; I held my breath in the renewed stillness of expectation; one wouldn't have thought that there was a single living soul on her decks. A sudden brisk shout, "Mainsail haul!" broke the spell, and in the noisy cries and rush overhead of the men running away with the main brace we two, down in my cabin, came together in our usual position by the bedplace.

He did not wait for my question. "I heard him fumbling here and just managed to squat myself down in the bath," he whispered to me. "The fellow only opened the door and put his arm in to hang the coat up. All the same. . . ."

"I never thought of that," I whispered back, even more appalled than before at the closeness of the shave, and marveling at the something unyielding in his character which was carrying him through so finely. There was no agitation in his whisper. Whoever was being driven distracted, it was not he. He was sane. And the proof of his sanity was continued when he took up the whispering again.

"It would never do for me to come to life again."

It was something that a ghost might have said. But what he was alluding to was his old captain's reluctant admission of the theory of suicide. It would obviously serve his turn—if I had understood at all the view which seemed to govern the unalterable purpose of his action.

"You must maroon me as soon as ever you can get amongst these islands off the Cambodje shore," he went on.

"Maroon you! We are not living in a boy's adventure tale," I protested. His scornful whispering took me up.

"We aren't indeed! There's nothing of a boy's tale in this. But there's nothing else for it. I want no more. You don't suppose I am afraid of what can be done to me? Prison or gallows or whatever they may please. But you don't see me coming back to explain such things to an old fellow in a wig and twelve respectable tradesmen, do you? What can they know whether I am guilty or not—or of *what* I am guilty, either? That's my affair. What does the Bible say? 'Driven off the face of the earth.' Very well. I am off the face of the earth now. As I came at night so I shall go."

"Impossible!" I murmured. "You can't."

"Can't? . . . Not naked like a soul on the Day of Judgment. I shall freeze on to this sleeping suit. The Last Day is not yet—and . . . you have understood thoroughly. Didn't you?"

I felt suddenly ashamed of myself. I may say truly that I understood—and my hesitation in letting that man swim away from my ship's side had been a mere sham sentiment, a sort of cowardice.

"It can't be done now till next night," I breathed out. "The ship is on the offshore tack and the wind may fail us."

"As long as I know that you understand," he whispered. "But of course you do. It's a great satisfaction to have got somebody to understand. You seem to have been there on purpose." And in the same whisper, as if we two whenever we talked had to say things to each other which were not fit for the world to hear, he added, "It's very wonderful."

We remained side by side talking in our secret way—but sometimes silent or just exchanging a whispered word or two at long intervals. And as usual he stared through the port. A breath of wind came now and again into our faces. The ship might have been moored in dock, so gently and on an even keel she slipped through the water, that did not murmur even at our passage, shadowy and silent like a phantom sea.

At midnight I went on deck, and to my mate's great surprise put the ship round on the other tack. His terrible whiskers flitted round me in silent criticism. I certainly should not have done it if it had been only a question of getting out of that sleepy gulf as quickly as possible. I believe he told the second mate, who relieved him, that it was a great want of judgment. The other only yawned. That intolerable cub shuffled about so sleepily and lolled against the rails in such a slack, improper fashion that I came down on him sharply.

"Aren't you properly awake yet?"

"Yes, sir! I am awake."

"Well, then, be good enough to hold yourself as if you were. And keep a look out. If there's any current we'll be closing with some islands long before daylight."

The east side of the gulf is fringed with islands, some solitary, others in groups. On the blue background of the high coast they seem to float on silvery patches of calm water, arid and gray, or dark green and rounded like clumps of evergreen bushes, with the larger ones, a mile or two long, showing the outlines of ridges, ribs of gray rock under the dank mantle of matted leafage. Unknown to trade, to travel, almost to geography, the manner of life they harbor is an unsolved secret. There must be villages—settlements of fishermen at least—on the largest of them, and some communication with the world is probably kept up by native craft. But all that forenoon, as we headed for them, fanned along by the faintest of breezes, I saw no sign of man or canoe in the field of the telescope I kept on pointing at the scattered group.

At noon I gave no orders for a change of course, and the mate's whiskers became much concerned and seemed to be offering themselves unduly to my notice. At last I said:

"I am going to stand[16] right in. Quite in—as far as I can take her."

The stare of extreme surprise imparted an air of ferocity also to his eyes, and he looked truly terrific for a moment.

"We're not doing well in the middle of the gulf," I continued casually. "I am going to look for the land breezes tonight."

"Bless my soul! Do you mean, sir, in the dark amongst the lot of all them islands and reefs and shoals?"

"Well, if there are any regular land breezes at all on this coast one must get close inshore to find them—mustn't one?"

"Bless my soul!" he exclaimed again under his breath. All that afternoon he wore a dreamy, contemplative appearance which in him was a mark of perplexity. After dinner I went into my stateroom as if I meant to take some rest. There we two bent our dark heads over a half-unrolled chart lying on my bed.

"There," I said. "It's got to be Koh-ring.[17] I've been looking at it ever since sunrise. It has got two hills and a low point. It must be inhabited. And on the coast opposite there is what looks like the mouth of a biggish river—with some town, no doubt, not far up. It's the best chance for you that I can see."

"Anything. Koh-ring let it be."

He looked thoughtfully at the chart as if surveying chances and distances from a lofty height—and following with his eyes his own figure wandering on the blank land of Cochin-China, and then passing off that piece of paper clean out of sight into uncharted regions. And it was as if the ship had two captains to plan her course for her. I had been so worried and restless running up and down that I had not had the patience to dress that day. I had remained in my sleeping suit, with straw slippers and a soft floppy hat. The closeness of the heat in the gulf had been most oppressive, and the crew were used to see me wandering in that airy attire.

"She will clear the south point as she heads now," I whispered into his ear. "Goodness only knows when, though—but certainly after dark. I'll edge her in to half a mile, as far as I may be able to judge in the dark . . ."

[16] Stand, in nautical termonology, means to take a particular course or direction.
[17] Koh-ring could be one of many possible islands at the head of the Gulf of Siam.

"Be careful," he murmured warningly—and I realized suddenly that all my future, the only future for which I was fit, would perhaps go irretrievably to pieces in any mishap to my first command.

I could not stop a moment longer in the room. I motioned him to get out of sight and made my way on the poop. That unplayful cub had the watch. I walked up and down for a while thinking things out, then beckoned him over.

"Send a couple of hands to open the two quarter-deck ports," I said mildly.

He actually had the impudence, or else so forgot himself in his wonder at such an incomprehensible order, as to repeat:

"Open the quarter-deck ports! For what, sir?"

"The only reason you need concern yourself about is because I tell you to do so. Have them opened wide and fastened properly."

He reddened and went off, but I believe made some jeering remark to the carpenter as to the sensible practice of ventilating a ship's quarter-deck. I know he popped into the mate's cabin to impart the fact to him, because the whiskers came on deck, as it were by chance, and stole glances at me from below—for signs of lunacy or drunkenness, I suppose.

A little before supper, feeling more restless than ever, I rejoined, for a moment, my second self. And to find him sitting so quietly was surprising, like something against nature, inhuman.

I developed my plan in a hurried whisper.

"I shall stand in as close as I dare and then put her round. I shall presently find means to smuggle you out of here into the sail-locker, which communicates with the lobby. But there is an opening, a sort of square for hauling the sails out, which gives straight on the quarter-deck and which is never closed in fine weather, so as to give air to the sails. When the ship's way is deadened in stays and all the hands are aft at the main braces you shall have a clear road to slip out and get overboard through the open quarter-deck port. I've had them both fastened up. Use a rope's end to lower yourself into the water so as to avoid a splash—you know. It could be heard and cause some beastly complication."

He kept silent for a while, then whispered, "I understand."

"I won't be there to see you go," I began with an effort. "The rest . . . I only hope I have understood too."

"You have. From first to last"—and for the first time there seemed to be a faltering, something strained in his whisper. He caught hold of my arm, but the ringing of the supper bell made me start. He didn't, though; he only released his grip.

After supper I didn't come below again till well past eight o'clock. The faint, steady breeze was loaded with dew; and the wet, darkened sails held all there was of propelling power in it. The night, clear and starry, sparkled darkly, and the opaque, lightless patches shifting slowly amongst the low stars were the drifting islets. On the port bow there was a big one more distant and shadowily imposing by the great space of sky it eclipsed.

On opening the door I had a back view of my very own self looking at a chart. He had come out of the recess and was standing near the table.

"Quite dark enough," I whispered.

He stepped back and leaned against my bed with a level, quiet glance. I sat on the couch. We had nothing to say to each other. Over our heads the officer of the watch moved here and there. Then I heard him move quickly. I knew what that meant. He was making for the companion; and presently his voice was outside my door.

"We are drawing in pretty fast, sir. Land looks rather close."

"Very well," I answered. "I am coming on deck directly."

I waited till he was gone out of the cuddy, then rose. My double moved too. The time had come to exchange our last whispers, for neither of us was ever to hear each other's natural voice.

"Look here!" I opened a drawer and took out three sovereigns. "Take this, anyhow. I've got six and I'd give you the lot, only I must keep a little money to buy some fruit and vegetables for the crew from native boats as we go through Sunda Straits."

He shook his head.

"Take it," I urged him, whispering desperately. "No one can tell what . . ."

He smiled and slapped meaningly the only pocket of the sleeping jacket. It was not safe, certainly. But I produced a large old silk handkerchief of mine, and tying the three pieces of gold in a corner, pressed it on him. He was touched, I suppose, because he took it at last and tied it quickly round his waist under the jacket, on his bare skin.

Our eyes met; several seconds elapsed, till, our glances still mingled, I extended my hand and turned the lamp out. Then I passed through the cuddy, leaving the door of my room wide open. . . . "Steward!"

He was still lingering in the pantry in the greatness of his zeal, giving a rub-up to a plated cruet stand the last thing before going to bed. Being careful not to wake up the mate, whose room was opposite, I spoke in an undertone.

He looked round anxiously. "Sir!"

"Can you get me a little hot water from the galley?"

"I am afraid, sir, the galley fire's been out for some time now."

"Go and see."

He fled up the stairs.

"Now," I whispered loudly into the saloon—too loudly, perhaps, but I was afraid I couldn't make a sound. He was by my side in an instant—the double captain slipped past the stairs—through a tiny dark passage . . . a sliding door. We were in the sail-locker, scrambling on our knees over the sails. A sudden thought struck me. I saw myself wandering barefooted, bareheaded, the sun beating on my dark poll. I snatched off my floppy hat and tried hurriedly in the dark to ram it on my other self. He dodged and fended off silently. I wonder what he thought had come to me before he understood and suddenly desisted. Our hands met gropingly, lingered united in a steady, motionless clasp for a second. . . . No word was breathed by either of us when they separated.

I was standing quietly by the pantry door when the steward returned.

"Sorry, sir. Kettle barely warm. Shall I light the spirit-lamp?"

"Never mind."

I came out on deck slowly. It was now a matter of conscience to shave the land as close as possible—for now he must go overboard whenever the ship was put in stays. Must! There could be no going back for him. After a moment I walked over to leeward and my heart flew into my mouth at the nearness of the land on the bow. Under any other circumstances I would not have held on a minute longer. The second mate had followed me anxiously.

I looked on till I felt I could command my voice.

"She will weather,"[18] I said then in a quiet tone.

"Are you going to try that, sir?" he stammered out incredulously.

I took no notice of him and raised my tone just enough to be heard by the helmsman.

"Keep her good full."

"Good full, sir."

The wind fanned my cheek, the sails slept, the world was silent. The strain of watching the dark loom of the land grow bigger and denser was too much for me. I had to shut my eyes—because the ship must go closer. She must! The stillness was intolerable. Were we standing still?

When I opened my eyes the second view started my heart with a thump. The black southern hill of Koh-ring seemed to hang right over the ship like a towering fragment of the everlasting night. On that enormous mass of blackness there was not a gleam to be seen, not a sound to be heard. It was gliding irresistibly towards us and yet seemed already within reach of the hand. I saw the vague figures of the watch grouped in the waist, gazing in awed silence.

"Are you going on, sir?" inquired an unsteady voice at my elbow.

I ignored it. I had to go on.

"Keep her full. Don't check her way. That won't do now," I said warningly.

"I can't see the sails very well," the helmsman answered me, in strange, quavering tones.

[18] Weather means to pass on the windward side of a marker—thus, to survive a dangerous situation.

Was she close enough? Already she was, I won't say in the shadow of the land, but in the very blackness of it, already swallowed up as it were, gone too close to be recalled, gone from me altogether.

"Give the mate a call," I said to the young man who stood at my elbow as still as death. "And turn all hands up."

My tone had a borrowed loudness reverberated from the height of the land. Several voices cried out together, "We are all on deck, sir."

Then stillness again, with the great shadow gliding closer, towering higher, without a light, without a sound. Such a hush had fallen on the ship that she might have been a bark of the dead floating in slowly under the very gate of Erebus.[19]

"My God! Where are we?"

It was the mate moaning at my elbow. He was thunderstruck, and as it were deprived of the moral support of his whiskers. He clapped his hands and absolutely cried out. "Lost!"

"Be quiet," I said sternly.

He lowered his tone, but I saw the shadowy gesture of his despair. "What are we doing here?"

"Looking for the land wind."

He made as if to tear his hair, and addressed me recklessly.

"She will never get out. You have done it, sir. I knew it'd end in something like this. She will never weather, and you are too close now to stay. She'll drift ashore before she's round. O my God!"

I caught his arm as he was raising it to batter his poor devoted head, and shook it violently.

"She's ashore already," he wailed, trying to tear himself away.

"Is she? . . . Keep good full there!"

"Good full, sir," cried the helmsman in a frightened, thin, childlike voice.

I hadn't let go the mate's arm and went on shaking it. "Ready about, do you hear? You go forward"—shake—"and stop there"—shake—"and hold your noise"—shake—"and see these head-sheets properly overhauled"—shake, shake—shake.

And all the time I dared not look towards the land lest my heart should fail me. I released my grip at last and he ran forward as if fleeing for dear life.

I wondered what my double there in the sail-locker thought of this commotion. He was able to hear everything—and perhaps he was able to understand why, on my conscience, it had to be thus close—no less. My first order "Hard alee!" re-echoed ominously under the towering shadow of Koh-ring as if I had shouted in a mountain gorge. And then I watched the land intently. In that smooth water and light wind it was impossible to feel the ship coming-to. No! I could not feel her.

[19] The gate of Erebus is the entrance to the underworld.

And my second self was making now ready to slip out and lower himself overboard. Perhaps he was gone already . . . ?

The great black mass brooding over our very mast-heads began to pivot away from the ship's side silently. And now I forgot the secret stranger ready to depart, and remembered only that I was a total stranger to the ship. I did not know her. Would she do it? How was she to be handled?

I swung the mainyard and waited helplessly. She was perhaps stopped, and her very fate hung in the balance, with the black mass of Koh-ring like the gate of the everlasting night towering over her taffrail. What would she do now? Had she way on her yet? I stepped to the side swiftly, and on the shadowy water I could see nothing except a faint phosphorescent flash revealing the glassy smoothness of the sleeping surface. It was impossible to tell—and I had not learned yet the feel of my ship. Was she moving? What I needed was something easily seen, a piece of paper, which I could throw overboard and watch. I had nothing on me. To run down for it I didn't dare. There was no time. All at once my strained, yearning stare distinguished a white object floating within a yard of the ship's side—white, on the black water. A phosphorescent flash passed under it. What was that thing? . . . I recognized my own floppy hat. It must have fallen off his head . . . and he didn't bother. Now I had what I wanted—the saving mark for my eyes. But I hardly thought of my other self, now gone from the ship, to be hidden for ever from all friendly faces, to be a fugitive and a vagabond on the earth, with no brand of the curse on his sane forehead to stay a slaying hand . . . too proud to explain.

And I watched the hat—the expression of my sudden pity for his mere flesh. It had been meant to save his homeless head from the dangers of the sun. And now—behold—it was saving the ship, by serving me for a mark to help out the ignorance of my strangeness. Ha! It was drifting forward, warning me just in time that the ship had gathered sternway.

"Shift the helm," I said in a low voice to the seaman standing still like a statue.

The man's eyes glistened wildly in the binnacle light as he jumped round to the other side and spun round the wheel.

I walked to the break of the poop. On the overshadowed deck all hands stood by the forebraces waiting for my order. The stars ahead seemed to be gliding from right to left. And all was so still in the world that I heard the quiet remark, "She's round," passed in a tone of intense relief between two seamen.

"Let go and haul."

The foreyards ran round with a great noise, amidst cheery cries. And now the frightful whiskers made themselves heard giving various orders. Already the ship was drawing ahead. And I was alone with her.

Nothing! no one in the world should stand now between us, throwing a shadow on the way of silent knowledge and mute affection; the perfect communion of a seaman with his first command.

Walking to the taffrail, I was in time to make out, on the very edge of a darkness thrown by a towering black mass like the very gateway of Erebus—yes, I was in time to catch an evanescent glimpse of my white hat left behind to mark the spot where the secret sharer of my cabin and of my thoughts, as though he were my second self, had lowered himself into the water to take his punishment: a free man, a proud swimmer striking out for a new destiny.

QUESTIONS

1. The narrator contrasts "the great security of the sea" with "the unrest of land." Is that a just comparison?
2. The narrator believes the sea has "an elemental moral beauty . . . by the singleness of its purpose." Does the story indicate that this is a truthful evaluation of the sea?
3. The narrator's goal is to find out "how far [he] should turn out faithful to that ideal conception of one's own personality every man sets up for himself secretly." Does he live up to that "ideal conception" at the end of the story?
4. What is the communion between a seaman and his first command that the narrator hopes he has achieved at the end of the story?

JOSEPH CONRAD

from PREFACE TO "THE SECRET SHARER"

The origins of the middle story, *The Secret Sharer,* are quite other. It was written much earlier and was published first in *Harper's Magazine,* during the early part, I think, of 1911. Or perhaps the latter part? My memory on that point is hazy. The basic fact of the tale I had in my possession for a good many years. It was in truth the common possession of the whole fleet of merchant ships trading to India, China, and Australia: a great company the last years of which coincided with my first years on the wider seas. The fact itself happened on board a very distinguished member of it, *Cutty Sark* by name and belonging to Mr. Willis, a notable shipowner in his day, one of the kind (they are all underground now) who used personally to see his ships start on their voyages to those distant shores where they showed worthily the honoured house-flag of their owner. I am glad I was not too late to get at least one glimpse of Mr. Willis on a very wet and gloomy morning watching from the pier head of the New South Dock one of his clippers starting on a China voyage—an imposing figure of a man under the invariable white hat so well known in the Port of London, waiting till the head of his ship had swung downstream before giving her a dignified wave of a big gloved hand. For all I know it may have been the *Cutty Sark* herself, though certainly not on that fatal voyage. I do not know the date of the occurrence on which the scheme of *The Secret Sharer* is founded; it came to light an even got into newspapers about the middle eighties, though I had heard of it before, as it were privately, among the officers of the great wool fleet in which my first years in deep water were served. It came to light under circumstances dramatic enough, I think, but which have nothing to do with my story. In the more specially maritime part of my writings this bit of presentation may take its place as one of my two Calm-pieces. For, if there is to be any classification by subjects, I have done two Storm-pieces in *The Nigger of the 'Narcissus'* and in *Typhoon;* and two Calm-pieces: this one and *The Shadow-Line,* a book which belongs to a later period.

Notwithstanding their autobiographical form the above are not the record of personal experience. Their quality, such as it is, depends on something larger if less precise: on the character, vision, and sentiment of the first twenty independent years of my life.

THINGS TO THINK ABOUT

1. In "The Secret Sharer" Conrad has taken a piece of history and written about it as though it were a personal experience. Why do you suppose writers do such things? Why hasn't Conrad written about the experience in the third person? Are there any recent events that you could imagine writing as a personal narrative?
2. In what sense is this a "Calm-piece"? Are the emotions of this piece calm? In what ways are the emotions of the participants contrasted to the environment?
3. Conrad speaks of ships like *Cutty Sark* making "voyages to those distant shores where they showed worthily the honored house–flag of their owner." Does Conrad believe such practices still exist? In what ways does he contrast personal entrepreneurship to corporate ownership?

FRANZ KAFKA

BEFORE THE LAW

Great art is frequently in danger of disappearing. Meville's work went through a period of almost total neglect before it was rediscovered. Vincent Van Gogh sold not one painting in his entire life, and died in poverty and neglect. Franz Kafka (1883–1924) published only a handful of stories before he died of tuberculosis at the age of forty and requested that his manuscripts be destroyed. Luckily his friend and fellow writer Max Brod not only saved Kafka's work, but saw it into publication.

Kafka was born to a wealthy Jewish family in Prague, Czechoslovakia. He became a lawyer after studying at the German University in his native city and worked for several years for an insurance company. His work is saturated by his experience of both the legal system (which forms the backdrop of "Before the Law") and the bureaucracy. More importantly he captures—as no writer before him had captured—the spiritual crisis of twentieth century humankind caught in a world whose complexity, barbarity, and emptiness were seemingly beyond comprehension or correction.

Photographs of Franz Kafka show a pale, sunken-eyed, painfully thin young man, with large pointy ears. Though he died before the Nazis came to power, he resembles—as his work anticipates—the victims of the Holocaust.

Before the law stands a doorkeeper. To this doorkeeper there comes a man from the country and prays for admittance to the Law. But the doorkeeper says that he cannot grant admittance at the moment. The man thinks it over and then asks if he will be allowed in later. "It is possible," says the doorkeeper, "but not at the moment." Since the gate stands open, as usual, and the doorkeeper steps to one side, the man stoops to peer through the gateway into the interior. Observing that, the doorkeeper laughs and says: "If you are so drawn to it, just try to go in despite my veto. But take note: I am powerful. And I am only the least of the doorkeepers. From hall to hall there is one doorkeeper after another, each more powerful than the last. The third doorkeeper is already so terrible that even I cannot bear to look at him." These are difficulties the man from the country has not expected; the Law, he thinks, should surely be accessible at all times and to everyone, but as he now takes a closer look at the doorkeeper in his fur coat, with his big sharp nose and long, thin, black Tartar beard, he decides that it is better to wait until he gets permission to enter. The doorkeeper gives him a stool and lets him sit down at one side of the door. There he sits for days and years. He makes many attempts to be admitted, and wearies the doorkeeper by his importunity. The doorkeeper frequently has little interviews with him, asking him questions about his home and many other things, but the questions are put indifferently, as great lords put them, and always finish with the statement that he cannot be let in yet. The man, who has furnished himself with many things for his journey, sacrifices all he has, however valuable, to bribe the doorkeeper. The doorkeeper accepts everything, but always with the remark: "I am only taking it to keep you from thinking you have omitted anything." During these many years the man fixes his attention almost continuously on the doorkeeper. He forgets the other doorkeepers, and this first one seems to him the sole obstacle preventing access to the Law. He curses his bad luck, in his early years boldly and loudly, later, as he grows old, he only grumbles to himself. He becomes childish, and since in his yearlong contemplation of the doorkeeper he has come to know even the fleas in his fur collar, he begs the fleas as well to help him and to change the doorkeeper's mind. At length his eyesight begins to fail, and he does not know whether the world is really darker or whether his eyes are only deceiving him. Yet in his darkness he is now aware of a radiance that streams inextinguishably from the gateway of the Law. Now he has not very long to live. Before he dies, all his experiences in these long years gather themselves in his head to one point, a question he has not yet asked the doorkeeper. He waves him nearer, since he can no longer raise his stiffening body. The doorkeeper has to bend low towards him, for the difference in height between them has altered much to the man's disadvantage. "What do you want to know now?" asks the doorkeeper; "you are insatiable." "Everyone strives to reach the Law," says the man, "so how does it happen that for all these many years no one but myself has ever begged for admittance?" The doorkeeper recognizes that the man has reached his end, and to let his failing senses catch the words roars in his ear: "No one else could ever be admitted here, since this gate was made only for you. I am now going to shut it."

QUESTIONS

1. What does the door of justice look like? Is the door open or closed? Is this a realistic or fantastic setting?
2. Why doesn't the man from the country enter the hall of justice?
3. Why is the man content to sit before the door of justice?
4. What by extension is Kafka saying that we must do to gain justice?

JOYCE CAROL OATES

THE THAW

Joyce Carol Oates (b. 1938) is one of the most prolific authors in America today. She has written over sixty books, including volumes of poetry, short stories, essays, plays, critical studies and novels. The pace of her remarkable productivity has not diminished over the years.

She was born in Millersport, New York and was educated at Syracuse University and the University of Wisconsin. For many years she lived in the Detroit area with her husband Raymond J. Smith, with whom she is the publisher of The Ontario Review. *Since 1978, she has been the writer-in-residence at Princeton University.*

Shortly after noon on their second day at Baylis Lake they encountered the girl: she passed them swiftly, headed in the direction of the lake, accompanied by a large sleek gray-furred dog. She was about eighteen years old, with loose, thick, shoulderlength blond hair of a striking dark gold, quite tall, nearly as tall as Scott. They were on their way to the village, to buy a newspaper and a few supplies. It was a mile's hike and the wind was rather chilly from the northeast, but they did not want to drive; they had come to the lake to get some exercise. When they saw the girl approaching, striding along the hard, frozen path, Ellen could sense her husband's surprise and then his interest and she could almost have said, to the instant, when he would raise a gloved hand and call out a greeting. He was a reticent man and so he sometimes forced himself at such times to be friendly; to behave in a friendly manner. She knew how vulnerable he was and she hoped the girl would respond.

At first she was not going to notice them. She walked hurriedly, eyes lowered, hands thrust into the pockets of her oversized wool jacket; she was very much alone, even with the dog beside her. But it really would have been impossible for her to ignore them. The lake was deserted at this time of year. Apart from the caretaker who lived in one of the smaller cabins on the far side of the lake, the three of them were probably the only people in the immediate vicinity. So it was quite natural for Scott to speak to her as they passed. His greeting was casual, cheerful. She glanced up at him and at Ellen, unsmiling, and murmured a few words, and continued on. Yet she had not been unfriendly. She had managed the encounter gracefully enough.

"What a pretty girl!" Ellen said warmly. "She didn't look familiar, though. Whose cabin do you suppose she's staying in?"

"She looked familiar," Scott said.

"Did she? Do you know her?"

"No."

"I wonder if she's here alone. We didn't notice anyone yesterday, there weren't any cars around yesterday. . . . It would be odd, wouldn't it, for her to be here alone?"

Her hair was so rich a color: her eyes deep-set and blue and thickly lashed, like a child's. Like a child she had had an open, frank, disingenuous stare, raised to them and then lowered, with that timid, clever grace, acknowledging them in one instant and in the next dismissing them.

"She looked familiar," Scott said. "Someone's daughter. Someone's daughter grown up, since we last saw her."

"A very pretty girl," Ellen said.

Scott said nothing.

They had driven up the day before, a Sunday; four hundred miles to the upper peninsula of the state, into the lake country. The roads had been nearly deserted. The drive had been long and exhausting and when they got to their cabin, it had seemed rather shabby and smaller than they remembered—hadn't it been more attractive last summer?—the summer before last? They had not been to Baylis Lake for a year and a half. As soon as they unlocked the door and went inside the cabin Scott said the trip had been a mistake. "Obviously we shouldn't have come. It's wrong. It feels wrong."

"But we thought. . . ."

"I didn't. I wasn't the one. You were the one who insisted."

"But. . . ."

"It's freezing in here," he said, his voice rising shrilly. "What are we going to do until it warms up? It might take hours. . . ."

"We could sit in the car."

"In the car! And risk being asphyxiated. . . ."

"We could drive around the lake. We could drive back to the village and stop somewhere . . . at the hotel, or the pub. . . ."

"It wasn't my idea to come here," he said.

It had been his idea from the first. But she would not challenge him.

"Everything seems so ugly, so muted at this time of year," he said helplessly. "Easter Sunday . . . Easter. . . . And the lake is icebound and there's snow everywhere and it's so cold in here in this ugly cabin, what are we going to do?"

"Would you like to go back home?"

"It's out of the question to go back home."

Dismay and anger had enlivened him. His cheeks were flushed, the very tip of his nose had reddened, his dark, almost black eyes were bright and glistening. He knew she was watching him and so he refused to look at her. He went to stand by the floor-to-ceiling plate-glass window that faced the lake, fifty yards away; even in his bulky, coarse-knit sweater he looked frail. His red-brown hair seemed to move, however, even to breathe, wisps of it stirring as if with his emotion. Ellen said, softly, "If you want to go back, I don't mind. I don't mind driving."

"You're being ridiculous."

"I don't mind. We could start out and stay in a motel."

"You're exhausted. You don't know what you're talking about," he said tonelessly. "We might as well stay."

After they unpacked and the cabin heated and Ellen fixed a light, warm meal—scrambled eggs with ham and cheese, and thick dark bread—the tension between them lessened. It had been a good idea to come north, after all. The stillness, the isolation, the view of the lake—the cold, harsh, fresh air—the occasional honking of mallards or geese and the sound of the wind in the pines: Ellen felt moved by these things, reassured. When the sun set, the sky and part of the lake were transformed, subtly, richly, a pale red-orange that accentuated the division between the open, choppy water and the jagged line of ice that edged the beach. They sat in silence, watching. "It's so beautiful here," Ellen whispered. "People can never imagine . . . can never remember, in that other life. . . ."

"Yes," Scott said. "It's beautiful. It always is."

The cabin belonged to Scott's uncle, now an elderly man in a nursing home in Ft. Lauderdale; it, and the fairly large lot that came with it, would go to Scott when the old man died. Scott had always liked their brief vacations here, though he had not liked the presence of other people, and had detested the noise of outboard motors on the lake. But now it was late winter and no one was around.

"Then you're happy we came? You don't think it was a mistake?" Ellen asked.

". . . as good a place as any to die," Scott said lightly.

"But you're not going to die," Ellen said. "That's ridiculous."

"I know. I know it is."

"It's ridiculous to talk like that," she said, blinking rapidly.

"I know. . . . But death is ridiculous in itself. It's ridiculous anywhere."

"Scott, please. . . ."

"I know, I know," he said quickly. "I *know*."

In the distance, the soft wheezy cry of an owl. A barn owl, probably. Closer, the calls of mourning doves, light, eerie, melodic, blending with the wind; and the abrupt, raucous cries of the mallards; and the chattering of smaller birds, primarily sparrows and juncos and cardinals. Ellen heard a red-winged blackbird, far away: so it was spring, it was going to turn warmer, it was going to thaw.

One day he had said to her: "I'm not what I appear to be."

She had laughed nervously. She had not understood.

"I appear to be well, don't I? In good health? Eh? I appear to resemble anybody, any normal man? Don't I? . . . But that's not the case. That's an illusion."

"I don't understand," she had said.

They had been married for many years. She would not have hesitated to say that they were happily married; she believed they were "happily married." But when he sat with her that day, holding both her hands in his, grave, decorous, faintly mocking, when he spoke in a deliberately casual voice of certain physical symptoms and a visit he had made to their doctor without telling her and the need for a few days' hospitalization in order for tests to be made, she had thought, suddenly, that she did not know him at all; she was terrified not to know him. The prospect of his being seriously ill, even the prospect of his death, did not seem so terrible to her at that moment as the realization that she hardly knew him.

"I appear to be absolutely normal," he said, chuckling. "I'm not much different—only a few pounds heavier—than the man you married, eh? I could fool anyone. I do. But not for much longer."

Now, eighteen months later, the pale skin stretched tight over his prominent cheekbones and there were bruiselike pockets beneath his eyes and faint, vexed lines on his face and throat; but he was still attractive. His brown hair was fine and silky, his eyes were sharp, alert, bright. He walked stiffly, carrying himself almost with a kind of awe or dread; sometimes he leaned upon Ellen involuntarily. He did look older now. He had lost weight. But he had triumphed; by his thirty-ninth birthday they were reasonably sure he had triumphed.

"I love you so much," he had said, weeping in her arms. "Without you I couldn't . . . I couldn't have. . . ."

"It's all right," she said. "It's over."

They met the girl again, on the beach. This time they stopped to talk, self-consciously, as the dog sniffed at them and circled them in silence and then trotted away. At first they spoke of the weather—a record cold for this time of the year, according to the news broadcast that morning—the coldest Easter Sunday in twenty-three years—and light snow flurries predicted for today. But it would thaw soon, it *must* thaw soon. Unless of course the North American climate were really changing, as some people claimed, and a new Ice Age was imminent. . . . "I believe that," the girl said. "I think that makes sense. . . . We deserve it, I mean, don't we? I think that makes sense." But she smiled. And her manner was rather gay, almost flippant. "I don't mind at all. I really don't. I came here on purpose because I knew it would be cold, I love it up here when the lake's frozen and no one's around and you can hear your footsteps crunching in the snow, breaking through the crust of the snow. . . ."

Then the dog trotted back and the girl bent to hug him and they complimented her on the dog: a Russian wolfhound, long-legged, silky, aristocratic, with a head so small and narrow as to seem unnatural. A handsome dog, though. Both Ellen and Scott patted him. The girl seemed pleased by their attention, still bent over the dog, fussing with him, even kissing his head. She was extraordinarily pretty, Ellen saw, with her wide, expressive blue gaze and her loose blond hair and her manner of bright, agreeable insouciance, her sense of being the center of attention, childlike and even innocent in her vanity. She chattered and they listened, warmed by her. Ellen felt a pang of emotion; nothing so simple or crude as jealousy, not even envy. . . .

"I'm here because I want to be alone," the girl announced. "I need to be alone. I need to think my life through . . . need to assess certain things that have happened to me recently . . . certain involvements I can't handle. I love to be alone. I don't mind at all. I could live alone for years like this, with Randy, without any human beings at all. . . . Why are you here? Just for a change?"

"For a change, yes," Scott said quickly. "A change in the pattern of our lives."

The girl looked from Scott to Ellen, smiling. The whites of her eyes were very white. Her skin glowed, her teeth were perfect. Strands of hair were blown into her face and she brushed them away, with a graceful flicking of her long fingers.

"For a change in the pattern of your lives," she repeated. "I think that's wonderful."

"She's very pretty," Ellen said.

"Very young and thinks awfully well of herself," Scott said.

". . . She's confident. She's evidently able to take control of her own life, her own feelings. It's confidence."

"It's arrogance," Scott said.

"But—don't you like her?" Ellen said, as if hurt. "I thought you liked her. We had a pleasant conversation."

"She's only a child," Scott said irritably.

"Do you know who she is? She's that Carlisle's daughter—the doctor—you remember, the doctor?—with the blue-striped sail? I saw her going into his cabin. I'm sure it's his. I remember his children being so young!—I'm sure I remember her, from years ago, as a skinny little girl."

"Does it matter?" Scott said evasively. "I don't think it matters."

Ellen stared at him, uncomprehending.

"Why do you hate me?" she whispered.

During the difficult time of his illness she had read many books and articles; most were on the subject of his illness, but some were by poets and mystics; even by saints—Saint John of the Cross, Saint Teresa. There seemed to be a great deal of time, once he was home from the hospital. There were many hours, one following another. A long stretch of hours broken only by nighttime and the possibility of sleep, hour following hour, endless. Sometimes she read aloud to her husband, in a girlish, quavering voice; almost at random she read to him—*Near is God, and hard to apprehend, but where danger is there arises salvation also*—grateful when he was struck by the wisdom or beauty of her offering. She searched through her college anthologies, discovered poems she had not read or recalled for fifteen years, some of them minutely annotated in her schoolgirl's hand; she came upon a poem she had loved and had forgotten, Hopkins's "As Kingfishers Catch Fire," and read it to Scott, deeply moved, almost euphoric, transported. He had not understood it, but had seemed to like it. Reserved, always a little secretive, he had become almost mute since the operation . . . though at times he would speak effusively, chattering of inconsequential matters.

He had triumphed and would continue to triumph.

"How wonderful to be alive!" he said often. And then again: "How queer, to be alive—how unreal it seems!—and not very important."

There were days of relative normality, peace, contentment. And then, unaccountably, a bad day. Two or three bad days. But he had triumphed and would continue to triumph, had endured a series of seven cobalt treatments, headaches and indigestion and temporary blindness the only side effects. He grew stronger. Gained a few pounds. Seemed to enjoy her reading to him when he was lying down, not quite in the mood to read for himself.

"There are times when your voice is so bell-like and reverent," he said. "You must love me . . . ?"

"Of course I love you."

"But it doesn't change anything, does it? It doesn't change me."

"Doesn't it?"

"Does it?"

"I wish you wouldn't joke, Scott."

"You're such a good, reverent wife," he murmured, taking her hands. "How could I joke with you? That would be cruel."

They walked to the village a second time, in jeans and boots and heavy belted sweaters bought in Scotland years ago. The air was wet, cold, sharply pleasant. The smells of spruce and yew were strong and Ellen would have liked to wander, alone, back into the woods; the trees were more impressive at this time of year than in the summer. Everything was strange, unsettling. There were patches and fingers of snow on the ground and yet the earth's axis had shifted and the days were noticeably longer, the pale sunlight more intense, concentrated. It was April. Snowflakes fell while the sun shone and vast areas of the sky were clear, so that the open waters of the lake were a deep, vivid blue, violent in motion. A small flock of mallards, males and females, rode the choppy waves placidly; Scott called her attention to them. He squeezed her hand. He mumbled something about being sorry for certain remarks he had made—being sorry he was an invalid, in ways he could not always control.

"You're not an invalid," Ellen said flatly.

They saw a deer several hundred feet away, motionless in a grove of yew trees, watching them. They saw rabbit tracks and what must have been raccoon tracks. They stood for several minutes watching three black squirrels high in an oak tree, involved in a noisy skirmish of some kind, agitated, manic. They held hands, laughing at the squirrels.

"Yes, it was a good idea to come here," Scott said.

In the village they went to Vic's Drugs, with its new mock-colonial façade, to buy a newspaper. A radio played rock music. Then there was a five-minute news break: an arms build-up somewhere in the Mideast, the first several indictments handed down by a grand jury investigating conflict of interest in the state legislature, a fourteen-year-old girl found dead in a field near Ypsilanti, having been raped and stabbed repeatedly. They paid for their newspaper and a bottle of hand lotion and left. The little town was fairly busy; the parking lot adjacent to the A&P was filled. Children rode bicycles, squealing, as if delighted with the snow flurries. They went to the Wellington Hotel, where there was a pleasant English-style pub, but it struck them as different from what they remembered—not quite so charming, rather chilly, shabby. And a television set was on above the bar. They did no more than glance in. "Just as well," Scott said. "I don't want to start drinking this early in the day."

They walked back down to the lake, both rather tired. From time to time Scott leaned against Ellen, his arm through hers. He was panting slightly and his breath steamed. There was an odd attentiveness in him, a tension she could not comprehend; he seemed expectant, apprehensive. When he spoke, it was absently, as if he were thinking of something else, not attending to his own words. When she spoke, she knew he wasn't listening. She knew from the past that there were reserves of blind, baffled rage in him, as if a complex story were working itself out inside him and only its outbursts were known to her; and she did not dare interrupt that story.

Nearing the path that led to the cabin both spoke at once, at the same moment. Ellen asked what he would like for dinner that night and Scott murmured: ". . . Carlisle place, did you say? Which one is that?"

Entering, she wore a crocheted cap of red wool and a long red scarf, wound about her neck; and a navy-blue jacket, sheepskinlined, shapeless. Beneath it she wore rather soiled jeans and an inexpensive jersey blouse, pale blue, which fitted her tightly. Her breasts were surprisingly full; her thighs and hips well-developed. Her name was Abigail. Her father was indeed Dr. Carlisle, of Grosse Pointe Farms, but she did not care to speak of her parents at the moment. "I came here for solitude," she said. "I came here to assess my life."

Her pronouncements were solemn and yet audacious, almost coquettish. She laughed quite a bit. The white wine went to her head and she laughed superbly, tilting her shoulders, showing her beautiful teeth. She complimented Ellen on the dinner several times; she wished she had the ability to cook but it was hopeless—she had no patience for that sort of thing. "Sometimes I wish, y'know what I wish?—that I was just like anyone else, that I would marry someone I loved and stay in one place and be content, you know, and live out my life like that."

There was a half-moon. Ellen stared at the lake, at the icy glinting waves, wondering why she felt so indifferent. The dinner had gone well and Scott was in an excellent mood, the happiest she had seen him in weeks, and Abigail was charming, really very sweet; but Ellen could not concentrate on their conversation. Scott was asking questions and the girl replied evasively, hinting of some disappointment, then laughing again, like a child eager to escape adult surveillance. Was she in love?—had she ever been in love? Scott did not quite ask this; and the girl managed to not quite answer. Ellen watched the moonlight on the water, hypnotized by its constant agitation. She had had only one glass of wine but she felt numbed. Abigail's dog lay asleep at Ellen's feet. The weight of its head was warm and pleasant, rather heavy.

Scott and the girl talked. They drank and talked. They laughed together, companionably. Ellen heard again her husband's young, vigorous voice and she did not dare look at him—did not dare see, again, the bold flush of youth in his wasted face. She remembered having seen him that morning, by accident, as she was about to leave the bedroom and he was crossing from the kitchen area to the side door: thinking himself alone, unobserved, he had been frowning, his face tight and pursed, his lips slightly moving as if he were whispering to himself, arguing. At such times his eyes narrowed and his jaw tensed, as if he were confronting an enemy. Who was the enemy? What was it?—But now he was transformed, now he was another man entirely. And she did not dare look.

It turned out that Abigail sang; that she took voice lessons. But she had no talent, she insisted. Her voice was weak.—Would she sing for them? No, no, her voice was weak, her breathing wasn't right, she hated herself.—Please, wouldn't she sing? It would be lovely to hear her sing!

She laughed in embarrassment. No, really she couldn't. She couldn't.

But it would mean so much, Scott insisted.

Abigail managed to change the subject and they talked for a while of the northern woods, and Scott gave Abigail a book to read or to keep if she liked—*The Great Lakes: From Pre-Historical Times to the Present.* It was one of the many old battered books Scott's uncle kept here in the cabin. Then they spoke of the weather again and Abigail thanked them once more for having invited her to dinner and then, adroitly, Scott shifted back to the subject of her singing; wouldn't she sing one song for them? Please?

So she sang. And it was quite a surprise: not a popular song, not even a ballad, but an art-song a friend of hers had composed, setting the words of a Hölderlin poem to music. She sang the German words in a strong, deep, thrilling voice, a woman's voice and not a girl's, not a child's. The effect was so startling that Ellen and Scott glanced at each other. Her shyness had misled them; they were really not prepared for the deep-voiced, mysterious power of what they were hearing, these incomprehensible and yet utterly convincing words—

Gröbers wolltest auch du, aber die Liebe zwingt
  All uns nieder, das Leid beuget gewaltiger,
    Doch es kehret umsonst nicht
      Unser Bogen, woher er kommt!
Aufwärts oder hinab. . . .[1]

When she stopped, they were silent for a moment; then Scott began to clap and Ellen joined in, self-consciously. The girl flicked her hair out of her face and grinned, with a curious reluctance, as if the song and their admiration had really given her no pleasure.

"Amazing," Scott said, staring at her. "I wouldn't have thought. . . . Yes, it's amazing. And very beautiful."

She shrugged her shoulders. "Thank you. You're very nice. A friend of mine set the poem to music, a close friend, someone who was a close friend at one time. . . . It has a private meaning to me and I wouldn't have sung it except it's the best thing I know, I feel closer to it than to anything else. . . ."

"What do the words mean? Ellen and I don't know German."

But the girl had turned away and was preparing to leave. She ignored Scott's question. He jumped to his feet, helped her with her chair, fussed over her. "Very nice of you to come . . . your voice is haunting, isn't it, Ellen? . . . and beautiful . . . powerful . . . you shouldn't underestimate yourself; modesty isn't always becoming. . . . Wait, I'll get my sweater. I can't allow you to walk back alone."

"It isn't far. There's no one around."

"Really, must you leave so soon? It's still early."

But she was waking the dog, hauling him playfully to his feet. "Randy is all the protection I need, aren't you? Hey? Wake up!"

"It's early, Ellen, isn't it! Tell Abigail she shouldn't leave so early. . . ."

Ellen forced herself to speak. She was still transfixed by the girl's voice and by the mysterious authority of the German words, only a few of which she recognized; the sudden intrusion of her husband's voice and the bustle of leave-taking disturbed her. "Yes? . . . Yes, it's early, it's still early . . . won't you stay a little longer? Shall I make coffee?"

[1] Frederick Holderlin (1770–1843) was a German poet who was friendly with many of the most important writers and thinkers of his time before he went insane in 1802. This poem "The Course of Life" was written before his illness. The lines read:

More you also desired, but every one of us
  Love draws earthward, and grief bends with still greater power;
Yet our arc not for nothing
Brings us back to our starting-place.

Whether upward or down—

Michael Hamberger (trans.)

But the evening was over; the girl was clearly anxious to leave. She slipped on her heavy jacket and wound the scarf about her neck and folded the red cap, not wanting to wear it, and slipped it into one of her pockets. Scott was muttering to himself, getting his sweater from the closet. "I really must leave," the girl said, edging toward the door. "Thank you very much. You were very kind to invite me over. . . ."

"I hope we'll see you again soon," Ellen said politely. "How long will you be staying here?"

"I can walk back alone," the girl said to Scott. She smiled brightly, showing her lovely teeth. "Really. Randy is all the protection I need. And no one's around, no one is staying here except us. . . ."

"Don't be silly, Abigail," Scott said shortly. "I'm certainly not going to let you walk a half-mile in this dark, even with your elegant wolfhound. Don't you agree, Ellen? . . . Of course."

Ellen agreed. She rose, watched them from the door, her arms folded across her thin chest. The girl, Scott, the slow-trotting dog; that mysterious song, the simple, almost plain melody, the precise progression of words. What did it mean? What did they mean? She was numb, as if her spirit had been drained from her. Not indifferent but numb, stricken. The girl's voice had been such a surprise, so beautiful, so compelling. . . .

She watched the three figures until they were out of sight, then she stood in the open doorway for a while longer, staring at the lake and the broken border of ice and the opaque line of trees on the opposite shore. She wondered how long her husband would be gone.

She had learned to nurse him many months ago. She had learned not to weep or to show exhaustion in his presence. Had she lied to him?—perhaps, but only occasionally. Never about anything serious. She lied about herself, about her own feelings; not about him.

She had followed him a great distance, along endless low-ceilinged corridors, between windowless walls. Her voice had echoed monstrously as she spoke his name, assured him he would not die, citing statistics, summarizing case histories, reporting doctors' pronouncements in her small clear voice. White-clad attendants, faceless, pushed the dying man on a hospital cart and she followed behind him, murmuring his name, trying not to scream. There were walls of antiseptic tile, doors that swung heavily to and fro, stairs that led into the cavernous earth or up into the shadows, out of the range of her vision. Except for her sobbing and the squeaking of the cart's wheels, all was silent. Perhaps he had already died: he lay on the cart motionless, beneath a thin white cloth.

There were enormous humming machines. There were unwinking lights. Transparent tubes fed him, by way of his blood-rimmed nostrils and the vein on the inside of his left arm. He groaned, stirred, breathed laboriously. He had not died. She watched over him, miraculously clear-headed, not at all afraid. It was a shock to see how wasted his arms and legs were and how pale his flesh, the papery-thin flesh of his face. But she withstood it. She had no choice. She learned to nurse him: how to sponge his body with warm water and a gentle, fragrant soap, how to help him with the bedpan and, later, how to walk with him to the bathroom, how exactly to hold him so that he would not bruise.

She was with him, always. When she was in another part of the house or outside, she was still with him—her mind circled him, always, absorbed by him. He had not died. He was not going to die. She read to him and brought the phonograph into his room and played records, the volume turned low. She measured out his capsules; she brought him food on a tray; she helped him exercise. Later, he would claim that he owed his life to her. She had always loved him and now she loved him more than ever. She did not speak of love, nor did he. But it was obvious that they loved each other very much, having come so close to death.

"It's been a year and a half," Scott said one day. "I'm not going to die, am I?" His voice was toneless.

"Of course you're not going to die."

"Am I going to live, though . . . ?"

He lay back on his pillows, watching her. He was the man she had married and yet a man she did not know, had never met. Her own husband had died and another man had slipped into his body. . . . But that was a ridiculous thought. She loved him just the same. Tears edged into her eyes, provoked by his rude stare. "Why do you hate me, Scott?" she whispered.

"You know too much," he said.

The day dawned like the others, dark and cold. But shortly after nine o'clock the sun shone and after an hour or so the eaves began dripping and there was the sense of change, of melting, of a thaw—though it was still quite cold and there was a northeastern wind so strong that tiny whitecaps appeared in the open water. Scott tossed down the book he had been trying to read and picked up yesterday's newspaper and, after a few seconds, tossed that down as well. "My mind is wrecked. My mind is broken," he said. "I can no longer concentrate on words."

He was slouched in the leather chair that faced the window and the lake, and Ellen was in the second bedroom, going through a pile of old books and magazines, and though she heard him clearly enough she pretended she had not.

"Ellen? I think I'll go out for a while."

"Yes?"

"I think I'll go out for a while."

He had no need to tell her, as if he were a child and she his mother, but it was an odd habit they had gotten into since his illness. Sometimes he made such announcements ironically, as if he were aware of what he did, aware that it was not really necessary, yet resentful that he must do it. Ellen murmured a reply.

He was going to the girl, of course.

But she did not mind. She was not going to mind. She continued working in the bedroom, listening to the dripping of the eaves and the excited chattering of birds close by, in the pines. The day was sunny and windy. There was excitement in it, an almost tangible sense of motion, change. Scott went out, wearing the handsome beige sweater she had bought him in Inverness and a cloth cap with earflaps, because of the wind. "Do you think I look ridiculous in this cap?" he said doubtfully. "I do. I look ridiculous. But I can't help it."

He did not head for the girl's cabin, however; surprisingly, he got a rake from the toolshed and began clearing the grassy patch and the stretch of sloping beach before the cabin, working briskly. Ellen watched him. He appeared to be absorbed in what he did. A tall, touchingly thin figure, rather awkward with the rake, but industrious. Ellen wondered if she should help him. She wondered if it might be too tiring for him, or too cold; he was susceptible to chest colds and the wind from the lake was strong. But she did not dare disturb him. When she looked out, after fifteen minutes, he had slowed considerably and she could see that his face was closed, pursed, his lips moving again in that ceaseless argument, his body stiff with antagonism. A story of some kind was telling itself in him, below his level of consciousness, erupting only occasionally into the world he shared with others. Sometimes he burst out, unaccountably, against members of his family or friends or business associates—sharp bitter denunciations, really inexplicable—and it seemed to Ellen that these remarks made reference to a level of discourse totally alien to her, coming from nowhere, fitting into no prior scheme of his. After the outburst he would seem to catch himself and say he hadn't meant it—hadn't even known what he was saying. The night before, returning from walking Abigail back to her cabin, he had said suddenly, undressing, "Do you think that was intentional, the German song? The German words?" and Ellen had not known what he meant, so he went on to say, with a peculiar anger that was half-apologetic, that maybe the girl had deliberately sung a song they wouldn't know, maybe she had wanted to put them in their place, let them *know.* "Know? Know what?" Ellen had asked. But Scott could not explain. "Let us know . . . who she is, who we are," he said vaguely. "The differences between us."

He had been gone no more than ten minutes, walking with Abigail and the dog. Probably less. Ellen had had time only to clear the table and rinse the dishes; time only to play back in her imagination the scene at the table—her husband's rapt gaze, the girl's smile and her paradoxical manner and her strong, deep, thrilling voice. Ellen hated the girl. She hated the girl and Scott both. Her heart seemed to stab at her, with the realization of her hatred. She was excluded from their pleasure in each other, from the easy intimacy that had grown between them . . . she would be excluded forever, set aside. Yet she worked mechanically at the sink, and when Scott returned, so soon, she felt an indefinable disappointment. He had seemed rather tired. He had remarked on the persistent cold—unnatural, freakish, maddening for April. Ellen said nothing, thinking of the girl singing, and of the dog at her own feet, and of her husband's transfixed face. She did hate them, hated even that elegant, comely dog, but it gave her pleasure to think of them. *Did you kiss her?* she wanted to ask, bitterly.

At the long walnut table they sat in silence, eating, facing the window as always. The sun was still shining. The water shone coldly, broken and agitated, hypnotic. On the far side of the lake the pines appeared to be of a uniform, rigid height. Everything was still except for the sound of dripping and the birds' cries and the wind, which had not died down. At the rear of the cabin something was scraping irritably against the roof.

"This is the edge of the world," Scott said in a queer hollow voice. "It was like this before we lived."

Ellen turned to him. *We* . . . ?"

"Our species."

She laughed. The sound surprised her, it was so joyless.

"Why don't you go to her?" she said softly after a moment. "That's what you want, isn't it?"

"It's beautiful here but it hurts. The air hurts. The sun. The water. It isn't human here," he said in the same hollow, bewildered voice.

"Go to her, why don't you? The girl. *Her*. She's waiting for you."

Her mouth twisted as she spoke. Her voice was ugly, not her own.

"She's waiting for me . . . ?" Scott said.

"I know what you want, what you've been thinking of. I know how you've been thinking of her."

"You do?"

His voice raised lightly, scornfully.

"I hate you both," Ellen whispered.

She rose blindly from the table and went into the bedroom.

At the window she half closed her eyes. She saw a man's figure on the beach, a man's figure cutting across the edge of the lake, risking the ice. He walked quickly, knowing his destination. Quickly. Confidently. He was young, energetic, shameless. She hated him. Yet she would watch: she would stand at the window and watch until he was out of sight.

She could hear again the girl's lovely calm mysterious voice. It had issued from her as if it were not her own possession, as if it were a bodiless sound, excruciatingly beautiful, indescribable, not hers, not even human. She could hear that voice, and she could see, again, her husband's face: the intensity of his emotion, the shameless blunt power of his lust.

"Why don't you go to her . . . ?" she whispered aloud.

It was horrible, hideous, that he should not, that he should remain in this place, fixed and helpless; merely her husband. That he should be himself and none other. That he should someday die.

They listened to the rhythmic dripping of the eaves. Harsh rude joyful dripping melting thawing: the entire world was thawing.

"Look at that sun!" Scott said.

Ellen shaded her eyes and squinted. It was true, the sun was enormous, powerful, almost intimidating. The thaw had begun. Something in her responded to it, some feeling too subtle, too deep, to be called an emotion. She wanted to cry, then again she wanted to laugh. She wanted to exclaim in vexation.

"She has a visitor anyway," Scott said. "Someone drove over there around noon."

"A visitor?"

"It looked like a man. A young man."

"Then we won't see her again . . . ?" Ellen said slowly.

Scott was lying on a sofa, facing the windows, propped against a pillow. He had pulled an old afghan of green and brown squares up to his chin. In the painful clarity of the sunshine he looked aged and yet peaceful, serene; for the first time Ellen saw him as an old man and realized that he would be—he would be beautiful. She stared at him, struck by her knowledge, and he must have felt her surprise because he turned to her, trying to smile. Yet he misunderstood. He said, "Do you forgive me?"

"Forgive you?"

"For the girl—for all that."

"Of course I forgive you," Ellen said, still in a slow, stricken voice. She took his hand and squeezed his cold fingers.

"If I had gone, I might never have come back. . . ."

"Yes, I know."

". . . you wouldn't have wanted me back, and I couldn't have come back. . . ."

"Of course I forgive you," she said.

She bent to kiss him. She hoped neither of them would draw away.

"I love you," one whispered.

And the other replied at once, "I love *you.*"

QUESTIONS

1. Why do Ellen and Scott go to Baylis Lake?
2. Why are Ellen and Scott attracted to Abigail Carlisle? What qualities does Abigail possess that disturbs them?
3. Is there any significance to the detail that the action of the story takes place during Easter, and that this Easter is the coldest one in over twenty years?
4. What are Ellen's feelings for Scott? Are love and hate necessarily opposite emotions?
5. What are Scott's feelings for Ellen? Why does he ask for forgiveness at the end of the story?
6. What is the significance of the title "The Thaw"?
7. Is this a hopeful or a pessimistic story?

F. SCOTT FITZGERALD

BABYLON REVISITED

No writer epitomized "The Roaring Twenties" as did F. Scott Fitzgerald (1896–1940), who achieved fame with his first novel This Side of Paradise, *published when he was twenty-four. But it was in his novel* The Great Gatsby *and in many of his short stories that he succeeded as a writer.*

With his wife Zelda, a fine novelist in her own right, he went to live in Paris where he became friendly with Ernest Hemingway and other expatriate Americans. With their fame, wealth, talent and beauty the Fitzgeralds were social favorites, and their revelries ended only after he had become an alcoholic and Zelda had suffered a breakdown from which she never recovered.

To make money, Fitzgerald went to Hollywood where he worked on several screenplays and began his last novel The Last Tycoon, *which he did not live to complete, though he had stopped drinking and begun putting his life back together.*

"And where's Mr. Campbell?" Charlie asked.

"Gone to Switzerland. Mr. Campbell's a pretty sick man, Mr. Wales."

"I'm sorry to hear that. And George Hardt?" Charlie inquired.

"Back in America, gone to work."

"And where is the Snow Bird?"

"He was in here last week. Anyway, his friend, Mr. Schaeffer, is in Paris."

Two familiar names from the long list of a year and a half ago. Charlie scribbled an address in his notebook and tore out the page.

"If you see Mr. Schaeffer, give him this," he said. "It's my brother-in-law's address. I haven't settled on a hotel yet."

He was not really disappointed to find Paris was so empty. But the stillness in the Ritz bar was strange and portentous. It was not an American bar any more—he felt polite in it, and not as if he owned it. It had gone back into France. He felt the stillness from the moment he got out of the taxi and saw the doorman, usually in a frenzy of activity at this hour, gossiping with a *chasseur* by the servants' entrance.

Passing through the corridor, he heard only a single, bored voice in the once-clamorous women's room. When he turned into the bar he traveled the twenty feet of green carpet with his eyes fixed straight ahead by old habit; and then, with his foot firmly on the rail, he turned and surveyed the room, encountering only a single pair of eyes that fluttered up from a newspaper in the corner. Charlie asked for the head barman, Paul, who in the latter days of the bull market had come to work in his own custom-built car—disembarking, however, with due nicety at the nearest corner. But Paul was at his country house today and Alix giving him information.

"No, no more," Charlie said, "I'm going slow these days."

Alix congratulated him: "You were going pretty strong a couple of years ago."

"I'll stick to it all right," Charlie assured him. "I've stuck to it for over a year and a half now."

"How do you find conditions in America?"

"I haven't been to America for months, I'm in business in Prague, representing a couple of concerns there. They don't know about me down there."

Alix smiled.

"Remember the night of George Hardt's bachelor dinner here?" said Charlie. "By the way, what's become of Claude Fessenden?"

Alix lowered his voice confidentially: "He's in Paris, but he doesn't come here any more. Paul doesn't allow it. He ran up a bill of thirty thousand francs, charging all his drinks and his lunches, and usually his dinner, for more than a year. And when Paul finally told him he had to pay, he gave him a bad check."

Alix shook his head sadly.

"I don't understand it, such a dandy fellow. Now he's all bloated up—" He made a plump apple of his hands.

Charlie watched a group of strident queens installing themselves in a corner.

"Nothing affects them," he thought. "Stocks rise and fall, people loaf or work, but they go on forever." The place oppressed him. He called for the dice and shook with Alix for the drink.

"Here for long, Mr. Wales?"

"I'm here for four or five days to see my little girl."

"Oh-h! You have a little girl?"

Outside, the fire-red, gas-blue, ghost-green signs shone smokily through the tranquil rain. It was late afternoon and the streets were in movement; the *bistros* gleamed. At the corner of the Boulevard des Capucines he took a taxi. The Place de la Concorde moved by in pink majesty;

they crossed the logical Seine, and Charlie felt the sudden provincial quality of the left bank.

Charlie directed his taxi to the Avenue de l'Opera, which was out of his way. But he wanted to see the blue hour spread over the magnificent façade, and imagine that the cab horns, playing endlessly the first few bars of *Le Plus que Lent,* were the trumpets of the Second Empire. They were closing the iron grill in front of Brentano's Book-store, and people were already at dinner behind the trim little bourgeois hedge of Duval's. He had never eaten at a really cheap restaurant in Paris. Five-course dinner, four francs fifty, eighteen cents, wine included. For some odd reason he wished that he had.

As they rolled on to the Left Bank and he felt its sudden provincialism, he thought, "I spoiled this city for myself. I didn't realize it, but the days came along one after another, and then two years were gone, and everything was gone, and I was gone."

He was thirty-five, and good to look at. The Irish mobility of his face was sobered by a deep wrinkle between his eyes. As he rang his brother-in-law's bell in the Rue Palatine, the wrinkle deepened till it pulled down his brows; he felt a cramping sensation in his belly. From behind the maid who opened the door darted a lovely little girl of nine who shrieked "Daddy!" and flew up, struggling like a fish, into his arms. She pulled his head around by one ear and set her cheek against his.

"My old pie," he said.

"Oh, daddy, daddy, daddy, daddy, dads, dads, dads!"

She drew him into the salon, where the family waited, a boy and a girl his daughter's age, his sister-in-law and her husband. He greeted Marion with his voice pitched carefully to avoid either feigned enthusiasm or dislike, but her response was more frankly tepid, though she minimized her expression of unalterable distrust by directing her regard toward his child. The two men clasped hands in a friendly way and Lincoln Peters rested his for a moment on Charlie's shoulder.

The room was warm and comfortably American. The three children moved intimately about, playing through the yellow oblongs that led to other rooms; the cheer of six o'clock spoke in the eager smacks of the fire and the sounds of French activity in the kitchen. But Charlie did not relax; his heart sat up rigidly in his body and he drew confidence from his daughter, who from time to time came close to him, holding in her arms the doll he had brought.

"Really extremely well," he declared in answer to Lincoln's question. "There's a lot of business there that isn't moving at all, but we're doing even better than ever. In fact, damn well. I'm bringing my sister over from America next month to keep house for me. My income last year was bigger than it was when I had money. You see, the Czechs——"

His boasting was for a specific purpose; but after a moment, seeing a faint restiveness in Lincoln's eye, he changed the subject:

"Those are fine children of yours, well brought up, good manners."

"We think Honoria's a great little girl too."

Marion Peters came back from the kitchen. She was a tall woman with worried eyes, who had once possessed a fresh American loveliness. Charlie had never been sensitive to it and was always surprised when people spoke of how pretty she had been. From the first there had been an instinctive antipathy between them.

"Well, how do you find Honoria?" she asked.

"Wonderful. I was astonished how much she's grown in ten months. All the children are looking well."

"We haven't had a doctor for a year. How do you like being back in Paris?"

"It seems very funny to see so few Americans around."

"I'm delighted," Marion said vehemently. "Now at least you can go into a store without their assuming you're a millionaire. We've suffered like everybody, but on the whole it's a good deal pleasanter."

"But it was nice while it lasted," Charlie said. "We were a sort of royalty, almost infallible, with a sort of magic around us. In the bar this afternoon"—he stumbled, seeing his mistake—"there wasn't a man I knew."

She looked at him keenly. "I should think you'd have had enough of bars."

"I only stayed a minute. I take one drink every afternoon, and no more."

"Don't you want a cocktail before dinner?" Lincoln asked.

"I take only one drink every afternoon, and I've had that."

"I hope you keep to it," said Marion.

Her dislike was evident in the coldness with which she spoke, but Charlie only smiled; he had larger plans. Her very aggressiveness gave him an advantage, and he knew enough to wait. He wanted them to initiate the discussion of what they knew had brought him to Paris.

At dinner he couldn't decide whether Honoria was most like him or her mother. Fortunate if she didn't combine the traits of both that had brought them to disaster. A great wave of protectiveness went over him. He thought he knew what to do for her. He believed in character; he wanted to jump back a whole generation and trust in character again as the eternally valuable element. Everything else wore out.

He left soon after dinner, but not to go home. He was curious to see Paris by night with clearer and more judicious eyes than those of other days. He bought a *strapontin* for the Casino and watched Josephine Baker go through her chocolate arabesques.

After an hour he left and strolled toward Montmartre, up the Rue Pigalle into the Place Blanche. The rain had stopped and there were a few people in evening clothes disembarking from taxis in front of cabarets, and *cocottes* prowling singly or in pairs, and many Negroes. He passed a lighted door from which issued music, and stopped with the sense of familiarity; it was Bricktop's, where he had parted with so many hours and so much money. A few doors farther on he found another ancient rendezvous and incautiously put his head inside. Immediately an eager orchestra burst into sound, a pair of professional dancers leaped to their feet and a maître d'hôtel swooped toward him, crying, "Crowd just arriving, sir!" But he withdrew quickly.

"You have to be damn drunk," he thought.

Zelli's was closed, the bleak and sinister cheap hotels surrounding it were dark; up in the Rue Blanche there was more light and a local, colloquial French crowd. The Poet's Cave had disappeared, but the two great mouths of the Café of Heaven and the Café of Hell still yawned—even devoured, as he watched, the meager contents of a tourist bus—a German, a Japanese, and an American couple who glanced at him with frightened eyes.

So much for the effort and ingenuity of Montmartre. All the catering to vice and waste was on an utterly childish scale, and he suddenly realized the meaning of the word "dissipate"—to dissipate into thin air; to make nothing out of something. In the little hours of the night every move from place to place was an enormous human jump, an increase of paying for the privilege of slower and slower motion.

He remembered thousand-franc notes given to an orchestra for playing a single number, hundred-franc notes tossed to a doorman for calling a cab.

But it hadn't been given for nothing.

It had been given, even the most wildly squandered sum, as an offering to destiny that he might not remember the things most worth remembering, the things that now he would always remember—his child taken from his control, his wife escaped to a grave in Vermont.

In the glare of a *brasserie* a woman spoke to him. He bought her some eggs and coffee, and then, eluding her encouraging stare, gave her a twenty-franc note and took a taxi to his hotel.

II

He woke upon a fine fall day—football weather. The depression of yesterday was gone and he liked the people on the streets. At noon he sat opposite Honoria at Le Grand Vatel, the only restaurant he could think of not reminiscent of champagne dinners and long luncheons that began at two and ended in a blurred and vague twilight.

"Now, how about vegetables? Oughtn't you to have some vegetables?"

"Well, yes."

"Here's *épinards* and *chou-fleur* and carrots and *baricots.*"

"I'd like *chou-fleur.*"

"Wouldn't you like to have two vegetables?"

"I usually only have one at lunch."

The waiter was pretending to be inordinately fond of children. *"Qu'elle est mignonne la petite! Elle parle exactement comme une Française."*

"How about dessert? Shall we wait and see?"

The waiter disappeared. Honoria looked at her father expectantly. "What are we going to do?"

"First, we're going to that toy store in the Rue Saint-Honoré and buy you anything you like. And then we're going to the vaudeville at the Empire."

She hesitated. "I like it about the vaudeville, but not the toy store."

"Why not?"

"Well, you brought me this doll." She had it with her. "And I've got lots of things. And we're not rich any more, are we?"

"We never were. But today you are to have anything you want."

"All right," she agreed resignedly.

When there had been her mother and a French nurse he had been inclined to be strict; now he extended himself, reached out for a new tolerance; he must be both parents to her and not shut any of her out of communication.

"I want to get to know you," he said gravely. "First let me introduce myself. My name is Charles J. Wales, of Prague."

"Oh, daddy!" her voice cracked with laughter.

"And who are you, please?" he persisted, and she accepted a rôle immediately: "Honoria Wales, Rue Palatine, Paris."

"Married or single?"

"No, not married. Single."

He indicated the doll. "But I see you have a child, madame."

Unwilling to disinherit it, she took it to her heart and thought quickly: "Yes, I've been married, but I'm not married now. My husband is dead."

He went on quickly, "And the child's name?"

"Simone. That's after my best friend at school."

"I'm very pleased that you're doing so well at school."

"I'm third this month," she boasted. "Elsie"—that was her cousin—"is only about eighteenth, and Richard is about at the bottom."

"You like Richard and Elsie, don't you?"

"Oh, yes. I like Richard quite well and I like her all right."

Cautiously and casually he asked: "And Aunt Marion and Uncle Lincoln—which do you like best?"

"Oh, Uncle Lincoln, I guess."

He was increasingly aware of her presence. As they came in, a murmur of ". . . adorable" followed them, and now the people at the next table bent all their silences upon her, staring as if she were something no more conscious than a flower.

"Why don't I live with you?" she asked suddenly. "Because mamma's dead?"

"You must stay here and learn more French. It would have been hard for daddy to take care of you so well."

"I don't really need much taking care of any more. I do everything for myself."

Going out of the restaurant, a man and a woman unexpectedly hailed him.

"Well, the old Wales!"

"Hello there, Lorraine. . . . Dunc."

Sudden ghosts out of the past: Duncan Schaeffer, a friend from college. Lorraine Quarrles, a lovely, pale blonde of thirty; one of a crowd who had helped them make months into days in the lavish times of three years ago.

"My husband couldn't come this year," she said, in answer to his question. "We're poor as hell. So he gave me two hundred a month and told me I could do my worst on that. . . . This your little girl?"

"What about coming back and sitting down?" Duncan asked.

"Can't do it." He was glad for an excuse. As always, he felt Lorraine's passionate, provocative attraction, but his own rhythm was different now.

"Well, how about dinner?" she asked.

"I'm not free. Give me your address and let me call you."

"Charlie, I believe you're sober," she said judicially. "I honestly believe he's sober, Dunc. Pinch him and see if he's sober."

Charlie indicated Honoria with his head. They both laughed.

"What's your address?" said Duncan skeptically.

He hesitated, unwilling to give the name of his hotel.

"I'm not settled yet. I'd better call you. We're going to see the vaudeville at the Empire."

"There! That's what I want to do," Lorraine said. "I want to see some clowns and acrobats and jugglers. That's just what we'll do, Dunc."

"We've got to do an errand first," said Charlie. "Perhaps we'll see you there."

"All right, you snob. . . . Good-by, beautiful little girl."

"Good-by."

Honoria bobbed politely.

Somehow, an unwelcome encounter. They liked him because he was functioning, because he was serious; they wanted to see him, because he was stronger than they were now, because they wanted to draw a certain sustenance from his strength.

At the Empire, Honoria proudly refused to sit upon her father's folded coat. She was already an individual with a code of her own, and Charlie was more and more absorbed by the desire of putting a little of himself into her before she crystallized utterly. It was hopeless to try to know her in so short a time.

Between the acts they came upon Duncan and Lorraine in the lobby where the band was playing.

"Have a drink?"

"All right, but not up at the bar. We'll take a table."

"The perfect father."

Listening abstractedly to Lorraine, Charlie watched Honoria's eyes leave their table, and he followed them wistfully about the room, wondering what they saw. He met her glance and she smiled.

"I liked that lemonade," she said.

What had she said? What had he expected? Going home in a taxi afterward, he pulled her over until her head rested against his chest.

"Darling, do you ever think about your mother?"

"Yes, sometimes," she answered vaguely.

"I don't want you to forget her. Have you got a picture of her?"

"Yes, I think so. Anyhow, Aunt Marion has. Why don't you want me to forget her?"

"She loved you very much."

"I loved her too."

They were silent for a moment.

"Daddy, I want to come and live with you," she said suddenly.

His heart leaped; he had wanted it to come like this.

"Aren't you perfectly happy?"

"Yes, but I love you better than anybody. And you love me better than anybody, don't you, now that mummy's dead?"

"Of course I do. But you won't always like me best, honey. You'll grow up and meet somebody your own age and go marry him and forget you ever had a daddy."

"Yes, that's true," she agreed tranquilly.

He didn't go in. He was coming back at nine o'clock and he wanted to keep himself fresh and new for the thing he must say then.

"When you're safe inside, just show yourself in that window."

"All right. Good-by, dads, dads, dads, dads."

He waited in the dark street until she appeared, all warm and glowing, in the window above and kissed her fingers out into the night.

III

They were waiting, Marion sat behind the coffee service in a dignified black dinner dress that just faintly suggested mourning. Lincoln was walking up and down with the animation of one who had already been talking. They were as anxious as he was to get into the question. He opened it almost immediately:

"I suppose you know what I want to see you about—why I really came to Paris."

Marion played with the black stars on her necklace and frowned.

"I'm awfully anxious to have a home," he continued. "And I'm awfully anxious to have Honoria in it. I appreciate your taking in Honoria for her mother's sake, but things have changed now"—he hesitated and then continued more forcibly—"changed radically with me, and I want to ask you to reconsider the matter. It would be silly for me to deny that about three years ago I was acting badly——"

Marion looked up at him with hard eyes.

"—but all that's over. As I told you, I haven't had more than a drink a day for over a year, and I take that drink deliberately, so that the idea of alcohol won't get too big in my imagination. You see the idea?"

"No," said Marion succinctly.

"It's a sort of stunt I set myself. It keeps the matter in proportion."

"I get you," said Lincoln. "You don't want to admit it's got any attraction for you."

"Something like that. Sometimes I forget and don't take it. But I try to take it. Anyhow, I couldn't afford to drink in my position. The people I represent are more than satisfied with what I've done, and I'm bringing my sister over from Burlington to keep house for me, and I want awfully to have Honoria too. You know that even when her mother and I weren't getting along well we never let anything that happened touch Honoria. I know she's fond of me and I know I'm able to take care of her and—well, there you are. How do you feel about it?"

He knew that now he would have to take a beating. It would last an hour or two hours, and it would be difficult, but if he modulated his inevitable resentment to the chastened attitude of the reformed sinner, he might win his point in the end.

Keep your temper, he told himself. You don't want to be justified. You want Honoria.

Lincoln spoke first: "We've been talking it over ever since we got your letter last month. We're happy to have Honoria here. She's a dear little thing, and we're glad to be able to help her, but of course that isn't the question——"

Marion interrupted suddenly. "How long are you going to stay sober, Charlie?" she asked.

"Permanently, I hope."

"How can anybody count on that?"

"You know I never did drink heavily until I gave up business and came over here with nothing to do. Then Helen and I began to run around with——"

"Please leave Helen out of it. I can't bear to hear you talk about her like that."

He stared at her grimly; he had never been certain how fond of each other the sisters were in life.

"My drinking only lasted about a year and a half—from the time we came over until I—collapsed."

"It was time enough."

"It was time enough," he agreed.

"My duty is entirely to Helen," she said. "I try to think what she would have wanted me to do. Frankly, from the night you did that terrible thing you haven't really existed for me. I can't help that. She was my sister."

"Yes."

"When she was dying she asked me to look out for Honoria. If you hadn't been in a sanitarium then, it might have helped matters."

He had no answer.

"I'll never in my life be able to forget the morning when Helen knocked at my door, soaked to the skin and shivering and said you'd locked her out."

Charlie gripped the sides of the chair. This was more difficult than he expected; he wanted to launch out into a long expostulation and explanation, but he only said: "The night I locked her out—" and she interrupted, "I don't feel up to going over that again."

After a moment's silence Lincoln said: "We're getting off the subject. You want Marion to set aside her legal guardianship and give you Honoria. I think the main point for her is whether she has confidence in you or not."

"I don't blame Marion," Charlie said slowly, "but I think she can have entire confidence in me. I had a good record up to three years ago. Of course, it's within human possibilities I might go wrong any time. But if we wait much longer I'll lose Honoria's childhood and my chance for a home." He shook his head, "I'll simply lose her, don't you see?"

"Yes, I see," said Lincoln.

"Why didn't you think of all this before?" Marion asked.

"I suppose I did, from time to time, but Helen and I were getting along badly. When I consented to the guardianship, I was flat on my back in a sanitarium and the market had cleaned me out. I knew I'd acted badly, and I thought if it would bring any peace to Helen, I'd agree to anything. But now it's different. I'm functioning, I'm behaving damn well, so far as——"

"Please don't swear at me," Marion said.

He looked at her, startled. With each remark the force of her dislike became more and more apparent. She had built up all her fear of life into one wall and faced it toward him. This trivial reproof was possibly the result of some trouble with the cook several hours before. Charlie became increasingly alarmed at leaving Honoria in this atmosphere of hostility against himself; sooner or later it would come out, in a word here, a shake of the head there, and some of that distrust would be irrevocably implanted in Honoria. But he pulled his temper down out of his face and shut it up inside him; he had won a point, for Lincoln realized the absurdity of Marion's remark and asked her lightly since when she had objected to the word "damn."

"Another thing," Charlie said: "I'm able to give her certain advantages now. I'm going to take a French governess to Prague with me. I've got a lease on a new apartment——"

He stopped, realizing that he was blundering. They couldn't be expected to accept with equanimity the fact that his income was again twice as large as their own.

"I suppose you can give her more luxuries than we can," said Marion. "When you were throwing away money we were living along watching every ten francs. . . . I suppose you'll start doing it again."

"Oh, no," he said. "I've learned. I worked hard for ten years, you know—until I got lucky in the market, like so many people. Terribly lucky. It won't happen again."

There was a long silence. All of them felt their nerves straining, and for the first time in a year Charlie wanted a drink. He was sure now that Lincoln Peters wanted him to have his child.

Marion shuddered suddenly; part of her saw that Charlie's feet were planted on the earth now, and her own maternal feeling recognized the naturalness of his desire; but she had lived for a long time with a prejudice—a prejudice founded on a curious disbelief in her sister's happiness, and which, in the shock of one terrible night, had turned to hatred for him. It had all happened at a point in her life where the discouragement of ill health and adverse circumstances made it necessary for her to believe in tangible villainy and a tangible villain.

"I can't help what I think!" she cried out suddenly. "How much you were responsible for Helen's death, I don't know. It's something you'll have to square with your own conscience."

An electric current of agony surged through him; for a moment he was almost on his feet, an unuttered sound echoing in his throat. He hung on to himself for a moment, another moment.

"Hold on there," said Lincoln uncomfortably. "I never thought you were responsible for that."

"Helen died of heart trouble," Charlie said dully.

"Yes, heart trouble," Marion spoke as if the phrase had another meaning for her.

Then, in the flatness that followed her outburst, she saw him plainly and she knew he had somehow arrived at control over the situation. Glancing at her husband, she found no help from him, and as abruptly as if it were a matter of no importance, she threw up the sponge.

"Do what you like!" she cried, springing up from her chair. "She's your child. I'm not the person to stand in your way. I think if it were my child I'd rather see her—" She managed to check herself. "You two decide it. I can't stand this. I'm sick. I'm going to bed."

She hurried from the room; after a moment Lincoln said:

"This has been a hard day for her. You know how strongly she feels—" His voice was almost apologetic: "When a woman gets an idea in her head."

"Of course."

"It's going to be all right. I think she sees now that you—can provide for the child, and so we can't very well stand in your way or Honoria's way."

"Thank you, Lincoln."

"I'd better go along and see how she is."

"I'm going."

He was still trembling when he reached the street, but a walk down the Rue Bonaparte to the *quais* set him up, and as he crossed the Seine, fresh and new by the *quai* lamps, he felt exultant. But back in his room he couldn't sleep. The image of Helen haunted him. Helen whom he had loved so until they had senselessly begun to abuse each other's love, tear it into shreds. On that terrible February night that Marion remembered so vividly, a slow quarrel had gone on for hours. There was a scene at the Florida, and then he attempted to take her home, and then she kissed young Webb at a table; after that there was what she had hysterically said. When he arrived home alone he turned the key in the lock in wild anger. How could he know she would arrive an hour later alone, that there would be a snowstorm in which she wandered about in slippers, too confused to find a taxi? Then the aftermath, her escaping pneumonia by a miracle, and all the attendant horror. They were "reconciled," but that was the beginning of the end, and Marion, who had seen with her own eyes and who imagined it to be one of many scenes from her sister's martyrdom, never forgot.

Going over it again brought Helen nearer, and in the white, soft light that steals upon half sleep near morning he found himself talking to her again. She said that he was perfectly right about Honoria and that she wanted Honoria to be with him. She said she was glad he was being good and doing better. She said a lot of other things—very friendly things—but she was in a swing in a white dress, and swinging faster and faster all the time, so that at the end he could not hear clearly all that she said.

IV

He woke up feeling happy. The door of the world was open again. He made plans, vistas, futures for Honoria and himself, but suddenly he grew sad, remembering all the plans he and Helen had made. She had not planned to die. The present was the thing—work to do and someone to love. But not to love too much, for he knew the injury that a father can do to a daughter or a mother to a son by attaching them too closely; afterward, out in the world, the child would seek in the marriage partner the same blind tenderness and, failing probably to find it, turn against love and life.

It was another bright, crisp day. He called Lincoln Peters at the bank where he worked and asked if he could count on taking Honoria when he left for Prague. Lincoln agreed that there was no reason for delay. One thing—the legal guardianship. Marion wanted to retain that a while longer. She was upset by the whole matter, and it would oil things if she felt that the situation was still in her control for another year. Charlie agreed, wanting only the tangible, visible child.

Then the question of a governess. Charles sat in a gloomy agency and talked to a cross Béarnaise and to a buxom Breton peasant, neither of whom he could have endured. There were others whom he would see tomorrow.

He lunched with Lincoln Peters at Griffons, trying to keep down his exultation.

"There's nothing quite like your own child," Lincoln said. "But you understand how Marion feels too."

"She's forgotten how hard I worked for seven years there," Charlie said. "She just remembers one night."

"There's another thing," Lincoln hesitated. "While you and Helen were tearing around Europe throwing money away, we were just getting along. I didn't touch any of the prosperity because I never got ahead enough to carry anything but my insurance. I think Marion felt there was some kind of injustice in it—you not even working toward the end, and getting richer and richer."

"It went just as quick as it came," said Charlie.

"Yes, a lot of it stayed in the hands of *chasseurs* and saxophone players and maîtres d'hótel—well, the big party's over now. I just said that to explain Marion's feeling about those crazy years. If you drop in about six o'clock tonight before Marion's too tired, we'll settle the details on the spot."

Back at his hotel, Charlie found a *pneumatique* that had been redirected from the Ritz bar where Charlie had left his address for the purpose of finding a certain man.

> "Dear Charlie:
> You were so strange when we saw you the other day that I wondered if I did something to offend you. If so, I'm not conscious of it. In fact, I have thought about you too much for the last year, and it's always been in the back of my mind that I might see you if I came over here. We *did* have such good times that crazy spring, like the night you and I stole the butcher's tricycle, and the time we tried to call on the president and you had the old derby rim and the wire cane. Everybody seems so old lately, but I don't feel old a bit. Couldn't we get together some time today for old time's sake? I've got a vile hang-over for the moment, but will be feeling better this afternoon and will look for you about five in the sweatshop at the Ritz.
>
> Always devotedly,
> Lorraine."

His first feeling was one of awe that he had actually, in his mature years, stolen a tricycle and pedaled Lorraine all over the Etoile between the small hours and dawn. In retrospect it was a nightmare. Locking out Helen didn't fit in with any other act of his life, but the tricycle incident did—it was one of many. How many weeks or months of dissipation to arrive at that condition of utter irresponsibility?

He tried to picture how Lorraine had appeared to him then—very attractive; Helen was unhappy about it, though she said nothing. Yesterday, in the restaurant, Lorraine had seemed trite, blurred, worn away. He emphatically did not want to see her, and he was glad Alix had not given away his hotel address. It was a relief to think, instead, of Honoria, to think of Sundays spent with her and of saying good morning to her and of knowing she was there in his house at night, drawing her breath in the darkness.

At five he took a taxi and bought presents for all the Peters—a piquant cloth doll, a box of Roman soldiers, flowers for Marion, big linen handkerchiefs for Lincoln.

He saw, when he arrived in the apartment, that Marion had accepted the inevitable. She greeted him now as though he were a recalcitrant member of the family, rather than a menacing outsider. Honoria had been told she was going; Charlie was glad to see that her tact made her conceal her excessive happiness. Only on his lap did she whisper her delight and the question "When?" before she slipped away with the other children.

He and Marion were alone for a minute in the room, and on an impulse he spoke out boldly:

"Family quarrels are bitter things. They don't go according to any rules. They're not like aches or wounds; they're more like splits in the skin that won't heal because there's not enough material. I wish you and I could be on better terms."

"Some things are hard to forget," she answered. "It's a question of confidence." There was no answer to this and presently she asked, "When do you propose to take her?"

"As soon as I can get a governess. I hoped the day after tomorrow."

"That's impossible. I've got to get her things in shape. Not before Saturday."

He yielded. Coming back into the room, Lincoln offered him a drink.

"I'll take my daily whisky," he said.

It was warm here, it was a home, people together by a fire. The children felt very safe and important; the mother and father were serious, watchful. They had things to do for the children more important than his visit here. A spoonful of medicine was, after all, more important than the strained relations between Marion and himself. They were not dull people, but they were very much in the grip of life and circumstances. He wondered if he couldn't do something to get Lincoln out of his rut at the bank.

A long peal at the door-bell; the *bonne à tout faire* passed through and went down the corridor. The door opened upon another long ring, and then voices, and the three in the salon looked up expectantly; Richard moved to bring the corridor within his range of vision, and Marion rose. Then the maid came back along the corridor, closely followed by the voices, which developed under the light into Duncan Schaeffer and Lorraine Quarrles.

They were gay, they were hilarious, they were roaring with laughter. For a moment Charlie was astounded; unable to understand how they ferreted out the Peters' address.

"Ah-h-h!" Duncan wagged his finger roguishly at Charlie. "Ah-h-h!"

They both slid down another cascade of laughter. Anxious and at a loss, Charlie shook hands with them quickly and presented them to Lincoln and Marion. Marion nodded, scarcely speaking. She had drawn back a step toward the fire; her little girl stood beside her, and Marion put an arm about her shoulder.

With growing annoyance at the intrusion, Charlie waited for them to explain themselves. After some concentration Duncan said: "We came to invite you out to dinner. Lorraine and I insist that all this shishi, cagy business 'bout your address got to stop."

Charlie came closer to them, as if to force them backward down the corridor.

"Sorry, but I can't. Tell me where you'll be and I'll phone you in half an hour."

This made no impression. Lorraine sat down suddenly on the side of a chair, and focusing her eyes on Richard, cried, "Oh, what a nice little boy! Come here, little boy," Richard glanced at his mother, but did not move. With a perceptible shrug of her shoulders, Lorraine turned back to Charlie:

"Come and dine. Sure your cousins won' mine. See you so sel'om. Or solemn."

"I can't," said Charlie sharply. "You two have dinner and I'll phone you."

Her voice became suddenly unpleasant. "All right, we'll go. But I remember once when you hammered on my door at four A.M. I was enough of a good sport to give you a drink. Come on, Dunc."

Still in slow motion, with blurred, angry faces, with uncertain feet, they retired along the corridor.

"Good night," Charlie said.

"Good night!" responded Lorraine emphatically.

When he went back into the salon Marion had not moved, only now her son was standing in the circle of her other arm. Lincoln was still swinging Honoria back and forth like a pendulum from side to side.

"What an outrage!" Charlie broke out. "What an absolute outrage!"

Neither of them answered, Charlie dropped into an armchair, picked up his drink, set it down again and said:

"People I haven't seen for two years having the colossal nerve——"

He broke off. Marion had made the sound "Oh!" in one swift, furious breath, turned her body from him with a jerk and left the room.

Lincoln set down Honoria carefully.

"You children go in and start your soup," he said, and when they obeyed, he said to Charlie:

"Marion's not well and she can't stand shocks. That kind of people make her really physically sick."

"I didn't tell them to come here. They wormed your name out of somebody. They deliberately——"

"Well, it's too bad. It doesn't help matters. Excuse me a minute."

Left alone, Charlie sat tense in his chair. In the next room he could hear the children eating, talking in monosyllables, already oblivious to the scene between their elders. He heard a murmur of conversation from a farther room and then the ticking bell of a telephone receiver picked up, and in a panic he moved to the other side of the room and out of earshot.

In a minute Lincoln came back. "Look here, Charlie. I think we'd better call off dinner for tonight. Marion's in bad shape."

"Is she angry with me?"

"Sort of," he said, almost roughly. "She's not strong and——"

"You mean she's changed her mind about Honoria?"

"She's pretty bitter right now. I don't know. You phone me at the bank tomorrow."

"I wish you'd explain to her I never dreamed these people would come here. I'm just as sore as you are."

"I couldn't explain anything to her now."

Charlie got up. He took his coat and hat and started down the corridor. Then he opened the door of the dining room and said in a strange voice, "Good night, children."

Honoria rose and ran around the table to hug him.

"Good night, sweetheart," he said vaguely, and then trying to make his voice more tender, trying to conciliate something, "Good night, dear children."

V

Charlie went directly to the Ritz bar with the furious idea of finding Lorraine and Duncan, but they were not there, and he realized that in any case there was nothing he could do. He had not touched his drink at the Peters, and now he ordered a whiskey-and-soda. Paul came over to say hello.

"It's a great change," he said sadly. "We do about half the business we did. So many fellows I hear about back in the States lost everything, maybe not in the first crash, but then in the second. Your friend George Hardt lost every cent, I hear. Are you back in the States?"

"No, I'm in business in Prague."

"I heard that you lost a lot in the crash."

"I did," and he added grimly, "but I lost everything I wanted in the boom." "Selling short."

"Something like that."

Again the memory of those days swept over him like a nightmare—the people they had met travelling; then people who couldn't add a row of figures or speak a coherent sentence. The little man Helen had consented to dance with at the ship's party, who had insulted her ten feet from the table; the women and girls carried screaming with drink or drugs out of public places——

—The men who locked their wives out in the snow, because the snow of twenty-nine wasn't real snow. If you didn't want it to be snow, you just paid some money.

He went to the phone and called the Peters' apartment; Lincoln answered.

"I called up because this thing is on my mind. Has Marion said anything definite?"

"Marion's sick," Lincoln answered shortly. "I know this thing isn't altogether your fault, but I can't have her go to pieces about it. I'm afraid we'll have to let it slide for six months; I can't take the chance of working her up to this state again."

"I see."

"I'm sorry, Charlie."

He went back to his table. His whisky glass was empty, but he shook his head when Alix looked at it questioningly. There wasn't much he could do now except send Honoria some things; he would send her a lot of things tomorrow. He thought rather angrily that this was just money—he had given so many people money. . . .

"No, no more," he said to another waiter. "What do I owe you?"

He would come back some day; they couldn't make him pay forever. But he wanted his child, and nothing was much good now, beside that fact. He wasn't young any more, with a lot of nice thoughts and dreams to have by himself. He was absolutely sure Helen wouldn't have wanted him to be so alone.

QUESTIONS

1. Charles Wales "believed in character . . . as the eternally valuable element. Everything else wore out." What does Charlie mean by "character"? Why has it become so important to him?

2. In what ways did Charles suffer from "dissipation"? Why does that word seem particularly fitting to him?
3. How has too much money led to Charles's dissipation? What value has money for Charles now?
4. F. Scott Fitzgerald is one of the writers of "The Lost Generation." In what ways are the characters of this story "lost"? How have they been affected by economic, political, and social factors out of their control?
5. Why does Charlie not want to love Honoria "too much"? Why is Charlie afraid of excessive affection? Does he see any examples of loving "too much"?
6. Charlie refers to "the lavish times three years ago." Contrast Paris and his life style of that period with the city and his situation at the present.

7
SYMBOLISM

I began reading literature seriously in high school. My teacher Mr. Enslow—a tall, thin man with owlish glasses and thinning hair—kept talking about symbols. Everything seemed to be a symbol of something else, and reading literature seemed to be the art of learning a new language in which common, ordinary words changed their meaning. I began to make for myself a little dictionary of symbolic meanings. But I soon encountered the problem that the same word seemed to have different symbolic meanings in different stories. I became frustrated. I thought Mr. Enslow either had an incredible fund of symbolic knowledge (which I was not old enough or smart enough to understand) or else he was making up these symbolic meanings as he went along. For a while I believed that symbol hunting and symbol making were games English teachers played with students.

Perhaps you have had a similar experience and shared the same frustration. When you come to read a story, you begin to look for equivalent meanings for what you read. I have learned, however, that Mr. Enslow was right. What I didn't understand was that his idea of symbolism and my idea were very different.

TRADITIONAL SYMBOLS

I originally thought of a symbol as a word, image or sign that stood for something else. For example, the dove was a stand-in for the idea of peace or the Holy Spirit. Tradition had anchored these symbols to specific meanings. There seemed to be a great number of these fixed traditional symbols:

light = God or wisdom
olive branch = peace
Old Glory = patriotism
crown = kingship
snakes = evil, Satan

The list could be much longer, but we can recognize that these symbols tend to be either religious or political symbols—symbols meant to be recognized by a large, varied audience. Religion and politics use symbols for many reasons. First, they are useful to give visible and tangible substance to an invisible and intangible spiritual reality. Many religions hold that we can not see God directly, but we can behold the divine presence through intermediary symbols. Second, symbols are an excellent way to communicate to a pre- or semi-literate population. Before children can read, they can often recognize the symbols for their favorite products, a bear that symbolizes a breakfast cereal or a red wave for a particular brand of soda, the golden arches of a restaurant. Symbols have vast appeal because they are easy to recognize and often quite beautiful. Your clothes, school, records and television shows are crowded with easily identifiable symbols.

Literature contains a good number of these fixed and traditional symbols. But the kind of symbol most frequently found in literature, the kind Mr. Enslow was pointing out to me, is a different kind. To understand this sort of symbol, we need to go back to the relationship between the writer and the reader.

THE CONCRETE AND THE ABSTRACT

At the beginning of this chapter I related a short anecdote about being a student in high school. The narrative, though sketchy, had several concrete details. For example, I gave the teacher a name and personal characteristics so you could visualize him better. I stated my feelings and a specific action—making a symbol dictionary—I adopted for solving my problem. Finally I stated that the action failed.

Why did I begin with this anecdote? First, it is appropriate. Both the chapter and my story are about symbols. Second, it is a story with which you, the reader, might identify because you might have had a teacher like Mr. Enslow who liked to hunt symbols. Or perhaps you had trouble in mathematics which also is indebted to symbols. Your teacher's discussions of X and Y and $<$ and % made your head spin. In short, you may have had your own Mr. Enslow.

What I was doing was using Mr. Enslow as a symbol of sorts. He came to represent—at least in my mind—the entire group of teachers who confused me. He is a concrete example of a larger, more abstract group. It is easier for me to talk about one person than it is to talk about an abstract class of persons, and it is easier for readers to visualize a single person than an abstract generalization. Thus, when I want to interest readers in a subject, I often start with a concrete anecdote that suggests a broader significance, or symbolizes an abstract, general concept.

DEFINITION OF SYMBOL

What is a symbol? It is an object, word or sign that has significance beyond its literal meaning. Take a star for example. A star is literally a distant sphere of burning gases, an object in the sky. When we put a representation of a star on an American flag, however, it represents more than a natural phenomenon—it stands for one state within the United States. When a star is put on the top of a steeple, it stands for hope. When it appears on a general's uniform, it indicates his or her rank, and when it appears on the door of a performer's dressing room, it means that he or she is an important cast member.

Mr. Enslow is not a symbol similar to that of a star. The symbolic meanings of a star has been established before a writer uses it. So if I wrote: "Uncle Sam took thirteen stars from the sky to establish his new country," I have assumed that my readers would already know that Uncle Sam is a pre-existing symbol for the United States and that the thirteen stars symbolized the original thirteen colonies. But when I wrote: "Mr. Enslow . . . kept talking about symbols," I knew that you did not have a pre-existing notion of what Mr. Enslow represented. Such a notion would have to arise from the anecdote itself. Mr. Enslow's significance is drawn from his specific context in the text while the star's significance precedes the text.

There is, moreover, another way in which the two symbols—the star and Mr. Enslow—differ. A star has nothing to do with colonies. A fairly arbitrary association has been drawn between the sign and its significance. Not all traditional symbols are so arbitrary. The cross, for example, has a close relationship with Jesus's life. But over time, the cross has come to represent all of Christianity and not just Christ's passion. Indeed when the symbol gets on band aid boxes as a red cross, it has lost virtually all of its original context and represents merely *first aid.* However, Mr. Enslow's significance is far less arbitrary. His significance grows out of the immediate context in which he appears. He is a single instance of an entire class of people with similar qualities. He symbolizes English teachers in a way similar to the manner that elected officials "represent" in legislative bodies the views of their constituents or as one student is chosen to represent his class at graduation.

In general we find in literature two sorts of symbols. First are *traditional symbols,* such as the star, the dove or the eagle, symbols that have a limited number of fixed and widely-recognized pre-existing meanings. The second kind of symbol is sometimes called a *romantic symbol* or *representative symbol* or *natural symbol.* Mr. Enslow is a representative symbol because (1) he stands for not a single fixed meaning, but a variety of different significances, (2) he did not have a pre-established symbolic significance, and (3) he acquired significance by being selected from a group to represent all the elements of that group in a particular context.

SELECTIVITY OF CONCRETE DETAILS

As readers move through a story, they encounter numbers of concrete details about the characters' physical appearances, their clothing, faces, actions and gestures. The writer has chosen those details because they make the character more vivid and individual. Such details help readers imagine the experience so they can visualize it in their mind's eye. Writers work hard to create this impression.

But as we reflect upon these particular and concrete details of the story, we often recognize that these concrete particulars are also examples of more general conditions or truths, which we might say the story "symbolizes." Beyond the differences of time, place and circumstance, we often can recognize more general sorts of experience that are true—if not for us—at least for others.

The details of a story often take on added significance. After all, they have been chosen because they seemed especially vivid or appropriate. I sometimes play a game with myself in order to appreciate the "rightness" of narrative detail and to locate its added significance. I try to imagine how the passage would change if the details were reversed or omitted. For example, James Joyce begins his story "Araby" with this particular detail: "North Richmond Street, being blind, was a quiet street." It may help us to know that there is in Dublin a North Richmond Street, which is "blind," or as we would say, "a dead end." How would the story be changed if Joyce had told us that North Richmond Street was a wide, open thoroughfare? Well, first, an open street would lead somewhere, but a dead end has no where to go. A thoroughfare would be busy with people and carriages. But North Richmond Street is quiet, and has little life to it. Dead end streets are out of the way, where only those with a specific purpose would enter. Thus, this very concrete detail about North Richmond Street not only helps readers to visualize the setting, but suggests "symbolically" some of the deeper significance of being a dead-end.

We might ask ourselves, "Why did Joyce choose this particular detail to start his story when he could have used some other? Is there some special significance to the fact that North Richmond Street is 'blind' or 'a dead end'? Is North Richmond Street the only dead-end element in the story?" After reading the story, we might recall that the narrator takes a train to Araby which is at the end of a special line. The narrator leaves one dead-end to arrive at another. In fact, we may say that his life is a dead-end. We now can see some of the extra significance the concrete detail about North Richmond Street has in the story; we now recognize its symbolic significance.

RECOGNIZING SYMBOLS

The impression I received from Mr. Enslow that everything is a symbol is in part correct. Everything appears in a story by design. Commas, periods, apostrophes don't just leap on to the page. An author or editor puts them there because they will add to the impact of the story. Similarly, all the narrative details have been selected because they bear the most significance. All the details of a story are charged with deeper (symbolic) meaning. We don't often speak of them as symbols—in fact, when writing about literature, I often steer clear of the term—but that's what they are.

Nevertheless, particularly important symbols often appear in key places in a story. Often they crop up at the beginnings and ends of works or at the climax of a story. Frequently, the most important symbols reappear, sometimes in slightly altered form, throughout a story.

For example, in Zora Neal Hurston's story "Sweat" we are told from the beginning that the central character Delia is afraid of snakes. Her cruel husband brings home a rattlesnake to frighten her, and eventually he is killed by that snake. A snake is literally a reptile, but we also know that snakes have traditional associations. A snake tricked Adam and Eve into eating the fruits of the knowledge of good and evil. Thus the snake is associated with evil, trickery and knowledge. But the snake has other associations. In Greek mythology two snakes are entwined on Hermes' staff, and his staff symbolizes medical care and healing. You may also recall a flag used during the American Revolution, a flag that bore a coiled rattlesnake and the motto "Don't Tread on Me." In that context the rattlesnake stood for fierce independence and freedom. Hurston uses the snake at all the key points of the story, and throughout "Sweat" its significance changes. At first Delia associates snakes only with what is evil, frightening and harmful. But towards the end of the story, she recognizes that the snake's power can be used to free her from the tyranny of her brutal husband and to gain her independence.

"Sweat" provides us with several important lessons on reading symbols. First one has to bear in mind the various meanings a symbol can have. Don't be too rigid, especially at first, in establishing a symbol's significance. Writers usually choose symbols that have a wealth of associations. Next let the context in which the symbol appears govern its meaning, but as the context changes, be ready to consider additional or variant meanings to the symbol. A symbol and its context interact with one another. While the context defines a symbol, so, too, a symbol gives meaning to its context. One does not operate independently of the other. It is this interactive and mutually modifying relationship between symbols and their narrative contexts that makes reading so complex, challenging and richly rewarding.

THE TRUTH OF FICTION

How can a story—which is purely imaginative—be said to contain truth? We usually think of truth and fiction as opposites, and yet we are also told that fiction contains truth. How can we resolve this paradox?

Would it make "Araby" any truer if we were presented with Mangan's sister's birth certificate and thus could verify that such a person actually existed? I don't think so. The story's success must stand or fall on what it contains, not on extraneous documentation.

The "truth" of "Araby" lies elsewhere. I have never been to Dublin, and I have never had quite the experience that the narrator has, but Joyce has made me feel that this is how a young man might actually experience the world. The feelings of the young man for the sister of a friend seem true to me. I can understand how a young man who feels his life is at a dead-end, might escape into romance and wish to bring back from some far away place an object of rare value. I have not had that particular daydream, but I have daydreamed, and I know what daydreams are like. The concrete details of "Araby"—many of which *are* factually accurate—are included in the story (1) to make the action more vivid, and (2) to suggest on a more general or symbolic level a larger experience that affects not just one particular young man, but people throughout the world.

THINGS TO THINK ABOUT

1. How are people's lives ruled by symbols? What sorts of status symbols do they hope to acquire? What sorts of symbols of femininity or masculinity do you recognize as governing people's behavior? Go through your day from the time you wake to the time you go to bed and list the symbols you encounter.
2. Consider how you draw inferences about people's behavior from a few incidents. In what way do these incidents become symbolic of general character traits? Is this sort of thinking fair? Is it unavoidable?
3. Many psychologists and psychiatrists maintain that dreams are made up of nothing but symbols. Narrate a dream you have had recently. Do you recognize any symbols in the dream—persons, actions, names or things that represent others?
4. Can we think without symbols? Can we live without symbols?

ESSAY TOPICS

1. We often try to communicate our love or affection for other people through symbolic gifts and ceremonies. Discuss the kinds of symbols that people use to indicate their feelings for one another.
2. The transition from childhood to adulthood is frequently marked by symbolic acts. Discuss the various ceremonies and symbols we use in this society to indicate the transition to adulthood.
3. Our environment is often quite literally filled with symbols. Discuss

the types of symbols you might find in your church, in school, in your city hall or in your home. What do these symbols mean? Why are they there?

4. The same symbol can have a different meaning in a different context. For example, a star on a church steeple has one meaning; a star on the American Flag has another meaning, and a star on over a gas station may have a third meaning. Choose a symbol such as a star and discuss the various meanings it can have and how the context alters its meaning.

CREATIVE WRITING EXERCISES

1. The Statue of Liberty is an excellent example of a public sculpture made to symbolize an abstract concept. Describe a Statue of Laziness, a Statue of Loyalty, a Statue of Good Teaching, or some other public monument commemorating an abstract quality, condition or institution.
2. We often save things for "sentimental reasons." These sentimental objects are more valuable for what they symbolize than for their immediate utility. Create a character whose personality the reader knows only through the objects he or she has kept for "sentimental reasons."
3. We often get a good idea about what people are like by their environments, their rooms, houses or offices. Present a character by describing a room in which he or she lives.

LITERARY ESSAYS

1. Discuss how the narrative gives small details or ordinary objects deeper significance. Discuss how the story heightened your awareness of the symbolic significance of everyday objects and occurrences.
2. Discuss how one symbol helps clarify other symbols in "The Birthmark" or "The Other Side of the Hedge."
3. We tend to think about symbols as objects, but there are symbolic actions such as saluting the flag or taking off a hat during solemn occasions. Discuss how actions become symbolic in one or more of the stories in this chapter.

NADINE GORDIMER

THE TRAIN FROM RHODESIA

Nadine Gordimer (b. 1923) is a native of South Africa where she continues to live with her husband and two children despite harassment and continual difficulty getting her works published in that country. Her short stories and novels—the most famous of which are Guest of Honor *and* Burger's Daughter*—are concerned with how apartheid affects the people, both white and black, in her troubled country.*

She has won many prizes including the Booker Prize (England's most prestigious award for fiction) and honorary membership to the American Academy of Arts and Science. Her style is marked by clarity, cleanliness and wit that penetrates into the core of her characters' emotional life and the political realities of South Africa.

The train came out of the red horizon and bore down toward them over the single straight track.

The stationmaster came out of his little brick station with its pointed chalet roof, feeling the creases in his serge uniform in his legs as well. A stir of preparedness rippled through the squatting native vendors waiting in the dust; the face of a carved wooden animal, eternally surprised, stuck out of a sack. The stationmaster's barefoot children wandered over. From the gray mud huts with the untidy heads that stood within a decorated mud wall, chickens, and dogs with their skin stretched like parchment over their bones, followed the piccanins down to the track. The flushed and perspiring west cast a reflection, faint, without heat, upon the station, upon the tin shed marked "Goods," upon the walled kraal, upon the gray tin house of the stationmaster and upon the sand, that lapped all around, from sky to sky, cast little rhythmical cups of shadow, so that the sand became the sea, and closed over the children's black feet softly and without imprint.

The stationmaster's wife sat behind the mesh of her verandah. Above her head the hunk of a sheep's carcass moved slightly, dangling in a current of air.

They waited.

The train called out, along the sky; but there was no answer; and the cry hung on: I'm coming . . . I'm coming . . .

The engine flared out now, big, whisking a dwindling body behind it; the track flared out to let it in.

Creaking, jerking, jostling, gasping, the train filled the station.

Here, let me see that one—the young woman curved her body further out of the corridor window. Missus? smiled the old boy, looking at the creatures he held in his hand. From a piece of string on his gray finger hung a tiny woven basket; he lifted it, questioning. No, no, she urged, leaning down toward him, across the height of the train, toward the man in the piece of old rug; that one, that one, her hand commanded. It was a lion, carved out of soft dry wood that looked like spongecake; heraldic, black and white, with impressionistic detail burnt in. The old man held it up to her still smiling, not from the heart, but at the customer.

Between its Vandyke teeth, in the mouth opened in an endless roar too terrible to be heard, it had a black tongue. Look, said the young husband, if you don't mind! And round the neck of the thing, a piece of fur (rat? rabbit? meerkat?); a real mane, majestic, telling you somehow that the artist had delight in the lion.

All up and down the length of the train in the dust the artists sprang, walking bent, like performing animals, the better to exhibit the fantasy held toward the faces on the train. Buck, startled and stiff, staring with round black and white eyes. More lions, standing erect, grappling with strange, thin, elongated warriors who clutched spears and showed no fear in their slits of eyes. How much, they asked from the train, how much?

Give me penny, said the little ones with nothing to sell. The dogs went and sat, quite still, under the dining car, where the train breathed out the smell of meat, cooking with onion.

A man passed beneath the arch of reaching arms meeting gray-black and white in the exchange of money for the staring wooden eyes, the stiff wooden legs sticking up in the air; went along under the voices and the bargaining, interrogating the wheels. Past the dogs; glancing up at the dining car where he could stare at the faces, behind glass, drinking beer, two by two, on either side of a uniform railway vase with its pale dead flower. Right to the end, to the guard's van, where the stationmaster's children had just collected their mother's two loaves of bread; to the engine itself, where the stationmaster and the driver stood talking against the steaming complaint of the resting beast.

The man called out to them, something loud and joking. They turned to laugh, in a twirl of steam. The two children careered over the sand, clutching the bread, and burst through the iron gate and up the path through the garden in which nothing grew.

Passengers drew themselves in at the corridor windows and turned into compartments to fetch money, to call someone to look. Those sitting inside looked up: suddenly different, caged faces, boxed in, cut off, after the contact of outside. There was an orange a piccanin would like. . . . What about that chocolate? It wasn't very nice. . . .

A young girl had collected a handful of the hard kind, that no one liked, out of the chocolate box, and was throwing them to the dogs, over at the dining car. But the hens darted in, and swallowed the chocolates, incredibly quick and accurate, before they had even dropped in the dust, and the dogs, a little bewildered, looked up with their brown eyes, not expecting anything.

—No, leave it, said the girl, don't take it. . . .

Too expensive, too much, she shook her head and raised her voice to the old boy, giving up the lion. He held it up where she had handed it to him. No, she said, shaking her head. Three-and-six? insisted her husband, loudly. Yes baas! laughed the boy. *Three-and-six?*—the young man was incredulous. Oh leave it—she said. The young man stopped. Don't you want it? he said, keeping his face closed to the boy. No, never mind, she said, leave it. The old native kept his head on one side, looking at them sideways, holding the lion. Three-and-six, he murmured, as old people repeat things to themselves.

The young woman drew her head in. She went into the coupé and sat down. Out of the window, on the other side, there was nothing; sand and bush; a thorn tree. Back through the open doorway, past the figure of her husband in the corridor, there was the station, the voices, wooden animals waving, running feet. Her eye followed the funny little valance of scrolled wood that outlined the chalet roof of the station; she thought of the lion and smiled. That bit of fur round the neck. But the wooden buck, the hippos, the elephants, the baskets that already bulked out of their brown paper under the seat and on the luggage rack! How will they look at home? Where will you put them? What will they mean away from the places you found them? Away from the unreality of the last few weeks? The man outside. But he is not part of the unreality; he is for good now. Odd . . . somewhere there was an idea that he, that living with him, was part of the holiday, the strange places.

Outside, a bell rang. The stationmaster was leaning against the end of the train, green flag rolled in readiness. A few men who had got down to stretch their legs sprang on to the train, clinging to the observation platforms, or perhaps merely standing on the iron step, holding the rail; but on the train, safe from the one dusty platform, the one tin house, the empty sand.

There was a grunt. The train jerked. Through the glass the beer drinkers looked out, as if they could not see beyond it. Behind the flyscreen, the stationmaster's wife sat facing back at them beneath the darkening hunt of meat.

There was a shout. The flag drooped out. Joints not yet coordinated, the segmented body of the train heaved and bumped back against itself. It began to move; slowly the scrolled chalet moved past it, the yells of the natives, running alongside, jetted up into the air, fell back at different levels. Staring wooden faces waved drunkenly, there, then gone, questioning for the last time at the windows. Here, one-and-six baas!—As one automatically opens a hand to catch a thrown ball, a man fumbled wildly down his pocket, brought up the shilling and sixpence and threw them out; the old native, gasping, his skinny toes splaying the sand, flung the lion.

The piccanins were waving, the dogs stood, tails uncertain, watching the train go: past the mud huts, where a woman turned to look, up from the smoke of the fire, her hand pausing on her hip.

The stationmaster went slowly in under the chalet.

The old native stood, breath blowing out the skin between his ribs, feet tense, balanced in the sand, smiling and shaking his head. In his opened palm, held in the attitude of receiving, was the retrieved shilling and sixpence.

The blind end of the train was being pulled helplessly out of the station.

The young man swung in from the corridor, breathless. He was shaking his head with laughter and triumph. Here! he said. And waggled the lion at her. One-and-six!

What? she said.

He laughed. I was arguing with him for fun, bargaining—when the train had pulled out already, he came tearing after. . . . One-and-six Baas! So there's your lion.

She was holding it away from her, the head with the open jaws, the pointed teeth, the black tongue, the wonderful ruff of fur facing her. She was looking at it with an expression of not seeing, of seeing something different. Her face was drawn up, wryly, like the face of a discomforted child. Her mouth lifted nervously at the corner. Very slowly, cautious, she lifted her finger and touched the mane, where it was joined to the wood.

But how could you, she said. He was shocked by the dismay of her face.

Good Lord, he said, what's the matter?

If you wanted the thing, she said, her voice rising and breaking with the shrill impotence of anger, why didn't you buy it in the first place? If you wanted it, why didn't you pay for it? Why didn't you take it decently, when he offered it? Why did you have to wait for him to run after the train with it, and give him one-and-six? One-and-six!

She was pushing it at him, trying to force him to take it. He stood astonished, his hands hanging at his sides.

But you wanted it! You liked it so much?

—It's a beautiful piece of work, she said fiercely, as if to protect it from him.

You liked it so much! You said yourself it was too expensive—

Oh *you*—she said, hopeless and furious. *You*. . . . She threw the lion on to the seat.

He stood looking at her.

She sat down again in the corner and, her face slumped in her hand, stared out of the window. Everything was turning round inside her. One-and-six. One-and-six. One-and-six for the wood and the carving and the sinews of the legs and the switch of the tail. The mouth open like that and the teeth. The black tongue, rolling, like a wave. The mane round the neck. To give one-and-six for that. The heat of shame mounted through her legs and body and sounded in her ears like the sound of sand pouring. Pouring, pouring. She sat there, sick. A weariness, a tastelessness, the discovery of a void made her hands slacken their grip, atrophy emptily, as if the hour was not worth their grasp. She was feeling like this again. She had thought it was something to do with singleness, with being alone and belonging too much to oneself.

She sat there not wanting to move or speak, or to look at anything, even; so that the mood should be associated with nothing, no object, word or sight that might recur and so recall the feeling again. . . . Smuts blew in grittily, settled on her hands. Her back remained at exactly the same angle, turned against the young man sitting with his hands drooping between his sprawled legs, and the lion, fallen on its side in the corner.

The train had cast the station like a skin. It called out to the sky, I'm coming, I'm coming; and again, there was no answer.

QUESTIONS

1. What is the significance of the creases in the pants legs of the stationmaster's uniform? How do his clothes contrast with the attire of others?
2. What is the symbolic significance of the carved lion?
3. Why does the young woman regard the "last few weeks" as "unreality"?
4. Why is the young woman so angry that the young man has bought her the lion for one-and-six?
5. What is the symbolic significance of the lion's having "fallen on its side in the corner"?
6. Why is there "no answer" to the train's call?
7. Why is the train compared to a snake in the last paragraph? Is the train elsewhere described as possessing snake-like qualities? Does this comparison have any symbolic significance?

NADINE GORDIMER

from AN INTERVIEW WITH NADINE GORDIMER

Q. What is your aesthetic motivation for this increasing exploration of the internal landscapes of character?

A. Insofar as it's aesthetic, it has to do with finding the right means to express what I am discovering. Perhaps it's got more to do with the degree to which we conceal ourselves here. It's part of living in South Africa, having these incredible layers of concealment, and I suppose I've become more and more conscious of them in relation to other people, and even to myself, I've always said, and I still feel, that style is something that is dictated by the subject; it comes about through looking for the right way to deal with a particular subject, or an aspect of a subject. This inner-directed style comes about from the feeling that what we say and do—well, it's always only half of what we mean, but in South Africa it's less than half. And this constant shifting of foothold is both in terms of our society—in terms of relations to other people around you—and in terms of your own self-respect and your own self-esteem. I want to convey this constant shifting along, on very uncertain and uneven ground.

Q. You've said elsewhere that Africa needs an "articulated consciousness" and that it's the novelist's job to provide it. Do you stick with that?

A. Yes, and I think that is what changes all the time in my own writing. My own consciousness has changed. I can certainly see that if I look at my early work. And, no doubt, if I keep my wits about me for a few more years, it'll keep on changing.

Q. Reaction to your work here is severely polarized between awards of the highest literary honors and reliable official execration, bannings, embargoes, and so on. How do you handle this invariably bizarre reception?

A. Well, I suppose I've never really thought about it, because I suppose I know it is going to happen. I have been protected all my life, and still am—after all this time and all these books and this middle age of mine—by such a fascination with what I'm trying to do, while I'm writing it, that I honestly don't think till afterwards, and sometimes in quite personal ways, of the consequences. I'm reckless when I write, and I always have the feeling that, oh well, it doesn't really matter, I'm *going* to do it. It's got to be done completely, or not at all.

Q. But when the book's out, published, then embargoed, next thing wins some prize, it's banned, it's unbanned—do you just take it? I know that as a public spokesperson you are powerfully against this censorship process. But I mean, how are you personally affected? Water off a duck's back?

A. Yes, because if you look at what happens to writers here, there's nothing unusual, really, about what happens to me.

Q. Has this recurring humiliation worn you down over the years?

A. No; but it depresses me. There's always this feeling about the book's life here, where it is so important to me. It's a platitude, but it's true; here you are among your own people, and you want to be read by them, and there's this grey area, this fog, that you struggle through to reach them. Indeed, you can't struggle through it, because there's nothing you can do—what *can* you do?—sell the damn thing on the street-corner? And be arrested for doing so?

THINGS TO THINK ABOUT

1. In what ways does Gordimer see the techniques of her stories related to political events in South Africa? Do you know of any American authors who relate political events in a similar way in their works?
2. Do American writers feel the need to develop an "articulated consciousness?" Why or why not?
3. Many American authors and works have been banned at various times in this country, including such writers as Mark Twain and Herman Melville, and such books as *The Wizard of Oz*. Why do some people consider these authors or books dangerous? Why do people ban books?
4. How does censorship affect Gordimer? How would censorship affect you? Are you conscious of the results of censorship?

NATHANIEL HAWTHORNE

THE BIRTHMARK

Nathaniel Hawthorne (1804–1864) was born in Salem, Massachusetts where his family had lived for generations. One of his relatives had been a judge at the infamous Salem Witch Trials, and Hawthorne, especially in "Young Goodman Brown" and The Scarlet Letter, *returns to the Puritan past in his stories and novels. In the Puritans, Hawthorne found the three elements that most interested him: psychological complexity, moral fervor, and grotesque and gothic imagery. Though "The Birthmark" is not set in the Puritan past, it does possess the three hallmarks of Hawthorne's imagination.*

Paintings of Hawthorne in his youth reveal that he was an exceptionally handsome man, and throughout his life he seems to have attracted admirers. Yet Hawthorne was a reclusive spirit. In the years between his graduation from college and the publication of his first stories, he lived in isolation, leaving his house only in the evenings when the streets were empty. Later when he achieved fame he settled in Tanglewood to escape visitors. However, in his later life, he travelled widely and for a number of years served as the American consul in Liverpool, England.

In the latter part of the last century there lived a man of science, an eminent proficient in every branch of natural philosophy, who not long before our story opens had made experience of a spiritual affinity more attractive than any chemical one. He had left his laboratory to the care of an assistant, cleared his fine countenance from the furnace smoke, washed the stain of acids from his fingers, and persuaded a beautiful woman to become his wife. In those days when the comparatively recent discovery of electricity and other kindred mysteries of Nature seemed to open paths into the region of miracle, it was not unusual for the love of science to rival the love of woman in its depth and absorbing energy. The higher intellect, the imagination, the spirit, and even the heart might all find their congenial aliment in pursuits which, as some of their ardent votaries believed, would ascend from one step of powerful intelligence to another, until the philosopher should lay his hand on the secret of creative force and perhaps make new worlds for himself. We know not whether Aylmer possessed this degree of faith in man's ultimate control over Nature. He had devoted himself, however, too unreservedly to scientific studies ever to be weaned from them by any second passion. His love for his young wife might prove the stronger of the two; but it could only be by intertwining itself with his love of science, and uniting the strength of the latter to his own.

Such a union accordingly took place, and was attended with truly remarkable consequences and a deeply impressive moral. One day, very soon after their marriage, Aylmer sat gazing at his wife with a trouble in his countenance that grew stronger until he spoke.

"Georgiana," said he, "has it never occurred to you that the mark upon your cheek might be removed?"

"No, indeed," said she, smiling; but perceiving the seriousness of his manner, she blushed deeply. "To tell you the truth it has been so often called a charm that I was simple enough to imagine it might be so."

"Ah, upon another face perhaps it might," replied her husband; "but never on yours. No, dearest Georgiana, you came so nearly perfect from the hand of Nature that this slightest possible defect, which we hesitate whether to term a defect or a beauty, shocks me, as being the visible mark of earthly imperfection."

"Shocks you, my husband!" cried Georgiana, deeply hurt; at first reddening with momentary anger, but then bursting into tears. "Then why did you take me from my mother's side? You cannot love what shocks you!"

To explain this conversation it must be mentioned that in the centre of Georgiana's left cheek there was a singular mark, deeply interwoven, as it were, with the texture and substance of her face. In the usual state of her complexion—a healthy though delicate bloom—the mark wore a tint of deeper crimson, which imperfectly defined its shape amid the surrounding rosiness. When she blushed it gradually became more indistinct, and finally vanished amid the triumphant rush of blood that bathed the whole cheek with its brilliant glow. But if any shifting motion caused her to turn pale there was the mark again, a crimson stain upon the snow, in which Aylmer sometimes deemed an almost fearful distinctness. Its shape bore not a little similarity to the human hand, though of the smallest pygmy size. Georgiana's loves were wont to say that some fairy at her birth hour had laid her tiny hand upon the infant's cheek, and left this impress there in token of the magic endowments that were to give her such sway over all hearts. Many a desperate swain would have risked life for the privilege of pressing his lips to the mysterious hand. It must not be concealed, however, that the impression wrought by this fairy sign manual varied exceedingly, according to the difference of temperament in the beholders. Some fastidious persons—but they were exclusively of her own sex—affirmed that the bloody hand, as they chose to call it, quite destroyed the effect of Georgiana's beauty, and rendered her countenance even hideous. But it would be as reasonable to say that one of those small blue stains which sometimes occur in the purest statuary marble would convert the Eve of Powers to a monster. Masculine observers, if the birthmark did not heighten their admiration, contented themselves with wishing it away, that the world might possess one living specimen of ideal loveliness without the semblance of a flaw. After his marriage—for he thought little or nothing of the matter before—Aylmer discovered that this was the case with himself.

Had she been less beautiful—if Envy's self could have found aught else to sneer at—he might have felt his affection heightened by the prettiness of this mimic hand, now vaguely portrayed, now lost, now stealing forth again and glimmering to and fro with every pulse of emotion that throbbed within her heart; but seeing her otherwise so perfect, he found this one defect grow more and more intolerable with every moment of their united lives. It was the fatal flaw of humanity which Nature, in one shape or another, stamps ineffaceably on all her productions, either to imply that they are temporary and finite, or that their perfection must be wrought by toil and pain. The crimson hand expressed the ineludible gripe in which mortality clutches the highest and purest of earthly mould, degrading them into kindred with the lowest, and even with the very brutes, like whom their visible frames return to dust. In this manner, selecting it as the symbol of his wife's liability to sin, sorrow, decay, and death, Aylmer's sombre imagination was not long in rendering the birthmark a frightful object, causing him more trouble and horror than ever Georgiana's beauty, whether of soul or sense, had given him delight.

At all the seasons which should have been their happiest, he invariably and without intending it, nay, in spite of a purpose to the contrary, reverted to this one disastrous topic. Trifling as it at first appeared, it so connected itself with innumerable trains of thought and modes of feeling that it became the central point of all. With the morning twilight Aylmer opened his eyes upon his wife's face and recognized the symbol of imperfection; and when they sat together at the evening hearth his eyes wandered stealthily to her cheek, and beheld, flickering with the blaze of the wood fire, the spectral hand that wrote mortality where he would fain have worshipped. Georgiana soon learned to shudder at his gaze. It needed but a glance with the peculiar expression that his face often wore to change the roses of her cheek into a deathlike paleness, amid which the crimson hand was brought strongly out, like bas-relief of ruby on the whitest marble.

Late one night when the lights were growing dim, so as hardly to betray the stain on the poor wife's cheek, she herself, for the first time, voluntarily took up the subject.

"Do you remember, my dear Aylmer," said she, with a feeble attempt at a smile, "have you any recollection of a dream last night about this odious hand?"

"None! none whatever!" replied Aylmer, starting; but then he added, in a dry, cold tone, affected for the sake of concealing the real depth of his emotion, "I might well dream of it; for before I fell asleep it had taken a pretty firm hold of my fancy."

"And you did dream of it?" continued Georgiana, hastily; for she dreaded lest a gush of tears should interrupt what she had to say. "A terrible dream! I wonder that you can forget it. Is it possible to forget this one expression?—'It is in her heart now; we must have it out!' Reflect, my husband; for by all means I would have you recall that dream."

The mind is in a sad state when Sleep, the all-involving, cannot confine her spectres within the dim region of her sway, but suffers them to break forth, affrighting this actual life with secrets that perchance belong to a deeper one. Aylmer now remembered his dream. He had fancied himself with his servant Aminadab, attempting an operation for the removal of the birthmark; but the deeper went the knife, the deeper sank the hand, until at length its tiny grasp appeared to have caught hold of Georgiana's heart; whence, however, her husband was inexorably resolved to cut or wrench it away.

When the dream had shaped itself perfectly in his memory, Aylmer sat in his wife's presence with a guilty feeling. Truth often finds its way to the mind close muffled in robes of sleep, and then speaks with uncompromising directness of matters in regard to which we practise an unconscious self-deception during our waking moments. Until now he had not been aware of the tyrannizing influence acquired by one idea over his mind, and of the lengths which he might find in his heart to go for the sake of giving himself peace.

"Aylmer," resumed Georgiana, solemnly, "I know not what may be the cost to both of us to rid me of this fatal birthmark. Perhaps its removal may cause cureless deformity; or it may be the stain goes as deep as life itself. Again: do we know that there is a possibility, on any terms, of unclasping the firm gripe of this little hand which was laid upon me before I came into the world?"

"Dearest Georgiana, I have spent much thought upon the subject," hastily interrupted Aylmer. "I am convinced of the perfect practicability of its removal."

"If there be the remotest possibility of it," continued Georgiana, "let the attempt be made at whatever risk. Danger is nothing to me; for life, while this hateful mark makes me the object of your horror and disgust—life is a burden which I would fling down with joy. Either remove this dreadful hand, or take my wretched life! You have deep science. All the world bears witness of it. You have achieved great wonders. Cannot you remove this little, little mark, which I cover with the tips of two small fingers? Is this beyond your power, for the sake of your own peace, and to save your poor wife from madness?"

"Noblest, dearest, tenderest wife," cried Aylmer, rapturously, "doubt not my power. I have already given this matter the deepest thought—thought which might almost have enlightened me to create a being less perfect than yourself. Georgiana, you have led deeper than ever into the heart of science. I feel myself fully competent to render this deer cheek as faultless as its fellow; and then, most beloved, what will be my triumph when I shall have corrected what Nature left imperfect in her fairest work! Even Pygmalion, when his sculptured woman assumed life, felt not greater ecstasy than mine will be."

"It is resolved, then," said Georgiana, faintly smiling. "And, Aylmer, spare me not, though you should find the birthmark take refuge in my heart at last."

Her husband tenderly kissed her cheek—her right cheek—not that which bore the impress of the crimson hand.

The next day Aylmer apprised his wife of a plan that he had formed whereby he might have opportunity for the intense thought and constant watchfulness which the proposed operation would require; while Georgiana, likewise, would enjoy the perfect repose essential to its success. They were to seclude themselves in the extensive apartments occupied by Aylmer as a laboratory, and where, during his toilsome youth, he had made discoveries in the elemental powers of Nature that had roused the admiration of all the learned societies in Europe. Seated calmly in this laboratory, the pale philosopher had investigated the secrets of the highest cloud region and of the profoundest mines; he had satisfied himself of the causes that kindled and kept alive the fires of the volcano; and had explained the mystery of the fountains, and how it is that they gush forth, some so bright and pure, and others with such rich medicinal virtues, from the dark bosom of the earth. Here, too, at an earlier period, he had studied the wonders of the human frame, and attempted to fathom the very process by which Nature assimilates all her precious influences from earth and air, and from the spiritual world, to create and foster man, her masterpiece. The latter pursuit, however, Aylmer had long laid aside in unwilling recognition of the truth—against which all seekers sooner or later stumble—that our great creative Mother, while she amuses us with apparently working in the broadest sunshine, is yet severely careful to keep her own secrets, and, in spite of her pretended openness, shows us nothing but results. She permits us, indeed, to mar, but seldom to mend, and, like a jealous patentee, on no account to make. Now, however, Aylmer resumed these half-forgotten investigations; not, of course, with such hopes or wishes as first suggested them; but because they involved much physiological truth and lay in the path of his proposed scheme for the treatment of Georgiana.

As he led her over the threshold of the laboratory, Georgiana was cold and tremulous. Aylmer looked cheerfully into her face, with intent to reassure her, but was so startled with the intense glow of the birthmark upon the whiteness of her cheek that he could not restrain a strong convulsive shudder. His wife fainted.

"Aminadab! Aminadab!" shouted Aylmer, stamping violently on the floor.

Forthwith there issued from an inner apartment a man of low stature, but bulky frame, with shaggy hair hanging about his visage, which was grimed with the vapors of the furnace. This personage had been Aylmer's underworker during his whole scientific career, and was admirably fitted for that office by his great mechanical readiness, and the skill with which, while incapable of comprehending a single principle, he executed all the details of his master's experiments. With his vast strength, his shaggy hair, his smoky aspect, and the indescribable earthiness that incrusted him, he seemed to represent man's physical nature; while Aylmer's slender figure, and pale, intellectual face, were no less apt a type of the spiritual element.

"Throw open the door of the boudoir, Aminadab," said Aylmer, "and burn a pastil."

"Yes, master," answered Aminadab, looking intently at the lifeless form of Georgiana; and then he muttered to himself, "If she were my wife, I'd never part with that birthmark."

When Georgiana recovered consciousness she found herself breathing an atmosphere of penetrating fragrance, the gentle potency of which had recalled her from her deathlike faintness. The scene around her looked like enchantment. Aylmer had converted those smoky, dingy, sombre rooms, where he had spent his brightest years in recondite pursuits, into a series of beautiful apartments not unfit to be the secluded abode of a lovely woman. The walls were hung with gorgeous curtains, which imparted the combination of grandeur and grace that no other species of adornment can achieve; and as they fell from the ceiling to the floor, their rich and ponderous folds, concealing all angles and straight lines, appeared to shut in the scene from infinite space. For aught Georgiana knew, it might be a pavilion among the clouds. And Aylmer, excluding the sunshine, which would have interfered with his chemical processes, had supplied its place with perfumed lamps, emitting flames of various hue, but all uniting in a soft, impurpled radiance. He now knelt by his wife's side, watching her earnestly, but without alarm; for he was confident in his science, and felt that he could draw a magic circle round her within which no evil might intrude.

"Where am I? Ah, I remember," said Georgiana, faintly; and she placed her hand over her cheek to hide the terrible mark from her husband's eyes.

"Fear not, dearest!" exclaimed he. "Do not shrink from me! Believe me, Georgiana, I even rejoice in this single imperfection, since it will be such a rapture to remove it."

"Oh, spare me!" sadly replied his wife. "Pray do not look at it again. I never can forget that convulsive shudder."

In order to soothe Georgiana, and, as it were, to release her mind from the burden of actual things, Aylmer now put in practice some of the light and playful secrets which science had taught him among its profounder lore. Airy figures, absolutely bodiless ideas, and forms of unsubstantial beauty came and danced before her, imprinting their momentary footsteps on beams of light. Though she had some indistinct idea of the method of these optical phenomena, still the illusion was almost perfect enough to warrant the belief that her husband possessed sway over the spiritual world. Then again, when she felt a wish to look forth from her seclusion, immediately, as if her thoughts were answered, the procession of external existence flitted across a screen. The scenery and the figures of actual life were perfectly represented, but with that bewitching, yet indescribable difference which always makes a picture, an image, or a shadow so much more attractive than the original. When wearied of this Aylmer bade her cast her eyes upon a vessel containing a quantity of earth. She did so, with little interest at first; but was soon startled to perceive the germ of a plant shooting upward from the soil. Then came the slender stalk; the leaves gradually unfolded themselves; and amid them was a perfect and lovely flower.

"It is magical!" cried Georgiana. "I dare not touch it."

"Nay, pluck it," answered Aylmer,—"pluck it, and inhale its brief perfume while you may. The flower will wither in a few moments and leave nothing save its brown seed vessels; but thence may be perpetuated a race as ephemeral as itself."

But Georgiana had no sooner touched the flower than the whole plant suffered a blight, its leaves turning coal-black as if by the agency of fire.

"There was too powerful a stimulus," said Aylmer, thoughtfully.

To make up for this abortive experiment, he proposed to take her portrait by a scientific process of his own invention. It was to be effected by rays of light striking upon a polished plate of metal. Georgiana assented; but, on looking at the result, was affrighted to find the features of the portrait blurred and indefinable; while the minute figure of a hand appeared where the cheek should have been. Aylmer snatched the metallic plate and threw it into a jar of corrosive acid.

Soon, however, he forgot these mortifying failures. In the intervals of study and chemical experiment he came to her flushed and exhausted, but seemed invigorated by her presence, and spoke in glowing language of the resources of his art. He gave a history of the long dynasty of the alchemists, who spent so many ages in quest of the universal solvent by which the golden principle might be elicited from all things vile and base. Aylmer appeared to believe that, by the plainest scientific logic, it was altogether within the limits of possibility to discover this long-sought medium; "but," he added, "a philosopher who should go deep enough to acquire the power would attain too lofty a wisdom to stoop to the exercise of it." Not less singular were his opinions in regard to the elixir vitae. He more than intimated that it was at his option to concoct a liquid that should prolong life for years, perhaps interminably; but that it would produce a discord in Nature which all the world, and chiefly the quaffer of the immortal nostrum, would find cause to curse.

"Aylmer, are you in earnest?" asked Georgiana, looking at him with amazement and fear. "It is terrible to possess such power, or even to dream of possessing it."

"Oh, do not tremble, my love," said her husband. "I would not wrong either you or myself by working such inharmonious effects upon our lives; but I would have you consider how trifling, in comparision, is the skill requisite to remove this little hand."

At the mention of the birthmark, Georgiana, as usual, shrank as if a redhot iron had touched her cheek.

Again Aylmer applied himself to his labors. She could hear his voice in the distant furnace room giving directions to Aminadab, whose harsh, uncouth, misshapen tones were audible in response, more like the grunt or growl of a brute than human speech. After hours of absence, Aylmer reappeared and proposed that she should now examine his cabinet of chemical products and natural treasures of the earth. Among the former he showed her a small vial, in which, he remarked, was contained a gentle yet most powerful fragrance, capable of impregnating all the breezes that blow across a kingdom. They were of inestimable value, the contents of that little vial; and, as he said so, he threw some of the perfume into the air and filled the room with piercing and invigorating delight.

"And what is this?" asked Georgiana, pointing to a small crystal globe containing a gold-colored liquid. "It is so beautiful to the eye that I could imagine it the elixir of life."

"In one sense it is," replied Aylmer; "or, rather, the elixir of immortality. It is the most precious poison that ever was concocted in this world. By its aid I could apportion the lifetime of any mortal at whom you might point your finger. The strength of the dose would determine whether he were to linger out years, or drop dead in the midst of a breath. No king on his guarded throne could keep his life if I, in my private station, should deem that the welfare of millions justified me in depriving him of it."

"Why do you keep such a terrific drug?" inquired Georgiana in horror.

"Do not mistrust me, dearest," said her husband, smiling; "its virtuous potency is yet greater than its harmful one. But see! here is a powerful cosmetic. With a few drops of this in a vase of water, freckles may be washed away as easily as the hands are cleansed. A stronger infusion would take the blood out of the cheek, and leave the rosiest beauty a pale ghost."

"Is it with this lotion that you intend to bathe my cheek?" asked Georgiana anxiously.

"Oh, no," hastily replied her husband; "this is merely superficial. Your case demands a remedy that shall go deeper."

In his interviews with Georgiana, Aylmer generally made minute inquiries as to her sensations and whether the confinement of the rooms and the temperature of the atmosphere agreed with her. These questions had such a particular drift that Georgiana began to conjecture that she was already subjected to certain physical influences, either breathed in with the fragrant air or taken with her food. She fancied likewise, but it might be altogether fancy, that there was a stirring up of her system—a strange, indefinite sensation creeping through her veins, and tingling, half painfully, half pleasurably, at her heart. Still, whenever she dared to look into the mirror, there she beheld herself pale as a white rose and with the crimson birthmark stamped upon her cheek. Not even Aylmer now hated it so much as she.

To dispel the tedium of the hours which her husband found it necessary to devote to the processes of combination and analysis, Georgiana turned over the volumes of his scientific library. In many dark old tomes she met with chapters full of romance and poetry. They were the works of philosophers of the middle ages, such as Albertus Magnus, Cornelius Agrippa, Paracelsus, and the famous friar who created the prophetic Brazen Head. All these antique naturalists stood in advance of their centuries, yet were imbued with some of their credulity, and therefore were believed, and perhaps imagined themselves to have acquired from the investigation of Nature a power above Nature, and from physics a sway over the spiritual world. Hardly less curious and imaginative were the early volumes of the Transactions of the Royal Society, in which the members, knowing little of the limits of natural possibility, were continually recording wonders or proposing methods whereby wonders might be wrought.

But to Georgiana the most engrossing volume was a large folio from her husband's own hand, in which he had recorded every experiment of his scientific career, its original aim, the methods adopted for its development, and its final success or failure, with the circumstances to which either event was attributable. The book, in truth, was both the history and emblem of his ardent, ambitious, imaginative, yet practical and laborious life. He handled physical details as if there were nothing beyond them; yet spiritualized them all, and redeemed himself from materialism by his strong and eager aspiration towards the infinite. In his grasp the veriest clod of earth assumed a soul. Georgiana, as she read, reverenced Aylmer and loved him more profoundly than ever, but with a less entire dependence on his judgment than heretofore. Much as he had accomplished, she could not but observe that his most splendid successes were almost invariably failures, if compared with the ideal at which he aimed. His brightest diamonds were the merest pebbles, and felt to be so by himself, in comparison with the inestimable gems which lay hidden beyond his reach. The volume, rich with achievements that had won renown for its author, was yet as melancholy a record as ever mortal hand had penned. It was the sad confession and continual exemplification of the shortcomings of the composite man, the spirit burdened with clay and working in matter, and of the despair that assails the higher nature at finding itself so miserably thwarted by the earthly part. Perhaps every man of genius in whatever sphere might recognize the image of his own experience in Aylmer's journal.

So deeply did these reflections affect Georgiana that she laid her face upon the open volume and burst into tears. In this situation she was found by her husband.

"It is dangerous to read in a sorcerer's books," said he with a smile, though his countenance was uneasy and displeased. "Georgiana, there are pages in that volume which I can scarcely glance over and keep my senses. Take heed lest it prove as detrimental to you."

"It has made me worship you more than ever," said she.

"Ah, wait for this one success," rejoined he, "then worship me if you will. I shall deem myself hardly unworthy of it. But come, I have sought you for the luxury of your voice. Sing to me, dearest."

So she poured out the liquid music of her voice to quench the thirst of his spirit. He then took his leave with a boyish exuberance of gayety, assuring her that her seclusion would endure but a little longer, and that the result was already certain. Scarcely had he departed when Georgiana felt irresistibly impelled to follow him. She had forgotten to inform Aylmer of a symptom which for two or three hours past had begun to excite her attention. It was a sensation in the fatal birthmark, not painful, but which induced a restlessness throughout her system. Hastening after her husband, she intruded for the first time into the laboratory.

The first thing that struck her eye was the furnace, that hot and feverish worker, with the intense glow of its fire, which by the quantities of soot clustered above it seemed to have been burning for ages. There was a distilling apparatus in full operation. Around the room were retorts, tubes, cylinders, crucibles, and other apparatus of chemical research. An electrical machine stood ready for immediate use. The atmosphere felt oppressively close, and was tainted with gaseous odors which had been tormented forth by the processes of science. The severe and homely simplicity of the apartment, with its naked walls and brick pavement, looked strange, accustomed as Georgiana had become to the fantastic elegance of her boudoir. But what chiefly, indeed almost solely, drew her attention, was the aspect of Aylmer himself.

He was pale as death, anxious and absorbed, and hung over the furnace as if it depended upon his utmost watchfulness whether the liquid which it was distilling should be the draught of immortal happiness or misery. How different from the sanguine and joyous mien that he had assumed for Georgiana's encouragement!

"Carefully now, Aminadab; carefully, thou human machine; carefully, thou man of clay!" muttered Aylmer, more to himself than his assistant. "Now if there be a thought too much or too little, it is all over."

"Ho! ho!" mumbled Aminadab. "Look, master! look!"

Aylmer raised his eyes hastily, and at first reddened, then grew paler than ever, on beholding Georgiana. He rushed towards her and seized her arm with a gripe that left the print of his fingers upon it.

"Why do you come hither? Have you no trust in your husband?" cried he, impetuously, "Would you throw the blight of that fatal birthmark over my labors? It is not well done. Go, prying woman, go!"

"Nay, Aylmer," said Georgiana with the firmness of which she possessed no stinted endowment, "it is not you that have a right to complain. You mistrust your wife; you have concealed the anxiety with which you watch the development of this experiment. Think not so unworthily of me, my husband. Tell me all the risk we run, and fear not that I shall shrink; for my share in it is far less than your own."

"No, no, Georgiana!" said Aylmer, impatiently; "it must not be."

"I submit," replied she calmly. "And, Aylmer, I shall quaff whatever draught you bring me; but it will be on the same principle that would induce me to take a dose of poison if offered by your hand."

"My noble wife," said Aylmer, deeply moved, "I knew not the height and depth of your nature until now. Nothing shall be concealed. Know, then, that this crimson hand, superficial as it seems, has clutched its grasp into your being with a strength of which I had no previous conception. I have already administered agents powerful enough to do aught except to change your entire physical system. Only one thing remains to be tried. If that fails us we are ruined."

"Why did you hesitate to tell me this?" asked she.

"Because, Georgiana," said Aylmer, in a low voice, "there is danger."

"Danger? There is but one danger—that this horrible stigma shall be left upon my cheek!" cried Georgiana. "Remove it, remove it, whatever be the cost, or we shall both go mad!"

"Heaven knows your words are too true," said Aylmer, sadly. "And now, dearest, return to your boudoir. In a little while all will be tested."

He conducted her back and took leave of her with a solemn tenderness which spoke far more than his words how much was now at stake. After his departure, Georgiana became rapt in musings. She considered the character of Aylmer, and did it completer justice than at any previous moment. Her heart exulted, while it trembled, at his honorable love—so pure and lofty that it would accept nothing less than perfection nor miserably make itself contented with an earthlier nature than he had dreamed of. She felt how much more precious was such a sentiment than that meaner kind which would have borne with the imperfection for her sake, and have been guilty of treason to holy love by degrading its perfect idea to the level of the actual; and with her whole spirit she prayed that, for a single moment, she might satisfy his highest and deepest conception. Longer than one moment she well knew it could not be; for his spirit was ever on the march, ever ascending, and each instant required something that was beyond the scope of the instant before.

The sound of her husband's footsteps aroused her. He bore a crystal goblet containing a liquor colorless as water, but bright enough to be the draught of immortality. Aylmer was pale; but it seemed rather the consequence of a highly-wrought state of mind and tension of spirit than of fear or doubt.

"The concoction of the draught has been perfect," said he, in answer to Georgiana's look. "Unless all my science have deceived me, it cannot fail."

"Save on your account, my dearest Aylmer," observed his wife, "I might wish to put off this birthmark of mortality by relinquishing mortality itself in preference to any other mode. Life is but a sad possession to those who have attained precisely the degree of moral advancement at which I stand. Were I weaker and blinder it might be happiness. Were I stronger, it might be endured hopefully. But being what I find myself, methinks I am of all mortals the most fit to die."

"You are fit for heaven without tasting death!" replied her husband. "But why do we speak of dying? The draught cannot fail. Behold its effect upon this plant."

On the window seat there stood a geranium diseased with yellow blotches, which had overspread all its leaves. Aylmer poured a small quantity of the liquid upon the soil in which it grew. In a little time, when the roots of the plant had taken up the moisture, the unsightly blotches began to be extinguished in a living verdure.

"There needed no proof," said Georgiana, quietly. "Give me the goblet. I joyfully stake all upon your word."

"Drink, then, thou lofty creature!" exclaimed Aylmer, with fervid admiration. "There is no taint of imperfection on thy spirit. Thy sensible frame, too, shall soon be all perfect."

She quaffed the liquid and returned the goblet to his hand.

"It is grateful," said she with a placid smile. "Methinks it is like water from a heavenly fountain; for it contains I know not what of unobtrusive fragrance and deliciousness. It allays a feverish thirst that had parched me for many days. Now, dearest, let me sleep. My earthly senses are closing over my spirit like the leaves around the heart of a rose at sunset."

She spoke the last words with a gentle reluctance, as if it required almost more energy than she could command to pronounce the faint and lingering syllables. Scarcely had they loitered through her lips ere she was lost in slumber. Aylmer sat by her side, watching her aspect with the emotions proper to a man the whole value of whose existence was involved in the process now to be tested. Mingled with this mood, however, was the philosophic investigation characteristic of the man of science. Not the minutest symptom escaped him. A heightened flush of the cheek, a slight irregularity of breath, a quiver of the eyelid, a hardly perceptible tremor through the frame—such were the details which, as the moments passed, he wrote down in his folio volume. Intense thought had set its stamp upon every previous page of that volume, but the thoughts of years were all concentrated upon the last.

While thus employed, he failed not to gaze often at the fatal hand, and not without a shudder. Yet once, by a strange and unaccountable impulse, he pressed it with his lips. His spirit recoiled, however, in the very act; and Georgiana, out of the midst of her deep sleep, moved uneasily and murmured as if in remonstrance. Again Aylmer resumed his watch. Nor was it without avail. The crimson hand, which at first had been strongly visible upon the marble paleness of Georgiana's cheek, now grew more faintly outlined. She remained not less pale than ever; but the birthmark, with every breath that came and went, lost somewhat of its former distinctness. Its presence had been awful; its departure was more awful still. Watch the stain of the rainbow fading out the sky, and you will know how the mysterious symbol passed away.

"By Heaven! it is well-nigh gone!" said Aylmer to himself, in almost irrepressible ecstasy. "I can scarcely trace it now. Success! success! And now it is like the faintest rose color. The lightest flush of blood across her cheek would overcome it. But she is so pale!"

He drew aside the window curtain and suffered the light of natural day to fall into the room and rest upon her cheek. At the same time he heard a gross, hoarse chuckle, which he had long known as his servant Aminadab's expression of delight.

"Ah, clod! ah, earthly mass!" cried Aylmer, laughing in a sort of frenzy, "you have served me well! Matter and spirit—earth and heaven—have both done their part in this! Laugh, thing of the senses! You have earned the right to laugh."

These exclamations broke Georgiana's sleep. She slowly unclosed her eyes and gazed into the mirror which her husband had arranged for that purpose. A faint smile flitted over her lips when she recognized how barely perceptible was now that crimson hand which had once blazed forth with such disastrous brilliancy as to scare away all their happiness. But then her eyes sought Aylmer's face with a trouble and anxiety that he could by no means account for.

"My poor Aylmer!" murmured she.

"Poor? Nay, richest, happiest, most favored!" exclaimed he. "My peerless bride, it is successful! You are perfect!"

"My poor Aylmer," she repeated, with a more than human tenderness, "you have aimed loftily; you have done nobly. Do not repent that with so high and pure a feeling, you have rejected the best the earth could offer. Alymer, dearest Aylmer, dearest Aylmer, I am dying!"

Alas! it was too true! the fatal hand had grappled with the mystery of life, and was the bond by which an angelic spirit kept itself in union with a mortal frame. As the last crimson tint of the birthmark—that sole token of human imperfection—faded from her cheek, the parting breath of the now perfect woman passed into the atmosphere, and her soul, lingering a moment near her husband, took its heavenward flight. Then a hoarse, chuckling laugh was heard again! Thus ever does the gross fatality of earth exult in its invariable triumph over the immortal essence which, in this dim sphere of half development, demands the completeness of a higher state. Yet, had Aylmer reached a profounder wisdom, he need not thus have flung away the happiness which would have woven his mortal life of the selfsame texture with the celestial. The momentary circumstance was too strong for him; he failed to look beyond the shadowy scope of time, and, living once for all in eternity, to find the perfect future in the present.

QUESTIONS

1. What are the symbolic significances of Georgiana's birthmark? Are any of the interpretations correct? Are they all correct? Can readers tell?
2. How does Aylmer conceive of nature?
3. Why does Aylmer wish to remove the birthmark? How do you assess his motives?
4. How does Georgiana feel about her birthmark? Why does she let Aylmer remove it?
5. How does Aylmer decorate the rooms where he secludes Georgiana? What is the significance of the decor?
6. To what extent does Georgiana wish to believe that "her husband possessed sway over the spiritual world"? Does Aylmer's demonstrations of his science justify Georgiana's faith in his abilities?
7. What does the narrator mean when he writes: "Perhaps every man of genius in whatever sphere might recognize the image of his own experience in Aylmer's journal"? What does such a statement reveal about Hawthorne's attitude toward his own work?
8. Is there any symbolic significance in the description of Aylmer's laboratory? How does it compare with Georgiana's boudoir?

9. Are you or have you known a perfectionist? What has been the result of the search for perfection?

E. M. FORSTER

THE OTHER SIDE OF THE HEDGE

E.M. Forster (1879–1970) was born in London and attended Cambridge University where he fell in with a crowd which became known as The Bloomsbury Group and included the historian Lytton Strachey, the economist John Maynard Keynes, and the novelist Virginia Woolf. He wrote four novels in relatively quick succession, and ended his novelistic career with his masterpiece, A Passage to India *(1924).* Maurice, *a novel of overt homosexual subject matter, was published only after his death. In all his work he emphasized the importance of genuine human relations over hollow social convention.*

From 1924 on, he devoted himself to essays, history and biography, authoring Two Cheers for Democracy, *a biography of his friend, the political theorist, Goldsworthy Lowes Dickinson, and the influential* Aspects of the Novel.

My pedometer told me that I was twenty-five; and, though it is a shocking thing to stop walking, I was so tired that I sat down on a milestone to rest. People outstripped me, jeering as they did so, but I was too apathetic to feel resentful, and even when Miss Eliza Dimbleby, the great educationist, swept past, exhorting me to persevere, I only smiled and raised my hat.

At first I thought I was going to be like my brother, whom I had had to leave by the roadside a year or two round the corner. He had wasted his breath on singing, and his strength on helping others. But I had travelled more wisely, and now it was only the monotony of the highway that oppressed me—dust under foot and brown crackling hedges on either side, ever since I could remember.

And I had already dropped several things—indeed, the road behind was strewn with the things we all had dropped; and the white dust was settling down on them, so that already they looked no better than stones. My muscles were so weary that I could not even bear the weight of those things I still carried. I slid off the milestone into the road, and lay there prostrate, with my face to the great parched hedge, praying that I might give up.

A little puff of air revived me. It seemed to come from the hedge; and, when I opened my eyes, there was a glint of light through the tangle of boughs and dead leaves. The hedge could not be as thick as usual. In my weak, morbid state, I longed to force my way in, and see what was on the other side. No one was in sight, or I should not have dared to try. For we of the road do not admit in conversation that there is another side at all.

I yielded to the temptation, saying to myself that I would come back in a minute. The thorns scratched my face, and I had to use my arms as a shield, depending on my feet alone to push me forward. Halfway through I would have gone back, for in the passage all the things I was carrying were scraped off me, and my clothes were torn. But I was so wedged that return was impossible, and I had to wriggle blindly forward, expecting every moment that my strength would fail me, and that I should perish in the undergrowth.

Suddenly cold water closed round my head, and I seemed sinking down for ever. I had fallen out of the hedge into a deep pool. I rose to the surface at last, crying for help, and I heard someone on the opposite bank laugh and say: "Another!" And then I was twitched out and laid panting on the dry ground.

Even when the water was out of my eyes, I was still dazed, for I had never been in so large a space, nor seen such grass and sunshine. The blue sky was no longer a strip, and beneath it the earth had risen grandly into hills—clean, bare buttresses, with beech trees in their folds, and meadows and clear pools at their feet. But the hills were not high, and there was in the landscape a sense of human occupation—so that one might have called it a park, or garden, if the words did not imply a certain triviality and constraint.

As soon as I got my breath, I turned to my rescuer and said:

"Where does this place lead to?"

"Nowhere, thank the Lord!" said he, and laughed. He was a man of fifty or sixty—just the kind of age we mistrust on the road—but there was no anxiety in his manner, and his voice was that of a boy of eighteen.

"But it must lead somewhere!" I cried, too much surprised at his answer to thank him for saving my life.

"He wants to know where it leads!" he shouted to some men on the hill side, and they laughed back, and waved their caps.

I noticed then that the pool into which I had fallen was really a moat which bent round to the left and to the right, and that the hedge followed it continually. The hedge was green on this side—its roots showed through the clear water, and fish swam about in them—and it was wreathed over with dog-roses and Traveller's Joy. But it was a barrier, and in a moment I lost all pleasure in the grass, the sky, the trees, the happy men and women, and realized that the place was but a prison, for all its beauty and extent.

We moved away from the boundary, and then followed a path almost parallel to it, across the meadows. I found it difficult walking, for I was always trying to out-distance my companion, and there was no advantage in doing this if the place led nowhere. I had never kept step with anyone since I left my brother.

I amused him by stopping suddenly and saying disconsolately, "This is perfectly terrible. One cannot advance: one cannot progress. Now we of the road—"

"Yes. I know."

"I was going to say, we advance continually."

"I know."

"We are always learning, expanding, developing. Why, even in my short life I have seen a great deal of advance—the Transvaal War, the Fiscal Question, Christian Science, Radium. Here for example—"

I took out my pedometer, but it still marked twenty-five, not a degree more.

"Oh, it's stopped! I meant to show you. It should have registered all the time I was walking with you. But it makes me only twenty-five."

"Many things don't work in here," he said. "One day a man brought in a Lee-Metford, and that wouldn't work."

"The laws of science are universal in their application. It must be the water in the moat that has injured the machinery. In normal conditions everything works. Science and the spirit of emulation—those are the forces that have made us what we are."

I had to break off and acknowledge the pleasant greetings of people whom we passed. Some of them were singing, some talking, some engaged in gardening, hay-making, or other rudimentary industries. They all seemed happy; and I might have been happy too, if I could have forgotten that the place led nowhere.

"The road sometimes doubles, to be sure, but that is part of our discipline. Who can doubt that its general tendency is onward? To what goal we know not—it may be to some mountain where we shall touch the sky, it may be over precipices into the sea. But that it goes forward—who can doubt that? It is the thought of that that makes us strive to excel, each in his own way, and gives us an impetus which is lacking with you. Now that man who passed us—it's true that he ran well, and jumped well, and swam well; but we have men who can run better, and men who can jump better, and who can swim better. Specialization has produced results which would surprise you. Similarly, that girl—"

Here I interrupted myself to exclaim: "Good gracious me! I could have sworn it was Miss Eliza Dimbleby over there, with her feet in the fountain!"

He believed that it was.

"Impossible! I left her on the road, and she is due to lecture this evening at Tunbridge Wells. Why, her train leaves Cannon Street in—of course my watch has stopped like everything else. She is the last person to be here."

"People always are astonished at meeting each other. All kinds come through the hedge, and come at all times—when they are drawing ahead in the race, when they are lagging behind, when they are left for dead. I often stand near the boundary listening to the sounds of the road—you know what they are—and wonder if anyone will turn aside. It is my great happiness to help someone out of the moat, as I helped you. For our country fills up slowly, though it was meant for all mankind."

"Mankind have other aims," I said gently, for I thought him well-meaning; "and I must join them." I bade him good evening, for the sun was declining, and I wished to be on the road by nightfall. To my alarm, he caught hold of me, crying: "You are not to go yet!" I tried to shake him off, for we had no interests in common, and his civility was becoming irksome to me. But for all my struggles the tiresome old man would not let go; and, as wrestling is not my speciality, I was obliged to follow him.

It was true that I could have never found alone the place where I came in, and I hoped that, when I had seen the other sights about which he was worrying, he would take me back to it. But I was determined not to sleep in the country, for I mistrusted it, and the people too, for all their friendliness. Hungry though I was, I would not join them in their evening meals of milk and fruit, and, when they gave me flowers, I flung them away as soon as I could do so unobserved. Already they were lying down for the night like cattle—some out on the bare hillside, others in groups under the beeches. In the light of an orange sunset I hurried on with my unwelcome guide, dead tired, faint for want of food, but murmuring indomitably: "Give me life, with its struggles and victories, with its failures and hatreds, with its deep moral meaning and its unknown goal!"

At last we came to a place where the encircling moat was spanned by another bridge, and where another gate interrupted the line of the boundary hedge. It was different from the first gate; for it was half transparent like horn, and opened inwards. But through it, in the waning light, I saw again just such a road as I had left—monotonous, dusty, with brown crackling hedges on either side, as far as the eye could reach.

I was strangely disquieted at the sight, which seemed to deprive me of all self-control. A man was passing us, returning for the night to the hills, with a scythe over his shoulder and a can of some liquid in his hand. I forgot the destiny of our race. I forgot the road that lay before my eyes, and I sprang at him, wrenched the can out of his hand, and began to drink.

It was nothing stronger than beer, but in my exhausted state it overcame me in a moment. As in a dream, I saw the old man shut the gate, and heard him say: "This is where your road ends, and through this gate humanity—all that is left of it—will come in to us."

Though my senses were sinking into oblivion, they seemed to expand ere they reached it. They perceived the magic song of nightingales, and the odour of invisible hay, and stars piercing the fading sky. The man whose beer I had stolen lowered me down gently to sleep off its effects, and, as he did so, I saw that he was my brother.

QUESTIONS

1. What is the narrator's attitude toward the road he was walking and the race in which he was engaged?
2. What is the symbolic significance of the road?
3. Why does the narrator refuse at first to believe that the road that doubles back is "never far from [the garden's] boundary?"
4. What is the narrator's attitude toward his brother? What is the symbolic significance of his brother's appearance at the end of the story?
5. Is the narrator reliable or unreliable? What is Forster's attitude toward the road and the garden? Can we tell?
6. What does the story say about progress? The value of competition? The value of deferred pleasure? Capitalism?

8
THEME

Some people do not learn from experience. They move from one event in their lives to another, but they never attempt to understand why they behave as they do, what is involved in the institutions and structures through which they pass, or how they relate to other people and the times in which they live. They live from moment to moment, either happy or sad, without any direction or illumination.

Literature is also an experience. Not only is it an experience in itself, but also it tries to bring us other people's experiences. And just as some people never reflect upon the lives they live, so, too, some readers never reflect upon the books they read. They live the stories moment to moment. Sometimes stories make them happy; at other times stories make them sad. But they never ask themselves, "What is happening in this experience? What are the broader, general issues that inform the literary experience?" In short, they never ask themselves, "What is the theme of this story?"

THEME IN FICTION VS. THEME IN ESSAYS

Essays, sermons, political speeches, usually make their themes clear to their audience or readers. They put forth a *thesis*—a position, attitude or belief they wish their readers to share. Essayists, politicians, sermonizers are all using some form of argument in which they try to convince their audience by logic, by appeals to emotions, or through evidence of the correctness of their positions and the truth of their beliefs.

Stories, poems and plays operate in a different way. They lead the reader through an experience which they try to make as vivid and engaging as possible. The reader of the story is "convinced" when the work becomes a vivid experience. Although the distinction is rough and one could find exceptions, we might say that generally authors of essays have ideas they want readers to accept, while authors of stories have events they want their readers to live through. Correct, reasonable ideas do not necessarily make a good story. Conversely, we may thoroughly disagree with an author's philosophy of life and still find his or her stories vivid, gripping and alive. Thus, we do not have to share authors' beliefs to admire their art, although it may be important to understand the ideas which inform a story and guide its selection of details.

THE THEME AND THE STORY

Some stories, called *didactic stories,* have a clear moral, a lesson that they wish to teach. We all know the story of the boy who cried "Wolf!" so often that when a wolf finally appeared at his door, no one would believe his cries of help and he was eaten alive. The lesson of this story is so clear that even as children we understood it. The lesson is habitual liars will not be believed even when they are telling the truth. But most stories do not have such clear and simple morals. In fact, most writers look down at stories that are so clearly didactic. Such stories usually lack the subtlety and complexity of real moral problems.

Indeed most writers don't have clear lessons to teach their readers. They don't want to put themselves in the position of telling people what to do and what not to do. Most writers prefer to have readers draw their own conclusions from their stories.

Let us imagine an author who has sat down at a desk. On it is a clean sheet of paper waiting to be written upon. Conceivably the author could write about anything that took place anywhere at any time. A writer has an infinite number of stories that could be told. But writers do not have an infinite amount of time and energy. They can write only one story at a time, and they must tell that story—by choosing from the enormous number of words at their disposal—word by word.

How then does a writer choose which story to write? Some writers are under contract to publishers or magazines to write certain stories. Some writers know that certain types of stories are popular and have a better chance of being published and making money. Such authors are ruled by the marketplace, and their choices are ruled by popular demand. Other writers tell stories that seem to haunt them, demanding to be written down, stories like a song you may hear all day in your head urging to be hummed, whistled or sung. Indeed, many writers claim they do not choose their stories as much as their stories choose them.

Yet in selecting which stories to narrate, authors—whether they recognize it or not—have begun to choose a theme. Thom Gunn, the poet, writes about the unconscious way events embody ideas:

> One day I was walking on a hill going down to the Pacific, which it met at a narrow, partly-sheltered beach. I came to the beach from some bushes and was confronted by a naked family—father, mother and small son. The son rushed up to me very excited, shouting 'hi there, hi there' in his shrill voice, and rushed away without waiting for an answer. I walked off and felt happy about the comeliness of the scene: it had, too, a kind of decorum that made my mind return to it several times in the next few hours. I mentioned it to some friends that evening and to others the next day, and the day after that I realized that I wanted to write a poem about the naked family.

> I didn't know any more than that I wanted to preserve them on paper in the best way I knew, as a kind of snapshot, getting my feeling from them into my description of them. It wasn't till the poem was finished that I realized I had among other things found an embodiment for my haunting cluster of concepts, though I hadn't known it at the time (*The Occasions of Poetry*, pp. 161–2).

Gunn was not at first aware that what he wrote included the themes that had concerned him at the time. "I did not know why [the naked family] satisfied me so much," he writes later in his essay, "But I did know that I had certain clear strong feelings about them that I wanted to preserve." What is true of Thom Gunn is also true of many other writers. Authors begin by wishing to record an experience—whether real or imaginary, or more often a combination of the two—and only later recognize why that story seemed so "right," so "urgently in need of telling," or so "satisfying."

Gunn talks about how the work is "an embodiment for my haunting cluster of concepts." The word "embodiment" is important. Good themes are not added on to a story, nor are they necessarily found in the character's or the narrator's moral statements. The entire narrative embodies the themes of a story; the themes are given concrete shape in the action and the characters. To put it yet another way, you cannot separate a theme from the action of the story because the theme is to be found embodied in the story itself.

One way to articulate the theme of a story is to look at the action in its abstract terms. In "Lappin and Lapinova," Virginia Woolf has chosen to write about marriage and the stories that a young couple tell each other at the beginning of their relationship. One might say that the imaginative world of Lappin and Lapinova brought the couple together and its dissolution pulls them apart. One might then say that the theme of "Lappin and Lapinova" is that marriages are held together by the mutually held fictions of the husband and wife.

THEME AND CONFLICT

In the chapter on plot, I discussed that the main characters of stories often develop purposes or goals. While working toward these goals, characters often run into obstacles that stand in their way. Conflict is a central ingredient of any plot. Writers about fiction often describe the themes of a story in terms of these conflicts. For example, in "The Dead Man's Path," the educated headmaster or principal runs into conflict with the tribal community. The headmaster believes he has "enlightened," "rational" ideas, while the community is filled with "superstition."

The community thinks of itself as maintaining "traditional" beliefs and piety toward its sacred places. We might describe the theme as the conflict between reason and superstition, or as rationality vs. religiousity. But there are other ways to describe the conflict. The headmaster thinks he is progressive. We might describe the theme as the conflict between progressiveness and traditionalism. Again, the headmaster's ideas are mostly European in origin. We might say the conflict is between imported European notions and domestic African notions. Indeed, there are many ways to conceptualize the conflicts in Achebe's story, and such diversity of conception makes "The Dead Man's Path" a particularly rich and challenging one.

Achebe has not, however, achieved this richness of significance by being vague or unspecific. Some young writers believe that their stories can be richer in meaning if they allow the action to be indefinite and foggy, covering over the narrative with a thick veil of language. Achebe's story is a model of clarity and simplicity. But the event he has chosen to narrate is one rich with significance and emotion. The various conflicts all work together to inform the story. In an essay, the author is obliged to separate these conflicts and handle them separately. But the power of literature is derived in part from the way various themes—what Gunn calls a "haunting cluster of concepts"—can be embodied simultaneously. Fiction writers can achieve this richness because they work on the concrete level, trying to make the action as clear and vivid as possible. With the action vividly in front of us, we as readers can then reflect on its significance.

THINGS TO THINK ABOUT

1. If a single story can embody several themes simultaneously, can a story embody all themes? How can we know whether a story actually embodies a theme? For example, could "The Dead Man's Path" mean anything a reader wishes it to mean? What right does a teacher or any reader have to stating the theme of a story?
2. What is more important—the concrete experience of a story or the thematic material embodied by the story? Do we need to decide? Can they be equally important?
3. In real life what lessons can we draw from our experience? Do you know anyone who seems to make the same mistakes over and over again? Why do they make those mistakes repeatedly? Why is it difficult to learn from experience?

ESSAY TOPICS

1. Narrate an experience that has taught you a particularly valuable lesson. Why was that experience so instructive? Why hadn't you learned that lesson before?

2. Have you ever had an experience you didn't understand until much later? For example, did you ever make anyone angry and recognize much later what you did that so infuriated the person? Narrate the incident, discuss why you were unable to understand it, and what finally prompted your realization.
3. Choose a basic moral lesson (such as "penny wise, pound foolish" or "a fool and his money are easily parted") and illustrate it with three anecdotes.

CREATIVE WRITING EXERCISES

1. Narrate an incident that has remained in your mind even though you don't know why it has stayed with you. As you narrate the incident, see if you can discover what lay behind the event.
2. Choose a basic moral lesson and stand it on its head (for example, "penny foolish, pound wise" or "a fool and his money are never parted" or "an apple a day keeps the doctor coming back"), and illustrate it with a story.
3. Create a character who does not learn from experience. What kind of things happen to your character? What becomes of the character at the end of your narrative?

LITERARY ESSAYS

1. We usually think that people grouped together share certain common ideas, values and/or myths. But in each of the stories in this chapter, people who are brought together because of marriage, nationality or religion find that they do not share basic beliefs and attitudes. Compare two or more of the stories and discuss what beliefs aren't shared, why they aren't shared, and what is the effect of not sharing these beliefs.
2. The desire for progress often divides people. Choose one or more stories and discuss the effects of social, economic or psychological progress.
3. Can people once divided ever be reunited? Compare the conclusions of these stories and discuss whether the authors hold out promises of reconciliation.

VIRGINIA WOOLF

LAPPIN AND LAPINOVA

Virginia Woolf (1882–1941) was born into English literary society. Her father was Sir Leslie Stephens, one of the more important men of letters and the editor of The Dictionary of National Biography. *Her godfather was Henry James, whose story "The Real Thing" is included in this volume. When she grew up she found herself in the center of what has been called The Bloomsbury Group, a circle of writers, painters, economists and political activists which included her husband Leonard Woolf, her sister Vanessa Bell, John Maynard Keynes, Lytton Strachey and E.M. Forster.*

Virginia Woolf was one of the developers of the psychological novel, and as one of the founders of the Hogarth Press was responsible for publishing the English edition of the complete works of Sigmund Freud. She herself suffered from repeated bouts of manic-depression and finally committed suicide in 1941.

They were married. The wedding march pealed out. The pigeons fluttered. Small boys in Eton jackets threw rice; a fox terrier sauntered across the path; and Ernest Thorburn led his bride to the car through that small inquisitive crowd of complete strangers which always collects in London to enjoy other people's happiness or unhappiness. Certainly he looked handsome and she looked shy. More rice was thrown, and the car moved off.

That was on Tuesday. Now it was Saturday. Rosalind had still to get used to the fact that she was Mrs. Ernest Thorburn. Perhaps she never would get used to the fact that she was Mrs. Ernest Anybody, she thought, as she sat in the bow window of the hotel looking over the lake to the mountains, and waited for her husband to come down to breakfast. Ernest was a difficult name to get used to. It was not the name she would have chosen. She would have preferred Timothy, Antony, or Peter. He did not look like Ernest either. The name suggested the Albert Memorial, mahogany sideboards, steel engravings of the Prince Consort with his family—her mother-in-law's dining-room in Porchester Terrace in short.

But here he was. Thank goodness he did not look like Ernest—no. But what did he look like? She glanced at him sideways. Well, when he was eating toast he looked like a rabbit. Not that anyone else would have seen a likeness to a creature so diminutive and timid in this spruce, muscular young man with the straight nose, the blue eyes, and the very firm mouth. But that made it all the more amusing. His nose twitched very slightly when he ate. So did her pet rabbit's. She kept watching his nose twitch; and then she had to explain, when he caught her looking at him, why she laughed.

"It's because you're like a rabbit, Ernest," she said. "Like a wild rabbit," she added, looking at him. "A hunting rabbit; a King Rabbit; a rabbit that makes laws for all the other rabbits."

Ernest had no objection to being that kind of rabbit, and since it amused her to see him twitch his nose—he had never known that his nose twitched—he twitched it on purpose. And she laughed and laughed; and he laughed too, so that the maiden ladies and the fishing man and the Swiss waiter in his greasy black jacket all guessed right; they were very happy. But how long does such happiness last? they asked themselves; and each answered according to his own circumstances.

At lunch time, seated on a clump of heather beside the lake, "Lettuce, rabbit?" said Rosalind, holding out the lettuce that had been provided to eat with the hard-boiled eggs. "Come and take it out of my hand," she added, and he stretched out and nibbled the lettuce and twitched his nose.

"Good rabbit, nice rabbit," she said, patting him, as she used to pat her tame rabbit at home. But that was absurd. He was not a tame rabbit, whatever he was. She turned it into French. "Lapin," she called him. But whatever he was, he was not a French rabbit. He was simply and solely English—born at Porchester Terrace, educated at Rugby; now a clerk in His Majesty's Civil Service. So she tried "Bunny" next; but that was worse. "Bunny" was someone plump and soft and comic; he was thin and hard and serious. Still, his nose twitched. "Lappin," she exclaimed suddenly; and gave a little cry as if she had found the very word she looked for.

"Lappin, Lappin, King Lappin," she repeated. It seemed to suit him exactly; he was not Ernest, he was King Lappin. Why? She did not know.

When there was nothing new to talk about on their long solitary walks—and it rained, as everyone had warned them that it would rain; or when they were sitting over the fire in the evening, for it was cold, and the maiden ladies had gone and the fishing man, and the waiter only came if you rang the bell for him, she let her fancy play with the story of the Lappin tribe. Under her hands—she was sewing; he was reading—they became very real, very vivid, very amusing. Ernest put down the paper and helped her. There were the black rabbits and the red; there were the enemy rabbits and the friendly. There were the wood in which they lived and the outlying prairies and the swamp. Above all there was King Lappin, who, far from having only the one trick—that he twitched his nose—became as the days passed an animal of the greatest character; Rosalind was always finding new qualities in him. But above all he was a great hunter.

"And what," said Rosalind, on the last day of the honeymoon, "did the King do to-day?"

In fact they had been climbing all day; and she had worn a blister on her heel; but she did not mean that.

"To-day," said Ernest, twitching his nose as he bit the end off his cigar, "he chased a hare." He paused; struck a match, and twitched again.

"A woman hare," he added.

"A white hare!" Rosalind exclaimed, as if she had been expecting this. "Rather a small hare; silver grey; with big bright eyes?"

"Yes," said Ernest, looking at her as she had looked at him, "a smallish animal; with eyes popping out of her head, and two little front paws dangling." It was exactly how she sat, with her sewing dangling in her hands; and her eyes, that were so big and bright, were certainly a little prominent.

"Ah, Lapinova," Rosalind murmured.

"Is that what she's called?" said Ernest—"the real Rosalind?" He looked at her. He felt very much in love with her.

"Yes; that's what she's called," said Rosalind. "Lapinova." And before they went to bed that night it was all settled. He was King Lappin; she was Queen Lapinova. They were the opposite of each other; he was bold and determined; she wary and undependable. He ruled over the busy world of rabbits; her world was a desolate, mysterious place, which she ranged mostly by moonlight. All the same, their territories touched; they were King and Queen.

Thus when they came back from their honeymoon they possessed a private world, inhabited, save for the one white hare, entirely by rabbits. No one guessed that there was such a place, and that of course made it all the more amusing. It made them feel, more even than most young married couples, in league together against the rest of the world. Often they looked slyly at each other when people talked about rabbits and woods and traps and shooting. Or they winked furtively across the table when Aunt Mary said that she could never bear to see a hare in a dish—it looked so like a baby: or when John, Ernest's sporting brother, told them what price rabbits were fetching that autumn in Wiltshire, skins and all. Sometimes when they wanted a gamekeeper, or a poacher or a Lord of the Manor, they amused themselves by distributing the parts among their friends. Ernest's mother, Mrs. Reginald Thorburn, for example, fitted the part of the Squire to perfection. But it was all secret—that was the point of it; nobody save themselves knew that such a world existed.

Without that world, how, Rosalind wondered, that winter could she have lived at all? For instance, there was the golden-wedding party, when all the Thorburns assembled at Porchester Terrace to celebrate the fiftieth anniversary of that union which had been so blessed—had it not produced Ernest Thorburn? and so fruitful—had it not produced nine other sons and daughters into the bargain, many themselves married and also fruitful? She dreaded that party. But it was inevitable. As she walked upstairs she felt bitterly that she was an only child and an orphan at that; a mere drop among all those Thorburns assembled in the great drawing-room with the shiny satin wallpaper and the lustrous family portraits. The living Thorburns much resembled the painted; save that instead of painted lips they had real lips; out of which came jokes; jokes about schoolrooms, and how they had pulled the chair from under the governess; jokes about frogs and how they had put them between the virgin sheets of maiden ladies. As for herself, she had never even made an apple-pie bed. Holding her present in her hand she advanced toward her mother-in-law sumptuous in yellow satin; and toward her father-in-law decorated with a rich yellow carnation. All round them on tables and chairs there were golden tributes, some nestling in cotton wool; others branching resplendent—candlesticks; cigar boxes; chains; each stamped with the goldsmith's proof that it was solid gold, hall-marked, authentic. But her present was only a little pinchbeck box pierced with holes; an old sand caster, an eighteenth-century relic, once used to sprinkle sand over wet ink. Rather a senseless present she felt—in an age of blotting paper; and as she proffered it, she saw in front of her the stubby black handwriting in which her mother-in-law when they were engaged had expressed the hope that "My son will make you happy." No, she was not happy. Not at all happy. She looked at Ernest, straight as a ramrod with a nose like all the noses in the family portraits; a nose that never twitched at all.

Then they went down to dinner. She was half hidden by the great chrysanthemums that curled their red and gold petals into large tight balls. Everything was gold. A gold-edged card with gold initials inter-twined recited the list of all the dishes that would be set one after another before them. She dipped her spoon in a plate of clear golden fluid. The raw white fog outside had been turned by the lamps into a golden mesh that blurred the edges of the plates and gave the pineapples a rough golden skin. Only she herself in her white wedding dress peering ahead of her with her prominent eyes seemed insoluble as an icicle.

As the dinner wore on, however, the room grew steamy with heat. Beads of perspiration stood out on the men's foreheads. She felt that her icicle was being turned to water. She was being melted; dispersed; dissolved into nothingness; and would soon faint. Then through the surge in her head and the din in her ears she heard a woman's voice exclaim, "But they breed so!"

The Thorburns—yes; they breed so, she echoed; looking at all the round red faces that seemed doubled in the giddiness that overcame her; and magnified in the gold mist that enhaloed them. "They breed so." Then John bawled:

"Little devils! . . . Shoot'em! Jump on'em with big boots! That's the only way to deal with 'em . . . rabbits!"

At that word, that magic word, she revived. Peeping between the chrysanthemums she saw Ernest's nose twitch. It rippled, it ran with successive twitches. And at that a mysterious catastrophe befell the Thorburns. The golden table became a moor with the gorse in full bloom; the din of voices turned to one peal of lark's laughter ringing down from the sky. It was a blue sky—clouds passed slowly. And they had all been changed—the Thorburns. She looked at her father-in-law, a furtive little man with dyed moustaches. His foible was collecting things—seals, enamel boxes, trifles from eighteenth-century dressing tables which he hid in the drawers of his study from his wife. Now she saw him as he was—a poacher, stealing off with his coat bulging with pheasants and partridges to drop them stealthily into a three-legged pot in his smoky little cottage. That was her real father-in-law—a poacher. And Celia, the unmarried daughter, who always nosed out other people's secrets, the little things they wished to hide—she was a white ferret with pink eyes, and a nose clotted with earth from her horrid underground nosings and pokings. Slung round men's shoulders, in a net, and thrust down a hole—it was a pitiable life—Celia's; it was none of her fault. So she saw Celia. And then she looked at her mother-in-law—whom they dubbed The Squire. Flushed, coarse, a bully—she was all that, as she stood returning thanks, but now that Rosalind—that is Lapinova—saw her, she saw behind her the decayed family mansion, the plaster peeling off the walls, and heard her, with a sob in her voice, giving thanks to her children (who hated her) for a world that had ceased to exist. There was a sudden silence. They all stood with their glasses raised; they all drank; then it was over.

"Oh, King Lappin!" she cried as they went home together in the fog, "if your nose hadn't twitched just at that moment, I should have been trapped!"

"But you're safe," said King Lappin, pressing her paw.

"Quite safe," she answered.

And they drove back through the Park, King and Queen of the marsh, of the mist, and of the gorse-scented moor.

Thus time passed; one year; two years of time. And on a winter's night, which happened by a coincidence to be the anniversary of the golden-wedding party—but Mrs. Reginald Thorburn was dead; the house was to let; and there was only a caretaker in residence—Ernest came home from the office. They had a nice little home; half a house above a saddler's shop in South Kensington, not far from the tube station. It was cold, with fog in the air, and Rosalind was sitting over the fire, sewing.

"What d'you think happened to me to-day?" she began as soon as he had settled himself down with his legs stretched to the blaze. "I was crossing the stream when—"

"What stream?" Ernest interrupted her.

"The stream at the bottom, where our wood meets the black wood," she explained.

Ernest looked completely blank for a moment.

"What the deuce are you talking about?" he asked.

"My dear Ernest!" she cried in dismay, "King Lappin," she added, dangling her little front paws in the firelight. But his nose did not twitch. Her hands—they turned to hands—clutched the stuff she was holding; her eyes popped half out of her head. It took him five minutes at least to change from Ernest Thorburn to King Lappin; and while she waited she felt a load on the back of her neck, as if somebody were about to wring it. At last he changed to King Lappin; his nose twitched; and they spent the evening roaming the woods much as usual.

But she slept badly. In the middle of the night she woke, feeling as if something strange had happened to her. She was stiff and cold. At last she turned on the light and looked at Ernest lying beside her. He was sound asleep. He snored. But even though he snored, his nose remained perfectly still. It looked as if it had never twitched at all. Was it possible that he was really Ernest; and that she was really married to Ernest? A vision of her mother-in-law's dining-room came before her; and there they sat, she and Ernest, grown old, under the engravings, in front of the sideboard. . . . It was their golden-wedding day. She could not bear it.

"Lappin, King Lappin!" she whispered, and for a moment his nose seemed to twitch of its own accord. But he still slept. "Wake up, Lappin, wake up!" she cried.

Ernest woke; and seeing her sitting bolt upright beside him he asked:

"What's the matter?"

"I thought my rabbit was dead!" she whimpered. Ernest was angry.

"Don't talk such rubbish, Rosalind," he said. "Lie down and go to sleep."

He turned over. In another moment he was sound asleep and snoring.

But she could not sleep. She lay curled up on her side of the bed, like a hare in its form. She had turned out the light, but the street lamp lit the ceiling faintly, and the trees outside made a lacy network over it as if there were a shadowy grove on the ceiling in which she wandered, turning, twisting, in and out, round and round, hunting, being hunted, hearing the bay of hounds and horns; flying, escaping . . . until the maid drew the blinds and brought their early tea.

Next day she could settle to nothing. She seemed to have lost something. She felt as if her body had shrunk; it had grown small, and black and hard. Her joints seemed stiff too, and when she looked in the glass, which she did several times as she wandered about the flat, her eyes seemed to burst out of her head, like currants in a bun. The rooms also seemed to have shrunk. Large pieces of furniture jutted out at odd angles and she found herself knocking against them. At last she put on her hat and went out. She walked along the Cromwell Road; and every room she passed and peered into seemed to be a dining-room where people sat eating under steel engravings, with thick yellow lace curtains, and mahogany sideboards. At last she reached the Natural History Museum; she used to like it when she was a child. But the first thing she saw when she went in was a stuffed hare standing on sham snow with pink glass eyes. Somehow it made her shiver all over. Perhaps it would be better when dusk fell. She went home and sat over the fire, without a light, and tried to imagine that she was out alone on a moor; and there was a stream rushing; and beyond the stream a dark wood. But she could get no further than the stream. At last she squatted down on the bank on the wet grass, and sat crouched in her chair, with her hands dangling empty, and her eyes glazed, like glass eyes, in the firelight. Then there was the crack of a gun. . . . She started as if she had been shot. It was only Ernest, turning his key in the door. She waited, trembling. He came in and switched on the light. There he stood, tall, handsome, rubbing his hands that were red with cold.

"Sitting in the dark?" he said.

"Oh, Ernest, Ernest!" she cried, starting up in her chair.

"Well, what's up now?" he asked briskly, warming his hands at the fire.

"It's Lapinova . . ." she faltered, glancing wildly at him out of her great started eyes. "She's gone, Ernest. I've lost her!"

Ernest frowned. He pressed his lips tight together.

"Oh, that's what's up, is it?" he said, smiling rather grimly at his wife. For ten seconds he stood there, silent; and she waited, feeling hands tightening at the back of her neck.

"Yes," he said at length. "Poor Lapinova . . ." He straightened his tie at the looking-glass over the mantelpiece.

"Caught in a trap," he said, "killed," and sat down and read the newspaper.

So that was the end of that marriage.

QUESTIONS

1. The narrator tells us that Ernest had no objections to being "a hunting rabbit, a King Rabbit, a rabbit that makes laws for all other rabbits." To what other kinds of rabbits might he have complained of being compared? Why would he have objected?
2. How do Rosalind and Ernest divide the work of the rabbit kingdom? Is it a fair division of labor?
3. Why is it important for Rosalind and Ernest to keep their stories of the animal kingdom secret?
4. Does Rosalind's present to Ernest's mother have any symbolic significance? How is it different from the other presents the Thorburns get?
5. Why is it significant that the Thorburns breed like rabbits? Does Rosalind?
6. In what sense is Lapinova "caught in a trap"? What does such an occurance say about Rosalind?
7. What is the significance of Rosalind's decision to use the French rather than the English word for rabbit?

VIRGINIA WOOLF

PROFESSIONS FOR WOMEN

When your secretary invited me to come here, she told me that your Society is concerned with the employment of women and she suggested that I might tell you something about my own professional experiences.

It is true I am a woman; it is true I am employed; but what professional experiences have I had? It is difficult to say. My profession is literature; and in that profession there are fewer experiences for women than in any other, with the exception of the stage—fewer, I mean, that are peculiar to women. For the road was cut many years ago—by Fanny Burney, by Aphra Behn, by Harriet Martineau, by Jane Austen, by George Eliot—many famous women, and many more unknown and forgotten, have been before me, making the path smooth, and regulating my steps. Thus, when I came to write, there were very few material obstacles in my way. Writing was a reputable and harmless occupation. The family peace was not broken by the scratching of a pen. No demand was made upon the family purse. For ten and sixpence one can buy paper enough to write all the plays of Shakespeare—if one has a mind that way. Pianos and models, Paris, Vienna and Berlin, masters and mistresses, are not needed by a writer. The cheapness of writing paper is, of course, the reason why women have succeeded as writers before they have succeeded in the other professions.

But to tell you my story—it is a simple one. You have only got to figure to yourselves a girl in a bedroom with a pen in her hand. She had only to move that pen from left to right—from ten o'clock to one. Then it occurred to her to do what is simple and cheap enough after all—to slip a few of those pages into an envelope, fix a penny stamp in the corner, and drop the envelope into the red box at the corner. It was thus that I became a journalist; and my effort was rewarded on the first day of the following month—a very glorious day it was for me—by a letter from an editor containing a cheque for one pound ten shillings and sixpence. But to show you how little I deserve to be called a professional woman, how little I know of the struggles and difficulties of such lives, I have to admit that instead of spending that sum upon bread and butter, rent, shoes and stockings, or butcher's bills, I went out and bought a cat—a beautiful cat, a Persian cat, which very soon involved me in bitter disputes with my neighbours.

What could be easier than to write articles and to buy Persian cats with the profits? But wait a moment. Articles have to be about something. Mine, I seem to remember, was about a novel by a famous man. And while I was writing this review, I discovered that if I were going to review books I should need to do battle with a certain phantom. And the phantom was a woman, and when I came to know her better I called her after the heroine of a famous poem, The Angel in the House. It was she who used to come between me and my paper when I was writing reviews. It was she who bothered me and wasted my time and so tormented me that at last I killed her. You who come of a younger and happier generation may not have heard of her—you may not know what I mean by the Angel in the House. I will describe her as shortly as I can. She was intensely sympathetic. She was immensely charming. She was utterly unselfish. She excelled in the difficult arts of family life. She sacrificed herself daily. If there was chicken, she took the leg; if there was a draught she sat in it—in short she was so constituted that she never had a mind or a wish of her own, but preferred to sympathize always with the minds and wishes of others. Above all—I need not say it—she was pure. Her purity was supposed to be her chief beauty—her blushes, her great grace. In those days—the last of Queen Victoria—every house had its Angel. And when I came to write I encountered her with the very first words. The shadow of her wings fell on my page; I heard the rustling of her skirts in the room. Directly, that is to say, I took my pen in hand to review that novel by a famous man, she slipped behind me and whispered: "My dear, you are a young woman. You are writing about a book that has been written by a man. Be sympathetic; be tender; flatter; deceive; use all the arts and wiles of our sex. Never let anybody guess that you have a mind of your own. Above all, be pure." And she made as if to guide my pen. I now record the one act for which I take some credit to myself, though the credit rightly belongs to some excellent ancestors of mine who left me a certain sum of money—shall we say five hundred pounds a year?—so that it was not necessary for me to depend solely on charm for my living. I turned upon her and caught her by the throat. I did my best to kill her. My excuse, if I were to be had up in a court of law, would be that I acted in self-defence. Had I not killed her she would have killed me. She would have plucked the heart out of my writing. For, as I found, directly I put pen to paper, you cannot review even a novel without having a mind of your own, without expressing what you think to be the truth about human relations, morality, sex. And all these questions, according to the Angel in the House, cannot be dealt with freely and openly by women; they must charm, they must conciliate, they must—to put it bluntly—tell lies if they are to succeed. Thus, whenever I felt the shadow of her wing or the radiance of her halo upon my page, I took up the inkpot and flung it at her. She died hard. Her fictitious nature was of great assistance to her. It is far harder to kill a phantom than a reality. She was always creeping back when I thought I had despatched her. Though I flatter myself that I killed her in the end, the struggle was severe; it took much time that had better have been spent upon learning Greek grammar; or in roaming the world in search of adventures. But it was a real experience; it was an experience that was bound to befall all women writers at that time. Killing the Angel in the House was part of the occupation of a woman writer.

But to continue my story. The Angel was dead; what then remained? You may say that what remained was a simple and common object—a young woman in a bedroom with an inkpot. In other words, now that she had rid herself of falsehood, that young woman had only to be herself. Ah, but what is "herself"? I mean, what is a woman? I assure you, I do not know. I do not believe that you know. I do not believe that anybody can know until she has expressed herself in all the arts and professions open to human skill. That indeed is one of the reasons why I have come here—out of respect for you, who are in process of showing us by your experiments what a woman is, who are in process of providing us, by your failures and successes, with that extremely important piece of information.

But to continue the story of my professional experiences. I made one pound ten and six by my first review; and I bought a Persian cat with the proceeds. Then I grew ambitious. A Persian cat is all very well, I said; but a Persian cat is not enough. I must have a motor car. And it was thus that I became a novelist—for it is a very strange thing that people will give you a motor car if you will tell them a story. It is a still stranger thing that there is nothing so delightful in the world as telling stories. It is far pleasanter than writing reviews of famous novels. And yet, if I am to obey your secretary and tell you my professional experiences as a novelist, I must tell you about a very strange experience that befell me as a novelist. And to understand it you must try first to imagine a novelist's state of mind. I hope I am not giving away professional secrets if I say that a novelist's chief desire is to be as unconscious as possible. He has to induce in himself a state of perpetual lethargy. He wants life to proceed with the utmost quiet and regularity. He wants to see the same faces, to read the same books, to do the same things day after day, month after month, while he is writing, so that nothing may break the illusion in which he is living—so that nothing may disturb or disquiet the mysterious nosings about, feelings round, darts, dashes and sudden discoveries of that very shy and illusive spirit, the imagination. I suspect that this state is the same both for men and women. Be that as it may, I want you to imagine me writing a novel in a state of trance. I want you to figure to yourselves a girl sitting with a pen in her hand, which for minutes, and indeed for hours, she never dips into the inkpot. The image that comes to my mind when I think of this girl is the image of a fisherman lying sunk in dreams on the verge of a deep lake with a rod held out over the water. She was letting her imagination sweep unchecked round every rock and cranny of the world that lies submerged in the depths of our unconscious being. Now came the experience, the experience that I believe to be far commoner with women writers than with men. The line raced through the girl's fingers. Her imagination had rushed away. It had sought the pools, and depths, the dark places where the largest fish slumber. And then there was a smash. There was an explosion. There was foam and confusion. The imagination had dashed itself against something hard. The girl was roused from her dream. She was indeed in a state of the most acute and difficult distress. To speak without figure she had thought of something, something about the body, about the passions which it was unfitting for her as a woman to say. Men, her reason told her, would be shocked. The consciousness of what men will say of a woman who speaks the truth about her passions had roused her from her artist's state of unconsciousness. She could write no more. The trance was over. Her imagination could work no longer. This I believe to be a very common experience with women writers—they are impeded by the extreme conventionality of the other sex. For though men sensibly allow themselves great freedom in these respects, I doubt that they realize or can control the extreme severity with which they condemn such freedom in women.

These then were two very genuine experiences of my own. These were two of the adventures of my professional life. The first—killing the Angel in the House—I think I solved. She died. But the second, telling the truth about my own experiences as a body, I do not think I solved. I doubt that any woman has solved it yet. The obstacles against her are still immensely powerful—and yet they are very difficult to define. Outwardly, what is simpler than to write books? Outwardly, what obstacles are there for a woman rather than for a man? Inwardly, I think, the case is very different; she has still many ghosts to fight, many prejudices to overcome. Indeed it will be a long time still, I think, before a woman can sit down to write a book without finding a phantom to be slain, a rock to be dashed against. And if this is so in literature, the freest of all professions for women, how is it in the new professions which you are now for the first time entering?

Those are the questions that I should like, had I time, to ask you. And indeed, if I have laid stress upon these professional experiences of mine, it is because I believe that they are, though in different forms, yours also. Even when the path is nominally open—when there is nothing to prevent a woman from being a doctor, a lawyer, a civil servant—there are many phantoms and obstacles, as I believe, looming in her way. To discuss and define them is I think of great value and importance; for thus only can the labour be shared, the difficulties be solved. But besides this, it is necessary also to discuss the ends and the aims for which we are fighting, for which we are doing battle with these formidable obstacles. Those aims cannot be taken for granted; they must be perpetually questioned and examined. The whole position, as I see it—here in this hall surrounded by women practising for the first time in history I know not how many different professions—is one of extraordinary interest and importance. You have won rooms of your own in the house hitherto exclusively owned by men. You are able, though not without great labour and effort, to pay the rent. You are earning your five hundred pounds a year. But this freedom is only a beginning; the room is your own, but it is still bare. It has to be furnished; it has to be decorated; it has to be shared. How are you going to furnish it, how are you going to decorate it? With whom are you going to share it, and upon what terms? These, I think are questions of the utmost importance and interest. For the first time in history you are able to ask them; for the first time you are able to decide for yourselves what the answers should be. Willingly would I stay and discuss those questions and answers—but not tonight. My time is up; and I must cease.

THINGS TO THINK ABOUT

1. According to Woolf, why could women become writers before they could take part in other arts and professions?
2. Why doesn't Woolf consider herself worthy of being called "a professional woman"?
3. Of what is the Angel of the House a symbol? Why was it necessary for Woolf to kill her? Do you see any evidence of the Angel's death in "Lappin and Lapinova"?
4. Woolf says that she has not been able to solve the problem of "telling the truth about my experience as a body." How has she tried to solve the problem in "Professions for Women"? Do you see any evidence of the problem in "Lappin and Lapinova"?
5. How does the heritage of The Angel of the House affect Rosalind in Woolf's story? How does it affect the men and women you know? Do you know any Angels of the House? Have you ever desired to kill one?

CHINUA ACHEBE

DEAD MEN'S PATH

Chinua Achebe (b. 1930) was born, raised and educated in Nigeria, but he has worked in England and the United States as a teacher and publisher. He is considered one of the finest African authors writing in English.

His writing, like his life, has been an encounter between two cultures: Euro-American culture and his native Ibo. (The Ibo are a loose confederation of tribes located in eastern Nigeria.) According to Achebe, the fundamental theme for all African writers must be "that African people did not hear of culture for the first time from Europeans; that [African societies] had a philosophy of great depth and value and beauty, that they had poetry and, above all, dignity."

Michael Obi's hopes were fulfilled much earlier than he had expected. He was appointed headmaster of Ndume Central School in January 1949. It had always been an unprogressive school, so the Mission authorities decided to send a young and energetic man to run it. Obi accepted this responsibility with enthusiasm. He had many wonderful ideas and this was an opportunity to put them into practice. He had had sound secondary school education which designated him a "pivotal teacher" in the official records and set him apart from the other headmasters in the mission field. He was outspoken in his condemnation of the narrow views of these older and often less-educated ones.

"We shall make a good job of it, shan't we?" he asked his young wife when they first heard the joyful news of his promotion.

"We shall do our best," she replied. "We shall have such beautiful gardens and everything will be just *modern* and delightful . . ." In their two years of married life she had become completely infected by his passion for "modern methods" and his denigration of "these old and superannuated people in the teaching field who would be better employed as traders in the Onitsha market." She began to see herself already as the admired wife of the young headmaster, the queen of the school.

The wives of the other teachers would envy her position. She would set the fashion in everything . . . Then, suddenly, it occurred to her that there might not be other wives. Wavering between hope and fear, she asked her husband, looking anxiously at him.

"All our colleagues are young and unmarried," he said with enthusiasm which for once she did not share. "Which is a good thing," he continued.

"Why?"

"Why? They will give all their time and energy to the school."

Nancy was downcast. For a few minutes she became sceptical about the new school; but it was only for a few minutes. Her little personal misfortune could not blind her to her husband's happy prospects. She looked at him as he sat folded up in a chair. He was stoop-shouldered and looked frail. But he sometimes surprised people with sudden bursts of physical energy. In his present posture, however, all his bodily strength seemed to have retired behind his deep-set eyes, giving them an extraordinary power of penetration. He was only twenty-six, but looked thirty or more. On the whole, he was not unhandsome.

"A penny for your thoughts, Mike," said Nancy after a while, imitating the woman's magazine she read.

"I was thinking what a grand opportunity we've got at last to show these people how a school should be run."

Ndume School was backward in every sense of the word. Mr. Obi put his whole life into the work, and his wife hers too. He had two aims. A high standard of teaching was insisted upon, and the school compound was to be turned into a place of beauty. Nancy's dream-gardens came to life with the coming of the rains, and blossomed. Beautiful hibiscus and allamanda hedges in brilliant red and yellow marked out the carefully tended school compound from the rank neighbourhood bushes.

One evening as Obi was admiring his work he was scandalized to see an old woman from the village hobble right across the compound, through a marigold flower-bed and the hedges. On going up there he found faint signs of an almost disused path from the village across the school compound to the bush on the other side.

"It amazes me," said Obi to one of his teachers who had been three years in the school, "that you people allowed the villagers to make use of this footpath. It is simply incredible." He shook his head.

"The path," said the teacher apologetically, "appears to be very important to them. Although it is hardly used, it connects the village shrine with their place of burial."

"And what has that got to do with the school?" asked the headmaster.

"Well, I don't know," replied the other with a shrug of the shoulders. "But I remember there was a big row some time ago when we attempted to close it."

"That was some time ago. But it will not be used now," said Obi as he walked away. "What will the Government Education Officer think of this when he comes to inspect the school next week? The villagers might, for all I know, decide to use the schoolroom for a pagan ritual during the inspection."

Heavy sticks were planted closely across the path at the two places where it entered and left the school premises. These were further strengthened with barbed wire.

Three days later the village priest of *Ani* called on the headmaster. He was an old man and walked with a slight stoop. He carried a stout walking-stick which he usually tapped on the floor, by way of emphasis, each time he made a new point in his argument.

"I have heard," he said after the usual exchange of cordialities, "that our ancestral footpath has recently been closed . . ."

"Yes," replied Mr. Obi. "We cannot allow people to make a highway of our school compound."

"Look here, my son," said the priest bringing down his walking-stick, "this path was here before you were born and before your father was born. The whole life of this village depends on it. Our dead relatives depart by it and our ancestors visit us by it. But most important, it is the path of children coming in to be born . . ."

Mr. Obi listened with a satisfied smile on his face.

"The whole purpose of our school," he said finally, "is to eradicate just such beliefs as that. Dead men do not require footpaths. The whole idea is just fantastic. Our duty is to teach your children to laugh at such ideas."

"What you say may be true," replied the priest, "but we follow the practices of our fathers. If you re-open the path we shall have nothing to quarrel about. What I always say is: let the hawk perch and let the eagle perch." He rose to go.

"I am sorry," said the young headmaster. "But the school compound cannot be a thoroughfare. It is against our regulations. I would suggest your constructing another path, skirting our premises. We can even get our boys to help in building it. I don't suppose the ancestors will find the little detour too burdensome."

"I have no more words to say," said the old priest, already outside.

Two days later a young woman in the village died in childbed. A diviner was immediately consulted and he prescribed heavy sacrifices to propitiate ancestors insulted by the fence.

Obi woke up next morning among the ruins of his work. The beautiful hedges were torn up not just near the path but right round the school, the flowers trampled to death and one of the school buildings pulled down . . . That day, the white Supervisor came to inspect the school and wrote a nasty report on the state of the premises but more seriously about the "tribal-war situation developing between the school and the village, arising in part from the misguided zeal of the new headmaster."

QUESTIONS

1. What were Michael Obi's career goals? How well did he think he had done in achieving them?
2. What are Obi's attitudes toward his teachers and the people in the community? Are his attitudes well founded?
3. Why does Obi close the path? Are his motives good or bad?
4. Why can't Obi and the village priest come to a compromise? What does the priest mean by saying "let the hawk perch and the eagle perch"?
5. What does the Supervisor think of Obi's administration of the school? Is there any significance in the race of the Supervisor?
6. What does the Supervisor mean by "misguided zeal"? Have you ever seen examples of "misguided zeal"? What happened?

BERNARD MALAMUD

THE JEWBIRD

Bernard Malamud (b. 1914) was born in New York City and attended City College and Columbia University. He has taught since 1961 at Bennington College in Vermont.

Malamud combines in his fiction two different traditions: the Jewish comic tradition of such authors as Sholem Aleichem and I.L. Peretz and the American fabulist tradition of Hawthorne and Mark Twain. His works include The Assistant, The Fixer, *and* The Natural *which was turned into a popular motion picture.*

The window was open so the skinny bird flew in. Flappity-flap with its frazzled black wings. That's how it goes. It's open, you're in. Closed, you're out and that's your fate. The bird wearily flapped through the open kitchen window of Harry Cohen's top-floor apartment on First Avenue near the lower East River.[1] On a rod on the wall hung an escaped canary cage, its door wide open, but this black-type longbeaked

[1] A section of New York City called the Lower East Side. This was a poor Jewish neighborhood.

bird—its ruffled head and small dull eyes, crossed a little, making it look like a dissipated crow—landed if not smack on Cohen's thick lamb chop, at least on the table, close by. The frozen foods salesman was sitting at supper with his wife and young son on a hot August evening a year ago. Cohen, a heavy man with hairy chest and beefy shorts; Edie, in skinny yellow shorts and red halter; and their ten-year-old Morris (after his father)—Maurie, they called him, a nice kid though not overly bright—were all in the city after two weeks out, because Cohen's mother was dying. They had been enjoying Kingston, New York, but drove back when Mama got sick in her flat in the Bronx.[2]

"Right on the table," said Cohen, putting down his beer glass and swatting at the bird. "Son of a bitch."

"Harry, take care with your language," Edie said, looking at Maurie, who watched every move.

The bird cawed hoarsely and with a flap of its bedraggled wings—feathers tufted this way and that—rose heavily to the top of the open kitchen door, where it perched staring down.

"Gevalt, a pogrom!"[3]

"It's a talking bird," said Edie in astonishment.

"In Jewish," said Maurie.

"Wise guy," muttered Cohen. He gnawed on his chop, then put down the bone. "So if you can talk, say what's your business. What do you want here?"

"If you can't spare a lamb chop," said the bird, "I'll settle for a piece of herring with a crust of bread. You can't live on your nerve forever."

"This ain't a restaurant," Cohen replied. "All I'm asking is what brings you to this address?"

"The window was open," the bird sighed; adding after a moment, "I'm running. I'm flying but I'm also running."

"From whom?" asked Edie with interest.

"Anti-Semeets."

"Anti-Semites?" they all said.

"That's from who."

"What kind of anti-Semites bother a bird?" Edie asked.

"Any kind," said the bird, "also including eagles, vultures, and hawks. And once in a while some crows will take your eyes out."

"But aren't you a crow?"

"Me? I'm a Jewbird."

Cohen laughed heartily. "What do you mean by that?"

[2] Kingston is a resort town in the Catskill Mountains. The Bronx is the northernmost borough of New York City.

[3] A pogrom is an organized slaughter of a minority group, especially Jews. Gevalt is a Yiddish exclamation of woe.

The bird began dovening. He prayed without Book or tallith,[4] but with passion. Edie bowed her head though not Cohen. And Maurie rocked back and forth with the prayer, looking up with one wide-open eye.

When the prayer was done Cohen remarked, "No hat, no phylacteries?"[5]

"I'm an old radical."

"You're sure you're not some kind of a ghost or dybbuk?"[6]

"Not a dybbuk," answered the bird, "though one of my relatives had such an experience once. It's all over now, thanks God. They freed her from a former lover, a crazy jealous man. She's now the mother of two wonderful children."

"Birds?" Cohen asked slyly.

"Why not?"

"What kind of birds?"

"Like me. Jewbirds."

Cohen tipped back in his chair and guffawed. "That's a big laugh. I've heard of a Jewfish but not a Jewbird."

"We're once removed." The bird rested on one skinny leg, then on the other. "Please, could you spare maybe a piece of herring with a small crust of bread?"

Edie got up from the table.

"What are you doing?" Cohen asked her.

"I'll clear the dishes."

Cohen turned to the bird. "So what's your name, if you don't mind saying?"

"Call me Schwartz."[7]

"He might be an old Jew changed into a bird by somebody," said Edie, removing a plate.

"Are you?" asked Harry, lighting a cigar.

"Who knows?" answered Schwartz. "Does God tell us everything?"

Maurie got up on his chair. "What kind of herring?" he asked the bird in excitement.

"Get down, Maurie, or you'll fall," ordered Cohen.

"If you haven't got matjes, I'll take schmaltz,"[8] said Schwartz.

"All we have is marinated, with slices of onion—in a jar," said Edie.

"If you'll open for me the jar I'll eat marinated. Do you have also, if you don't mind, a piece of rye bread—the spitz?"[9]

[4] Dovening is praying, especially softly and to oneself. A tallith is a prayer shawl.

[5] Phylacteries are leather-covered boxes containing scriptural passages that are worn on the left arm and forehead during prayers.

[6] A dybbuk is an evil spirit.

[7] Schwartz is German for "black," an appropriate name for a blackbird.

[8] Matjes is a better sort of herring; schmaltz herring is cheaper and greasier.

[9] The spitz is the heel of a bread loaf.

Edie thought she had.

"Feed him out on the balcony," Cohen said. He spoke to the bird. "After that take off."

Schwartz closed both bird eyes. "I'm tired and it's a long way."

"Which direction are you headed, north or south?"

Schwartz, barely lifting his wings, shrugged.

"You don't know where you're going?"

"Where there's charity I'll go."

"Let him stay, papa," said Maurie. "He's only a bird."

"So stay the night," Cohen said, "but no longer."

In the morning Cohen ordered the bird out of the house but Maurie cried, so Schwartz stayed for a while. Maurie was still on vacation from school and his friends were away. He was lonely and Edie enjoyed the fun he had, playing with the bird.

"He's no trouble at all," she told Cohen, "and besides his appetite is very small."

"What'll you do when he makes dirty?"

"He flies across the street in a tree when he makes dirty, and if nobody passes below, who notices?"

"So all right," said Cohen, "but I'm dead set against it. I warn you he ain't gonna stay here long."

"What have you got against the poor bird?"

"Poor bird, my ass. He's a foxy bastard. He thinks he's a Jew."

"What difference does it make what he thinks?"

"A Jewbird, what chutzpah.[10] One false move and he's out on his drumsticks."

At Cohen's insistence Schwartz lived out on the balcony in a new wooden birdhouse Edie had bought him.

"With many thanks," said Schwartz, "though I would rather have a human roof over my head. You know how it is at my age. I like the warm, the windows, the smell of cooking. I would also be glad to see once in a while the *Jewish Morning Journal* and have now and then a schnapps[11] because it helps my breathing, thanks God. But whatever you give me, you won't hear complaints."

However, when Cohen brought home a bird feeder full of dried corn, Schwartz said, "Impossible."

Cohen was annoyed. "What's the matter, crosseyes, is your life getting too good for you? Are you forgetting what it means to be migratory? I'll bet a helluva lot of crows you happen to be acquainted with, Jews or otherwise, would give their eyeteeth to eat this corn."

Schwartz did not answer. What can you say to a grubber yung?[12]

[10] Chutzpah is Yiddish for "pushiness."
[11] Schnapps is a strong liquor.
[12] Grubber yung is Yiddish for "moocher."

"Not for my digestion," he later explained to Edie. "Cramps. Herring is better even if it makes you thirsty. At least rainwater don't cost anything." He laughed sadly in breathy caws.

And herring, thanks to Edie, who knew where to shop, was what Schwartz got, with an occasional piece of potato pancake, and even a bit of soupmeat when Cohen wasn't looking.

When school began in September, before Cohen would once again suggest giving the bird the boot, Edie prevailed on him to wait a little while until Maurie adjusted.

"To deprive him right now might hurt his school work, and you know what trouble we had last year."

"So okay, but sooner or later the bird goes. That I promise you."

Schwartz, though nobody had asked him, took on full responsibility for Maurie's performance in school. In return for favors granted, when he was let in for an hour or two at night, he spent most of his time overseeing the boy's lessons. He sat on top of the dresser near Maurie's desk as he laboriously wrote out his homework. Maurie was a restless type and Schwartz gently kept him to his studies. He also listened to him practice his screechy violin, taking a few minutes off now and then to rest his ears in the bathroom. And they afterwards played dominoes. The boy was an indifferent checker player and it was impossible to teach him chess. When he was sick, Schwartz read him comic books though he personally disliked them. But Maurie's work improved in school and even his violin teacher admitted his playing was better. Edie gave Schwartz credit for these improvements though the bird pooh-poohed them.

Yet he was proud there was nothing lower than C minuses on Maurie's report card, and on Edie's insistence celebrated with a little schnapps.

"If he keeps up like this," Cohen said, "I'll get him in an Ivy League college for sure."

"Oh I hope so," sighed Edie.

But Schwartz shook his head. "He's a good boy—you don't have to worry. He won't be a shicker[13] or a wifebeater, God forbid, but a scholar he'll never be, if you know what I mean, although maybe a good mechanic. It's no disgrace in these times."

"If I were you," Cohen said, angered, "I'd keep my big snoot out of other people's private business."

"Harry, please," said Edie.

"My goddamn patience is wearing out. That crosseyes butts into everything."

Though he wasn't exactly a welcome guest in the house, Schwartz gained a few ounces although he did not improve in appearance. He

[13] A shicker is a drunkard.

looked bedraggled as ever, his feathers unkempt, as though he had just flown out of a snowstorm. He spent, he admitted, little time taking care of himself. Too much to think about. "Also outside plumbing," he told Edie. Still there was more glow to his eyes so that though Cohen went on calling him crosseyes he said it less emphatically.

Liking his situation, Schwartz tried tactfully to stay out of Cohen's way, but one night when Edie was at the movies and Maurie was taking a hot shower, the frozen foods salesman began a quarrel with the bird.

"For Christ sake, why don't you wash yourself sometimes? Why must you always stink like a dead fish?"

"Mr. Cohen, if you'll pardon me, if somebody eats garlic he will smell from garlic. I eat herring three times a day. Feed me flowers and I will smell like flowers."

"Who's obligated to feed you anything at all? You're lucky to get herring."

"Excuse me, I'm not complaining," said the bird. "You're complaining."

"What's more," said Cohen, "even from out on the balcony I can hear you snoring away like a pig. It keeps me awake at night."

"Snoring," said Schwartz, "isn't a crime, thanks God."

"All in all you are a goddamn pest and free loader. Next thing you'll want to sleep in bed next to my wife."

"Mr. Cohen," said Schwartz, "on this rest assured. A bird is a bird."

"So you say, but how do I know you're a bird and not some kind of a goddamn devil?"

"If I was a devil you would know already. And I don't mean because your son's good marks."

"Shut up, you bastard bird," shouted Cohen.

"Grubber yung," cawed Schwartz, rising to the tips of his talons, his long wings outstretched.

Cohen was about to lunge for the bird's scrawny neck but Maurie came out of the bathroom, and for the rest of the evening until Schwartz's bedtime on the balcony, there was pretended peace.

But the quarrel had deeply disturbed Schwartz and he slept badly. His snoring woke him, and awake, he was fearful of what would become of him. Wanting to stay out of Cohen's way, he kept to the birdhouse as much as possible. Cramped by it, he paced back and forth on the balcony ledge, or sat on the birdhouse roof, staring into space. In the evenings, while overseeing Maurie's lessons, he often fell asleep. Awakening, he nervously hopped around exploring the four corners of the room. He spent much time in Maurie's closet, and carefully examined his bureau drawers when they were left open. And once when he found a large paper bag on the floor, Schwartz poked his way into it to investigate what possibilities were. The boy was amused to see the bird in the paper bag.

"He wants to build a nest," he said to his mother.

Edie, sensing Schwartz's unhappiness, spoke to him quietly.

"Maybe if you did some of the things my husband wants you, you would get along better with him."

"Give me a for instance," Schwartz said.

"Like take a bath, for instance."

"I'm too old for baths," said the bird. "My feathers fall out without baths."

"He says you have a bad smell."

"Everybody smells. Some people smell because of their thoughts or because who they are. My bad smell comes from the food I eat. What does his come from?"

"I better not ask him or it might make him mad," said Edie.

In late November Schwartz froze on the balcony in the fog and cold, and especially on rainy days he woke with stiff joints and could barely move his wings. Already he felt twinges of rheumatism. He would have liked to spend more time in the warm house, particularly when Maurie was in school and Cohen at work. But though Edie was good-hearted and might have sneaked him in in the morning, just to thaw out, he was afraid to ask her. In the meantime Cohen, who had been reading articles about the migration of birds, came out on the balcony one night after work when Edie was in the kitchen preparing pot roast, and peeking into the birdhouse, warned Schwartz to be on his way soon if he knew what was good for him. "Time to hit the flyways."

"Mr. Cohen, why do you hate me so much?" asked the bird. "What did I do to you?"

"Because you're an A-number-one trouble maker, that's why. What's more, whoever heard of a Jewbird! Now scat or it's open war."

But Schwartz stubbornly refused to depart so Cohen embarked on a campaign of harassing him, meanwhile hiding it from Edie and Maurie. Maurie hated violence and Cohen didn't want to leave a bad impression. He thought maybe if he played dirty tricks on the bird he would fly off without being physically kicked out. The vacation was over, let him make his easy living off the fat of somebody else's land. Cohen worried about the effect of the bird's departure on Maurie's schooling but decided to take the chance, first, because the boy now seemed to have the knack of studying—give the black bird-bastard credit—and second, because Schwartz was driving him bats by being there always, even in his dreams.

The frozen foods salesman began his campaign against the bird by mixing watery cat food with the herring slices in Schwartz's dish. He also blew up and popped numerous paper bags outside the birdhouse as the bird slept, and when he had got Schwartz good and nervous, though not enough to leave, he brought a full-grown cat into the house, supposedly a gift for little Maurie, who had always wanted a pussy. The cat never stopped springing up at Schwartz whenever he saw him, one day managing to claw out several of his tailfeathers. And even at lesson time, when the cat was usually excluded from Maurie's room, though somehow or other he quickly found his way in at the end of the lesson, Schwartz was desperately fearful of his life and flew from pinnacle to pinnacle—light fixture to clothes tree to door-top—in order to elude the beast's wet jaws.

Once when the bird complained to Edie how hazardous his existence was, she said, "Be patient, Mr. Schwartz. When the cat gets to know you better he won't try to catch you any more."

"When he stops trying we will both be in Paradise," Schwartz answered. "Do me a favor and get rid of him. He makes my whole life worry. I'm losing feathers like a tree loses leaves."

"I'm awfully sorry but Maurie likes the pussy and sleeps with it."

What could Schwartz do? He worried but came to no decision, being afraid to leave. So he ate the herring garnished with cat food, tried hard not to hear the paper bags bursting like fire crackers outside the birdhouse at night, and lived terror-stricken closer to the ceiling than the floor, as the cat, his tail flicking, endlessly watched him.

Weeks went by. Then on the day after Cohen's mother had died in her flat in the Bronx, when Maurie came home with a zero on an arithmetic test, Cohen, enraged, waited until Edie had taken the boy to his violin lesson, then openly attacked the bird. He chased him with a broom on the balcony and Schwartz frantically flew back and forth, finally escaping into his birdhouse. Cohen triumphantly reached in, and grabbing both skinny legs, dragged the bird out, cawing loudly, his wings wildly beating. He whirled the bird around and around his head. But Schwartz, as he moved in circles, managed to swoop down and catch Cohen's nose in his beak, and hung on for dear life. Cohen cried out in great pain, punched the bird with his fist, and tugging at his legs with all his might, pulled his nose free. Again he swung the yawking Schwartz around until the bird grew dizzy, then with a furious heave, flung him into the night. Schwartz sank like stone into the street. Cohen then tossed the birdhouse and feeder after him, listening at the ledge until they crashed on the sidewalk below. For a full hour, broom in hand, his heart palpitating and nose throbbing with pain, Cohen waited for Schwartz to return but the broken-hearted bird didn't.

That's the end of that dirty bastard, the salesman thought and went in. Edie and Maurie had come home.

"Look," said Cohen, pointing to his bloody nose swollen three times its normal size, "what that sonofabitchy bird did. It's a permanent scar."

"Where is he now?" Edie asked, frightened.

"I threw him out and he flew away. Good riddance."

Nobody said no, though Edie touched a handkerchief to her eyes and Maurie rapidly tried the nine times table and found he knew approximately half.

In the spring when the winter's snow had melted, the boy, moved by a memory, wandered in the neighborhood, looking for Schwartz. He found a dead black bird in a small lot near the river, his two wings broken, neck twisted, and both bird-eyes plucked clean.

"Who did it to you, Mr. Schwartz?" Maurie wept.

"Anti-Semeets," Edie said later.

QUESTIONS

1. Although Edie and Maurie are astonished by the talking bird, Cohen is unimpressed. How do you account for that difference?
2. Why does Cohen dislike the bird? Does he have good reasons?
3. From whom and from what is Schwartz running away?
4. Schwarts is a Jewbird, but does his name and color have other significance?
5. Why does Cohen finally attack the bird? Is his attack justified?
6. Edie says "Anti-Semeets" killed Schwartz. What does she mean? Is she correct?

BERNARD MALAMUD

from AN INTERVIEW WITH BERNARD MALAMUD

INTERVIEWER: What about a little personal history? There's been little written about your life.

MALAMUD: That's how I wanted it—I like privacy, and as much as possible to stay out of my books. I know that's disadvantageous to certain legitimate kinds of criticism of literature, but my needs come first. Still, I have here and there talked a little about my life: My father was a grocer; my mother, who helped him, after a long illness, died young. I had a younger brother who lived a hard and lonely life and died in his fifties. My mother and father were gentle, honest, kindly people, and who they were and their affection for me to some degree made up for the cultural deprivation I felt as a child. They weren't educated, but their values were stable. Though my father always managed to make a living, they were comparatively poor, especially in the Depression, and yet I never heard a word in praise of the buck. On the other hand, there were no books that I remember in the house, no records, music, pictures on the wall. On Sundays I listened to somebody's piano through the window. At nine I caught pneumonia, and when I was convalescing my father bought me *The Book of Knowledge,* twenty volumes where there had been none. That was, considering the circumstances, an act of great generosity. When I was in high school he bought a radio. As a kid, for entertainment I turned to the movies and dime novels. Maybe *The Natural* derives from Frank Merriwell as well as the adventures of the Brooklyn Dodgers in Ebbets Field. Anyway, my parents stayed close to the store. Once in a while, on Jewish holidays, we went visiting, or saw a Jewish play—Sholem Aleichem, Peretz, and others. My mother's brother,

Charles Fidelman, and their cousin, Isidore Cashier, were in the Yiddish theatre.

Around the neighborhood the kids played Chase the White Horse, Ringolevio, Buck-Buck, punchball and one o'cat. Occasionally we stole tomatoes from the Italian dirt farmers, gypped the El to ride to Coney Island, smoked in cellars, and played blackjack. I wore sneakers every summer. My education at home derived mostly from the presence and example of good, feelingful, hard-working people. They were worriers, with other faults I wasn't much conscious of until I recognized them in myself. I learned from books, in the public schools. I had some fine teachers in grammar school, Erasmus Hall High School, and later in City College, in New York. I took to literature and early wanted to be a writer.

INTERVIEWER: How early?

MALAMUD: At eight or nine I was writing little stories in school and feeling the glow. To anyone of my friends who'd listen I'd recapitulate at tedious length the story of the last movie I'd seen. The movies tickled my imagination. As a writer I learned from Charlie Chaplin.

INTERVIEWER: What in particular?

MALAMUD: Let's say the rhythm, the snap of comedy; the reserved comic presence—that beautiful distancing; the funny with sad; the surprise of surprise.

INTERVIEWER: Humor is so much a part of your work. Is this an easy quality to deal with? Is one problem that the response to humor is so much a question of individual taste?

MALAMUD: The funny bone is universal. I doubt humorists think of individual taste when they're enticing the laugh. With me humor comes unexpectedly, usually in defense of a character, sometimes because I need cheering up. When something starts funny I can feel my imagination eating and running. I love the distancing—the guise of invention—that humor gives fiction. Comedy, I imagine, is harder to do consistently than tragedy, but I like it spiced in the wine of sadness.

INTERVIEWER: What about suffering? It's a subject much in your early work.

MALAMUD: I'm against it, but when it occurs, why waste the experience?

INTERVIEWER: Are you a Jewish writer?

MALAMUD: What is the question asking?

INTERVIEWER: One hears various definitions and insistences, for instance, that one is primarily a writer and any subject matter is secondary; or that one is an American-Jewish writer. There are qualifications, by Bellow, Roth, others.

MALAMUD: I'm an American, I'm a Jew, and I write for all men. A novelist has to, or he's built himself a cage. I write about Jews, when I write about Jews, because they set my imagination going. I know something about their history, the quality of their experience and belief, and of their literature, though not as much as I would like. Like many writers I'm influenced especially by the Bible, both Testaments. I respond in particular to the East European immigrants of my father's and mother's generation; many of them were Jews of the Pale as described by the classic Yiddish writers. And of course I've been deeply moved by the Jews of the concentration camps, and the refugees wandering from nowhere to nowhere. I'm concerned about Israel. Sometimes I make characters Jewish because I think I will understand them better as people, not because I am out to prove anything. That's a qualification. Still another is that I know that, as a writer, I've been influenced by Hawthorne, James, Mark Twain, Hemingway, more than I have been by Sholem Aleichem and I. L. Peretz, whom I read with pleasure. Of course I admire and have been moved by other writers, Dostoyevsky and Chekhov, for instance, but the point I'm making is that I was born in America and respond, in American life, to more than Jewish experience. I wrote for those who read.

THINGS TO THINK ABOUT

1. Is there anything in Malamud's childhood that would especially prepare him as a writer? Must writers come from a particularly privileged background to write good literature? Is there anything in your background that would keep you from being a good writer?
2. Malamud says he learned humor from Charlie Chaplin? Is there anything Chaplinesque in "The Jewbird"? Are there any comedians today that might influence you as a writer?
3. How does Malamud balance his ethnic background against his sense of being American? In the Black-American stories in this volume is there a similar balance? How do you regard your ethnic or regional heritage? How does it color your perceptions of America?

9
STYLE

One of the more elusive terms in the study of literature is style because the word is used in so many ways. People refer to national or regional styles; they speak of British styles of writing or Southern styles. Often people speak about a period or historical styles. "This language is very Elizabethian," they might say, or "This is a very Victorian story." Still at other times, people will refer to a journalistic style, or a poetic style. And finally people will say, "This is not a very effective style." With so many ways of using the word, no wonder students get confused.

STYLE DEFINED

To understand style, we must return to our portrait of the writer. There she or he sits before the desk, a blank page of paper ready to be written upon. Now the writer must choose one story to write from the infinite number of possible stories and from the vast—though not infinite—number of possible words. The act of writing demands the constant making of choices, choices about content, choices about organization, choices about point-of-view, choices about language. We might call style the basis upon which an author makes choices, or the pattern that emerges from those choices. For example, let us suppose an author wishes to describe a stain on a carpet. The author might have three possible ways of describing the color of the stain: red, blood-red, carmine. Which is best?

If the author has decided to choose the simplest words, he or she would probably decide on just "red" as the most appropriate term. If the author wanted to be a bit more specific and graphic, the color might be described as "blood-red." If the author wanted more variety of language or more elevated diction, then "carmine" might be the best choice. As you can see, the choices are determined either consciously or unconsciously on some principle. These principles of selection can be identified as the author's style. Of course, we can not determine an author's style from one sentence (though we may on occasion be able to illustrate the style with one sentence); rather it is the larger patterns of choice that reveal an author's style.

REGIONAL STYLES

So far we have been talking about style as an individual choice, but what we as individuals choose to do is often limited, if not determined by, what those around us do. For example, when you got dressed this morning, you probably didn't consider all the pieces in your wardrobe before selecting what you wore to class. The men probably didn't consider wearing suits or sports jackets, and the women probably didn't consider wearing long gowns or business suits. There is no law against wearing a tuxedo to class, but I have never seen a student wear one. The reason is that such clothing is considered inappropriate. But why is it inappropriate? Because other people don't wear tuxedos to class. Before the 1960's, wearing jeans and tee shirts to class was considered inappropriate attire in most colleges and universities, and many schools had dress codes which forbade the wearing of such clothing. Today, such dress is standard at most schools.

My point is simple: what we consider an appropriate or inappropriate style is not solely an individual choice. It is based in part on the choices other people make. People in certain places, at certain periods of time, and in certain professions and occupations establish different styles that they consider appropriate and which the majority follows. But it is important to recognize the difference between a style and a uniform. A uniform allows no range of difference. Everyone must dress alike. A style permits a range of individual differences. People can select from a number of limited options.

The same is true of writing. Writers from a certain region, or from a certain time period make similar choices in subject matter, language, and organization, and are said to possess a style. The novelist Susan Kenney wrote in a recent review: "It has been suggested before that there is a similarity between recent Maine fiction and the tough and earthy, often sensational yet sensitive, fiction known as Southern Gothic written from the 1930's on" (NYTBR, 6/1/86, p. 7). What Kenney means is that some of the same features that tend to appear in Southern writing also tend to appear in recent fiction of novelists from Maine. These qualities include toughness, earthiness, sensationalism and sensitivity. This book contains stories by Flannery O'Connor, William Faulkner and Eudora Welty—three of the major Southern writers Kenney refers to later in her review—and you may judge for yourself how accurately Kenney describes their work.

But let us consider a group of similarities in these stories. Both O'Connor's and Faulkner's stories contain murders—murder is usually considered "sensational" subject matter. The murderer in O'Connor's story is called The Misfit, and we might say that misfits appear in all three stories where they are handled with a kind of earthy humor and sensitivity. Does this mean that all Southern stories are about murderers and misfits, and are "tough and earthy, sensational yet sensitive"? No. It merely means that Southern writers tend to choose such characters and such features for their works. Kenney is making a generalization, and for all such broad generalizations there are always exceptions.

GOOD STYLES AND BAD STYLES

Just as there is no one style of clothing good for all occasions, so there is no one style of writing appropriate for all occasions. Lawyers do not wear to tennis courts what they wear to courts of law, and surgeons do not wear to the operating table the same clothes they wear to the dinner table. We judge literary style in much the same way that we judge clothing styles by appropriateness, accuracy, and attractiveness.

Writers choose a style after considering, either consciously or unconsciously, several factors: (1) the subject, (2) the audience, (3) the effect they wish to have on the audience, (4) their own personal preferences and capacities. These factors are not independent of one another. For example, let us say you were writing a manual about a computer language. Your subject matter has already limited your audience to those people with enough knowledge about computers that they would want to learn one of their languages. In addition, the kinds of effect you could have on your audience are also limited because writers of computer manuals don't usually want to shock, sadden, arouse, or convulse their readers with laughter. Their job is usually to inform as clearly and as quickly as possible.

RESISTING READERS

One of the difficult stylistic problems a writer is faced with is the audience's resistance to certain ideas or emotions. If you want to borrow money, for example, you anticipate resistance on the part of the person from whom you wish to obtain the loan. Before speaking to the person, you would probably try to formulate a strategy or plan to increase your chances of getting the money. In literature, the same process occurs.

For example, in her story "Giving Birth," Margaret Atwood wishes to explore some of the mixed feelings pregnant women have toward childbirth. Most of us like to consider childbirth a wonderful, miraculous and joyous event. In general, the reading public does not want to think about the pain, the worry, the fear, or the anger that sometimes accompanies giving birth. In order for the typical reader to consider these unpleasant feelings, Atwood develops certain procedures to break down the readers' resistance. Most people are better able to confront unpleasantness when they are given time to prepare for it. Atwood does not plunge the reader directly into the action of the story. First the narrator begins with a meditation about the oddness of the expression "giving birth," and then she discusses her own experiences as a mother. Only gradually does she lead up to Jeanie's experience. Another technique Atwood uses is distancing the reader from the most unpleasant feelings. Not only does the narrator attempt to distance herself from Jeanie, but Jeanie distances herself from her own worst feeling by creating the nameless woman who follows her, a woman "who did not wish to become pregnant . . . who did not choose any of these ordeals." In these, and in other ways, Atwood acknowledges the resistance of her readers and attempts to breakdown or circumvent their resistance.

THREE IMPORTANT ASPECTS OF STYLE

When people talk about style they often concentrate on the language that the author employs, and especially on matters of tone, diction and sentence construction.

Tone

Actors sometimes play a game taking a simple sentence such as "I think that story is beautiful" and by changing their tone of voice, alter the meaning of the sentence. One actor might say the sentence sarcastically, indicating the story is anything but beautiful. Another might say it defiantly to indicate that "I don't care what the rest of you believe, *I* think the story is beautiful!" Another might say it romantically, as if half in love with the "beautiful" story. The meaning of a sentence depends in part on the tone of the speaker's voice.

Writers do the same, although they cannot signal changes in tone as quickly or as clearly as actors. Sometimes writers are clearly emotionally involved in their stories, but many times they are matter-of-fact, merely stating in a detached way the facts of the story. Tone is the result of the author's attitude toward the narrative events and the audience.

Diction

Diction is the author's choice of words. Some authors prefer to tell their stories as if they were sitting down talking to us. Such a style is called *colloquial,* and Eudora Welty's "Why I Live at the P.O." and John Barth's "Autobiography" are colloquial.

At the other end of the stylistic spectrum is the elevated style of Henry James, who uses a broader, more colorful, more formal and richer vocabulary than most people use in ordinary speech. It should be noted, however, that according to his friends, James spoke in much the same style as he wrote, and toward the end of his life actually dictated his elaborate and highly literary novels to a secretary. Thus even the most formal and elaborate style is not always entirely divorced from the oral tradition of storytelling.

Sentence Structure

Critics often characterize writing styles by the author's general pattern of sentence structure. Some authors use short, simple sentences combined with simple conjunctions such as "and" or "but." This style is called *paratactic,* and it is used not only for the simplest subjects and the least sophisticated readers (it is the basic style of children's books), but the most elevated subjects as well. The following passage in praise of wisdom is from The Book of Samuel. Notice the independent clauses linked together by semi-colons and co-ordinate conjunctions.

> Wisdom shines bright and never fades; she is easily discerned by those who love her, and by those who seek her she is found. She is quick to make herself known to those who desire knowledge of her; the man who rises early in search of her will not grow weary in the quest, for he will find her seated at his door. To set all one's thoughts on her is prudence in its perfect shape, and to lie wakeful in her cause is the short way to peace of mind. For she herself ranges in search of those who are worthy of her; on their daily path she appears to them with kindly intent, and in all their purposes meets them half–way. The true beginning of wisdom is the desire to learn, and a concern for learning means love toward her; the love of her means the keeping of her laws; to keep her laws is a warrant of immortality; and immortality brings a man near God.

The paratactic style is capable of deep feeling and great eloquence as well as simplicity.

The opposite of the paratactic style is the *hypotactic* style which uses many subordinate or dependent clauses, parenthetical thoughts and appositives. Hypotactic sentences tend to be longer and more complicated than paratactic ones. The following passage is from Marcel Proust's story "A Dinner in Society." He is describing Madame Fremer, a banker's wife and the hostess of a large dinner party which is the setting of the story.

> Madame Fremer presided over the conversation with a visible satisfaction due to her consciousness of the high mission she was accomplishing. Accustomed to presenting noted writers to duchess, she seemed in her own eyes a sort of all powerful Foreign Minister exercising, even over the protocol, her sovereign judgment, just as

> a spectator at the theatre, as he digests his dinner, looks down upon, since he judges them, actors, audience, author, the rules of dramatic art, genius. As a matter of fact the conversation was going along smoothly enough.

Proust's long, complicated sentences are especially appropriate for the elegant, sophisticated and complex people in the story. It may be useful to compare Proust's prose style with V.S. Naipaul's. Proust adopts a highly hypotactic style for his portraits of Parisian aristocratic society. Naipaul adopts a highly paratactic style for his portrait of a poor man in Trinidad's Miguel Street. But notice not all of Proust's sentences are long. The final sentence of the above passage is short. Writers tend to try to gain variety in their writing, so the most hypotactic styles will have short, clipped sentences in them, and the most paratactic of styles will allow an occasional long, complex sentence.

EVALUATING STYLE

In evaluating style, one should consider several questions: (1) How appropriate is the style to the subject matter and the audience? (2) How effective is the style in achieving the author's purposes or in satisfying and accommodating the needs of the readers?

When choosing styles for your own writing, you must consider the same sorts of questions. What is the subject? Who are my readers? What are their expectations and presuppositions about the subject? What do I want to happen to them as they read? What sorts of language, sentence structure, tonality and content will achieve the intellectual and emotional effects I desire?

THINGS TO THINK ABOUT

1. In writing this textbook I have spent a great deal of time considering its style. What sort of style have I employed in this book? What sort of readers have I anticipated? Is this style appropriate? What changes, if any, would you make to the style of the book?
2. What sort of style do you use in your papers? Is the style appropriate to your audience? Is it appropriate to the subject? Does it feel comfortable to you? How would you describe your own writing style?
3. People adopt certain dress styles. For whom do they dress? What message do they wish to convey with their clothing? Is the style appropriate?
4. We talk about life styles? In what way are life styles like literary styles?

Do they have a particular audience? Subject matter? Tone? In what way can we call life styles good or bad? In what ways are they expressive or inexpressive?

ESSAY TOPICS

1. Compare the style of a paper you wrote in grade school with the style you use now. How has your style changed? How has it remained the same? Does your style reflect your personality?
2. There is an old saying, "Style is the man." Is this saying true? Is it always true? Is it true of women?
3. Compare the style of two musicians. How do their styles differ? In what ways are they the same? In what ways do their styles express something of their individuality? In what way does their style reflect a tradition?

CREATIVE WRITING EXERCISES

1. Narrate an incident first in a paratactic style, and then in a hypotactic style. Which is more effective? Which seems more appropriate?
2. Narrate the same incident first using sentences of the same general length and then in sentences of widely varying lengths. How did you choose which details should be in long sentences and which should be in short ones? Which narrative is most effective and appropriate?
3. Analyze the style of a writer you particularly admire, and write a parody of the style.

LITERARY ESSAYS

1. All of "The Jilting of Granny Weatherall" may be said to be written with the stream-of-consciousness technique. But within this general style there are many variations. Does the style of the story change in the course of its telling? If so, what is the significance of the change?
2. The hero of Vladimir Nabokov's "Cloud, Castle, Lake" is attracting to a certain style of living, a style that runs counter to the style of his fellow travellers. Contrast these styles and tell whether the style of the narrative reflects Ivanovich's style or the style of his companions.
3. If style is choice, then we must consider not only what is selected, but also what is rejected, not only what's said, but also what's unsaid. Discuss how the "unsaid" becomes both a theme of Doerr's story "Parts of Speech" and an aspect of its narrative style.

RAYMOND CARVER

THE STUDENT'S WIFE

Raymond Carver (b. 1938) was raised in an unlikely home for a writer. His father was an alcoholic saw-filer in an Oregon lumber mill and his mother worked as a waitress. A year after graduating high school he married his sixteen-year-old girlfriend, and a few months later—having moved to California—he started college where he was taught by the novelist John Gardner, who recognized Carver's talent. But it took ten years before he began to gain a reputation as a writer, during which time he worked as a hospital janitor and textbook editor.

Since the publication of his first book of short stories Will You Please Be Quiet, Please, *Carver has gained a reputation for his hard, but lyric narratives that capture the lives of poor, hardworking, often inarticulate people.*

He had been reading to her from Rilke, a poet he admired, when she fell asleep with her head on his pillow. He liked reading aloud, and he read well—a confident sonorous voice, now pitched low and somber, now rising, now thrilling. He never looked away from the page when he read and stopped only to reach to the nightstand for a cigaret. It was a rich voice that spilled her into a dream of caravans just setting out from walled cities and bearded men in robes. She had listened to him for a few minutes, then she had closed her eyes and drifted off.

He went on reading aloud. The children had been asleep for hours, and outside a car rubbered by now and then on the wet pavement. After a while he put down the book and turned in the bed to reach for the lamp. She opened her eyes suddenly, as if frightened, and blinked two or three times. Her eyelids looked oddly dark and fleshy to him as they flicked up and down over her fixed glassy eyes. He stared at her.

"Are you dreaming?" he asked.

She nodded and brought her hand up and touched her fingers to the plastic curlers at each side of her head. Tomorrow would be Friday, her day for all the four-to-seven-year-olds in the Woodlawn Apartments. He kept looking at her, leaning on his elbow, at the same time trying to straighten the spread with his free hand. She had a smooth-skinned face with prominent cheekbones; the cheekbones, she sometimes insisted to friends, were from her father, who had been one-quarter Nez Perce.

Then: "Make me a little sandwich of something, Mike. With butter and lettuce and salt on the bread."

He did nothing and he said nothing because he wanted to go to sleep. But when he opened his eyes she was still awake, watching him.

"Can't you go to sleep, Nan?" he said, very solemnly. "It's late."

"I'd like something to eat first," she said. "My legs and arms hurt for some reason, and I'm hungry."

He groaned extravagantly as he rolled out of bed.

He fixed her the sandwich and brought it in on a saucer. She sat up in bed and smiled when he came into the bedroom, then slipped a pillow behind her back as she took the saucer. He thought she looked like a hospital patient in her white nightgown.

"What a funny little dream I had."

"What were you dreaming?" he said, getting into bed and turning over onto his side away from her. He stared at the nightstand waiting. Then he closed his eyes slowly.

"Do you really want to hear it?" she said.

"Sure," he said.

She settled back comfortably on the pillow and picked a crumb from her lip.

"Well. It seemed like a real long drawn-out kind of dream, you know, with all kinds of relationships going on, but I can't remember everything now. It was all very clear when I woke up, but it's beginning to fade now. How long have I been asleep, Mike? It doesn't really matter, I guess. Anyway, I think it was that we were staying someplace overnight. I don't know where the kids were, but it was just the two of us at some little hotel or something. It was on some lake that wasn't familiar. There was another, older, couple there and they wanted to take us for a ride in their motorboat." She laughed, remembering, and leaned forward off the pillow. "The next thing I recall is we were down at the boat landing. Only the way it turned out, they had just one seat in the boat, a kind of bench up in the front, and it was only big enough for three. You and I started arguing about who was going to sacrifice and sit all cooped up in the back. You said you were, and I said I was. But I finally squeezed in the back of the boat. It was so narrow it hurt my legs, and I was afraid the water was going to come in over the sides. Then I woke up."

"That's some dream," he managed to say and felt drowsily that he should say something more. "You remember Bonnie Travis? Fred Travis' wife? She used to have *color* dreams, she said."

She looked at the sandwich in her hand and took a bite. When she had swallowed, she ran her tongue in behind her lips and balanced the saucer on her lap as she reached behind and plumped up the pillow. Then she smiled and leaned back against the pillow again.

"Do you remember that time we stayed overnight on the Tilton River, Mike? When you caught that big fish the next morning?" She placed her hand on his shoulder. "Do you remember that?" she said.

She did. After scarcely thinking about it these last years, it had begun coming back to her lately. It was a month or two after they'd married and gone away for a weekend. They had sat by a little campfire that night, a watermelon in the snow-cold river, and she'd fried Spam and eggs and canned beans for supper and pancakes and Spam and eggs in the same blackened pan the next morning. She had burned the pan both times she cooked, and they could never get the coffee to boil, but it was one of the best times they'd ever had. She remembered he had read to her that night as well: Elizabeth Browning and a few poems from the *Rubáiyát.* They had had so many covers over them that she could hardly turn her feet under all the weight. The next morning he had hooked a big trout, and people stopped their cars on the road across the river to watch him play it in.

"Well? Do you remember or not?" she said, patting him on the shoulder. "Mike?"

"I remember," he said. He shifted a little on his side, opened his eyes. He did not remember very well, he thought. What he did remember was very carefully combed hair and loud half-baked ideas about life and art, and he did not want to remember that.

"That was a long time ago, Nan," he said.

"We'd just got out of high school. You hadn't started to college," she said.

He waited, and then he raised up onto his arm and turned his head to look at her over his shoulder. "You about finished with that sandwich, Nan?" She was still sitting up in the bed.

She nodded and gave him the saucer.

"I'll turn off the light," he said.

"If you want," she said.

Then he pulled down into the bed again and extended his foot until it touched against hers. He lay still for a minute and then tried to relax.

"Mike, you're not asleep, are you?"

"No," he said. "Nothing like that."

"Well, don't go to sleep before me," she said. "I don't want to be awake by myself."

He didn't answer, but he inched a little closer to her on his side. When she put her arm over him and planted her hand flat against his chest, he took her fingers and squeezed them lightly. But in moments his hand dropped away to the bed, and he sighed.

"Mike? Honey? I wish you'd rub my legs. My legs hurt," she said.

"God," he said softly. "I was sound asleep."

"Well, I wish you'd rub my legs and talk to me. My shoulders hurt, too. But my legs especially."

He turned over and began rubbing her legs, then fell asleep again with his hand on her hip.

"Mike?"

"What is it, Nan? Tell me what it *is.*"

"I wish you'd rub me all over," she said, turning onto her back. "My legs and arms both hurt tonight." She raised her knees to make a tower with the covers.

He opened his eyes briefly in the dark and then shut them. "Growing pains, huh?

"O God, yes," she said, wiggling her toes, glad she had drawn him out. "When I was ten or eleven years old I was as big then as I am now. You should've seen me! I grew so fast in those days my legs and arms hurt me all the time. Didn't you?"

"Didn't I what?"

"Didn't you ever feel yourself growing?"

"Not that I remember," he said.

At last he raised up on his elbow, struck a match, and looked at the clock. He turned his pillow over to the cooler side and lay down again.

She said, "You're asleep, Mike. I wish you'd want to talk."

"All right," he said, not moving.

"Just hold me and get me off to sleep. I can't go to sleep," she said.

He turned over and put his arm over her shoulder as she turned onto her side to face the wall.

"Mike?"

He tapped his toes against her foot.

"Why don't you tell me all the things you like and the things you don't like."

"Don't know any right now," he said. "Tell me if you want," he said.

"If you promise to tell *me.* Is that a promise?"

He tapped her foot again.

"Well . . ." she said and turned onto her back, pleased. "I like good foods, steaks and hash-brown potatoes, things like that. I like good books and magazines, riding on trains at night, and those times I flew in an airplane." She stopped. "Of course none of this is in order of preference. I'd have to think about it if it was in the order of preference. But I like that, flying in airplanes. There's a moment as you leave the ground you feel whatever happens is all right." She put her leg across his ankle. "I like staying up late at night and then staying in bed the next morning. I wish we could do that all the time, not just once in a while. And I like sex. I like to be touched now and then when I'm not expecting it. I like going to movies and drinking beer with friends afterwards. I like to have friends. I like Janice Hendricks very much. I'd like to go dancing at least once a week. I'd like to have nice clothes all the time. I'd like to be able to buy the kids nice clothes every time they need it without having to wait. Laurie needs a new little outfit right now for Easter. And I'd like to get Gary a little suit or something. He's old enough. I'd like you to have a new suit, too. You really need a new suit more than he does. And I'd like us to have a place of our own. I'd like to stop moving around every year, or every other year. Most of all," she said, "I'd like us both just to live a good honest life without having to worry about money and bills and things like that. You're asleep," she said.

"I'm not," he said.

"I can't think of anything else. You go now. Tell me what you'd like."

"I don't know. Lots of things," he mumbled.

"Well, tell me. We're just talking, aren't we?"

"I wish you'd leave me alone, Nan." He turned over to his side of the bed again and let his arm rest off the edge. She turned too and pressed against him.

"Mike?"

"Jesus," he said. Then: "All right. Let me stretch my legs a minute, then I'll wake up."

In a while she said, "Mike? Are you asleep?" She shook his shoulder gently, but there was no response. She lay there for a time huddled against his body, trying to sleep. She lay quietly at first, without moving, crowded against him and taking only very small, very even breaths. But she could not sleep.

She tried not to listen to his breathing, but it began to make her uncomfortable. There was a sound coming from inside his nose when he breathed. She tried to regulate her breathing so that she could breathe in and out at the same rhythm he did. It was no use. The little sound in his nose made everything no use. There was a webby squeak in his chest too. She turned again and nestled her bottom against his, stretched her arm over to the edge and cautiously put her fingertips against the cold wall. The covers had pulled up at the foot of the bed, and she could feel a draft when she moved her legs. She heard two people coming up the stairs to the apartment next door. Someone gave a throaty laugh before opening the door. Then she heard a chair drag on the floor. She turned again. The toilet flushed next door, and then it flushed again. Again she turned, onto her back this time, and tried to relax. She remembered an article she'd once read in a magazine: If all the bones and muscles and joints in the body could join together in perfect relaxation, sleep would almost certainly come. She took a long breath, closed her eyes, and lay perfectly still, arms straight along her sides. She tried to relax. She tried to imagine her legs suspended, bathed in something gauze-like. She turned onto her stomach. She closed her eyes, then she opened them. She thought of the fingers of her hand lying curled on the sheet in front of her lips. She raised a finger and lowered it to the sheet. She touched the wedding band on her ring finger with her thumb. She turned onto her side and then onto her back again. And then she began to feel afraid, and in one unreasoning moment of longing she prayed to go to sleep.

Please, God, let me go to sleep.

She tried to sleep.

"Mike," she whispered.

There was no answer.

She heard one of the children turn over in the bed and bump against the wall in the next room. She listened and listened but there was no other sound. She laid her hand under her left breast and felt the beat of her heart rising into her fingers. She turned onto her stomach and began to cry, her head off the pillow, her mouth against the sheet. She cried. And then she climbed out over the foot of the bed.

She washed her hands and face in the bathroom. She brushed her teeth. She brushed her teeth and watched her face in the mirror. In the living room she turned up the heat. Then she sat down at the kitchen table, drawing her feet up underneath the nightgown. She cried again. She lit a cigaret from the pack on the table. After a time she walked back to the bedroom and got her robe.

She looked in on the children. She pulled the covers up over her son's shoulders. She went back to the living room and sat in the big chair. She paged through a magazine and tried to read. She gazed at the photographs and then she tried to read again. Now and then a car went by on the street outside and she looked up. As each car passed she waited, listening. And then she looked down at the magazine again. There was a stack of magazines in the rack by the big chair. She paged through them all.

When it began to be light outside she got up. She walked to the window. The cloudless sky over the hills was beginning to turn white. The trees and the row of two-story apartment houses across the street were beginning to take shape as she watched. The sky grew whiter, the light expanding rapidly up from behind the hills. Except for the times she had been up with one or another of the children (which she did not count because she had never looked outside, only hurried back to bed or to the kitchen), she had seen few sunrises in her life and those when she was little. She knew that none of them had been like this. Not in pictures she had seen nor in any book she had read had she learned a sunrise was so terrible as this.

She waited and then she moved over to the door and turned the lock and stepped out onto the porch. She closed the robe at her throat. The air was wet and cold. By stages things were becoming very visible. She let her eyes see everything until they fastened on the red winking light atop the radio tower atop the opposite hill.

She went through the dim apartment, back into the bedroom. He was knotted up in the center of the bed, the covers bunched over his shoulders, his head half under the pillow. He looked desperate in his heavy sleep, his arm flung out across her side of the bed, his jaws clenched. As she looked, the room grew very light and the pale sheets whitened grossly before her eyes.

She wet her lips with a sticking sound and got down on her knees. She put her hands out on the bed.

"God," she said. "God, will you help us, God?" she said.

QUESTIONS

1. What is the dominant style of this story? Is it colloquial or elevated in tone? Is the diction simple or elaborate? Is the sentence structure paratactic or hypotactic?
2. From the first two or three paragraphs what sort of marriage did you think the couple had? Happy or unhappy? Peaceful or conflicted? Close or distant? Was your reaction supported by the end of the story?
3. What sort of life does Nan want to have? What sort of life does she have?
4. What does Mike want? Does he get it?
5. Why can't Nan sleep?
6. Why does she pray to God? What kind of help do you think Nan wants?

HARRIET DOERR

PARTS OF SPEECH

A literary career can begin at any age. Harriet Doerr (b. 1910) published her first novel Stones of Ibarra *when she was seventy-three years old. The novel won her an American Book Award and a National Book Critics Circle Award.*

During her third Mexican autumn, when there was still a nuns' school in Ibarra, Sara walked through the plaza and along the alameda every Thursday to take Spanish lessons from Madre Petra. A few years later, accredited government teachers would supplant the nuns, and a new cura would pasture his cows in the convent patios and store his fodder in the classrooms. After that, there was no school where the children of Ibarra could learn both to spell their names and understand religion.

While Richard spoke more and more fluently in the accents of the miners who worked with him, Sara continued to speak incorrectly and without embarrassment her own flawed version of the language. When at last she noticed the grammatical precision of Mexican children barely able to walk, when she heard them utter their first word, "Mamá," and follow it soon after with the subjunctive, she arranged for weekly sessions with the madre.

To reach the nuns' school and its *sala,* narrow as a closet and cold as a cave, Sara picked her way between the ruts of a wagon road to the edge of the village. Once there, she had to pass two dozen adobe houses whose doorsteps lined the ditches as close as park benches bordering promenades. From behind fences of organ cactus patched with tangles of thorns, the family watchdogs ran out to bark. On the morning of her first lesson many housewives, unprepared, failed to reach their doors in time to observe her. But every Thursday after that they were waiting on their thresholds at eleven o'clock to watch her pass in one direction and again at twelve to see her return by the other. At each separate house, greetings were exchanged.

As a result of this, Sara said *"Buenos días"* twenty-four times on her way to school and *"Buenas tardes"* twenty-four times on her way home.

Madre Petra was seventy years old and had rheumatism. She walked with a cane. After inquiring for Richard and hearing Sara's quick answer, "He is well," the nun explained the parts of speech.

"These are nouns, señora." The madre pointed at the page with her left hand, from which the third and fourth fingers were missing. An accident with a door, Sara thought, or a windowpane.

"These are the verbs," said Madre Petra. "This is a list of possessive pronouns." Then she read examples of them all as if in English there were no such things.

The two women sat on stiff chairs at a blue table under pictures of the Sacred Heart, the Virgin of Guadalupe, and the pope. Sara, even at midday, was buttoned into a sweater. The nun wore a plain black dress and flat black shoes. A square of black cotton covered her head. Gone were the starched white wimple and bib, torn loose by the constitutional reforms of 1857, snatched off by the Revolution of 1910. Sara made slow sentences.

"My house is one kilometer from your school. Our well is dry. A burro brings our water from the Drunk Man's Spring."

"This water you and your señor boil and drink."

"No, it is too muddy. We drive to Loreto to buy bottles of pure water and tanks of butane gas. The water from the spring is for the bougainvillea and the Castile rose." Sara averted her eyes from the nun's maimed hand. "Loreto is a town so new it has no history, it has no trees. Have you been there?"

"Please write a sentence using the preterit tense," said the madre, and Sara put down in her notebook, The father of my husband was born in Ibarra and lived here as a boy.

Outside the single window a peach tree, still in October leaf, insulated a small patio and the *sala* itself from warmth. Under her scarf the nun's eyes gazed serenely out of her creased face, two stillnesses at the center of a hurricane.

"Where were you born?" asked Sara.

"For your next lesson please write a paragraph on an event of the coming week," said the nun.

As simply as this, without method or rules, the line of skirmish was drawn between the two women, one resolved to close off the past, the other to reject the future.

It was noon and the children dismissed by the mother superior had gathered to form a frieze at the window. Whole classes crowded at the entrance to watch the American woman leave, and the boldest among them followed her as far as the plaza. A few told her their names. Most of the rest clasped their homework to their chests in silence. But there were one or two who for no reason burst into such sudden laughter that they stumbled and fell down on the road.

By the end of a month Sara had written paragraphs about the explosion of the water heater and the strangling of the drains by pepper-tree roots. She read her compositions to the nun.

Madre Petra made corrections. "Your house, as well as the copper mine, suffered from disuse during the years since your husband's family left Ibarra."

Sara stared through the window at the peach tree which interfered with daylight as effectively as a palm-thatched roof. "But this house," she began. "The one Richard's grandfather built," and she tried to find words. "The walls and floors of it," she began again, and wanted to say, Richard scarcely sees their cracks and splinters. She was at a loss to explain. "And this town," she went on, and sensed its desolate, flat, earth-colored presence behind her. "Ibarra," she said, and stopped. She had wanted to say, If my husband could choose any place to live on the face of the globe, this is where he would put his finger.

"Let us turn to irregular verbs," said Madre Petra. "Please conjugate the verb, to know."

"Sé," said Sara. Then she said, *"No sé."*

Later the same morning she interrupted a discussion of geography to ask, for the second time, "In what part of the country were you born?"

The madre hesitated. "On an hacienda."

"Which one?"

"The hacienda called Cinco Cerros." And, in case she had implied wealth of her own, added, "My father was a groom in the stables."

"And were there actually five hills?"

"Señora, you must try to roll your *r*'s," said the nun.

That evening Sara told Richard that the nun was born on an hacienda between five hills, and each one named for a bird. So that there were the Eagle, the Dove, the Vulture, and the Quail, and one more, the Lark. The original owner, who was granted the land from the king of Spain, believed the names would bring the birds. But of them all only the vulture flew over the hills.

Richard listened to all this. "You've learned more words," he said.

"Is it possible to visit the hacienda?" Sara asked the madre at her next lesson.

"The hacienda perished with the family who owned it."

"But the five hills, where are they?"

Madre Petra closed her notebook. "Until next Thursday," she said.

* * *

"The Spaniard and his descendants lie twice buried, in the ground and under their fallen walls," Sara told Richard that night in the kitchen. He measured rum into two glasses and filled them with ice.

"Twice buried," he repeated. "Fallen walls." He sat on the kitchen table and handed his wife a glass. "The madre's a poet," he said. *"Salud."*

Week by week, between the study of accents and adverbial clauses, the indicative and conditional tenses, between diminutives and *ísimos,* Sara pried at the doors the madre had locked behind her. At the end of three months, in December, she pried one open.

When she asked if the hacienda workers were allowed holidays, the nun looked up from the page she was correcting and said, "Yes. There was a particular celebration every year, though I did not see the first one. I happened to be born the same day as the hacienda owner's only son. The fiesta that took place then was described to me so often I used to think I remembered it." She returned Sara's notebook and, to her pupil's surprise, went on. "Because of a coincidence all my birthdays were observed with fireworks and songs meant for someone else. Until the revolutionaries came." Then she found a list of abstract nouns and the lesson continued.

Sara believed there was more to be told. Details had been omitted. What of the flags and the tissue-paper garlands, the tuberoses on the chapel altar? Band music that shook ripe figs from trees?

Later on she described these things to her husband. "The *hacendado* himself hung a cedar wreath around the coat of arms carved above his door. The *mayordomo* fired off a thousand rockets between one morning and the next."

Richard examined her face. "Are you sure this is what Madre Petra told you?"

Sara thought of the convent *sala,* its sparse furnishings, the nun's seamed face, her crippled hand.

"It's what I heard her say."

As the lessons progressed Sara became uneasily aware of the erosion of areas she herself had sealed off. Within these guarded places were hidden all matters connected with Richard's health, and with the counting off of days and the sharpening of fear. When she spoke again of a trip to Loreto, the madre said, "It must be troublesome to drive so far simply to procure drinking water and gas." Without thinking, Sara answered, "This time I went alone. To place a telephone call." She was astonished to hear herself go on. "To a doctor in the United States."

Madre Petra was concerned. "Have you been ill?"

"No." Then, instead of suggesting, as the nun would in her place, Let us review the idioms, Sara recklessly continued. "I called about my husband."

"Is the senor ill?"

"No," said Sara. "He is working as usual at the mine. But last week he had an infection and a fever."

"You do not trust the doctors in Concepción to care for don Ricardo."

"They are excellent and highly trained. But the North American doctor is a specialist." And she almost added, impelled by her familiarity with the words, A specialist in diseases of the blood. *Enfermedades de la sangre,* she translated to herself.

"I will pray for him," said the madre.

Sara protested. "But he is well now." Through an open classroom door she heard the voices of children reciting multiplication tables in unison.

"Did the *hacendado's* son like to ride?" she suddenly asked.

The nun was caught by surprise. "Yes. From the moment the child Alejandro was first handed up to his father, Captain Velasco de Aragón, and the two rode down the avenue to the gates." The madre was quick to forestall further questions. "Señora, those years belonged to another life. The old images have faded, as God intended."

* * *

But on her way home Sara sketched in new outlines and filled the spaces with primary colors. At dinner she described the child's first ride to Richard. She said that when the captain's son was still an infant he rode in his father's arm through plantations of corn and alfalfa, through pastures where humped cattle buried their heads in grass, and up to the bullring. Here the father lifted his son to watch the apprentices wave red rags at the yearlings. At the house, servants collected on the steps to see for themselves if it was a braver child that returned than the one who had started out.

Richard tried to break in.

"No, let me tell you." Sara paused for the words she needed. "When the boy was six, he rode every day on his pony with the groom, Madre Petra's father. From the tops of the hills named for birds he looked out over the twenty thousand *hectáreas* of land and the house, built like a pink stone fortress, that would be his. He saw Indians clearing the plain, watched them chop cactus and walk barefoot through the spines."

Richard's hand was on her arm to stop her.

"But wait," she said. "When they returned to the house, the groom lifted the child down to his mother. 'What did you see?' she asked. And the boy said, 'Two rabbits and one iguana.' "

Richard stared. "Is that what the madre told you? In those words?"

"Almost," she said.

They had finished their fruit and their wine. Sara pulled Richard back as he started to leave the table, but she confessed to no fabrication. She simply held him there.

"Are you all right?"
"Yes," he said. "Why?"

By March and the twentieth lesson Sara had found out that Madre Petra lost two fingers of her hand when she was thrown from a horse.
"Did you ride much?"
"Only rarely, behind the stables."
"How old were you when the accident occurred?"
"Eighteen years. Señora, please give an example of the subjunctive used in a phrase contrary to fact."
"If it were still winter, the tree would not have flowered." Both women looked outside where a fading mat of petals covered the space between the walls.
"The haciendas were no better than feudal estates," said Sara. "It was time for a revolution."
"We in religion do not discuss the politics of Mexico," said the nun. "Is your husband in good health?"
"Naturally," said Sara. She did not say, Three more years remain of the time the doctor promised.

That night she told Richard, "As a girl Madre Petra helped her father exercise the horses. She rode sidesaddle in a long green skirt and embroidered blouse. She wore a man's sombrero."
"How do you know?" Richard sounded impatient.
They were sitting on the porch under Orion and a sky of other stars. When there was no answer, Richard went on. "Even assuming some of it's true, the rest is your invention."
His annoyance was clear. Sara stretched her hand toward him.
"The madre asked how you were."
"Did you tell her?" said Richard.

Sara studied with Madre Petra for ten months, her lessons interrupted twice by vacation weeks and twice by visits to the North American doctor. In Morelia, Michoacán, where the vacations were spent, streams rushed down hillsides and wild orchids grew from trees.
"Morelia is a city of carved wood and stone," she told the nun. "In spring the streets turn purple with jacarandas. For each rainstorm we have here, there are five in Morelia."
"Then, thanks to God, here in Ibarra we are permitted more sun."
Sara thought of reservoirs drying in from the edge and street dogs panting with thirst. "The animals," she said, and had started to speak of their plight when a new idea came to her.
"Perhaps your accident happened when one of the captain's hunting dogs frightened your horse."
"No," said the madre. "Not a dog."

"Were you alone? With no one to help you?"

"I was not alone." The nun looked from the *sala* window into the curling summer foliage of the peach tree, which had already been stripped of its hard pale fruit. "Is the North American doctor satisfied with don Ricardo's recovery from his recent infection?" asked the madre.

In the second before she answered the nun's question Sara had time to travel two thousand miles and enter the hematologist's office, time to sit for half an hour with the silent relatives of other patients. When Richard emerged from the laboratory rolling down his left sleeve, he held a slip of paper in his hand. Outside the office he and Sara read the report. "Only 22,000," they said of the white count. Or, on another occasion, "58,000. But there's the new medication."

Resuming her place in the convent *sala* after this second's lapse, Sara answered the nun. "Yes, he is," she said. "The doctor is quite satisfied."

She told her husband at dinner it was not a dog that had caused the madre's horse to shy. Therefore it was a rattlesnake or a coyote. The girl Petra was thrown, not in the exercise ring behind the stables, but somewhere out on the plain that stretched to the five hills.

"I see," said Richard.

"She was not alone at the time," his wife went on. "Eighteen years old and beautiful as the Malinche of Cortés. Her father saw to it that none of the laborers' sons approached her. He broke the nose of one and loosened the teeth of another."

"That's what the madre told you," said Richard. He pushed back his chair.

"Listen," she said. "The only son of Captain Velasco de Aragón was a boy Petra's father couldn't hit." Sara watched a candle burn bright, dim, then bright again. "This is what happened." And she explained to Richard that on the day of the accident a horse was saddled and ready to mount when the *hacendado's* son sent the groom off for a riding crop. When Petra's father returned, the horse was gone, also his daughter, also the captain's son.

"You heard this from the nun." His voice had hardened.

Sara leaned toward him across the table. "But surely you can see that this is how it must have been."

Richard stood up. His eyes had turned marine blue and the old scar across his cheek stood out white against his skin.

Sara was late for her next lesson and half ran the kilometer between her house and the school. She stumbled into ditches and slid on gravel, and finally tripped over the root of a stump and fell to her hands and knees. Her notebook and dictionary lay open in the dirt, exposing their rules and definitions to a red flycatcher in passage from a roof to a huisache tree.

From where he lay against the threshold, Remedios Acosta's blind old dog, El Tigre, lifted his head to listen. Remedios herself stepped from her dooryard to the road. "What a barbarity," she said. "Look at your torn skirt. Look at your scraped palms."

Five minutes later, sitting discomposed and grimy in the habitual twilight of the *sala,* Sara told the nun that the lesson after this one must be her last.

"So you believe you understand the language and its irregularities," said the madre. She laid both her hands with their eight fingers on the table as if it were a trunk she had packed and locked.

"You have taught me the usages most important for communication." Sara noticed that the leaves of the peach tree were powdered with the dust of June. "I must stop because during the next weeks visitors are coming, geologists and engineers."

"And when will you travel next across the frontier?"

"Not for several months." And once again Sara removed herself to the doctor's waiting room two thousand miles away and watched Richard come out of the laboratory rolling down his sleeve.

"Don Ricardo is well then," said the nun.

Sara listened for a child's recitation from a classroom but the doors were closed. "On the hacienda, when you were a girl, did you ever ride as far as the hills?"

"The horses were for the pleasure of the *hacendado's* family."

"Was the captain's son a good rider?"

"I used to see him on his buckskin," the nun began. Then she stopped and said only, "Yes. Both were fine horsemen, the captain and his son."

"Did you ever ride the buckskin?"

"Señora, it is as difficult to recapture the past as it is to prefigure the future."

At eleven o'clock that night the Evertons were reading in bed. Sara closed her book on one finger and said, "Now I have found out everything."

"Good," said Richard, without looking up.

"About the madre and the *hacendado's* son."

Richard laid his open book, pages down, on the blanket. He said, "I see."

"The day the groom discovered the buckskin horse and both of them gone was in July and hot. Mirage pools formed and dissolved on the plain." Sara said that Alejandro, as he rode off, had pulled Petra up in front of him and that her skirt whipped back like a green flag against his leg. Her hair came loose, her hat blew off, and the groom's daughter held tight to the captain's son until they reached the farthest hill, the one where the lark was never seen. Under an oak behind this hill Alejandro and Petra lay together until evening.

Richard made no comment.

"All one afternoon they lay there," said Sara.

When Richard spoke, there was something unfamiliar in his tone, an edge of outrage. "It's unthinkable that the madre told you this," he said. "Either in these words or any others."

"But let me tell you." Sara sat straight up and faced him. "It was on their way back to the stables that a coyote broke out of the brush like a running gray mist and crossed in front of them. The buckskin shied and they were thrown. Alejandro released the reins, but Petra couldn't let go. That's how she lost two fingers."

Richard turned away from her. He said, "I'm married to a clairvoyant," and picked up his book. They read for half an hour without speaking, and both at the same time put out their separate lamps.

For five minutes they lay silent in the dark. Then Richard spoke. "Do you believe the doctor will find a cure for me?"

Sara drew a long, careful breath. "He might."

"Don't count on it," said Richard. He turned and reached for her. "Please don't count on it."

On the Thursday of her last lesson Sara cut a sprig of mint and a rose from her garden and tied them with a twist of purple string for the nun. At each house she passed that morning, the woman sitting at the door or sweeping the empty dirt in front of it said, "Wait." Then each of them, understanding the flowers were for the madre, picked a nasturtium or a lily from her row of pots and thrust it out to Sara. There were so many of these offerings that when she entered the *sala* and presented them to Madre Petra they seemed to kindle in her hand.

Sara read her homework, a paragraph describing preparations for the visitors. At the nun's request, she composed a sentence including both the perfect and imperfect tenses. "While I was driving to Loreto yesterday, a bird flew into my windshield and was killed."

"You have had to telephone again from Loreto," said the madre.

Sara picked up a fiery geranium, considered it, and put it down. "When did the revolutionary armies seize the captain's house?"

"Only a few days after my accident. My hand was still bandaged."

"Couldn't the hacienda protect itself behind its own walls with its own guns?"

"Señora, I remember this. That when the first rebel shot was fired, the Indians who had worked whole lifetimes for a sack of corn and one pesa a week ran in from the fields waving pitchforks and hoes. Side by side with the insurgent cavalry they attacked the house of Velasco de Aragón."

"And the captain's son, was he saved?"

But the madre only said, "That same day the hacienda priest, whose parish was about to be stripped from him, took me to the nuns in the provincial capital. It was there, señora, more than fifty years ago, that I learned the rules of grammar I have been teaching you."

Outside the *sala* the peach tree scattered down its wilted leaves. Inside the room the two women seemed to have nothing more to say. The silver ringing of the mother superior's bell announced noon, and half a minute later the window was fringed with children's faces.

Madre Petra paused at the *sala* door. "I prayed for your husband in our chapel this morning. For his lasting good health."

"You are kind," said Sara. But she was not grateful. She was angry. She considered the nun's prayers an intrusion, a threat to the act of will she herself daily performed on Richard's behalf. Remote as from another planet, she heard her own voice stiffly thank the madre for the lessons, her time, her patience.

As Sara walked away from the school with the second and third grades trailing behind, the nun called after her. "Review the idioms with your husband. Practice the parts of speech."

By the time the last child had dropped from the procession and the last "*Adiós*" been spoken, Sara's fury had subsided.

But no more than halfway home here was Remedios Acosta at the roadside, holding out a glass jar. It was filled with a cloudy liquid and rich beads of fat. Floating in it was a chicken's foot, crusted with scales.

"Broth for don Ricardo," said Remedios. "To prevent another attack of grippe."

Sara acknowledged the jar as she had the madre's prayers, in a flat tone that was not hers. And to the same extent that she rejected the prayers, she rejected the broth.

Beyond the edge of the village and as if in answer to her dilemma she encountered Remedios's blind dog, El Tigre, rubbing his back against the rough bark of a tree. When she spoke to him, he turned slow, white-filmed eyes in her direction. But she called his name until he followed her behind a wall of rubble. Here she opened the jar. The dog lapped ravenously at its contents, but in the end she had to spill the liquid out and reach in with her fingers for the hen's foot. El Tigre swallowed it with a single contortion of his throat and his tail wagged of its own accord.

"Now you will see again," she told him, and his the jar under some broken adobes.

She had passed the water carrier and his burro at the Drunk Man's Spring and almost reached the corner of her own high wall when she began to narrate to herself the details of the storming of the hacienda. As though Madre Petra had described it all, Sara knew that five hundred shouting insurgents had galloped in, half of them bareback. Within ten minutes they had killed the guards, two house servants, and an Indian *peón* who crossed the line of fire as he rushed from the threshing room to join the revolution.

The *hácendado,* Captain Velasco de Aragón, was disarmed at his iron-grilled outer door. From here he witnessed the ravaging of his house and the liberation of his serfs. He saw his mother's portrait slashed and bottles from his wine cellar broken open on the keyboard of the Bechstein piano. After the rebels had drunk, they handed the bottles to the Indians, who washed the dirt from their tongues and the grit from their throats and for the first time laid their hands on cut velvet and set their feet on tapestried rugs.

Velasco de Aragón, held at gunpoint, looked on as the ragtag troops led his horses, tossing and dancing, from the stables. The groom, as he had on occasions of house parties, carried out silver-trimmed saddles, two at a time. Alejandro had come to his father's side to watch the new masters mount.

When at last the buckskin was brought to be saddled, the captain's son stepped forward. He still believed his word had power. He shouted, "Stop!" A dozen pistols took aim in warning. Alejandro, as if he had inherited immunity from his ancestors, ignored them. "Get back," ordered the soldiers of the people's army. He advanced in spite of them and they shot him.

At this, the captain, too, disobeyed commands and ran out to his son. Because of his own obstinacy, he also was killed. Hours later, when the girl Petra was taken away by the priest, the two still lay not far apart on ground that had blackened with their blood.

By now Sara had arrived at her gates. Between them and her front door she confronted and stripped off illusion. The scene she just created may have revealed itself as myth. Or it may have been that for the first time, having found herself too occupied before, she noticed how a month's drought had reduced the countryside. Up and down the face of the hill, goats cropped dry stems and thorns. The arroyo had run dry. Long after a truck passed on the road, dust hung in the hot, still air.

She would say no more to Richard of the hacienda's pink bastions and its hopeless fields and paths. And, together with one fantasy, she renounced another.

Until this moment she had refused to consider the sort of future that included hospital rooms and nurses, that threatened emergencies and an ambulance. She had denied a whole vocabulary of words: radiation, transfusion, hemorrhage. Until today she had convinced herself Richard might be spared them all.

Standing here at noon on the long covered porch, with her lists of double negatives and dependent clauses, she relinquished her right to have her way. None of it would happen as she had willed it. The magic pill would not be found. Richard would not recover.

And she knew it was unlikely that some windless morning or brilliant afternoon he would simply get up from the desk or come in from the road, lie down on the window seat, the bench, or the bed, and without even closing his eyes say, "Now."

QUESTIONS

1. The narrator describes that a "line of skirmish was drawn between the two women." What is the struggle between them about?
2. Sara recounts to Richard what Madre Petra said about birthday celebrations. Richard asks Sara, "Are you sure that is what Madre Petra told you." Sara replies, "It's what I heard her say." What is the difference between Richard's question and Sara's answer? Is Sara a reliable narrator of Madre Petra's life?
3. How do the two women both reveal and conceal their secrets? How does Sara try to reconstruct the Madre's past? How does the nun try to understand don Ricardo's future?
4. Has Madre Petra taught Sara more than the Spanish language? Is learning a language just learning grammar and vocabulary? Are there other things involved in learning a language?
5. Why can Sara accept at last her husband's forthcoming death?

KATHERINE ANNE PORTER

THE JILTING OF GRANNY WEATHERALL

Katherine Anne Porter (1890–1980) was a scrupulous artist who published relatively little in her long career. Her one long work of fiction Ship of Fools *won the Pulitzer Prize. She is remembered mostly for her short fiction and its remarkable style—dense, intense, lyric and penetrating. Her major collections include* Flowering Judas, Pale Horse, Pale Rider *and* A Defense of Circe.

She flicked her wrist neatly out of Doctor Harry's pudgy careful fingers and pulled the sheet up to her chin. The brat ought to be in knee breeches. Doctoring around the country with spectacles on his nose! "Get along now, take your schoolbooks and go. There's nothing wrong with me."

Doctor Harry spread a warm paw like a cushion on her forehead where the forked green vein danced and made her eyelids twitch. "Now, now, be a good girl, and we'll have you up in no time."

"That's no way to speak to a woman nearly eighty years old just because she's down. I'd have you respect your elders, young man."

"Well, Missy, excuse me." Doctor Harry patted her cheek. "But I've got to warn you, haven't I? You're a marvel, but you must be careful or you're going to be good and sorry."

"Don't tell me what I'm going to be. I'm on my feet now, morally speaking. It's Cornelia. I had to go to bed to get rid of her."

Her bones felt loose, and floated around in her skin, and Doctor Harry floated like a balloon around the foot of the bed. He floated and pulled down his waistcoat and swung his glasses on a cord. "Well, stay where you are, it certainly can't hurt you."

"Get along and doctor your sick," said Granny Weatherall. "Leave a well woman alone. I'll call for you when I want you. . . . Where were you forty years ago when I pulled through milk-leg[1] and double pneumonia? You weren't even born. Don't let Cornelia lead you on," she shouted, because Doctor Harry appeared to float up the ceiling and out. "I pay my own bills, and I don't throw my money away on nonsense!"

She meant to wave good-by, but it was too much trouble. Her eyes closed of themselves, it was like a dark curtain drawn around the bed. The pillow rose and floated under her, pleasant as a hammock in a light wind. She listened to the leaves rustling outside the window. No, somebody was swishing newspapers: no, Cornelia and Doctor Harry were whispering together. She leaped broad awake, thinking they whispered in her ear.

"She was never like this, *never* like this!" "Well, what can we expect?" "Yes, eighty years old. . . ."

Well, and what if she was? She still had ears. It was like Cornelia to whisper around doors. She always kept things secret in such a public way. She was always being tactful and kind. Cornelia was dutiful; that was the trouble with her. Dutiful and good: "So good and dutiful," said Granny, "and I'd like to spank her." She saw herself spanking Cornelia and making a fine job of it.

"What'd you say, Mother?"

Granny felt her face tying up in hard knots.

"Can't a body think, I'd like to know?"

"I thought you might want something."

"I do. I want a lot of things. First off, go away and don't whisper."

She lay and drowsed, hoping in her sleep that the children would keep out and let her rest a minute. It had been a long day. Not that she was tired. It was always pleasant to snatch a minute now and then. There was always so much to be done, let me see: tomorrow.

Tomorrow was far away and there was nothing to trouble about. Things were finished somehow when the time came; thank God there was always a little margin over for peace: then a person could spread out the plan of life and tuck in the edges orderly. It was good to have everything clean and folded away, with the hair brushes and tonic bottles sitting straight on the white embroidered linen: the day started without fuss and the pantry shelves laid out with rows of jelly glasses and brown jugs and white stone-china jars with blue whirligigs and words painted on them: coffee, tea, sugar, ginger, cinnamon, allspice: and the bronze

[1] Milk-leg is a swelling of the leg caused by childbirth.

clock with the lion on top nicely dusted off. The dust that lion could collect in twenty-four hours! The box in the attic with all those letters tied up, well, she'd have to go through that tomorrow. All those letters—George's letters and John's letters and her letters to them both—lying around for the children to find afterwards made her uneasy. Yes, that would be tomorrow's business. No use to let them know how silly she had been once.

While she was rummaging around she found death in her mind and it felt clammy and unfamiliar. She had spent so much time preparing for death there was no need for bringing it up again. Let it take care of itself now. When she was sixty she had felt very old, finished, and went around making farewell trips to see her children and grandchildren, with a secret in her mind: This is the very last of your mother, children! Then she made her will and came down with a long fever. That was all just a notion like a lot of other things, but it was lucky too, for she had once for all got over the idea of dying for a long time. Now she couldn't be worried. She hoped she had better sense now. Her father had lived to be one hundred and two years old and had drunk a noggin of strong hot toddy on his last birthday. He told the reporters it was his daily habit, and he owed his long life to that. He had made quite a scandal and was very pleased about it. She believed she'd just plague Cornelia a little.

"Cornelia! Cornelia!" No footsteps, but a sudden hand on her cheek. "Bless you, where have you been?"

"Here, Mother."

"Well, Cornelia, I want a noggin of hot toddy."

"Are you cold, darling?"

"I'm chilly, Cornelia. Lying in bed stops the circulation. I must have told you that a thousand times."

Well, she could just hear Cornelia telling her husband that Mother was getting a little childish and they'd have to humor her. The thing that most annoyed her was that Cornelia thought she was deaf, dumb, and blind. Little hasty glances and tiny gestures tossed around her and over her head saying, "Don't cross her, let her have her way, she's eighty years old," and she sitting there as if she lived in a thin glass cage. Sometimes Granny almost made up her mind to pack up and move back to her own house where nobody could remind her every minute that she was old. Wait, wait, Cornelia, till your own children whisper behind your back!

In her day she had kept a better house and had got more work done. She wasn't too old yet for Lydia to be driving eighty miles for advice when one of the children jumped the track, and Jimmy still dropped in and talked things over: "Now, Mammy, you've a good business head, I want to know what you think of this? . . ." Old. Cornelia couldn't change the furniture around without asking. Little things, little things!

They had been so sweet when they were little. Granny wished the old days were back again with the children young and everything to be done over. It had been a hard pull, but not too much for her. When she thought of all the food she had cooked, and all the clothes she had cut and sewed, and all the gardens she had made—well, the children showed it. There they were, made out of her, and they couldn't get away from that. Sometimes she wanted to see John again and point to them and say, Well, I didn't do so badly, did I? But that would have to wait. That was for tomorrow. She used to think of him as a man, but now all the children were older than their father, and he would be a child beside her if she saw him now. It seemed strange and there was something wrong in the idea. Why, he couldn't possibly recognize her. She had fenced in a hundred acres once, digging the post holes herself and clamping the wires with just a negro boy to help. That changed a woman. John would be looking for a young woman with the peaked Spanish comb in her hair and the painted fan. Digging post holes changed a woman. Riding country roads in the winter when women had their babies was another thing: sitting up nights with sick horses and sick negroes and sick children and hardly ever losing one. John, I hardly ever lost one of them! John would see that in a minute, that would be something he could understand, she wouldn't have to explain anything!

It made her feel like rolling up her sleeves and putting the whole place to rights again. No matter if Cornelia was determined to be everywhere at once, there were a great many things left undone on this place. She would start tomorrow and do them. It was good to be strong enough for everything, even if all you made melted and changed and slipped under your hands, so that by the time you finished you almost forgot what you were working for. What was it I set out to do? she asked herself intently, but she could not remember. A fog rose over the valley, she saw it marching across the creek swallowing the trees and moving up the hill like an army of ghosts. Soon it would be at the near edge of the orchard, and then it was time to go in and light the lamps. Come in, children, don't stay out in the night air.

Lighting the lamps had been beautiful. The children huddled up to her and breathed like little calves waiting at the bars in the twilight. Their eyes followed the match and watched the flame rise and settle in a blue curve, then they moved away from her. The lamp was lit, they didn't have to be scared and hang on to mother any more. Never, never, never more. God, for all my life I thank Thee. Without Thee, my God, I could never have done it. Hail, Mary, full of grace.

I want you to pick all the fruit this year and see that nothing is wasted. There's always someone who can use it. Don't let good things rot for want of using. You waste life when you waste good food. Don't let things get lost. It's bitter to lose things. Now, don't let me get to thinking, not when I am tired and taking a little nap before supper. . . .

The pillow rose about her shoulders and pressed against her heart and the memory was being squeezed out of it: oh, push down the pillow, somebody: it would smother her if she tried to hold it. Such a fresh breeze blowing and such a green day with no threats in it. But he had not come, just the same. What does a woman do when she has put on the white veil and set out the white cake for man and he doesn't come? She tried to remember. No, I swear he never harmed me but in that. He never harmed me but in that . . . and what if he did? There was the day, the day, but a whirl of dark smoke rose and covered it, crept up and over into the bright field where everything was planted so carefully in orderly rows. That was hell, she knew hell when she saw it. For sixty years she had prayed against remembering him and against losing her soul in the deep pit of hell, and now the two things were mingled in one and the thought of him was a smoky cloud from hell that moved and crept in her head when she had just got rid of Doctor Harry and was trying to rest a minute. Wounded vanity, Ellen, said a sharp voice in the top of her mind. Don't let your wounded vanity get the upper hand of you. Plenty of girls get jilted. You were jilted, weren't you? Then stand up to it. Her eyelids wavered and let in streamers of blue-gray light like tissue paper over her eyes. She must get up and pull the shades down or she'd never sleep. She was in bed again and the shades were not down. How could that happen? Better turn over, hide from the light, sleeping in the light gave you nightmares. "Mother, how do you feel now?" and a stinging wetness on her forehead. But I don't like having my face washed in cold water!

Hapsy? George? Lydia? Jimmy? No, Cornelia, and her features were swollen and full of little puddles. "They're coming, darling, they'll all be here soon." Go wash your face, child, you look funny.

Instead of obeying, Cornelia knelt down and put her head on the pillow. She seemed to be talking but there was no sound. "Well, are you tongue-tied? Whose birthday is it? Are you going to give a party?"

Cornelia's mouth moved urgently in strange shapes. "Don't do that, you bother me, daughter."

"Oh, no, Mother. Oh, no. . . ."

Nonsense. It was strange about children. They disputed your every word. "No what, Cornelia?"

"Here's Doctor Harry."

"I won't see that boy again. He just left five minutes ago."

"That was this morning, Mother. It's night now. Here's the nurse."

"This is Doctor Harry, Mrs. Weatherall. I never saw you look so young and happy!"

"Ah, I'll never be young again—but I'd be happy if they'd let me lie in peace and get rested."

She thought she spoke up loudly, but no one answered. A warm weight on her forehead, a warm bracelet on her wrist, and a breeze went on whispering, trying to tell her something. A shuffle of leaves in the everlasting hand of God. He blew on them and they danced and rattled. "Mother, don't mind, we're going to give you a little hypodermic." "Look here, daughter, how do ants get in this bed? I saw sugar ants yesterday." Did you send for Hapsy too?

It was Hapsy she really wanted. She had to go a long way back through a great many rooms to find Hapsy standing with a baby on her arm. She seemed to herself to be Hapsy also, and the baby on Hapsy's arm was Hapsy and himself and herself, all at once, and there was no surprise in the meeting. Then Hapsy melted from within and turned flimsy as gray gauze and the baby was a gauzy shadow, and Hapsy came up close and said, "I thought you'd never come," and looked at her very searchingly and said, "You haven't changed a bit!" They leaned forward to kiss, when Cornelia began whispering from a long way off, "Oh, is there anything you want to tell me? Is there anything I can do for you?"

Yes, she had changed her mind after sixty years and she would like to see George. I want you to find George. Find him and be sure to tell him I forgot him. I want him to know I had my husband just the same and my children and my house like any other woman. A good house too and a good husband that I loved and fine children out of him. Better than I hoped for even. Tell him I was given back everything he took away and more. Oh, no, oh, God, no, there was something else besides the house and the man and the children. Oh, surely they were not all? What was it? Something not given back. . . . Her breath crowded down under her ribs and grew into a monstrous frightening shape with cutting edges; it bored up into her head, and the agony was unbelievable: Yes, John, get the doctor now, no more talk, my time has come.

When this one was born it should be the last. The last. It should have been born first, for it was the one she had truly wanted. Everything came in good time. Nothing left out, left over. She was strong, in three days she would be as well as ever. Better. A woman needed milk in her to have her full health.

"Mother, do you hear me?"

"I've been telling you—"

"Mother, Father Connolly's here."

"I went to Holy Communion only last week. Tell him I'm not so sinful as all that."

"Father just wants to speak to you."

He could speak as much as he pleased. It was like him to drop in and inquire about her soul as if it were a teething baby, and then stay on for a cup of tea and a round of cards and gossip. He always had a funny story of some sort, usually about an Irishman who made his little mistakes and confessed them, and the point lay in some absurd thing he would blurt out in the confessional showing his struggles between native piety and original sin. Granny felt easy about her soul. Cornelia, where are your manners? Give Father Connolly a chair. She had her secret comfortable understanding with a few favorite saints who cleared a straight road to God for her. All as surely signed and sealed as the papers for the new Forty Acres. Forever . . . heirs and assigns forever. Since the day the wedding cake was not cut, but thrown out and wasted. The whole bottom dropped out of the world, and there she was blind and sweating with nothing under her feet and the walls falling away. His hand had caught her under the breast, she had not fallen, there was the freshly polished floor with the green rug on it, just as before. He had cursed like a sailor's parrot and said, "I'll kill him for you." Don't lay a hand on him, for my sake leave something to God. "Now, Ellen, you must believe what I tell you. . . ."

So there was nothing, nothing to worry about any more, except sometimes in the night one of the children screamed in a nightmare, and they both hustled out shaking and hunting for the matches and calling, "There, wait a minute, here we are!" John, get the doctor now, Hapsy's time has come. But there was Hapsy standing by the bed in a white cap. "Cornelia, tell Hapsy to take off her cap. I can't see her plain."

Her eyes opened very wide and the room stood out like a picture she had seen somewhere. Dark colors with the shadows rising towards the ceiling in long angles. The tall black dresser gleamed with nothing on it but John's picture, enlarged from a little one, with John's eyes very black when they should have been blue. You never saw him, so how do you know how he looked? But the man insisted the copy was perfect, it was very rich and handsome. For a picture, yes, but it's not my husband. The table by the bed had a linen cover and a candle and a crucifix. The light was blue from Cornelia's silk lampshades. No sort of light at all, just frippery. You had to live forty years with kerosene lamps to appreciate honest electricity. She felt very strong and she saw Doctor Harry with a rosy nimbus around him.

"You look like a saint, Doctor Harry, and I vow that's as near as you'll ever come to it."

"She's saying something."

"I heard you, Cornelia. What's all this carrying on?"

"Father Connolly's saying—"

Cornelia's voice staggered and bumped like a cart in a bad road. It rounded corners and turned back again and arrived nowhere. Granny stepped up in the cart very lightly and reached for the reins, but a man sat beside her and she knew him by his hands, driving the cart. She did not look in his face, for she knew without seeing, but looked instead down the road where the trees leaned over and bowed to each other and a thousand birds were singing a Mass. She felt like singing too, but she put her hand in the bosom of her dress and pulled out a rosary, and Father Connolly murmured Latin in a very solemn voice and tickled her feet. My God, will you stop that nonsense? I'm a married woman. What if he did run away and leave me to face the priest by myself? I found another a whole world better. I wouldn't have exchanged my husband for anybody except St. Michael himself, and you may tell him that for me with a thank you in the bargain.

Light flashed on her closed eyelids, and a deep roaring shook her. Cornelia, is that lightning? I hear thunder. There's going to be a storm. Close all the windows. Call the children in. . . ." Mother, here we are, all of us." "Is that you, Hapsy?" "Oh, no, I'm Lydia. We drove as fast as we could." Their faces drifted above her, drifted away. The rosary fell out of her hands and Lydia put it back. Jimmy tried to help, their hands fumbled together, and Granny closed two fingers around Jimmy's thumb. Beads wouldn't do, it must be something alive. She was so amazed her thoughts ran round and round. So, my dear Lord, this is my death and I wasn't even thinking about it. My children have come to see me die. But I can't, it's not time. Oh, I always hated surprises. I wanted to give Cornelia the amethyst set—Cornelia, you're to have the amethyst set, but Hapsy's to wear it when she wants, and, Doctor Harry, do shut up. Nobody sent for you. Oh my dear Lord, do wait a minute. I meant to do something about the Forty Acres, Jimmy doesn't need it and Lydia will later on, with that worthless husband of hers. I meant to finish the altar cloth and send six bottles of wine to Sister Borgia for her dyspepsia. I want to send six bottles of wine to Sister Borgia, Father Connolly, now don't let me forget.

Cornelia's voice made short turns and tilted over and crashed. "Oh, Mother, oh, Mother, oh, Mother. . . ."

"I'm not going, Cornelia. I'm taken by surprise. I can't go."

You'll see Hapsy again. What about her? "I thought you'd never come." Granny made a long journey outward, looking for Hapsy. What if I don't find her? What then? Her heart sank down and down, there was no bottom to death, she couldn't come to the end of it. The blue light from Cornelia's lampshade drew into a tiny point in the center of her brain, it flickered and winked like an eye, quietly it fluttered and dwindled. Granny lay curled down within herself, amazed and watchful, staring at the point of light that was herself; her body was now only a deeper mass of shadow in an endless darkness and this darkness would curl around the light and swallow it up. God, give a sign!

For the second time there was no sign. Again no bridegroom and the priest in the house. She could not remember any other sorrow because this grief wiped them all away. Oh, no, there's nothing more cruel than this—I'll never forgive it. She stretched herself with a deep breath and blew out the light.

QUESTIONS

1. What is the style of this story? Is the language colloquial or elevated? Is the tone comic, serious or both. Is the sentence structure paratactic or hypotactic? Are the sentences always grammatical?
2. Is the style appropriate to the story?
3. What kind of character is Granny Weatherall? Loving or distant? Independent or dependent? Happy or unhappy? Flexible or rigid? Approachable or inapproachable? Does the style reflect the character?
4. Who are John and George? Why does Granny want to see George?
5. Who is Hapsy? Why does Granny confuse herself with Hapsy?
6. Who is the bridegroom in the last paragraph? Is there both a literal and symbolic bridegroom for whom Granny is waiting? Why won't she forgive him?
7. Granny says, "I'm on my feet now, morally speaking." Is she?

KATHERINE ANNE PORTER

from THREE STATEMENTS ABOUT WRITING

Q. *Have you found it possible to make a living by writing the sort of thing you want to, and without the aid of such crutches as teaching and editorial work? Do you think there is any place in our present economic system for literature as a profession?*

No, there has not been a living in it, so far. The history of literature, musical composition, painting shows there has never been a living in art, except by flukes of fortune; by weight of long, cumulative reputation, or generosity of a patron; a prize, a subsidy, a commission of some kind; or (in the American style) anonymous and shamefaced hackwork; in the English style, a tradition of hackwork, openly acknowledged if deplored. The grand old English hack is a melancholy spectacle perhaps, but a figure not without dignity. He is a man who sticks by his trade, does the best he can with it on its own terms, and abides by the consequences of his choice, with a kind of confidence in his way of life that has some merit, certainly.

Literature as a profession? It *is* a profession, and the professional literary man is on his own as any other professional man is.

If you mean, is there any place in our present economic system for the practice of literature as a source of steady income and economic security, I should say, no. There never has been, in any system, any guarantee of economic security for the artist, unless he took a job and worked under orders as other men do for a steady living. In the arts, you simply cannot secure your bread and your freedom of action too. You cannot be a hostile critic of society and expect society to feed you regularly. The artist of the present day is demanding (I think childishly) that he be given, free, a great many irreconcilable rights and privileges. He wants as a right freedoms which the great spirits of all time have had to fight and often to die for. If he wants freedom, let him fight and die for it too, if he must, and not expect it to be handed to him on a silver plate.

Q. *Do you find, in retrospect, that your writing reveals any allegiance to any group, class, organization, region, religion, or system of thought, or do you conceive of it as mainly the expression of yourself as an individual?*

I find my writing reveals all sorts of sympathies and interests which I had not formulated exactly to myself; "the expression of myself as an individual" has never been my aim. My whole attempt has been to discover and understand human motives, human feelings, to make a distillation of what human relations and experiences my mind has been able to absorb. I have never known an uninteresting human being, and I have never known two alike; there are broad classifications and deep similarities, but I am interested in the thumbprint. I am passionately involved with these individuals who populate all these enormous migrations, calamities; who fight wars and furnish life for the future; these beings without which, one by one, all the "broad movements of history" could never take place. One by one—as they were born.

THINGS TO THINK ABOUT

1. What does Porter mean when she says "in the arts, you simply cannot secure your bread and your freedom of action too." In what ways are freedom and financial success opposed for the artist? Does Porter think the opposition is bad?
2. Porter distinguishes between the artist and the professional hack. According to Porter what is the difference? What is Porter's attitude toward the professional hack? Do you think hers is a fair distinction? Should there be such a distinction?
3. Many people suppose that the two main reasons authors write are (1) to make money, or (2) to express themselves. Does Porter write for money or for self-expression? Why does she write? Do her reasons surprise you? Do you think they are typical?

VLADIMIR NABOKOV

CLOUD, CASTLE, LAKE

Vladimir Nabokov (1899–1977) was a truly international writer. Born in St. Petersburg, Russia (now Leningrad), he left his homeland in 1919 to settle with his family in Germany. With the rise of Hitler, he next resided in France, and when that country too fell to the Nazis, he emigrated to the United States and became an American citizen in 1945. At the end of his life, he made his home in Switzerland.

Nabokov came from wealthy, socially prominent family. His father was a statesman, and he was taught English and French before he learned Russian. Later he was to write works in all three languages, and major works in Russian (Invitation to a Beheading) *and English* (Lolita, Pale Fire, *and* Pnin). *In addition he wrote plays, poetry, translations, critical works, and was a chess expert and an authority on butterflies, working as a research fellow during the forties at Harvard's Museum of Comparative Zoology.*

One of my representatives—a modest, mild bachelor, very efficient—happened to win a pleasure trip at a charity ball given by Russian refugees. That was in 1936 or 1937. The Berlin summer was in full flood (it was the second week of damp and cold, so that it was a pity to look at everything which had turned green in vain, and only the sparrows kept cheerful); he did not care to go anywhere, but when he tried to sell his ticket at the office of the Bureau of Pleasantrips he was told that to do so he would have to have special permission from the Ministry of Transportation; when he tried them, it turned out that first he would have to draw up a complicated petition at a notary's on stamped paper; and besides, a so-called "certificate of non-absence from the city for the summertime" had to be obtained from the police.

So he sighed a little, and decided to go. He borrowed an aluminum flask from friends, repaired his soles, bought a belt and a fancy-style flannel shirt—one of those cowardly things which shrink in the first wash. Incidentally, it was too large for that likable little man, his hair always neatly trimmed, his eyes so intelligent and kind. I cannot remember his name at the moment. I think it was Vasili Ivanovich.

He slept badly the night before the departure. And why? Because he had to get up unusually early, and hence took along into his dreams the delicate face of the watch ticking on his night table; but mainly because that very night, for no reason at all, he began to imagine that this trip, thrust upon him by a feminine Fate in a low-cut gown, this trip which he had accepted so reluctantly, would bring him some wonderful, tremulous happiness. This happiness would have something in common with his childhood, and with the excitement aroused in him by Russian lyrical poetry, and with some evening sky line once seen in a dream, and with that lady, another man's wife, whom he had hopelessly loved for seven years—but it would be even fuller and more significant than all that. And besides, he felt that the really good life must be oriented toward something or someone.

The morning was dull, but steam-warm and close, with an inner sun, and it was quite pleasant to rattle in a streetcar to the distant railway station where the gathering place was: several people, alas, were taking part in the excursion. Who would they be, these drowsy beings, drowsy as seem all creatures still unknown to us? By Window No. 6, at 7 A.M., as was indicated in the directions appended to the ticket, he saw them (they were already waiting; he had managed to be late by about three minutes).

A lanky blond young man in Tyrolese garb stood out at once. He was burned the color of a cockscomb, had huge brick-red knees with golden hairs, and his nose looked lacquered. He was the leader furnished by the Bureau, and as soon as the newcomer had joined the group (which consisted of four women and as many men) he led it off toward a train lurking behind other trains, carrying his monstrous knapsack with terrifying ease, and firmly clanking with his hobnailed boots.

Everyone found a place in an empty car, unmistakably third-class, and Vasili Ivanovich, having sat down by himself and put a peppermint into his mouth, opened a little volume of Tyutchev, whom he had long intended to reread; but he was requested to put the book aside and join the group. An elderly bespectacled post-office clerk, with skull, chin, and upper lip a bristly blue as if he had shaved off some extraordinarily luxuriant and tough growth especially for this trip, immediately announced that he had been to Russia and knew some Russian—for instance, *patzlui*—and, recalling philanderings in Tsaritsya, winked in such a manner that his fat wife sketched out in the air the outline of a backhand box on the ear. The company was getting noisy. Four employees of the same building firm were tossing each other heavyweight jokes: a middle-aged man, Schultz; a younger man, Schultz also, and two fidgety young women with big mouths and big rumps. The red-headed, rather burlesque widow in a sport skirt knew something too about Russia (the Riga beaches). There was also a dark young man by the name of Schramm, with lusterless eyes and a vague velvety vileness about his person and manners, who constantly switched the conversation to this or that attractive aspect of the excursion, and who gave the first signal for rapturous appreciation; he was, as it turned out later, a special stimulator from the Bureau of Pleasantrips.

The locomotive, working rapidly with its elbows, hurried through a pine forest, then—with relief—among fields. Only dimly realizing as yet all the absurdity and horror of the situation, and perhaps attempting to persuade himself that everything was very nice, Vasili Ivanovich contrived to enjoy the fleeting gifts of the road. And indeed, how enticing it all is, what charm the world acquires when it is wound up and moving like a merry-go-round! The sun crept toward a corner of the window and suddenly spilled over the yellow bench. The badly pressed shadow of the car sped madly along the grassy bank, where flowers blended into colored streaks. A crossing: a cyclist was waiting, one foot resting on the ground. Trees appeared in groups and singly, revolving coolly and blandly, displaying the latest fashions. The blue dampness of a ravine. A memory of love, disguised as a meadow. Wispy clouds—greyhounds of heaven.

We both, Vasili Ivanovich and I, have always been impressed by the anonymity of all the parts of a landscape, so dangerous for the soul, the impossibility of ever finding out where that path you see leads—

and look, what a tempting thicket! It happened that on a distant slope or in a gap in the trees there would appear and, as it were, stop for an instant, like air retained in the lungs, a spot so enchanting—a lawn, a terrace—such perfect expression of tender well-meaning beauty—that it seemed that if one could stop the train and go thither, forever, to you, my love . . . But a thousand beech trunks were already madly leaping by, whirling in a sizzling sun pool, and again the chance for happiness was gone.

At the stations, Vasili Ivanovich would look at the configuration of some entirely insignificant objects—a smear on the platform, a cherry stone, a cigarette butt—and would say to himself that never, never would he remember these three little things here in that particular interrelation, this pattern, which he now could see with such deathless precision; or again, looking at a group of children waiting for a train, he would try with all his might to single out at least one remarkable destiny—in the form of a violin or a crown, a propeller or a lyre—and would gaze until the whole party of village schoolboys appeared as on an old photograph, now reproduced with a little white cross above the face of the last boy on the right: the hero's childhood.

But one could look out of the window only by snatches. All had been given sheet music with verses from the Bureau:

Stop that worrying and moping,
Take a knotted stick and rise,
Come a-tramping in the open
With the good, the hearty guys!

Tramp your country's grass and stubble,
With the good, the hearty guys,
Kill the hermit and his trouble
And to hell with doubts and sighs!

In a paradise of heather
Where the field mouse screams and dies,
Let us march and sweat together
With the steel-and-leather guys!

This was to be sung in chorus: Vasili Ivanovich, who not only could not sing but could not even pronounce German words clearly, took advantage of the drowning roar of mingling voices and merely opened his mouth while swaying slightly, as if he were really singing—but the leader, at a sign from the subtle Schramm, suddenly stopped the general singing and, squinting askance at Vasili Ivanovich, demanded that he sing solo. Vasili Ivanovich cleared his throat, timidly began, and after a minute of solitary torment all joined in; but he did not dare thereafter to drop out.

He had with him his favorite cucumber from the Russian store, a loaf of bread, and three eggs. When evening came, and the low crimson sun entered wholly the soiled seasick car, stunned by its own din, all were invited to hand over their provisions, in order to divide them evenly—this was particularly easy, as all except Vasili Ivanovich had the same things. The cucumber amused everybody, was pronounced inedible, and was thrown out of the window. In view of the insufficiency of his contribution, Vasili Ivanovich got a smaller portion of sausage.

He was made to play cards. They pulled him about, questioned him, verified whether he could show the route of the trip on a map—in a word, all busied themselves with him, at first good-naturedly, then with malevolence, which grew with the approach of night. Both girls were called Greta; the redheaded widow somehow resembled the rooster-leader; Schramm, Schultz, and the other Schultz, the post-office clerk and his wife, all gradually melted together, merged together, forming one collective, wobbly, many-handed being, from which one could not escape. It pressed upon him from all sides. But suddenly at some station all climbed out, and it was already dark, although in the west there still hung a very long, very pink cloud, and farther along the track, with a soul-piercing light, the star of a lamp trembled through the slow smoke of the engine, and crickets chirped in the dark, and from somewhere there came the odor of jasmine and hay, my love.

They spent the night in a tumble-down inn. A mature bedbug is awful, but there is a certain grace in the motions of silky silverfish. The post-office clerk was separated from his wife, who was put with the widow; he was given to Vasili Ivanovich for the night. The two beds took up the whole room. Quilt on top, chamber pot below. The clerk said that somehow he did not feel sleepy, and began to talk of his Russian adventures, rather more circumstantially than in the train. He was a great bully of a man, thorough and obstinate, clad in long cotton drawers, with mother-of-pearl claws on his dirty toes, and bear's fur between fat breasts. A moth dashed about the ceiling, hobnobbing with its shadow. "In Tsaritsyn," the clerk was saying, "there are now three schools, a German, a Czech, and a Chinese one. At any rate, that is what my brother-in-law says; he went there to build tractors."

Next day, from early morning to five o'clock in the afternoon, they raised dust along a highway, which undulated from hill to hill; then they took a green road through a dense fir wood. Vasili Ivanovich, as the least burdened, was given an enormous round loaf of bread to carry under his arm. How I hate you, our daily! But still his precious, experienced eyes noted what was necessary. Against the background of fir-tree gloom a dry needle was hanging vertically on an invisible thread.

Again they piled into a train, and again the small partitionless car was empty. The other Schultz began to teach Vasili Ivanovich how to play the mandolin. There was much laughter. When they got tired of that, they thought up a capital game, which was supervised by Schramm.

It consisted of the following: the women would lie down on the benches they chose, under which the men were already hidden, and when from under one of the benches there would emerge a ruddy face with ears, or a big outspread hand, with a skirt-lifting curve of the fingers (which would provoke much squealing), then it would be revealed who was paired off with whom. Three times Vasili Ivanovich lay down in filthy darkness, and three times it turned out that there was no one on the bench when he crawled out from under. He was acknowledged the loser and was forced to eat a cigarette butt.

They spent the night on straw mattresses in a barn, and early in the morning set out again on foot. Firs, ravines, foamy streams. From the heat, from the songs which one had constantly to bawl, Vasili Ivanovich became so exhausted that during the midday halt he fell asleep at once, and awoke only when they began to slap at imaginary horseflies on him. But after another hour of marching, that very happiness of which he had once half dreamt was suddenly discovered.

It was a pure, blue lake, with an unusual expression of its water. In the middle, a large cloud was reflected in its entirety. On the other side, on a hill thickly covered with verdure (and the darker the verdure, the more poetic it is), towered, arising from dactyl to dactyl, an ancient black castle. Of course, there are plenty of such views in Central Europe, but just this one—in the inexpressible and unique harmoniousness of its three principal parts, in its smile, in some mysterious innocence it had, my love! my obedient one!—was something so unique, and so familiar, and so long-promised, and it so *understood* the beholder that Vasili Ivanovich even pressed his hand to his heart, as if to see whether his heart was there in order to give it away.

At some distance, Schramm, poking into the air with the leader's alpenstock, was calling the attention of the excursionists to something or other; they had settled themselves around on the grass in poses seen in amateur snapshots, while the leader sat on a stump, his behind to the lake, and was having a snack. Quietly, concealing himself in his own shadow, Vasili Ivanovich followed the shore, and came to a kind of inn. A dog still quite young greeted him; it crept on its belly, its jaws laughing, its tail fervently beating the ground. Vasili Ivanovich accompanied the dog into the house, a piebald two-storied dwelling with a winking window beneath a convex tiled eyelid; and he found the owner, a tall old man vaguely resembling a Russian war veteran, who spoke German so poorly and with such a soft drawl that Vasili Ivanovich changed to his own tongue, but the man understood as in a dream and continued in the language of his environment, his family.

Upstairs was a room for travelers. "You know, I shall take it for the rest of my life," Vasili Ivanovich is reported to have said as soon as he had entered it. The room itself had nothing remarkable about it. On the contrary, it was a most ordinary room, with a red floor, daisies daubed on the white walls, and a small mirror half filled with the yellow infusion of the reflected flowers—but from the window one could clearly see the lake with its cloud and its castle, in a motionless and perfect correlation of happiness. Without reasoning, without considering, only entirely surrendering to an attraction the truth of which consisted in its own strength, a strength which he had never experienced before, Vasili Ivanovich in one radiant second realized that here in this little room with that view, beautiful to the verge of tears, life would at last be what he had always wished it to be. What exactly it would be like, what would take place here, that of course he did not know, but all around him were help, promise, and consolation—so that there could not be any doubt that he must live here. In a moment he figured out how he would manage it so as not to have to return to Berlin again, how to get the few possessions that he had—books, the blue suit, her photograph. How simple it was turning out! As my representative, he was earning enough for the modest life of a refugee Russian.

"My friends," he cried, having run down again to the meadow by the shore, "my friends, good-by. I shall remain for good in that house over there. We can't travel together any longer. I shall go no farther. I am not going anywhere. Good-by!"

"How is that?" said the leader in a queer voice, after a short pause, during which the smile on the lips of Vasili Ivanovich slowly faded, while the people who had been sitting on the grass half rose and stared at him with stony eyes.

"But why?" he faltered. "It is here that . . ."

"Silence!" the post-office clerk suddenly bellowed with extraordinary force. "Come to your senses, you drunken swine!"

"Wait a moment, gentlemen," said the leader, and, having passed his tongue over his lips, he turned to Vasili Ivanovich.

"You probably have been drinking," he said quietly. "Or have gone out of your mind. You are taking a pleasure trip with us. Tomorrow, according to the appointed itinerary—look at your ticket—we are all returning to Berlin. There can be no question of anyone—in this case you—refusing to continue this communal journey. We were singing today a certain song—try and remember what it said. That's enough now! Come, children, we are going on."

"There will be beer at Ewald," said Schramm in a caressing voice. "Five hours by train. Hikes. A hunting lodge. Coal mines. Lots of interesting things."

"I shall complain," wailed Vasili Ivanovich. "Give me back my bag. I have the right to remain where I want. Oh, but this is nothing less than an invitation to a beheading"—he told me he cried when they seized him by the arms.

"If necessary we shall carry you," said the leader grimly, "but that is not likely to be pleasant. I am responsible for each of you, and shall bring back each of you, alive or dead."

Swept along a forest road as in a hideous fairy tale, squeezed, twisted, Vasili Ivanovich could not even turn around, and only felt how the radiance behind his back receded, fractured by trees, and then it was no longer there, and all around the dark firs fretted but could not interfere. As soon as everyone had got into the car and the train had pulled off, they began to beat him—they beat him a long time, and with a good deal of inventiveness. It occurred to them, among other things, to use a corkscrew on his palms; then on his feet. The post-office clerk, who had been to Russia, fashioned a knout out of a stick and a belt, and began to use it with devilish dexterity. Atta boy! The other men relied more on their iron heels, whereas the women were satisfied to pinch and slap. All had a wonderful time.

After returning to Berlin, he called on me, was much changed, sat down quietly, putting his hands on his knees, told his story; kept on repeating that he must resign his position, begged me to let him go, insisted that he could not continue, that he had not the strength to belong to mankind any longer. Of course, I let him go.

QUESTIONS

1. What is the setting of the story's opening? In what year is the story set? What country? Is anything of political or historical significance happening at that time? Does the story reflect those political or historical events?
2. Is there anything significant in the fact that two of the men are named Schultz and two of the women Greta? Is there any significance that everyone but Ivanovich brings the same meal on board the train?
3. The narrator tells us that Ivanovich's "precious, experienced eyes noted what was necessary." Yet what Ivanovich notices is "a dry needle . . . hanging vertically on an invisible thread." What is so important about this perception? Does this detail have any symbolic significance? Or is the narrator being ironic?
4. Why is Ivanovich so attracted to the house by the lake?
5. Why do his fellow travellers beat him when Ivanovich announces that he is not returning with them?
6. What is the style of the story? What is the diction of the story? What is the tone of the story?
7. Why do you suppose Nabokov has Ivanovich's employer tell the story and not Ivanovich himself?
8. "Cloud, Castle, Lake" was written in 1937. What political events were happening in Germany in 1937? In what way can the style itself be considered a political statement?

10
LITERARY JUDGMENTS

Judging anyone's work is always a hard task if we take the job seriously. Snap judgments formed by first impressions, long held prejudices or sheer intuition are not reliable guides to lasting excellence. The best literary judgments emerge only after many years of consideration and reading, and even then the best critics are limited. The history of literature is filled with examples of writers who were ignored until long after their deaths and of once-praised authors whose fame and reputation quickly faded.

Why then make judgments at all? One reason is that with the ever-increasing number of published books and stories, a reader could not finish everything. We must decide what to read, and that requires making judgments and listening to others whose judgments we trust. But there are other, more important reasons. One of the ways we improve ourselves as individuals is to have models of excellence in front of us. The person who finds everything of equal value will have nothing to strive for, to cherish or to value, and no way to make improvements. Judgments are necessary for growth, and one of the signs of maturity is the wisdom of our judgments.

In determining the success of a literary work, the reader must examine many factors. (1) How well does the story fulfill the requirements of its genre or literary type? (2) How well does it serve its intended or implied readers? (3) How well does the story serve the writer's purpose insofar as we can determine that purpose?

THE DEMANDS OF FORM

When people go to see a comedy they have certain expectations. They expect to laugh or, at the very least, be amused. The audience at a horror film has very different expectations. It expects to be filled with fear and terror, which can be pleasurable experiences in the proper setting. These theatrical or literary types or *genres* evoke certain audience expectations, and a work that fails to satisfy the expectations or provide compensating pleasures will disappoint its audience. When readers come to a short story, they expect—depending on the story's genre—certain elements of style and content. A good author recognizes those reader expectations and either satisfies them or provides a suitable alternative. For example, Mel Brook's film *Young Frankenstein* does not fill us with horror, but it does make us laugh.

Yet it is important not to have notions that are too rigid about what a story should contain. If you are open to only one type of story, you may miss tales that are equally as pleasurable, if not more pleasurable. Some people only like stories with happy endings, or clearly resolved endings. They cheat themselves of the enjoyment of the tragic and the ambiguous. Rigid and limited expectations lead to rigid and limited judgments.

PLAYING WITH AUDIENCE EXPECTATIONS

Writers often rebel against the rigid expectations of readers. Experimental writers such as Robbe-Grillet in France and John Barth in the United States have written stories that completely abandon our conventional expectations of plot, character and setting. In the Barth story included in this volume, "Autobiography: A Self-Recorded Experience," Barth plays with the reader's tendency to think of the narrative as a real human being talking to us as though it had an actual life before the story began and one that will continue after the story is finished. But the narrator only exists on paper and for as long as the story lasts. Barth has a lot of fun playing with this idea, but his game has serious consequences: it should help us become more aware that any storyteller is constructing him- or herself before us as a fictional character.

Herman Melville plays with the audience's expectations in a more subtle way in "Bartleby the Scrivener." When we are presented with such a strange and interesting character such as Bartleby, we come to expect that the author will reveal by the story's end an explanation of the character's bizarre behavior. V.S. Naipaul in "Bogart" illustrates the usual pattern of such stories. By the end of the story, Naipaul explains both Bogart's mysterious disappearance and the reason for his change in character. But in "Bartleby" neither the narrator nor the reader ever is allowed to understand why Bartleby behaves as he does, or what Bartleby is thinking. Why does Melville frustrate our desire to know? A reason may be that Melville wants us to consider why we need such information. Can't we accept human beings as they are? Must those who act oddly always justify and defend their behavior when it is causing no one else difficulty? Notice that neither Barth nor Melville play with expectations simply to frustrate the reader. Both have good reasons for what they do.

Good writing, we might say, falls into two categories: (1) those works which satisfy reader expectations and the requirements of their genre, and (2) those works that expand or alter our expectations and thereby bring something new to literature and our consciousness.

Those works that expand our awareness, our "horizon of expectation"—to use the term of the critic Hans Robert Jauss—are especially valuable. Many of the greatest works of literature not only altered the expectations of readers in their own day, but continue to challenge the way readers and writers view their world.

Do readers especially *like* these works? To be honest, I must say that the greatest works such as *Hamlet* or John Milton's *Paradise Lost* or Melville's *Moby Dick* or James Joyce's *Ulysses* are profoundly discomforting works that challenge our perceptions and understanding. They question—and often leave unresolved—many of our long held assumptions. But it is their very power to make us uneasy, to force us to rethink, relearn, reevaluate, and re-feel that makes them great and exciting works to read for those who like challenges and are unafraid of exploring new thoughts and emotions. Many great works give us comfort, but feeling comfortable is not the only purpose of literature. To arouse us to think for ourselves, to break open our prejudices and examine our limitations, to release our unexpressed emotions and to give us an awareness of other people's thoughts and feelings—these are but a few of the other purposes of literature, purposes that may be disquieting, uncomfortable and startling.

THE AUTHOR'S PURPOSE

We forget that people write for a purpose, and the purpose may vary from author to author and from work to work. I can't imagine a situation when someone *accidentally* writes a poem, story or play, when a pen just happens to fall into a person's hands and the text is produced unconsciously.

Why do people write? Frequently people write to make money. Writers are hired by industry and government, public relations and advertising forms, newspapers, magazines and the electronic media. As professional writers their purpose may be to sell a product or service, to explain a procedure or process, to report an event, to present a new idea, to win friends and to influence public opinion. A few novelists and playwrights make their living writing, but their numbers are very small. Most write for other reasons than monetary gain.

Readers frequently believe that people write stories if not for money, then to convince others of their opinions. But fiction writers rarely speak about their art as a tool to alter public opinion. "Poetry makes nothing happen," declares W.H. Auden, one of the most influential poets of his generation, and he might have said the same of fiction. Fiction writers scoff at the notion of stories as propaganda.

Writers most frequently speak of their works as explorations, explorations of an idea, an image, a situation, a mood or feeling. Writers ask themselves "What if . . ." What if an angel fell to earth? What would it look like? How would people respond? Out of such questions could emerge a story like "A Very Old Man with Enormous Wings." What would a proud Southern lady do if a man whom she loved rejected her? "A Rose for Emily" is one answer; Katherine Anne Porter's "The Jilting of Granny Weatherall" is another answer. If we look at stories as explorations, we will recognize several important aspects of storytelling. The writer does not necessarily believe that the resolution of the story is the only right resolution, or the best one, or even the most preferable one. Under different circumstances and different characters, the resolution of the story may be different. For the writer who is truly exploring characters, or issues, cannot guarantee what will be found at the end of the search, whether the result will be pleasant, comforting, affirming, or terrifying, horrible, and discouraging. Moreover, the truly interesting questions can be explored over and over with different characters and slightly different situations. Writers are motivated by the pleasures of the hunt, the same sort of excitement that explorers feel. And the reader who travels along with the writer in exploring these questions can experience some of the same pleasures, excitement, delight and satisfaction.

Consequently, when judging works of literature, we must see if we can discover the author's purpose for writing. Was this purpose worthy of serious consideration? Was the purpose achieved against unusual odds? Did the writer expand the realms of literature or achieve something new?

FINAL JUDGMENTS

As a reader you don't have to decide once and for all whether a story is good or bad. Several of the works of literature, theatre and the cinema that I now most admire, I started out disliking. Instead of setting up a rigid system of rules through which you pass every story, it may be more valuable to ask a series of questions, the answers to which may change over time and as your judgment matures.

GENRE

1. What sort of story is this?
2. Does the story live up to my expectations?
3. If not, are my expectations fair? Does it supply something to compensate me?

READER

1. For what sort of reader was this story intended?

2. How would the story affect such readers?
3. Would the intended reader be satisfied with such a story?
4. Would its readers be challenged by such a story?
5. Does the story meet the needs and abilities of its readers?

AUTHOR

1. Can we determine the author's purpose in writing the story?
2. Does the author achieve the purpose?
3. Does the author give the reader a reason for reading the story?
4. Is the author's purpose worthwhile? Is the author attempting anything unusual or particularly difficult?

THINGS TO THINK ABOUT

1. Have women in the past had the same access to publishing as males? Have women had to overcome any particular obstacles to write? Have blacks and other minorities had the same access to literature? Have those experiences altered their goals in writing? Does it alter the way we might judge their works?
2. Is formal perfection the only criteria for judging the worth of a piece of literature? Is a graceful work on a trivial matter as valuable as a rather clumsy work on a serious or difficult matter?
3. Is there a difference between personal preference and literary excellence? Does it make any sense to say, "I like this story even though I know it is not very good," or "I don't like this story even though I know it is excellent"? Are literary judgments merely an expression of personal preference?

ESSAY TOPICS

1. Evaluate a movie you have recently seen. What criteria do you use for judging a movie? Are those criteria fair? How do you judge the movie against the criteria?
2. Discuss how your opinions have changed. Have you ever come to value a person, institution or object that at one point you did not value? Why has your opinion changed? Have you changed criteria? Or have you re–evaluated the person against the same criteria?
3. Do you like things because they are truly excellent or because they are comfortable? Discuss an occasion when you pursued excellence even though it meant some discomfort.

CREATIVE WRITING EXERCISES

1. Write a formal critique of one of your own stories pretending that it has been written by another person.

2. Write up a list of ten elements that you want to see in your own writing. Then re–write a story trying to bring it closer to your own conception of excellence.
3. What do you think would make you a better writer? What would you have to do to become a better writer? Have you tried doing those things that you think would improve your writing? Discuss the results of trying to achieve excellence.
4. Write a story about someone writing the perfect story. What does the character do to write the perfect story? How do people respond to the perfect story? What does the writer do *after* he or she has written the perfect story?

LITERARY ESSAYS

1. In "A Conversation with My Father" the father articulates certain criteria for a good story. What are these criteria? Are they reasonable? To what extent do the inner stories embody these values? To what extent does the entire story both embody and challenge the father's aesthetic criteria?
2. As the title indicates, "Homage to Isaac Babel" is written in honor of the Russian author. But to what extent does Lessing's tale put into practice the stylistic features praised in Babel's work?
3. Which of the stories in this chapter do you think is the best? Justify your choice.

GRACE PALEY

A CONVERSATION WITH MY FATHER

Grace Paley (b. 1922) is a perfectionist. She has produced only three collections of short stories, The Little Disturbances of Man, Enormous Changes at the Last Minute, *and* Later that Day, *and a slim volume of poetry. But the quality of her writing has never been in doubt. A political activist all her life, she brings to all her relations a gentle, but passionate response leavened by a keen sense of humor and morality.*

Paley was born in New York City to Dr. Isaac and Mary Goodside and has two children. She was educated at Hunter College and New York University and teaches at Sarah Lawrence College.

My father is eighty-six years old and in bed. His heart, that bloody motor, is equally old and will not do certain jobs any more. It still floods his head with brainy light. But it won't let his legs carry the weight of his body around the house. Despite my metaphors, this muscle failure is not due to his old heart, he says, but to a potassium shortage. Sitting on one pillow, leaning on three, he offers last-minute advice and makes a request.

"I would like you to write a simple story just once more," he says, "the kind de Maupassant wrote, or Chekhov,[1] the kind you used to write. Just recognizable people and then write down what happened to·them next."

I say, "Yes, why not? That's possible." I want to please him, though I don't remember writing that way. I *would* like to try to tell such a story, if he means the kind that begins: "There was a woman . . ." followed by plot, the absolute line between two points which I've always despised. Not for literary reasons, but because it takes all hope away. Everyone, real or invented, deserves the open destiny of life.

Finally I thought of a story that had been happening for a couple of years right across the street. I wrote it down, then read it aloud, "Pa," I said, "how about this? Do you mean something like this?"

> Once in my time there was a woman and she had a son. They lived nicely, in a small apartment in Manhattan. This boy at about fifteen became a junkie,[2] which is not unusual in our neighborhood. In order to maintain her close friendship with him, she became a junkie too. She said it was part of the youth culture, with which she felt very much at home. After a while, for a number of reasons, the boy gave it all up and left the city and his mother in disgust. Hopeless and alone, she grieved. We all visit her.

"O.K., Pa, that's it," I said, "an unadorned and miserable tale."

"But that's not what I mean," my father said. "You misunderstood me on purpose. You know there's a lot more to it. You know that. You left everything out. Turgenev[3] wouldn't do that. Chekhov wouldn't do that. There are in fact Russian writers you never heard of, you don't have an inkling of, as good as anyone, who can write a plain ordinary story, who would not leave out what you have left out. I object not to facts but to people sitting in trees talking senselessly, voices from who knows where[4] . . ."

"Forget that one, Pa, what have I left out now? In this one?"

"Her looks, for instance."

"Oh. Quite handsome, I think. Yes."

"Her hair?"

"Dark, with heavy braids, as though she were a girl or a foreigner."

"What were her parents like, her stock? That she became such a person. It's interesting, you know."

[1] Guy de Maupassant (1850–1893) and Anton Chekhov (1860–1904) were two masters of short fiction whose works developed finely drawn psychological characters in realistic settings. One of Chekhov's stories, "Lady with Lapdog," appears on p. 483.

[2] A junkie is a heroin user.

[3] Ivan Turgenev (1818–1883) is a precursor of the psychological-realist school of Chekhov and Maupassant.

[4] Paley is alluding to her story "Faith in a Tree."

"From out of town. Professional people. The first to be divorced in their county. How's that? Enough?" I asked.

"With you, it's all a joke," he said. "What about the boy's father? Why didn't you mention him? Who was he? Or was the boy born out of wedlock?"

"Yes," I said. "He was born out of wedlock."

"For Godsakes, doesn't anyone in your stories get married? Doesn't anyone have the time to run down to City Hall before they jump into bed?"

"No," I said. "In real life, yes. But in my stories, no."

"Why do you answer me like that?"

"Oh, Pa, this is a simple story about a smart woman who came to N.Y.C. full of interest love trust excitement very up to date, and about her son, what a hard time she had in this world. Married or not, it's of small consequence."

"It is of great consequence," he said.

"O.K.," I said.

"O.K. O.K. yourself," he said, "but listen. I believe you that she's good-looking, but I don't think she was so smart."

"That's true," I said. "Actually that's the trouble with stories. People start out fantastic. You think they're extraordinary, but it turns out as the work goes along, they're just average with a good education. Sometimes the other way around, the person's a kind of dumb innocent, but he outwits you and you can't even think of an ending good enough."

"What do you do then?" he asked. He had been a doctor for a couple of decades and then an artist for a couple of decades and he's still interested in details, craft, technique.

"Well, you just have to let the story lie around till some agreement can be reached between you and the stubborn hero."

"Aren't you talking silly, now?" he asked. "Start again," he said. "It so happens I'm not going out this evening. Tell *the story* again. See what you can do this time."

"O.K.," I said. "But it's not a five-minute job." Second attempt:

> Once, across the street from us, there was a fine handsome woman, our neighbor. She had a son whom she loved because she'd known him since birth (in helpless chubby infancy, and in the wrestling, hugging ages, seven to ten, as well as earlier and later). This boy, when he fell into the fist of adolescence, became a junkie. He was not a hopeless one. He was in fact hopeful, an ideologue and successful converter. With his busy brilliance, he wrote persuasive articles for his highschool newspaper. Seeking a wider audience, using important connections, he drummed into Lower Manhattan newsstand distribution a periodical called *Oh! Golden Horse!*[5]

[5] Horse is a slang term for heroin.

In order to keep him from feeling guilty (because guilt is the stony heart of nine tenths of all clinically diagnosed cancers in America today, she said), and because she had always believed in giving bad habits room at home where one could keep an eye on them, she too became a junkie. Her kitchen was famous for a while—a center for intellectual addicts who knew what they were doing. A few felt artistic like Coleridge and others were scientific and revolutionary like Leary.[6] Although she was often high herself, certain good mothering reflexes remained, and she saw to it that there was lots of orange juice around and honey and milk and vitamin pills. However, she never cooked anything but chili, and that no more than once a week. She explained, when we talked to her, seriously, with neighborly concern, that it was her part in the youth culture and she would rather be with the young, it was an honor, than with her own generation.

One week, while nodding through an Antonioni[7] film, this boy was severely jabbed by the elbow of a stern and proselytizing girl, sitting beside him. She offered immediate apricots and nuts for his sugar level, spoke to him sharply, and took him home.

She had heard of him and his work and she herself published, edited, and wrote a competitive journal called *Man Does Live By Bread Alone.* In the organic heat of her continuous presence he could not help but become interested once more in his muscles, his arteries, and nerve connections. In fact he began to love them, treasure them, praise them with funny little songs in *Man Does Live* . . .

the fingers of my flesh transcend
my transcendental soul
the tightness in my shoulders end
my teeth have made me whole

To the mouth of his head (that glory of will and determination) he brought hard apples, nuts, wheat germ, and soybean oil. He said to his old friends, From now on, I guess I'll keep my wits about me. I'm going on the natch. He said he was about to begin a spiritual deep-breathing journey. How about you too, Mom? he asked kindly.

His conversion was so radiant, splendid, that neighborhood kids his age began to say that he had never been a real addict at all, only a journalist along for the smell of the story. The mother tried several times to give up what had become without her son and his friends a lonely habit. This effort only brought it to supportable levels. The boy and his girl took their electronic mimeograph and

[6] Samuel Taylor Coleridge (1772–1834) was an English poet and essayist who suffered from opium addiction. Dr. Timothy Leary (1920–), former Harvard lecturer in psychology, became known during the 1960s for his experiments with psychedelic drugs.
[7] Michelangelo Antonioni (1912–) is an experimental Italian filmmaker, *Blow-up* (1966) made him famous in the United States.

> moved to the bushy edge of another borough. They were very strict. They said they would not see her again until she had been off drugs for sixty days.
>
> At home alone in the evening, weeping, the mother read and reread the seven issues of *Oh! Golden Horse!* They seemed to her as truthful as ever. We often crossed the street to visit and console. But if we mentioned any of our children who were at college or in the hospital or dropouts at home, she would cry out, My baby! My baby! and burst into terrible, face-scarring, time-consuming tears. The End.

First my father was silent, then he said, "Number One: You have a nice sense of humor. Number Two: I see you can't tell a plain story. So don't waste time." Then he said sadly, "Number Three: I suppose that means she was alone, she was left like that, his mother. Alone. Probably sick?"

I said, "Yes."

"Poor woman. Poor girl, to be born in a time of fools, to live among fools. The end. The end. You were right to put that down. The end."

I didn't want to argue, but I had to say, "Well, it is not necessarily the end, Pa."

"Yes," he said, "what a tragedy. The end of a person."

"No, Pa," I begged him. "It doesn't have to be. She's only about forty. She could be a hundred different things in this world as time goes on. A teacher or a social worker. An ex-junkie! Sometimes it's better than having a master's in education."

"Jokes," he said. "As a writer that's your main trouble. You don't want to recognize it. Tragedy! Plain tragedy! Historical tragedy! No hope. The end."

"Oh, Pa," I said. "She could change."

"In your own life, too, you have to look it in the face." He took a couple of nitroglycerin.[8] "Turn to five," he said, pointing to the dial on the oxygen tank. He inserted the tubes into his nostrils and breathed deep. He closed his eyes and said, "No."

I had promised the family to always let him have the last word when arguing, but in this case I had a different responsibility. That woman lives across the street. She's my knowledge and my invention. I'm sorry for her. I'm not going to leave her there in that house crying. (Actually neither would Life, which unlike me has no pity.)

Therefore: She did change. Of course her son never came home again. But right now, she's the receptionist in a storefront community

[8] Nitroglycerine is not only an explosive but also a drug for the treatment of some types of heart disease.

clinic in the East Village.[9] Most of the customers are young people, some old friends. The head doctor has said to her, "If we only had three people in this clinic with your experiences . . ."

"The doctor said that?" My father took the oxygen tubes out of his nostrils and said, "Jokes. Jokes again."

"No, Pa, it could really happen that way, it's a funny world nowadays."

"No," he said. "Truth first. She will slide back. A person must have character. She does not."

"No, Pa," I said. "That's it. She's got a job. Forget it. She's in that storefront working."

"How long will it be?" he asked. "Tragedy! You too. When will you look it in the face?"

QUESTIONS

1. What sort of aesthetic expectations does the narrator's father hold? Does the narrator hold the same values?
2. How do the two versions of the addict story try to accommodate the views on fiction held by the narrator's father.
3. What version do you prefer? Why?
4. What is the relationship between the addict story and the frame around it, the conversation between the narrator and her father?
5. Does the story as a whole confirm the narrator's belief that "everyone, real or invented, deserves the open destiny of life"?
6. How would you evaluate this story? Why?

ISAAC BABEL

MY FIRST GOOSE

Isaac Babel (1894–1941) suffered a fate typical of many artists—especially Jewish artists—in Stalinist Russia. After a period of great popular and critical success, he was denounced for defaming the Communist state and thrown into a Siberian concentration camp where he died.

Born to a shopkeeper in Odessa, he studied Hebrew and scripture at home and law at the University of Saratov. He served during the revolution with the revolutionary forces and the secret police. A meticulous craftsman who went through numerous drafts before he was satisfied, he left behind a few volumes of short stories, Odessa Tales *and* Red Cavalry, *a few plays, and a film script.*

Savitsky, Commander of the VI Division, rose when he saw me, and I wondered at the beauty of his giant's body. He rose, the purple of his riding breeches and the crimson of his little tilted cap and the decorations stuck on his chest cleaving the hut as a standard cleaves the sky. A smell of scent and the sickly sweet freshness of soap emanated from

[9] The East Village, a poor section of New York City, was one of the centers of the youth movement.

him. His long legs were like girls sheathed to the neck in shining riding boots.

He smiled at me, struck his riding whip on the table, and drew toward him an order that the Chief of Staff had just finished dictating. It was an order for Ivan Chesnokov to advance on Chugunov-Dobryvodka with the regiment entrusted to him, to make contact with the enemy and destroy the same.

"For which destruction," the Commander began to write, smearing the whole sheet, "I make this same Chesnokov entirely responsible, up to and including the supreme penalty, and will if necessary strike him down on the spot; which you, Chesnokov, who have been working with me at the front for some months now, cannot doubt."

The Commander signed the order with a flourish, tossed it to his orderlies and turned upon me gray eyes that danced with merriment.

I handed him a paper with my appointment to the Staff of the Division.

"Put it down in the Order of the Day," said the Commander. "Put him down for every satisfaction save the front one. Can you read and write?"

"Yes, I can read and write," I replied, envying the flower and iron of that youthfulness. "I graduated in law from St. Petersburg University."

"Oh, are you one of those grinds?"[1] he laughed. "Specs on your nose, too! What a nasty little object! They've sent you along without making any enquiries; and this is a hot place for specs. Think you'll get on with us?"

"I'll get on all right," I answered, and went off to the village with the quartermaster to find a billet for the night.

The quartermaster carried my trunk on his shoulder. Before us stretched the village street. The dying sun, round and yellow as a pumpkin, was giving up its roseate ghost to the skies.

We went up to a hut painted over with garlands. The quartermaster stopped, and said suddenly, with a guilty smile:

"Nuisance with specs. Can't do anything to stop it, either. Not a life for the brainy type here. But you go and mess up a lady, and a good lady too, and you'll have the boys patting you on the back."

He hesitated, my little trunk on his shoulder; then he came quite close to me, only to dart away again despairingly and run to the nearest yard. Cossacks[2] were sitting there, shaving one another.

"Here, you soldiers," said the quartermaster, setting my little trunk down on the ground. "Comrade Savitsky's orders are that you're to take this chap in your billets, so no nonsense about it, because the chap's been through a lot in the learning line."

The quartermaster, purple in the face, left us without looking back.

[1] A grind is a hard-working student.

[2] The Cossacks were a warlike tribe, in marked contrast to the narrator, a Jewish lawyer.

I raised my hand to my cap and saluted the Cossacks. A lad with long straight flaxen hair and the handsome face of the Ryazan Cossacks[3] went over to my little trunk and tossed it out at the gate. Then he turned his back on me and with remarkable skill emitted a series of shameful noises.

"To your guns—number double-zero!" an older Cossack shouted at him, and burst out laughing. "Running fire!"

His guileless art exhausted, the lad made off. Then, crawling over the ground, I began to gather together the manuscript and tattered garments that had fallen out of the trunk. I gathered them up and carried them to the other end of the yard. Near the hut, on a brick stove, stood a cauldron in which pork was cooking. The steam that rose from it was like the far-off smoke of home in the village, and it mingled hunger with desperate loneliness in my head. Then I covered my little broken trunk with hay, turning it into a pillow, and lay down on the ground to read in *Pravda* Lenin's speech at the Second Congress of the Comintern.[4] The sun fell upon me from behind the toothed hillocks, the Cossacks trod on my feet, the lad made fun of me untiringly, the beloved lines came toward me along a thorny path and could not reach me. Then I put aside the paper and went out to the landlady, who was spinning on the porch.

"Landlady," I said, "I've got to eat."

The old woman raised to me the diffused whites of her purblind eyes and lowered them again.

"Comrade," she said, after a pause, "what with all this going on, I want to go and hang myself."

"Christ!" I muttered, and pushed the old woman in the chest with my fist. "You don't suppose I'm going to go into explanations with you, do you?"

And turning around I saw somebody's sword lying within reach. A severe-looking goose was waddling about the yard, inoffensively preening its feathers. I overtook it and pressed it to the ground. Its head cracked beneath my boot, cracked and emptied itself. The white neck lay stretched out in the dung, the wings twitched.

"Christ!" I said, digging into the goose with my sword. "Go and cook it for me, landlady."

Her blind eyes and glasses glistening, the old woman picked up the slaughtered bird, wrapped it in her apron, and started to bear it off toward the kitchen.

[3] Cossacks from Ryazan, a former principality in central Russia, southeast of Moscow.

[4] The Comintern is an acronym for the Communist International, a worldwide organization of Communist parties. The Comintern was under the direction of V. I. Lenin (1870–1924), one of the founders of the Communist Revolution and virtual dictator of the Soviet Union. He called the Second Congress of Comintern (1920) to wage a world communist revolution. *Pravda* is the official Communist Party newspaper.

"Comrade," she said to me, after a while, "I want to go and hang myself." And she closed the door behind her.

The Cossacks in the yard were already sitting around their cauldron. They sat motionless, stiff as heathen priests at a sacrifice, and had not looked at the goose.

"The lad's all right," one of them said, winking and scooping up the cabbage soup with his spoon.

The Cossacks commenced their supper with all the elegance and restraint of peasants who respect one another. And I wiped the sword with sand, went out at the gate, and came in again, depressed. Already the moon hung above the yard like a cheap earring.

"Hey, you," suddenly said Surovkov, an older Cossack. "Sit down and feed with us till your goose is done."

He produced a spare spoon from his boot and handed it to me. We supped up the cabbage soup they had made, and ate the pork.

"What's in the newspaper?" asked the flaxen-haired lad, making room for me.

"Lenin writes in the paper," I said, pulling out *Pravda*. "Lenin writes that there's a shortage of everything."

And loudly, like a triumphant man hard of hearing, I read Lenin's speech out to the Cossacks.

Evening wrapped about me the quickening moisture of its twilight sheets; evening laid a mother's hand upon my burning forehead. I read on and rejoiced, spying out exultingly the secret curve of Lenin's straight line.

"Truth tickles everyone's nostrils," said Surovkov, when I had come to the end. "The question is, how's it to be pulled from the heap. But he goes and strikes at it straight off like a hen pecking at a grain!"

This remark about Lenin was made by Surovkov, platoon commander of the Staff Squadron; after which we lay down to sleep in the hayloft. We slept, all six of us, beneath a wooden roof that let in the stars, warming one another, our legs intermingled. I dreamed, and in my dreams saw women. But my heart, stained with bloodshed, grated and brimmed over.

QUESTIONS

1. Why does the narrator kill the goose? Does the act achieve its goal?
2. Legs are mentioned at least three times in the story. Where are they referred to either directly or indirectly? Is there any reason for this unusual number of references?
3. How would you describe the style of this story? Is it appropriate? Is it effective?
4. Are the characters suitably drawn? Do you need to know more about them in order to understand the story? Would additional information clarify their motives?

5. Does the action properly make Babel's thematic point?
6. How would you evaluate this story?

DORIS LESSING

HOMAGE FOR ISAAC BABEL

The British critic Richard Locke has written of Doris Lessing (b. 1919) that she "is the foremost creative descendant of that 'great tradition' which includes George Eliot, Conrad and D.H. Lawrence: a tradition of intense social concerns and moral realism." No one could doubt her energy and power. In a steady stream of books of fiction, drama, essays and poetry, she has shown herself as perhaps the most ambitious and unpredictable author in Great Britain, writing realistic novels, satires of ideas, and a science fiction tetralogy.

Born in Persia (now Iran), she moved to Rhodesia (now Zimbabwe) as a girl, and was educated in a Catholic girls' schools in Africa. She worked as a nurse maid, typist and secretary. Not until the publication of her first novel The Grass is Singing *in 1950 did she move to England where she still lives. Her major works include the five novels of her* Children of Violence *series and* The Golden Notebook.

The day I had promised to take Catherine down to visit my young friend Philip at his school in the country, we were to leave at eleven, but she arrived at nine. Her blue dress was new, and so were her fashionable shoes. Her hair had just been done. She looked more than ever like a pink-and-gold Renoir[1] girl who expects everything from life.

Catherine lives in a white house overlooking the sweeping brown tides of the river. She helped me clean up my flat with a devotion which said that she felt small flats were altogether more romantic than large houses. We drank tea, and talked mainly about Philip, who, being fifteen, has pure stern tastes in everything from food to music. Catherine looked at the books lying around his room, and asked if she might borrow the stories of Isaac Babel to read on the train. Catherine is thirteen. I suggested she might find them difficult, but she said: "Philip reads them, doesn't he?"

During the journey I read newspapers and watched her pretty frowning face as she turned the pages of Babel, for she was determined to let nothing get between her and her ambition to be worthy of Philip.

At the school, which is charming, civilised, and expensive, the two children walked together across green fields, and I followed, seeing how the sun gilded their bright friendly heads turned towards each other as they talked. In Catherine's left hand she carried the stories of Isaac Babel.

After lunch we went to the pictures. Philip allowed it to be seen

[1] Pierre-Auguste Renoir (1841–1919) was a French impressionist painter known for his lovely pictures of French family life which included many rosy-cheeked young girls.

that he thought going to the pictures just for the fun of it was not worthy of intelligent people, but he made the concession, for our sakes. For his sake we chose the more serious of the two films that were showing in the little town. It was about a good priest who helped criminals in New York. His goodness, however, was not enough to prevent one of them from being sent to the gas chamber; and Philip and I waited with Catherine in the dark until she had stopped crying and could face the light of a golden evening.

At the entrance of the cinema the doorman was lying in wait for anyone who had red eyes. Grasping Catherine by her suffering arm, he said bitterly: "Yes, why are you crying? He had to be punished for his crime, didn't he?" Catherine stared at him, incredulous. Philip rescued her by saying with disdain: "Some people don't know right from wrong even when it's *demonstrated* to them." The doorman turned his attention to the next red-eyed emerger from the dark; and we went on together to the station, the children silent because of the cruelty of the world.

Finally Catherine said, her eyes wet again: "I think it's all absolutely beastly, and I can't bear to think about it." And Philip said: "But we've got to think about it, don't you see, because if we don't it'll just go on and on, don't you see?"

In the train going back to London I sat beside Catherine. She had the stories open in front of her, but she said: "Philip's awfully lucky. I wish I went to that school. Did you notice that girl who said hullo to him in the garden? They must be great friends. I wish my mother would let me have a dress like that, it's *not* fair."

"I thought it was too old for her."

"Oh, *did* you?"

Soon she bent her head again over the book, but almost at once lifted it to say: "Is he a very famous writer?"

"He's a marvellous writer, brilliant, one of the very best."

"Why?"

"Well, for one thing he's so simple. Look how few words he uses, and how strong his stories are."

"I see. Do you know him? Does he live in London?"

"Oh no, he's dead."

"Oh. Then why did you—I thought he was alive, the way you talked."

"I'm sorry, I suppose I wasn't thinking of him as dead."

"When did he die?"

"He was murdered. About twenty years ago, I suppose."

"Twenty years." Her hands began the movement of pushing the book over to me, but then relaxed. "I'll be fourteen in November," she stated, sounding threatened, while her eyes challenged me.

I found it hard to express my need to apologise, but before I could speak, she said, patiently attentive again: "You said he was murdered?"

"Yes."

"I expect the person who murdered him felt sorry when he discovered he had murdered a famous writer."

"Yes, I expect so."

"Was he old when he was murdered?"

"No, quite young really."

"Well, that was bad luck, wasn't it?"

"Yes, I suppose it was bad luck."

"Which do you think is the very best story here? I mean, in your honest opinion, the very very best one."

I chose the story about killing the goose. She read it slowly, while I sat waiting, wishing to take it from her, wishing to protect this charming little person from Isaac Babel.

When she had finished, she said: "Well, some if it I don't understand. He's got a funny way of looking at things. Why should a man's legs in boots look like *girls?*" She finally pushed the book over at me, and said: "I think it's all morbid."

"But you have to understand the kind of life he had. First, he was a Jew in Russia. That was bad enough. Then his experience was all revolution and civil war and . . ."

But I could see these words bouncing off the clear glass of her fiercely denying gaze; and I said: "Look, Catherine, why don't you try again when you're older? Perhaps you'll like him better then?"

She said gratefully: "Yes, perhaps that would be best. After all, Philip is two years older than me, isn't he?"

A week later I got a letter from Catherine.

> Thank you very much for being kind enough to take me to visit Philip at his school. It was the most lovely day in my whole life. I am extremely grateful to you for taking me. I have been thinking about the Hoodlum Priest. That was a film which demonstrated to me beyond any shadow of doubt that Capital Punishment is a Wicked Thing, and I shall never forget what I learned that afternoon, and the lessons of it will be with me all my life. I have been meditating about what you said about Isaac Babel, the famed Russian short story writer, and I now see that the conscious simplicity of his style is what makes him, beyond the shadow of a doubt, the great writer that he is, and now in my school compositions I am endeavoring to emulate him so as to learn a conscious simplicity which is the only basis for a really brilliant writing style. Love, Catherine. P.S. Has Philip said anything about my party? I wrote but he hasn't answered. Please find out if he is coming or if he just forgot to answer my letter. I hope he comes, because sometimes I feel I shall die if he doesn't. P.P.S. Please don't tell him I said anything, because I should die if he knew. Love, Catherine.

QUESTIONS

1. What are the narrator's aesthetic values and how are they embodied in the story?
2. What are the aesthetic values Catherine espouses in her letter? Does she really believe them? How are they reflected in her letter?
3. Why is it difficult for Catherine to understand the Babel story? What does she indicate about her aesthetic values by crying over the Hoodlum Priest movie and finding "My First Goose" "morbid"?
4. Why does the narrator wish to "protect" Catherine from Isaac Babel? From what in the story does Catherine need protection?
5. Is Philip's attitude more mature? Does Philip hold the same views as the narrator? Does he hold the same view as Isaac Babel?
6. How does Lessing's story compare to "My First Goose"? How would evaluate Lessing's story?

11

WRITING ABOUT FICTION

Every writer goes about the business of writing in his or her own way. Thomas Wolfe is said to have written on the top of a refrigerator. Pushkin, the great Russian poet, kept rotting apples in his desk drawer because the smell reminded him of his childhood. I know a novelist who can write only with a mechanical pencil, and a critic who writes on a certain kind of expensive paper. I have written this book on a word processor, but I write poetry in long hand usually on small scraps of paper. My point is a simple one: no one can teach you the way you can write most comfortably and effectively. You must find your own way yourself. Teachers can show you only those ways that have worked well for others and that might keep you from making bad mistakes. But in the end, you alone hold the key to your own way of writing.

Nevertheless, through the years I have asked students who write well how they go about composing their papers and what pointers they might give to other students who needed to write about literature. This chapter contains their advice mixed in with suggestions of my own. I hope our collective minds might give you some suggestions that would be useful and make the task of writing, easier, more enjoyable and satisfying.

HOW MUCH TIME DOES WRITING TAKE?

When I was an undergraduate, there always seemed to be a student in my class who could sit down at the typewriter, grind out a paper in a single draft, hand it in, and get a B. Why couldn't I do that? Why did the Fates decree that I would have to sit at my desk for hours writing and crossing out page after page, revising what I'd written, then correcting the essay once more as I typed the final version? Why wasn't I blessed with a quick tongue and a facile mind? The truth is that while some students can get away with their first drafts some of the time, no one can do it all the time. Writing—even for professional writers—is an often frustrating, difficult, time-consuming process. Though years of practice can make it easier, good writers never find it easy.

My student writers tell me that all of them take too much time. Not one of them seems to think that he or she writes quickly or easily enough. "I struggle with writing more than I think I should," writes one excellent student, and another finds it "impossible not to panic" when she learns about an assignments. "To a student in a writing course, a blank piece of paper is the most terrifying thing on earth. As in the story of creation, an essay begins in the void."

A student who didn't do as well as she knew she could have done wrote: "The first bit of advice that I would give to students is to make sure to allow enough time for writing their essays. My failing this semester was procrastination. By putting papers off until the last minute; I didn't have enough time to rewrite or even closely examine the stories I was writing about. It is really unfortunate when one turns in poor quality work done with little effort and receives a deservedly low grade, because the only person one cheats is oneself."

The students have generally two ways of making the writing of an essay quicker and less terrifying. They start thinking about the paper long before they sit down to write, and they have developed certain tricks that give them comfort and confidence.

Almost all of the students claim that a good essay starts off with changing the way they read. They usually break down the process into a number of smaller steps: (1) reading, (2) meditating on the essay, (3) formulating a central idea, thesis, question or task, (4) developing evidence, (5) writing the essay, and finally, (6) revising the paper into a final draft.

Clearly if you go through all of these steps, writing a paper will take a long time. But as these students have found out, there is no quick way to write well. Writing is simply one of those jobs that suffers from being rushed. Students who are realistic will set aside ample time for writing. However several steps can be taken to make the job less anxious. Breaking the big task down into smaller, more manageable jobs, not only helps writers avoid the panic, but gives writers opportunities for reward themselves for the work they've finished. As one student wrote, "It's a whole lot easier to write an outline when I've saved a candy bar as my reward for completing it."

Reading

"I have found that the way in which I read a story is the most important factor affecting the production of a reasonable essay," wrote a student. You can't write well on a story unless you have read it carefully.

"My advice," writes another student, "is to reread the story several times." One student makes a practice of reading stories at least three times. Another reads them five times. But all the students read in different ways each time they go through a story.

The students usually read a story quickly the first time through. One student got her best ideas for papers during her first reading, but most of the students needed several readings before they could formulate ideas. Thus, they simply let themselves in the first reading respond freely to the story, letting it leave its impressions. During that first reading they sometimes would circle words they didn't know or things they didn't understand. But they didn't stop to look the words up until after they had finished the first reading.

When they returned for a second reading, they had pencil in hand. "If a passage strikes me as being significant or if it relates to another passage, I underline it or make a note in the margin," explains one student. "I find these notes very helpful when I'm trying to think of ideas for my papers."

Another student advises, "As you read a work and come across something that bothers you, don't doubt yourself and dismiss it from your mind as I used to do. Instead jot down the problem and continue reading. The problem might end up being a great topic for a paper."

"I think in terms of connections when I reread a story," a very good student informs me. "I assume that to some degree everything in a story influences everything else so I pay attention to how things are linked together and also what at first doesn't seem to fit in. I know it should fit in somehow. You should also pay close attention to your emotions. What moves you? How did it get you emotionally involved?"

"I read whatever it is I want to write about—short story, poem, novel or essay—with a sharp eye on both the writer's style and the writer's message. I think about what the piece is trying to say and how it is saying it even if it involves reading the piece three or four times. Become an expert on that particular piece of writing."

Disliking a story should not be an obstacle to writing about it. As one student noted, "I encounter a number of works that I do not like or do not understand. *This is allowed!* No one likes everything; everyone has his or her own likes and dislikes. But your reaction can work to your advantage. Write about what you don't like or understand. You may very well raise questions even your instructor has not thought about."

Thinking Space

In the opinion of one student, "The most important part of writing for me is giving myself time between reading a work and writing the essay to think, to stir up ideas. Just casually push ideas around inside your head for a couple of days before getting serious. This relieves the anxiety of writing and really gets thoughts flowing. I also usually give myself time before I write the conclusion. The extra time helps me see my ideas objectively so I can tie things together."

Another student writes: "Before I start writing a rough draft, I brainstorm. I know for myself, when I start brainstorming, all sorts of new ideas pop into my head, and I usually end up with a better idea of what I want to write about. When I brainstorm, I write down everything that comes to my mind about the work, whether or not the ideas seem intelligent. Who knows whether a dumb idea will lead to something better. And I don't worry about grammar, spelling or style. I just write."

"Once you have read a work," yet another student advises, "let the experience of reading it—the images and emotions it has instilled in you—sit for a while in your thoughts."

But your success rests not only on *what* you do, but also on *how* you do it. My students are very aware of how their own attitudes often undermine their efforts to write. Hostility to an assignment can boobytrap any effort. According to one student "the most important change in my writing came when I got over my attitude about 'the stupid story' I had to write about. If I continued with that negative attitude, I probably would have never written a good essay. Chances are the detested story has some literary value or you wouldn't have to read and write about it. So I try to find out what might be worthwhile about the story even when I don't like it."

"One thing I needed to overcome," writes another student, "is the feeling of being abandoned when writing a paper. I always felt that my teachers never gave me enough direction either about writing or the meaning of a work. Won't someone tell me what to do! I would say to myself. Now, if I really feel lost I go and ask the teacher for advice, a place to start. But I also recognize that if I don't panic, I can figure things out for myself. I don't start looking for 'hidden messages' in the work because there probably aren't any, and if there are, they are probably too hidden for me to see. Once I allow myself to see what's there, I see a whole lot. Once I let myself open up to the work, answers to my questions come to me."

Finally, a student advises to trust yourself when reading. "No doubt you have read enough to know what you like or dislike, what satisfies you or leaves you hanging, or what seems problematic to you in a work. Trust your instincts. As you read a work and come across something that bothers you, don't doubt yourself and dismiss it from your mind as I did. Jot it down."

Developing a Thesis

All of this thinking should lead you to a particular question you want to answer, an issue you want to explore, and a point you wish to make. In other words you should be ready to formulate a thesis.

The traditional way of defining "thesis" is that it is an intellectual position that needs to be defended; in short, it is a controversial statement about the work of literature. The military metaphors suggest the ways people traditionally thought about a thesis. The writer was a general who staked out a "position" against various enemy readers who wanted to shoot him or her down. The best positions were highly defendable. The writer then collected an army of facts and quotations as supporting ammunition. Each paragraph would send out attacking squadrons against those who dared to disagree. By thinking of an essay as a war fought against those who disagreed, writers often chose positions that were easy to defend or invented weak antagonists. Some writers, the peace-loving ones, found it difficult to come up with a thesis. It was hard for them to imagine fighting over a story.

Most of my students did not find it useful to think of the essay as a battle against those who disagreed. They preferred to think of themselves as questioners or problem-solvers. "It is often helpful," one student found, "to ask in your paper the same questions you asked yourself when thinking about the work. An interesting way is to use a question to lead to your thesis or make the thesis a question." For example, instead of stating "At the end of 'A Good Man is Hard to Find,' Grandma finally recognizes her kinship with all humanity," one could ask the question "Does Grandma at the end of the story really recognize her kinship with the Misfit or is she only trying to stay alive?" The question focuses the issue more clearly than the statement and better indicates alternative ways of viewing the story. The writer of the essay who asks a question doesn't have to defend a predetermined position, but instead can search out various answers and try to determine which answer might be the most fitting.

Another student searches out patterns that appear in stories. She advises: "Look for recurring actions, repetition of words, reappearing symbols. Then try to find out why the author has used these." One of the student essays at the end of this chapter is a good example of this method. The writer notices that at both the beginning and end of Chekhov's story "Lady With Lapdog" the character Anna cries while Gurov watches her. The student wonders why these scenes frame the story. What do they share in common? How do they differ? The answers to the questions produces an interesting and important understanding of the story.

Yet another student uses a formula to generate papers. "I have found it helpful to use a formula sentence that defines exactly what in a story I want to write about. Here is the formula: 'In story __________, author __________ does __________ by using technique __________.' While this formula doesn't work for all stories, I have found that it is frequently helpful in focusing my thoughts into a manageable but interesting point. It forces me to choose a single aspect of the story and to develop specific examples of supportive evidence."

All of these methods of developing a thesis have certain common elements. The students don't start with a big idea, some enormously original grand notion about life and literature. They all begin by looking carefully at the particular story and noticing particular things about the story. Why is this here? How is this effect achieved? What do these two incidents have in common? Moreover they look for answers not in the clouds, but by carefully examining the story.

A good thesis or good questions arise from being specific. The more specifically you can focus a thesis or question the better your answer or support can be. You might start with the question "Why don't I like this story?" But such a vague question is going to have vague answers. Try to narrow the question down. For example, one of the students did not like "Lady with Lapdog." When he asked himself why it seemed so uninteresting, he realized it was the ending that he found disappointing. But then the student asked himself what sort of ending would have satisfied him? He realized that the sort of ending he was expecting was far less interesting and believable than the ending Chekhov actually wrote. By trying to pinpoint your questions or thesis, you uncover a lot more in a story than you might expect.

Developing Evidence

Once you have developed a good thesis or have a good question you want to ask, most students return to the story for a last good reading. But this reading is different from all the rest. This time they are looking for evidence that will either support their thesis, answer the question or help solve the literary problem they gave themselves.

"After I get a noteworthy idea," a student tells me, "I go through the text again and see what I can find that contributes to that noteworthy character development, or symbolic structure, or whatever it is I have noticed. Only then do I organize the paper."

An excellent student warned her friends: "Even if you have a clear idea of what you want to write about and the sorts of evidence that could support your ideas, reread the story anyway. With this clear perspective, you'll find all kinds of evidence you never realized. If you don't, then you might need to rethink your idea."

Outlines often help students put together their ideas and show them where they have to find supporting evidence. It's just common sense, says one student, "that when you sit down to write that you have a clear picture in your mind of what you mean to say. This clarity is much easier to achieve if you have an outline. A topic outline is enough, but a sentence outline may help you find the words you need to get going."

"If organizing ideas is easy for you, you're lucky!" says another student. "I have to keep my ideas in the back of my mind for days, and while I do mundane, mindless chores, I think about the paper. Then if I'm still not clear, I write my thoughts and quotations on note cards and shuffle them into the best order I can think of."

Still another student writes: "I find it useful to make very specific outlines that tend to be very long. That way when I get to write I can concentrate on writing correctly. I can be more certain of choosing the best word because I know already what I want to say. I have this feeling when I finish a detailed outline that my paper is really finished, and I can relax and enjoy the writing."

But another student says, "Once you start writing your paper, don't be alarmed if your thesis and organization change. This is natural. Writing is, after all, a process of thinking—an idea doesn't really exist until you've put it into words, so until you write it down you can't really tell whether an idea will strike you as valid. But don't try to twist little bits of evidence to support a thesis you no longer believe in. Go with your new idea, and then go back and rework your paper from the beginning. Reworking the opening will take time, but it's always necessary for me. When ever I change something in a paper, no matter how small, I have to change something else. Every element affects the whole. If not, something's wrong."

Writing

Most of my students find that they do their best writing when they set aside a block of uninterrupted time and put themselves in an environment that is comfortable but not sleep-inducing.

The best advice I've heard came from a student who likes to write. "Have a nice place in which to write. Libraries tend to put me to sleep because they're so sterile. I like to write in my bedroom, but first I have to tidy things up. Having my room organized makes me believe that my brain is organized. Have roomates turn down distractions such as the tv or stereo. Plan to settle in for a couple of hours. But give yourself breaks when you feel blocked. Accompany breaks with food, but not too much because it will make you drowsy. I like to drink hot liquids. I alternate between coffee and herbal tea. The coffee perks me up and the tea soothes me."

Students don't often realize that mental activity (especially writing) consumes a lot of calories. You need energy to write. Consequently your writing will improve when you're alert and well fed.

Some students like to spend a lot of time writing a first draft. They can't go on until they have everything they've already written in top notch shape. Others like to write very quickly, unconcerned about grammar, sentence structure or paragraph organization. Getting a draft down helps them avoid writer's block. Then they go back, virtually rewriting the entire paper, correcting errors and filling in the places where their explanations were incomplete or the evidence weak. Remember, there's no single way to write. Every writer must find the method that best suits him or her.

The Finished Product

As a teacher I see many students who have done a lot of thinking about literature, and have given a good deal of time to writing their papers, but their finished product is hurriedly put together. Making a clearly written copy, or typing the final draft is an important part of the process—perhaps for some people the most important part, because it is the part they will be graded on.

Don't short change your hard work by ignoring this final step. By now, you will probably be sick of looking at the paper. Most people just want to hand in their essays and get the process completed. But take the time to read the typed version carefully. If you have written your paper on a word processor, be certain to check spelling and that all the parts of the essay have come out of the printer in the correct order. Don't just make changes on your CRT, but pull a hard copy and check the work in black and white. Errors are much easier to catch in print than when projected on a screen. If your software contains a speller, don't trust it. Most computer spellers aren't sophisticated enough to tell the difference between homonyms or to detect when you should have used an apostrophe to show possession. They are best for catching typos.

What happens if you notice an error just before you hand in your paper? Most teachers would prefer that you make the correction in ink (perhaps messing up your clean copy) than to leave in a mistake. No one is perfect. No typist is perfect. Errors occur. No doubt there will be errors in this book that I did not catch in the countless times I've gone through it or that the professional proofreaders missed. But if you find an error before it's too late, ink in the correction.

QUOTING AND DOCUMENTING

As the students have indicated, one of the stages of preparing a literary essay is to locate all the quotations that support or illustrate the points you wish to make. You should say nothing about the story that you couldn't illustrate with an appropriate quotation either from the story itself or from a reputable critic or scholar. In fact one of the reasons writing literary essays is considered so valuable a discipline for any career is that it forces you to read carefully and avoid unsupported statements and vague impressions. Writers of good literary essays quote frequently and well. They choose quotations that are clear illustrations of their point or eloquent statements of critical support.

After you have quoted, you must document your quotation, that is, indicate where the quotation comes from. There are several reasons proper documentation is necessary: (1) It promotes intellectual honesty.

Students who might make up evidence and quotations are less likely to fabricate sources if they know that it will be easy for readers to check up on them. (2) Documentation helps readers who are interested locate the quotation's context. (3) Most important of all is that documentation helps researchers locate material which might contain other passages of interest.

Quoting

There are two sorts of quotations: long and short quotations. A short quotation can be a single word, and a long quotation several pages. Usually any passage over three sentences is considered a long quotation.

Short quotations are integrated into your sentences and are indicated by quotation marks at their beginning and end. Long quotations are normally separated from the text and indented. You should *not* enclose long quotations in quotation marks. By separating them from the rest of the text, you have already indicated that they are quotations.

Even though you will document quotations, you should still introduce them carefully. The first time you cite an author you should state his or her name. You might also indicate from which work you have taken the quotation especially if you will be refering to multiple works by the same author. You should also place the quotation in context and indicate its significance.

Brenda Piskor is a student who wrote an essay "Anton Chekhov's Subtlety in 'Lady with Lapdog.' " She quotes well and often in her essay. Study, for example, this passage:

> During her first display of emotion Girov exhibits impatience; he is "irritated by her naive tone of voice and her repentence, which was so unexpected and so out of place" (487). Girov acts as though Anna Sergeyevna's inexperience with affairs spoils his intended, detached enjoyment of the evening.

Notice how smoothly Brenda Piskor introduces the quotation by setting it in its narrative context, then she follows the quotation with a sentence that beautifully states how it illuminates Girov's psychology.

The way I have handled Piskor's passage shows how longer quotations should be treated. I have separated the long quotation by skipping a line before and after the quotation and indenting it (usually five spaces) from the left hand margin.

Quoting precisely

All quotations must be quoted precisely as they appeared originally. Any alterations must be clearly indicated by either an ellipsis (. . .) or brackets ([ ]).

Ellipsis are used to indicate where words have been left out. An ellipsis is usually three dots unless the portion left out includes a period, in which case the ommission should be indicated with a four dots. Brackets indicate an addition or minor alteration of wording. Here, for example, is another portion from Brenda Piskor's essay:

> They believe they belong rightfully with each other, "that fate itself . . . intended them for one another, and they [are] unable to understand why he should have a wife and she a husband" (496).

Chekhov originally wrote "they could not help feeling that fate itself had intended them for one another, and they were unable to understand why he should have a wife and she a husband." To shift the sentence into the present tense, Piskor has dropped the word "had" and altered the word "were." She has marked these changes even though they are minor and in no way alter the essential meaning of the text.

Documentation

Documentation should give the reader all the necessary information to locate the source of the quotation. Complete documentation should contain the standard bibliographic information. For books you should include author, title, place of publication, publisher and publishing date as well as page number. For articles you should include besides the author and title of the article, the magazine's name, volume and issue number, year and page numbers.

To make documentation easier for the reader, the information is divided into two places: (1) in parenthesis directly after the quotation and (2) in a list at the end of the paper.

The documentation in the essay appears in parenthesis directly after the quotation. If the author and the source are clear (and in the student papers that follow all the quotations are from Chekhov's "Lady with Lapdog"), all you need to do is place the page number in parenthesis. If the author isn't clear, place it and the page number in parenthesis. If the author is represented by several books and it isn't clear which is the source of the quotation, place a shortened version of the title and the page number in parenthesis.

At the end of the essay, head a list with the title "Works Cited." The list in alphabetical order of the author's last names all the books and articles you referred to in your essay. My commentary in this book, for example, would be listed in this way:

> Bergman, David. *The Story: Readers and Writers of Fiction.* New York: Macmillan, 1988.

A story from this book should be cited this way:

> Chekhov, Anton. "Lady with Lapdog." *The Story: Readers and Writers of Fiction.* Ed. David Bergman. New York: Macmillan, 1988. 482–496.

For a complete discussion of how to quote and document consult the latest edition of the *MLA Handbook for Writers of Research Papers.*

SOME SAMPLE ESSAYS

Over the years I have collected a number of student essays that are particularly good at showing students what sort of work they can accomplish. None of these essays is perfect. Paul Valery said that "a poem is never completed, only abandoned," and the same is true of any piece of writing. I present these essays because I think they are worthy of consideration and because seeing what other have done is often a constructive way to develop one's own skills and abilities.

All three essays are about Anton Chekhov's story "Lady With Lapdog." By choosing three essays on the same story, I hope to show you several different things. First, a good story is open to a number of different critical, intellectual and emotional approaches. "Lady With Lapdog" is considered one of the great short stories, and it is particularly open to different forms of analysis and response. Second, I wanted to show you three different types of essays. Randall Ails discusses how his responses were modified by closely reading the story. He indicates that his first response was inappropriate, and that by frustrating Ails's initial expectations, Chekhov led Ails to a deeper understanding of human relations. Brenda Piskor compares two similar scenes—one that appears at the story's opening and one at its end. By examining these scenes closely, Piskor shows how Chekhov subtlely indicates character development. Her essay compares and contrasts the two scenes in order to show the dynamics of the characters. The last essay by Michael Kliewer is a critical essay. Kliewer does not like the story because he does not think the characters are motivated clearly enough. Kliewer is not in awe of Chekhov's reputation, and he is willing to judge the work by his own lights. Thus we have three different approaches: an analysis of reader's response, a formal analysis, and a critical analysis. Finally, I have chosen these essays because they demonstrate how attitudes toward the work can influence what readers get out of the work. As writers we should be aware that what we say often is a mirror more of our own minds and emotions than the thoughts and feelings in the work.

BRENDA PISKOR
ANTON CHEKHOV'S SUBTLETY IN "LADY WITH LAPDOG"

Some readers of Anton Chekhov's short story, "Lady with Lapdog," have voiced dissatisfaction with the growth of Gurov and Anna Sergeyevna's love for each other. The readers feel that, at the end of the story, Chekhov merely states the characters are in love, and neglects to show the growth of their affection. Chekhov may have left out a scene in which the couple's love blooms; however, by closely parallelling two scenes within the story, Chekhov shows how the couple's attitudes toward each other change throughout the course of their relationship. The second and fifth parts of "Lady with Lapdog" contain similar incidents in a hotel room; however, one takes place at the beginning of the couple's relationship, and the other approximately one year later: both are scenes in which Anna Sergeyevna cries to Gurov.

The reason for Anna Sergeyevna's first outburst focuses on her guilt for committing adultery for the first time. She fears she has become " 'a vulgar worthless woman whom everyone has a right to despise' " (487). She pleads for God's forgiveness and worries about her society's view of adulterous women like herself. She does not consider the effect her deception may have on her husband: " 'I haven't deceived my husband,' " she says, " 'I have deceived myself' " (487). Her tears in this scene are purely selfish; she has no concern for anyone else whom her sin may hurt, except herself.

In contrast, Anna Sergeyevna weeps at the conclusion of the story not only for herself, but also for Gurov: ". . . She was bitterly conscious of the fact that their life was so sad: they could only meet in secret, they had to hide from people, like thieves!" (495). Anna Sergeyevna desperately wants Gurov and herself to be together always, without the need for hiding and lying. The inclusion of Gurov in her concerns shows she has abandoned her self-centered attitude; Anna Sergeyevna grew to love Gurov in the time that lapsed between her first and second displays of emotion. At the conclusion of the story, she displays no guilt for their affair, only remorse that they cannot remain always together.

Likewise, Gurov displays changes in his attitude from the second part of the story to the conclusion; his reactions to Anna Sergeyevna's emotional outbursts differ from one scene to the next. During her first display of emotion, Gurov exhibits impatience; he is "irritated by her naive tone of voice and her repentance, which was so unexpected and so out of place" (487). Gurov acts as though Anna Sergeyevna's inexperience with affairs spoils his intended, detached enjoyment of the evening. He ignores her at first, waiting a full half an hour before responding to her statement that he will no longer respect her, and he only tries to console her after he becomes bored with her weeping.

At the conclusion of the story, however, Gurov displays no impatience at Anna Sergeyevna's crying: " 'Well, let her have her cry,' he thought. 'I'll wait' " (495). He shows consideration for her feelings, and does not seem to care that her outburst infringes on the little time they have to spend peacefully with each other. Also, contrary to his actions when Anna Sergeyevna first cried to him, Gurov desires to comfort her; he feels "profound compassion" and longs "to be sincere, tender . . ." (496). Love has softened his heart; now that he has "fallen in love properly," Gurov displays patience, compassion, and sincerity (496).

Expectedly, the couple's view of their relationship changes from the second chapter to the fifth. As Anna Sergeyevna leaves Yalta on the train, she tells Gurov, " 'It's fate . . . We are parting for ever. Yes, it must be so, for we should never have met' " (489). Both she and Gurov believe her departure from Yalta signifies the end of their association with each other, but she feels their separation is for the best.

Nevertheless, the couple's outlook on their relationship changes considerably by the conclusion of the story; they no longer feel they must discourage their mutual attraction, for they feel "that their love would not come to an end for a long time, if ever" (495). They believe they belong rightfully with each other, "that fate itself . . . intended them for one another, and they [are] unable to understand why he should have a wife and she a husband" (496). They attempt to formulate a plan which would free themselves from their personal constraints and allow themselves to be together forever.

Contrary to some readers' opinions, Chekhov does show how Gurov and Anna Sergeyevna's love progresses in "Lady with Lapdog," but he does it subtly by closely parallelling two incidents in the story which take place at significant points in their relationship. The subtlety employed by Chekhov increases the story's literary value; Chekhov wrote each scene economically, omitting any superfluous details. Instead of merely telling the reader Gurov and Anna Sergeyevna love each other, he artfully shows the development of their personalities throughout their relationship. By examining and comparing both of Anna Sergeyevna's crying scenes, the reader can clearly see that, by the conclusion of the story, Gurov and Anna Sergeyevna learn to love and grow close to each other. The couple themselves are aware of the change; they "felt that this love of theirs had changed them both".

RANDALL C. AILS ON ANTON CHEKHOV'S "LADY WITH LAPDOG"

Finding a piece of literature to be "good" or "bad" through judging the degree of reader response it evokes is a subjective method of evaluation. Stories affect different readers in different ways. If the work affects us, and we see some degree of merit in it, then the work can be said to be a "good" piece of literature. *In Lady With Lapdog,* the author wishes for us to understand *his view* on finding meaningfulness in life through true love and uses the story as his medium to communicate this idea to us. Anton Chekhov's *Lady With Lapdog* is a good piece of literature because the reader recognizes and responds to the theme of the relationship between love and the meaningfulness in life.

As the many characters are introduced in the opening of the story, we see each of them as separate, with their own lives and views. Chekhov gives us an overview of Dimitry Gurov as a married man who sees his wife as "not particularly intelligent, narrow minded, and inelegant" (483), in addition to being an unsatisfying lover. We also learn that Gurov is fond of having an occasional love affair, but always leaves when the situation becomes "an extremely complicated problem . . . rather cumbersome (484)." This description of Gurov shows a character who's untouched by love in his present life. He neither loves his wife, nor his mistresses.

Anna Sergeyevna is introduced as a woman "of good social standing . . . , married," (484), and attractive to Gurov. Anna appears to be bored with her life at home and is searching for some stimulation in the resort town of Yalta. Her life too lacks love as we see her opinion of her husband as a "flunkey" (487). We learn of Anna's desire for a higher meaning in life as she states, "I wanted to live. To live, to live! I was burning with curiosity. I don't think you know what I'm talking about, but I swear I could no longer control myself, something was happening to me, I could not be held back, I told my husband I was ill, and I came here" (487). Anna tells Gurov that she wants "a pure, honest life" (487).

The idea of true love between the characters is suggested as they continue to meet and kiss. Eventually, Gurov displays his love for Anna to us: "he told Anna Sergeyevna that she was beautiful, that she was desirable, made passionate love to her, never left her side (488)." After the characters return to their separate homes, they fully realize the importance of their love for their immediate lives. Chekhov shows us Gurov's mental turmoil as Anna is remembered. "Another month and, he thought, nothing but a memory would remain of Anna Sergeyevna, he would remember her as through a haze, and only occasionally dream of her with a wistful smile, as he did the others before her" (490). And then, "closing his eyes, he saw her as clearly as if she were before him, and she seemed to him lovelier, younger, and tenderer than she had been" (490). Unable to share his thoughts with anyone, Gurov seeks out the woman of his obsession, taking the train to see Anna in her hometown. She is shocked to see him when they meet, and she tells him, "I've suffered so much . . . I've been thinking of you all the time. The thought of you kept me alive. And yet I tried so hard to forget you—why, oh why did you come?" (494) Through their actions and statements, Gurov and Anna confirm their true love for one another.

Having found in their love a source of meaningfulness, Anna and Gurov meet regularly though they are married. The two look forward to their meetings. As Gurov takes his daughter to school, he thinks, "he was going to meet his mistress and not a living soul knew about it" (494). When he arrives at Anna's hotel room, she is "wearing the grey dress he liked most" (495).

In the final scene of the story when the lovers meet at a hotel in Moscow, we learn that they both understand the depth of their love and the sadness of their adulterous situation. Gurov holds Anna while she weeps. "She wept because she could not control her emotions, because she was bitterly conscious of the fact that their life was so sad: they could only meet in secret, they had to hide from people, like thieves! Was not their life ruined?" (495). Here, Gurov sees his love and his sadness as he comforts Anna. He makes the connection between his love and the degree of meaningfulness in his life. "It was only now, when his hair was beginning to grey, that he had fallen in love properly, in good earnest—for the first time in his life" (496).

In realizing their love for one another, Anna and Gurov find meaningfulness in their lives. This meaningfulness stems from their emotions, and they are the ones who assign this love this great meaning. It is in this realization that the story closes, with Anna and Gurov motivated to solve their dilemma in order to bring happiness into their meaningful, but sad, lives. "They tried to think how they could get rid of the necessity of hiding, telling lies, living in different towns, not seeing one another for so long. How were they to free themselves from their intolerable chains?" (496). Motivated by their new perspective, Gurov and Anna begin to seek their freedom.

As the story concludes, the reader, while slightly surprised that no solution to Anna and Gurov's dilemma is presented, realizes that the main point of the story is that the lovers understand that they find true meaning in their love for one another. Their situation is ironic, but it is also secondary in importance to the love theme. Anna and Gurov could be any two lovers, in any situation, and while the degree of their overall happiness would vary, they would center their lives around each other. Chekhov offers no solution to the lovers' problem because he wants the reader to respond not to some future outcome of the lovers' lives, but to the fact that the characters are truly in love.

MICHAEL KLIEWER
LADY WITH LAPDOG: A TRAGEDY

"Lady with Lapdog," although meant to be a story of romance, turns out for the reader to be a tragedy. This is not to imply that structurally there is anything wrong with the story, only that for me the scenario and characters do not make the story believable.

Anton Chekhov, in writing this story, has, in my opinion, written in a very austere and in a high browed manner. There seems to be a lack of strong emotion in the story. The characters are flat and one dimensional. Even when describing the couple's clandestine meetings, Chekhov refrains from letting the reader attain any kind of cathartic feeling from the character's actions. For example, Gurov is described as gazing into Anna's eyes, having kissed her, speaking to her gently and affectionately, and in the next short paragraph makes small talk about finding out her surname (485). To me there seems to be a less than arousing relationship going on here.

The character of Gurov is pathetic. He uses people to his own ends, and women are nothing more than a brief amusement. How are we to believe in his growth and transformation at the end when we are given such a cold and unfeeling description of the man. Chekhov allows for too many extremes in a very short amount of time. No one changes from "male chauvanist" to "prince charming" overnight, so to speak. Chekhov sets the premise that this man does not really like women as human beings. Gurov almost always spoke ill of women, and when discussed in his presence, he described them as a "lower breed" (483).

Anna is no better than Gurov as far as character growth is concerned although her character's change makes more sense. Anna has just finished boarding school and has married quite early. Her naîveté is understandable and admirable, but even she is stock and flat. She has said that the only reason she married in the first place was out of curiosity. One would expect more of a rush of emotion in a young girl who is truly attracted to a man, as she is to Gurov.

In real life the situation of married people having affairs and falling in love with that person is a very common occurrence. But can we relate to a whirlwind romance on holiday that is everlasting? They play victims of life and don't really understand that the banality that they see is only due to themselves. Chekhov does not let us inside the character's mind and emotions to fully comprehend their supposed desperation. The reader is left wanting for sincerity and warmth and even sensuality in a experience which is so filled with passion.

We as readers are only given a glimpse of what we seek at the very end of the story. There is an intensity implied as the lovers frantically search for answers to their problems. The frustration and feeling of being denied the opportunity for "real love" allows the reader finally to sympathize with the characters' situation. But in the progression of emotion throughout the story there is no indication that this relationship is anything more than a casual fling. The transformation of attitudes in the characters is too drastic and unbelievable. Even when Gurov speaks to Anna in a consoling tone and uses the words "my sweet," the statement comes off weak and patronizing.

For me, the story would have held more meaning if Chekhov had let the reader into the characters emotions earlier and with greater intensity. A love story demands passion not only from the characters but also from the writer. If a story is written in the framework of the writers own emotions and experiences this will transfer itself into the story. This story seems almost trite in its depiction of clandestine love and the frustration of fulfilling one's desires.

12

MORE STORIES

KATE CHOPIN

DÉSIRÉE'S BABY

Although Kate Chopin (1851–1904) was born and raised in St. Louis, Missouri, most of her work is set among the Creoles of Louisiana, a world she discovered when at the age of nineteen she married a Louisiana banker and heir to the plantation that served as the model of Uncle Tom's Cabin. When he died twelve years later, leaving her with six children, she returned to St. Louis, a woman of independent wealth, free to write what she wanted.

Even before her husband's death, Chopin had published her first novel At Fault *(1890) and followed it up with two well received collections of short stories. But her masterpiece* The Awakening *(1899) was a scandal because its adulterous heroine makes no apologies for her behavior and experiences no remorse.* The Awakening *was banned from libraries, and Chopin was ostracized from polite society. She died from a stroke after visiting the World's Fair.*

As the day was pleasant, Madame Valmondé drove over to L'Abri to see Désirée and the baby.

It made her laugh to think of Désirée with a baby. Why, it seemed but yesterday that Désirée was little more than a baby herself; when Monsieur in riding through the gateway of Valmondé had found her lying asleep in the shadow of the big stone pillar.

The little one awoke in his arms and began to cry for "Dada." That was as much as she could do or say. Some people thought she might have strayed there of her own accord, for she was of the toddling age. The prevailing belief was that she had been purposely left by a party of Texans, whose canvas-covered wagon, late in the day, had crossed the ferry that Coton Maïs kept, just below the plantation. In time Madame Valmondé abandoned every speculation but the one that Désirée had been sent to her by a beneficent Providence to be the child of her affection, seeing that she was without child of the flesh. For the girl grew to be beautiful and gentle, affectionate and sincere,—the idol of Valmondé.

It was no wonder, when she stood one day against the stone pillar in whose shadow she had lain asleep, eighteen years before, that Armand Aubigny riding by and seeing her there, had fallen in love with her. That was the way all the Aubignys fell in love, as if struck by a pistol shot. The wonder was that he had not loved her before; for he had known her since his father brought him home from Paris, a boy of eight, after his mother died there. The passion that awoke in him that day, when he saw her at the gate, swept along like an avalanche, or like a prairie fire, or like anything that drives headlong over all obstacles.

Monsieur Valmondé grew practical and wanted things well considered: that is, the girl's obscure origin. Armand looked into her eyes and did not care. He was reminded that she was nameless. What did it matter about a name when he could give her one of the oldest and proudest in Louisiana? He ordered the *corbeille* from Paris, and contained himself with what patience he could until it arrived; then they were married.

Madame Valmondé had not seen Désirée and the baby for four weeks. When she reached L'Abri she shuddered at the first sight of it, as she always did. It was a sad looking place, which for many years had not known the gentle presence of a mistress, old Monsieur Aubigny having married and buried his wife in France, and she having loved her own land too well ever to leave it. The roof came down steep and black like a cowl, reaching out beyond the wide galleries that encircled the yellow stuccoed house. Big solemn oaks grew close to it, and their thick-leaved, far-reaching branches shadowed it like a pall. Young Aubigny's rule was a strict one, too, and under it his negroes had forgotten how to be gay, as they had been during the old master's easy-going and indulgent lifetime.

The young mother was recovering slowly, and lay full length, in her soft white muslins and laces, upon a couch. The baby was beside her, upon her arm, where he had fallen asleep, at her breast. The yellow nurse woman sat beside a window fanning herself.

Madame Valmondé bent her portly figure over Désirée and kissed her, holding her an instant tenderly in her arms. Then she turned to the child.

"This is not the baby!" she exclaimed, in startled tones. French was the language spoken at Valmondé in those days.

"I knew you would be astonished," laughed Désirée, "at the way he has grown. The little *cochon de lait!* Look at his legs, mamma, and his hands and fingernails,—real finger-nails. Zandrine had to cut them this morning. Isn't it true, Zandrine?"

The woman bowed her turbaned head majestically, "Mais si, Madame."

"And the way he cries," went on Désirée, "is deafening. Armand heard him the other day as far away as La Blanche's cabin."

Madame Valmondé had never removed her eyes from the child. She lifted it and walked with it over to the window that was lightest. She scanned the baby narrowly, then looked as searchingly at Zandrine, whose face was turned to gaze across the fields.

"Yes, the child has grown, has changed," said Madame Valmondé, slowly, as she replaced it beside its mother. "What does Armand say?"

Désirée's face became suffused with a glow that was happiness itself.

"Oh, Armand is the proudest father in the parish, I believe, chiefly because it is a boy, to bear his name; though he says not,—that he would have loved a girl as well. But I know it isn't true. I know he says that to please me. And mamma," she added, drawing Madame Valmondé's head down to her, and speaking in a whisper, "he hasn't punished one of them—not one of them—since baby is born. Even Négrillon, who pretended to have burnt his leg that he might rest from work—he only laughed, and said Négrillon was a great scamp. Oh, mamma, I'm so happy; it frightens me."

What Désirée said was true. Marriage, and later the birth of his son had softened Armand Aubigny's imperious and exacting nature greatly. This was what made the gentle Désirée so happy, for she loved him desperately. When he frowned she trembled, but loved him. When he smiled, she asked no greater blessing of God. But Armand's dark, handsome face had not often been disfigured by frowns since the day he fell in love with her.

When the baby was about three months old, Désirée awoke one day to the conviction that there was something in the air menacing her peace. It was at first too subtle to grasp. It had only been a disquieting suggestion; an air of mystery among the blacks; unexpected visits from far-off neighbors who could hardly account for their coming. Then a strange, an awful change in her husband's manner, which she dared not ask him to explain. When he spoke to her, it was with averted eyes, from which the old love-light seemed to have gone out. He absented himself from home; and when there, avoided her presence and that of her child, without excuse. And the very spirit of Satan seemed suddenly to take hold of him in his dealings with the slaves. Désirée was miserable enough to die.

She sat in her room, one hot afternoon, in her *peignoir,* listlessly drawing through her fingers the strands of her long, silky brown hair that hung about her shoulders. The baby, half naked, lay asleep upon her own great mahogany bed, that was like a sumptuous throne, with its satin-lined half-canopy. One of La Blanche's little quadroon boys—half naked too—stood fanning the child slowly with a fan of peacock feathers. Désirée's eyes had been fixed absently and sadly upon the baby, while she was striving to penetrate the threatening mist that she felt closing about her. She looked from her child to the boy who stood beside him, and back again; over and over. "Ah!" It was a cry that she could not help; which she was not conscious of having uttered. The blood turned like ice in her veins, and a clammy moisture gathered upon her face.

She tried to speak to the little quadroon boy; but no sound would come, at first. When he heard his name uttered, he looked up, and his mistress was pointing to the door. He laid aside the great, soft fan, and obediently stole away, over the polished floor, on his bare tiptoes.

She stayed motionless, with gaze riveted upon her child, and her face the picture of fright.

Presently her husband entered the room, and without noticing her, went to a table and began to search among some papers which covered it.

"Armand," she called to him, in a voice which must have stabbed him, if he was human. But he did not notice. "Armand," she said again. Then she rose and tottered towards him. "Armand," she panted once more, clutching his arm, "look at our child. What does it mean? tell me."

He coldly but gently loosened her fingers from about his arm and thrust the hand away from him. "Tell me what it means!" she cried despairingly.

"It means," he answered lightly, "that the child is not white; it means that you are not white."

A quick conception of all that this accusation meant for her nerved her with unwonted courage to deny it. "It is a lie; it is not true, I am white! Look at my hair, it is brown; and my eyes are gray, Armand, you know they are gray. And my skin is fair," seizing his wrist. "Look at my hand; whiter than yours, Armand," she laughed hysterically.

"As white as La Blanche's," he returned cruelly; and went away leaving her alone with their child.

When she could hold a pen in her hand, she sent a despairing letter to Madame Valmondé.

"My mother, they tell me I am not white. Armand has told me I am not white. For God's sake tell them it is not true. You must know it is not true. I shall die. I must die. I cannot be so unhappy, and live."

The answer that came was as brief:

"My own Désirée: Come home to Valmondé; back to your mother who loves you. Come with your child."

When the letter reached Désirée she went with it to her husband's study, and laid it open upon the desk before which he sat. She was like a stone image: silent, white, motionless after she placed it there.

In silence he ran his cold eyes over the written words. He said nothing. "Shall I go, Armand?" she asked in tones sharp with agonized suspense.

"Yes, go."

"Do you want me to go?"

"Yes, I want you to go."

He thought Almighty God had dealt cruelly and unjustly with him; and felt, somehow, that he was paying Him back in kind when he stabbed thus into his wife's soul. Moreover he no longer loved her, because of the unconscious injury she had brought upon his home and his name.

She turned away like one stunned by a blow, and walked slowly toward the door, hoping he would call her back.

"Good-by, Armand," she moaned.

He did not answer her. That was his last blow at fate.

Désirée went in search of her child. Zandrine was pacing the sombre gallery with it. She took the little one from the nurse's arms with no word of explanation, and descending the steps, walked away, under the live-oak branches.

It was an October afternoon; the sun was just sinking. Out in the still fields the negroes were picking cotton.

Désirée had not changed the thin white garment nor the slippers which she wore. Her hair was uncovered and the sun's rays brought a golden gleam from its brown meshes. She did not take the broad, beaten road which led to the far-off plantation of Valmondé. She walked across a deserted field, where the stubble bruised her tender feet, so delicately shod, and tore her thin gown to shreds.

She disappeared among the reeds and willows that grew thick along the banks of the deep, sluggish bayou; and she did not come back again.

Some weeks later there was a curious scene enacted at L'Abri. In the centre of the smoothly swept back yard was a great bonfire. Armand Aubigny sat in the wide hallway that commanded a view of the spectacle; and it was he who dealt out to a half dozen negroes the material which kept this fire ablaze.

A graceful cradle of willow, with all its dainty furbishings, was laid upon the pyre, which had already been fed with the richness of a priceless *layette.* Then there were silk gowns, and velvet and satin ones added to these; laces, too, and embroideries; bonnets and gloves; for the *corbeille* had been of rare quality.

The last thing to go was a tiny bundle of letters; innocent little scribblings that Désirée had sent to him during the days of their espousal. There was the remnant of one back in the drawer from which he took them. But it was not Désirée's; it was part of an old letter from his mother to his father. He read it. She was thanking God for the blessing of her husband's love:—

"But, above all," she wrote, "night and day, I thank the good God for having so arranged our lives that our dear Armand will never know that his mother, who adores him, belongs to the race that is cursed with the brand of slavery."

STEPHEN CRANE

THE BRIDE COMES TO YELLOW SKY

Since he achieved so much in his short life, one wonders what Stephen Crane (1871–1900) might have achieved had he lived past his twenties. As it is he published two short novels (Maggie: A Girl of the Streets *and the hyper-realistic* The Red Badge of Courage) *collections of short stories and journalistic pieces and two volumes of poetry.*

Born in New Jersey, the son of a Methodist preacher, he attended Lafayette

College before starting his career as a journalist. His last years were spent in England where he became a friend of Henry James and Joseph Conrad. He died of tuberculosis at the age of twenty-nine.

I

The great Pullman was whirling onward with such dignity of motion that a glance from the window seemed simply to prove that the plains of Texas were pouring eastward. Vast flats of green grass, dull-hued spaces of mesquit and cactus, little groups of frame houses, woods of light and tender trees, all were sweeping into the east, sweeping over the horizon, a precipice.

A newly married pair had boarded this coach at San Antonio. The man's face was reddened from many days in the wind and sun, and a direct result of his new black clothes was that his brick-colored hands were constantly performing in a most conscious fashion. From time to time he looked down respectfully at his attire. He sat with a hand on each knee, like a man waiting in a barber's shop. The glances he devoted to other passengers were furtive and shy.

The bride was not pretty, nor was she very young. She wore a dress of blue cashmere, with small reservations of velvet here and there, and with steel buttons abounding. She continually twisted her head to regard her puff sleeves, very stiff, straight, and high. They embarrassed her. It was quite apparent that she had cooked, and that she expected to cook, dutifully. The blushes caused by the careless scrutiny of some passengers as she had entered the car were strange to see upon this plain, under-class countenance, which was drawn in placid, almost emotionless lines.

They were evidently very happy. "Ever been in a parlor-car before?" he asked, smiling with delight.

"No," she answered; "I never was. It's fine, ain't it?"

"Great! And then after a while we'll go forward to the diner, and get a big lay-out. Finest meal in the world. Charge a dollar."

"Oh, do they?" cried the bride. "Charge a dollar? Why, that's too much—for us—ain't it, Jack?"

"Not this trip, anyhow," he answered bravely. "We're going to go the whole thing."

Later he explained to her about the trains. "You see, it's a thousand miles from one end of Texas to the other; and this train runs right across it, and never stops but for four times." He had the pride of an owner. He pointed out to her the dazzling fittings of the coach; and in truth her eyes opened wider as she contemplated the sea-green figured velvet, the shining brass, silver, and glass, the wood that gleamed as darkly brilliant as the surface of a pool of oil. At one end a bronze figure sturdily held a support for a separated chamber, and at convenient places on the ceiling were frescos in olive and silver.

To the minds of the pair, their surroundings reflected the glory of their marriage that morning in San Antonio; this was the environment of their new estate; and the man's face in particular beamed with an elation that made him appear ridiculous to the negro porter. This individual at times surveyed them from afar with an amused and superior grin. On other occasions he bullied them with skill in ways that did not make it exactly plain to them that they were being bullied. He subtly used all the manners of the most unconquerable kind of snobbery. He oppressed them; but of this oppression they had small knowledge, and they speedily forgot that infrequently a number of travellers covered them with stares of derisive enjoyment. Historically there was supposed to be something infinitely humorous in their situation.

"We are due in Yellow Sky at 3:42," he said, looking tenderly into her eyes.

"Oh, are we?" she said, as if she had not been aware of it. To evince surprise at her husband's statement was part of her wifely amiability. She took from a pocket a little silver watch; and as she held it before her, and stared at it with a frown of attention, the new husband's face shone.

"I bought it in San Anton' from a friend of mine," he told her gleefully.

"It's seventeen minutes past twelve," she said, looking up at him with a kind of shy and clumsy coquetry. A passenger, noting this play, grew excessively sardonic, and winked at himself in one of the numerous mirrors.

At last they went to the dining-car. Two rows of negro waiters, in glowing white suits, surveyed their entrance with the interest, and also the equanimity, of men who had been forewarned. The pair fell to the lot of a waiter who happened to feel pleasure in steering them through their meal. He viewed them with the manner of a fatherly pilot, his countenance radiant with benevolence. The patronage, entwined with the ordinary deference, was not plain to them. And yet, as they returned to their coach, they showed in their faces a sense of escape.

To the left, miles down a long purple slope, was a little ribbon of mist where moved the keening Rio Grande. The train was approaching it at an angle, and the apex was Yellow Sky. Presently it was apparent that, as the distance from Yellow Sky grew shorter, the husband became commensurately restless. His brick-red hands were more insistent in their prominence. Occasionally he was even rather absent-minded and far-away when the bride leaned forward and addressed him.

As a matter of truth, Jack Potter was beginning to find the shadow of a deed weigh upon him like a leaden slab. He, the town marshal of Yellow Sky, a man known, liked, and feared in his corner, a prominent person, had gone to San Antonio to meet a girl he believed he loved, and there, after the usual prayers, had actually induced her to marry him, without consulting Yellow Sky for any part of the transaction. He was now bringing his bride before an innocent and unsuspecting community.

Of course people in Yellow Sky married as it pleased them, in accordance with a general custom; but such was Potter's thought of his duty to his friends, or of their idea of his duty, or of an unspoken form which does not control men in these matters, that he felt he was heinous. He had committed an extraordinary crime. Face to face with this girl in San Antonio, and spurred by his sharp impulse, he had gone headlong over all the social hedges. At San Antonio he was like a man hidden in the dark. A knife to sever any friendly duty, any form, was easy to his hand in that remote city. But the hour of Yellow Sky—the hour of daylight—was approaching.

He knew full well that his marriage was an important thing to his town. It could only be exceeded by the burning of the new hotel. His friends could not forgive him. Frequently he had reflected on the advisability of telling them by telegraph, but a new cowardice had been upon him. He feared to do it. And now the train was hurrying him toward a scene of amazement, glee, and reproach. He glanced out of the window at the line of haze swinging slowly in toward the train.

Yellow Sky had a kind of brass band, which played painfully, to the delight of the populace. He laughed without heart as he thought of it. If the citizens could dream of his prospective arrival with his bride, they would parade the band at the station and escort them, amid cheers and laughing congratulations, to his adobe home.

He resolved that he would use all the devices of speed and plainscraft in making the journey from the station to his house. Once within that safe citadel, he could issue some sort of vocal bulletin, and then not go among the citizens until they had time to wear off a little of their enthusiasm.

The bride looked anxiously at him. "What's worrying you, Jack?"

He laughed again. "I'm not worrying, girl; I'm only thinking of Yellow Sky."

She flushed in comprehension.

A sense of mutual guilt invaded their minds and developed a finer tenderness. They looked at each other with eyes softly aglow. But Potter often laughed the same nervous laugh; the flush upon the bride's face seemed quite permanent.

The traitor to the feelings of Yellow Sky narrowly watched the speeding landscape. "We're nearly there," he said.

Presently the porter came and announced the proximity of Potter's home. He held a brush in his hand, and, with all his airy superiority gone, he brushed Potter's new clothes as the latter slowly turned this way and that way. Potter fumbled out a coin and gave it to the porter, as he had seen others do. It was a heavy and muscle-bound business, as that of a man shoeing his first horse.

The porter took their bag, and as the train began to slow they moved forward to the hooded platform of the car. Presently the two engines and their long string of coaches rushed into the station of Yellow Sky.

"They have to take water here," said Potter, from a constricted throat and in mournful cadence, as one announcing death. Before the train stopped his eye had swept the length of the platform, and he was glad and astonished to see there was none upon it but the station-agent, who, with a slightly hurried and anxious air, was walking toward the water-tanks. When the train had halted, the porter alighted first, and placed in position a little temporary step.

"Come on, girl," said Potter, hoarsely. As he helped her down they each laughed on a false note. He took the bag from the negro, and bade his wife cling to his arm. As they slunk rapidly away, his hang-dog glance perceived that they were unloading the two trunks, and also that the station agent, far ahead near the baggage car, had turned and was running towards him, making gestures. He laughed, and groaned as he laughed, when he noted the first effect of his marital bliss upon Yellow Sky. He gripped his wife's arm firmly to his side, and they fled. Behind them the porter stood, chuckling fatuously.

II

The California express on the Southern Railway was due at Yellow Sky in twenty-one minutes. There were six men at the bar of the Weary Gentleman Saloon. One was a drummer who talked a great deal and rapidly; three were Texans who did not care to talk at that time; and two were Mexican sheep-herders, who did not talk as a general practice in the Weary Gentleman Saloon. The barkeeper's dog lay on the board walk that crossed in front of the door. His head was on his paws, and he glanced drowsily here and there with the constant vigilance of a dog that is kicked on occasion. Across the sandy street were some vivid green grass-plots, so wonderful in appearance, amid the sands that burned near them in a blazing sun, that they caused a doubt in the mind. They exactly resembled the grass mats used to represent lawns on the stage. At the cooler end of the railway station, a man without a coat sat in a tilted chair and smoked his pipe. The fresh-cut bank of the Rio Grande circled near the town, and there could be seen beyond it a great plum-colored plain of mesquit.

Save for the busy drummer and his companions in the saloon, Yellow Sky was dozing. The newcomer leaned gracefully upon the bar, and recited many tales with the confidence of a bard who has come upon a new field.

"—and at the moment that the old man fell downstairs with the bureau in his arms, the old woman was coming up with two scuttles of coal, and of course—"

The drummer's tale was interrupted by a young man who suddenly appeared in the open door. He cried: "Scratchy Wilson's drunk, and has turned loose with both hands." The two Mexicans at once set down their glasses and faded out of the rear entrance of the saloon.

The drummer, innocent and jocular, answered: "All right, old man. S'pose he has? Come in and have a drink, anyhow."

But the information had made such an obvious cleft in every skull in the room that the drummer was obliged to see its importance. All had become instantly solemn. "Say," said he, mystified, "what is this?" His three companions made the introductory gesture of eloquent speech; but the young man at the door forestalled them.

"It means, my friend," he answered, as he came into the saloon, "that for the next two hours this town won't be a health resort."

The barkeeper went to the door, and locked and barred it; reaching out of the window, he pulled in heavy wooden shutters, and barred them. Immediately a solemn, chapel-like gloom was upon the place. The drummer was looking from one to another.

"But say," he cried, "what is this anyhow? You don't mean there is going to be a gun-fight?"

"Don't know whether there'll be a fight or not," answered one man, grimly; "but there'll be some shootin'—some good shootin'."

The young man who had warned them waved his hand. "Oh, there'll be a fight fast enough, if any one wants it. Anybody can get a fight out there in the street. There's a fight just waiting."

The drummer seemed to be swayed between the interest of a foreigner and a perception of personal danger.

"What did you say his name was?" he asked.

"Scratchy Wilson," they answered in chorus.

"And will he kill anybody? What are you going to do? Does this happen often? Does he rampage around like this once a week or so? Can he break in that door?"

"No; he can't break down that door," replied the barkeeper. "He's tried it three times. But when he comes you'd better lay down on the floor, stranger. He's dead sure to shoot at it, and a bullet may come through."

Thereafter the drummer kept a strict eye upon the door. The time had not yet been called for him to hug the floor, but, as a minor precaution, he sidled near to the wall. "Will he kill anybody?" he said again.

The men laughed low and scornfully at the question.

"He's out to shoot, and he's out for trouble. Don't see any good in experimentin' with him."

"But what do you do in a case like this? What do you do?"

A man responded: "Why, he and Jack Potter—"

"But," in chorus the other men interrupted, "Jack Potter's in San Anton'."

"Well, who is he? What's he got to do with it?"

"Oh, he's the town marshal. He goes out and fights Scratchy when he gets on one of these tears."

"Wow!" said the drummer, mopping his brow. "Nice job he's got."

The voices had toned away to mere whisperings. The drummer wished to ask further questions, which were born of an increasing anxiety and bewilderment; but when he attempted them, the men merely looked at him in irritation and motioned him to remain silent. A tense waiting hush was upon them. In the deep shadows of the room their eyes shone as they listened for sounds from the street. One man made three gestures at the barkeeper; and the latter moving like a ghost, handed him a glass and a bottle. The man poured a full glass of whiskey, and set down the bottle noiselessly. He gulped the whiskey in a swallow, and turned again toward the door in immovable silence. The drummer saw that the barkeeper, without a sound, had taken a Winchester from beneath the bar. Later he saw this individual beckoning to him, so he tiptoed across the room.

"You better come with me back of the bar."

"No, thanks," said the drummer, perspiring; "I'd rather be where I can make a break for the back door."

Whereupon the man of bottles made a kindly but peremptory gesture. The drummer obeyed it, and, finding himself seated on a box with his head below the level of the bar, balm was laid upon his soul at sight of various zinc and copper fittings that bore a resemblance to armor-plate. The barkeeper took a seat comfortably upon an adjacent box.

"You see," he whispered, "this here Scratchy Wilson is a wonder with a gun—a perfect wonder; and when he goes on the wartrail, we hunt our holes—naturally. He's about the last one of the old gang that used to hang out along the river here. He's a terror when he's drunk. When he's sober he's all right—kind of simple—wouldn't hurt a fly—nicest fellow in town. But when he's drunk—whoo!"

There were periods of stillness. "I wish Jack Potter was back from San Anton'," said the barkeeper. "He shot Wilson up once—in the leg—and he would sail in and pull out the kinks in this thing."

Presently they heard from a distance the sound of a shot, followed by three wild yowls. It instantly removed a bond from the men in the darkened saloon. There was a shuffling of feet. They looked at each other. "Here he comes," they said.

III

A man in a maroon-colored flannel shirt, which had been purchased for purposes of decoration, and made principally by some Jewish women on the East Side of New York, rounded a corner and walked into the middle of the main street of Yellow Sky. In either hand the man held a long, heavy, blue-black revolver. Often he yelled, and these cries rang through a semblance of a deserted village, shrilly flying over the roofs in a volume that seemed to have no relation to the ordinary vocal strength of a man. It was as if the surrounding stillness formed the arch of a tomb over him. These cries of ferocious challenge rang against walls of silence. And his boots had red tops with gilded imprints, of the kind beloved in winter by little sledding boys on the hillsides of New England.

The man's face flamed in a rage begot of whiskey. His eyes, rolling, and yet keen for ambush, hunted the still doorways and windows. He walked with the creeping movement of the midnight cat. As it occurred to him, he roared menacing information. The long revolvers in his hands were as easy as straws; they were moved with an electric swiftness. The little fingers of each hand played sometimes in a musician's way. Plain from the low collar of the shirt, the cords of his neck straightened and sank, straightened and sank as passion moved him. The only sounds were his terrible invitations. The calm adobes preserved their demeanor at the passing of this small thing in the middle of the street.

There was no offer of fight—no offer of fight. The man called to the sky. There were no attractions. He bellowed and fumed and swayed his revolvers here and everywhere.

The dog of the barkeeper of the Weary Gentleman Saloon had not appreciated the advance of events. He yet lay dozing in front of his master's door. At sight of the dog, the man paused and raised his revolver humorously. At sight of the man, the dog sprang up and walked diagonally away, with a sullen head, and growling. The man yelled, and the dog broke into a gallop. As it was about to enter an alley, there was a loud noise, a whistling, and something spat the ground directly before it. The dog screamed, and, wheeling in terror, galloped headlong in a new direction. Again there was a noise, a whistling, and sand was kicked viciously before it. Fear-stricken, the dog turned and flurried like an animal in a pen. The man stood laughing, his weapons at his hips.

Ultimately the man was attracted by the closed door of the Weary Gentleman Saloon. He went to it and, hammering with a revolver, demanded drink.

The door remaining imperturbable, he picked a bit of paper from the walk, and nailed it to the framework with a knife. He then turned his back contemptuously upon this popular resort, and, walking to the opposite side of the street and spinning there on his heel quickly and lithely, fired at the bit of paper. He missed it by a half-inch. He swore at himself, and went away. Later he comfortably fusilladed the windows of his most intimate friend. The man was playing with this town; it was a toy for him.

But still there was no offer of fight. The name of Jack Potter, his ancient antagonist, entered his mind, and he concluded that it would be a glad thing if he should go to Potter's house, and by bombardment induce him to come out and fight. He moved in the direction of his desire, chanting Apache scalp-music.

When he arrived at it, Potter's house presented the same still front as had the other adobes. Taking up a strategic position, the man howled a challenge. But this house regarded him as might a great stone god. It gave no sign. After a decent wait, the man howled further challenges, mingling with them wonderful epithets.

Presently there came the spectacle of a man churning himself into deepest rage over the immobility of a house. He fumed at it as the winter wind attacks a prairie cabin in the North. To the distance there should have gone the sound of a tumult like the fighting of two hundred Mexicans. As necessity bade him, he paused for breath or to reload his revolvers.

IV

Potter and his bride walked sheepishly and with speed. Sometimes they laughed together shamefacedly and low.

"Next corner, dear," he said finally.

They put forth the efforts of a pair walking bowed against a strong wind. Potter was about to raise a finger to point the first appearance of the new home when, as they circled the corner, they came face to face with a man in a maroon-colored shirt, who was feverishly pushing cartridges into a large revolver. Upon the instant the man dropped his revolver to the ground, and, like lightning, whipped another from its holster. The second weapon was aimed at the bridegroom's chest.

There was a silence. Potter's mouth seemed to be merely a grave for his tongue. He exhibited an instinct to at once loosen his arm from the woman's grip, and he dropped the bag to the sand. As for the bride, her face had gone as yellow as old cloth. She was a slave to hideous rites, gazing at the apparitional snake.

The two men faced each other at a distance of three paces. He of the revolver smiled with a new and quiet ferocity.

"Tried to sneak up on me," he said. "Tried to sneak up on me!" His eyes grew more baleful. As Potter made a slight movement, the man thrust his revolver venomously forward. "No; don't you do it, Jack Potter. Don't you move a finger toward a gun just yet. Don't you move an eyelash. The time has come for me to settle with you, and I'm goin' to do it my own way, and loaf along with no interferin'. So if you don't want a gun bent on you, just mind what I tell you."

Potter looked at his enemy. "I ain't got a gun on me, Scratchy," he said. "Honest, I ain't." He was stiffening and steadying, but yet somewhere at the back of his mind a vision of the Pullman floated: the sea-green figured velvet, the shining brass, silver, and glass, the wood that gleamed as darkly brilliant as the surface of a pool of oil—all the glory of the marriage, the environment of the new estate. "You know I fight when it comes to fighting, Scratchy Wilson; but I ain't got a gun on me. You'll have to do all the shootin' yourself."

His enemy's face went livid. He stepped forward, and lashed his weapon to and fro before Potter's chest. "Don't you tell me you ain't got no gun on you, you whelp. Don't tell me no lie like that. There ain't a man in Texas ever seen you without no gun. Don't take me for no kid." His eyes blazed with light, and his throat worked like a pump.

"I ain't takin' you for no kid," answered Potter. His heels had not moved an inch backward. "I'm takin' you for a—fool. I tell you I ain't got a gun, and I ain't. If you're goin' to shoot me up, you better begin now; you'll never get a chance like this again."

So much enforced reasoning had told on Wilson's rage; he was calmer. "If you ain't got a gun, why ain't you got a gun?" he sneered. "Been to Sunday school?"

"I ain't got a gun because I've just come from San Anton' with my wife. I'm married," said Potter. "And if I'd thought there was going to be any galoots like you prowling around when I brought my wife home, I'd had a gun, and don't you forget it."

"Married!" said Scratchy, not at all comprehending.

"Yes, married. I'm married," said Potter, distinctly.

"Married?" said Scratchy. Seemingly for the first time, he saw the drooping, drowning woman at the other man's side. "No!" he said. He was like a creature allowed a glimpse of another world. He moved a pace backward, and his arm, with the revolver, dropped to his side. "Is this the lady?" he asked.

"Yes; this is the lady," answered Potter.

There was another period of silence.

"Well," said Wilson at last, slowly, "I s'pose it's all off now."

"It's all off if you say so, Scratchy. You know I didn't make the trouble." Potter lifted his valise.

"Well, I 'low it's off, Jack," said Wilson. He was looking at the ground. "Married!" He was not a student of chivalry; it was merely that in the presence of this foreign condition he was a simple child of the earlier plains. He picked up his starboard revolver, and, placing both weapons in their holsters, he went away. His feet made funnel-shaped tracks in the heavy sand.

ANTON CHEKHOV

LADY WITH LAPDOG

Anton Chekhov (1860–1904) studied at Moscow University to become not a writer, but a doctor. His medical training had a deep influence on his writing for it not only filled him with sympathy for the suffering and weak, but also taught him the need to view such conditions straightforwardly and honestly. He wrote in a letter once, "You confuse two things: solving a problem and stating a problem correctly. It is only the second that is obligatory for the artist." Chekhov diagnoses his characters as he would patients, but he does not prescribe for them.

Chekhov began his literary career writing comic sketches, but he soon moved into more serious work. He wrote nearly six hundred stories, but he is equally famous for his plays. The psychological complexity and social criticism of Uncle Vanya, The Three Sisters *and* The Cherry Orchard *altered the direction of Western theatre. "Lady With Lapdog" begins in a resort city; it was in such a city that he died of tuberculosis at the age of forty-four. Chekhov is buried in Moscow.*

I

The appearance on the front of a new arrival—a lady with a lapdog—became the topic of general conversation. Dimitry Dmitrich Gurov, who had been a fortnight in Yalta[1] and got used to its ways, was also interested in new arrivals. One day, sitting on the terrace of Vernet's restaurant, he saw a young woman walking along the promenade; she was fair, not very tall, and wore a toque; behind her trotted a white pomeranian.

Later he came across her in the park and in the square several times a day. She was always alone, always wearing the same toque, followed by the white pomeranian. No one knew who she was, and she became known simply as the lady with the lapdog.

"If she's here without her husband and without any friends," thought Gurov, "it wouldn't be a bad idea to strike up an acquaintance with her."

He was not yet forty, but he had a twelve-year-old daughter and two schoolboy sons. He had been married off when he was still in his second year at the university, and his wife seemed to him now to be almost twice his age. She was a tall, black-browed woman, erect, dignified, austere, and, as she liked to describe herself, a "thinking person." She was a great reader, preferred the new "advanced" spelling, called her husband by the more formal "Dimitry" and not the familiar "Dmitry"; and though he secretly considered her not particularly intelligent, narrow-minded, and inelegant, he was afraid of her and disliked being at home. He had been unfaithful to her for a long time, he was often unfaithful to her, and that was why, perhaps, he almost always spoke ill of women, and when men discussed women in his presence, he described them as *the lower breed.*

He could not help feeling that he had had enough bitter experience to have the right to call them as he pleased, but all the same without *the lower breed* he could not have existed a couple of days. He was bored

[1] Yalta is located on the Black Sea in southwestern Russia and is one of the biggest resort areas in the Soviet Union.

and ill at ease among men, with whom he was reticent and cold, but when he was among women he felt at ease, he knew what to talk about with them and how to behave; even when he was silent in their company he experienced no feeling of constraint. There was something attractive, something elusive in his appearance, in his character and his whole person, that women found interesting and irresistible; he was aware of it, and was himself drawn to them by some irresistible force.

Long and indeed bitter experience had taught him that every new affair, which at first relieved the monotony of life so pleasantly and appeared to be such a charming and light adventure, among decent people and especially among Muscovites, who are so irresolute and so hard to rouse, inevitably developed into an extremely complicated problem and finally the whole situation became rather cumbersome. But at every new meeting with an attractive woman he forgot all about this experience, he wanted to enjoy life so badly and it all seemed so simple and amusing.

And so one afternoon, while he was having dinner at a restaurant in the park, the woman in the toque walked in unhurriedly and took a seat at the table next to him. The way she looked, walked, and dressed, wore her hair, told him that she was of good social standing, that she was married, that she was in Yalta for the first time, that she was alone and bored. . . . There was a great deal of exaggeration in the stories about the laxity of morals among the Yalta visitors, and he dismissed them with contempt, for he knew that such stories were mostly made up by people who would gladly have sinned themselves if they had had any idea how to go about it; but when the woman sat down at the table three yards away from him he remembered these stories of easy conquests and excursions to the mountains and the tempting thought of a quick and fleeting affair, an affair with a strange woman whose very name he did not know, suddenly took possession of him.

He tried to attract the attention of the dog by calling softly to it, and when the pomeranian came up to him he shook a finger at it. The pomeranian growled. Gurov again shook a finger at it.

The woman looked up at him and immediately lowered her eyes.

"He doesn't bite," she said and blushed.

"May I give him a bone?" he asked, and when she nodded, he said amiably: "Have you been long in Yalta?"

"About five days."

"And I am just finishing my second week here."

They said nothing for the next few minutes.

"Time flies," she said without looking at him, "and yet it's so boring here."

"That's what one usually hears people saying here. A man may be living in Belev and Zhizdra or some other God-forsaken hole and he isn't bored, but the moment he comes here all you hear from him is

'Oh, it's so boring! Oh, the dust!' You'd think he'd come from Granada!"

She laughed. Then both went on eating in silence, like complete strangers; but after dinner they strolled off together, and they embarked on the light playful conversation of free and contented people who do not care where they go or what they talk about. They walked, and talked about the strange light that fell on the sea; the water was of such a soft and warm lilac, and the moon threw a shaft of gold across it. They talked about how close it was after a hot day. Gurov told her that he lived in Moscow, that he was a graduate in philology but worked in a bank, that he had at one time thought of singing in a private opera company but had given up the idea, that he owned two houses in Moscow. . . . From her he learnt that she had grown up in Petersburg, but had got married in the town of S—, where she had been living for the past two years, that she would stay another month in Yalta, and that her husband, who also needed a rest, might join her. She was quite unable to tell him what her husband's job was, whether he served in the offices of the provincial governor or the rural council, and she found this rather amusing herself. Gurov also found out that her name and patronymic were Anna Sergeyevna.

Later, in his hotel room, he thought about her and felt sure that he would meet her again the next day. It had to be. As he went to bed he remembered that she had only recently left her boarding school, that she had been a schoolgirl like his own daughter; he recalled how much diffidence and angularity there was in her laughter and her conversation with a stranger—it was probably the first time in her life she had found herself alone, in a situation when men followed her, looked at her, and spoke to her with only one secret intention, an intention she could hardly fail to guess. He remembered her slender, weak neck, her beautiful grey eyes.

"There's something pathetic about her, all the same," he thought as he fell asleep.

II

A week had passed since their first meeting. It was a holiday. It was close indoors, while in the streets a strong wind raised clouds of dust and tore off people's hats. All day long one felt thirsty, and Gurov kept going to the terrace of the restaurant, offering Anna Sergeyevna fruit drinks and ices. There was nowhere to go.

In the evening, when the wind had dropped a little, they went to the pier to watch the arrival of the steamer. There were a great many people taking a walk on the landing pier; some were meeting friends, they had bunches of flowers in their hands. It was there that two peculiarities of the Yalta smart set at once arrested attention: the middle-aged women dressed as if they were still young girls and there was a great number of generals.

Because of the rough sea the steamer arrived late, after the sun had set, and she had to swing backwards and forwards several times before getting alongside the pier. Anna Sergeyevna looked at the steamer and the passengers through her lorgnette, as though trying to make out some friends, and when she turned to Gurov her eyes were sparkling. She talked a lot, asked many abrupt questions, and immediately forgot what it was she had wanted to know; then she lost her lorgnette in the crowd of people.

The smartly dressed crowd dispersed; soon they were all gone, the wind had dropped completely, but Gurov and Anna were still standing there as though waiting to see if someone else would come off the boat. Anna Sergeyevna was no longer talking. She was smelling her flowers without looking at Gurov.

"It's a nice evening," he said. "Where shall we go now? Shall we go for a drive?"

She made no answer.

Then he looked keenly at her and suddenly put his arms round her and kissed her on the mouth. He felt the fragrance and dampness of the flowers and immediately looked round him fearfully: had anyone seen them?

"Let's go to your room," he said softly.

And both walked off quickly.

It was very close in her hotel room, which was full of the smell of the scents she had bought in a Japanese shop. Looking at her now, Gurov thought: "Life is full of strange encounters!" From his past he preserved the memory of carefree, good-natured women, whom love had made gay and who were grateful to him for the happiness he gave them, however short-lived; and of women like his wife, who made love without sincerity, with unnecessary talk, affectedly, hysterically, with such an expression, as though it were not love or passion, but something much more significant; and of two or three very beautiful, frigid women, whose faces suddenly lit up with a predatory expression, an obstinate desire to take, to snatch from life more than it could give; these were women no longer in their first youth, capricious, unreasoning, despotic, unintelligent women, and when Gurov lost interest in them, their beauty merely aroused hatred in him and the lace trimmings on their négligés looked to him then like the scales of a snake.

But here there was still the same diffidence and angularity of inexperienced youth—an awkward feeling; and there was also the impression of embarrassment, as if someone had just knocked at the door. Anna Sergeyevna, this lady with the lapdog, apparently regarded what had happened in a peculiar sort of way, very seriously, as though she had become a fallen woman—so it seemed to him, and he found it odd and disconcerting. Her features lengthened and drooped, and her long hair hung mournfully on either side of her face; she sank into thought in a despondent pose, like a woman taken in adultery in an old painting.

"It's wrong," she said. "You'll be the first not to respect me now."

There was a water-melon on the table. Gurov cut himself a slice and began to eat it slowly. At least half an hour passed in silence.

Anna Sergeyevna was very touching; there was an air of a pure, decent, naïve woman about her, a woman who had very little experience of life; the solitary candle burning on the table scarcely lighted up her face, but it was obvious that she was unhappy.

"But, darling, why should I stop respecting you?" Gurov asked. "You don't know yourself what you're saying."

"May God forgive me," she said, and her eyes filled with tears. "It's terrible."

"You seem to wish to justify yourself."

"How can I justify myself? I am a bad, despicable creature. I despise myself and have no thought of justifying myself. I haven't deceived my husband, I've deceived myself. And not only now. I've been deceiving myself for a long time. My husband is, I'm sure, a good and honest man, but, you see, he is a flunkey. I don't know what he does at his office, all I know is that he is a flunkey. I was only twenty when I married him, I was eaten up by curiosity, I wanted something better. There surely must be a different kind of life, I said to myself. I wanted to live. To live, to live! I was burning with curiosity. I don't think you know what I am talking about, but I swear I could no longer control myself, something was happening to me, I could not be held back, I told my husband I was ill, and I came here. . . . Here too I was going about as though in a daze, as though I was mad, and now I've become a vulgar worthless woman whom everyone has a right to despise."

Gurov could not help feeling bored as he listened to her; he was irritated by her naïve tone of voice and her repentance, which was so unexpected and so out of place; but for the tears in her eyes, he might have thought that she was joking or play-acting.

"I don't understand," he said gently, "what it is you want."

She buried her face on his chest and clung close to him.

"Please, please believe me," she said. "I love a pure, honest life. I hate immorality. I don't know myself what I am doing. The common people say 'the devil led her astray.' I too can now say about myself that the devil has led me astray."

"There, there . . ." he murmured.

He gazed into her staring, frightened eyes, kissed her, spoke gently and affectionately to her, and gradually she calmed down and her cheerfulness returned; both of them were soon laughing.

Later, when they went out, there was not a soul on the promenade, the town with its cypresses looked quite dead, but the sea was still roaring and dashing itself against the shore; a single launch tossed on the waves, its lamp flickering sleepily.

They hailed a cab and drove to Oreanda.

"I've just found out your surname, downstairs in the lobby," said Gurov. "Von Diederitz. Is your husband a German?"

"No. I believe his grandfather was German. He is of the Orthodox faith himself."

In Oreanda they sat on a bench not far from the church, looked down on the sea, and were silent. Yalta could scarcely be seen through the morning mist. White clouds lay motionless on the mountain tops. Not a leaf stirred on the trees, the cicadas chirped, and the monotonous, hollow roar of the sea, coming up from below, spoke of rest, of eternal sleep awaiting us all. The sea had roared like that down below when there was no Yalta or Oreanda, it was roaring now, and it would go on roaring as indifferently and hollowly when we were here no more. And in this constancy, in this complete indifference to the life and death of each one of us, there is perhaps hidden the guarantee of our eternal salvation, the never-ceasing movement of life on earth, the never-ceasing movement towards perfection. Sitting beside a young woman who looked so beautiful at the break of day, soothed and enchanted by the sight of all that fairy-land scenery—the sea, the mountains, the clouds, the wide sky—Gurov reflected that, when you came to think of it, everything in the world was really beautiful, everything but our own thoughts and actions when we lose sight of the higher aims of existence and our dignity as human beings.

Someone walked up to them, a watchman probably, looked at them, and went away. And there seemed to be something mysterious and also beautiful in this fact, too. They could see the Theodosia boat coming towards the pier, lit up by the sunrise, and with no lights.

"There's dew on the grass," said Anna Sergeyevna, breaking the silence.

"Yes. Time to go home."

They went back to the town.

After that they met on the front every day at twelve o'clock, had lunch and dinner together, went for walks, admired the sea. She complained of sleeping badly and of her heart beating uneasily, asked the same questions, alternately worried by feelings of jealousy and by fear that he did not respect her sufficiently. And again and again in the park or in the square, when there was no one in sight, he would draw her to him and kiss her passionately. The complete idleness, these kisses in broad daylight, always having to look round for fear of someone watching them, the heat, the smell of the sea, and the constant looming into sight of idle, well-dressed, and well-fed people seemed to have made a new man of him; he told Anna Sergeyevna that she was beautiful, that she was desirable, made passionate love to her, never left her side, while she was often lost in thought and kept asking him to admit that he did not really respect her, that he was not in the least in love with her and only saw in her a vulgar woman. Almost every night they drove out of town, to Oreanda or to the waterfall; the excursion was always a success, and every time their impressions were invariably grand and beautiful.

They kept expecting her husband to arrive. But a letter came from him in which he wrote that he was having trouble with his eyes and implored his wife to return home as soon as possible. Anna Sergeyevna lost no time in getting ready for her journey home.

"It's a good thing I'm going," she said to Gurov. "It's fate."

She took a carriage to the railway station, and he saw her off. The drive took a whole day. When she got into the express train, after the second bell, she said:

"Let me have another look at you. . . . One last look. So."

She did not cry, but looked sad, just as if she were ill, and her face quivered.

"I'll be thinking of you, remembering you," she said. "Good-bye. You're staying, aren't you? Don't think badly of me. We are parting for ever. Yes, it must be so, for we should never have met. Well, good-bye. . . ."

The train moved rapidly out of the station; its lights soon disappeared, and a minute later it could not even be heard, just as though everything had conspired to put a quick end to this sweet trance, this madness. And standing alone on the platform gazing into the dark distance, Gurov listened to the churring of the grasshoppers and the humming of the telegraph wires with a feeling as though he had just woken up. He told himself that this had been just one more affair in his life, just one more adventure, and that it too was over, leaving nothing but a memory. He was moved and sad, and felt a little penitent that the young woman, whom he would never see again, had not been happy with him; he had been amiable and affectionate with her, but all the same in his behaviour to her, in the tone of his voice and in his caresses, there was a suspicion of light irony, the somewhat coarse arrogance of the successful male, who was, moreover, almost twice her age. All the time she called him good, wonderful, high-minded; evidently she must have taken him to be quite different from what he really was, which meant that he had involuntarily deceived her.

At the railway station there was already a whiff of autumn in the air; the evening was chilly.

"Time I went north too," thought Gurov, as he walked off the platform. "High time!"

III

At home in Moscow everything was already like winter: the stoves were heated, and it was still dark in the morning when the children were getting ready to go to school and having breakfast, so that the nurse had to light the lamp for a short time. The frosts had set in. When the first snow falls and the first day one goes out for a ride in a sleigh, one is glad to see the white ground, the white roofs, the air is so soft and wonderful to breathe, and one remembers the days of one's youth. The old lime trees and birches, white with rime, have such a benignant look, they are nearer to one's heart than cypresses and palms, and beside them one no longer wants to think of mountains and the sea.

Gurov had been born and bred in Moscow, and he returned to Moscow on a fine frosty day; and when he put on his fur coat and warm gloves and took a walk down Petrovka Street, and when on Saturday evening he heard the church bells ringing, his recent holiday trip and the places he had visited lost their charm for him. Gradually he became immersed in Moscow life, eagerly reading three newspapers a day and declaring that he never read Moscow papers on principle. Once more he could not resist the attraction of restaurants, clubs, banquets, and anniversary celebrations, and once more he felt flattered that well-known lawyers and actors came to see him and that in the Medical Club he played cards with a professor as his partner. Once again he was capable of eating a whole portion of the Moscow speciality of sour cabbage and meat served in a frying-pan.

Another month and, he thought, nothing but a memory would remain of Anna Sergeyevna; he would remember her as through a haze and only occasionally dream of her with a wistful smile, as he did of the others before her. But over a month passed, winter was at its height, and he remembered her as clearly as though he had only parted from her the day before. His memories haunted him more and more persistently. Every time the voices of his children doing their homework reached him in his study in the stillness of the evening, every time he heard a popular song or some music in a restaurant, every time the wind howled in the chimney—it all came back to him: their walks on the pier, early morning with the mist on the mountains, the Theodosia boat, and the kisses. He kept pacing the room for hours remembering it all and smiling, and then his memories turned into daydreams and the past mingled in his imagination with what was going to happen. He did not dream of Anna Sergeyevna, she accompanied him everywhere like his shadow and followed him wherever he went. Closing his eyes, he saw her as clearly as if she were before him, and she seemed to him lovelier, younger, and tenderer than she had been; and he thought that he too was much better than he had been in Yalta. In the evenings she gazed at him from the bookcase, from the fireplace, from the corner—he heard her breathing, the sweet rustle of her dress. In the street he followed women with his eyes, looking for anyone who resembled her. . . .

He was beginning to be overcome by an overwhelming desire to share his memories with someone. But at home it was impossible to talk of his love, and outside his home there was no one he could talk to. Not the tenants who lived in his house, and certainly not his colleagues in the bank. And what was he to tell them? Had he been in love then? Had there been anything beautiful, poetic, edifying, or even anything interesting about his relations with Anna Sergeyevna? So he had to talk in general terms about love and women, and no one guessed what he was driving at, and his wife merely raised her black eyebrows and said:

"Really, Dimitry, the role of a coxcomb doesn't suit you at all!"

One evening, as he left the Medical Club with his partner, a civil servant, he could not restrain himself, and said:

"If you knew what a fascinating woman I met in Yalta!"

The civil servant got into his sleigh and was about to be driven off, but suddenly he turned round and called out:

"I say!"

"Yes?"

"You were quite right: the sturgeon *was* a bit off."

These words, so ordinary in themselves, for some reason hurt Gurov's feelings: they seemed to him humiliating and indecent. What savage manners! What faces! What stupid nights! What uninteresting, wasted days! Crazy gambling at cards, gluttony, drunkenness, endless talk about one and the same thing. Business that was of no use to anyone and talk about one and the same thing absorbed the greater part of one's time and energy, and what was left in the end was a sort of dock-tailed, barren life, a sort of nonsensical existence, and it was impossible to escape from it, just as though you were in a lunatic asylum or a convict chain-gang!

Gurov lay awake all night, fretting and fuming, and had a splitting headache the whole of the next day. The following nights too he slept badly, sitting up in bed thinking, or walking up and down his room. He was tired of his children, tired of the bank, he did not feel like going out anywhere or talking about anything.

In December, during the Christmas holidays, he packed his things, told his wife that he was going to Petersburg to get a job for a young man he knew, and set off for the town of S—. Why? He had no very clear idea himself. He wanted to see Anna Sergeyevna, to talk to her, to arrange a meeting, if possible.

He arrived in S—in the morning and took the best room in a hotel, with a fitted carpet of military grey cloth and an inkstand grey with dust on the table, surmounted by a horseman with raised hand and no head. The hall porter supplied him with all the necessary information: Von Diederitz lived in a house of his own in Old Potter's Street, not far from the hotel. He lived well, was rich, kept his own carriage horses, the whole town knew him. The hall-porter pronounced the name: Dridir-itz.

Gurov took a leisurely walk down Old Potter's Street and found the house. In front of it was a long grey fence studded with upturned nails.

"A fence like that would make anyone wish to run away," thought Gurov, scanning the windows and the fence.

As it was a holiday, he thought, her husband was probably at home. It did not matter either way, though, for he could not very well embarrass her by calling at the house. If he were to send in a note it might fall into the hands of the husband and ruin everything. The best thing was to rely on chance. And he kept walking up and down the street and along the fence, waiting for his chance. He watched a beggar enter the gate and the dogs attack him; then, an hour later, he heard the faint indistinct sounds of a piano. That must have been Anna Sergeyevna playing. Suddenly the front door opened and an old woman came out, followed by the familiar white pomeranian. Gurov was about to call to the dog, but his heart began to beat violently and in his excitement he could not remember its name.

He went on walking up and down the street, hating the grey fence more and more, and he was already saying to himself that Anna Sergeyevna had forgotten him and had perhaps been having a good time with someone else, which was indeed quite natural for a young woman who had to look at that damned fence from morning till night. He went back to his hotel room and sat on the sofa for a long time, not knowing what to do, then he had dinner and after dinner a long sleep.

"How stupid and disturbing it all is," he thought, waking up and staring at the dark windows: it was already evening. "Well, I've had a good sleep, so what now? What am I going to do tonight?"

He sat on a bed covered by a cheap grey blanket looking exactly like a hospital blanket, and taunted himself in vexation:

"A *lady* with a lapdog! Some adventure, I must say! Serves you right!"

At the railway station that morning he had noticed a poster announcing in huge letters the first performance of *The Geisha Girl* at the local theatre. He recalled it now, and decided to go to the theatre.

"Quite possibly she goes to first nights," he thought.

The theatre was full. As in all provincial theatres, there was a mist over the chandeliers and the people in the gallery kept up a noisy and excited conversation; in the first row of the stalls stood the local dandies with their hands crossed behind their backs; here, too, in the front seat of the Governor's box, sat the Governor's daughter, wearing a feather boa, while the Governor himself hid modestly behind the portière so that only his hands were visible; the curtain stirred, the orchestra took a long time tuning up. Gurov scanned the audience eagerly as they filed in and occupied their seats.

Anna Sergeyevna came in too. She took her seat in the third row, and when Gurov glanced at her his heart missed a beat and he realized clearly that there was no one in the world nearer and dearer or more important to him than that little woman with the stupid lorgnette in her hand, who was in no way remarkable. That woman lost in a provincial crowd now filled his whole life, was his misfortune, his joy, and the only happiness that he wished for himself. Listening to the bad orchestra and the wretched violins played by second-rate musicians, he thought how beautiful she was. He thought and dreamed.

A very tall, round-shouldered young man with small whiskers had come in with Anna Sergeyevna and sat down beside her; he nodded at every step he took and seemed to be continually bowing to someone. This was probably her husband, whom in a fit of bitterness at Yalta she had called a flunkey. And indeed there was something of a lackey's obsequiousness in his lank figure, his whiskers, and the little bald spot on the top of his head. He smiled sweetly, and the gleaming insignia of some scientific society which he wore in his buttonhole looked like the number on a waiter's coat.

In the first interval the husband went out to smoke and she was left in her seat. Gurov, who also had a seat in the stalls, went up to her and said in a trembling voice and with a forced smile:

"Good evening!"

She looked up at him and turned pale, then looked at him again in panic, unable to believe her eyes, clenching her fan and lorgnette in her hand and apparently trying hard not to fall into a dead faint. Both were silent. She sat and he stood, frightened by her embarrassment and not daring to sit down beside her. The violinists and the flautist began tuning their instruments, and they suddenly felt terrified, as though they were being watched from all the boxes. But a moment later she got up and walked rapidly towards one of the exits; he followed her, and both of them walked aimlessly along corridors and up and down stairs. Figures in all sorts of uniforms—lawyers, teachers, civil servants, all wearing badges—flashed by them; ladies, fur coats hanging on pegs, the cold draught bringing with it the odour of cigarette-ends. Gurov, whose heart was beating violently, thought:

"Oh Lord, what are all these people, that orchestra, doing here?"

At that moment he suddenly remembered how after seeing Anna Sergeyevna off he had told himself that evening at the station that all was over and that they would never meet again. But how far they still were from the end!

She stopped on a dark, narrow staircase with a notice over it: "To the Upper Circle."

"How you frightened me!" she said, breathing heavily, still looking pale and stunned. "Oh dear, how you frightened me! I'm scarcely alive. Why did you come? Why?!"

"But, please, try to understand, Anna," he murmured hurriedly. "I beg you, please, try to understand. . . ."

She looked at him with fear, entreaty, love, looked at him intently, so as to fix his features firmly in her mind.

"I've suffered so much," she went on, without listening to him. "I've been thinking of you all the time. The thought of you kept me alive. And yet I tried so hard to forget you—why, oh why did you come?"

On the landing above two schoolboys were smoking and looking down, but Gurov did not care. He drew Anna Sergeyevna towards him and began kissing her face, her lips, her hands.

"What are you doing? What are you doing?" she said in horror, pushing him away. "We've both gone mad. You must go back tonight, this minute. I implore you, by all that's sacred . . . Somebody's coming!"

Somebody was coming up the stairs.

"You must go back," continued Anna Sergeyevna in a whisper. "Do you hear? I'll come to you in Moscow. I've never been happy, I'm unhappy now, and I shall never be happy, never! So please don't make me suffer still more. I swear I'll come to you in Moscow. But now you must part. Oh, my sweet, my darling, we must part!"

She pressed his hand and went quickly down the stairs, looking back at him all the time, and he could see from the expression in her eyes that she really was unhappy. Gurov stood listening for a short time, and when all was quiet he went to look for his coat and left the theatre.

IV

Anna Sergeyevna began going to Moscow to see him. Every two or three months she left the town of S—, telling her husband that she was going to consult a Moscow gynaecologist, and her husband believed and did not believe her. In Moscow she stayed at the Slav Bazaar and immediately sent a porter in a red cap to inform Gurov of her arrival. Gurov went to her hotel, and no one in Moscow knew about it.

One winter morning he went to her hotel as usual (the porter had called with his message at his house the evening before, but he had not been in). He had his daughter with him, and he was glad of the opportunity of taking her to school, which was on the way to the hotel. Snow was falling in thick wet flakes.

"It's three degrees above zero," Gurov was saying to his daughter, "and yet it's snowing. But then, you see, it's only warm on the earth's surface, in the upper layers of the atmosphere the temperature's quite different."

"Why isn't there any thunder in winter, Daddy?"

He explained that, too. As he was speaking, he kept thinking that he was going to meet his mistress and not a living soul knew about it. He led a double life: one for all who were interested to see, full of conventional truth and conventional deception, exactly like the lives of his friends and acquaintances; and another which went on in secret. And by a kind of strange concatenation of circumstances, possibly quite by accident, everything that was important, interesting, essential, everything about which he was sincere and did not deceive himself, everything that made up the quintessence of his life, went on in secret, while everything that was a lie, everything that was merely the husk in which he hid himself to conceal the truth, like his work at the bank, for instance, his discussions at the club, his ideas of the lower breed, his going to anniversary functions with his wife—all that happened in the sight of all. He judged others by himself, did not believe what he saw, and was always of the opinion that every man's real and most interesting life went on in secret, under cover of night. The personal, private life of an individual was kept a secret, and perhaps that was partly the reason why civilized man was so anxious that his personal secrets should be respected.

Having seen his daughter off to her school, Gurov went to the Slav Bazaar. He took off his fur coat in the cloakroom, went upstairs, and knocked softly on the door. Anna Sergeyevna, wearing the grey dress he liked most, tired out by her journey and by the suspense of waiting for him, had been expecting him since the evening before; she was pale, looked at him without smiling, but was in his arms the moment he went into the room. This kiss was long and lingering as if they had not seen each other for two years.

"Well," he asked, "how are you getting on there? Anything new?"

"Wait, I'll tell you in a moment. . . . I can't . . ."

She could not speak because she was crying. She turned away from him and pressed her handkerchief to her eyes.

"Well, let her have her cry," he thought, sitting down in an armchair. "I'll wait."

Then he rang the bell and ordered tea; while he was having his tea, she was still standing there with her face to the window. She wept because she could not control her emotions, because she was bitterly conscious of the fact that their life was so sad: they could only meet in secret, they had to hide from people, like thieves! Was not their life ruined?

"Please, stop crying!" he said.

It was quite clear to him that their love would not come to an end for a long time, if ever. Anna Sergeyevna was getting attached to him more and more strongly, she worshipped him, and it would have been absurd to tell her that all this would have to come to an end one day. She would not have believed it, anyway.

He went up to her and took her by the shoulders, wishing to be nice to her, to make her smile; and at that moment he caught sight of himself in the looking glass.

His hair was already beginning to turn grey. It struck him as strange that he should have aged so much, that he should have lost his good looks in the last few years. The shoulders on which his hands lay were warm and quivering. He felt so sorry for this life, still so warm and beautiful, but probably soon to fade and wilt like his own. Why did she love him so? To women he always seemed different from what he was, and they loved in him not himself, but the man their imagination conjured up and whom they had eagerly been looking for all their lives; and when they discovered their mistake they still loved him. And not one of them had ever been happy with him. Time had passed, he had met women, made love to them, parted from them, but not once had he been in love; there had been everything between them, but no love.

It was only now, when his hair was beginning to turn grey, that he had fallen in love properly, in good earnest—for the first time in his life.

He and Anna Sergeyevna loved each other as people do who are very dear and near, as man and wife or close friends love each other; they could not help feeling that fate itself had intended them for one another, and they were unable to understand why he should have a wife and she a husband; they were like two migrating birds, male and female, who had been caught and forced to live in separate cages. They had forgiven each other what they had been ashamed of in the past, and forgave each other everything in their present, and felt that this love of theirs had changed them both.

Before, when he felt depressed, he had comforted himself by all sorts of arguments that happened to occur to him on the spur of the moment, but now he had more serious things to think of, he felt profound compassion, he longed to be sincere, tender. . . .

"Don't cry, my sweet," he said. "That'll do, you've had your cry. . . . Let's talk now, let's think of something."

Then they had a long talk. They tried to think how they could get rid of the necessity of hiding, telling lies, living in different towns, not seeing one another for so long. How were they to free themselves from their intolerable chains?

"How? How?" he asked himself, clutching at his head. "How?"

And it seemed to them that in only a few more minutes a solution would be found and a new, beautiful life would begin; but both of them knew very well that the end was still a long, long way away and that the most complicated and difficult part was only just beginning.

F. SCOTT FITZGERALD

THE DIAMOND AS BIG AS THE RITZ

John T. Unger came from a family that had been well known in Hades—a small town on the Mississippi River—for several generations. John's father had held the amateur gold championship through many a heated contest; Mrs. Unger was known "from hot-box to hot-bed," as the local phrase went, for her political addresses; and young John T. Unger, who had just turned sixteen, had danced all the latest dances from

New York before he put on long trousers. And now, for a certain time, he was to be away from home. That respect for a New England education which is the bane of all provincial places, which drains them yearly of their most promising young men, had seized upon his parents. Nothing would suit them but that he should go to St. Midas' School near Boston—Hades was too small to hold their darling and gifted son.

Now in Hades—as you know if you ever have been there—the names of the more fashionable preparatory schools and colleges mean very little. The inhabitants have been so long out of the world that, though they make a show of keeping up to date in dress and manners and literature, they depend to a great extent on hearsay, and a function that in Hades would be considered elaborate would doubtless be hailed by a Chicago beef-princess as "perhaps a little tacky."

John T. Unger was on the eve of departure. Mrs. Unger, with maternal fatuity, packed his trunks full of linen suits and electric fans, and Mr. Unger presented his son with an asbestos pocket-book stuffed with money.

"Remember, you are always welcome here," he said. "You can be sure, boy, that we'll keep the home fires burning."

"I know," answered John huskily.

"Don't forget who you are and where you come from," continued his father proudly, "and you can do nothing to harm you. You are an Unger—from Hades."

So the old man and the young shook hands and John walked away with tears streaming from his eyes. Ten minutes later he had passed outside the city limits, and he stopped to glance back for the last time. Over the gates the old-fashioned Victorian motto seemed strangely attractive to him. His father had tried time and time again to have it changed to something with a little more push and verve about it, such as "Hades—Your Opportunity," or else a plain "Welcome" sign set over a hearty handshake pricked out in electric lights. The old motto was a little depressing, Mr. Unger had thought—but now. . . .

So John took his look and then set his face resolutely toward his destination. And, as he turned away, the lights of Hades against the sky seemed full of a warm and passionate beauty.

St. Midas' School is half an hour from Boston in a Rolls-Pierce motor-car. The actual distance will never be known, for no one, except John T. Unger, had ever arrived there save in a Rolls-Pierce and probably no one ever will again. St. Midas' is the most expensive and the most exclusive boys' preparatory school in the world.

John's first two years there passed pleasantly. The fathers of all the boys were money-kings and John spent his summers visiting at fashionable resorts. While he was very fond of all the boys he visited, their fathers struck him as being much of a piece, and in his boyish way he often wondered at their exceeding sameness. When he told them where his home was they would ask jovially, "Pretty hot down there?" and John would muster a faint smile and answer, "It certainly is." His response would have been heartier had they not all made this joke—at best varying it with, "Is it hot enough for you down there?" which he hated just as much.

In the middle of his second year at school, a quiet, handsome boy named Percy Washington had been put in John's form. The newcomer was pleasant in his manner and exceedingly well dressed even for St. Midas', but for some reason he kept aloof from the other boys. The only person with whom he was intimate was John T. Unger, but even to John he was entirely uncommunicative concerning his home or his family. That he was wealthy went without saying, but beyond a few such deductions John knew little of his friend, so it promised rich confectionery for his curiosity when Percy invited him to spend the summer at his home "in the West." He accepted, without hesitation.

It was only when they were in the train that Percy became, for the first time, rather communicative. One day while they were eating lunch in the dining-car and discussing the imperfect characters of several of the boys at school, Percy suddenly changed his tone and made an abrupt remark.

"My father," he said, "is by far the richest man in the world."

"Oh," said John, politely. He could think of no answer to make to this confidence. He considered "That's very nice," but it sounded hollow and was on the point of saying, "Really?" but refrained since it would seem to question Percy's statement. And such an astounding statement could scarcely be questioned.

"By far the richest," repeated Percy.

"I was reading in the *World Almanac,*" began John, "that there was one man in America with an income of over five million a year and four men with incomes of over three million a year, and——"

"Oh, they're nothing," Percy's mouth was a half-moon of scorn. "Catchpenny capitalists, financial small-fry, petty merchants and money-lenders. My father could buy them out and not know he'd done it."

"But how does he——"

"Why haven't they put down *his* income tax? Because he doesn't pay any. At least he pays a little one—but he doesn't pay any on his *real* income."

"He must be very rich," said John simply. "I'm glad. I like very rich people."

"The richer a fella is, the better I like him." There was a look of passionate frankness upon his dark face. "I visited the Schnlitzer-Murphys last Easter. Vivian Schnlitzer-Murphy had rubies as big as hen's eggs, and sapphires that were like globes with lights inside them——"

"I love jewels," agreed Percy enthusiastically. "Of course I wouldn't want any one at school to know about it, but I've got quite a collection myself. I used to collect them instead of stamps."

"And diamonds," continued John eagerly. "The Schnlitzer-Murphys had diamonds as big as walnuts——"

"That's nothing." Percy had leaned forward and dropped his voice to a low whisper. "That's nothing at all. My father has a diamond bigger than the Ritz-Carlton Hotel."

II

The Montana sunset lay between two mountains like a gigantic bruise from which dark arteries spread themselves over a poisoned sky. An immense distance under the sky crouched the village of Fish, minute, dismal, and forgotten. There were twelve men, so it was said, in the village of Fish, twelve sombre and inexplicable souls who sucked a lean milk from the almost literally bare rock upon which a mysterious populatory force had begotten them. They had become a race apart, these twelve men of Fish, like some species developed by an early whim of nature, which on second thought had abandoned them to struggle and extermination.

Out of the blue-black bruise in the distance crept a long line of moving lights upon the desolation of the land, and the twelve men of Fish gathered like ghosts at the shanty depot to watch the passing of the seven o'clock train, the Transcontinental Express from Chicago. Six times or so a year the Transcontinental Express, through some inconceivable jurisdiction, stopped at the village of Fish, and when this occurred a figure or so would disembark, mount into a buggy that always appeared from out of the dusk, and drive off toward the bruised sunset. The observation of this pointless and preposterous phenomenon had become a sort of cult among the men of Fish. To observe, that was all; there remained in them none of the vital quality of illusion which would make them wonder or speculate, else a religion might have grown up around these mysterious visitations. But the men of Fish were beyond all religion—the barest and most savage tenets of even Christianity could gain no foothold on that barren rock—so there was no altar, no priest, no sacrifice; only each night at seven the silent concourse by the shanty depot, a congregation who lifted up a prayer of dim, anaemic wonder.

On this June night, the Great Brakeman, whom, had they deified any one, they might well have chosen as their celestial protagonist, had ordained that the seven o'clock train should leave its human (or inhuman) deposit at Fish. At two minutes after seven Percy Washington and John T. Unger disembarked, hurried past the spellbound, the agape, the fearsome eyes of the twelve men of Fish, mounted into a buggy which had obviously appeared from nowhere, and drove away.

After half an hour, when the twilight had coagulated into dark, the silent negro who was driving the buggy hailed an opaque body somewhere ahead of them in the gloom. In response to his cry, it turned upon them a luminous disk which regarded them like a malignant eye out of the unfathomable night. As they came closer, John saw that it was the tail-light of an immense automobile, larger and more magnificent than any he had ever seen. Its body was of gleaming metal richer than nickel and lighter than silver, and the hubs of the wheels were studded with iridescent geometric figures of green and yellow—John did not dare to guess whether they were glass or jewel.

Two negroes, dressed in glittering livery such as one sees in pictures of royal processions in London, were standing at attention beside the car and as the two young men dismounted from the buggy they were greeted in some language which the guest could not understand, but which seemed to be an extreme form of the Southern negro's dialect.

"Get in," said Percy to his friend, as their trunks were tossed to the ebony roof of the limousine. "Sorry we had to bring you this far in that buggy, but of course it wouldn't do for the people on the train or those Godforsaken fellas in Fish to see this automobile."

"Gosh! What a car!" This ejaculation was provoked by its interior. John saw that the upholstery consisted of a thousand minute and exquisite tapestries of silk, woven with jewels and embroideries, and set upon a background of cloth of gold. The two armchair seats in which the boys luxuriated were covered with stuff that resembled duvetyn, but seemed woven in numberless colors of the ends of ostrich feathers.

"What a car!" cried John again, in amazement.

"This thing?" Percy laughed. "Why, it's just an old junk we use for a station wagon."

By this time they were gliding along through the darkness toward the break between the two mountains.

"We'll be there in an hour and a half," said Percy, looking at the clock. "I may as well tell you it's not going to be like anything you ever saw before."

If the car was any indication of what John would see, he was prepared to be astonished indeed. The simple piety prevalent in Hades has the earnest worship of and respect for riches as the first article of its creed—had John felt otherwise than radiantly humble before them, his parents would have turned away in horror at the blasphemy.

They had now reached and were entering the break between the two mountains and almost immediately the way became much rougher.

"If the moon shone down here, you'd see that we're in a big gulch," said Percy, trying to peer out of the window. He spoke a few words into the mouthpiece and immediately the footman turned on a searchlight and swept the hillsides with an immense beam.

"Rocky, you see. An ordinary car would be knocked to pieces in half an hour. In fact, it'd take a tank to navigate it unless you knew the way. You notice we're going uphill now."

They were obviously ascending, and within a few minutes the car was crossing a high rise, where they caught a glimpse of a pale moon newly risen in the distance. The car stopped suddenly and several figures took shape out of the dark beside it—these were negroes also. Again the two young men were saluted in the same dimly recognizable dialect; then the negroes set to work and four immense cables dangling from overhead were attached with hooks to the hubs of the great jeweled wheels. At a resounding "Hey-yah!" John felt the car being lifted slowly from the ground—up and up—clear of the tallest rocks on both sides—then higher, until he could see a wavy, moonlit valley stretched out before him in sharp contrast to the quagmire of rocks that they had just left. Only on one side was there still rock—and then suddenly there was no rock beside them or anywhere around.

It was apparent that they had surmounted some immense knifeblade of stone, projecting perpendicularly into the air. In a moment they were going down again, and finally with a soft bump they were landed upon the smooth earth.

"The worst is over," said Percy, squinting out the window. "It's only five miles from here, and our own road—tapestry brick—all the way. This belongs to us. This is where the United States ends, father says."

"Are we in Canada?"

"We are not. We're in the middle of the Montana Rockies. But you are now on the only five square miles of land in the country that's never been surveyed."

"Why hasn't it? Did they forget it?"

"No," said Percy, grinning, "they tried to do it three times. The first time my grandfather corrupted a whole department of the State survey; the second time he had the official maps of the United States tinkered with—that held them for fifteen years. The last time was harder. My father fixed it so that their compasses were in the strongest magnetic field ever artificially set up. He had a whole set of surveying instruments made with a slight defection that would allow for this territory not to appear, and he substituted them for the ones that were to be used. Then he had a river deflected and he had what looked like a village built up on its banks—so that they'd see it, and think it was a town ten miles farther up the valley. There's only one thing my father's afraid of," he concluded, "only one thing in the world that could be used to find us out."

"What's that?"

Percy sank his voice to a whisper.

"Aeroplanes," he breathed. "We've got half a dozen anti-aircraft guns and we've arranged it so far—but there've been a few deaths and a great many prisoners. Not that we mind *that,* you know, father and I, but it upsets mother and the girls, and there's always the chance that some time we won't be able to arrange it."

Shreds and tatters of chinchilla, courtesy clouds in the green moon's heaven, were passing the green moon like precious Eastern stuffs paraded for the inspection of some Tartar Khan. It seemed to John that it was day, and that he was looking at some lads sailing above him in the air, showering down tracts and patent medicine circulars, with their messages of hope for despairing, rockbound hamlets. It seemed to him that he could see them look down out of the clouds and stare—and stare at whatever there was to stare at in this place whither he was bound—What then? Were they induced to land by some insidious device there to be immured far from patent medicines and from tracts until the judgment day—or, should they fail to fall into the trap, did a quick puff of smoke and the sharp round of a splitting shell bring them drooping to earth—and "upset" Percy's mother and sisters. John shook his head and the wraith of a hollow laugh issued silently from his parted lips. What desperate transaction lay hidden here? What a moral expedient of a bizarre Croesus? What terrible and golden mystery? . . .

The chinchilla clouds had drifted past now and outside the Montana night was bright as day. The tapestry brick of the road was smooth to the tread of the great tires as they rounded a still, moonlit lake; they passed into darkness for a moment, a pine grove, pungent and cool, then they came out into a broad avenue of lawn and John's exclamation of pleasure was simultaneous with Percy's taciturn "We're home."

Full in the light of the stars, an exquisite château rose from the borders of the lake, climbed in marble radiance half the height of an adjoining mountain, then melted in grace, in perfect symmetry, in translucent feminine languor, into the massed darkness of a forest of pine. The many towers, the slender tracery of the sloping parapets, the chiselled wonder of a thousand yellow windows with their oblongs and hectagons and triangles of golden light, the shattered softness of the intersecting planes of star-shine and blue shade, all trembled on John's spirit like a chord of music. On one of the towers, the tallest, the blackest at its base, an arrangement of exterior lights at the top made a sort of floating fairyland—and as John gazed up in warm enchantment the faint acciaccare sound of violins drifted down in a rococo harmony that was like nothing he had ever heard before. Then in a moment the car stopped before wide, high marble steps around which the night air was fragrant with a host of flowers. At the top of the steps two great doors swung silently open and amber light flooded out upon the darkness, silhouetting the figure of an exquisite lady with black, high-piled hair, who held out her arms toward them.

"Mother," Percy was saying, "this is my friend, John Unger, from Hades."

Afterward John remembered that first night as a daze of many colors, of quick sensory impressions, of music soft as a voice in love, and of the beauty of things, lights and shadows, and motions and faces. There was a white-haired man who stood drinking a many-hued cordial from a crystal thimble set on a golden stem. There was a girl with a flowery face, dressed like Titania with braided sapphires in her hair. There was a room where the solid, soft gold of the walls yielded to the pressure of his hand, and a room that was like a platonic conception of the ultimate prison—ceiling, floor, and all, it was lined with an unbroken mass of diamonds, diamonds of every size and shape, until, lit with tall violet lamps in the corners, it dazzled the eyes with a whiteness that could be compared only with itself, beyond human wish or dream.

Through a maze of these rooms the two boys wandered. Sometimes the floor under their feet would flame in brilliant patterns from lighting below, patterns of barbaric clashing colors, of pastel delicacy, of sheer whiteness, or of subtle and intricate mosaic, surely from some mosque on the Adriatic Sea. Sometimes beneath layers of thick crystal he would see blue or green water swirling, inhabited by vivid fish and growths of rainbow foliage. Then they would be treading on furs of every texture and color or along corridors of palest ivory, unbroken as though carved complete from the gigantic tusks of dinosaurs extinct before the age of man. . . .

Then a hazily remembered transition, and they were at dinner—where each plate was of two almost imperceptible layers of solid diamond between which was curiously worked a filigree of emerald design, a shaving sliced from green air. Music, plangent and unobtrusive, drifted down through far corridors—his chair, feathered and curved insidiously to his back, seemed to engulf and overpower him as he drank his first glass of port. He tried drowsily to answer a question that had been asked him, but the honeyed luxury that clasped his body added to the illusion of sleep—jewels, fabrics, wines, and metals blurred before his eyes into a sweet mist. . . .

"Yes," he replied with a polite effort, "it certainly is hot enough for me down there."

He managed to add a ghostly laugh; then, without movement, without resistance, he seemed to float off and away, leaving an iced dessert that was pink as a dream. . . . He fell asleep.

When he awoke he knew that several hours had passed. He was in a great quiet room with ebony walls and a dull illumination that was too faint, too subtle, to be called a light. His young host was standing over him.

"You fell asleep at dinner," Percy was saying. "I nearly did, too—it was such a treat to be comfortable again after this year of school. Servants undressed and bathed you while you were sleeping."

"Is this a bed or a cloud?" sighed John. "Percy, Percy—before you go, I want to apologize."

"For what?"

"For doubting you when you said you had a diamond as big as the Ritz-Carlton Hotel."

Percy smiled.

"I thought you didn't believe me. It's that mountain, you know."

"What mountain?"

"The mountain the château rests on. It's not very big for a mountain. But except about fifty feet of sod and gravel on top it's solid diamond. *One* diamond, one cubic mile without a flaw. Aren't you listening? Say——"

But John T. Unger had again fallen asleep.

III

Morning. As he awoke he perceived drowsily that the room had at the same moment become dense with sunlight. The ebony panels of one wall had slid aside on a sort of track, leaving his chamber half open to the day. A large negro in a white uniform stood beside his bed.

"Good-evening," muttered John, summoning his brains from the wild places.

"Good-morning, sir. Are you ready for your bath, sir? Oh, don't get up—I'll put you in, if you'll just unbutton your pajamas—there. Thank you, sir."

John lay quietly as his pajamas were removed—he was amused and delighted; he expected to be lifted like a child by this black Gargantua who was tending him, but nothing of the sort happened; instead he felt the bed tilt up slowly on its side—he began to roll, startled at first, in the direction of the wall, but when he reached the wall its drapery gave way, and sliding two yards farther down a fleecy incline he plumped gently into water the same temperature as his body.

He looked about him. The runway or rollway on which he had arrived had folded gently back into place. He had been projected into another chamber and was sitting in a sunken bath with his head just above the level of the floor. All about him, lining the walls of the room and the sides and bottom of the bath itself, was a blue aquarium, and gazing through the crystal surface on which he sat, he could see fish swimming among amber lights and even gliding without curiosity past his outstretched toes, which were separated from them only by the thickness of the crystal. From overhead, sunlight came down through sea-green glass.

"I suppose, sir, that you'd like hot rosewater and soapsuds this morning, sir—and perhaps cold salt water to finish."

The negro was standing beside him.

"Yes," agreed John, smiling inanely, "as you please." Any idea of ordering this bath according to his own meagre standards of living would have been priggish and not a little wicked.

The negro pressed a button and a warm rain began to fall, apparently from overhead, but really, so John discovered after a moment, from a fountain arrangement near by. The water turned to a pale rose color and jets of liquid soap spurted into it from four miniature walrus heads at the corners of the bath. In a moment a dozen little paddle-wheels, fixed to the sides, had churned the mixture into a radiant rainbow of pink foam which enveloped him softly with its delicious lightness, and burst in shining, rosy bubbles here and there about him.

"Shall I turn on the moving-picture machine, sir?" suggested the negro deferentially. "There's a good one-reel comedy in this machine to-day, or I can put in a serious piece in a moment, if you prefer it."

"No, thanks," answered John, politely but firmly. He was enjoying his bath too much to desire any distraction. But distraction came. In a moment he was listening intently to the sound of flutes from just outside, flutes dripping a melody that was like a waterfall, cool and green as the room itself, accompanying a frothy piccolo, in play more fragile than the lace of suds that covered and charmed him.

After a cold salt-water bracer and a cold fresh finish, he stepped out and into a fleecy robe, and upon a couch covered with the same material he was rubbed with oil, alcohol, and spice. Later he sat in a voluptuous chair while he was shaved and his hair was trimmed.

"Mr. Percy is waiting in your sitting-room," said the negro, when these operations were finished. "My name is Gygsum, Mr. Unger, sir. I am to see to Mr. Unger every morning."

John walked out into the brisk sunshine of his living-room, where he found breakfast waiting for him and Percy, gorgeous in white kid knickerbockers, smoking in an easy chair.

IV

This is a story of the Washington family as Percy sketched it for John during breakfast.

The father of the present Mr. Washington had been a Virginian, a direct descendant of George Washington, and Lord Baltimore. At the close of the Civil War he was a twenty-five-year-old Colonel with a played-out plantation and about a thousand dollars in gold.

Fitz-Norman Culpepper Washington, for that was the young Colonel's name, decided to present the Virginia estate to his younger brother and go West. He selected two dozen of the most faithful blacks, who, of course, worshipped him, and bought twenty-five tickets to the West, where he intended to take out land in their names and start a sheep and cattle ranch.

When he had been in Montana for less than a month and things were going very poorly indeed, he stumbled on his great discovery. He had lost his way when riding in the hills, and after a day without food he began to grow hungry. As he was without his rifle, he was forced to pursue a squirrel, and in the course of the pursuit he noticed that it was carrying something shiny in its mouth. Just before it vanished into its hole—for Providence did not intend that this squirrel should alleviate his hunger—it dropped its burden. Sitting down to consider the situation Fitz-Norman's eye was caught by a gleam in the grass beside him. In ten seconds he had completely lost his appetite and gained one hundred thousand dollars. The squirrel, which had refused with annoying persistence to become food, had made him a present of a large and perfect diamond.

Late that night he found his way to camp and twelve hours later all the males among his darkies were back by the squirrel hole digging furiously at the side of the mountain. He told them he had discovered a rhinestone mine, and, as only one or two of them had ever seen even a small diamond before, they believed him, without question. When the magnitude of his discovery became apparent to him, he found himself in a quandary. The mountain was *a* diamond—it was literally nothing else but solid diamond. He filled four saddle bags full of glittering samples and started on horseback for St. Paul. There he managed to dispose of half a dozen small stones—when he tried a larger one a storekeeper fainted and Fitz-Norman was arrested as a public disturber. He escaped from jail and caught the train for New York, where he sold a few medium-sized diamonds and received in exchange about two hundred thousand dollars in gold. But he did not dare to produce any exceptional gems—in fact, he left New York just in time. Tremendous excitement had been created in jewelry circles, not so much by the size of his diamonds as by their appearance in the city from mysterious sources. Wild rumors became current that a diamond mine had been discovered in the Catskills, on the Jersey coast, on Long Island, beneath Washington Square. Excursion trains, packed with men carrying picks and shovels began to leave New York hourly, bound for various neighboring El Dorados. But by that time young Fitz-Norman was on his way back to Montana.

By the end of a fortnight he had estimated that the diamond in the mountain was approximately equal in quantity to all the rest of the diamonds known to exist in the world. There was no valuing it by any regular computation, however, for it was *one solid diamond*—and if it were offered for sale not only would the bottom fall out of the market, but also, if the value should vary with its size in the usual arithmetical progression, there would not be enough gold in the world to buy a tenth part of it. And what could any one do with a diamond that size?

It was an amazing predicament. He was, in one sense, the richest man that ever lived—and yet was he worth anything at all? If his secret should transpire there was no telling to what measures the Government might resort in order to prevent a panic, in gold as well as in jewels. They might take over the claim immediately and institute a monopoly.

There was no alternative—he must market his mountain in secret. He sent South for his younger brother and put him in charge of his colored following—darkies who had never realized that slavery was abolished. To make sure of this, he read them a proclamation that he had composed, which announced that General Forrest had reorganized the shattered Southern armies and defeated the North in one pitched battle. The negroes believed him implicitly. They passed a vote declaring it a good thing and held revival services immediately.

Fitz-Norman himself set out for foreign parts with one hundred thousand dollars and two trunks filled with rough diamonds of all sizes. He sailed for Russia in a Chinese junk and six months after his departure from Montana he was in St. Petersburg. He took obscure lodgings and called immediately upon the court jeweller, announcing that he had a diamond for the Czar. He remained in St. Petersburg for two weeks, in constant danger of being murdered, living from lodging to lodging, and afraid to visit his trunks more than three or four times during the whole fortnight.

On his promise to return in a year with larger and finer stones, he was allowed to leave for India. Before he left, however, the Court Treasurers had deposited to his credit, in American banks, the sum of fifteen million dollars—under four different aliases.

He returned to America in 1868, having been gone a little over two years. He had visited the capitals of twenty-two countries and talked with five emperors, eleven kings, three princes, a shah, a khan, and a sultan. At that time Fitz-Norman estimated his own wealth at one billion dollars. One fact worked consistently against the disclosure of his secret. No one of his larger diamonds remained in the public eye for a week before being invested with a history of enough fatalities, amours, revolutions, and wars to have occupied it from the days of the first Babylonian Empire.

From 1870 until his death in 1900, the history of Fitz-Norman Washington was a long epic in gold. There were side issues, of course—he evaded the surveys, he married a Virginia lady, by whom he had a single son, and he was compelled, due to a series of unfortunate complications, to murder his brother, whose unfortunate habit of drinking himself into an indiscreet stupor had several times endangered their safety. But very few other murders stained these happy years of progress and expansion.

Just before he died he changed his policy, and with all but a few million dollars of his outside wealth bought up rare minerals in bulk, which he deposited in the safety vaults of banks all over the world, marked as bric-à-brac. His son, Braddock Tarleton Washington, followed this policy on an even more intensive scale. The minerals were converted into the rarest of all elements—radium—so that the equivalent of a billion dollars in gold could be placed in a receptacle no bigger than a cigar box.

When Fitz-Norman had been dead three years his son, Braddock, decided that the business had gone far enough. The amount of wealth that he and his father had taken out of the mountain was beyond all exact computation. He kept a note-book in cipher in which he set down the approximate quantity of radium in each of the thousand banks he patronized, and recorded the alias under which it was held. Then he did a very simple thing—he sealed up the mine.

He sealed up the mine. What had been taken out of it would support all the Washingtons yet to be born in unparalleled luxury for generations. His one care must be the protection of his secret, lest in the possible panic attendant on its discovery he should be reduced with all the property-holders in the world to utter poverty.

This was the family among whom John T. Unger was staying. This was the story he heard in his silver-walled living-room the morning after his arrival.

V

After breakfast, John found his way out the great marble entrance, and looked curiously at the scene before him. The whole valley, from the diamond mountain to the steep granite cliff five miles away, still gave off a breath of golden haze which hovered idly above the fine sweep of lawns and lakes and gardens. Here and there clusters of elms made delicate groves of shade, contrasting strangely with the tough masses of pine forest that held the hills in a grip of dark-blue green. Even as John looked he saw three fawns in single file patter out from one clump about a half mile away and disappear with awkward gayety into the black-ribbed half-light of another. John would not have been surprised to see a goat-foot piping his way among the trees or to catch a glimpse of pink nymph-skin and flying yellow hair between the greenest of the green leaves.

In some such cool hope he descended the marble steps, disturbing faintly the sleep of two silky Russian wolfhounds at the bottom, and set off along a walk of white and blue brick that seemed to lead in no particular direction.

He was enjoying himself as much as he was able. It is youth's felicity as well as its insufficiency that it can never live in the present, but must always be measuring up the day against its own radiantly imagined future—flowers and gold, girls and stars, they are only prefigurations and prophecies of that incomparable, unattainable young dream.

John rounded a soft corner where the massed rosebushes filled the air with heavy scent, and struck off across a park toward a patch of moss under some trees. He had never lain upon moss, and he wanted to see whether it was really soft enough to justify the use of its name as an adjective. Then he saw a girl coming toward him over the grass. She was the most beautiful person he had ever seen.

She was dressed in a white little gown that came just below her knees, and a wreath of mignonettes clasped with blue slices of sapphire bound up her hair. Her pink bare feet scattered the dew before them as she came. She was younger than John—not more than sixteen.

"Hello," she cried softly, "I'm Kismine."

She was much more than that to John already. He advanced toward her, scarcely moving as he drew near lest he should tread on her bare toes.

"You haven't met me," said her soft voice. Her blue eyes added, "Oh, but you've missed a great deal!" . . . "You met my sister, Jasmine, last night. I was sick with lettuce poisoning," went on her soft voice, and her eyes continued, "and when I'm sick I'm sweet—and when I'm well."

"You have made an enormous impression on me," said John's eyes, "and I'm not so slow myself"—"How do you do?" said his voice. "I hope you're better this morning."—"You darling," added his eyes tremulously.

John observed that they had been walking along the path. On her suggestion they sat down together upon the moss, the softness of which he failed to determine.

He was critical about women. A single defect—a thick ankle, a hoarse voice, a glass eye—was enough to make him utterly indifferent. And here for the first time in his life he was beside a girl who seemed to him the incarnation of physical perfection.

"Are you from the East?" asked Kismine with charming interest.

"No," answered John simply. "I'm from Hades."

Either she had never heard of Hades, or she could think of no pleasant comment to make upon it, for she did not discuss it further.

"I'm going East to school this fall," she said. "D'you think I'll like it? I'm going to New York to Miss Bulge's. It's very strict, but you see over the weekends I'm going to live at home with the family in our New York house, because father heard that the girls had to go walking two by two."

"Your father wants you to be proud," observed John.

"We are," she answered, her eyes shining with dignity. "None of us has ever been punished. Father said we never should be. Once when my sister Jasmine was a little girl she pushed him down-stairs and he just got up and limped away.

"Mother was—well, a little startled," continued Kismine, "when she heard that you were from—from where you *are* from, you know. She said that when she was a young girl—but then, you see, she's a Spaniard and old-fashioned."

"Do you spend much time out here?" asked John, to conceal the fact that he was somewhat hurt by this remark. It seemed an unkind allusion to his provincialism.

"Percy and Jasmine and I are here every summer, but next summer Jasmine is going to Newport. She's coming out in London a year from this fall. She'll be presented at court."

"Do you know," began John hesitantly, "you're much more sophisticated than I thought you were when I first saw you?"

"Oh, no, I'm not," she exclaimed hurriedly. "Oh, I wouldn't think of being. I think that sophisticated young people are *terribly* common, don't you? I'm not at all, really. If you say I am, I'm going to cry."

She was so distressed that her lip was trembling. John was impelled to protest:

"I didn't mean that; I only said it to tease you."

"Because I wouldn't mind if I *were,*" she persisted "but I'm *not.* I'm very innocent and girlish. I never smoke, or drink, or read anything except poetry. I know scarcely any mathematics or chemistry. I dress *very* simply—in fact, I scarcely dress at all. I think sophisticated is the last thing you can say about me. I believe that girls ought to enjoy their youths in a wholesome way."

"I do too," said John heartily.

Kismine was cheerful again. She smiled at him, and a still-born tear dripped from the corner of one blue eye.

"I like you," she whispered, intimately. "Are you going to spend all your time with Percy while you're here, or will you be nice to me? Just think—I'm absolutely fresh ground. I've never had a boy in love with me in all my life. I've never been allowed even to *see* boys alone—except Percy. I came all the way out here into this grove hoping to run into you, where the family wouldn't be around."

Deeply flattered, John bowed from the hips as he had been taught at dancing school in Hades.

"We'd better go now," said Kismine sweetly. "I have to be with mother at eleven. You haven't asked me to kiss you once. I thought boys always did that nowadays."

John drew himself up proudly.

"Some of them do," he answered, "but not me. Girls don't do that sort of thing—in Hades."

Side by side they walked back toward the house.

VI

John stood facing Mr. Braddock Washington in the full sunlight. The elder man was about forty with a proud, vacuous face, intelligent eyes, and a robust figure. In the mornings he smelt of horses—the best horses. He carried a plain walking-stick of gray birch with a single large opal for a grip. He and Percy were showing John around.

"The slaves' quarters are there." His walking-stick indicated a cloister of marble on their left that ran in graceful Gothic along the side of the mountain. "In my youth I was distracted for a while from the business of life by a period of absurd idealism. During that time they lived in luxury. For instance, I equipped every one of their rooms with a tile bath."

"I suppose," ventured John, with an ingratiating laugh, "that they used the bathtubs to keep coal in. Mr. Schnlitzer-Murphy told me that once he——"

"The opinions of Mr. Schnlitzer-Murphy are of little importance, I should imagine," interrupted Braddock Washington, coldly. "My slaves did not keep coal in their bathtubs. They had orders to bathe every day, and they did. If they hadn't I might have ordered a sulphuric acid shampoo. I discontinued the baths for quite another reason. Several of them caught cold and died. Water is not good for certain races—except as a beverage."

John laughed, and then decided to nod his head in sober agreement. Braddock Washington made him uncomfortable.

"All these negroes are descendants of the ones my father brought North with him. There are about two hundred and fifty now. You notice that they've lived so long apart from the world that their original dialect has become an almost indistinguishable patois. We bring a few of them up to speak English—my secretary and two or three of the house servants.

"This is the golf course," he continued, as they strolled along the velvet winter grass. "It's all a green, you see—no fairway, no rough, no hazards."

He smiled pleasantly at John.

"Many men in the cage, father?" asked Percy suddenly.

Braddock Washington stumbled, and let forth an involuntary curse.

"One less than there should be," he ejaculated darkly—and then added after a moment, "We've had difficulties."

"Mother was telling me," exclaimed Percy, "that Italian teacher——"

"A ghastly error," said Braddock Washington angrily. "But of course there's a good chance that we may have got him. Perhaps he fell somewhere in the woods or stumbled over a cliff. And then there's always the probability that if he did get away his story wouldn't be believed. Nevertheless, I've had two dozen men looking for him in different towns around here."

"And no luck?"

"Some. Fourteen of them reported to my agent that they'd each killed a man answering to that description, but of course it was probably only the reward they were after——"

He broke off. They had come to a large cavity in the earth about the circumference of a merry-go-round and covered by a strong iron grating. Braddock Washington beckoned to John, and pointed his cane down through the grating. John stepped to the edge and gazed. Immediately his ears were assailed by a wild clamor from below.

"Come on down to Hell!"

"Hello, kiddo, how's the air up there?"

"Hey! Throw us a rope!"

"Got an old doughnut, Buddy, or a couple of second-hand sandwiches?"

"Say, fella, if you'll push down that guy you're with, we'll show you a quick disappearance scene."

"Paste him one for me, will you?"

It was too dark to see clearly into the pit below, but John could tell from the coarse optimism and rugged vitality of the remarks and voices that they proceeded from middle-class Americans of the more spirited type. Then Mr. Washington put out his cane and touched a button in the grass, and the scene below sprang into light.

"These are some adventurous mariners who had the misfortune to discover El Dorado," he remarked.

Below them there had appeared a large hollow in the earth shaped like the interior of a bowl. The sides were steep and apparently of polished glass, and on its slightly concave surface stood about two dozen men clad in the half costume, half uniform, of aviators. Their upturned faces, lit with wrath, with malice, with despair, with cynical humor, were covered by long growths of beard, but with the exception of a few who had pined perceptibly away, they seemed to be a well-fed, healthy lot.

Braddock Washington drew a garden chair to the edge of the pit and sat down.

"Well, how are you, boys?" he inquired genially.

A chorus of execration in which all joined except a few too dispirited to cry out, rose up into the sunny air, but Braddock Washington heard it with unruffled composure. When its last echo had died away he spoke again.

"Have you thought up a way out of your difficulty?"

From here and there among them a remark floated up.

"We decided to stay here for love!"

"Bring us up there and we'll find us a way!"

Braddock Washington waited until they were again quiet. Then he said:

"I've told you the situation. I don't want you here. I wish to heaven I'd never seen you. Your own curiosity got you here, and any time that you can think of a way out which protects me and my interests I'll be glad to consider it. But so long as you confine your efforts to digging tunnels—yes, I know about the new one you've started—you won't get very far. This isn't as hard on you as you make it out, with all your howling for the loved ones at home. If you were the type who worried much about the loved ones at home, you'd never have taken up aviation."

A tall man moved apart from the others, and held up his hand to call his captor's attention to what he was about to say.

"Let me ask you a few questions!" he cried. "You pretend to be a fair-minded man."

"How absurd. How could a man of *my* position be fair-minded toward *you?* You might as well speak of a Spaniard being fair-minded toward a piece of steak."

At this harsh observation the faces of the two dozen steaks fell, but the tall man continued:

"All right!" he cried. "We've argued this out before. You're not a humanitarian and you're not fair-minded, but you're human—at least you say you are—and you ought to be able to put yourself in our place for long enough to think how—how—how——"

"How what?" demanded Washington, coldly.

"—how unnecessary——"

"Not to me."

"Well,—how cruel——"

"We've covered that. Cruelty doesn't exist where self-preservation is involved. You've been soldiers; you know that. Try another."

"Well, then, how stupid."

"There," admitted Washington, "I grant you that. But try to think of an alternative. I've offered to have all or any of you painlessly executed if you wish. I've offered to have your wives, sweethearts, children, and mothers kidnapped and brought out here. I'll enlarge your place down there and feed and clothe you the rest of your lives. If there was some method of producing permanent amnesia I'd have all of you operated on and released immediately, somewhere outside of my preserves. But that's as far as my ideas go."

"How about trusting us not to peach on you?" cried some one.

"You don't proffer that suggestion seriously," said Washington, with an expression of scorn. "I did take out one man to teach my daughter Italian. Last week he got away."

A wild yell of jubilation went up suddenly from two dozen throats and a pandemonium of joy ensued. The prisoners clog-danced and cheered and yodled and wrestled with one another in a sudden uprush of animal spirits. They even ran up the glass sides of the bowl as far as they could, and slid back to the bottom upon the natural-cushions of their bodies. The tall man started a song in which they all joined——

"Oh, we'll hang the kaiser"
On a sour apple tree——"

Braddock Washington sat in inscrutable silence until the song was over.

"You see," he remarked, when he could gain a modicum of attention. "I bear you no ill-will. I like to see you enjoying yourselves. That's why I didn't tell you the whole story at once. The man—what was his name? Critchtichiello?—was shot by some of my agents in fourteen different places."

Not guessing that the places referred to were cities, the tumult of rejoicing subsided immediately.

"Nevertheless," cried Washington with a touch of anger, "he tried to run away. Do you expect me to take chances with any of you after an experience like that?"

Again a series of ejaculations went up.

"Sure!"

"Would your daughter like to learn Chinese?"

"Hey, I can speak Italian! My mother was a wop."

"Maybe she'd like t'learna speak N'Yawk!"

"If she's the little one with the big blue eyes I can teach her a lot of things better than Italian."

"I know some Irish songs—and I could hammer brass once't."

Mr. Washington reached forward suddenly with his cane and pushed the button in the grass so that the picture below went out instantly, and there remained only that great dark mouth covered dismally with the black teeth of the grating.

"Hey!" called a single voice from below, "you ain't goin' away without givin' us your blessing?"

But Mr. Washington, followed by the two boys, was already strolling on toward the ninth hole of the golf course, as though the pit and its contents were no more than a hazard over which his facile iron had triumphed with ease.

VII

July under the lee of the diamond mountain was a month of blanket nights and of warm, glowing days. John and Kismine were in love. He did not know that the little gold football (inscribed with the legend *Pro deo et patria et St. Mida*) which he had given her rested on a platinum chain next to her bosom. But it did. And she for her part was not aware that a large sapphire which had dropped one day from her simple coiffure was stowed away tenderly in John's jewel box.

Late one afternoon when the ruby and ermine music room was quiet, they spent an hour there together. He held her hand and she gave him such a look that he whispered her name aloud. She bent toward him—then hesitated.

"Did you say 'Kismine'?" she asked softly, "or——"

She had wanted to be sure. She thought she might have misunderstood.

Neither of them had ever kissed before, but in the course of an hour it seemed to make little difference.

The afternoon drifted away. That night when a last breath of music drifted down from the highest tower, they each lay awake, happily dreaming over the separate minutes of the day. They had decided to be married as soon as possible.

VIII

Every day Mr. Washington and the two young men went hunting or fishing in the deep forests or played golf around the somnolent course—games which John diplomatically allowed his host to win—or swam in the mountain coolness of the lake. John found Mr. Washington a somewhat exacting personality—utterly uninterested in any ideas or opinions except his own. Mrs. Washington was aloof and reserved at all times. She was apparently indifferent to her two daughters, and entirely absorbed in her son Percy, with whom she held interminable conversations in rapid Spanish at dinner.

Jasmine, the elder daughter, resembled Kismine in appearance—except that she was somewhat bow-legged, and terminated in large hands and feet—but was utterly unlike her in temperament. Her favorite books had to do with poor girls who kept house for widowed fathers. John learned from Kismine that Jasmine had never recovered from the shock and disappointment caused her by the termination of the World War, just as she was about to start for Europe as a canteen expert. She had even pined away for a time, and Braddock Washington had taken steps to promote a new war in the Balkans—but she had seen a photograph of some wounded Serbian soldiers and lost interest in the whole proceedings. But Percy and Kismine seemed to have inherited the arrogant attitude in all its harsh magnificence from their father. A chaste and consistent selfishness ran like a pattern through their every idea.

John was enchanted by the wonders of the château and the valley. Braddock Washington, so Percy told him, had caused to be kidnapped a landscape gardener, an architect, a designer of state settings, and a French decadent poet left over from the last century. He had put his entire force of negroes at their disposal, guaranteed to supply them with any materials that the world could offer, and left them to work out some ideas of their own. But one by one they had shown their uselessness. The decadent poet had at once begun bewailing his separation from the boulevards in spring—he made some vague remarks about spices, apes, and ivories, but said nothing that was of any practical value. The stage designer on his part wanted to make the whole valley a series of tricks and sensational effects—a state of things that the Washingtons would soon have grown tired of. And as for the architect and the landscape gardener, they thought only in terms of convention. They must make this like this and that like that.

But they had, at least, solved the problem of what was to be done with them—they all went mad early one morning after spending the night in a single room trying to agree upon the location of a fountain, and were now confined comfortably in an insane asylum at Westport, Connecticut.

"But," inquired John curiously, "who did plan all your wonderful reception rooms and halls, and approaches and bathrooms——?"

"Well," answered Percy, "I blush to tell you, but it was a moving-picture fella. He was the only man we found who was used to playing with an unlimited amount of money, though he did tuck his napkin in his collar and couldn't read or write."

As August drew to a close John began to regret that he must soon go back to school. He and Kismine had decided to elope the following June.

"It would be nicer to be married here," Kismine confessed, "but of course I could never get father's permission to marry you at all. Next to that I'd rather elope. It's terrible for wealthy people to be married in America at present—they always have to send out bulletins to the press saying that they're going to be married in remnants, when what they mean is just a peck of old second-hand pearls and some used lace worn once by the Empress Eugénie."

"I know," agreed John fervently. "When I was visiting the Schnlitzer-Murphys, the eldest daughter, Gwendolyn, married a man whose father owns half of West Virginia. She wrote home saying what a tough struggle she was carrying on on his salary as a bank clerk—and then she ended up by saying that 'Thank God, I have four good maids anyhow, and that helps a little.' "

"It's absurd," commented Kismine. "Think of the millions and millions of people in the world, laborers and all, who get along with only two maids."

One afternoon late in August a chance remark of Kismine's changed the face of the entire situation, and threw John into a state of terror.

They were in their favorite grove, and between kisses John was indulging in some romantic forebodings which he fancied added poignancy to their relations.

"Sometimes I think we'll never marry," he said sadly. "You're too wealthy, too magnificent. No one as rich as you are can be like other girls. I should marry the daughter of some well-to-do wholesale hardware man from Omaha or Sioux City, and be content with her half-million."

"I knew the daughter of a wholesale hardware man once," remarked Kismine. "I don't think you'd have been contented with her. She was a friend of my sister's. She visited here."

"Oh, then you've had other guests?" exclaimed John in surprise.

Kismine seemed to regret her words.

"Oh, yes," she said hurriedly, "we've had a few."

"But aren't you—wasn't your father afraid they'd talk outside?"

"Oh, to some extent, to some extent," she answered. "Let's talk about something pleasanter."

But John's curiosity was aroused.

"Something pleasanter!" he demanded. "What's unpleasant about that? Weren't they nice girls?"

To his great surprise Kismine began to weep.

"Yes—th—that's the—the whole t-trouble. I grew qu-quite attached to some of them. So did Jasmine, but she kept inv-viting them anyway. I couldn't under*stand* it."

A dark suspicion was born in John's heart.

"Do you mean that they *told,* and your father had them—removed?"

"Worse than that," she muttered brokenly. "Father took no chances—and Jasmine kept writing them to come, and they had *such* a good time!"

She was overcome by a paroxysm of grief.

Stunned with the horror of this revelation, John sat there open-mouthed, feeling the nerves of his body twitter like so many sparrows perched upon his spinal column.

"Now, I've told you, and I shouldn't have," she said, calming suddenly and drying her dark blue eyes.

"Do you mean to say that your father had them *murdered* before they left?"

She nodded.

"In August usually—or early in September. It's only natural for us to get all the pleasure out of them that we can first."

"How abominable! How—why, I must be going crazy! Did you really admit that——"

"I did," interrupted Kismine, shrugging her shoulders. "We can't very well imprison them like those aviators, where they'd be a continual reproach to us every day. And it's always been made easier for Jasmine and me, because father had it done sooner than we expected. In that way we avoided any farewell scene——"

"So you murdered them! Uh!" cried John.

"It was done very nicely. They were drugged while they were asleep—and their families were always told that they died of scarlet fever in Butte."

"But—I fail to understand why you kept on inviting them!"

"I didn't," burst out Kismine. "I never invited one. Jasmine did. And they always had a very good time. She'd give them the nicest presents toward the last. I shall probably have visitors too—I'll harden up to it. We can't let such an inevitable thing as death stand in the way of enjoying life while we have it. Think how lonesome it'd be out here if we never had *any* one. Why, father and mother have sacrificed some of their best friends just as we have."

"And so," cried John accusingly, "and so you were letting me make love to you and pretending to return it, and talking about marriage, all the time knowing perfectly well that I'd never get out of here alive——"

"No," she protested passionately. "Not any more. I did at first. You were here. I couldn't help that, and I thought your last days might as well be pleasant for both of us. But then I fell in love with you, and—and I'm honestly sorry you're going to—going to be put away—though I'd rather you'd be put away than ever kiss another girl."

"Oh, you would, would you?" cried John ferociously.

"Much rather. Besides, I've always heard that a girl can have more fun with a man whom she knows she can never marry. Oh, why did I tell you? I've probably spoiled your whole good time now, and we were really enjoying things when you didn't know it. I knew it would make things sort of depressing for you."

"Oh, you did, did you?" John's voice trembled with anger. "I've heard about enough of this. If you haven't any more pride and decency than to have an affair with a fellow that you know isn't much better than a corpse, I don't want to have any more to do with you!"

"You're not a corpse!" she protested in horror. "You're not a corpse! I won't have you saying that I kissed a corpse!"

"I said nothing of the sort!"

"You did! You said I kissed a corpse!"

"I didn't!"

Their voices had risen, but upon a sudden interruption they both subsided into immediate silence. Footsteps were coming along the path in their direction, and a moment later the rose bushes were parted displaying Braddock Washington, whose intelligent eyes set in his good-looking vacuous face were peering in at them.

"Who kissed a corpse?" he demanded in obvious disapproval.

"Nobody," answered Kismine quickly. "We were just joking."

"What are you two doing here, anyhow?" he demanded gruffly. "Kismine, you ought to be—to be reading or playing golf with your sister. Go read! Go play golf! Don't let me find you here when I come back!"

Then he bowed at John and went up the path.

"See?" said Kismine crossly, when he was out of hearing. "You've spoiled it all. We can never meet any more. He won't let me meet you. He'd have you poisoned if he thought we were in love."

"We're not, any more!" cried John fiercely, "so he can set his mind at rest upon that. Moreover, don't fool yourself that I'm going to stay around here. Inside of six hours I'll be over those mountains, if I have to gnaw a passage through them, and on my way East."

They had both got to their feet, and at this remark Kismine came close and put her arm through his.

"I'm going, too."

"You must be crazy——"

"Of course I'm going," she interrupted impatiently.

"You most certainly are not. You——"

"Very well," she said quietly, "we'll catch up with father now and talk it over with him."

Defeated, John mustered a sickly smile.

"Very well, dearest," he agreed, with pale and unconvincing affection, "we'll go together."

His love for her returned and settled placidly on his heart. She was his—she would go with him to share his dangers. He put his arms about her and kissed her fervently. After all she loved him; she had saved him, in fact.

Discussing the matter, they walked slowly back toward the château. They decided that since Braddock Washington had seen them together they had best depart the next night. Nevertheless, John's lips were unusually dry at dinner, and he nervously emptied a great spoonful of peacock soup into his left lung. He had to be carried into the turquoise and sable card-room and pounded on the back by one of the under-butlers, which Percy considered a great joke.

IX

Long after midnight John's body gave a nervous jerk, and he sat suddenly upright, staring into the veils of somnolence that draped the room. Through the squares of blue darkness that were his open windows, he had heard a faint far-away sound that died upon a bed of wind before identifying itself on his memory, clouded with uneasy dreams. But the sharp noise that had succeeded it was nearer, was just outside the room—the click of a turned knob, a footstep, a whisper, he could not tell; a hard lump gathered in the pit of his stomach, and his whole body ached in the moment that he strained agonizingly to hear. Then one of the veils seemed to dissolve, and he saw a vague figure standing by the door, a figure only faintly limned and blocked in upon the darkness, mingled so with the folds of the drapery as to seem distorted, like a reflection seen in a dirty pane of glass.

With a sudden movement of fright or resolution John pressed the button by his bedside, and the next moment he was sitting in the green sunken bath of the adjoining room, waked into alertness by the shock of the cold water which half filled it.

He sprang out, and, his wet pajamas scattering a heavy trickle of water behind him, ran for the aquamarine door which he knew led out onto the ivory landing of the second floor. The door opened noiselessly. A single crimson lamp burning in a great dome above lit the magnificent sweep of the carved stairways with a poignant beauty. For a moment John hesitated, appalled by the silent splendor massed about him, seeming to envelop in its gigantic folds and contours the solitary drenched little figure shivering upon the ivory landing. Then simultaneously two things happened. The door of his own sitting-room swung open, precipitating three naked negroes into the hall—and, as John swayed in wild terror toward the stairway, another door slid back in the wall on the other side of the corridor, and John saw Braddock Washington standing in the lighted lift, wearing a fur coat and a pair of riding boots which reached to his knees and displayed, above, the glow of his rose-colored pajamas.

On the instant the three negroes—John had never seen any of them before, and it flashed through his mind that they must be the professional executioners—paused in their movement toward John, and turned expectantly to the man in the lift, who burst out with an imperious command:

"Get in here! All three of you! Quick as hell!"

Then, within the instant, the three negroes darted into the cage, the oblong of light was blotted out as the lift door slid shut, and John was again alone in the hall. He slumped weakly down against an ivory stair.

It was apparent that something portentous had occurred, something which, for the moment at least, had postponed his own petty disaster. What was it? Had the negroes risen in revolt? Had the aviators forced aside the iron bars of the grating? Or had the men of Fish stumbled blindly through the hills and gazed with bleak, joyless eyes upon the gaudy valley? John did not know. He heard a faint whir of air as the lift whizzed up again, and then, a moment later, as it descended. It was probable that Percy was hurrying to his father's assistance, and it occurred to John that this was his opportunity to join Kismine and plan an immediate escape. He waited until the lift had been silent for several minutes; shivering a little with the night cool that whipped in through his wet pajamas, he returned to his room and dressed himself quickly. Then he mounted a long flight of stairs and turned down the corridor carpeted with Russian sable which led to Kismine's suite.

The door of her sitting-room was open and the lamps were lighted. Kismine, in an angora kimono, stood near the window of the room in a listening attitude, and as John entered noiselessly, she turned toward him.

"Oh, it's you!" she whispered, crossing the room to him. "Did you hear them?"

"I heard your father's slaves in my——"

"No," she interrupted excitedly. "Aeroplanes!"

"Aeroplanes? Perhaps that was the sound that woke me."

"There're at least a dozen. I saw one a few moments ago dead against the moon. The guard back by the cliff fired his rifle and that's what roused father. We're going to open on them right away."

"Are they here on purpose?"

"Yes—it's that Italian who got away——"

Simultaneously with her last word, a succession of sharp cracks tumbled in through the open window. Kismine uttered a little cry, took a penny with fumbling fingers from a box on her dresser, and ran to one of the electric lights. In an instant the entire château was in darkness—she had blown out the fuse.

"Come on!" she cried to him. "We'll go up to the roof garden, and watch it from there!"

Drawing a cape about her, she took his hand, and they found their way out the door. It was only a step to the tower lift, and as she pressed the button that shot them upward he put his arms around her in the darkness and kissed her mouth. Romance had come to John Unger at last. A minute later they had stepped out upon the star-white platform. Above, under the misty moon, sliding in and out of the patches of cloud that eddied below it, floated a dozen darkwinged bodies in a constant circling course. From here and there in the valley flashes of fire leaped toward them, followed by sharp detonations. Kismine clapped her hands with pleasure, which a moment later, turned to dismay as the aeroplanes at some prearranged signal, began to release their bombs and the whole of the valley became a panorama of deep reverberate sound and lurid light.

Before long the aim of the attackers became concentrated upon the points where the anti-aircraft guns were situated, and one of them was almost immediately reduced to a giant cinder to lie smouldering in a park of rose bushes.

"Kismine," begged John, "you'll be glad when I tell you that this attack came on the eve of my murder. If I hadn't heard that guard shoot off his gun back by the pass I should now be stone dead——"

"I can't hear you!" cried Kismine, intent on the scene before her. "You'll have to talk louder!"

"I simply said," shouted John, "that we'd better get out before they begin to shell the Château!"

Suddenly the whole portico of the negro quarters cracked asunder, a geyser of flame shot up from under the colonnades, and great fragments of jagged marble were hurled as far as the borders of the lake.

"There go fifty thousand dollars' worth of slaves," cried Kismine, "at prewar prices. So few Americans have any respect for property."

John renewed his efforts to compel her to leave. The aim of the aeroplanes was becoming more precise minute by minute, and only two of the anti-aircraft guns were still retaliating. It was obvious that the garrison, encircled with fire, could not hold out much longer.

"Come on!" cried John, pulling Kismine's arm, "we've got to go. Do you realize that those aviators will kill you without question if they find you?"

She consented reluctantly.

"We'll have to wake Jasmine!" she said, as they hurried toward the lift. Then she added in a sort of childish delight: "We'll be poor, won't we? Like people in books. And I'll be an orphan and utterly free. Free and poor! What fun!" She stopped and raised her lips to him in a delighted kiss.

"It's impossible to be both together," said John grimly. "People have found that out. And I should choose to be free as preferable of the two. As an extra caution you'd better dump the contents of your jewel box into your pockets."

Ten minutes later the two girls met John in the dark corridor and they descended to the main floor of the chateau. Passing for the last time through the magnificence of the splendid halls, they stood for a moment out on the terrace, watching the burning negro quarters and the flaming embers of two planes which had fallen on the other side of the lake. A solitary gun was still keeping up a sturdy popping, and the attackers seemed timorous about descending lower, but sent their thunderous fireworks in a circle around it, until any chance shot might annihilate its Ethiopian crew.

John and the two sisters passed down the marble steps, turned sharply to the left, and began to ascend a narrow path that wound like a garter about the diamond mountain. Kismine knew a heavily wooded spot half-way up where they could lie concealed and yet be able to observe the wild night in the valley—finally to make an escape, when it should be necessary, along a secret path laid in a rocky gully.

X

It was three o'clock when they attained their destination. The obliging and phlegmatic Jasmine fell off to sleep immediately, leaning against the trunk of a large tree, while John and Kismine sat, his arm around her, and watched the desperate ebb and flow of the dying battle among the ruins of a vista that had been a garden spot that morning. Shortly after four o'clock the last remaining gun gave out a clanging sound and went out of action in a swift tongue of red smoke. Though the moon was down, they saw that the flying bodies were circling closer to the earth. When the planes had made certain that the beleaguered possessed no further resources, they would land and the dark and glittering reign of the Washingtons would be over.

With the cessation of the firing the valley grew quiet. The embers of the two aeroplanes glowed like the eyes of some monster crouching in the grass. The château stood dark and silent, beautiful without light as it had been beautiful in the sun, while the woody rattles of Nemesis filled the air above with a growing and receding complaint. Then John perceived that Kismine, like her sister, had fallen sound asleep.

It was long after four when he became aware of footsteps along the path they had lately followed, and he waited in breathless silence until the persons to whom they belonged had passed the vantage-point he occupied. There was a faint stir in the air now that was not of human origin, and the dew was cold; he knew that the dawn would break soon. John waited until the steps had gone a safe distance up the mountain and were inaudible. Then he followed. About half-way to the steep summit the trees fell away and a hard saddle of rock spread itself over the diamond beneath. Just before he reached this point he slowed down his pace, warned by an animal sense that there was life just ahead of him. Coming to a high boulder, he lifted his head gradually above its edge. His curiosity was rewarded; this is what he saw:

Braddock Washington was standing there motionless, silhouetted against the gray sky without sound or sign of life. As the dawn came up out of the east, lending a cold green color to the earth, it brought the solitary figure into insignificant contrast with the new day.

While John watched, his host remained for a few moments absorbed in some inscrutable contemplation; then he signalled to the two negroes who crouched at his feet to lift the burden which lay between them. As they struggled upright, the first yellow beam of the sun struck through the innumerable prisms of an immense and exquisitely chiselled diamond—and a white radiance was kindled that glowed upon the air like a fragment of the morning star. The bearers staggered beneath its weight for a moment—then their rippling muscles caught and hardened under the wet shine of the skins and the three figures were again motionless in their defiant impotency before the heavens.

After a while the white man lifted his head and slowly raised his arms in a gesture of attention, as one who would call a great crowd to hear—but there was no crowd, only the vast silence of the mountain and the sky, broken by faint bird voices down among the trees. The figure on the saddle of rock began to speak ponderously and with an inextinguishable pride.

"You out there—" he cried in a trembling voice. "You—there—!" He paused, his arms still uplifted, his head held attentively as though he were expecting an answer. John strained his eyes to see whether there might be men coming down the mountain, but the mountain was bare of human life. There was only sky and a mocking flute of wind along the tree-tops. Could Washington be praying? For a moment John wondered. Then the illusion passed—there was something in the man's whole attitude antithetical to prayer.

"Oh, you above there!"

The voice was become strong and confident. This was no forlorn supplication. If anything, there was in it a quality of monstrous condescension.

"You there——"

Words, too quickly uttered to be understood, flowing one into the other. . . . John listened breathlessly, catching a phrase here and there, while the voice broke off, resumed, broke off again—now strong and argumentative, now colored with a slow, puzzled impatience. Then a conviction commenced to dawn on the single listener, and as realization crept over him a spray of quick blood rushed through his arteries. Braddock Washington was offering a bribe to God!

That was it—there was no doubt. The diamond in the arms of his slaves was some advance sample, a promise of more to follow.

That, John perceived after a time, was the thread running through his sentences. Prometheus Enriched was calling to witness forgotten sacrifices, forgotten rituals, prayers obsolete before the birth of Christ. For a while his discourse took the form of reminding God of this gift or that which Divinity had deigned to accept from men—great churches if he would rescue cities from the plague, gifts of myrrh and gold, of human lives and beautiful women and captive armies, of children and queens, of beasts of the forest and field, sheep and goats, harvests and cities, whole conquered lands that had been offered up in lust or blood for His appeasal, buying a meed's worth of alleviation from the Divine wrath—and now he, Braddock Washington, Emperor of Diamonds, king and priest of the age of gold, arbiter of splendor and luxury, would offer up a treasure such as princes before him had never dreamed of, offer it up not in suppliance, but in pride.

He would give to God, he continued, getting down to specifications, the greatest diamond in the world. This diamond would be cut with many more thousand facets than there were leaves on a tree, and yet the whole diamond would be shaped with the perfection of a stone no bigger than a fly. Many men would work upon it for many years. It would be set in a great dome of beaten gold, wonderfully carved and equipped with gates of opal and crusted sapphire. In the middle would be hollowed out a chapel presided over by an altar of iridescent, decomposing, ever-changing radium which would burn out the eyes of any worshipper who lifted up his head from prayer—and on this altar there would be slain for the amusement of the Divine Benefactor any victim He should choose, even though it should be the greatest and most powerful man alive.

In return he asked only a simple thing, a thing that for God would be absurdly easy—only that matters should be as they were yesterday at this hour and that they should so remain. So very simple! Let but the heavens open, swallowing these men and their aeroplanes—and then close again. Let him have his slaves once more, restored to life and well.

There was no one else with whom he had ever needed to treat or bargain.

He doubted only whether he had made his bribe big enough. God had His price, of course. God was made in man's image, so it had been said: He must have His price. And the price would be rare—no cathedral whose building consumed many years, no pyramid constructed by ten thousand workmen, would be like this cathedral, this pyramid.

He paused here. That was his proposition. Everything would be up to specifications and there was nothing vulgar in his assertion that it would be cheap at the price. He implied that Providence could take it or leave it.

As he approached the end his sentences became broken, became short and uncertain, and his body seemed tense, seemed strained to catch the slightest pressure or whisper of life in the spaces around him. His hair had turned gradually white as he talked, and now he lifted his head high to the heavens like a prophet of old—magnificently mad.

Then, as John stared in giddy fascination, it seemed to him that a curious phenomenon took place somewhere around him. It was as though the sky had darkened for an instant, as though there had been a sudden murmur in a gust of wind, a sound of far-away trumpets, a sighing like the rustle of a great silken robe—for a time the whole of nature round about partook of this darkness: the birds' song ceased; the trees were still, and far over the mountain there was a mutter of dull, menacing thunder.

That was all. The wind died along the tall grasses of the valley. The dawn and the day resumed their place in a time, and the risen sun sent hot waves of yellow mist that made its path bright before it. The leaves laughed in the sun, and their laughter shook the trees until each bough was like a girl's school in fairyland. God had refused to accept the bribe.

For another moment John watched the triumph of the day. Then, turning, he saw a flutter of brown down by the lake, then another flutter, then another, like the dance of golden angels alighting from the clouds. The aeroplanes had come to earth.

John slid off the boulder and ran down the side of the mountain to the clump of trees, where the two girls were awake and waiting for him. Kismine sprang to her feet, the jewels in her pockets jingling, a question on her parted lips, but instinct told John that there was no time for words. They must get off the mountain without losing a moment. He seized a hand of each, and in silence they threaded the tree-trunks, washed with light now and with the rising mist. Behind them from the valley came no sound at all, except the complaint of the peacocks far away and the pleasant undertone of morning.

When they had gone about half a mile, they avoided the park land and entered a narrow path that led over the next rise of ground. At the highest point of this they paused and turned around. Their eyes rested upon the mountainside they had just left—oppressed by some dark sense of tragic impendency.

Clear against the sky a broken, white-haired man was slowly descending the steep slope, followed by two gigantic and emotionless negroes, who carried a burden between them which still flashed and glittered in the sun. Half-way down two other figures joined them—John could see that they were Mrs. Washington and her son, upon whose arm she leaned. The aviators had clambered from their machines to the sweeping lawn in front of the château, and with rifles in hand were starting up the diamond mountain in skirmishing formation.

But the little group of five which had formed farther up and was engrossing all the watchers' attention had stopped upon a ledge of rock. The negroes stooped and pulled up what appeared to be a trapdoor in the side of the mountain. Into this they all disappeared, the white-haired man first, then his wife and son, finally the two negroes, the glittering tips of whose jeweled head-dresses caught the sun for a moment before the trap-door descended and engulfed them all.

Kismine clutched John's arm.

"Oh," she cried wildly, "where are they going? What are they going to do?"

"It must be some underground way of escape——"

A little scream from the two girls interrupted his sentence.

"Don't you see?" sobbed Kismine hysterically. "The mountain is wired!"

Even as she spoke John put up his hands to shield his sight. Before their eyes the whole surface of the mountain had changed suddenly to a dazzling burning yellow, which showed up through the jacket of turf as light shows through a human hand. For a moment the intolerable glow continued, and then like an extinguished filament it disappeared, revealing a black waste from which blue smoke arose slowly, carrying off with it what remained of vegetation and of human flesh. Of the aviators there was left neither blood nor bone—they were consumed as completely as the five souls who had gone inside.

Simultaneously, and with an immense concussion, the château literally threw itself into the air, bursting into flaming fragments as it rose, and then tumbling back upon itself in a smoking pile that lay projecting half into the water of the lake. There was no fire—what smoke there was drifted off mingling with the sunshine, and for a few minutes longer a powdery dust of marble drifted from the great featureless pile that had once been the house of jewels. There was no more sound and the three people were alone in the valley.

XI

At sunset John and his two companions reached the high cliff which had marked the boundaries of the Washingtons' dominion, and looking back found the valley tranquil and lovely in the dusk. They sat down to finish the food which Jasmine had brought with her in a basket.

"There!" she said, as she spread the table-cloth and put the sandwiches in a neat pile upon it. "Don't they look tempting? I always think that food tastes better outdoors."

"With that remark," remarked Kismine, "Jasmine enters the middle class."

"Now," said John eagerly, "turn out your pocket and let's see what jewels you brought along. If you made a good selection we three ought to live comfortably all the rest of our lives."

Obediently Kismine put her hand in her pocket and tossed two handfuls of glittering stones before him.

"Not so bad," cried John, enthusiastically. "They aren't very big, but—Hello!" His expression changed as he held one of them up to the declining sun. "Why, these aren't diamonds! There's something the matter!"

"By golly!" exclaimed Kismine, with a startled look. "What an idiot I am!"

"Why, these are rhinestones!" cried John.

"I know." She broke into a laugh. "I opened the wrong drawer. They belonged on the dress of a girl who visited Jasmine. I got her to give them to me in exchange for diamonds. I'd never seen anything but precious stones before."

"And this is what you brought?"

"I'm afraid so." She fingered the brilliants wistfully. "I think I like these better. I'm a little tired of diamonds."

"Very well," said John gloomily. "We'll have to live in Hades. And you will grow old telling incredulous women that you got the wrong drawer. Unfortunately your father's bank-books were consumed with him."

"Well, what's the matter with Hades?"

"If I come home with a wife at my age my father is just as liable as not to cut me off with a hot coal, as they say down there."

Jasmine spoke up.

"I love washing," she said quietly. "I have always washed my own handkerchiefs. I'll take in laundry and support you both."

"Do they have washwomen in Hades?" asked Kismine innocently.

"Of course," answered John. "It's just like anywhere else."

"I thought—perhaps it was too hot to wear any clothes."

John laughed.

"Just try it!" he suggested. "They'll run you out before you're half started."

"Will father be there?" she asked.

John turned to her in astonishment.

"Your father is dead," he replied somberly. "Why should he go to Hades? You have it confused with another place that was abolished long ago."

After supper they folded up the table-cloth and spread their blankets for the night.

"What a dream it was," Kismine sighed, gazing up at the stars. "How strange it seems to be here with one dress and a penniless fiancé!

"Under the stars," she repeated. "I never noticed the stars before. I always thought of them as great big diamonds that belonged to some one. Now they frighten me. They make me feel that it was all a dream, all my youth."

"It *was* a dream," said John quietly. "Everybody's youth is a dream, a form of chemical madness."

"How pleasant then to be insane!"

"So I'm told," said John gloomily. "I don't know any longer. At any rate, let us love for a while, for a year or so, you and me. That's a form of divine drunkenness that we can all try. There are only diamonds in the whole world, diamonds and perhaps the shabby gift of disillusion. Well, I have that last and I will make the usual nothing of it." He shivered. "Turn up your coat collar, little girl, the night's full of chill and you'll get pneumonia. His was a great sin who first invented consciousness. Let us lose it for a few hours."

So wrapping himself in his blanket he fell off to sleep.

ERNEST HEMINGWAY

THE KILLERS

Writing is often a dull, private affair, and writers often live quiet uneventful lives. Ernest Hemingway (1899–1961) was an exception. His books were not only the most popular (and critically acclaimed) works of the 1930s and 1940s, but he was an international celebrity whose movements were recorded in the daily newspapers. Hemingway came to represent "The Lost Generation," the generation which came to adulthood in the twenty years between the First and Second World Wars.

Born in Oak Park, Illinois—a prosperous and quiet suburb of Chicago—Hemingway began as a reporter. He served in Italy during World War I, then lived in Paris during the roaring twenties. A sportsman and traveller, he fought bulls in Spain, tigers in Africa, sharks in the Caribbean and F. Scott Fitzgerald in France and wrote about all these encounters. In 1954, he was awarded the Nobel Prize in Literature, and in 1961, having developed cancer, committed suicide. His major works include The Sun Also Rises *and* A Farewell to Arms.

The door of Henry's lunch-room opened and two men came in. They sat down at the counter.

"What's yours?" George asked them.

"I don't know," one of the men said. "What do you want to eat, Al?"

"I don't know," said Al. "I don't know what I want to eat."

Outside it was getting dark. The street-light came on outside the window. The two men at the counter read the menu. From the other end of the counter Nick Adams watched them. He had been talking to George when they came in.

"I'll have a roast pork tenderloin with apple sauce and mashed potatoes," the first man said.

"It isn't ready yet."

"What the hell do you put it on the card for?"

"That's the dinner," George explained. "You can get that at six o'clock."

George looked at the clock on the wall behind the counter.

"It's five o'clock."

"The clock says twenty minutes past five," the second man said.

"It's twenty minutes fast."

"Oh, to hell with the clock," the first man said. "What have you got to eat?"

"I can give you any kind of sandwiches," George said. "You can have ham and eggs, bacon and eggs, liver and bacon, or a steak."

"Give me chicken croquettes with green peas and cream sauce and mashed potatoes."

"That's the dinner."

"Everything we want's the dinner, eh? That's the way you work it."

"I can give you ham and eggs, bacon and eggs, liver——"

"I'll take ham and eggs," the man called Al said. He wore a derby hat and a black overcoat buttoned across the chest. His face was small and white and he had tight lips. He wore a silk muffler and gloves.

"Give me bacon and eggs," said the other man. He was about the same size as Al. Their faces were different, but they were dressed like twins. Both wore overcoats too tight for them. They sat leaning forward, their elbows on the counter.

"Got anything to drink?" Al asked.

"Silver beer, bevo, ginger-ale," George said.

"I mean you got anything to *drink?*"

"Just those I said."

"This is a hot town," said the other. "What do they call it?"

"Summit."

"Ever hear of it?" Al asked his friend.

"No," said the friend.

"What do you do here nights?" Al asked.

"They eat the dinner," his friend said. "They all come here and eat the big dinner."

"That's right," George said.

"So you think that's right?" Al asked George.

"Sure."

"You're a pretty bright boy, aren't you?"

"Sure," said George.

"Well, you're not," said the other little man. "Is he, Al?"

"He's dumb," said Al. He turned to Nick. "What's your name?"

"Adams."

"Another bright boy," Al said. "Ain't he a bright boy, Max?"

"The town's full of bright boys," Max said.

George put the two platters, one of ham and eggs, the other of bacon and eggs, on the counter. He set down two side-dishes of fried potatoes and closed the wicket into the kitchen.

"Which is yours?" he asked Al.

"Don't you remember?"

"Ham and eggs."

"Just a bright boy," Max said. He leaned forward and took the ham and eggs. Both men ate with their gloves on. George watched them eat.

"What are *you* looking it?" Max looked at George.

"Nothing."

"The hell you were. You were looking at me."

"Maybe the boy meant it for a joke, Max," Al said.

George laughed.

"*You* don't have to laugh," Max said to him. "*You* don't have to laugh at all, see?"

"All right," said George.

"So he thinks it's all right." Max turned to Al. "He thinks it's all right. That's a good one."

"Oh, he's a thinker," Al said. They went on eating.

"What's the bright boy's name down the counter?" Al asked Max.

"Hey, bright boy," Max said to Nick. "You go around on the other side of the counter with your boy friend."

"What's the idea?" Nick asked.

"There isn't any idea."

"You better go around, bright boy," Al said. Nick went around behind the counter.

"What's the idea?" George asked.

"None of your damn business," Al said. "Who's out in the kitchen?"

"The nigger."

"What do you mean the nigger?"

"The nigger that cooks."

"Tell him to come in."

"What's the idea?"

"Tell him to come in."

"Where do you think you are?"

"We know damn well where we are," the man called Max said. "Do we look silly?"

"You talk silly," Al said to him. "What the hell do you argue with this kid for? Listen," he said to George, "tell the nigger to come out here."

"What are you going to do to him?"

"Nothing. Use your head, bright boy. What would we do to a nigger?"

George opened the slit that opened back into the kitchen. "Sam," he called. "Come in here a minute."

The door to the kitchen opened and the nigger came in. "What was it?" he asked. The two men at the counter took a look at him.

"All right, nigger. You stand right there," Al said.

Sam, the nigger, standing in his apron, looked at the two men sitting at the counter. "Yes, sir," he said. Al got down from his stool.

"I'm going back to the kitchen with the nigger and bright boy," he said. "Go on back to the kitchen, nigger. You go with him, bright boy." The little man walked after Nick and Sam, the cook, back into the kitchen. The door shut after them. The man called Max sat at the counter opposite George. He didn't look at George but looked in the mirror that ran along back of the counter. Henry's had been made over from a saloon into a lunch-counter.

"Well, bright boy," Max said, looking into the mirror, "why don't you say something?"

"What's it all about?"

"Hey, Al," Max called, "bright boy wants to know what it's all about."

"Why don't you tell him?" Al's voice came from the kitchen.

"What do you think it's all about?"

"I don't know."

"What do you think?"

Max looked into the mirror all the time he was talking.

"I wouldn't say."

"Hey, Al, bright boy says he wouldn't say what he thinks it's all about."

"I can hear you, all right," Al said from the kitchen. He had propped open the slit that dishes passed through into the kitchen with a catsup bottle. "Listen, bright boy," he said from the kitchen to George. "Stand a little further along the bar. You move a little to the left, Max." He was like a photographer arranging for a group picture.

"Talk to me, bright boy," Max said. "What do you think's going to happen?"

George did not say anything.

"I'll tell you," Max said. "We're going to kill a Swede. Do you know a big Swede named Ole Andreson?"

"Yes."

"He comes here to eat every night, don't he?"

"Sometimes he comes here."

"He comes here at six o'clock, don't he?"

"If he comes."

"We know all that, bright boy," Max said. "Talk about something else. Ever go to the movies?"

"Once in a while."

"You ought to go to the movies more. The movies are fine for a bright boy like you."

"What are you going to kill Ole Andreson for? What did he ever do to you?"

"He never had a chance to do anything to us. He never even seen us."

"And he's only going to see us once," Al said from the kitchen.

"What are you going to kill him for, then?" George asked.

"We're killing him for a friend. Just to oblige a friend, bright boy."

"Shut up," said Al from the kitchen. "You talk too goddam much."

"Well, I got to keep bright boy amused. Don't I, bright boy?"

"You talk too damn much," Al said. "The nigger and my bright boy are amused by themselves. I got them tied up like a couple of girl friends in the convent."

"I suppose you were in a convent?"

"You never know."

"You were in a kosher convent. That's where you were."

George looked up at the clock.

"If anybody comes in you tell them the cook is off, and if they keep after it, you tell them you'll go back and cook yourself. Do you get that, bright boy?"

"All right," George said. "What you going to do with us afterward?"

"That'll depend," Max said. "That's one of those things you never know at the time."

George looked up at the clock. It was a quarter past six. The door from the street opened. A street-car motorman came in.

"Hello, George," he said. "Can I get supper?"

"Sam's gone out," George said. "He'll be back in about half an hour."

"I'd better go up the street," the motorman said. George looked at the clock. It was twenty minutes past six.

"That was nice, bright boy," Max said. "You're a regular little gentleman."

"He knew I'd blow his head off," Al said from the kitchen.

'No," said Max. "It ain't that. Bright boy is nice. He's a nice boy. I like him."

At six-fifty-five George said: "He's not coming."

Two other people had been in the lunch-room. Once George had gone out to the kitchen and made a ham-and-egg sandwich "to go" that a man wanted to take with him. Inside the kitchen he saw Al, his derby hat tipped back, sitting on a stool beside the wicket with the muzzle of a sawed-off shotgun resting on the ledge. Nick and the cook were back to back in the corner, a towel tied in each of their mouths. George had cooked the sandwich, wrapped it up in oiled paper, put it in a bag, brought it in, and the man had paid for it and gone out.

"Bright boy can do everything," Max said. "He can cook and everything. You'd make some girl a nice wife, bright boy."

"Yes?" George said. "Your friend, Ole Andreson, isn't going to come."

"We'll give him ten minutes," Max said.

Max watched the mirror and the clock. The hands of the clock marked seven o'clock, and then five minutes past seven.

"Come on, Al," said Max. "We better go. He's not coming."

"Better give him five minutes," Al said from the kitchen.

In the five minutes a man came in, and George explained that the cook was sick.

"Why the hell don't you get another cook?" the man asked. "Aren't you running a lunch-counter?" He went out.

"Come on, Al," Max said.

"What about the two bright boys and the nigger?"

"They're all right."

"You think so?"

"Sure. We're through with it."

"I don't like it," said Al. "It's sloppy. You talk too much."

"Oh, what the hell," said Max. "We got to keep amused, haven't we?"

"You talk too much, all the same," Al said. He came out from the kitchen. The cut-off barrels of the shotgun made a slight bulge under the waist of his too tight-fitting overcoat. He straightened his coat with his gloved hands.

"So long, bright boy," he said to George. "You got a lot of luck."

"That's the truth," Max said. "You ought to play the races, bright boy."

The two of them went out the door. George watched them, through the window, pass under the arc-light and cross the street. In their tight overcoats and derby hats they looked like a vaudeville team. George went back through the swinging-door into the kitchen and untied Nick and the cook.

"I don't want any more of that," said Sam, the cook. "I don't want any more of that."

Nick stood up. He had never had a towel in his mouth before.

"Say," he said. "What the hell?" He was trying to swagger it off.

"They were going to kill Ole Andreson," George said. "They were going to shoot him when he came in to eat."

"Ole Andreson?"

"Sure."

The cook felt the corners of his mouth with his thumbs.

"They all gone?" he asked.

"Yeah," said George. "They're gone now."

"I don't like it," said the cook. "I don't like any of it at all."

"Listen," George said to Nick. "You better go see Ole Andreson."

"All right."

"You better not have anything to do with it at all," Sam, the cook, said. "You better stay way out of it."

"Don't go if you don't want to," George said.

"Mixing up in this ain't going to get you anywhere," the cook said. "You stay out of it."

"I'll go see him," Nick said to George. "Where does he live?"

The cook turned away.

"Little boys always know what they want to do," he said.

"He lives up at Hirsch's rooming-house," George said to Nick.

"I'll go up there."

Outside the arc-light shone through the bare branches of a tree. Nick walked up the street beside the car-tracks and turned at the next arc-light down a side-street. Three houses up the street was Hirsch's rooming-house. Nick walked up the two steps and pushed the bell. A woman came to the door.

"Is Ole Andreson here?"

"Do you want to see him?"

"Yes, if he's in."

Nick followed the woman up a flight of stairs and back to the end of a corridor. She knocked on the door.

"Who is it?"

"It's somebody to see you, Mr. Andreson," the woman said.

"It's Nick Adams."

"Come in."

Nick opened the door and went into the room. Ole Andreson was lying on the bed with all his clothes on. He had been a heavyweight prizefighter and he was too long for the bed. He lay with his head on two pillows. He did not look at Nick.

"What was it?" he asked.

"I was up at Henry's," Nick said, "and two fellows came in and tied up me and the cook, and they said they were going to kill you."

It sounded silly when he said it. Ole Andreson said nothing.

"They put us out in the kitchen," Nick went on. "They were going to shoot you when you came in to supper."

Ole Andreson looked at the wall and did not say anything.

"George thought I better come and tell you about it."

"There isn't anything I can do about it," Ole Andreson said.

"I'll tell you what they were like."

"I don't want to know what they were like," Ole Andreson said. He looked at the wall. "Thanks for coming to tell me about it."

"That's all right."

Nick looked at the big man lying on the bed.

"Don't you want me to go and see the police?"

"No," Ole Andreson said. "That wouldn't do any good."

"Isn't there something I could do?"

"No. There ain't anything to do."

"Maybe it was just a bluff."

"No. It ain't just a bluff."

Ole Andreson rolled over toward the wall.

"The only thing is," he said, talking toward the wall, "I just can't make up my mind to go out. I been in here all day."

"Couldn't you get out of town?"

"No," Ole Andreson said. "I'm through with all that running around."

He looked at the wall.

"There ain't anything to do now."

"Couldn't you fix it up some way?"

"No. I got in wrong." He talked in the same flat voice. "There ain't anything to do. After a while I'll make up my mind to go out."

"I better go back and see George," Nick said.

"So long," said Ole Andreson. He did not look toward Nick. "Thanks for coming around."

Nick went out. As he shut the door he saw Ole Andreson with all his clothes on, lying on the bed looking at the wall.

"He's been in his room all day," the landlady said down-stairs. "I guess he don't feel well. I said to him: 'Mr. Andreson, you ought to go out and take a walk on a nice fall day like this,' but he didn't feel like it."

"He doesn't want to go out."

"I'm sorry he don't feel well," the woman said. "He's an awfully nice man. He was in the ring, you know."

"I know it."

"You'd never know it except from the way his face is," the woman said. They stood talking just inside the street door. "He's just as gentle."

"Well, good-night, Mrs. Hirsch," Nick said.

"I'm not Mrs. Hirsch," the woman said. "She owns the place. I just look after it for her. I'm Mrs. Bell."

"Well, good-night, Mrs. Bell," Nick said.

"Good-night," the woman said.

Nick walked up the dark street to the corner under the arc-light, and then along the car-tracks to Henry's eating-house. George was inside, back of the counter.

"Did you see Ole?"

"Yes," said Nick. "He's in his room and he won't go out."

The cook opened the door from the kitchen when he heard Nick's voice.

"I don't even listen to it," he said and shut the door.

"Did you tell him about it?" George asked.

"Sure. I told him but he knows what it's all about."

"What's he going to do?"

"Nothing."

"They'll kill him."

"I guess they will."

"He must have got mixed up in something in Chicago."

"I guess so," said Nick.

"It's a hell of a thing."

"It's an awful thing," Nick said.

They did not say anything. George reached down for a towel and wiped the counter.

"I wonder what he did?" Nick said.

"Double-crossed somebody. That's what they kill them for."

"I'm going go get out of this town," Nick said.

"Yes," said George. "That's a good thing to do."

"I can't stand to think about him waiting in the room and knowing he's going to get it. It's too damned awful."

"Well," said George, "you better not think about it."

ERNEST HEMINGWAY

THE SHORT HAPPY LIFE OF FRANCIS MACOMBER

It was now lunch time and they were all sitting under the double green fly of the dining tent pretending that nothing had happened.

"Will you have lime juice or lemon squash?" Macomber asked.

"I'll have a gimlet," Robert Wilson told him.

"I'll have a gimlet too. I need something," Macomber's wife said.

"I suppose it's the thing to do," Macomber agreed. "Tell him to make three gimlets."

The mess boy had started them already, lifting the bottles out of the canvas cooling bags that sweated wet in the wind that blew through the trees that shaded the tents.

"What had I ought to give them?" Macomber asked.

"A quid would be plenty," Wilson told him. "You don't want to spoil them."

"Will the headman distribute it?"

"Absolutely."

Francis Macomber had, half an hour before, been carried to his tent from the edge of the camp in triumph on the arms and shoulders of the cook, the personal boys, the skinner and the porters. The gun-bearers had taken no part in the demonstration. When the native boys put him down at the door of his tent, he had shaken all their hands, received their congratulations, and then gone into the tent and sat on the bed until his wife came in. She did not speak to him when she came in and he left the tent at once to wash his face and hands in the portable wash basin outside and go over to the dining tent to sit in a comfortable canvas chair in the breeze and the shade.

"You've got your lion," Robert Wilson said to him, "and a damned fine one too."

Mrs. Macomber looked at Wilson quickly. She was an extremely handsome and well-kept woman of the beauty and social position which had, five years before, commanded five thousand dollars as the price of endorsing, with photographs, a beauty product which she had never used. She had been married to Francis Macomber for eleven years.

"He is a good lion, isn't he?" Macomber said. His wife looked at him now. She looked at both these men as though she had never seen them before.

One, Wilson, the white hunter, she knew she had never truly seen before. He was about middle height with sandy hair, a stubby mustache, a very red face and extremely cold blue eyes with faint white wrinkles at the corners that grooved merrily when he smiled. He smiled at her now and she looked away from his face at the way his shoulders sloped in the loose tunic he wore with the four big cartridges held in loops where the left breast pocket should have been, at his big brown hands, his old slacks, his very dirty boots and back to his red face again. She noticed where the baked red of his face stopped in a white line that marked the circle left by his Stetson hat that hung now from one of the pegs of the tent pole.

"Well, here's to the lion," Robert Wilson said. He smiled at her again and, not smiling, she looked curiously at her husband.

Francis Macomber was very tall, very well built if you did not mind that length of bone, dark, his hair cropped like an oarsman, rather thin-lipped, and was considered handsome. He was dressed in the same sort of safari clothes that Wilson wore except that his were new, he was thirty-five years old, kept himself very fit, was good at court games, had a number of big-game fishing records, and had just shown himself, very publicly, to be a coward.

"Here's to the lion," he said. "I can't ever thank you for what you did."

Margaret, his wife, looked away from him and back to Wilson.

"Let's not talk about the lion," she said.

Wilson looked over at her without smiling and now she smiled at him.

"It's been a very strange day," she said. "Hadn't you ought to put your hat on even under the canvas at noon? You told me that, you know."

"Might put it on," said Wilson.

"You know you have a very red face, Mr. Wilson," she told him and smiled again.

"Drink," said Wilson.

"I don't think so," she said. "Francis drinks a great deal, but his face is never red."

"It's red today," Macomber tried a joke.

"No," said Margaret. "It's mine that's red today. But Mr. Wilson's is always red."

"Must be racial," said Wilson. "I say, you wouldn't like to drop my beauty as a topic, would you?"

"I've just started on it."

"Let's chuck it," said Wilson.

"Conversation is going to be so difficult," Margaret said.

"Don't be silly, Margot," her husband said.

"No difficulty," Wilson said. "Got a damn fine lion."

Margot looked at them both and they both saw that she was going to cry. Wilson had seen it coming for a long time and he dreaded it. Macomber was past dreading it.

"I wish it hadn't happened. Oh, I wish it hadn't happened," she said and started for her tent. She made no noise of crying but they could see that her shoulders were shaking under the rose-colored, sun-proofed shirt she wore.

"Women upset," said Wilson to the tall man. "Amounts to nothing. Strain on the nerves and one thing'n another."

"No," said Macomber. "I suppose that I rate that for the rest of my life now."

"Nonsense. Let's have a spot of the giant killer," said Wilson. "Forget the whole thing. Nothing to it anyway."

"We might try," said Macomber. "I won't forget what you did for me though."

"Nothing," said Wilson. "All nonsense."

So they sat there in the shade where the camp was pitched under some wide-topped acacia trees with a boulder-strewn cliff behind them, and a stretch of grass that ran to the bank of a boulder-filled stream in front with forest beyond it, and drank their just-cool lime drinks and avoided one another's eyes while the boys set the table for lunch. Wilson could tell that the boys all knew about it now and when he saw Macomber's personal boy looking curiously at his master while he was putting dishes on the table he snapped at him in Swahili. The boy turned away with his face blank.

"What were you telling him?" Macomber asked.

"Nothing. Told him to look alive or I'd see he got about fifteen of the best."

"What's that? Lashes?"

"It's quite illegal," Wilson said. "You're supposed to fine them."

"Do you still have them whipped?"

"Oh, yes. They could raise a row if they chose to complain. But they don't. They prefer it to the fines."

"How strange!" said Macomber.

"Not strange, really," Wilson said. "Which would you rather do? Take a good birching or lose your pay?"

Then he felt embarrassed at asking it and before Macomber could answer he went on, "We all take a beating every day, you know, one way or another."

This was no better. "Good God," he thought. "I am a diplomat, aren't I?"

"Yes, we take a beating," said Macomber, still not looking at him. "I'm awfully sorry about that lion business. It doesn't have to go any further, does it? I mean no one will hear about it, will they?"

"You mean will I tell it at the Mathaiga Club?" Wilson looked at him now coldly. He had not expected this. So he's a bloody four-letter man as well as a bloody coward, he thought. I rather liked him too until today. But how is one to know about an American?

"No," said Wilson. "I'm a professional hunter. We never talk about our clients. You can be quite easy on that. It's supposed to be bad form to ask us not to talk though."

He had decided now that to break would be much easier. He would eat, then, by himself and could read a book with his meals. They would eat by themselves. He would see them through the safari on a very formal basis—what was it the French called it? Distinguished consideration—and it would be a damn sight easier than having to go through this emotional trash. He'd insult him and make a good clean break. Then he could read a book with his meals and he'd still be drinking their whisky. That was the phrase for it when a safari went bad. You ran into another white hunter and you asked, "How is everything going?" and he answered, "Oh, I'm still drinking their whisky," and you knew everything had gone to pot.

"I'm sorry," Macomber said and looked at him with his American face that would stay adolescent until it became middle-aged, and Wilson noted his crew-cropped hair, fine eyes only faintly shifty, good nose, thin lips and handsome jaw. "I'm sorry I didn't realize that. There are lots of things I don't know."

So what could he do, Wilson thought. He was all ready to break it off quickly and neatly and here the beggar was apologizing after he had just insulted him. He made one more attempt. "Don't worry about me talking," he said. "I have a living to make. You know in Africa no woman ever misses her lion and no white man ever bolts."

"I bolted like a rabbit," Macomber said.

Now what in hell were you going to do about a man who talked like that, Wilson wondered.

Wilson looked at Macomber with his flat, blue, machine-gunner's eyes and the other smiled back at him. He had a pleasant smile if you did not notice how his eyes showed when he was hurt.

"Maybe I can fix it up on buffalo," he said. "We're after them next, aren't we?"

"In the morning if you like," Wilson told him. Perhaps he had been wrong. This was certainly the way to take it. You most certainly could not tell a damned thing about an American. He was all for Macomber again. If you could forget the morning. But, of course, you couldn't. The morning had been about as bad as they come.

"Here comes the Memsahib," he said. She was walking over from her tent looking refreshed and cheerful and quite lovely. She had a very perfect oval face, so perfect that you expected her to be stupid. But she wasn't stupid, Wilson thought, no, not stupid.

"How is the beautiful red-faced Mr. Wilson? Are you feeling better, Francis, my pearl?"

"Oh, much," said Macomber.

"I've dropped the whole thing," she said, sitting down at the table. "What importance is there to whether Francis is any good at killing lions? That's not his trade. That's Mr. Wilson's trade. Mr. Wilson is really very impressive killing anything. You do kill anything, don't you?"

"Oh, anything," said Wilson. "Simply anything." They are, he thought, the hardest in the world; the hardest, the cruelest, the most predatory and the most attractive and their men have softened or gone to pieces nervously as they have hardened. Or is it that they pick men they can handle? They can't know that much at the age they marry, he thought. He was grateful that he had gone through his education on American women before now because this was a very attractive one.

"We're going after buff in the morning," he told her.

"I'm coming," she said.

"No, you're not."

"Oh, yes, I am. Mayn't I, Francis?"

"Why not stay in camp?"

"Not for anything," she said. "I wouldn't miss something like today for anything."

When she left, Wilson was thinking, when she went off to cry, she seemed a hell of a fine woman. She seemed to understand, to realize, to be hurt for him and for herself and to know how things really stood. She is away for twenty minutes and now she is back, simply enamelled in that American female cruelty. They are the damnedest women. Really the damnedest.

"We'll put on another show for you tomorrow," Francis Macomber said.

"You're not coming," Wilson said.

"You're very mistaken," she told him. "And I want *so* to see you perform again. You were lovely this morning. That is if blowing things' heads off is lovely."

"Here's the lunch," said Wilson. "You're very merry, aren't you?"

"Why not? I didn't come out here to be dull."

"Well, it hasn't been dull," Wilson said. He could see the boulders in the river and the high bank beyond with the trees and he remembered the morning.

"Oh, no," she said. "It's been charming. And tomorrow. You don't know how I look forward to tomorrow."

"That's eland he's offering you," Wilson said.

"They're the big cowy things that jump like hares, aren't they?"

"I suppose that describes them," Wilson said.

"It's very good meat," Macomber said.

"Did you shoot it, Francis?" she asked.

"Yes."

"They're not dangerous, are they?"

"Only if they fall on you," Wilson told her.

"I'm so glad."

"Why not let up on the bitchery just a little, Margot," Macomber said, cutting the eland steak and putting some mashed potato, gravy and carrot on the down-turned fork that tined through the piece of meat.

"I suppose I could," she said, "since you put it so prettily."

"Tonight we'll have champagne for the lion," Wilson said. "It's a bit too hot at noon."

"Oh, the lion," Margot said. "I'd forgotten the lion!"

So, Robert Wilson thought to himself, she *is* giving him a ride, isn't she? Or do you suppose that's her idea of putting up a good show? How should a woman act when she discovers her husband is a bloody coward? She's damn cruel but they're all cruel. They govern, of course, and to govern one has to be cruel sometimes. Still, I've seen enough of their damn terrorism.

"Have some more eland," he said to her politely.

That afternoon, late, Wilson and Macomber went out in the motor car with the native driver and the two gun-bearers. Mrs. Macomber stayed in the camp. It was too hot to go out, she said, and she was going with them in the early morning. As they drove off Wilson saw her standing under the big tree, looking pretty rather than beautiful in her faintly rosy khaki, her dark hair drawn back off her forehead and gathered in a knot low on her neck, her face as fresh, he thought, as though she were in England. She waved to them as the car went off through the swale of high grass and curved around through the trees into the small hills of orchard bush.

In the orchard bush they found a herd of impala, and leaving the car they stalked one old ram with long, wide-spread horns and Macomber killed it with a very creditable shot that knocked the buck down at a good two hundred yards and sent the herd off bounding wildly and leaping over one another's backs in long, leg-drawn-up leaps as unbelievable and as floating as those one makes sometimes in dreams.

"That was a good shot," Wilson said. "They're a small target."

"Is it a worth-while head?" Macomber asked.

"It's excellent," Wilson told him. "You shoot like that and you'll have no trouble."

"Do you think we'll find buffalo tomorrow?"

"There's a good chance of it. They feed out early in the morning and with luck we may catch them in the open."

"I'd like to clear away that lion business," Macomber said. "It's not very pleasant to have your wife see you do something like that."

I should think it would be even more unpleasant to do it, Wilson thought, wife or no wife, or to talk about it having done it. But he said, "I wouldn't think about that any more. Any one could be upset by his first lion. That's all over."

But that night after dinner and a whisky and soda by the fire before going to bed, as Francis Macomber lay on his cot with the mosquito bar over him and listened to the night noises it was not all over. It was neither all over nor was it beginning. It was there exactly as it happened with some parts of it indelibly emphasized and he was miserably ashamed at it. But more than shame he felt cold, hollow fear in him. The fear was still there like a cold slimy hollow in all the emptiness where once his confidence had been and it made him feel sick. It was still there with him now.

It had started the night before when he had wakened and heard the lion roaring somewhere up along the river. It was a deep sound and at the end there were sort of coughing grunts that made him seem just outside the tent, and when Francis Macomber woke in the night to hear it he was afraid. He could hear his wife breathing quietly, asleep. There was no one to tell he was afraid, nor to be afraid with him, and, lying alone, he did not know the Somali proverb that says a brave man is always frightened three times by a lion; when he first sees his track, when he first hears him roar and when he first confronts him. Then while they were eating breakfast by lantern light out in the dining tent, before the sun was up, the lion roared again and Francis thought he was just at the edge of camp.

"Sounds like an old-timer," Robert Wilson said, looking up from his kippers and coffee. "Listen to him cough."

"Is he very close?"

"A mile or so up the stream."

"Will we see him?"

"We'll have a look."

"Does his roaring carry that far? It sounds as though he were right in camp."

"Carries a hell of a long way," said Robert Wilson. "It's strange the way it carries. Hope he's a shootable cat. The boys said there was a very big one about here."

"If I get a shot, where should I hit him," Macomber asked, "to stop him?"

"In the shoulders," Wilson said. "In the neck if you can make it. Shoot for bone. Break him down."

"I hope I can place it properly," Macomber said.

"You shoot very well," Wilson told him. "Take your time. Make sure of him. The first one in is the one that counts."

"What range will it be?"

"Can't tell. Lion has something to say about that. Won't shoot unless it's close enough so you can make sure."

"At under a hundred yards?" Macomber asked.

Wilson looked at him quickly.

"Hundred's about right. Might have to take him a bit under. Shouldn't chance a shot at much over that. A hundred's a decent range. You can hit him wherever you want at that. Here comes the Memsahib."

"Good morning," she said. "Are we going after that lion?"

"As soon as you deal with your breakfast," Wilson said. "How are you feeling?"

"Marvellous," she said. "I'm very excited."

"I'll just go and see that everything is ready." Wilson went off. As he left the lion roared again.

"Noisy beggar," Wilson said. "We'll put a stop to that."

"What's the matter, Francis?" his wife asked him.

"Nothing," Macomber said.

"Yes, there is," she said. "What are you upset about?"

"Nothing," he said.

"Tell me," she looked at him. "Don't you feel well?"

"It's that damned roaring," he said. "It's been going on all night, you know."

"Why didn't you wake me," she said. "I'd love to have heard it."

"I've got to kill the damned thing," Macomber said, miserably.

"Well, that's what you're out here for, isn't it?"

"Yes. But I'm nervous. Hearing the thing roar gets on my nerves."

"Well then, as Wilson said, kill him and stop his roaring."

"Yes, darling," said Francis Macomber. "It sounds easy, doesn't it?"

"You're not afraid, are you?"

"Of course not. But I'm nervous from hearing him roar all night."

"You'll kill him marvellously," she said. "I know you will. I'm awfully anxious to see it."

"Finish your breakfast and we'll be starting."

"It's not light yet," she said. "This is a ridiculous hour."

Just then the lion roared in a deep-chested moaning, suddenly guttural, ascending vibration that seemed to shake the air and ended in a sigh and a heavy, deep-chested grunt.

"He sounds almost here," Macomber's wife said.

"My God," said Macomber. "I hate that damned noise."

"It's very impressive."

"Impressive. It's frightful."

Robert Wilson came up then carrying his short, ugly, shockingly big-bored .505 Gibbs and grinning.

"Come on," he said. "Your gun-bearer has your Springfield and the big gun. Everything's in the car. Have you solids?"

"Yes."

"I'm ready," Mrs. Macomber said.

"Must make him stop that racket," Wilson said. "You get in front. The Memsahib can sit back here with me."

They climbed into the motor car and, in the gray first daylight, moved off up the river through the trees. Macomber opened the breech of his rifle and saw he had metal-cased bullets, shut the bolt and put the rifle on safety. He saw his hand was trembling. He felt in his pocket for more cartridges and moved his fingers over the cartridges in the loops of his tunic front. He turned back to where Wilson sat in the rear seat of the doorless, box-bodied motor car beside his wife, them both grinning with excitement, and Wilson leaned forward and whispered,

"See the birds dropping. Means the old boy has left his kill."

On the far bank of the stream Macomber could see, above the trees, vultures circling and plummeting down.

"Chances are he'll come to drink along here," Wilson whispered. "Before he goes to lay up. Keep an eye out."

They were driving slowly along the high bank of the stream which here cut deeply to its boulder-filled bed, and they wound in and out through big trees as they drove. Macomber was watching the opposite bank when he felt Wilson take hold of his arm. The car stopped.

"There he is," he heard the whisper. "Ahead and to the right. Get out and take him. He's a marvellous lion."

Macomber saw the lion now. He was standing almost broadside, his great head up and turned toward them. The early morning breeze that blew toward them was just stirring his dark mane, and the lion looked huge, silhouetted on the rise of bank in the gray morning light, his shoulders heavy, his barrel of a body bulking smoothly.

"How far is he?" asked Macomber, raising his rifle.

"About seventy-five. Get out and take him."

"Why not shoot from where I am?"

"You don't shoot them from cars," he heard Wilson saying in his ear. "Get out. He's not going to stay there all day."

Macomber stepped out of the curved opening at the side of the front seat, onto the step and down onto the ground. The lion still stood looking majestically and coolly toward this object that his eyes only showed in silhouette, bulking like some super-rhino. There was no man smell carried toward him and he watched the object, moving his great head a little from side to side. Then watching the object, not afraid, but hesitating before going down the bank to drink with such a thing opposite him, he saw a man figure detach itself from it and he turned his heavy head and swung away toward the cover of the trees as he heard a cracking crash and felt the slam of a .30–06 220-grain solid bullet that bit his flank and ripped in sudden hot scalding nausea through his stomach. He trotted, heavy, big-footed, swinging wounded full-bellied, through the trees toward the tall grass and cover, and the crash came again to go past him ripping the air apart. Then it crashed again and he felt the blow as it hit his lower ribs and ripped on through, blood sudden hot and frothy in his mouth, and he galloped toward the high grass where he could crouch and not be seen and make them bring the crashing thing close enough so he could make a rush and get the man that held it.

Macomber had not thought how the lion felt as he got out of the car. He only knew his hands were shaking and as he walked away from the car it was almost impossible for him to make his legs move. They were stiff in the thighs, but he could feel the muscles fluttering. He raised the rifle, sighted on the junction of the lion's head and shoulders and pulled the trigger. Nothing happened though he pulled until he thought his finger would break. Then he knew he had the safety on and as he lowered the rifle to move the safety over he moved another frozen pace forward, and the lion seeing his silhouette now clear of the silhouette of the car, turned and started off at a trot, and, as Macomber fired, he heard a whunk that meant that the bullet was home; but the lion kept on going. Macomber shot again and every one saw the bullet throw a spout of dirt beyond the trotting lion. He shot again, remembering to lower his aim, and they all heard the bullet hit, and the lion went into a gallop and was in the tall grass before he had the bolt pushed forward.

Macomber stood there feeling sick at his stomach, his hands that held the Springfield still cocked, shaking, and his wife and Robert Wilson were standing by him. Beside him too were the two gun-bearers chattering in Wakamba.

"I hit him," Macomber said. "I hit him twice."

"You gut-shot him and you hit him somewhere forward," Wilson said without enthusiasm. The gun-bearers looked very grave. They were silent now.

"You may have killed him," Wilson went on. "We'll have to wait a while before we go in to find out."

"What do you mean?"

"Let him get sick before we follow him up."

"Oh," said Macomber.

"He's a hell of a fine lion," Wilson said cheerfully. "He's gotten into a bad place though."

"Why is it bad?"

"Can't see him until you're on him."

"Oh," said Macomber.

"Come on," said Wilson. "The Memsahib can stay here in the car. We'll go to have a look at the blood spoor."

"Stay here, Margot," Macomber said to his wife. His mouth was very dry and it was hard for him to talk.

"Why?" she asked.

"Wilson says to."

"We're going to have a look," Wilson said. "You stay here. You can see even better from here."

"All right."

Wilson spoke in Swahili to the driver. He nodded and said, "Yes, Bwana."

Then they went down the steep bank and across the stream, climbing over and around the boulders and up the other bank, pulling up by some projecting roots, and along it until they found where the lion had been trotting when Macomber first shot. There was dark blood on the short grass that the gun-bearers pointed out with grass stems, and that ran away behind the river bank trees.

"What do we do?" asked Macomber.

"Not much choice," said Wilson. "We can't bring the car over. Bank's too steep. We'll let him stiffen up a bit and then you and I'll go in and have a look for him."

"Can't we set the grass on fire?" Macomber asked.

"Too green."

"Can't we send beaters?"

Wilson looked at him appraisingly. "Of course we can," he said. "But it's just a touch murderous. You see we know the lion's wounded. You can drive an unwounded lion—he'll move on ahead of a noise—but a wounded lion's going to charge. You can't see him until you're right on him. He'll make himself perfectly flat in cover you wouldn't think would hide a hare. You can't very well send boys in there to that sort of a show. Somebody bound to get mauled."

"What about the gun-bearers?"

"Oh, they'll go with us. It's their *shauri.* You see, they signed on for it. They don't look too happy though, do they?"

"I don't want to go in there," said Macomber. It was out before he knew he'd said it.

"Neither do I," said Wilson very cheerily. "Really no choice though." Then, as an afterthought, he glanced at Macomber and saw suddenly how he was trembling and the pitiful look on his face.

"You don't have to go in, of course," he said. "That's what I'm hired for, you know. That's why I'm so expensive."

"You mean you'd go in by yourself? Why not leave him there?"

Robert Wilson, whose entire occupation had been with the lion and the problem he presented, and who had not been thinking about Macomber except to note that he was rather windy, suddenly felt as though he had opened the wrong door in a hotel and seen something shameful.

"What do you mean?"

"Why not just leave him?"

"You mean pretend to ourselves he hasn't been hit?"

"No. Just drop it."

"It isn't done."

"Why not?"

"For one thing, he's certain to be suffering. For another, some one else might run onto him."

"I see."

"But you don't have to have anything to do with it."

"I'd like to," Macomber said. "I'm just scared, you know."

"I'll go ahead when we go in," Wilson said, "with Kongoni tracking. You keep behind me and a little to one side. Chances are we'll hear him growl. If we see him we'll both shoot. Don't worry about anything. I'll keep you backed up. As a matter of fact, you know, perhaps you'd better not go. It might be much better. Why don't you go over and join the Memsahib while I just get it over with?"

"No, I want to go."

"All right," said Wilson. "But don't go in if you don't want to. This is my *shauri* now, you know."

"I want to go," said Macomber.

They sat under a tree and smoked.

"Want to go back and speak to the Memsahib while we're waiting?" Wilson asked.

"No."

"I'll just step back and tell her to be patient."

"Good," said Macomber. He sat there, sweating under his arms, his mouth dry, his stomach hollow feeling, wanting to find courage to tell Wilson to go on and finish off the lion without him. He could not know that Wilson was furious because he had not noticed the state he was in earlier and sent him back to his wife. While he sat there Wilson came up. "I have your big gun," he said. "Take it. We've given him time, I think. Come on."

Macomber took the big gun and Wilson said:

"Keep behind me and about five yards to the right and do exactly as I tell you." Then he spoke in Swahili to the two gun-bearers who looked the picture of gloom.

"Let's go," he said.

"Could I have a drink of water?" Macomber asked. Wilson spoke to the older gun-bearer, who wore a canteen on his belt, and the man unbuckled it, unscrewed the top and handed it to Macomber, who took it noticing how heavy it seemed and how hairy and shoddy the felt covering was in his hand. He raised it to drink and looked ahead at the high grass with the flat-topped trees behind it. A breeze was blowing toward them and the grass rippled gently in the wind. He looked at the gun-bearer and he could see the gun-bearer was suffering too with fear.

Thirty-five yards into the grass the big lion lay flattened out along the ground. His ears were back and his only movement was a slight twitching up and down of his long, black-tufted tail. He had turned at bay as soon as he had reached this cover and he was sick with the wound through his full belly, and weakening with the wound through his lungs that brought a thin foamy red to his mouth each time he breathed. His flanks were wet and hot and flies were on the little openings the solid bullets had made in his tawny hide, and his big yellow eyes, narrowed with hate, looked straight ahead, only blinking when the pain came as he breathed, and his claws dug in the soft baked earth. All of him, pain, sickness, hatred and all of his remaining strength, was tightening into an absolute concentration for a rush. He could hear the men talking and he waited, gathering all of himself into this preparation for a charge as soon as the men would come into the grass. As he heard their voices his tail stiffened to twitch up and down, and, as they came into the edge of the grass, he made a coughing grunt and charged.

Kongoni, the old gun-bearer, in the lead watching the blood spoor, Wilson watching the grass for any movement, his big gun ready, the second gun-bearer looking ahead and listening, Macomber close to Wilson, his rifle cocked, they had just moved into the grass when Macomber heard the blood-choked coughing grunt, and saw the swishing rush in the grass. The next thing he knew he was running; running wildly, in panic in the open, running toward the stream.

He heard the *ca-ra-wong!* of Wilson's big rifle, and again in a second crashing *carawong!* and turning saw the lion, horrible-looking now, with half his head seeming to be gone, crawling toward Wilson in the edge of the tall grass while the red-faced man worked the bolt on the short ugly rifle and aimed carefully as another blasting *carawong!* came from the muzzle, and the crawling, heavy, yellow bulk of the lion stiffened and the huge, mutilated head slid forward and Macomber, standing by himself in the clearing where he had run, holding a loaded rifle, while two black men and a white man looked back at him in contempt, knew the lion was dead. He came toward Wilson, his tallness all seeming a naked reproach, and Wilson looked at him and said:

"Want to take pictures?"

"No," he said.

That was all any one had said until they reached the motor car. Then Wilson had said:

"Hell of a fine lion. Boys will skin him out. We might as well stay here in the shade."

Macomber's wife had not looked at him nor he at her and he had sat by her in the back seat with Wilson sitting in the front seat. Once he had reached over and taken his wife's hand without looking at her and she had removed her hand from his. Looking across the stream to where the gun-bearers were skinning out the lion he could see that she had been able to see the whole thing. While they sat there his wife had reached forward and put her hand on Wilson's shoulder. He turned and she had leaned forward over the low seat and kissed him on the mouth.

"Oh, I say," said Wilson, going redder than his natural baked color.

"Mr. Robert Wilson," she said. "The beautiful red-faced Mr. Robert Wilson."

Then she sat down beside Macomber again and looked away across the stream to where the lion lay, with uplifted, white-muscled, tendon-marked naked forearms, and white bloating belly, as the black men fleshed away the skin. Finally the gun-bearers brought the skin over, wet and heavy, and climbed in behind with it, rolling it up before they got in, and the motor car started. No one had said anything more until they were back in camp.

That was the story of the lion. Macomber did not know how the lion had felt before he started his rush, nor during it when the unbelievable smash of the .505 with a muzzle velocity of two tons had hit him in the mouth, nor what kept him coming after that, when the second ripping crash had smashed his hind quarters and he had come crawling on toward the crashing, blasting thing that had destroyed him. Wilson knew something about it and only expressed it by saying, "Damned fine lion," but Macomber did not know how Wilson felt about things either. He did not know how his wife felt except that she was through with him.

His wife had been through with him before but it never lasted. He was very wealthy, and would be much wealthier, and he knew she would not leave him ever now. That was one of the few things that he really knew. He knew about that, about motor cycles—that was earliest—about motor cars, about duck-shooting, about fishing, trout, salmon and big-sea, about sex in books, many books, too many books, about all court games, about dogs, not much about horses, about hanging on to his money, about most of the other things his world dealt in, and about his wife not leaving him. His wife had been a great beauty and she was still a great beauty in Africa, but she was not a great enough beauty any more at home to be able to leave him and better herself and she knew it and he knew it. She had missed the chance to leave him and he knew it. If he had been better with women she would probably have started to worry about him getting another new, beautiful wife; but she knew too much about him to worry about him either. Also, he had always had a great tolerance which seemed the nicest thing about him if it were not the most sinister.

All in all they were known as a comparatively happily married couple, one of those whose disruption is often rumored but never occurs, and as the society columnist put it, they were adding more than a spice of *adventure* to their much envied and ever-enduring *Romance* by a *Safari* in what was known as *Darkest Africa* until the Martin Johnsons lighted it on so many silver screens where they were pursuing *Old Simba* the lion, the buffalo, *Tembo* the elephant and as well collecting specimens for the Museum of Natural History. This same columnist had reported them *on the verge* at least three times in the past and they had been. But they always made it up. They had a sound basis of union. Margot was too beautiful for Macomber to divorce her and Macomber had too much money for Margot ever to leave him.

It was now about three o'clock in the morning and Francis Macomber, who had been asleep a little while after he had stopped thinking about the lion, wakened and then slept again, woke suddenly, frightened in a dream of the bloody-headed lion standing over him, and listening while his heart pounded, he realized that his wife was not in the other cot in the tent. He lay awake with that knowledge for two hours.

At the end of that time his wife came into the tent, lifted her mosquito bar and crawled cozily into bed.

"Where have you been?" Macomber asked in the darkness.

"Hello," she said. "Are you awake?"

"Where have you been?"

"I just went out to get a breath of air."

"You did, like hell."

"What do you want me to say, darling?"

"Where have you been?"

"Out to get a breath of air."

"That's a new name for it. You *are* a bitch."

"Well, you're a coward."

"All right," he said. "What of it?"

"Nothing as far as I'm concerned. But please let's not talk, darling, because I'm very sleepy."

"You think that I'll take anything."

"I know you will, sweet."

"Well, I won't."

"Please, darling, let's not talk. I'm so very sleepy."

"There wasn't going to be any of that. You promised there wouldn't be."

"Well, there is now," she said sweetly.

"You said if we made this trip that there would be none of that. You promised."

"Yes, darling. That's the way I meant it to be. But the trip was spoiled yesterday. We don't have to talk about it, do we?"

"You don't wait long when you have an advantage, do you?"

"Please let's not talk. I'm so sleepy, darling."

"I'm going to talk."

"Don't mind me then, because I'm going to sleep." And she did.

At breakfast they were all three at the table before daylight and Francis Macomber found that, of all the many men that he had hated, he hated Robert Wilson the most.

"Sleep well?" Wilson asked in his throaty voice, filling a pipe.

"Did you?"

"Topping," the white hunter told him.

You bastard, thought Macomber, you insolent bastard.

So she woke him when she came in, Wilson thought, looking at them both with his flat, cold eyes. Well, why doesn't he keep his wife where she belongs? What does he think I am, a bloody plaster saint? Let him keep her where she belongs. It's his own fault.

"Do you think we'll find buffalo?" Margot asked, pushing away a dish of apricots.

"Chance of it," Wilson said and smiled at her. "Why don't you stay in camp?"

"Not for anything," she told him.

"Why not order her to stay in camp?" Wilson said to Macomber.

"You order her," said Macomber coldly.

"Let's not have any ordering, nor," turning to Macomber, "any silliness, Francis," Margot said quite pleasantly.

"Are you ready to start?" Macomber asked.

"Any time," Wilson told him. "Do you want the Memsahib to go?"

"Does it make any difference whether I do or not?"

The hell with it, thought Robert Wilson. The utter complete hell with it. So this is what it's going to be like. Well, this is what it's going to be like, then.

"Makes no difference," he said.

"You're sure you wouldn't like to stay in camp with her yourself and let me go out and hunt the buffalo?" Macomber asked.

"Can't do that," said Wilson. "Wouldn't talk rot if I were you."

"I'm not talking rot. I'm disgusted."

"Bad word, disgusted."

"Francis, will you please try to speak sensibly!" his wife said.

"I speak too damned sensibly," Macomber said. "Did you ever eat such filthy food?"

"Something wrong with the food?" asked Wilson quietly.

"No more than with everything else."

"I'd pull yourself together, laddybuck," Wilson said very quietly. "There's a boy waits at table that understands a little English."

"The hell with him."

Wilson stood up and puffing on his pipe strolled away, speaking a few words in Swahili to one of the gun-bearers who was standing waiting for him. Macomber and his wife sat on at the table. He was staring at his coffee cup.

"If you make a scene I'll leave you, darling," Margot said quietly.

"No, you won't."

"You can try it and see."

"You won't leave me."

"No," she said. "I won't leave you and you'll behave your self."

"Behave myself? That's a way to talk. Behave myself."

"Yes. Behave yourself."

"Why don't *you* try behaving?"

"I've tried it so long. So very long."

"I hate that red-faced swine," Macomber said. "I loathe the sight of him."

"He's really *very* nice."

"Oh, *shut up,*" Macomber almost shouted. Just then the car came up and stopped in front of the dining tent and the driver and the two gun-bearers got out. Wilson walked over and looked at the husband and wife sitting there at the table.

"Going shooting?" he asked.

"Yes," said Macomber, standing up. "Yes."

"Better bring a woolly. It will be cool in the car," Wilson said.

"I'll get my leather jacket," Margot said.

"The boy has it," Wilson told her. He climbed into the front with the driver and Francis Macomber and his wife sat, not speaking, in the back seat.

Hope the silly beggar doesn't take a notion to blow the back of my head off, Wilson thought to himself. Women *are* a nuisance on safari.

The car was grinding down to cross the river at a pebbly ford in the gray daylight and then climbed, angling up the steep bank, where Wilson had ordered a way shovelled out the day before so they could reach the parklike wooded rolling country on the far side.

It was a good morning, Wilson thought. There was a heavy dew and as the wheels went through the grass and low bushes he could smell the odor of the crushed fronds. It was an odor like verbena and he liked this early morning smell of the dew, the crushed bracken and the look of the tree trunks showing black through the early morning mist, as the car made its way through the untracked, parklike country. He had put the two in the back seat out of his mind now and was thinking about buffalo. The buffalo that he was after stayed in the daytime in a thick swamp where it was impossible to get a shot, but in the night they fed out into an open stretch of country and if he could come between them and their swamp with the car, Macomber would have a good chance at them in the open. He did not want to hunt buff with Macomber in thick cover. He did not want to hunt buff or anything else with Macomber at all, but he was a professional hunter and he had hunted with some rare ones in his time. If they got buff today there would only be rhino to come and the poor man would have gone through his dangerous game and things might pick up. He'd have nothing more to do with the woman and Macomber would get over that too. He must have gone through plenty of that before by the look of things. Poor beggar. He must have a way of getting over it. Well, it was the poor sod's own bloody fault.

He, Robert Wilson, carried a double size cot on safari to accommodate any windfalls he might receive. He had hunted for a certain clientele, the international, fast, sporting set, where the women did not feel they were getting their money's worth unless they had shared that cot with the white hunter. He despised them when he was away from them although he liked some of them well enough at the time, but he made his living by them; and their standards were his standards as long as they were hiring him.

They were his standards in all except the shooting. He had his own standards about the killing and they could live up to them or get some one else to hunt them. He knew, too, that they all respected him for this. This Macomber was an odd one though. Damned if he wasn't. Now the wife. Well, the wife. Yes, the wife. Hm, the wife. Well he'd dropped all that. He looked around at them. Macomber sat grim and furious. Margot smiled at him. She looked younger today, more innocent and fresher and not so professionally beautiful. What's in her heart God knows, Wilson thought. She hadn't talked much last night. At that it was a pleasure to see her.

The motor car climbed up a slight rise and went on through the trees and then out into a grassy prairie-like opening and kept in the shelter of the trees along the edge, the driver going slowly and Wilson looking carefully out across the prairie and all along its far side. He stopped the car and studied the opening with his field glasses. Then he motioned to the driver to go on and the car moved slowly along, the driver avoiding wart-hog holes and driving around the mud castles ants had built. Then, looking across the opening, Wilson suddenly turned and said,

"By God, there they are!"

And looking where he pointed, while the car jumped forward and Wilson spoke in rapid Swahili to the driver, Macomber saw three huge, black animals looking almost cylindrical in their long heaviness, like big black tank cars, moving at a gallop across the far edge of the open prairie. They moved at a stiff-necked, stiff bodied gallop and he could see the upswept wide black horns on their heads as they galloped heads out; the heads not moving.

"They're three old bulls," Wilson said. "We'll cut them off before they get to the swamp."

The car was going a wild forty-five miles an hour across the open and as Macomber watched, the buffalo got bigger and bigger until he could see the gray, hairless, scabby look of one huge bull and how his neck was a part of his shoulders and the shiny black of his horns as he galloped a little behind the others that were strung out in that steady plunging gait; and then, the car swaying as though it had just jumped a road, they drew up close and he could see the plunging hugeness of the bull, and the dust in his sparsely haired hide, the wide boss of horn and his outstretched, wide-nostrilled muzzle, and he was raising his rifle when Wilson shouted, "Not from the car, you fool!" and he had no fear, only hatred of Wilson, while the brakes clamped on and the car skidded, plowing sideways to an almost stop and Wilson was out on one side and he on the other, stumbling as his feet hit the still speeding-by of the earth, and then he was shooting at the bull as he moved away, hearing the bullets whunk into him, emptying his rifle at him as he moved steadily away, finally remembering to get his shots forward into the shoulder, and as he fumbled to re-load, he saw the bull was down. Down on his knees, his big head tossing, and seeing the other two still galloping he shot at the leader and hit him. He shot again and missed and he heard the *carawonging* roar as Wilson shot and saw the leading bull slide forward onto his nose.

"Get that other," Wilson said. "Now you're shooting!"

But the other bull was moving steadily at the same gallop and he missed, throwing a spout of dirt, and Wilson missed and the dust rose in a cloud and Wilson shouted, "Come on. He's too far!" and grabbed his arm and they were in the car again, Macomber and Wilson hanging on the sides and rocketing swayingly over the uneven ground, drawing up on the steady, plunging, heavy-necked, straight-moving gallop of the bull.

They were behind him and Macomber was filling his rifle, dropping shells onto the ground, jamming it, clearing the jam, then they were almost up with the bull when Wilson yelled "Stop," and the car skidded so that it almost swung over and Macomber fell forward onto his feet, slammed his bolt forward and fired as far forward as he could aim into the galloping, rounded black back, aimed and shot again, then again, then again, and the bullets, all of them hitting, had no effect on the buffalo that he could see. Then Wilson shot, the roar deafening him, and he could see the bull stagger. Macomber shot again, aiming carefully, and down he came, onto his knees.

"All right," Wilson said. "Nice work. That's the three."

Macomber felt a drunken elation.

"How many times did you shoot?" he asked.

"Just three," Wilson said. "You killed the first bull. The biggest one. I helped you finish the other two. Afraid they might have got into cover. You had them killed. I was just mopping up a little. You shot damn well."

"Let's go to the car," said Macomber. "I want a drink."

"Got to finish off that buff first," Wilson told him. The buffalo was on his knees and he jerked his head furiously and bellowed in pig-eyed, roaring rage as they came toward him.

"Watch he doesn't get up," Wilson said. Then, "Get a little broadside and take him in the neck just behind the ear."

Macomber aimed carefully at the center of the huge, jerking, rage-driven neck and shot. At the shot the head dropped forward.

"That does it," said Wilson. "Got the spine. They're a hell of a looking thing, aren't they?"

"Let's get the drink," said Macomber. In his life he had never felt so good.

In the car Macomber's wife sat very white faced. "You were marvelous, darling," she said to Macomber. "What a ride."

"Was it rough?" Wilson asked.

"It was frightful. I've never been more frightened in my life."

"Let's all have a drink," Macomber said.

"By all means," said Wilson. "Give it to the Memsahib." She drank the neat whisky from the flask and shuddered a little when she swallowed. She handed the flask to Macomber who handed it to Wilson.

"It was frightfully exciting," she said. "It's given me a dreadful headache. I didn't know you were allowed to shoot them from cars though.

"No one shot from cars," said Wilson coldly.

"I mean chase them from cars."

"Wouldn't ordinarily," Wilson said. "Seemed sporting enough to me though while we were doing it. Taking more chance driving that way across the plain full of holes and one thing and another than hunting on foot. Buffalo could have charged us each time we shot if he liked. Gave him every chance. Wouldn't mention it to any one though. It's illegal if that's what you mean."

"It seemed very unfair to me," Margot said, "chasing those big helpless things in a motor car."

"Did it?" said Wilson.

"What would happen if they heard about it in Nairobi?"

"I'd lose my licence for one thing. Other unpleasantnesses," Wilson said, taking a drink from the flask. "I'd be out of business."

"Really?"

"Yes, really."

"Well," said Macomber, and he smiled for the first time all day. "Now she has something on you."

"You have such a pretty way of putting things, Francis," Margot Macomber said. Wilson looked at them both. If a four-letter man marries a five-letter woman, he was thinking, what number of letters would their children be? What he said was, "We lost a gun-bearer. Did you notice it?"

"My God, no," Macomber said.

"Here he comes," Wilson said. "He's all right. He must have fallen off when we left the first bull."

Approaching them was the middle-aged gun-bearer, limping along in his knitted cap, khaki tunic, shorts and rubber sandals, gloomy-faced and disgusted looking. As he came up he called out to Wilson in Swahili and they all saw the change in the white hunter's face.

"What does he say?" asked Margot.

"He says the first bull got up and went into the bush," Wilson said with no expression in his voice.

"Oh," said Macomber blankly.

"Then it's going to be just like the lion," said Margot, full of anticipation.

"It's not going to be a damned bit like the lion," Wilson told her. "Did you want another drink, Macomber?"

"Thanks, yes," Macomber said. He expected the feeling he had had about the lion to come back but it did not. For the first time in his life he really felt wholly without fear. Instead of fear he had a feeling of definite elation.

"We'll go and have a look at the second bull," Wilson said. "I'll tell the driver to put the car in the shade."

"What are you going to do?" asked Margaret Macomber.

"Take a look at the buff," Wilson said.

"I'll come."

"Come along."

The three of them walked over to where the second buffalo bulked blackly in the open, head forward on the grass, the massive horns swung wide.

"He's a very good head," Wilson said. "That's close to a fifty-inch spread."

Macomber was looking at him with delight.

"He's hateful looking," said Margot. "Can't we go into the shade?"

"Of course," Wilson said. "Look," he said to Macomber, and pointed. "See that patch of bush?"

"Yes."

"That's where the first bull went in. The gun-bearer said when he fell off the bull was down. He was watching us helling along and the other two buff galloping. When he looked up there was the bull up and looking at him. Gun-bearer ran like hell and the bull went off slowly into that bush."

"Can we go in after him now?" asked Macomber eagerly.

Wilson looked at him appraisingly. Damned if this isn't a strange one, he thought. Yesterday he's scared sick and today he's a ruddy fire eater.

"No, we'll give him a while."

"Let's please go into the shade," Margot said. Her face was white and she looked ill.

They made their way to the car where it stood under a single, wide-spreading tree and all climbed in.

"Chances are he's dead in there," Wilson remarked. "After a little we'll have a look."

Macomber felt a wild unreasonable happiness that he had never known before.

"By God, that was a chase," he said. "I've never felt any such feeling. Wasn't it marvellous, Margot?"

"I hated it."

"Why?"

"I hated it," she said bitterly. "I loathed it."

"You know I don't think I'd ever be afraid of anything again," Macomber said to Wilson. "Something happened in me after we first saw the buff and started after him. Like a dam bursting. It was pure excitement."

"Cleans out your liver," said Wilson. "Damn funny things happen to people."

Macomber's face was shining. "You know something did happen to me," he said. "I feel absolutely different."

His wife said nothing and eyed him strangely. She was sitting far back in the seat and Macomber was sitting forward talking to Wilson who turned sideways talking over the back of the front seat.

"You know, I'd like to try another lion," Macomber said. "I'm really not afraid of them now. After all, what can they do to you?"

"That's it," said Wilson. "Worst one can do is kill you. How does it go? Shakespeare. Damned good. See if I can remember. Oh, damned good. Used to quote it to myself at one time. Let's see. 'By my troth, I care not; a man can die but once; we owe God a death and let it go which way it will, he that dies this year is quit for the next.' Damned fine, eh?"

He was very embarrassed, having brought out this thing he had lived by, but he had seen men come of age before and it always moved him. It was not a matter of their twenty-first birthday.

It had taken a strange chance of hunting, a sudden precipitation into action without opportunity for worrying beforehand, to bring this about with Macomber, but regardless of how it had happened it had most certainly happened. Look at the beggar now, Wilson thought. It's that some of them stay little boys so long, Wilson thought. Sometimes all their lives. Their figures stay boyish when they're fifty. The great American boy-men. Damned strange people. But he liked this Macomber now. Damned strange fellow. Probably meant the end of cuckoldry too. Well, that would be a damned good thing. Damned good thing. Beggar had probably been afraid all his life. Don't know what started it. But over now. Hadn't had time to be afraid with the buff. That and being angry too. Motor car too. Motor cars made it familiar. Be a damn fire eater now. He'd seen it in the war work the same way. More of a change than any loss of virginity. Fear gone like an operation. Something else grew in its place. Main thing a man had. Made him into a man. Women knew it too. No bloody fear.

From the far corner of the seat Margaret Macomber looked at the two of them. There was no change in Wilson. She saw Wilson as she had seen him the day before when she had first realized what his great talent was. But she saw the change in Francis Macomber now.

"Do you have that feeling of happiness about what's going to happen?" Macomber asked, still exploring his new wealth.

"You're not supposed to mention it," Wilson said, looking in the other's face. "Much more fashionable to say you're scared. Mind you, you'll be scared too, plenty of times."

"But you *have* a feeling of happiness about action to come?"

"Yes," said Wilson. "There's that. Doesn't do to talk too much about all this. Talk the whole thing away. No pleasure in anything if you mouth it up too much."

"You're both talking rot," said Margot. "Just because you've chased some helpless animals in a motor car you talk like heroes."

"Sorry," said Wilson. "I have been gassing too much." She's worried about it already, he thought.

"If you don't know what we're talking about why not keep out of it?" Macomber asked his wife.

"You've gotten awfully brave, awfully suddenly," his wife said contemptuously, but her contempt was not secure. She was very afraid of something.

Macomber laughed, a very natural hearty laugh. "You know I *have,*" he said. "I really have."

"Isn't it sort of late?" Margot said bitterly. Because she had done the best she could for many years back and the way they were together now was no one person's fault.

"Not for me," said Macomber.

Margot said nothing but sat back in the corner of the seat.

"Do you think we've given him time enough?" Macomber asked Wilson cheerfully.

"We might have a look," Wilson said. "Have you any solids left?"

"The gun-bearer has some."

Wilson called in Swahili and the older gun-bearer, who was skinning out one of the heads, straightened up, pulled a box of solids out of his pocket and brought them over to Macomber, who filled his magazine and put the remaining shells in his pocket.

"You might as well shoot the Springfield," Wilson said. "You're used to it. We'll leave the Mannlicher in the car with the Memsahib. Your gun-bearer can carry your heavy gun. I've this damned cannon. Now let me tell you about them." He had saved this until the last because he did not want to worry Macomber. "When a buff comes he comes with his head high and thrust straight out. The boss of the horns covers any sort of a brain shot. The only shot is straight into the nose. The only other shot is into his chest or, if you're to one side, into the neck or the shoulders. After they've been hit once they take a hell of a lot of killing. Don't try anything fancy. Take the easiest shot there is. They've finished skinning out that head now. Should we get started?"

He called to the gun-bearers, who came up wiping their hands, and the older one got into the back.

"I'll only take Kongoni," Wilson said. "The other can watch to keep the birds away."

As the car moved slowly across the open space toward the island of brushy trees that ran in a tongue of foliage along a dry water course that cut the open swale, Macomber felt his heart pounding and his mouth was dry again, but it was excitement, not fear.

"Here's where he went in," Wilson said. Then to the gun-bearer in Swahili, "Take the blood spoor."

The car was parallel to the patch of bush. Macomber, Wilson and the gun-bearer got down. Macomber, looking back, saw his wife, with the rifle by her side, looking at him. He waved to her and she did not wave back.

The brush was very thick ahead and the ground was dry. The middle-aged gun-bearer was sweating heavily and Wilson had his hat down over his eyes and his red neck showed just ahead of Macomber. Suddenly the gun-bearer said something in Swahili to Wilson and ran forward.

"He's dead in there," Wilson said. "Good work," and he turned to grip Macomber's hand and as they shook hands, grinning at each other, the gun-bearer shouted wildly and they saw him coming out of the bush sideways, fast as a crab, and the bull coming, nose out, mouth tight closed, blood dripping, massive head straight out, coming in a charge, his little pig eyes bloodshot as he looked at them. Wilson, who was ahead was kneeling shooting, and Macomber, as he fired, unhearing his shot in the roaring of Wilson's gun, saw fragments like slate burst from the huge boss of the horns, and the head jerked, he shot again at the wide nostrils and saw the horns jolt again and fragments fly, and he did not see Wilson now and, aiming carefully, shot again with the buffalo's huge bulk almost on him and his rifle almost level with the on-coming head, nose out, and he could see the little wicked eyes and the head started to lower and he felt a sudden white-hot, blinding flash explode inside his head and that was all he ever felt.

Wilson had ducked to one side to get in a shoulder shot. Macomber had stood solid and shot for the nose, shooting a touch high each time and hitting the heavy horns, splintering and chipping them like hitting a slate roof, and Mrs. Macomber, in the car, had shot at the buffalo with the 6.5 Mannlicher as it seemed about to gore Macomber and had hit her husband about two inches up and a little to one side of the base of his skull.

Francis Macomber lay now, face down, not two yards from where the buffalo lay on his side and his wife knelt over him with Wilson beside her.

"I wouldn't turn him over," Wilson said.

The woman was crying hysterically.

"I'd get back in the car," Wilson said. "Where's the rifle?"

She shook her head, her face contorted. The gun-bearer picked up the rifle.

"Leave it as it is," said Wilson. Then, "Go get Abdulla so that he may witness the manner of the accident."

He knelt down, took a handkerchief from his pocket, and spread it over Francis Macomber's crew-cropped head where it lay. The blood sank into the dry, loose earth.

Wilson stood up and saw the buffalo on his side, his legs out, his thinly-haired belly crawling with ticks. "Hell of a good bull," his brain registered automatically. "A good fifty inches, or better. Better." He called to the driver and told him to spread a blanket over the body and stay by it. Then he walked over to the motor car where the woman sat crying in the corner.

"That was a pretty thing to do," he said in a toneless voice. "He *would* have left you too."

"Stop it," she said.

"Of course it's an accident," he said. "I know that."

"Stop it," she said.

"Don't worry," he said. "There will be a certain amount of unpleasantness but I will have some photographs taken that will be very useful at the inquest. There's the testimony of the gun-bearers and the driver too. You're perfectly all right."

"Stop it," she said.

"There's a hell of a lot to be done," he said. "And I'll have to send a truck off to the lake to wireless for a plane to take the three of us into Nairobi. Why didn't you poison him? That's what they do in England."

"Stop it. Stop it. Stop it," the woman cried.

Wilson looked at her with his flat blue eyes.

"I'm through now," he said. "I was a little angry. I'd begun to like your husband."

"Oh, please stop it," she said. "Please, please stop it."

"That's better," Wilson said. "Please is much better. Now I'll stop."

MILAN KUNDERA

THE GOLDEN APPLE OF ETERNAL DESIRE

Milan Kundera (b. 1929) was born in Brno, Czechoslovakia and studied film making at the Academy of Music and Dramatic Arts in the capital, Prague, where later he taught. During the "Prague Spring" of 1968, he took a major part in the cultural and political liberalization, but when the Soviets invaded Czechoslovakia, his books were banned, and he lost his job. In 1975, he obtained permission to leave his country and has become a French citizen teaching at the University of Rennes.

In addition to his novels, which include the unforgettable Book of Laughter and Forgetting *and* The Unbearable Lightness of Being, *he has written poetry, plays, short stories and nonfiction. His work is known for its wild, often dreamlike, events, his understanding of human and political psychology, and an irresistible sense of humor and rebellion.*

> . . . they do not know that they seek only the chase and not the quarry.
>
> *Blaise Pascal*

MARTIN

Martin is able to do something I'm incapable of—to stop any woman on any street. I must say that during the time I've known Martin I've greatly profited by this skill of his, for I like women not a whit less than he, but I wasn't granted his reckless audacity. On the other hand, through an error of Martin the so-called *arresting* of a woman itself sometimes became the goal of his virtuosity and he would very often stop at that. For this reason he used to say, not without a certain bitterness, that he was like a forward, who unselfishly passes certain balls to his teammate, who then shoots cheap goals and reaps cheap glory.

Last Monday afternoon after work I was waiting for him in a cafe on Vaclav Square, looking through a thick German book on ancient Etruscan culture. It had taken several months for the university library to negotiate its loan from Germany, and now that it had finally come just that day, I carried it off as if it were a relic, and I was actually quite pleased that Martin had kept me waiting for him, and that I could leaf through the book I'd long wanted at a cafe table.

Whenever I think about ancient cultures nostalgia seizes me. Perhaps this is nothing but envy of the sweet slowness of the history of that time: the era of ancient Egyptian culture lasted for several thousand years; the era of Greek antiquity for almost a thousand. In this respect, a single human life imitates the history of mankind; at first it is plunged into immobile slowness and only then gradually does it accelerate more and more. Martin and I unfortunately already found ourselves in that phase, when the days, the months, and the years pass in a mad rush. Just two months ago Martin had turned forty.

But: "Everything depends," Martin would say, "on one's ability to resist the laws." By this he doesn't mean so much the laws of the land as rather more general laws—such as perhaps the laws of biology or time. Martin resists his forty years: his élan, his restlessness, and his incorrigible childishness are his main supports in the resistance.

THE ADVENTURE BEGINS

It was he who disturbed my thoughtful mood. He appeared suddenly in the glass door of the cafe and headed for me, making expressive gestures and grimaces in the direction of a table at which a woman was sitting over a cup of coffee. Without taking his eyes off her, he sat down beside me and said, "What do you say about that?"

I felt humiliated; I'd actually been so engrossed in my thick volume that only now did I notice the girl. I had to admit that she was pretty. And at that moment the girl straightened up and called the man with the black bowtie, saying that she wished to pay.

"Pay too!" ordered Martin.

We thought that we would have to run after the girl, but luckily she was detained at the cloakroom. She had left a shopping bag there and the cloakroom attendant had to hunt for a while before placing it on the counter in front of the girl. As the girl gave the cloakroom attendant a couple of ten-haller pieces, Martin snatched the German book out of my hands.

"It will be better to put it in here," he said with daredevil nonchalance, and slipped the book carefully into the girl's bag. The girl looked surprised, but didn't know what she was supposed to say.

"It's uncomfortable to carry in one's hand," continued Martin, and when the girl went to pick up the bag herself, he told me off for not knowing how to behave.

The young woman was a nurse in a country hospital. She was in Prague, she said, only for a look around and was hurrying on to the Florents bus terminal. The short distance to the streetcar stop was enough for us to say everything essential and to agree that on Saturday we would come to B. to visit this lovely young woman, who, as Martin meaningfully pointed out, would certainly have some pretty colleague.

The streetcar arrived, I handed the young woman her bag, and she began to take the book out of it, but Martin prevented her with a grand gesture, saying we would come for it on Saturday, and that she should read through it carefully in the meantime. The young woman smiled in a bewildered fashion, the streetcar carried her away, and we waved.

What sense was there in this. The book, which I'd been looking forward to for so long, suddenly found itself in a faraway place. When you came to think of it, it was quite annoying. But nonetheless a certain lunacy happily uplifted me on the wings it promptly provided. Martin immediately began thinking about how to make an excuse for Saturday afternoon and night to his young wife (for this is how things stand: at home he has a young wife; and what is worse, he loves her; and what is still worse, he is afraid of her; and what is still far worse, he is anxious about her).

A SUCCESSFUL REGISTRATION

For our excursion I borrowed a neat little Fiat for a small sum and on Saturday at two o'clock I drove up in front of Martin's apartment; Martin was waiting for me and we set off. It was July and oppressively hot.

We wanted to get to B. as soon as possible, but when we saw, in a village through which we were driving, two young men only in swimming trunks and with eloquently wet hair, I stopped the car. The lake was actually not far away, a few paces, a mere stone's throw. I'm no longer able to sleep as I once was, the night before I'd tossed about on account of God knows what worries until three o'clock. I needed to be refreshed. Martin was also for swimming.

We changed into our swimming trunks and leaped into the water. I dove into the water and swam quickly to the other side. Martin, however, barely took a dip, washed himself off, and came out again. When I'd had a good swim and returned to shore, I caught sight of him in a state of intent absorption. On the shore a crowd of kids was yelling; somewhere further off the local young people were playing ball, but Martin was staring at the sturdy little figure of a young girl, who was perhaps fifty feet away with her back toward us. Totally motionless, she was observing the water.

"Look," said Martin.

"I am looking."

"And what do you say?"

"What should I say?"

"You don't know what you should say about that?"

"We'll have to wait until she turns round," I suggested.

"Not at all. We don't have to wait until she turns round. What's showing from this side is quite enough for me."

"At least let's get her registered," said Martin, and turned to a little boy a short distance away who was putting on his swimming trunks: "Say, kid, d'you know the name of that girl over there?" and he pointed to the girl, who, apparently in some curious state of apathy, went on standing in the same position.

"That one there?"

"Yeah, that one there."

"That one is not from here," said the little boy.

Martin turned to a little girl of about twelve, who was sunbathing close by:

"Say, kid, d'you know who that girl over there is, the one standing on the edge?"

The little girl obediently sat up. "That one there?"

"Yeah, that one."

"That's Manka . . ."

"Manka? Manka what?"

"Manka Panku . . . from Traplitse. . . ."

And the girl still stood with her back to us looking at the water. Now she bent down for her swimming cap and when she straightened up again, putting it on her head as she did so, Martin was already at my side saying, "That's a certain Manka Panku from Traplitse. Now we can drive on."

He was completely calmed down and satisfied, and obviously no longer thinking of anything but the rest of the journey.

A LITTLE THEORY

That's what Martin calls *registration.* From his vast experience, he has come to the conclusion that it is not so difficult to seduce a girl—if in this area we have high quantitative pretensions—as it is always to know enough girls whom we have not yet seduced.

Therefore, he asserts that it is necessary always, no matter where, and at every opportunity, to compile a wide registration, i.e., to record in a notebook or in our memories (Martin usually relies upon his memory), the names of women who have attracted us and whom we could contact sometime.

Contact is a higher level of activity and means that we will get in touch with a particular woman, make her acquaintance, and gain access to her.

He who likes to look back boastfully will stress the names of the women he's made love to, but he who looks forward, toward the future, must above all see to it that he has plenty of *registered* and *contacted* women.

Above contact there exists only one last level of activity, and I am happy to point out, in deference to Martin, that those who do not go after anything but this last level are wretched, primitive men, who remind me of village footballers, pressing forward thoughtlessly toward the rival goal and forgetting that a rash desire to shoot will not necessarily lead to this goal (or many further goals), but that a competent and fair game on the field will.

"Do you think that you'll go look her up in Traplitse sometime?" I asked Martin, when we were driving again.

"One can never know . . ." said Martin.

Then I said, "In any case the day is beginning propitiously for us."

GAME AND NECESSITY

We arrived at the hospital in B. in excellent spirits. It was about three-thirty. We called our nurse on the phone in the lobby. Before long she came down in her cap and white uniform; I noticed that she was blushing and I took this to be a good sign.

Martin began to talk right away and the girl informed us that she finished work at seven and that we should wait for her at that time in front of the hospital.

"Have you already arranged it with your girl friend?" asked Martin and the girl nodded:

"Yes, we'll both come."

"Fine," said Martin, "but we can't confront my colleague here with a fait accompli."

"O.K.," said the girl, "we can drop in on her; Bozhena is in the internal medicine ward."

As we walked slowly across the hospital courtyard I shyly said: "I wonder if you still have that thick book?"

The nurse nodded, saying that she did and in fact it was right here at the hospital. A weight fell from my heart and I insisted that we had to get it first.

Of course it seemed improper to Martin that I should openly give preference to a book over a woman about to be presented to me, but I just couldn't help it.

I confess that I had suffered greatly during those few days, having the book on Etruscan culture out of my sight. And it was only through great self-restraint that I had stoically put up with this, not wishing under any circumstances to spoil the Game, which has such value for me. Over the years I've learned to appreciate the Game and to subordinate to it all my personal interests and desires.

While I was having a touching reunion with my book, Martin continued his conversation with the pretty nurse, and got as far as getting her to promise that she would borrow a cabin by the nearby Hotersky Lake from a colleague for the evening. We were all perfectly happy. Finally we went across the hospital courtyard to a small green building, where the internal medicine ward was.

A nurse and a doctor were just walking toward us. The doctor was a funny-looking bean pole with protruding ears, which fascinated me all the more because at this moment our nurse elbowed me. I let out a short laugh. When they had passed us Martin turned to me: "So you're in luck, fella. You don't deserve such a gorgeous young woman."

I was ashamed to say that I had only looked at the bean pole, so I simulated approbation. After all, there wasn't any hypocrisy on my part. That is to say, I trust in Martin's taste more than in my own, because I believe that his taste is supported by a much greater *interest* than mine. I like objectivity and order in everything, even in love affairs—which only through error are held to be the exclusive realm of caprice. Consequently I have more respect for the opinion of a connoisseur than for that of a dilettante.

Someone might consider it hypocritical for me to call myself a dilettante—I a divorced man who is right now relating one of his (obviously in no way exceptional) affairs. But still I am a dilettante. It could be said that I am *playing* at something which Martin *lives*. Sometimes I have the feeling that the whole of my polygamous life is a consequence of nothing but my imitation of other men; although I am not denying that I take a liking to this imitation. But I cannot rid myself of the feeling that in this liking there remains, all the same, something entirely free, playful, and revocable. It is the same thing that perhaps characterizes visits to art galleries or foreign countries and is in no way reducible to the unconditional imperative which I have suspected at the back of Martin's erotic life. It is precisely the presence of this unconditional imperative that has raised Martin in my eyes. His judgment about a woman seems to me to be that of Nature herself, Necessity herself speaking through his lips.

HOME SWEET HOME

When we found ourselves outside the hospital Martin pointed out that everything was going tremendously well for us, and then added: "Of course we'll have to hurry this evening. I want to be home by nine."

I was amazed: "By nine? That means we'll have to leave here at eight. But then we came here for no reason! I counted on having the whole night!"

"Why should you want to waste time!"

"But what sense is there in driving here for one hour? What can you do between seven and eight?"

"Everything. As you noticed I got hold of the cabin, so that everything will go swimmingly. It will depend only on you, you'll have to show that you're sufficiently determined."

"But why, I ask, must you be home at nine?"

"I promised Jirzhinka. She's used to playing a game of rummy before going to bed on Saturdays."

"Oh God . . ." I sighed.

"Yesterday again Jirzhinka had a bad time at the office, so I should give her this little bit of joy on Saturday, shouldn't I? You know, she's the best woman I've ever had. After all," he added, "you should be pleased anyway that you'll still have the whole night before you in Prague."

I understood that it was useless to object. Martin's misgivings about his wife's peace of mind could never be appeased, and his faith in the endless erotic possibilities of every hour or minute could never be shaken by anything.

"Come," said Martin, "there are still three hours till seven! We won't be idle!"

A DELUSION

We started on our way along the broad path of the local park, which served the inhabitants as a promenade. We inspected several pairs of girls who walked by us or were sitting on the benches, but we didn't like the look of them too well.

Martin, it must be admitted, accosted two of them, entered into conversation with them, and finally arranged a meeting with them, but I knew that he didn't mean it seriously. This was a so-called *practice contact,* which Martin performed from time to time in order to stay in practice.

Dissatisfied, we went out of the park into the streets, which yawned with small-town vacuity and boredom.

"Let's get something to drink, I'm thirsty," I said to Martin.

We found an establishment above which was the sign CAFE. We entered, but inside there was only self-service. It was a tiled room that gave off an air of coldness and hostility. We went over to the counter and bought ourselves watered-down lemonades from a sullen woman, and then carried them over to a table, which being moist with gravy, invited us to depart hastily.

"Don't worry about it," said Martin. "In our world ugliness has its positive function. No one feels like staying anywhere, people hurry on and thus arises the desirable pace of life. But we won't let ourselves be provoked by this. We can now talk about all sorts of things in the safety of this ugly place." He drank some lemonade and asked: "Have you contacted that medical student yet?"

"Naturally," I replied.

"And what's she like then? Describe to me exactly how she looks!"

I described the medical student to him. This was not very difficult for me to do, even though no medical student existed. Yes. Perhaps this puts me in a bad light, but it's like this: *I invented her.*

I give my word that I didn't do it maliciously, neither to show off in front of Martin nor because I wanted to lead him by the nose. I invented the medical student simply because I couldn't resist Martin's insistence.

Martin's claims about my activities were boundless. Martin was convinced that I met new women every day. He saw me as other than I am, and if I had truthfully told him that not only had I not possessed any new women for a week, but hadn't even come close, he would have taken me for a hypocrite.

For this reason, about a week earlier, I had been forced to dream up my registration of some medical student. Martin was satisfied and he urged me to contact her. And today he was checking up on my progress.

"And about what level is she on? Is she on the level . . ." He closed his eyes and in the darkness searched for a standard of measure: then he remembered a mutual friend: ". . . is she on Marketa's level?"

"She's far better," I said.

"Don't say . . . ," marveled Martin.

"She's on your Jirzhinka's level."

For Martin his own wife was the highest standard of measure. Martin was greatly pleased by my news and fell into a dreamlike state.

A SUCCESSFUL CONTACT

Then some girl in corduroy pants and a short jacket walked into the room. She went to the counter, waited for a soda, and took it away to drink. She approached a table adjoining ours, put the glass to her lips, and drank without sitting down.

Martin turned to her: "Miss," he said, "we're strangers here and we'd like to ask you a question."

The girl smiled. She was rather pretty.

"We are terribly hot and we don't know what we should do."

"Go and take a swim."

"That's just it. We don't know where to go swimming around here."

"There isn't any swimming here."

"How is that possible?"

"There's one swimming pool, but it's been empty for a month now."

"And what about the river?"

"It's being dredged."

"So where do you go swimming?"

"Only at Hotersky Lake, but it's at least five miles away."

"That's a small matter, we have a car, it would be very nice if you'd accompany us."

"As our guide," I said.

"Rather our guiding light," Martin corrected me.

"Then why not our starlight," said I.

"Our North Star," said Martin.

"And in that case may I say that our star is brighter than Venus," I replied.

"You're simply our constellation and you should go with us," said Martin.

The girl was confused by our foolish banter and finally said that she would go, but that she had to take care of something first and then she'd pick up her bathing suit; she said that we should be waiting for her in exactly an hour at this same spot.

We were glad. We watched her as she walked away, cutely swinging her backside and tossing her black curls.

"You see," said Martin, "life is short. We must take advantage of every minute."

IN PRAISE OF FRIENDSHIP

We went once again into the park. Once again we examined several pairs of girls on the benches; it happened that many a young woman was good-looking, but it never happened that her companion was also good-looking.

"In this there is some special law," I said to Martin. "An ugly woman hopes to gain something from the luster of her pretty friend; a pretty woman, for her part, hopes that she will stand out more lustrously against the background of the ugly woman; and for us it follows from this that our friendship is subjected to continuous trials. And it is precisely this that I value, that we will never leave the choice to the random development of events, nor even to some mutual struggle; choice for us is always a matter of courtesy. We'd offer each other the prettier girl like two old-fashioned gentlemen who can never enter a room because neither wants to be the one who goes first."

"Yes," said Martin with emotion. "You're a great buddy. Come, let's go sit down for a while, my legs are aching."

And thus we sat comfortably with our faces turned up toward the face of the sun, and we let the world around us rush on unnoticed.

THE GIRL IN WHITE

All of a sudden Martin got up (moved evidently by some mysterious sense) and stared along a secluded path of the park. A girl in a white dress was coming our way. Already from afar, before it was possible to ascertain with complete confidence the proportions of her body or the features of her face, we saw that she possessed unmistakable, special, and very perceptible charm, that there was a certain purity or tenderness in her appearance.

When the girl was fairly close to us, we realized that she was quite young, something between a child and a young woman, and this at once threw us into a state of complete agitation. Martin shot up off the bench: "Miss, I am the director Jasny, the film director; you must help us."

He gave her his hand and the young girl with an utterly astonished expression shook it.

Martin nodded in my direction and said: "This is my cameraman."

"Kalish," I offered my hand.

The girl nodded.

"We are in an awkward situation here. I am looking for outdoor locations for my film. Our assistant, who knows this area well, was supposed to meet us here, but he hasn't arrived, so that right now we are wondering how to get about in this town and in the surrounding countryside. My friend Kalish here," joked Martin, "is always studying his fat German book, but unfortunately it is not to be found in there."

The allusion to the book, which I had been deprived of for the whole week, somehow irritated me all of a sudden: "It's a pity that you don't take a greater interest in this book," I attacked my director. "If you prepared thoroughly and didn't leave the studying to your cameramen maybe your films wouldn't be so superficial and there wouldn't be so much nonsense in them . . . forgive me." I turned then to the girl with an apology. "Anyhow, we won't bother you with our quarrels about our work; our film is to be a historical film and will touch upon Etruscan culture in Bohemia. . . ."

"Yes," the girl nodded.

"It's a rather interesting book—look." I handed the girl the book and she took it in her hands with a certain religious awe, and when she saw that I wanted her to, turned the pages lightly.

"The Phachek castle must surely not be far from here," I continued. "It was the center of the Bohemian Etruscans . . . but how can we get there?"

"It's only a little way," said the girl and beamed all over, because her secure knowledge of the road to Phachek gave her a little bit of firm ground in the somewhat obscure conversation that we were carrying on with her.

"Yes? Do you know the area around there?" asked Martin, feigning great relief.

"Sure I know it!" said the girl. "It's an hour away!"

"On foot?" asked Martin.

"Yes, on foot," said the girl.

"But luckily we have a car here," I said.

"Wouldn't you like to be our guide?" said Martin, but I didn't continue the customary ritual of witticisms, because I have a more precise sense of psychological judgment than Martin, and I felt that frivolous joking would be more inclined to harm us in this case and that our best weapon was absolute propriety.

"We do not want, miss, to disturb you in any way," I said, "but if you would be so kind as to devote a short time to us and show us some of the places we're looking for, you would help us a great deal—and we would both be very grateful."

"But yes," the girl nodded again, "I am happy . . . but I . . ." Only now did we notice that she had a shopping bag in her hand and in it two heads of lettuce. "I must take Mom the lettuce, but it's only a little way away and I would come right back . . ."

"Of course you must take the lettuce to Mom on time and intact," I said. "We will be happy to wait here."

"Yes. It won't take more than ten minutes," said the girl and once again she nodded, and then she walked off quickly and anxiously.

"God!" said Martin and sat down.

"Isn't it great, eh?"

"I should say so. For this I'd be willing to sacrifice our two female barber surgeons."

DECEIVED BY EXCESSIVE FAITH

But ten minutes passed, a quarter of an hour, and the girl didn't come.

"Don't be afraid," Martin consoled me. "If anything is certain, then it's this, that she'll come. Our performance was completely plausible and the girl was in raptures."

I too was of this opinion, and so we went on waiting, with each moment becoming more and more eager for this childish young girl. In the meanwhile, also, the time appointed for our meeting with the girl in corduroy pants went by, but we were so set on our little girl in white that it didn't even occur to us to leave.

And time was passing.

"Listen, Martin, I think that she won't come now," I said at last.

"How do you explain it? After all, that girl believed in us as in God Himself."

"Yes," I said, "and in that lies our misfortune. That is to say she believed us only too well!"

"What? Perhaps you'd have wanted her not to believe us?"

"It would perhaps have been better like that. Too much faith is the worst ally." A thought took my fancy; I got really involved in it: "When you believe in something literally, through your faith you'll turn it into something absurd. One who is a genuine adherent, if you like, of some political outlook, never takes its *sophistries* seriously, but only its practical aims, which are concealed beneath these sophistries. Political rhetoric and sophistries do not exist, after all, in order that they be believed; rather, they have to serve as a *common and agreed upon alibi.* Foolish people, who take them in earnest, sooner or later discover inconsistencies in them, begin to protest, and finish finally and infamously as heretics and apostates. No, too much faith never brings anything good—and not only to political or religious systems but even to our own system, the one we used to convince the girl."

"Somehow I'm not quite following you any more."

"It's quite simple: for the girl we were actually two serious and respectable gentlemen, and she, like a well-behaved child who offers her seat to an older person on a streetcar, wanted to please us."

"So why didn't she please us?"

"Because she believed us so completely. She gave Mom the lettuce and at once told her enthusiastically all about us: about the historical film, about the Etruscans in Bohemia, and Mom . . ."

"Yes, the rest is perfectly clear to me . . ." Martin interrupted me and got up from the bench.

THE BETRAYAL

The sun was already slowly going down over the roofs of the town. It was cooling off a bit and we felt sad. We went to the cafe just in case the girl in the corduroy pants was by some mistake still waiting for us. Of course she wasn't there. It was six-thirty. We walked down to the car, and feeling all of a sudden like two people who had been banished from a foreign city and its pleasures, we said to ourselves that nothing remained for us but to retire to the extraterritorial domain of our own car.

"Come on!" remonstrated Martin in the car. "Anyhow, don't look so gloomy! We don't have any reason for that! The most important thing is still before us!"

I wanted to object that we had no more than an hour for this most important thing, because of Jirzhinka and her rummy—but I chose to keep silent.

"Anyway," continued Martin, "it was a fruitful day; the registration of that girl from Traplitse, contact with the girl in the corduroy pants; after all, we have it all set up whenever we feel like it. We don't have to do anything but drive here again!"

I didn't object at all. Yes. The registration and the contact had been excellently brought off. This was quite in order. But at this moment it occurred to me that for the last year, apart from countless registrations and contacts, Martin had not come by anything more worthwhile.

I looked at him. As always his eyes shone with a lustful glow. I felt at that moment that I liked Martin and that I also liked the banner under which he had been marching all his life: the banner of the eternal pursuit of women.

Time was passing and Martin said, "It's seven o'clock."

We drove to within about thirty feet of the hospital gates, so that in the rear-view mirror I could safely observe who was coming out.

I was still thinking about that banner. And also about the fact that in this pursuit of women from year to year it had become less a matter of women and much more a matter of the pursuit itself. Assuming that the pursuit is known to be *vain* in advance, it is possible to pursue any number of women and thus to make the pursuit *an absolute pursuit.* Yes, Martin had attained the state of being in absolute pursuit.

We waited five minutes. The girls didn't come.

It didn't put me out in the least. It was a matter of complete indifference to me whether they came or not. Even if they came, could we in a mere hour drive with them to the isolated cabin, become intimate with them, make love to them, and at eight o'clock say goodbye pleasantly and take off? No, at that moment when Martin limited our available time to ending on the stroke of eight, he had shifted the whole affair to the sphere of a self-deluding game. Yes, that is the word for it! All these registrations and contacts are nothing but a *self-deluding game* with which Martin wants to retain for himself the illusion that nothing has changed, that the beloved comedy of youth continues to be played, that the labyrinth of women is endless, and that it is still his preserve.

Ten minutes went by. No one appeared at the gates.

Martin became indignant and almost yelled: "I'll give them five more minutes! I won't wait any longer!"

Martin hasn't been young for quite a while now. I speculated further—he truly loves his wife, as a matter of fact he has the most regular sort of marriage. This is a fact. And yet—above this (and simultaneously with it), Martin's youth continues on the level of touchingly innocent self-deception: a restless, gay, and erring youth transformed into a mere game, a game that was no longer in any way up to crossing the line into real life and realizing itself as a fact. And because Martin is the knight obsessed by Necessity, he has transformed his love affairs into the harmlessness of a game, *without knowing it.* So he continues to put his whole inflamed soul into them.

O.K., I said to myself. Martin is the captive of his self-deception, but what am I? What am I? Why do I assist him in this ridiculous game? Why do I, who know that all of this is a delusion, pretend along with him? Am I not then still more ridiculous than Martin? Why at this time should I behave as if an amorous adventure lay before me, when I know that at most a single aimless hour with unknown and indifferent girls awaits me.

At that moment in the mirror I caught sight of two young women at the hospital gates. Even from that distance they gave off a glow of powder and rouge. They were strikingly chic and their delay was obviously connected with their well made-up appearance. They looked around and headed toward our car.

"Martin, there's nothing to be done." I renounced the girls. "It's over a quarter of an hour. Let's go." And I put my foot on the gas.

REPENTANCE

We drove out of B. We passed the last little houses and drove into the countryside through fields and woods, toward whose treetops a large sun was sinking.

We were silent.

I thought about Judas Iscariot, about whom a brilliant author relates that he betrayed Jesus just because he *believed* in him infinitely: he couldn't wait for the miracle through which Jesus was to have shown all the Jews his divine power. So he handed Him over to His tormentors in order to provoke Him at last to action. He betrayed Him, because he longed to hasten His victory.

Oh God, I said to myself, I've betrayed Martin from far less noble motives. I betrayed him in fact just because I stopped believing in him (and in the divine power of his womanizing). I am a vile compound of Judas Iscariot and of the man whom they called Doubting Thomas. I felt that as a result of my wrongdoing my sympathy for Martin was growing and that his banner of the eternal chase (which was to be heard still fluttering above us) was reducing me to tears. I began to reproach myself for my overhasty action.

Does perhaps some magnet not attract me to lead expeditions back to the time of freedom and wandering, of choice and searching, to the time of lack of commitment and initial choice? Shall I be in a position more easily to part with these gestures which signify youth for me? And will there remain for me perhaps something other than a feeling that I should at least *imitate* them and endeavor to find a small, safe place for this foolish activity within my otherwise sensible life?

What does it matter that it's all a futile game? What does it matter that I *know* it. Will I stop playing the game just because it is futile?

I knew that this would not be the case; I knew that soon we'd drive out of Prague again, we'd stop girls and think up new escapades.

In all this I shall rightly remain a split character, doubting and vacillating, while Martin, like a character from mythology, will forever be an internally integrated being, fighting the great metaphysical battle against time and against those damnably narrow confines, within which our life cowers.

THE GOLDEN APPLE OF ETERNAL DESIRE

He was sitting beside me and little by little his indignation subsided.

"Listen," he said, "is that medical student really so high-class?"

"I'm telling you she's on Jirzhinka's level."

Martin put further questions to me. I had to describe the medical student to him once again.

Then he said: "Perhaps you could hand her over to me afterward, eh?"

I wanted to appear plausible. "That may be quite difficult. It would bother her that you're my buddy. She has firm principles . . ."

"She has firm principles . . . ," said Martin sadly, and it was plain that he was upset by this.

I didn't want to upset him.

"Unless I could pretend I don't know you," I said. "Perhaps you could pass yourself off as someone else."

"Fine! Perhaps as Jasny, like today!"

"She doesn't give a damn about film directors. She prefers athletes."

"Why not?" said Martin, "it's all within the realm of possibility," and we spent some time involved in this discussion. From moment to moment the plan became clearer and after a while it dangled before us in the advancing twilight like a beautiful, ripe, shining apple.

Permit me to name this apple with a certain ceremoniousness The Golden Apple of Eternal Desire.

HERMAN MELVILLE

BARTLEBY THE SCRIVENER

Herman Melville (1819–1891) is now recognized as one of the greatest writers in American literature. It was not always so. Melville began as an enormously popular writer, penning romantic tales about the South Seas. But after the publication of Moby Dick, *his masterwork in the view of many critics, his popularity declined, and he died poor and forgotten. Melville wrote "Bartleby, The Scrivener" during his period of neglect, and the character of Bartleby—insistently holding on to his anonymity and pride—may reflect some of Melville's own resistance to social norms.*

Melville was born in New York City and raised in upstate New York. After a number of jobs including teaching, he set sail as a cabin boy. He was twenty, and for the next fifteen or so years he worked as a sailor. Like Joseph Conrad, Melville knew the sea first hand. But he also knew the dull routine of offices because like Nathaniel Hawthorne, he worked in a customs house for the last nineteen years of his life.

I am a rather elderly man. The nature of my avocations, for the last thirty years, has brought me into more than ordinary contact with what would seem an interesting and somewhat singular set of men, of whom, as yet, nothing, that I know of, has ever been written—I mean, the law-copyists, or scriveners. I have known very many of them, professionally and privately, and, if I pleased, could relate divers histories, at which good-natured gentlemen might smile, and sentimental souls might weep. But I waive the biographies of all other scriveners, for a few passages in the life of Bartleby, who was a scrivener, the strangest I ever saw, or heard of. While, of other law-copyists, I might write the complete life, of Bartleby nothing of that sort can be done. I believe that no materials exist, for a full and satisfactory biography of this man. It is an irreparable loss to literature. Bartleby was one of those beings of whom nothing is ascertainable, except from the original sources, and, in his case, those are very small. What my own astonished eyes saw of Bartleby, *that* is all I know of him, except, indeed, one vague report, which will appear in the sequel.

Ere introducing the scrivener, as he first appeared to me, it is fit I make some mention of myself, my *employés,* my business, my chambers, and general surroundings; because some such description is indispensable to an adequate understanding of the chief character about to be presented. Imprimis:[1] I am a man who, from his youth upwards has been filled with a profound conviction that the easiest way of life is the best. Hence, though I belong to a profession proverbially energetic and nervous, even to turbulence, at times, yet nothing of that sort have I ever suffered to invade my peace. I am one of those unambitious lawyers who never addresses a jury, or in any way draws down public applause; but, in the cool tranquillity of a snug retreat, do a snug business among the rich men's bonds, and mortgages, and title-deeds. All who know me, consider me an eminently *safe* man. The late John Jacob Astor,[2] a personage little given to poetic enthusiasm, had no hesitation in pronouncing my first grand point to be prudence; my next, method. I do not speak it in vanity, but simply record the fact, that I was not unemployed in my profession by the late John Jacob Astor, a name which, I admit, I love to repeat; for it hath a rounded and orbicular[3]

[1] Imprimis is Latin for "in the first place." The word is used to begin a list.
[2] John Jacob Astor (1763–1848) was the founder of a family fortune based on fur trading and real estate.
[3] Orbicular means to be rounded like a sphere.

sound to it, and rings like unto bullion.[4] I will freely add, that I was not insensible to the late John Jacob Astor's good opinion.

Some time prior to the period at which this little history begins, my avocations had been largely increased. The good old office, now extinct in the State of New York, of a Master in Chancery, had been conferred upon me. It was not rather than spoken, in the heat of business; and especially by a continual discontent with the height of the table where he worked. Though of a very ingenious mechanical turn, Nippers could never get this table to suit him. He put chips under it, blocks of various sorts, bits of pasteboard, and at last went so far as to attempt an exquisite adjustment, by final pieces of folded blotting-paper. But no invention would answer. If, for the sake of easing his back, he brought the table lid at a sharp angle well up towards his chin, and wrote there like a man using the steep roof of a Dutch house for his desk, then he declared that it stopped the circulation in his arms. If now he lowered the table to his waistbands, and stooped over it in writing, then there was a sore aching in his back. In short, the truth of the matter was, Nippers knew not what he wanted. Or, if he wanted anything, it was to be rid of a scrivener's table altogether. Among the manifestations of his diseased ambition was a fondness he had for receiving visits from certain ambiguous-looking fellows in seedy coats, whom he called his clients. Indeed, I was aware that not only was he, at times, considerable of a ward-politician, but he occasionally did a little business at the Justices' courts, and was not unknown on the steps of the Tombs.[6] I have good reason to believe, however, that one individual who called upon him at my chambers, and who, with a grand air, he insisted was his client, was no other than a dun, and the alleged title-deed, a bill. But, with all his failings, and the annoyances he caused me, Nippers, like his compatriot Turkey, was a very useful man to me; wrote a neat, swift hand; and, when he chose, was not deficient in a gentlemanly sort of deportment. Added to this, he always dressed in a gentlemanly sort of way; and so, incidentally, reflected credit upon my chambers. Whereas, with respect to Turkey, I had much ado to keep him from being a reproach to me. His clothes were apt to look oily, and smell of eating-houses. He wore his pantaloons very loose and baggy in summer. His coats were execrable; his hat not to be handled. But while the hat was a thing of indifference to me, inasmuch as his natural civility and deference, as a dependent Englishman, always led him to doff it the moment he entered the room, yet his coat was another matter. Concerning his coats, I reasoned with him; but with no effect. The truth was, I suppose, that a man with so small an income could not afford to sport such a lustrous face and a lustrous coat at one and the same time. As Nippers once observed,

[4] Bullion is coined gold or silver in bars.
[6] The Tombs is the name given to the New York City Jail located in lower Manhattan.

Turkey's money went chiefly for red ink. One winter day, I presented Turkey with a highly respectable-looking coat of my own—a padded gray coat, of a most comfortable warmth, and which buttoned straight up from the knee to the neck. I thought Turkey would appreciate the favor, and abate his rashness and obstreperousness of afternoons. But no; I verily believe that buttoning himself up in so downy and blanket-like a coat had a pernicious effect upon him—upon the same principle that too much oats are bad for horses. In fact, precisely as a rash, restive horse is said to feel his oats, so Turkey felt his coat. It made him insolent. He was a man whom prosperity harmed.

Though, concerning the self-indulgent habits of Turkey, I had my own private surmises, yet, touching Nippers, I was well persuaded that, whatever might be his faults in other respects, he was, at least, a temperate young man. But, indeed, nature herself seemed to have been his vintner, and, at his birth, charged him so thoroughly with an irritable, brandy-like disposition, that all subsequent potations were needless. When I consider how, amid the stillness of my chambers, Nippers would sometimes impatiently rise from his seat, and stooping over his table, spread his arms wide apart, seize the whole desk, and move it, and jerk it, with a grim, grinding motion on the floor, as if the table were a perverse voluntary agent, intent on thwarting and vexing him, I plainly perceive that, for Nippers, brandy-and-water were altogether superfluous.

It was fortunate for me that, owing to its peculiar cause—indigestion—the irritability and consequent nervousness of Nippers were mainly observable in the morning, while in the afternoon he was comparatively mild. So that, Turkey's paroxysms only coming on about twelve o'clock, I never had to do with their eccentricities at one time. Their fits relieved each other, like guards. When Nippers' was on, Turkey's was off; and *vice versa.* This was a good natural arrangement, under the circumstances.

Ginger Nut, the third on my list, was a lad, some twelve years old. His father was a car-man, ambitious of seeing his son on the bench instead of a cart, before he died. So he sent him to my office, as student at law, errand-boy, cleaner and sweeper, at the rate of one dollar a week. He had a little desk to himself, but he did not use it much. Upon inspection, the drawer exhibited a great array of the shells of various sorts of nuts. Indeed, to this quick-witted youth, the whole noble science of the law was contained in a nut-shell. Not the least among the employments of Ginger Nut, as well as one which he discharged with the most alacrity, was his duty as cake and apple purveyor for Turkey and Nippers. Copying law-papers being proverbially a dry, husky sort of business, my two scriveners were fain to moisten their mouths very often with Spitzenbergs,[7] to be had at the numerous stalls nigh the Custom House and the Post Office. Also, they sent Ginger Nut very frequently for that peculiar cake—small, flat, round, and very spicy—after which he

[7] Spitzenbergs are a variety of apple native to New York State.

had been named by them. Of a cold morning, when business was but dull, Turkey would gobble up scores of these cakes, as if they were mere wafers—indeed, they sell them at the rate of six or eight for a penny—the scrape of his pen blending with the crunching of the crisp particles in his mouth. Of all the fiery afternoon blunders and flurried rashnesses of Turkey, was his once moistening a ginger-cake between his lips, and clapping it on to a mortgage, for a seal. I came within an ace of dismissing him then. But he mollified me by making an oriental bow, and saying—

"With submission, sir, it was generous of me to find you in stationery on my own account."

Now my original business—that of a conveyancer and title hunter, and drawer-up of recondite documents of all sorts—was considerably increased by receiving the master's office. There was now great work for scriveners. Not only must I push the clerks already with me, but I must have additional help.

In answer to my advertisement, a motionless young man one morning stood upon my office threshold, the door being open, for it was summer. I can see that figure now—pallidly neat, pitiably respectable, incurably forlorn! It was Bartleby.

After a few words touching his qualifications, I engaged him, glad to have among my corps of copyists a man of so singularly sedate an aspect, which I thought might operate beneficially upon the flighty temper of Turkey, and the fiery one of Nippers.

I should have stated before that ground glass folding-doors divided my premises into two parts, one of which was occupied by my scriveners, the other by myself. According to my humor, I threw open these doors, or closed them. I resolved to assign Bartleby a corner by the folding-doors, but on my side of them, so as to have this quiet man within easy call, in case any trifling thing was to be done. I placed his desk close up to a small side-window in that part of the room, a window which originally had afforded a lateral view of certain grimy backyards and bricks, but which, owing to subsequent erections, commanded at present no view at all, though it gave some light. Within three feet of the panes was a wall, and the light came down from far above, between two lofty buildings, as from a very small opening in a dome. Still further to a satisfactory arrangement, I procured a high green folding screen, which might entirely isolate Bartleby from my sight, though not remove him from my voice. And thus, in a manner, privacy and society were conjoined.

At first, Bartleby did an extraordinary quantity of writing. As if long famishing for something to copy, he seemed to gorge himself on my documents. There was no pause for digestion. He ran a day and night line, copying by sun-light and by candle-light. I should have been quite delighted with his application, had he been cheerfully industrious. But he wrote on silently, palely, mechanically.

It is, of course, an indispensable part of a scrivener's business to verify the accuracy of his copy, word by word. Where there are two or more scriveners in an office, they assist each other in this examination, one reading from the copy, the other holding the original. It is a very dull, wearisome, and lethargic affair. I can readily imagine that, to some sanguine temperaments, it would be altogether intolerable. For example, I cannot credit that the mettlesome poet, Byron, would have contentedly sat down with Bartleby to examine a law document of say five hundred pages, closely written in a crimpy hand.

Now and then, in the haste of business, it had been my habit to assist in comparing some brief document myself, calling Turkey or Nippers for this purpose. One object I had, in placing Bartleby so handy to me behind the screen, was, to avail myself of his services on such trivial occasions. It was on the third day, I think, of his being with me, and before any necessity had arisen for having his own writing examined, that, being much hurried to complete a small affair I had in hand, I abruptly called to Bartleby. In my haste and natural expectancy of instant compliance, I sat with my head bent over the original on my desk, and my right hand sideways, and somewhat nervously extended with the copy, so that, immediately upon emerging from his retreat, Bartleby might snatch it and proceed to business without the least delay.

In this very attitude did I sit when I called to him, rapidly stating what it was I wanted him to do—namely, to examine a small paper with me. Imagine my surprise, nay, my consternation, when, without moving from his privacy, Bartleby, in a singularly mild, firm voice, replied, "I would prefer not to."

I sat awhile in perfect silence, rallying my stunned faculties. Immediately it occurred to me that my ears had deceived me, or Bartleby had entirely misunderstood my meaning. I repeated my request in the clearest tone I could assume; but in quite as clear a one came the previous reply, "I would prefer not to."

"Prefer not to," echoed I, rising in high excitement, and crossing the room with a stride. "What do you mean? Are you moon-struck? I want you to help me compare this sheet here—take it," and I thrust it towards him.

"I would prefer not to," said he.

I looked at him steadfastly. His face was leanly composed; his gray eye dimly calm. Not a wrinkle of agitation rippled him. Had there been the least uneasiness, anger, impatience or impertinence in his manner; in other words, had there been any thing ordinarily human about him, doubtless I should have violently dismissed him from the premises. But as it was, I should have as soon thought of turning my pale plaster-of-paris bust of Cicero[8] out of doors. I stood gazing at him awhile, as he went on with his own writing, and then reseated myself at my desk.

[8] Cicero (106–43 B.C.) was a Roman orator, statesman, and philosopher.

This is very strange, thought I. What had one best do? But my business hurried me. I concluded to forget the matter for the present, reserving it for my future leisure. So calling Nippers from the other room, the paper was speedily examined.

A few days after this, Bartleby concluded four lengthy documents, being quadruplicates of a week's testimony taken before me in my High Court of Chancery. It became necessary to examine them. It was an important suit, and great accuracy was imperative. Having all things arranged, I called Turkey, Nippers, and Ginger Nut, from the next room, meaning to place the four copies in the hands of my four clerks, while I should read from the original. Accordingly, Turkey, Nippers, and Ginger Nut had taken their seats in a row, each with his document in his hand, when I called to Bartleby to join this interesting group.

"Bartleby! quick, I am waiting."

I heard a slow scrape of his chairlegs on the uncarpeted floor, and soon he appeared standing at the entrance of his hermitage.

"What is wanted?" said he, mildly.

"The copies, the copies," said I, hurriedly. "We are going to examine them. There"—and I held towards him the fourth quadruplicate.

"I would prefer not to," he said, and gently disappeared behind the screen.

For a few moments I was turned into a pillar of salt, standing at the head of my seated column of clerks. Recovering myself, I advanced towards the screen, and demanded the reason for such extraordinary conduct.

"*Why* do you refuse?"

"I would prefer not to."

With any other man I should have flown outright into a dreadful passion, scorned all further words, and thrust him ignominiously from my presence. But there was something about Bartleby that not only strangely disarmed me, but, in a wonderful manner, touched and disconcerted me. I began to reason with him.

"These are your own copies we are about to examine. It is labor saving to you, because one examination will answer for your four papers. It is common usage. Every copyist is bound to help examine his copy. Is it not so? Will you not speak? Answer!"

"I prefer not to," he replied in a flutelike tone. It seemed to me that, while I had been addressing him, he carefully revolved every statement that I made; fully comprehended the meaning; could not gainsay the irresistible conclusion; but, at the same time, some paramount consideration prevailed with him to reply as he did.

"You are decided, then, not to comply with my request—a request made according to common usage and common sense?"

He briefly gave me to understand, that on that point my judgment was sound. Yes: his decision was irreversible.

It is not seldom the case that, when a man is browbeaten in some unprecedented and violently unreasonable way, he begins to stagger in his own plainest faith. He begins, as it were, vaguely to surmise that, wonderful as it may be, all the justice and all the reason is on the other side. Accordingly, if any disinterested persons are present, he turns to them for some reinforcement of his own faltering mind.

"Turkey," said I, "what do you think of this? Am I not right?"

"With submission, sir," said Turkey, in his blandest tone, "I think that you are."

"Nippers," said I, "what do *you* think of it?"

"I think I should kick him out of the office."

(The reader, of nice perceptions, will here perceive that, it being morning, Turkey's answer is couched in polite and tranquil terms, but Nippers' replies in ill-tempered ones. Or, to repeat a previous sentence, Nippers' ugly mood was on duty, and Turkey's off.)

"Ginger Nut," said I, willing to enlist the smallest suffrage in my behalf, "what do *you* think of it?"

"I think, sir, he's a little *luny*," replied Ginger Nut, with a grin.

"You hear what they say," said I, turning towards the screen, "come forth and do your duty."

But he vouchsafed no reply. I pondered a moment in sore perplexity. But once more business hurried me. I determined again to postpone the consideration of this dilemma to my future leisure. With a little trouble we made out to examine the papers without Bartleby, though at every page or two Turkey deferentially dropped his opinion, that this proceeding was quite out of the common; while Nippers, twitching in his chair with a dyspeptic[9] nervousness, ground out, between his set teeth, occasional hissing maledictions against the stubborn oaf behind the screen. And for his (Nippers') part, this was the first and the last time he would do another man's business without pay.

Meanwhile Bartleby sat in his hermitage, oblivious to everything but his own peculiar business there.

Some days passed, the scrivener being employed upon another lengthy work. His late remarkable conduct led me to regard his ways narrowly. I observed that he never went to dinner; indeed, that he never went anywhere. As yet I had never, of my personal knowledge, known him to be outside of my office. He was a perpetual sentry in the corner. At about eleven o'clock though, in the morning, I noticed that Ginger Nut would advance toward the opening in Bartleby's screen, as if silently beckoned thither by a gesture invisible to me where I sat. The boy would then leave the office, jingling a few pence, and reappear with a handful of ginger-nuts, which he delivered in the hermitage, receiving two of the cakes for his trouble.

He lives, then, on ginger-nuts, thought I; never eats a dinner, properly speaking; he must be a vegetarian, then; but no; he never eats even

[9] Dyspeptic refers to indigestion.

vegetables, he eats nothing but ginger-nuts. My mind then ran on in reveries concerning the probable effects upon the human constitution of living entirely on ginger-nuts. Ginger-nuts are so called, because they contain ginger as one of their peculiar constituents, and the final flavoring one. Now, what was ginger? A hot, spicy thing. Was Bartleby hot and spicy? Not at all. Ginger, then, had no effect upon Bartleby. Probably he preferred it should have none.

Nothing so aggravates an earnest person as a passive resistance. If the individual so resisted be of a not inhumane temper, and the resisting one perfectly harmless in his passivity, then, in the better moods of the former, he will endeavor charitably to construe to his imagination what proves impossible to be solved by his judgment. Even so, for the most part, I regarded Bartleby and his ways. Poor fellow! thought I, he means no mischief; it is plain he intends no insolence; his aspect sufficiently evinces that his eccentricities are involuntary. He is useful to me. I can get along with him. If I turn him away, the chances are he will fall in with some less-indulgent employer, and then he will be rudely treated, and perhaps driven forth miserably to starve. Yes. Here I can cheaply purchase a delicious self-approval. To befriend Bartleby; to humor him in his strange willfulness, will cost me little or nothing, while I lay up in my soul what will eventually prove a sweet morsel for my conscience. But this mood was not invariable with me. The passiveness of Bartleby sometimes irritated me. I felt strangely goaded on to encounter him in new opposition—to elicit some angry spark from him answerable to my own. But, indeed, I might as well have essayed to strike fire with my knuckles against a bit of Windsor soap. But one afternoon the evil impulse in me mastered me, and the following little scene ensued:

"Bartleby," said I, "when those papers are all copied, I will compare them with you."

"I would prefer not to."

"How? Surely you do not mean to persist in that mulish vagary?"

No answer.

I threw open the folding-doors near by, and, turning upon Turkey and Nippers, exclaimed:

"Bartleby a second time says, he won't examine his papers. What do you think of it, Turkey?"

It was afternoon, be it remembered. Turkey sat glowing like a brass boiler; his bald head steaming; his hands reeling among his blotted papers.

"Think if it?" roared Turkey; "I think I'll just step behind his screen, and black his eyes for him!"

So saying, Turkey rose to his feet and threw his arms into a pugilistic position. He was hurrying away to make good his promise, when I detained him, alarmed at the effect of incautiously rousing Turkey's combativeness after dinner.

"Sit down, Turkey," said I, "and hear what Nippers has to say. What do you think of it, Nippers? Would I not be justified in immediately dismissing Bartleby?"

"Excuse me, that is for you to decide, sir. I think his conduct quite unusual, and, indeed, unjust, as regards Turkey and myself. But it may only be a passing whim."

"Ah," exclaimed I, "you have strangely changed your mind, then—you speak very gently of him now."

"All beer," cried Turkey; "gentleness is effects of beer—Nippers and I dined together to-day. You see how gentle *I* am, sir. Shall I go and black his eyes?"

"You refer to Bartleby, I suppose. No, not to-day, Turkey," I replied; "pray, put up your fists."

I closed the doors, and again advanced towards Bartleby. I felt additional incentives tempting me to my fate. I burned to be rebelled against again. I remember that Bartleby never left the office.

"Bartleby," said I, "Ginger Nut is away; just step around to the Post Office, won't you? (it was but a three minutes' walk), and see if there is anything for me."

"I would prefer not to."

"You *will* not?"

"I *prefer* not."

I staggered to my desk, and sat there in a deep study. My blind inveteracy returned. Was there any other thing in which I could procure myself to be ignominiously repulsed by this lean, penniless wight?—my hired clerk? What added thing is there, perfectly reasonable, that he will be sure to refuse to do?

"Bartleby!"

No answer.

"Bartleby," in a louder tone.

No answer.

"Bartleby," I roared.

Like a very ghost, agreeably to the laws of magical invocation, at the third summons, he appeared at the entrance of his hermitage.

"Go to the next room, and tell Nippers to come to me."

"I prefer not to," he respectfully and slowly said, and mildly disappeared.

"Very good, Bartleby," said I, in a quiet sort of serenely-severe self-possessed tone, intimating the unalterable purpose of some terrible retribution very close at hand. But upon the whole, as it was drawing towards my dinner-hour, I thought it best to put on my hat and walk home for the day, suffering much from perplexity and distress of mind.

Shall I acknowledge it? The conclusion of this whole business was, that it soon became a fixed fact of my chambers, that a pale young scrivener, by the name of Bartleby, had a desk there; that he copied for me at the usual rate of four cents a folio (one hundred words); but he was permanently exempt from examining the work done by him, that duty being transferred to Turkey and Nippers, out of compliment, doubtless, to their superior acuteness; moreover, said Bartleby was never, on any account, to be dispatched on the most trivial errand of any sort; and that even if entreated to take upon him such a matter, it was generally understood that he would "prefer not to"—in other words, that he would refuse point-blank.

As days passed on, I became considerably reconciled to Bartleby. His steadiness, his freedom from all dissipation, his incessant industry (except when he chose to throw himself into a standing revery behind his screen), his great stillness, his unalterableness of demeanor under all circumstances, made him a valuable acquisition. One prime thing was this—*he was always there*—first in the morning, continually through the day, and the last at night. I had a singular confidence in his honesty. I felt my most precious papers perfectly safe in his hands. Sometimes, to be sure, I could not, for the very soul of me, avoid falling into sudden spasmodic passions with him. For it was exceeding difficult to bear in mind all the time those strange peculiarities, privileges, and unheard of exemptions, forming the tacit stipulations on Bartleby's part under which he remained in my office. Now and then, in the eagerness of dispatching pressing business, I would inadvertently summon Bartleby, in a short, rapid tone, to put his finger, say, on the incipient tie of a bit of red tape with which I was about compressing some papers. Of course, from behind the screen the usual answer, "I prefer not to," was sure to come; and then, how could a human creature, with the common infirmities of our nature, refrain from bitterly exclaiming upon such perverseness—such unreasonableness. However, every added repulse of this sort which I received only tended to lessen the probability of my repeating the inadvertence.

Here it must be said, that according to the custom of most legal gentlemen occupying chambers in densely-populated law buildings, there were several keys to my door. One was kept by a woman residing in the attic, which person weekly scrubbed and daily swept and dusted my apartments. Another was kept by Turkey for convenience sake. The third I sometimes carried in my own pocket. The fourth I knew not who had.

Now, one Sunday morning I happened to go to Trinity Church, to hear a celebrated preacher, and finding myself rather early on the ground I thought I would walk around to my chambers for a while. Luckily I had my key with me, but upon applying it to the lock, I found it resisted by something inserted from the inside. Quite surprised, I called out; when to my consternation a key was turned from within; and thrusting his lean visage at me, and holding the door ajar, the apparition of Bartleby appeared in his shirt sleeves, and otherwise in a strangely tattered deshabille,[10] saying quietly that he was sorry, but he was deeply engaged just then, and—preferred not admitting me at present. In a brief word or two, he moreover added, that perhaps I had better walk around the block two or three times, and by that time he would probably have concluded his affairs.

Now, the utterly unsurmised appearance of Bartleby, tenanting my law-chambers of a Sunday morning, with his cadaverously gentlemanly *nonchalance,* yet withal firm and self-possessed, had such a strange effect upon me, that incontinently I slunk away from my own door, and did as desired. But not without sundry twinges of impotent rebellion against the mild effrontery of this unaccountable scrivener. Indeed, it was his wonderful mildness chiefly, which not only disarmed me, but unmanned me as it were. For I consider that one, for the time, is somehow unmanned when he tranquilly permits his hired clerk to dictate to him, and order him away from his own premises. Furthermore, I was full of uneasiness as to what Bartleby could possibly be doing in my office in his shirt sleeves, and in an otherwise dismantled condition of a Sunday morning. Was anything amiss going on? Nay, that was out of the question. It was not to be thought of for a moment that Bartleby was an immoral person. But what could he be doing there?—copying? Nay again, whatever might be his eccentricities, Bartleby was an eminently decorous person. He would be the last man to sit down to his desk in any state approaching to nudity. Besides, it was Sunday, and there was something about Bartleby that forbade the supposition that he would by any secular occupation violate the proprieties of the day.

Nevertheless, my mind was not pacified; and full of a restless curiosity, at last I returned to the door. Without hindrance I inserted my key, opened it, and entered. Bartleby was not to be seen. I looked round anxiously, peeped behind his screen; but it was very plain that he was gone. Upon more closely examining the place, I surmised that for an indefinite period Bartleby must have ate, dressed, and slept in my office, and that, too, without plate, mirror, or bed. The cushioned seat of a rickety old sofa in one corner bore the faint impression of a lean, reclining form. Rolled away under his desk, I found a blanket; on a chair, a tin basin, with soap and a ragged towel; in a newspaper a few crumbs of ginger-nuts and a morsel of cheese. Yes, thought I, it is evident enough that Bartleby has been making his home here, keeping bachelor's hall all by himself. Immediately then the thought came sweeping across me, what miserable friendlessness and loneliness are here revealed! His poverty is great; but his solitude, how horrible! Think of it. Of a Sunday, Wall Street is deserted as Petra;[11] and every night of every day it is an

[10] Deshabille (dishabille) is the state of being partially dressed.

[11] Petra was a city in southwestern Jordan captured by the Muslims in the 7th century and the crusaders in the 12th. Johann Ludwig Burckhardt (1784–1817) discovered its ruins in 1812.

emptiness. This building, too, which of weekdays hums with industry and life, at nightfall echoes with sheer vacancy, and all through Sunday is forlorn. And here Bartleby makes his home; sole spectator of a solitude which he has seen all populous—a sort of innocent and transformed Marius[12] brooding among the ruins of Carthage!

For the first time in my life a feeling of over-powering stinging melancholy seized me. Before, I had never experienced aught but a not unpleasing sadness. The bond of a common humanity now drew me irresistibly to gloom. A fraternal melancholy! For both I and Bartleby were sons of Adam. I remembered the bright silks and sparkling faces I had seen that day, in gala trim, swan-like sailing down the Mississippi of Broadway; and I contrasted them with the pallid copyist, and thought to myself, Ah, happiness courts the light, so we deem the world is gay; but misery hides aloof, so we deem that misery there is none. These sad fancyings—chimeras, doubtless, of a sick and silly brain—led on to other and more special thoughts, concerning the eccentricities of Bartleby. Presentiments of strange discoveries hovered round me. The scrivener's pale form appeared to me laid out, among uncaring strangers, in its shivering winding sheet.

Suddenly I was attracted by Bartleby's closed desk, the key in open sight left in the lock.

I mean no mischief, seek the gratification of no heartless curiosity, thought I; besides, the desk is mine, and its contents, too, so I will make bold to look within. Everything was methodically arranged, the papers smoothly placed. The pigeon holes were deep, and removing the files of documents, I groped into their recesses. Presently I felt something there, and dragged it out. It was an old bandanna handkerchief, heavy and knotted. I opened it, and saw it was a saving's bank.

I now recalled all the quiet mysteries which I had noted in the man. I remembered that he never spoke but to answer; that, though at intervals he had considerable time to himself, yet I had never seen him reading—no, not even a newspaper; that for long periods he would stand looking out, at his pale window behind the screen, upon a dead brick wall; I was quite sure he never visited any refectory or eating house; while his pale face clearly indicated that he never drank beer like Turkey, or tea and coffee even, like other men; that he never went anywhere in particular that I could learn; never went out for a walk, unless, indeed, that was the case at present; that he had declined telling who he was, or whence he came, or whether he had any relatives in the world; that though so thin and pale, he never complained of ill health. And more than all, I remembered a certain unconscious air of pallid—how shall I

[12] Marius (155?–86 B.C.) was a Roman general driven from Rome during a civil war. Carthage was a city whose battles with Rome led to its total destruction in 146 B.C.

call it?—of pallid haughtiness, say, or rather an austere reserve about him, which had positively awed me into my tame compliance with his eccentricities, when I had feared to ask him to do the slightest incidental thing for me, even though I might know, from his long-continued motionlessness, that behind his screen he must be standing in one of those dead-wall reveries of his.

Revolving all these things, and coupling them with the recently discovered fact, that he made my office his constant abiding place and home, and not forgetful of his morbid moodiness; revolving all these things, a prudential feeling began to steal over me. My first emotions had been those of pure melancholy and sincerest pity; but just in proportion as the forlornness of Bartleby grew and grew to my imagination, did that same melancholy merge into fear, that pity into repulsion. So true it is, and so terrible, too, that up to a certain point the thought or sight of misery enlists our best affections; but, in certain special cases, beyond that point it does not. They err who would assert that invariably this is owing to the inherent selfishness of the human heart. It rather proceeds from a certain hopelessness of remedying excessive and organic ill. To a sensitive being, pity is not seldom pain. And when at last it is perceived that such pity cannot lead to effectual succor, common sense bids the soul be rid of it. What I saw that morning persuaded me that the scrivener was the victim of innate and incurable disorder. I might give alms to his body; but his body did not pain him; it was his soul that suffered, and his soul I could not reach.

I did not accomplish the purpose of going to Trinity Church that morning. Somehow, the things I had seen disqualified me for the time from church-going. I walked homeward, thinking what I would do with Bartleby. Finally, I resolved upon this—I would put certain calm questions to him the next morning, touching his history, etc., and if he declined to answer them openly and unreservedly (and I supposed he would prefer not), then to give him a twenty dollar bill over and above whatever I might owe him, and tell him his services were no longer required; but that if in any other way I could assist him, I would be happy to do so, especially if he desired to return to his native place, wherever that might be, I would willingly help to defray the expenses. Moreover, if, after reaching home, he found himself at any time in want of aid, a letter from him would be sure of a reply.

The next morning came.

"Bartleby," said I, gently calling to him behind his screen.

No reply.

"Bartleby," said I, in a still gentler tone, "Come here; I am not going to ask you to do anything you would prefer not to do—I simply wish to speak to you."

Upon this he noiselessly slid into view.

"Will you tell me, Bartleby, where you were born?"

"I would prefer not to."

"Will you tell me *anything* about yourself?"

"I would prefer not to."

"But what reasonable objection can you have to speak to me? I feel friendly towards you."

He did not look at me while I spoke, but kept his glance fixed upon my bust of Cicero, which, as I then sat, was directly behind me, some six inches above my head.

"What is your answer, Bartleby," said I, after waiting a considerable time for a reply, during which his countenance remained immovable, only there was the faintest conceivable tremor of the white attenuated mouth.

"At present I prefer to give no answer," he said, and retired into his hermitage.

It was rather weak in me I confess, but his manner, on this occasion, nettled me. Not only did there seem to lurk in it a certain calm disdain, but his perverseness seemed ungrateful, considering the undeniable good usage and indulgence he had received from me.

Again I sat ruminating what I should do. Mortified as I was at his behavior, and resolved as I had been to dismiss him when I entered my office, nevertheless I strangely felt something superstitious knocking at my heart, and forbidding me to carry out my purpose, and denouncing me for a villain if I dared to breathe one bitter word against this forlornest of mankind. At last, familiarly drawing my chair behind his screen, I sat down and said: "Bartleby, never mind, then, about revealing your history; but let me entreat you, as a friend, to comply as far as may be with the usages of this office. Say now, you will help to examine papers to-morrow or next day: in short, say now, that in a day or two you will begin to be a little reasonable:—say so, Bartleby."

"At present I would prefer not to be a little reasonable," was his mildly cadaverous reply.

Just then the folding-doors opened, and Nippers approached. He seemed suffering from an unusually bad night's rest, induced by severer indigestion than common. He overheard those final words of Bartleby.

"Prefer not, eh?" gritted Nippers—"I'd *prefer* him, if I were you, sir," addressing me—"I'd *prefer* him; I'd give him preferences, the stubborn mule! What is it, sir, pray, that he *prefers* not to do now?"

Bartleby moved not a limb.

"Mr. Nippers," said I, "I'd prefer that you would withdraw for the present."

Somehow, of late, I had got into the way of involuntarily using this word "prefer" upon all sorts of not exactly suitable occasions. And I trembled to think that my contact with the scrivener had already and seriously affected me in a mental way. And what further and deeper aberration might it not yet produce? This apprehension had not been without efficacy in determining me to summary measures.

As Nippers, looking very sour and sulky, was departing, Turkey blandly and deferentially approached.

"With submission, sir," said he, "yesterday I was thinking abut Bartleby here, and I think that if he would but prefer to take a quart of good ale every day, it would do much towards mending him, and enabling him to assist in examining his papers."

"So you have got the word, too," said I, slightly excited.

"With submission, what word, sir," asked Turkey, respectfully crowding himself into the contracted space behind the screen, and by so doing, making me jostle the scrivener. "What word, sir?"

"I would prefer to be left alone here," said Bartleby, as if offended at being mobbed in his privacy.

"That's the word, Turkey," said I—*"that's* it."

"Oh, *prefer?* oh yes—queer word. I never use it myself. But, sir, as I was saying, if he would but prefer—"

"Turkey," interrupted I, "you will please withdraw."

"Oh, certainly, sir, if you prefer that I should."

As he opened the folding-door to retire, Nippers at his desk caught a glimpse of me, and asked whether I would prefer to have a certain paper copied on blue paper or white. He did not in the least roguishly accent the word prefer. It was plain that it involuntarily rolled from his tongue. I thought to myself, surely I must get rid of a demented man, who already has in some degree turned the tongues, if not the heads of myself and clerks. But I thought it prudent not to break the dismission at once.

The next day I noticed that Bartleby did nothing but stand at his window in his dead-wall revery. Upon asking him why he did not write, he said that he had decided upon doing no more writing.

"Why, how now? what next?" exclaimed I, "do no more writing?"

"No more."

"And what is the reason?"

"Do you not see the reason for yourself," he indifferently replied.

I looked steadfastly at him, and perceived that his eyes looked dull and glazed. Instantly it occurred to me, that his unexampled diligence in copying by his dim window for the first few weeks of his stay with me might have temporarily impaired his vision.

I was touched. I said something in condolence with him. I hinted that of course he did wisely in abstaining from writing for a while; and urged him to embrace that opportunity of taking wholesome exercise in the open air. This, however, he did not do. A few days after this, my other clerks being absent, and being in a great hurry to dispatch certain letters by the mail, I thought that, having nothing else earthly to do, Bartleby would surely be less inflexible than usual, and carry these letters to the post-office. But he blankly declined. So, much to my inconvenience, I went myself.

Still added days went by. Whether Bartleby's eyes improved or not, I could not say. To all appearance, I thought they did. But when I asked him if they did, he vouchsafed no answer. At all events, he would do no copying. At last, in reply to my urgings, he informed me that he had permanently given up copying.

"What!" exclaimed I; "suppose your eyes should get entirely well—better than ever before—would you not copy then?"

"I have given up copying," he answered, and slid aside.

He remained as ever, a fixture in my chamber. Nay—if that were possible—he became still more of a fixture than before. What was to be done? He would do nothing in the office; why should he stay there? In plain fact, he had now become a millstone to me, not only useless as a necklace, but afflictive to bear. Yet I was sorry for him. I speak less than truth when I say that, on his own account, he occasioned me uneasiness. If he would but have named a single relative or friend, I would instantly have written, and urged their taking the poor fellow away to some convenient retreat. But he seemed alone, absolutely alone in the universe. A bit of wreck in the mid Atlantic. At length, necessities connected with my business tyrannized over all other considerations. Decently as I could, I told Bartleby that in six days time he must unconditionally leave the office. I warned him to take measures, in the interval, for procuring some other abode. I offered to assist him in this endeavor, if he himself would but take the first step towards a removal. "And when you finally quit me, Bartleby," added I, "I shall see that you go not away entirely unprovided. Six days from this hour, remember."

At the expiration of that period, I peeped behind the screen, and lo! Bartleby was there.

I buttoned up my coat, balanced myself; advanced slowly towards him, touched his shoulder, and said, "The time has come; you must quit this place; I am sorry for you; here is money; but you must go."

"I would prefer not," he replied, with his back still towards me.

"You *must.*"

He remained silent.

Now I had an unbounded confidence in this man's common honesty. He had frequently restored to me sixpences and shillings carelessly dropped upon the floor, for I am apt to be very reckless in such shirt-button affairs. The proceeding, then, which followed will not be deemed extraordinary.

"Bartleby," said I, "I owe you twelve dollars on account; here are thirty-two; the odd twenty are yours—Will you take it?" and I handed the bills towards him.

But he made no motion.

"I will leave them here, then," putting them under a weight on the table. Then taking my hat and cane and going to the door, I tranquilly turned and added—"After you have removed your things from these offices, Bartleby, you will of course lock the door—since every one is now gone for the day but you—and if you please, slip your key underneath the mat, so that I may have it in the morning. I shall not see you again; so good-by to you. If, hereafter, in your new place of abode, I can be of any service to you, do not fail to advise me by letter. Good-by, Bartleby, and fare you well."

But he answered not a word; like the last column of some ruined temple, he remained standing mute and solitary in the middle of the otherwise deserted room.

As I walked home in a pensive mood, my vanity got the better of my pity. I could not but highly plume myself on my masterly management in getting rid of Bartleby. Masterly I call it, and such it must appear to any dispassionate thinker. The beauty of my procedure seemed to consist in its perfect quietness. There was no vulgar bullying, no bravado of any sort, no choleric hectoring, and striding to and fro across the apartment, jerking out vehement commands for Bartleby to bundle himself off with his beggarly traps. Nothing of the kind. Without loudly bidding Bartleby depart—as an inferior genius might have done—I *assumed* the ground that depart he must; and upon that assumption built all I had to say. The more I thought over my procedure, the more I was charmed with it. Nevertheless, next morning, upon awakening, I had my doubts—I had somehow slept off the fumes of vanity. One of the coolest and wisest hours a man has, is just after he awakes in the morning. My procedure seemed as sagacious as ever—but only in theory. How it would prove in practice—there was the rub. It was truly a beautiful thought to have assumed Bartleby's departure; but after all, that assumption was simply my own, and none of Bartleby's. The great point was, not whether I had assumed that he would quit me, but whether he would prefer so to do. He was more a man of preferences than assumptions.

After breakfast, I walked down town, arguing the probabilities *pro* and *con.* One moment I thought it would prove a miserable failure, and Bartleby would be found all alive at my office as usual; the next moment it seemed certain that I should find his chair empty. And so I kept veering about. At the corner of Broadway and Canal Street, I saw quite an excited group of people standing in earnest conversation.

"I'll take odds he doesn't," said a voice as I passed.

"Doesn't go?—done!" said I, "put up your money."

I was instinctively putting my hand in my pocket to produce my own, when I remembered that this was an election day. The words I had overheard bore no reference to Bartleby, but to the success or nonsuccess of some candidate for the mayoralty. In my intent frame of mind, I had, as it were, imagined that all Broadway shared in my excitement, and were debating the same question with me. I passed on, very thankful that the uproar of the street screened my momentary absent-mindedness.

As I had intended, I was earlier than usual at my office door. I stood listening for a moment. All was still. He must be gone. I tried the knob. The door was locked. Yes, my procedure had worked to a charm; he indeed must be vanished. Yet a certain melancholy mixed with this: I was almost sorry for my brilliant success. I was fumbling under the door mat for the key, which Bartleby was to have left there for me, when accidentally my knee knocked against a panel, producing a summoning sound, and in response a voice came to me from within—"Not yet; I am occupied."

It was Bartleby.

I was thunderstruck. For an instant I stood like the man who, pipe in mouth, was killed one cloudless afternoon long ago in Virginia, by summer lightning; at his own warm open window he was killed, and remained leaning out there upon the dreamy afternoon, till some one touched him, when he fell.

"Not gone!" I murmured at last. But again obeying that wondrous ascendancy which the inscrutable scrivener had over me, and from which ascendancy, for all my chafing, I could not completely escape, I slowly went down stairs and out into the street, and while walking round the block, considered what I should next do in this unheard-of perplexity. Turn the man out by an actual thrusting I could not; to drive him away by calling him hard names would not do; calling in the police was an unpleasant idea; and yet, permit him to enjoy his cadaverous triumph over me—this too, I could not think of. What was to be done? or, if nothing could be done, was there anything further that I could *assume* in the matter? Yes, as before I had prospectively assumed that Bartleby would depart, so now I might retrospectively assume that departed he was. In the legitimate carrying out of this assumption, I might enter my office in a great hurry, and pretending not to see Bartleby at all, walk straight against him as if he were air. Such a proceeding would in a singular degree have the appearance of homethrust. It was hardly possible that Bartleby could withstand such an application of the doctrine of assumptions. But upon second thoughts the success of the plan seemed rather dubious. I resolved to argue the matter over with him again.

"Bartleby," said I, entering the office, with a quietly severe expression, "I am seriously displeased. I am pained, Bartleby. I had thought better of you. I had imagined you of such a gentlemanly organization, that in any delicate dilemma a slight hint would suffice—in short, an assumption. But it appears I am deceived. Why," I added, unaffectedly starting, "you have not even touched that money yet," pointing to it, just where I had left it the evening previous.

He answered nothing.

"Will you, or will you not, quit me?" I now demanded in a sudden passion, advancing close to him.

"I would prefer *not* to quit you," he replied, gently emphasizing the *not*.

"What earthly right have you to stay here? Do you pay any rent? Do you pay my taxes? Or is this property yours?"

He answered nothing.

"Are you ready to go on and write now? Are your eyes recovered? Could you copy a small paper for me this morning? or help examine a few lines? or step round to the post-office? In a word, will you do anything at all, to give a coloring to your refusal to depart the premises?"

He silently retired into his hermitage.

I was now in such a state of nervous resentment that I thought it but prudent to check myself at present from further demonstrations. Bartleby and I were alone. I remembered the tragedy of the unfortunate Adams and the still more unfortunate Colt in the solitary office of the latter; and how poor Colt, being dreadfully incensed by Adams, and imprudently permitting himself to get wildly excited, was at unawares hurried into his fatal act—an act which certainly no man could possibly deplore more than the actor himself. Often it had occurred to me in my ponderings upon the subject, that had that altercation taken place in the public street, or at a private residence, it would not have terminated as it did. It was the circumstance of being alone in a solitary office, up stairs, of a building entirely unhallowed by humanizing domestic associations—an uncarpeted office, doubtless, of a dusty, haggard sort of appearance—this it must have been, which greatly helped to enhance the irritable desperation of the hapless Colt.[13]

But when this old Adam of resentment rose in me and tempted me concerning Bartleby, I grappled him and threw him. How? Why, simply by recalling the divine injunction: "A new commandment give I unto you, that ye love one another." Yes, this it was that saved me. Aside from higher considerations, charity often operates as a vastly wise and prudent principle—a great safeguard to its possessor. Men have committed murder for jealousy's sake, and anger's sake, and hatred's sake, and selfishness' sake, and spiritual pride's sake; but no man, that ever I heard of, ever committed a diabolical murder for sweet charity's sake. Mere self-interest, then, if no better motive can be enlisted, should, especially with high-tempered men, prompt all beings to charity and philanthropy. At any rate, upon the occasion in question, I strove to drown my exasperated feelings towards the scrivener by benevolently

[13] In January, 1842, John C. Colt killed Samuel Adams in a notorious New York City murder case.

construing his conduct. Poor fellow, poor fellow! thought I, he don't mean anything; and besides, he has seen hard times, and ought to be indulged.

I endeavored, also, immediately to occupy myself, and at the same time to comfort my despondency. I tried to fancy, that in the course of the morning, at such time as might prove agreeable to him, Bartleby, of his own free accord, would emerge from his hermitage and take up some decided line of march in the direction of the door. But no. Half-past twelve o'clock came; Turkey began to glow in the face, overturn his inkstand, and become generally obstreperous; Nippers abated down into quietude and courtesy; Ginger Nut munched his noon apple; and Bartleby remained standing at his window in one of his profoundest dead-wall reveries. Will it be credited? Ought I to acknowledge it? That afternoon I left the office without saying one further word to him.

Some days now passed, during which, at leisure intervals I looked a little into "Edwards on the Will," and "Priestley on Necessity."[14] Under the circumstances, those books induced a salutary feeling. Gradually I slid into the persuasion that these troubles of mine, touching the scrivener, had been all predestinated from eternity, and Bartleby was billeted upon me for some mysterious purpose of an allwise Providence, which it was not for a mere mortal like me to fathom. Yes, Bartleby, stay there behind your screen, thought I; I shall persecute you no more; you are harmless and noiseless as any of these old chairs; in short, I never feel so private as when I know you are here. At last I see it. I feel it; I penetrate to the predestinated purpose of my life. I am content. Others may have loftier parts to enact; but my mission in this world, Bartleby, is to furnish you with officeroom for such period as you may see fit to remain.

I believe that this wise and blessed frame of mind would have continued with me, had it not been for the unsolicited and uncharitable remarks obtruded upon me by my professional friends who visited the rooms. But thus it often is, that the constant friction of illiberal minds wears out at last the best resolves of the more generous. Though to be sure, when I reflected upon it, it was not strange that people entering my office should be struck by the peculiar aspect of the unaccountable Bartleby, and so be tempted to throw out some sinister observations concerning him. Sometimes an attorney, having business with me, and calling at my office, and finding no one but the scrivener there, would undertake to obtain some sort of precise information from him touching my whereabouts; but without heeding his idle talk, Bartleby would remain standing

[14] These are two philosophic books. "Edwards on the Will" refers to *Freedom of the Will* (1754) by Jonathan Edwards (1703–1758), an American theologian. "Priestley on Necessity" refers to an essay by Joseph Priestley (1733–1804), the British clergyman and scientist.

immovable in the middle of the room. So after contemplating him in that position for a time, the attorney would depart, no wiser than he came.

Also, when a reference was going on, and the room full of lawyers and witnesses, and business driving fast, some deeply-occupied legal gentleman present, seeing Bartleby wholly unemployed, would request him to run round to his (the legal gentleman's) office and fetch some papers for him. Thereupon, Bartleby would tranquilly decline, and yet remain idle as before. Then the lawyer would give a great stare, and turn to me. And what could I say? At last I was made aware that all through the circle of my professional acquaintance, a whisper of wonder was running round, having reference to the strange creature I kept at my office. This worried me very much. And as the idea came upon me of his possibly turning out a long-lived man, and keep occupying my chambers, and denying my authority; and perplexing my visitors; and scandalizing my professional reputation; and casting a general gloom over the premises; keeping soul and body together to the last upon his savings (for doubtless he spent but half a dime a day), and in the end perhaps outlive me, and claim possession of my office by right of his perpetual occupancy: as all these dark anticipations crowded upon me more and more, and my friends continually intruded their relentless remarks upon the apparition in my room; a great change was wrought in me. I resolved to gather all my faculties together, and forever rid me of this intolerable incubus.

Ere revolving any complicated project, however, adapted to this end, I first simply suggested to Bartleby the propriety of his permanent departure. In a calm and serious tone, I commended the idea to his careful and mature consideration. But, having taken three days to meditate upon it, he apprised me, that his original determination remained the same; in short, that he still preferred to abide with me.

What shall I do? I now said to myself, buttoning up my coat to the last button. What shall I do? what ought I to do? what does conscience say I *should* do with this man, or, rather, ghost. Rid myself of him, I must; go, he shall. But how? You will not thrust him, the poor, pale, passive mortal—you will not thrust such a helpless creature out of your door? you will not dishonor yourself by such cruelty? No, I will not, I cannot do that. Rather would I let him live and die here, and then mason up his remains in the wall. What, then, will you do? For all your coaxing, he will not budge. Bribes he leaves under your own paper-weight on your table; in short, it is quite plain that he prefers to cling to you.

Then something severe, something unusual must be done. What! surely you will not have him collared by a constable, and commit his innocent pallor to the common jail? And upon what ground could you procure such a thing to be done?—a vagrant, is he? What! he a vagrant, a wanderer, who refuses to budge? It is because he will *not* be a vagrant, then, that you seek to count him *as* a vagrant. That is too absurd. No visible means of support: there I have him. Wrong again: for indubitably he *does* support himself, and that is the only unanswerable proof that any man can show of his possessing the means so to do. No more, then. Since he will not quit me, I must quit him. I will change my offices; I will move elsewhere, and give him fair notice, that if I find him on my new premises I will then proceed against him as a common trespasser.

Acting accordingly, next day I thus addressed him: "I find these chambers too far from the City Hall; the air is unwholesome. In a word, I propose to remove my offices next week, and shall no longer require your services. I tell you this now, in order that you may seek another place."

He made no reply, and nothing more was said.

On the appointed day I engaged carts and men, proceeded to my chambers, and, having but little furniture, everything was removed in a few hours. Throughout, the scrivener remained standing behind the screen, which I directed to be removed the last thing. It was withdrawn; and, being folded up like a huge folio, left him the motionless occupant of a naked room. I stood in the entry watching him a moment, while something from within me upbraided me.

I re-entered, with my hand in my pocket—and—and my heart in my mouth.

"Good-by, Bartleby; I am going—good-by, and God some way bless you; and take that," slipping something in his hand. But it dropped upon the floor, and then—strange to say—I tore myself from him whom I had so longed to be rid of.

Established in my new quarters, for a day or two I kept the door locked, and started at every footfall in the passages. When I returned to my rooms, after any little absence, I would pause at the threshold for an instant, and attentively listen, ere applying my key. But these fears were needless. Bartleby never came nigh me.

I thought all was going well, when a perturbed-looking stranger visited me, inquiring whether I was the person who had recently occupied rooms at No.——Wall Street.

Full of forebodings, I replied that I was.

"Then, sir," said the stranger, who proved a lawyer, "you are responsible for the man you left there. He refuses to do any copying; he refuses to do anything; he says he prefers not to; and he refuses to quit the premises."

"I am very sorry, sir," said I, with assumed tranquillity, but an inward tremor, "but, really, the man you allude to is nothing to me—he is no relation or apprentice of mine, that you should hold me responsible for him."

"In mercy's name, who is he?"

"I certainly cannot inform you. I know nothing about him. Formerly I employed him as a copyist; but he has done nothing for me now for some time past."

"I shall settle him, then—good morning, sir."

Several days passed, and I heard nothing more; and, though I often felt a charitable prompting to call at the place and see poor Bartleby, yet a certain squeamishness, of I know not what, withheld me.

All is over with him, by this time, thought I, at last, when, through another week, no further intelligence reached me. But, coming to my room the day after, I found several persons waiting at my door in a high state of nervous excitement.

"That's the man—here he comes," cried the foremost one, whom I recognized as the lawyer who had previously called upon me alone.

"You must take him away, sir, at once," cried a portly person among them, advancing upon me, and whom I knew to be the landlord of No. – Wall Street. "These gentlemen, my tenants, cannot stand it any longer; Mr. B—," pointing to the lawyer, "has turned him out of his room, and he now persists in haunting the building generally, sitting upon the banisters of the stairs by day, and sleeping in the entry by night. Everybody is concerned; clients are leaving the offices; some fears are entertained of a mob; something you must do, and that without delay."

Aghast at this torrent, I fell back before it, and would fain have locked myself in my new quarters. In vain I persisted that Bartleby was nothing to me—no more than to any one else. In vain—I was the last person known to have anything to do with him, and they held me to the terrible account. Fearful, then, of being exposed in the papers (as one person present obscurely threatened), I considered the matter, and, at length, said, that if the lawyer would give me a confidential interview with the scrivener, in his (the lawyer's) own room, I would, that afternoon, strive my best to rid them of the nuisance they complained of.

Going up stairs to my old haunt, there was Bartleby silently sitting upon the banister at the landing.

"What are you doing here, Bartleby?" said I.

"Sitting upon the banister," he mildly replied.

I motioned him into the lawyer's room, who then left us.

"Bartleby," said I, "are you aware that you are the cause of great tribulation to me, by persisting in occupying entry after being dismissed from the office?"

No answer.

"Now one of two things must take place. Either you must do something, or something must be done to you. Now what sort of business would you like to engage in? Would you like to re-engage in copying for some one?"

"No; I would prefer not to make any change."

"Would you like a clerkship in a dry-goods store?"

"There is too much confinement about that. No, I would not like a clerkship; but I am not particular."

"Too much confinement," I cried, "why you keep yourself confined all the time!"

"I would prefer not to take a clerkship," he rejoined, as if to settle that little item at once.

"How would a bar-tender's business suit you? There is no trying of the eyesight in that."

"I would not like it at all; though, as I said before, I am not particular."

His unwonted wordiness inspirited me. I returned to the charge.

"Well, then, would you like to travel through the country collecting bills for the merchants? That would improve your health."

"No, I would prefer to be doing something else."

"How, then, would going as a companion to Europe, to entertain some young gentleman with your conversation—how would that suit you?"

"Not at all. It does not strike me that there is anything definite about that. I like to be stationary. But I am not particular."

"Stationary you shall be, then," I cried, now losing all patience, and, for the first time in all my exasperating connection with him, fairly flying into a passion. "If you do not go away from these premises before night, I shall feel bound—indeed, I *am* bound—*to—to—to* quit the premises myself!" I rather absurdly concluded, knowing not with what possible threat to try to frighten his immobility into compliance. Despairing of all further efforts, I was precipitately leaving him, when a final thought occurred to me—one which had not been wholly unindulged before.

"Bartleby," said I, in the kindest tone I could assume under such exciting circumstances, "will you go home with me now—not to my office, but my dwelling—and remain there till we can conclude upon some convenient arrangement for you at our leisure? Come, let us start now, right away."

"No: at present I would prefer not to make any change at all."

I answered nothing; but, effectually dodging every one by the suddenness and rapidity of my flight, rushed from the building, ran up Wall Street towards Broadway, and, jumping into the first omnibus, was soon removed from pursuit. As soon as tranquillity returned, I distinctly perceived that I had now done all that I possibly could, both in respect to the demands of the landlord and his tenants, and with regard to my own desire and sense of duty, to benefit Bartleby, and shield him from rude persecution. I now strove to be entirely care-free and quiescent;

and my conscience justified me in the attempt; though, indeed, it was not so successful as I could have wished. So fearful was I of being again hunted out by the incensed landlord and his exasperated tenants, that, surrendering my business to Nippers, for a few days, I drove about the upper part of the town and through the suburbs, in my rockaway;[15] crossed over to Jersey City and Hoboken, and paid fugitive visits to Manhattanville and Astoria. In fact, I almost lived in my rockaway for the time.

When again I entered my office, lo, a note from the landlord lay upon the desk. I opened it with trembling hands. It informed me that the writer had sent to the police, and had Bartleby removed to the Tombs as a vagrant. Moreover, since I knew more about him than any one else, he wished me to appear at that place, and make a suitable statement of the facts. These tidings had a conflicting effect upon me. At first I was indignant; but, at last, almost approved. The landlord's energetic, summary disposition, had led him to adopt a procedure which I do not think I would have decided upon myself; and yet, as a last resort, under such peculiar circumstances, it seemed the only plan.

As I afterwards learned, the poor scrivener, when told that he must be conducted to the Tombs, offered not the slightest obstacle, but, in his pale, unmoving way, silently acquiesced.

Some of the compassionate and curious bystanders joined the party; and headed by one of the constables arm in arm with Bartleby, the silent procession filed its way through all the noise, and heat, and joy of the roaring thoroughfares at noon.

The same day I received the note, I went to the Tombs, or, to speak more properly, the Hall of Justice. Seeking the right officer, I stated the purpose of my call, and was informed that the individual I described was, indeed, within. I then assured the functionary that Bartleby was a perfectly honest man, and greatly to be compassionated, however unaccountably eccentric. I narrated all I knew, and closed by suggesting the idea of letting him remain in as indulgent confinement as possible, till something less harsh might be done—though, indeed, I hardly knew what. At all events, if nothing else could be decided upon, the almshouse must receive him. I then begged to have an interview.

Being under no disgraceful charge, and quite serene and harmless in all his ways, they had permitted him freely to wander about the prison, and, especially, in the inclosed grass-platted yards thereof. And so I found him there, standing all alone in the quietest of the yards, his face towards a high wall, while all around, from the narrow slits of the jail windows, I thought I saw peering out upon him the eyes of murderers and thieves.

"Bartleby!"

[15] A rockaway is a four-wheeled, two-door carriage open only in the front.

"I know you," he said without looking round—"and I want nothing to say to you."

"It was not I that brought you here, Bartleby," said I, keenly pained at his implied suspicion. "And to you, this should not be so vile a place. Nothing reproachful attaches to you by being here. And see, it is not so sad a place as one might think. Look, there is the sky, and here is the grass."

"I know where I am," he replied, but would say nothing more, and so I left him.

As I entered the corridor again, a broad mean-like man, in an apron, accosted me, and, jerking his thumb over his shoulder, said—"Is that your friend?"

"Yes."

"Does he want to starve? If he does, let him live on the prison fare, that's all."

"Who are you?" asked I, not knowing what to make of such an unofficially speaking person in such a place.

"I am the grub-man. Such gentlemen as have friends here, hire me to provide them with something good to eat."

"Is this so?" said I, turning to the turnkey.

He said it was.

"Well, then," said I, slipping some silver into the grub-man's hands (for so they called him), "I want you to give particular attention to my friend there; let him have the best dinner you can get. And you must be as polite to him as possible."

"Introduce me, will you?" said the grub-man, looking at me with an expression which seemed to say he was all impatience for an opportunity to give a specimen of his breeding.

Thinking it would prove of benefit to the scrivener, I acquiesced; and, asking the grub-man his name, went up with him to Bartleby.

"Bartleby, this is a friend; you will find him very useful to you."

"Your sarvant, sir, your sarvant," said the grub-man, making a low salutation behind his apron. "Hope you find it pleasant here, sir; nice grounds—cool apartments—hope you'll stay with us sometime—try to make it agreeable. What will you have for dinner to-day?"

"I prefer not to dine to-day," said Bartleby, turning away. "It would disagree with me; I am unused to dinners." So saying, he slowly moved to the other side of the inclosure, and took up a position fronting the dead-wall.

"How's this?" said the grub-man, addressing me with a stare of astonishment. "He's odd, ain't he?"

"I think he is a little deranged," said I, sadly.

"Deranged? deranged is it? Well, now, upon my word, I thought that friend of yourn was a gentleman forger; they are always pale and genteel-like, them forgers. I can't help pity 'em—can't help it, sir. Did you know Monroe Edwards?" he added, touchingly, and paused. Then, laying his hand piteously on my shoulder, sighed, "he died of consumption at Sing-Sing.[16] So you weren't acquainted with Monroe?"

"No, I was never socially acquainted with any forgers. But I cannot stop longer. Look to my friend yonder. You will not lose by it. I will see you again."

Some few days after this, I again obtained admission to the Tombs, and went through the corridors in quest of Bartleby; but without finding him.

"I saw him coming from his cell not long ago," said a turnkey, "may be he's gone to loiter in the yards."

So I went in that direction.

"Are you looking for the silent man?" said another turnkey, passing me. "Yonder he lies—sleeping in the yard there. 'Tis not twenty minutes since I saw him lie down."

The yard was entirely quiet. It was not accessible to the common prisoners. The surrounding walls, of amazing thickness, kept off all sounds behind them. The Egyptian character of the masonry weighed upon me with its gloom. But a soft imprisoned turf grew under foot. The heart of the eternal pyramids, it seemed, wherein, by some strange magic, through the clefts, grass-seed, dropped by birds, had sprung.

Strangely huddled at the base of the wall, his knees drawn up, and lying on his side, his head touching the cold stones, I saw the wasted Bartleby. But nothing stirred. I paused; then went close up to him; stooped over, and saw that his dim eyes were open; otherwise he seemed profoundly sleeping. Something prompted me to touch him. I felt his hand, when a tingling shiver ran up my arm and down my spine to my feet.

The round face of the grub-man peered upon me now. "His dinner is ready. Won't he dine to-day, either? Or does he live without dining?"

"Lives without dining," said I, and closed the eyes.

"Eh!—He's asleep, ain't he?"

"With kings and counselors," murmured I.

There would seem little need for proceeding further in this history. Imagination will readily supply the meagre recital of poor Bartleby's interment. But, ere parting with the reader, let me say, that if this little narrative has sufficiently interested him, to awaken curiosity as to who Bartleby was, and what manner of life he led prior to the present narrator's making his acquaintance, I can only reply, that in such curiosity I fully share, but am wholly unable to gratify it. Yet here I hardly know whether I should divulge one little item of rumor, which came to my ear a few months after the scrivener's decease. Upon what basis it rested,

[16] Sing-Sing is now the State Prison at Ossining, New York.

I could never ascertain; and hence, how true it is I cannot now tell. But, inasmuch as this vague report has not been without a certain suggestive interest to me, however sad, it may prove the same with some others; and so I will briefly mention it. The report was this: that Bartleby had been a subordinate clerk in the Dead Letter Office at Washington, from which he had been suddenly removed by a change in the administration. When I think over this rumor, hardly can I express the emotions which seize me. Dead letters! does it not sound like dead men? Conceive a man by nature and misfortune prone to a pallid hopelessness, can any business seem more fitted to heighten it than that of continually handling these dead letters, and assorting them for the flames? For by the cartload they are annually burned. Sometimes from out the folded paper the pale clerk takes a ring—the finger it was meant for, perhaps, moulders in the grave; a bank-note sent in swiftest charity—he whom it would relieve, nor eats nor hungers any more; pardon for those who died despairing; hope for those who died unhoping; good tidings for those who died stifled by unrelieved calamities. On errands of life, these letters speed to death.

Ah, Bartleby! Ah, humanity!

RICHARD WRIGHT

THE MAN WHO WAS ALMOST A MAN

Richard Wright (1908–1960) was the first black writer to win a major reputation outside of black literary circles. In his books Uncle Tom's Children *(1938),* Native Son *(1940), and* Black Boy *(1945), he placed himself among the forefront of American authors of his day.*

Wright was largely self-educated, leaving school at the age of fifteen. But he continued to read widely, even though this meant the difficult task of obtaining books from the "whites only" libraries in the South. Politically active, he wrote essays, plays, film scripts and poems depicting the difficulties both psychological and sociological of being oppressed. Though born in Natchez, Mississippi, he died in Paris where he had lived for many years.

Dave struck out across the fields, looking homeward through paling light. Whuts the usa talkin wid em niggers in the field? Anyhow, his mother was putting supper on the table. Them niggers can't understand *nothing*. One of these days he was going to get a gun and practice shooting, then they can't talk to him as though he were a little boy. He slowed, looking at the ground. Shucks, Ah ain scareda them even ef they are biggern me! Aw, Ah know whut Ahma do. . . . Ahm going by ol Joe's sto n git that Sears Roebuck catlog n look at them guns. Mabbe Ma will lemme buy one when she gits mah pay from ol man Hawkins. Ahma beg her t gimme some money. Ahm ol ernough to hava gun. Ahm seventeen. Almos a man. He strode, feeling his long, loose-jointed limbs. Shucks, a man oughta hava little gun aftah he done worked hard all day. . . .

He came in sight of Joe's store. A yellow lantern glowed on the front porch. He mounted steps and went through the screen door, hearing it bang behind him. There was a strong smell of coal oil and mackerel fish. He felt very confident until he saw fat Joe walk in through the rear door, then his courage began to ooze.

'Howdy, Dave! Whutcha want?'

'How yuh, Mistah Joe? Aw, Ah don wanna buy nothing. Ah jus wanted t see ef yuhd lemme look at tha ol catlog erwhile.'

'Sure! You wanna see it here?'

'Nawsuh. Ah wans t take it home wid me. Ahll bring it back termorrow when Ah come in from the fiels.'

'You plannin on buyin something?'

'Yessuh.'

'Your ma letting you have your own money now?'

'Shucks. Mistah Joe, Ahm gittin t be a man like anybody else!'

Joe laughed and wiped his greasy white face with a red bandanna.

'Whut you plannin on buyin?'

Dave looked at the floor, scratched his head, scratched his thigh, and smiled. Then he looked up shyly.

'Ahll tell yuh, Mistah Joe, ef yuh promise yuh won't tell.'

'I promise.'

'Waal, Ahma buy a gun.'

'A gun? Whut you want with a gun?'

'Ah wanna keep it.'

'You ain't nothing but a boy. You don't need a gun.'

'Aw, lemme have the catalog, Mistah Joe. Ahll bring it back.'

Joe walked through the rear door. Dave was elated. He looked around at barrels of sugar and flour. He heard Joe coming back. He craned his neck to see if he were bringing the book. Yeah, he's got it! Gawddog, he's got it!

'Here; but be sure you bring it back. It's the only one I got.'

'Sho, Mistah Joe.'

'Say, if you wanna buy a gun, why don't you buy one from me. I gotta gun to sell.'

'Will it shoot?'

'Sure it'll shoot.'

'Whut kind is it?'

'Oh, it's kinda old. . . . A Lefthand Wheeler. A pistol. A big one.'

'Is it got bullets in it?'

'It's loaded.'

'Kin Ah see it?'

'Where's your money?'

'Whut yuh wan fer it?'

'I'll let you have it for two dollars.'

'Just *two* dollahs? Shucks, Ah could buy tha when Ah git mah pay.'

'I'll have it here when you want it.'

'Awright, suh. Ah be in fer it.'

He went through the door, hearing it slam again behind him. Ahma git some money from Ma n buy me a gun! Only *two* dollahs! He tucked the thick catalogue under his arm and hurried.

'Where yuh been, boy?' His mother held a steaming dish of black-eyed peas.

'Aw, Ma, Ah jus stopped down the road t talk wid th boys.'

'Yuh know bettah than t keep suppah waitin.'

He sat down, resting the catalogue on the edge of the table.

'Yuh git up from there and git to the well n wash yosef! Ah ain feedin no hogs in mah house!'

She grabbed his shoulder and pushed him. He stumbled out of the room, then came back to get the catalogue.

'Whut this?'

'Aw, Ma, it's jusa catlog.'

'Who yuh git it from?'

'From Joe, down at the sto.'

'Waal, thas good. We kin use it around the house.'

'Naw, Ma.' He grabbed for it. 'Gimme mah catlog, Ma.'

She held onto it and glared at him.

'Quit hollerin at me! Whuts wrong wid yuh? Yuh crazy?'

'But Ma, please. It ain mine! It's Joe's! He tol me t bring it back t im termorrow.'

She gave up the book. He stumbled down the back steps, hugging the thick book under his arm. When he had splashed water on his face and hands, he groped back to the kitchen and fumbled in a corner for the towel. He bumped into a chair; it clattered to the floor. The catalogue sprawled at his feet. When he had dried his eyes he snatched up the book and held it again under his arm. His mother stood watching him.

'Now, ef yuh gonna acka fool over that ol book, Ahll take it n burn it up.'

'Naw, Ma, please.'

'Waal, set down n be still!'

He sat and drew the oil lamp close. He thumbed page after page, unaware of the food his mother set on the table. His father came in. Then his small brother.

'Whutcha got there, Dave?' his father asked.

'Jusa catlog,' he answered, not looking up.

'Ywah, here they is!' His eyes glowed at blue and black revolvers. He glanced up, feeling sudden guilt. His father was watching him. He eased the book under the table and rested it on his knees. After the blessing was asked, he ate. He scooped up peas and swallowed fat meat without chewing. Buttermilk helped to wash it down. He did not want to mention money before his father. He would do much better by cornering his mother when she was alone. He looked at his father uneasily out of the edge of his eye.

'Boy, how come yuh don quit foolin wid tha book n eat yo suppah?'

'Yessuh.'

'How yuh n ol man Hawkins gittin erlong?'

'Suh?'

'Can't yuh hear? Why don yuh lissen? Ah ast yuh how wuz yuh n ol man Hawkins gittin erlong?'

'Oh, swell, Pa. Ah plows mo lan than anybody over there.'

'Waal, yuh oughta keep yo min on whut yuh doin.'

'Yessuh.'

He poured his plate full of molasses and sopped at it slowly with a chunk of cornbread. When all but his mother had left the kitchen, he still sat and looked again at the guns in the catalogue. Lawd, ef Ah only had tha pretty one! He could almost feel the slickness of the weapon with his fingers. If he had a gun like that he would polish it and keep it shining so it would never rust. N Ahd keep it loaded, by Gawd!

'Ma?'

'Hunh?'

'Ol man Hawkins give yuh mah money yit?'

'Yeah, but ain no usa yuh thinkin bout thowin nona it erway. Ahm keepin tha money sos yuh kin have cloes t go to school this winter.'

He rose and went to her side with the open catalogue in his palms. She was washing dishes, her head bent low over a pan. Shyly he raised the open book. When he spoke his voice was husky, faint.

'Ma, Gawd knows Ah wans one of these.'

'One of whut?' she asked, not raising her eyes.

'One of *these,*' he said again, not daring even to point. She glanced up at the page, then at him with wide eyes.

'Nigger is yuh gone plum crazy?'

'Ah, Ma——'

'Git outta here! Don yuh talk t me bout no gun! Yuh a fool!'

'Ma, Ah kin buy one fer *two* dollahs.'

'Not ef Ah knows it yuh ain!'

'But yuh promised me one——'

'Ah don care whut Ah promised! Yuh ain nothing but a boy yit!'

'Ma, ef yuh lemme buy one Ahll *never* ask yuh fer nothing no mo.'

'Ah tol yuh t git outta here! Yuh ain gonna toucha penny of tha money fer no gun! Thas how come Ah has Mistah Hawkins t pay yo wages t me, cause Ah knows yuh ain got no sense.'

'But Ma, we needa gun. Pa ain got no gun. We needa gun in the house. Yuh kin never tell whut might happen.'

'Now don yuh try to maka fool outta me, boy! Ef we did hava gun yuh wouldn't have it!'

He laid the catalogue down and slipped his arm around her waist.

'Aw, Ma, Ah done worked hard alla summer n ain ast yuh fer nothin, is Ah, now?'

'Thas whut yuh spose t do!'

'But Ma, Ah wans a gun. Yuh kin lemme have two dollahs outta mah money. Please, Ma. I kin give it to Pa . . . Please, Ma! Ah loves yuh, Ma.'

When she spoke her voice came soft and low.

'Whut yuh wan wida gun, Dave? Yuh don need no gun. Yuhll git in trouble. N ef yo Pa jus *thought* Ah let yuh have money t buy a gun he'd hava fit.'

'Ahll hide it, Ma, it ain but two dollahs.'

'Lawd, chil, whuts wrong wid yuh?'

'Ain nothing wrong, Ma. Ahm almos a man now. Ah wans a gun.'

'Who gonna sell yuh a gun?'

'Ol Joe at the sto.'

'N it don cos but two dollahs?'

'Thas all, Ma. Just two dollahs. Please, Ma.'

She was stacking the plates away; her hands moved slowly, reflectively. Dave kept an anxious silence. Finally, she turned to him.

'Ahll let yuh git tha gun ef yuh promise me one thing.'

'Whuts tha, Ma?'

'Yuh bring it straight back t *me,* yuh hear? Itll be fer Pa.'

'Yessum! Lemme go now, Ma.'

She stooped, turned slightly to one side, raised the hem of her dress, rolled down the top of her stocking, and came up with a slender wad of bills.

'Here,' she said. 'Lawd knows yuh don need no gun. But yer Pa does. Yuh bring it right back t *me,* yuh hear? Ahma put it up. Now ef yuh don, Ahma have yuh Pa lick yuh so hard yuh won ferget it.'

'Yessum.'

He took the money, ran down the steps, and across the yard.

'Dave! Yuuuuuh Daaaaave!'

He heard, but he was not going to stop now. 'Naw, Lawd!'

The first movement he made the following morning was to reach under his pillow for the gun. In the gray light of dawn he held it loosely, feeling a sense of power. Could killa man wida gun like this. Kill anybody, black er white. And if he were holding his gun in his hand nobody could run over him; they would have to respect him. It was a big gun, with a long barrel and a heavy handle. He raised and lowered it in his hand, marveling at its weight.

He had not come straight home with it as his mother had asked;

instead he had stayed out in the fields, holding the weapon in his hand, aiming it now and then at some imaginary foe. But he had not fired it; he had been afraid that his father might hear. Also he was not sure he knew how to fire it.

To avoid surrendering the pistol he had not come into the house until he knew that all were asleep. When his mother had tiptoed to his bedside late that night and demanded the gun, he had first played 'possum; then he had told her that the gun was hidden outdoors, that he would bring it to her in the morning. Now he lay turning it slowly in his hands. He broke it, took out the cartridges, felt them, and then put them back.

He slid out of bed, got a long strip of old flannel from a trunk, wrapped the gun in it, and tied it to his naked thigh while it was still loaded. He did not go in to breakfast. Even though it was not yet daylight, he started for Jim Hawkins' plantation. Just as the sun was rising he reached the barns where the mules and plows were kept.

'Hey! That you, Dave?'

He turned. Jim Hawkins stood eying him suspiciously.

'Whatre yuh doing here so early?'

'Ah didn't know Ah wuz gittin up so early, Mistah Hawkins. Ah wuz fixin t hitch up ol Jenny n take her t the fiels.'

'Good. Since you're here so early, how about plowing that stretch down by the woods?'

'Suits me. Mistah Hawkins.'

'O.K. Go to it!'

He hitched Jenny to a plow and started across the fields. Hot dog! This was just what he wanted. If he could get down by the woods, he could shoot his gun and nobody would hear. He walked behind the plow, hearing the traces creaking, feeling the gun tied tight to his thigh.

When he reached the woods, he plowed two whole rows before he decided to take out the gun. Finally, he stopped, looked in all directions, then untied the gun and held it in his hand. He turned to the mule and smiled.

'Know whut this is, Jenny? Naw, yuh wouldn't know! Yuhs jusa ol mule! Anyhow, this is a gun, n it kin shoot, by Gawd!'

He held the gun at arm's length. Whut t hell, Ahma shoot this thing! He looked at Jenny again.

'Lissen here, Jenny! When Ah pull this ol trigger Ah don wan yuh t run n acka fool now.'

Jenny stood with head down, her short ears pricked straight. Dave walked off about twenty feet, held the gun far out from him, at arm's length, and turned his head. Hell, he told himself, Ah ain afraid. The gun felt loose in his fingers; he waved it wildly for a moment. Then he shut his eyes and tightened his forefinger. *Blooom!* A report half-deafened him and he thought his right hand was torn from his arm.

He heard Jenny whinnying and galloping over the field, and he found himself on his knees, squeezing his fingers hard between his legs. His hand was numb; he jammed it into his mouth, trying to warm it, trying to stop the pain. The gun lay at his feet. He did not quite know what had happened. He stood up and stared at the gun as though it were a live thing. He gritted his teeth and kicked the gun. Yuh almos broke mah arm! He turned to look for Jenny; she was far over the fields, tossing her head and kicking wildly.

'Hol on there, ol mule!'

When he caught up with her she stood trembling, walling her big white eyes at him. The plow was far away; the traces had broken. Then Dave stopped short, looking, not believing. Jenny was bleeding. Her left side was red and wet with blood. He went closer. Lawd have mercy! Wondah did Ah shoot this mule? He grabbed for Jenny's mane. She flinched, snorted, whirled, tossing her head.

'Hol on now! Hol on.'

Then he saw the hole in Jenny's side, right between the ribs. It was round, wet, red. A crimson stream streaked down the front leg, flowing fast. Good Gawd! Ah wuznt shootin at tha mule. . . . He felt panic. He knew he had to stop that blood, or Jenny would bleed to death. He had never seen so much blood in all his life. He ran the mule for half a mile, trying to catch her. Finally she stopped, breathing hard, stumpy tail half arched. He caught her mane and led her back to where the plow and gun lay. Then he stopped and grabbed handfuls of damp black earth and tried to plug the bullet hole. Jenny shuddered, whinnied, and broke from him.

'Hol on! Hol on now!'

He tried to plug it again, but blood came anyhow. His fingers were hot and sticky. He rubbed dirt hard into his palms, trying to dry them. Then again he attempted to plug the bullet hole, but Jenny shied away, kicking her heels high. He stood helpless. He had to do something. He ran at Jenny; she dodged him. He watched a red stream of blood flow down Jenny's leg and form a bright pool at her feet.

'Jenny . . . Jenny . . .' he called weakly.

His lips trembled. She's bleeding t death! He looked in the direction of home, wanting to go back, wanting to get help. But he saw the pistol lying in the damp black clay. He had a queer feeling that if he only did something, this would not be; Jenny would not be there bleeding to death.

When he went to her this time, she did not move. She stood with sleepy, dreamy eyes; and when he touched her she gave a low-pitched whinny and knelt to the ground, her front knees slopping in blood.

'Jenny . . . Jenny . . .' he whispered.

For a long time she held her neck erect; then her head sank, slowly. Her ribs swelled with a mighty heave and she went over.

Dave's stomach felt empty, very empty. He picked up the gun and held it gingerly between his thumb and forefinger. He buried it at the foot of a tree. He took a stick and tried to cover the pool of blood with dirt—but what was the use? There was Jenny lying with her mouth open and her eyes walled and glassy. He could not tell Jim Hawkins he had shot his mule. But he had to tell something. Yeah, Ahll tell em Jenny started gittin wil n fell on the joint of the plow. . . . But that would hardly happen to a mule. He walked across the field slowly, head down.

It was sunset. Two of Jim Hawkins' men were over near the edge of the woods digging a hole in which to bury Jenny. Dave was surrounded by a knot of people; all of them were looking down at the dead mule.

'I don't see how in the world it happened,' said Jim Hawkins for the tenth time.

The crowd parted and Dave's mother, father, and small brother pushed into the center.

'Where Dave?' his mother called.

'There he is,' said Jim Hawkins.

His mother grabbed him.

'Whut happened, Dave? Whut yuh done?'

'Nothing.'

'C'mon, boy, talk,' his father said.

Dave took a deep breath and told the story he knew nobody believed.

'Waal,' he drawled. 'Ah brung ol Jenny down here sos Ah could do mah plowin. Ah plowed bout two rows, just like yuh see.' He stopped and pointed at the long rows of upturned earth. 'Then something musta been wrong wid ol Jenny. She wouldn't ack right atall. She started snortin n kickin her heels. Ah tried to hol her, but she pulled erway, rearin n goin on. Then when the point of the plow was stickin up in the air, she swung erroun n twisted hersef back on it. . . . She stuck hersef n started t bleed. N fo Ah could do anything, she wuz dead.'

'Did you ever hear of anything like that in all your life?' asked Jim Hawkins.

There were white and black standing in the crowd. They murmured. Dave's mother came close to him and looked hard into his face.

'Tell the truth, Dave,' she said.

'Looks like a bullet hole ter me,' said one man.

'Dave, whut yuh do wid tha gun?' his mother asked.

The crowd surged in, looking at him. He jammed his hands into his pockets, shook his head slowly from left to right, and backed away. His eyes were wide and painful.

'Did he hava gun?' asked Jim Hawkins.

'By Gawd, Ah tol yuh tha wuz a *gun* wound,' said a man, slapping his thigh.

His father caught his shoulders and shook him till his teeth rattled.

'Tell whut happened, yuh rascal! Tell whut . . .'

Dave looked at Jenny's stiff legs and began to cry.

'Whut yuh do wid tha gun?' his mother asked.

'Whut wuz he doin wida gun?' his father asked.

'Come on and tell the truth,' said Hawkins. 'Ain't nobody going to hurt you . . .'

His mother crowded close to him.

'Did yuh shoot tha mule, Dave?'

Dave cried, seeing blurred white and black faces.

'Ahh ddinnt gggo tt sshooooot hher. . . . Ah ssswear off Gawd Ahh ddint. . . . Ah wuz a-tryin t sssee ef the ol gggun would sshoot——'

'Where yuh git the gun from?' his father asked.

'Ah got it from Joe, at the sto.'

'Where yuh git the money?'

'Ma give it t me.'

'He kept worryin me, Bob. . . . Ah had t. . . . Ah tol im t bring the gun right back t me. . . . It was fer yuh, the gun.'

'But how yuh happen to shoot that mule?' asked Jim Hawkins.

'Ah wuznt shootin at the mule, Mistah Hawkins. The gun jumped when Ah pulled the trigger . . . N fo Ah knowed anything Jenny wuz there a-bleedin.'

Somebody in the crowd laughed. Jim Hawkins walked close to Dave and looked into his face.

'Well, looks like you have bought you a mule, Dave.'

'Ah swear fo Gawd, Ah didn't go t kill the mule, Mistah Hawkins!'

'But you killed her!'

All the crowd was laughing now. They stood on tiptoe and poked heads over one another's shoulders.

'Well, boy, looks like yuh done bought a dead mule! Hahaha!'

'Ain tha ershame.'

'Hohohohoho.'

Dave stood head down, twisting his feet in the dirt.

'Well, you needn't worry about it, Bob,' said Jim Hawkins to Dave's father. 'Just let the boy keep on working and pay me two dollars a month.'

'Whut yuh wan fer yo mule, Mistah Hawkins?'

Jim Hawkins screwed up his eyes.

'Fifty dollars.'

'Whut yuh do wid tha gun?' Dave's father demanded.

Dave said nothing.

'Yuh wan me t take a tree lim n beat yuh till yuh talk!'

'Nawsuh!'

'Whut yuh do wid it?'

'Ah thowed it erway.'

'Where?'

'Ah . . . Ah thowed it in the creek.'

'Waal, c mon home. N firs thing in the mawnin git to tha creek n fin tha gun.'

'Yessuh.'

'Whut yuh pay fer it?'

'Two dollahs.'

'Take tha gun n git yo money back n carry it t Mistah Hawkins, yuh hear? N don fergit Ahma lam yo black bottom good fer this! Now march yosef on home, suh!'

Dave turned and walked slowly. He heard people laughing. Dave glared, his eyes welling with tears. Hot anger bubbled in him. Then he swallowed and stumbled on.

That night Dave did not sleep. He was glad that he had gotten out of killing the mule so easily, but he was hurt. Something hot seemed to turn over inside him each time he remembered how they had laughed. He tossed on his bed, feeling his hard pillow. N Pa says he's gonna beat me. . . . He remembered other beatings, and his back quivered. Naw, naw, Ah sho don wan im t beat me tha way no mo. . . . Dam em *all!* Nobody ever gave him anything. All he did was work. They treat me lika mule. . . . N then they beat me. . . . He gritted his teeth. N Ma had t tell on me.

Well, if he had to, he would take old man Hawkins that two dollars. But that meant selling the gun. And he wanted to keep that gun. Fifty dollahs fer a dead mule.

He turned over, thinking of how he had fired the gun. He had an itch to fire it again. Ef other men kin shoota gun, by Gawd, Ah kin! He was still listening. Mebbe they all sleepin now. . . . The house was still. He heard the soft breathing of his brother. Yes, now! He would go down and get that gun and see if he could fire it! He eased out of bed and slipped into overalls.

The moon was bright. He ran almost all the way to the edge of the woods. He stumbled over the ground, looking for the spot where he had buried the gun. Yeah, here it is. Like a hungry dog scratching for a bone he pawed it up. He puffed his black cheeks and blew dirt from the trigger and barrel. He broke it and found four cartridges unshot. He looked around; the fields were filled with silence and moonlight. He clutched the gun stiff and hard in his fingers. But as soon as he wanted to pull the trigger, he shut his eyes and turned his head. Naw, Ah can't shoot wid mah eyes closed n mah head turned. With effort he held his eyes open; then he squeezed. *Blooooom!* He was stiff, not breathing. The gun was still in his hands. Dammit, he'd done it! He fired again. *Bloooom!* He smiled. *Bloooom! Bloooom! Click, click.* There! It was empty. If anybody could shoot a gun, he could. He put the gun into his hip pocket and started across the fields.

When he reached the top of a ridge he stood straight and proud in the moonlight, looking at Jim Hawkins' big white house, feeling the gun sagging in his pocket. Lawd, ef Ah had jus one mo bullet Ahd taka shot at tha house. Ahd like t scare ol man Hawkins jusa little. . . . Jussa enough t let im know Dave Sanders is a man.

To his left the road curved, running to the tracks of the Illinois Central. He jerked his head, listening. From far off came a faint *hoooof-hoooof; hoooof-hoooof; hoooof-hoooof* . . . Tha's number eight. He took a swift look at Jim Hawkins' white house; he thought of pa, of ma, of his little brother, and the boys. He thought of the dead mule and heard *hoooof-hoooof; hoooof-hoooof; hoooof-hoooof* . . . He stood rigid. Two dollahs a mont. Les see now. . . . Tha means itll take bout two years. Shucks! Ahll be dam!

He started down the road, toward the tracks. Yeah, here she comes! He stood beside the track and held himself stiffly. Here she comes, erroun the ben. . . . C mon, yuh slow poke! C mon! He had his hand on his gun; something quivered in his stomach. Then the train thundered past, the gray and brown box cars rumbling and clinking. He gripped the gun tightly; then he jerked his hand out of his pocket. Ah betcha Bill wouldn't do it! Ah betcha. . . . The cars slid past, steel grinding upon steel. Ahm riding yuh ternight so hep me Gawd! He was hot all over. He hesitated just a moment; then he grabbed, pulled atop of a car, and lay flat. He felt his pocket; the gun was still there. Ahead the long rails were glinting in the moonlight, stretching away, away to somewhere, somewhere where he could be a man. . . .

GLOSSARY

Antagonist A character who is an obstacle to the protagonist's goals, an adversary of the protagonist. Villains are antagonists.

Audience The receiver(s) of a message, particularly the onlookers of a play or performance. In literature, the audience is the potential or actual readers of a work.

Colloquial style A style that imitates people's speech, particularly their casual or informal conversation.

Conflict The condition in which a protagonist meets obstacles to his or her goals. The actions that occur between or within characters with differing goals, opinions or desires.

Diction The general pattern of word choice, often classified into high or low diction. High diction is a pattern of formal, elaborate words. Low diction includes street talk, slang, regional expressions and other colloquial words and expressions.

Didactic story A story told to illustrate or promote a particular lesson or moral. Fiction designed to teach.

Dynamic character A character that changes within the course of a story usually as a result of the events narrated.

Empathy The ability of the reader to experience the same or similar emotions of another person or character; the ability to put oneself in another person's position. Usually empathy is distinguished from sympathy. When we sympathize with people or characters we may feel pity for them, be moved by their plight, or supportive in a struggle they are going through, but we remain outside of their emotions and do not enter into their feelings.

Exposition The opening of a story when the major characters, situation and setting are presented and identified.

First person narration A story told by one of the characters who identifies him or herself in the first person, namely, using the pronoun "I."

Flat character A character whose personality traits can be summarized in one sentence; in short, a simple, stereotypical figure.

Formula fiction Stories that have a set of rules of composition more specific than those of fiction in general. Formula fiction is usually popular in nature—detective novels, spy thrillers or romances.

Genre A general type of literary work. There are generally four major genres: (1) prose fiction, (2) prose nonfiction (essays, biographies, memoirs etc.), (3) poetry, and (4) drama. These major categories can be broken down into *sub-genres:* comic novels, tragedies, romance novels, farces, lyrics, etc.

Horizon of expectation A term developed by the German critic Hans Robert Jauss refering to the expectations held by the reading public which an author anticipates in preparing the literary work. An author can determine these expectations by considering the genre of his work, the literary tradition in which the author operates, and the relationship between the work and the social reality in which it is to appear.

Hyperbole The use of exaggeration as a figure of speech; for example, "This essay will be remembered throughout the universe," "Leslie was the smartest student in the entire continent."

Hypotactic style A style that uses long sentences built up from subordinate or dependent clauses, phrases, or adverbial elements.

Limited third person narration A narrative perspective in which the narrator is not a participant in the action but limits what is told to what a single character experiences. *See also* Omniscient narrator and Reflector.

Magic realism A term to describe the style of several Latin American writers who give the works the drama of dreams, and the clarity and simplicity of folk tales. A style of heightened reality where supernatural occurrences take place. See especially "The Old Man with Enormous Wings."

Narrator The voice that tells the story. The narrator may either be a character in the story or a person outside of the story. Stories may have more than one narrator.

Natural symbol *see* Representative symbol.

Omniscient third person narration A narrative perspective or point-of-view in which the narrator is not a participant in the action and, thus, can tell the reader events that occurred before or after the action of the story, what happens in all of the character's minds and in any setting.

Paratactic style A literary style that uses mostly short sentences or independent clauses linked by simple coordinate conjunctions. Hemingway stories, for example, make particular use of the paratactic style.

Personification A figure of speech in which inanimate objects are given human properties. The following are examples of personification: "The sun smiled down on us," "Death walked into the room."

Protagonist The main character in a story. In most stories, it is the central character with whom the reader empathizes or supports. When the character is unusually brave, good or adventurous, the protagonist is called a hero.

Realism A fictional practice in which the writer limits the action to events that could actually occur, follows the rules of nature, and depicts characters who are in their motivation and thoughts like actual humans (as opposed to superheroes or gods).

Reflector The character through whom a story is viewed by a limited third person narrator.

Regional style A linguistic or narrative style that predominates among writers from a certain region, for example; properties that can be found in a number of Southern writers make up that region's style.

Reliable narrator A narrator who gives the reader an accurate account of the fictional action and whose judgment of character and morals is meant to be trusted.

Representative symbol One of a set of similar items that represents the whole class of things. For example, The Tomb of the Unknown Soldier symbolizes all the soldiers who have been anonymously killed in battle or whose fate remains unknown. Though only one soldier is buried there, he represents symbolically all such soldiers.

Resolution A point that occurs at the end of a story and indicates whether the protagonist has achieved his or her goal and what is the outcome of the narrative action. Many stories are not fully resolved, that is, the fates of the characters are not absolutely certain and are left at the end of the story undetermined.

Romantic symbol *see* Representative symbol

Round character A character whose various traits cannot be summarized in a single sentence; indeed, some characters are so full and varied they cannot be summed up at all. Round characters tend to avoid stereotypes and frequently seem to readers like actual people with all their complexities and internal contradictions.

Static character A character who stays unchanged throughout the course of the story.

Style The pattern of the author's choices on words, sentence structure, content and organization.

Surprise A narrative technique whereby events occur without the readers' knowledge that such events were in the offing.

Suspense A narrative technique in which readers are aware of some impending action but are unsure of its outcome or time of arrival.

Symbol A word, object, or action that signifies more than its actual self. For example, a dove in many contexts signifies not only a physical bird but the idea of peace.

Theme An abstract statement that the action of the entire story embodies, the thesis or doctrine contained within the story. Crudely considered, what a story "means."

Thesis A particular and controversial intellectual position that a story may attempt to illustrate or an essay attempt to prove. A proposition in need of support.

Tone The author's attitude toward the work or subject as revealed primarily in word choice and narrative point of view.

Traditional symbol Object, words, or images that have fairly fixed meanings, for example, the cross as a symbol of Christianity or stars and stripes as a symbol of the United States.

Turning point The part of the story in which the fortune of the protagonist changes or when it begins to become clear whether he or she will achieve the goal. Often this involves moving from seeming defeat to apparent victory or the other way around.

Unreliable narrator A speaker whose account of events we may doubt and whose judgments of character and morals are suspicious. "The Yellow Wallpaper" is a classic example of a narrator whose judgment and accuracy the reader comes to question.

INDEX OF AUTHORS AND TITLES

Authors' names appear in capitals and titles of stories in italics. Numbers in roman type indicate the page of the selection, and italic numbers indicate discussion of the story.

INDEX OF TERMS